**FIFTH EDITION**

# Introduction
## — to —
# Business Decision Making

TEXT *and* CASES

**Marilyn Campbell**

**Elizabeth Grasby**

**John Haywood-Farmer**

**Sonya Head**

**John Humphrey**

The Western Business School
**The University of Western Ontario**

**Nelson Canada**

I(T)P  An International Thomson Publishing Company

Toronto • Albany • Bonn • Boston • Cincinnati • Detroit • London • Madrid
Melbourne • Mexico City • New York • Pacific Grove • Paris
San Francisco • Singapore • Tokyo • Washington

I⬤P™
International Thomson Publishing

© Nelson Canada,
A Division of Thomson Canada Limited

Published in 1996 by
Nelson Canada,
A Division of Thomson Canada Limited
1120 Birchmount Road
Scarborough, Ontario M1K 5G4

**Canadian Cataloguing in Publication Data**
Main entry under title:

An introduction to business decision making

5th ed.
First ed. by M.R. Pearce, D.G. Burgoyne and
J.A. Humphrey.
Includes index.
ISBN 0-17-605573-8

1. Business – Case studies.  2. Industrial
management – Canada – Case studies.  3. Business –
Decision making – Case studies.  I. Campbell,
Marilyn.

HF5351.P42 1996      658.4′03      C95-932822-X

| | |
|---|---|
| **Publisher/Acquisitions Editor** | Jackie Wood |
| **Project Coordinator** | Edward Ikeda |
| **Production Editor** | Jill Young |
| **Senior Production Coordinator** | Carol Tong |
| **Art Director/Cover Design** | Stuart Knox |
| **Lead Composition Analyst** | Zenaida Diores |

3   4      EB      99  98

*To the Memory of*
*David G. Burgoyne and*
*John J. Wettlaufer*

# CONTENTS

# PREFACE TO THE FIFTH EDITION

A number of cases from the fourth edition have been replaced by newer and more relevant cases in this edition of *An Introduction to Business Decision Making: Text and Cases*. This edition has 32 new cases and retains 23 cases from the fourth edition. Most of the introductory material to the Parts of this edition have been extensively revised. These changes reflect a large investment of time and money by a great number of people over the past few years in case writing activities at the Western Business School. The authors would like to thank the instructors who have been teaching at the School over the past few years, without whom this edition would not exist. Their enthusiasm, dedication to students and teaching, and the energy they have brought to the task have been outstanding. In particular, we would like to thank the following past and current faculty members who have used the fourth edition at both Western and its affiliated colleges:

| | |
|---|---|
| Chris Albinson | Ken Bowlby |
| Michael Carter | Andrew Fletcher |
| Leo Klus | Stephannie Larocque |
| Chuck Lemmon | Michelle Linton |
| Lisa Luinenburg | Leena Malik |
| Lisa Melnychyn | Mitchell Orr |
| Tracy Paul | Paul Peters |
| John Siambani | Dave Town |
| Krista Wylie | |

A number of current and past members at the Western Business School have co-authored earlier editions of this book. The fifth edition owes a great deal to David Burgoyne, James Erskine, John Graham, Richard Mimick, and Michael Pearce who, along with Marilyn Campbell, John Haywood-Farmer, and John Humphrey, were responsible for the first four editions of the book. We thank them for their support and encouragement and for letting us build on the firm foundation they established.

We would also like to acknowledge the ongoing support of Renata Djurfeldt, the Business 020 teaching group support assistant. In addition to typing many of the new case and text material, Renata happily undertook many of the support tasks that enabled us to complete this edition. Carol Fuller and Sue LeMoine also aided in the typing.

We would also like to thank Adrian Ryans, Dean of the Western Business School, and Ken Hardy, Associate Dean & Research Director, for their support of this project. Financial assistance for case writing was provided through the Plan for Excellence. Several colleagues — including Joe DiStefano, Nick Fry, Mike Leenders, and Al Mikalachki — gave us significant assistance with textual material in this and previous editions.

One of the joys of being involved in the Business 020 course at Western is the opportunity to work with young people, both students who take the course, and the instructors who deliver it. They keep all of us challenged and stimulated. We hope that our future students will find this new edition one that actively involves them in the exciting task of decision making.

MARILYN M. CAMPBELL
ELIZABETH GRASBY
JOHN S. HAYWOOD-FARMER
SONYA HEAD
JOHN A. HUMPHREY

# PART

# AN INTRODUCTION TO
# THE CASE METHOD

## WHAT IS A CASE?

In this text, we use the term *case* to refer to a written description of "an actual administrative situation commonly involving a decision or problem."[1] Although in some cases the authors may have disguised names, places, and other facts at the request of the organizations involved, the cases in this book are real situations that real people have faced. The objective of each case is to leave you at a point much like the one that the individual in the case actually confronted — you must make a decision.

In each case situation, the decision maker was expected to determine what problems and opportunities existed, to analyze the situation, to generate and evaluate alternative courses of action, and to recommend and implement a plan of action. Except for the fact that you will not have the actual opportunity to implement the plan of action and see the results, we expect that you will go through this same process.

As they grapple with problems, decision makers encounter a number of common frustrations: a shortage of good information on which to base decisions, a shortage of time in which to make decisions, uncertainty about how plans will work out, and the lack of opportunity to reduce this uncertainty at a reasonable cost. You will experience these same frustrations because the cases give you the same information time pressures, and so on, that the decision maker had. In

1

short, you will simulate the experience of decision making. However, cases do simplify the task somewhat: someone has already collected and sorted all the available data for you. In real life the decision maker also faces the task of collecting the data that might be relevant for making a decision.

## THE CASE METHOD

The case method is not a single approach, but rather several variations. The general theme, however, is to learn by doing rather than by listening. Class sessions are not lectures but discussions that emphasize the development of skills in problem solving and decision making. In a typical case discussion everyone in the room works toward a solution to the particular problem being addressed. Consequently, students will interact with one another as well as with the instructor. The student's role, then, is one of participation — active listening and talking with others in the class. The instructor's role is not to lecture the group but to guide the discussion by probing, questioning, and adding some input.

Cases can be used in several ways. You will probably be asked to deal with them in some or all of the following ways:

1. a. Individual preparation for a class discussion, followed by
   b. Small group discussion in preparation for a class discussion, followed by
   c. Class discussion
2. A written report or in-class presentation of a case
3. A written examination of your ability to handle a case

Each of these methods is somewhat different and will require some variation in your approach. Also, your instructor will undoubtedly have his or her own comments to add to the following general remarks about approaches to cases.

## INDIVIDUAL PREPARATION FOR CLASS

Cases can be complicated and controversial. In reality, they are unstructured problems. Watch out — the process of case preparation can be deceiving! Some students think they are on top of the situation without really having done much work. They read over cases casually once or twice, jot down a few ideas, go to class, and listen to the discussion. As points come up they think, "I touched on that," or "I would have reached the same conclusion if I had pushed the data a little further." However, when exam, report, or presentation time arrives and they must do a case thoroughly on their own, they find themselves in serious difficulty. These students spend all their time in the exam trying to learn how to deal with a case, rather than tackling the case issues upon which they are being tested. Because this is the first case these students have really tried to do from beginning to end, this situation is not surprising. Their position is similar to that of someone who trained by watching others practise for a number of months and then entered a 100-metre race at an official track meet.

To help provide you with some structure, your instructor may assign specific questions to be addressed as you work on a case. You should consider such assignment questions as a means to assist you in getting into the case and *not* as the limits of your preparation. When your instructor assigns no questions, it is up to you to develop the structure. In class, your instructor will still expect you to be ready to give a supported decision concerning what you would do as the decision maker in the case. Accordingly, you should regard each case as a challenge to your ability to:

1. Define a problem,
2. Sort relevant from irrelevant information,
3. Separate fact from opinion,
4. Interpret and analyze information,
5. Come to a reasoned decision and course of action, and
6. Communicate your thoughts clearly and persuasively to others during class discussions.

Cases also serve to communicate a good deal of descriptive information about a wide variety of institutions and business practices. Many cases are sufficiently complex to absorb all the preparation time you have — and then some! Thus, it is extremely important that you develop skill in using your preparation time efficiently.

Much of your preparation time should be spent analyzing and interpreting information. In effect, the case presents facts and opinions. Your job is to become acquainted with those facts and opinions and to know how they relate to the decision.

We offer the following steps to help you in your individual case preparation:

1. Read the case once quickly to get an overview.
2. Skim any exhibits in the case just to see what information is available.
3. Find out — frequently from the first and last few paragraphs of the case — who the decision maker is (this will be your role); what his or her immediate concern, problem, or issue appears to be; why this concern has arisen; and when the decision must be made.
4. Read the case again, more carefully. This time highlight key information, make notes to yourself in the margin, and write down ideas as they occur to you. At this stage you are trying to familiarize yourself as thoroughly as possible with the case information. Having done so, you are ready to begin your analysis.

5. Try to answer at least the following questions:

   a. What business is the organization in? What are its objectives? What are its strengths and weaknesses? What opportunities and threats exist? Who are its customers? What does it have to do well to satisfy customers? How do you know?

   b. What is the decision to be made, problem to be solved, or issue to be resolved? How do you know — what is your evidence? (Let the case data guide you — most cases will have sufficient data for you to "solve" the problems and are unlikely to contain vast amounts of completely irrelevant data.)

   c. What facts are relevant and key to a solution? Are they symptoms? Causes? What is your quantitative and qualitative evaluation of the organization's strengths and weaknesses?

   d. What do the facts mean for the problem? Here, learn to analyze — ask and answer lots of questions.

   e. What are the decision criteria?

   f. What are the alternatives? Are they relevant to the problem at hand? It is usually unwise to ignore the ones spelled out in a case, although most instructors appreciate creative solutions, provided they are sensible and supported by reasonable data.

   g. What is your evaluation of the alternatives in view of the decision criteria? What are the pros and cons of each?

   h. Which alternative or combination of alternatives would you choose? Why?

   i. What is your plan of action? Outline your plan by answering the questions: who, when, what, where, why, and how.

   j. What results do you expect? Why?

## SMALL GROUP PREPARATION FOR CLASS

If possible, prior to class you should informally discuss your preparation of each case with some of your classmates. Many students find such study group sessions to be the most rewarding part of case method learning. A good group session is a sharing experience in which you discover ideas you may have missed or to which you did not give enough weight. Your colleagues will also benefit from your input.

The effectiveness of a small group case discussion can be increased substantially if you and the other members of the group adhere to the following guidelines:

1. Each student must come to the group meeting with a thorough knowledge of any assigned readings and analysis of the case. The small group session is not the place to start case preparation.

2. Each group member is expected to participate actively in the discussion — it is an excellent place to check your analysis before going into class.

3. It is not necessary to have a group leader. All members of the group are responsible for making their own decisions based on what is said plus their own case analysis.

4. It is also not necessary to have a recording secretary. Participants are responsible for their own notes. It is important to be able to recognize a good idea when you hear one.

5. Consensus is normally not necessary. No one has to agree with anyone else.

6. If it is important to you, work at clarifying individual disagreements after the small group discussion, especially if only one or two people are involved.

7. Set a time limit for discussion and stick to it. Effective small group case discussions can take less than 30 minutes and, because of your workload, 30 minutes will have to be adequate for most cases.

Remember, a group can be as small as two people. If you cannot get together in one place, spend some time with a classmate over the phone reviewing your respective case analyses. You will be more confident, feel better about your own preparation, and probably contribute more to the class discussion.

## CLASS DISCUSSION

Cases are complex and there are never any completely right or wrong answers. Consequently, groups of managers who address the kinds of issues represented by this book's cases nearly always express different views on how to interpret the data and what action could and should be taken. They see the world differently. That is one reason management is worth studying. You should expect something similar: during discussion of a case, your classmates will express several different views. The essence of the case method is the process of putting forward different points of view, defending your position, and listening actively to others in order to understand and criticize constructively others' points of view. Only rarely will you leave the classroom with your position or perspective unchanged after discussing a case; indeed, if you do so, it was a waste of your time to go to class.

However, despite the common interest of all class members in resolving the case issues, and regardless of guidance from the instructor, class discussions sometimes will seem repetitious and unorganized. This is an unavoidable and natural situation, especially during the early stages of a course. Over time, as a group develops its group decision-making ability, case discussions will become more orderly, effective, efficient, and satisfying to all.

The need to be a skilful communicator arises repeatedly in management. The case method presents an ideal opportunity to practise communication — both talking and listening skills. Some people, because they find talking in a group difficult and threatening, avoid talking in class even though they may realize that by being silent they are not getting full value out of the experience. If you are one of these individuals, the only way to overcome this problem is to jump in and begin. Make a habit of participating regularly in class. Do not wait until you have a major presentation to make in which you will hold the floor for a lengthy period. You can add a key piece of information or question something in just a few sentences and this may be the best way for you to begin active involvement. Your instructor and your classmates will support your efforts. Remember, the classroom is a place where we can learn from one another's mistakes as much as, and often more than, from one another's solutions. The cost of making a mistake in class is very small compared to making it in an actual situation. Other people have poorly developed listening skills. Some individuals do not listen: they simply wait for their turn to talk. The case method depends on the willing two-way interaction of the students. Without that essential ingredient, the cases become interesting stories rather than opportunities to develop the ability to make and argue for and against management decisions.

Not surprisingly, students are interested in finding out what actually happened in a case or what the instructor would do. Only rarely will you be provided with this information. Learning comes from the process and habit of making decisions, not in reviewing what others decided to do.

## AFTER CLASS

After class take a few minutes to assess your preparation by comparing it to what happened in class. Were you in the ball park or completely off base? Did you spend enough time preparing on your own? Was your small group session effective? What can you do better next time? What *general* lessons did you learn? For example, although you may not be interested in remembering how the market for athletic shoes is segmented, you should want to remember how to segment a market.

## EVALUATING PERFORMANCE

In a typical class discussion of a case, exactly what gets done depends not only on the work done by the students — what preparation they did, who actively participated in the discussion, how well people related their comments to previous discussion — but also on the instructor's pedagogical objectives and performance as a moderator and discussion leader. Instructors view case courses as sequences of problems that gradually foster the development of decision-making skills. With this longer time horizon, instructors often find it advisable to emphasize a specific analytical technique on one occasion, stress problem identification on another, and so on. Thus, it is possible that many class sessions will seem to be incomplete, unbalanced developments of a case analysis and plan of action. Although this may frustrate you, have faith that your instructor is trying to develop your skills over one or more terms.

How do instructors assess performance? The answer, of course, varies from one instructor to another. However, we suggest that there are some common factors. Above all, instructors develop your ability to demonstrate that you can think logically and consistently by being able to:

1. Identify, prioritize, and deal with issues and problems;
2. Judge the quality and relevance of information — fact, opinion, hearsay, lies, and so on;
3. Make and assess necessary assumptions;
4. Relate the information to the issues, problems, and decisions in the case;
5. Resolve conflicting information;
6. Analyze by asking and answering the right questions and correctly using appropriate analytical tools;
7. Determine and rank appropriate criteria for making decisions;
8. Generate and evaluate alternative courses of action;
9. Make a decision (take a stand) and defend it with persuasive, well-ordered convincing argument;
10. Develop a reasonably detailed action plan showing an awareness of what might happen;
11. Build on other students' arguments to advance the discussion towards a coherent conclusion rather than making unrelated points or repeating ones already made; and
12. Generalize: in traditional lectures instructors expect students to take the general lessons from the lecture and apply them to specific problems; case method instructors expect students to go from the specific lessons in a case to more general lessons.

In addition to assessing performance in class on a daily basis, most instructors will provide some opportunities for more complete, balanced treatment of cases. Sometimes instructors allow extra preparation time and ask for an oral presentation of a case by an individual or group. Sometimes instructors require students to prepare a written report on how they would handle a particular situation and why. Frequently, case method courses have cases as examinations: students are given a case and asked to do whatever analysis and make whatever recommendations they deem appropriate.

In reports, presentations, and examinations, instructors expect a more complete, balanced argument for a particular course of action. Such exercises are not usually intended to result in a diary of how a student or group looked at a case or in a rewritten version of the case. A report, presentation, or examination is supposed to be a concise, coherent exposition of what to do and why — it usually starts where most students leave off in their regular individual preparation for a case class. Think of a report, presentation, or examination as an organized, more fully developed (and perhaps rewritten) version of your regular class preparation notes.

You will find that your audience — instructor, business executive, or whoever — has particular ideas about how a report, presentation, or examination should be organized. We urge you to find out as much as you can about format expectations before embarking on your task. In general, we suggest that students use the following general outline:

1. Executive summary (written last but appearing first),
2. Statement of problem, opportunity, and objectives,
3. Analysis of the situation,
4. Identification and evaluation of alternatives, and
5. Decision, course of action, and implementation.

## Concluding Remarks

We are not really interested in the relatively straightforward problems typically found at the ends of chapters in most texts. Instead, we are interested in the unstructured problems more typical of real situations and exemplified in this text by cases. The key to dealing with unstructured problems is to learn what questions to ask. Ironically, answering the questions is usually easier than asking them because the questions focus thinking. It is like trying to find your way in the wilderness. Almost anyone can follow a trail; the key skill is knowing what trail to follow.

We believe that you will find case study a very rewarding way to learn. Good luck with it!

### Notes

1. J.A. Erskine, M.R. Leenders, and L.A. Mauffette-Leenders, *Teaching with Cases* (London, Ontario: The University of Western Ontario, 1981).

# PART

# AN INTRODUCTION TO
# FINANCIAL STATEMENTS

The purpose of this chapter is to introduce and explain financial statements, which give a picture of a company's operating results and its financial condition. The topics that will be discussed are:

- The balance sheet
- The income statement
- The statement of retained earnings
- The auditor's report and footnotes

All incorporated companies are obliged by law to provide annual financial statements to their shareholders. This information is usually presented in a firm's annual report. In addition to financial statements, these reports often contain a message from the president describing the corporation's past and planned activities, including new product developments, plant expansion, and assessment of changes in market conditions.

The balance sheet, the income statement, and the statement of retained earnings provide the basic information that a business person, investor, lender, or shareholder needs to gauge the financial well-being of a company. Learning to understand financial statements is not difficult.

Part 2 concentrates on the definition of the three financial statements. Part 3, "An Introduction to Financial Management," analyzes these statements and the cash sources and uses statement. Proper use of financial tools aids financial decision making. However, before analytical concepts can be used for decision making, you must understand the basic financial vocabulary, the relationships among the different financial statements, and the terms used in them.

## THE BALANCE SHEET

The balance sheet presents the financial position of an enterprise as of a particular day, such as December 31, 1995. It is like a photograph of a firm's financial condition at a particular point in time.

The purpose of a balance sheet is to show what a company owns and what it owes. *Assets* represent economic benefits. The assets — what a company owns — are listed on the left side of the statement. The liabilities — what a company owes — are listed on the right side. The net worth, which is known as shareholders' equity for incorporated companies, represents the difference between what a company owns and what it owes, and it is also listed on the right side. Both sides are always in balance.

Assets represent all the physical goods and things of value "owned" by the company, including finished and unfinished inventory, land, buildings, equipment, cash, and money owed to the company from credit sales or money lent to others. Liabilities consist of all debts or claims "owed" by the company, such as loans from the bank, and unpaid accounts due to suppliers.

Shareholders' equity (net worth) represents the interest, stake, or claim the owners have in the company. It is the owners' original investment plus (or minus) the accumulation of all profits (or losses) that have been retained in the firm since the company's inception.

Individuals can develop personal balance sheets. Before studying a business balance sheet, try to develop your own personal balance sheet. As a suggestion, first list your assets or things of value. Then after adding them up, list the credit claims against those assets. Such claims may be government loans to further your education or loans to purchase some of the assets you have listed previously. Subtract the total of the liabilities from your assets. The residual is your net worth, or equity. The net worth represents your claim as owner against the assets.

A more complicated balance sheet is presented for XYZ Manufacturing Co. as at December 31, 1995 (Exhibit 1). Each of the XYZ accounts will be discussed in turn.

### ASSETS

The size of the company is often measured in terms of its assets. Two major categories of assets are current assets and property, plant, and equipment (or fixed assets).

### Current Assets

Current assets include cash and items that in the normal course of business will be converted into cash within an operating cycle, which usually takes a year from the date of the balance sheet. Each current asset item should be listed in order of liquidity (ease of conversion to cash). Current assets generally consist of cash, marketable securities, receivables, inventories, and prepayments (prepaid expenses).

### Cash

Cash is the money that is on hand and the money on deposit in the bank.

| | |
|---|---|
| Cash | $30,000 |

### Marketable Securities

This asset represents investment of temporary cash surpluses in some form of short-term interest-earning instrument. Because these funds may be needed on short notice, it is usually considered wise to make investments that are readily convertible to cash and subject to minimum price fluctuations (such as certificates of deposit, commercial paper, and short-term government notes). The general practice is to show marketable securities at the lower of cost or market value. If market value differs from lower of cost or market, it is also shown, usually parenthetically.

| | |
|---|---|
| Marketable securities at cost | |
| (Market value, $230,000) | $225,000 |

### Accounts Receivable

Accounts receivable are amounts owed to the company by customers who have purchased on credit and usually have 30, 60, or 90 days in which to pay. The total amount due from customers as shown in the balance sheet is $555,000. However, some customers fail to pay their bills. Therefore, a provision for doubtful accounts is estimated (based on previous experience), so that the net accounts receivable amount will represent the actual amount that is expected to be collected. The balance of $530,000 is thus shown as the net accounts receivable on the balance sheet.

| | |
|---|---|
| Accounts receivable | $555,000 |
| Less: Allowance for doubtful accounts | 25,000 |
| Net accounts receivable | $530,000 |

### Inventory

Retailers' and wholesalers' inventories consist of the goods they have for sale to their customers. The functions these companies perform are to store, promote,

*Exhibit 1*

XYZ Manufacturing Company Ltd.
Balance Sheet
As at December 31, 1995

ASSETS

Current assets:

| | | | |
|---|---|---|---|
| Cash | | | $ 30,000 |
| Marketable securities at cost | | | 225,000 |
| (Market value $230,000) | | | |
| Accounts receivable | | $555,000 | |
| Less: Allowance for doubtful accounts | | 25,000 | |
| Net accounts receivable | | | 530,000 |
| Raw materials inventory | | $260,000 | |
| Work-in-process inventory | | 163,000 | |
| Finished goods inventory | | 285,000 | |
| Total inventories | | | 708,000 |
| Prepayments | | | 31,000 |
| Total current assets | | | $1,524,000 |
| | | | |
| Investment in subsidiaries | | | 200,000 |
| Other investments (Market value $30,000) | | | 40,000 |
| | | | |
| Property, plant, and equipment: | | | |
| Land | | $120,000 | |
| Plant | $1,000,000 | | |
| Less: Accumulated depreciation | 370,000 | 630,000 | |
| | | | |
| Machinery | $ 250,000 | | |
| Less: Accumulated depreciation | 95,000 | 155,000 | |
| | | | |
| Office equipment | $ 26,000 | | |
| Less: Accumulated depreciation | 9,000 | 17,000 | |
| Total property, plant, and equipment | | | 922,000 |
| | | | |
| Intangibles: | | | |
| Goodwill | | $ 20,000 | |
| Patents | | 140,000 | |
| Organization expenses | | 15,000 | |
| Total intangibles | | | 175,000 |
| | | | |
| TOTAL ASSETS | | | $2,861,000 |

**EXHIBIT 1**
*(cont'd)*

LIABILITIES

Current liabilities:

| | |
|---|---|
| Notes payable (demand note) | $ 225,000 |
| Accounts payable | 265,000 |
| Accrued expenses payable | 85,000 |
| Taxes payable | 40,000 |
| Current portion of long-term debt | 50,000 |
| Total current liabilities | $ 665,000 |

Long-term liabilities:

| | |
|---|---|
| First mortgage bonds (10% interest, due 2000) | 200,000 |
| Debentures (12% interest, due 2005) | 650,000 |
| Deferred taxes | 100,000 |
| TOTAL LIABILITIES | $1,615,000 |

SHAREHOLDERS' EQUITY

Capital stock:

| | | |
|---|---|---|
| Preferred shares, 5% cumulative, $100 par value; authorized, issued, and outstanding 1,400 shares | $140,000 | |
| Common shares, $5 stated value; authorized, issued, and outstanding 70,000 shares | 350,000 | |
| Premium on stock | 230,000 | $720,000 |
| Retained earnings | | 526,000 |

| | |
|---|---|
| TOTAL SHAREHOLDERS' EQUITY | 1,246,000 |
| TOTAL LIABILITIES AND SHAREHOLDERS' EQUITY | $2,861,000 |

sell, and distribute goods. The goods themselves are not changed in any major way from the time they are received to the time they are sold. The inventory is valued at its original cost or its present market value, whichever is lower.

A manufacturing company's inventory will consist of raw materials, work in process (subassemblies and partially completed products), and finished products that are manufactured but not yet sold. Finished and semifinished products are given a higher unit cost than the raw material: the cost of labour content, the cost of energy consumed in production, and other manufacturing costs are to be added to the raw material cost. Inventory, like marketable securities above, is generally shown at the lower of cost or market value (also known as net realizable value).

| | |
|---|---|
| Raw materials inventory | $260,000 |
| Work-in-process inventory | 163,000 |
| Finished inventory | 285,000 |
| Total inventories | $708,000 |

### Prepayments (Prepaid Expenses)

At times, it is necessary or convenient to pay for items in advance. When the items are meant for short-term purposes, such as property or equipment rental and fire insurance, they are called prepayments or prepaid expenses.

Although the payment is made at one time, the contract (in the case of rent) or the anticipated benefit or reward (in the case of insurance) is expected to last over a span of time. As the "value" is not fully received when the payment is made, the "unused" portion, or the benefit to come, is considered an asset of the company. For example, if two years of insurance are still unused on a five-year policy that originally cost $1,000, then $400 will be shown on the balance sheet as prepaid expense.

| | |
|---|---|
| Prepaid expenses | $31,000 |

To summarize, current assets include cash, marketable securities, accounts receivable, inventories, and prepaid expenses.

| | |
|---|---|
| Total current assets | $1,524,000 |

## Investment in Subsidiaries

XYZ Manufacturing Co. Ltd. owns two small businesses, one a wholesale business that aids in the distribution of its manufactured products, the other providing repair services for selected products. Investments in subsidiaries in both cases represent a controlling interest, more than 50 percent of the common stock. The common stock is not a tangible asset, and therefore not included with property, plant, and equipment. XYZ Manufacturing Co. Ltd. has no intention of selling its investment. As a consequence, the investment is listed in this separate category after current assets.

| | |
|---|---|
| Investment in subsidiaries | $200,000 |

## Other Investments

XYZ Manufacturing Co. has invested in other business operations and processes. None of the investments represents a controlling interest in the project; consequently they are listed separately. Also, XYZ Manufacturing Co. has no intention of selling the investments. Therefore, the other investments are listed in this separate category, setting it apart from investment in subsidiaries; marketable securities in current assets; and property, plant and equipment. Other investments are listed at cost, *not* lower of cost or market, unless a decline in value is considered permanent.

Other investments (market value $30,000)      $40,000

## Property, Plant, and Equipment

Property, plant, and equipment (or fixed assets) are physical items that will last more than one year. They include those items not intended for resale that will be used in the operation of the company, such as land, buildings, machinery, equipment, furniture, automobiles, and trucks. All fixed assets, with the exception of land, are shown at their original cost, less accumulated depreciation. Land is not depreciated: only its original cost is shown. This presentation may be conservative: the original cost may well be lower than either present market value or replacement cost. For example, land which appears on the books as $120,000 may actually be worth $200,000. Fixed assets should be stated in order of "permanence," with land generally considered the most permanent.

### Depreciation

Plant and equipment become useless over the years through wear or obsolescence. In order to allow for this loss of use, the asset is "written-down," or depreciated. These reductions are based on the expected useful life of the asset and estimated salvage value. The allowances for depreciation are usually accumulated separately so that the asset's original cost figure on the balance sheet is preserved. The accumulated depreciation amount then reflects that part of the original cost of the asset which has been depreciated and charged to the company as an expense. Thus, the net balance after accumulated depreciation (net book value) is not intended to reflect current or market value of an asset as of the balance sheet date, but rather the original cost less the accumulated depreciation to date.

There are a number of ways to calculate depreciation. The simplest is a straight-line method whereby the cost of the fixed asset is allocated evenly over its useful life. For example, suppose a machine is bought for $100,000 and it has an estimated life of 10 years, and zero salvage value. Its cost will be allocated at the rate of $10,000 each year. The accumulated depreciation would be $10,000 at the end of the first year; $20,000 at the end of the second year; $30,000 at the end of the third year, etc. By the end of the tenth year, the net book value of the machine would be zero. Other methods are also used; one, percentage declining balance, is a model for the calculation of depreciation for tax purposes.

The accumulated depreciation for each fixed asset is best shown separately, though usually only one total is shown for all the fixed assets.

| | | |
|---|---:|---:|
| Land | | $120,000 |
| Plant | $1,000,000 | |
| Less: Accumulated depreciation | 370,000 | |
| | | $630,000 |
| Machinery | $ 250,000 | |
| Less: Accumulated depreciation | 95,000 | |
| | | $155,000 |
| Office equipment | $ 26,000 | |
| Less: Accumulated depreciation | 9,000 | |
| | | $ 17,000 |

If only totals are shown, it would be:

| | | |
|---|---:|---:|
| Land | | $120,000 |
| Plant and equipment | $1,276,000 | |
| Less: Accumulated depreciation | 474,000 | 802,000 |

Fixed assets, in summary, are the investments in property, plant, and equipment. As explained, they are generally expressed in terms of their cost, diminished by the depreciation accumulated as of the date of the financial statement.

| | |
|---|---:|
| Total property, plant, and equipment | $922,000 |

### Intangibles

Most of the company's assets can be seen and touched. There are, however, some items of value that are not tangible yet are customarily recorded as assets. For example, patents and franchise rights are intangible assets. The amounts listed for patents and franchise rights are actual amounts paid. Some companies expense their research and development expenses as incurred. Others, such as XYZ Manufacturing Co., capitalize theirs (set them up as an asset).

Another item in intangibles is organization expenses. These refer to the cost of the legal formation of the enterprise. In setting up a corporation, there are fees that are owed to the jurisdiction that grants the incorporation, plus legal fees associated with preparing the documentation for incorporation. Another intangible, "goodwill," is encountered only when companies change hands. When a company is purchased, establishing a price for it is difficult. Often a purchaser will pay more for a company than it seems worth, according to the balance sheet, because he or she believes that the loyalty of existing customers, or the company's reputation, for example, are worth a premium over the tangible assets. The purchaser's balance sheet for the company after it is purchased will include an amount called goodwill that reflects the premium paid. Over time, usually over 40 years, goodwill is amortized, which means it is written down in a manner similar to depreciation on a tangible fixed asset. One might expect to find listed under intangibles the value of trained, competent personnel, but the human resources of a company are not typically valued and reported on the balance sheet, primarily because there is no agreement on how to arrive at an appropriate value.

| **Intangibles:** | |
| --- | --- |
| Goodwill | $ 20,000 |
| Patents | 140,000 |
| Organization intangibles | 15,000 |
| Total intangibles | $175,000 |

The total intangibles figure is net of amortization. All the assets are added together.

| TOTAL ASSETS | $2,861,000 |
| --- | --- |

## LIABILITIES

Liabilities refer to all the debts a company owes. They are categorized into current liabilities and long-term liabilities.

### Current Liabilities

Current liabilities reflect the amount of money the company owes and must pay within the coming year. Some of these debts include debt due within a year; amounts owed to material and service suppliers; and unpaid wages, bond interest, legal fees, pension payments, and taxes. In addition, it is usual to include in current liabilities the portion of long-term debts due within the year.

**Notes Payable**
Companies often need additional cash to operate. Thus, money is borrowed from banks or other lenders, such as suppliers, who usually demand formal recognition of amounts owed them. On receipt of cash, the borrower gives the lender a written promissory note, stating that borrowed funds will be returned within a year (plus any other agreed-upon arrangements, such as interest, etc.). These are called notes payable. The term "demand note" means the lender may demand repayment at any time.

| Notes payable (demand note) | $225,000 |
| --- | --- |

**Accounts Payable**
Funds owned by the company for goods and services provided on credit by its suppliers are accounts payable. The company usually has 30, 60, or 90 days in which to pay. Sometimes the suppliers offer a cash discount of, say, 2 percent, as an inducement to pay promptly.

| Accounts payable | $265,000 |
| --- | --- |

### Accrued Expenses Payable (Accruals)

In addition to its debt to suppliers and lenders, a company may owe for various goods not yet delivered in full or for services not yet fully performed. Examples are salaries and wages earned prior to payday; interest; and fees to lawyers, architects, etc., for partially completed undertakings. Accrued expenses are expenses that have been incurred, but because of an incomplete transaction, have not been recorded.

Accrued expenses payable                                      $85,000

### Taxes Payable

If a corporation's tax bill is high enough, the corporation must pay its taxes monthly. The tax payments may be based either on the estimate of the current year's taxes owed or the previous year's taxes. The general practice is for corporations to choose the lower of the two bases to determine their monthly payment. Within two months after the end of the fiscal year, the final payment for the estimated taxes owed is due. As a consequence, taxes payable will have a balance in it as long as there is a difference between the base used for payment and the estimated tax liability that is determined when the company draws up its financial statements at the end of its fiscal year.

Taxes payable                                                 $40,000

### Current Portion of Long-term Debt

Long-term debt contracts specify repayment terms. Of XYZ's long-term debts, the first mortgage bonds have a principal repayment of $50,000 due within one year. This portion of the long-term debt is added to current liabilities, or debts due within one year. The 12 percent debentures have no principal payments until 2000.

Current portion of long-term debt                            $50,000

To review, total current liabilities is the sum of all the debts that the company will have to pay within one year from the balance sheet date.

Total current liabilities                                     $665,000

### *Long-term Liabilities*

Current liabilities were defined as debts due within one year. Long-term liabilities are debts due after one year from the date of the balance sheet. The principal portions of mortgages, bonds, and some loans are examples. The interest on these items may be payable monthly, quarterly, semiannually, or annually. This year's or any previous year's interest, if not yet paid, would therefore be shown as an accrued expense payable, a current liability. Interest is charged against only those periods that have already passed. The interest that will be payable for the future may be known, but is not considered a debt until it has been incurred (but not paid). Therefore, future interest does not appear as a liability on the balance sheet.

### First Mortgage Bonds

In the sample balance sheet, one long-term liability is the 10 percent first mortgage bonds due in 2000. The money was received by the company as a loan from the bond holders, who in turn were given a certificate called a bond as evidence of the loan. The bond is really a formal promissory note issued by the company, which agreed to repay the debt at maturity in 2000 and agreed also to pay interest at the rate of 10 percent per year. The term *first mortgage* is a safeguard initiated by the lenders. This means that if the company is unable to pay off the bonds in cash when they are due, the bondholders have a claim, or lien, before other creditors on the mortgaged assets. The mortgaged assets may be sold and the proceeds used to satisfy the debt.

First mortgage bonds (10% interest, due 2000)     $200,000

### Debentures

The debentures (or bonds) are a certificate of debt. The security of the debenture is the general credit standing of the company. In other words, the debenture holders rank equally with the other general creditors, such as the trade creditors and nonsecured creditors.

Debentures 12%, due 2005                          $650,000

### Deferred Taxes

Sometimes the accounting principles for the determination of net earnings, set by the Canadian Institute of Chartered Accountants, and the law for the determination of taxable income, as set by the government, are in conflict. As a consequence, the taxpayer, in establishing financial statements, may estimate one level of income tax payable, and when filing taxable income according to government regulations, set a different level of tax liability. The difference between the two amounts is put in this account.

It may be useful to give an illustration. Most of the cases with deferred tax credit arise because of the different rules for depreciation. For example, XYZ may have purchased new machinery in 1994 worth $10,000. XYZ's normal accounting practice is to depreciate the $10,000 over its useful life, 10 years. As a consequence, it would deduct from income for depreciation, $1,000 per year. However, the government regulations allow for 10 percent depreciation, or $1,000, in 1994; and 20 percent on the declining balance in 1995 and thereafter, or $1,800 for 1995 [(i.e., $0.20 \times (\$10,000 - \$1,000)$)]. This means that in 1995, for this asset alone, the taxable income as reported on XYZ's tax form would be less than it reports on its financial statements. The difference would be $800 ($1,800 – $1,000). With a 22 percent tax rate, the difference in income tax expense for 1995 is $176 (22 × $800). The reduction in income tax expense is added to the deferred taxes account. In later years, when the net book value of the asset for tax regulations is below $5,000, the situation will be reversed.

Deferred taxes                                           $100,000

Finally, all liabilities, current and long-term, are added and listed under the heading of total liabilities.

TOTAL LIABILITIES                                    $1,615,000

## SHAREHOLDERS' EQUITY

The total equity interest that all stockholders (owners of the company) have in a corporation is called shareholders' equity, or net worth. It is what is left after subtracting total liabilities from total assets. For corporations, equity is separated into two categories — capital stock and retained earnings — while the capital structure for proprietors and partnerships is somewhat different.

### Capital Stock

The capital stock account reflects the owners' initial equity investment in the company. This account is treated differently depending on the company's form of ownership. (Forms of ownership will be discussed in more detail in Part 3.) In a sole proprietorship, this will appear as a single account, which includes both invested capital and retained profits; for example:

Scott Meddick, capital                                 $50,000

In a partnership, the accounts will show the respective amounts of the partners' shares of the ownership equity, which also includes both invested capital and retained profits; for example:

Scott Meddick, capital                                 $50,000

Bill West, capital                                        30,000

Total capital                                          $80,000

In a public or private company, the shares of ownership are called capital stock. A company often issues more than one kind of stock in order to appeal to as many investors as possible. Anyone can purchase shares in a public firm, whereas the sale of a private company's shares is restricted. Shares are represented by stock certificates issued by the company to its shareholders.

The number of shares of capital stock that a company is authorized to issue and the par value, if any, of these shares is specified in the articles of incorporation. The company usually requests authorization of a larger number of shares than it will issue immediately. Thus, if more capital is needed in future years, the company will not have to change its charter by increasing the number of authorized shares. *Issued* means the number of shares sold, while outstanding shares represent the shares that are still in the hands of shareholders. The term *par value* is the dollar value given to each share of stock on authorization. No par value shares have no such declared value, but may have a stated value, usually the original issue price. Although par value still appears on balance sheets, it is no longer required to issue par value stocks. Federally incorporated companies are not allowed to issue par value common stock, but most provinces permit a choice between par and no par stock.

### Preferred Shares

Normally, dividends are not declared on common shares until preferred shareholders have received their full dividend. If the company should be liquidated, preferred shareholders have first claim on remaining assets, after its creditors (those to whom the company owes money as shown in the liabilities section) have been repaid. Dividends to preferred shareholders are normally limited to a stated percentage of share value and are not related to the level of profit. In the XYZ Manufacturing Co. example, the preferred stock is designated 5 percent cumulative, $100 par value each; this means that each share is entitled to $5 in dividends a year when declared by the board of directors. Cumulative here means that, if in any year the dividend is not paid, it accumulates in favour of the preferred shareholders and must be paid to them before any dividends are distributed to common stock shareholders. In general, preferred shareholders do not have voting rights in the company, unless dividends are in arrears, i.e., have not been paid. Since there are many different kinds of preferred shares, the terms are specified on the balance sheet.

Preferred shares, 5% cumulative, $100 par value;

 authorized, issued, and outstanding 1,400 shares   $140,000

### Common Shares

Common shareholders control the company because the shareholders vote for a board of directors and vote on other management issues at shareholders' meetings. Common shares can be either par value or no par value. Dividends are not preset or guaranteed. When company earnings are high, dividends may be high; when earnings drop, so may dividends.

Common shares, $5 stated value;

 authorized, issued, and outstanding 70,000 shares   $350,000

### Premium on Stock

When a company sells shares, the buyers' investment is recorded under capital stock. However, shares may be sold for different prices at different times. To simplify the recording procedure, all shares sold are recorded at the price of the first shares sold (original issue) in a common shares account. When shares are sold at higher prices than the original issue, the difference is considered a premium and listed in "Premium on Stock." For example, if 20,000 common shares were sold at $5 each when the company was incorporated, this would have been recorded under common shares stock as $100,000. If at a later date, 50,000 additional common shares were issued and sold at $9.60 per share, then $50,000 \times \$5 = \$250,000$ would be added to common shares. The additional capital [$50,000 \times (\$9.60 - \$5) = 50,000 \times \$4.60 = \$230,000$] would be recorded as premium on stock. (Underwriter's fees would normally be deducted, but for simplicity this detail is omitted here.)

| | |
|---|---|
| Premium on stock | $230,000 |

The amounts in the capital stock accounts — preferred shares, common shares, and premium on stock — are added.

| | |
|---|---|
| Total Capital Stock | $720,000 |

### Retained Earnings

The second component of equity is retained earnings. This represents the accumulated total of after-tax profits and losses from operations over the life of the corporation that have been retained in the enterprise, in other words not paid out in dividends. Profits add to retained earnings, while losses reduce it. If a corporation has had more losses than profits, the amount in retained earnings will be negative (usually shown in brackets) and labelled "Retained Deficit." Any dividends paid are also subtracted from the running total through a statement of retained earnings which is discussed later in Section Three. XYZ Manufacturing Co., since it started, has retained a net total of $526,000 from its operations.

| | |
|---|---|
| Retained earnings | $526,000 |

The shareholders' equity accounts are then totalled.

| | |
|---|---|
| TOTAL SHAREHOLDERS' EQUITY | $1,246,000 |

All liabilities and shareholders' equity items are added together. This amount balances with the total assets.

| | |
|---|---|
| TOTAL LIABILITIES AND SHAREHOLDERS' EQUITY | $2,861,000 |

## FACTS TO REMEMBER ABOUT THE BALANCE SHEET

1. The balance sheet shows the financial picture as at a certain point in time.
2. The company name and date must appear in the title.
3. Assets are listed on the left, liabilities and shareholders' equity are on the right. (Sometimes they are listed one after another on a page.)
4. Current assets are shown first, followed by fixed assets.
5. Current assets are listed in order of liquidity, from most liquid to least liquid.

6. Fixed assets are listed in order of permanence, from the most permanent to the least.

7. Current liabilities are listed first, followed by long-term liabilities.

8. Liabilities are listed in terms of due dates.

9. Shareholders' equity is capital stock + retained earnings.

10. Assets = Liabilities + Equity. A balance sheet always balances.

## SECTION TWO

## THE INCOME STATEMENT

The income statement, also referred to as a profit and loss statement or statement of earnings, shows how much money the corporation made or lost during a particular period. While the balance sheet shows the financial position of a company at a given date, the income statement often is of greater interest to investors because it shows the record of the company's activities for an operating cycle, normally a year.

An income statement matches the revenue generated from selling goods or services against all the expenses incurred during the same period to generate these revenues. The difference is a net profit or loss for the period. The phrase "for the period" in the previous sentence is important. For example, if the period ended December 31 and a sale was made on December 30, it would be recorded as a revenue for the period even if the customer did not pay for the product until January. Similarly, expenses incurred but not yet paid, such as an employees' wages, are recorded for the appropriate period. Thus, the income statement does not relate to the actual movement of cash in a company, only to generating revenues and incurring expenses.

Examine the components and format of the income statement for XYZ Manufacturing Co. Ltd. in Exhibit 2.

### NET SALES

Net sales represent revenue earned by the company from its customers for goods sold or services rendered. When a company sells services rather than goods (e.g., a railroad, theatre, or dry cleaners), its net sales are usually called *operating revenues*. The net sales item covers the amount received after taking into consideration the value of returned goods and the amount of discounts for quick payment. Remember, net sales refer to sales made during the period, not cash collected.

| | | |
|---|---|---|
| Sales | | $3,000,000 |
| Less: Sales returns and allowances | $60,000 | |
| Sales discounts | 40,000 | 100,000 |
| Net sales | | $2,900,000 |

*EXHIBIT 2*

XYZ Manufacturing Company Ltd.
Statement of Earnings
for the Year Ending December 31, 1995

| | | |
|---|---:|---:|
| Sales | | $ 3,000,000 |
| Less: Sales returns and allowances | $    60,000 | |
|     Sales discounts | 40,000 | 100,000 |
| Net sales | | $ 2,900,000 |
| | | |
| Cost of goods sold: | | |
|     Finished goods inventory, December 31, 1994 | $  247,000 | |
|     Cost of goods manufactured (Exhibit 3) | 2,200,000 | |
|     Cost of goods available for sale | $2,447,000 | |
|     Less: finished goods inventory, December 31, 1995 | 285,000 | |
| Cost of goods sold | | 2,162,000 |
| Gross profit | | $   738,000 |
| | | |
| Operating expenses: | | |
|     General and administrative expenses | $  145,000 | |
|     Selling expenses | 225,000 | |
|     Depreciation expense | 80,000 | |
|     Total operating expenses | | 450,000 |
| | | |
| Operating profit | | $   288,000 |
| Plus: other income | | 20,000 |
| Less: other expenses, interest | | 100,000 |
| | | |
| Net profit before tax | | $   208,000 |
| Estimated income tax expense | | 46,000 |
| Net earnings | | $   162,000 |

## COST OF GOODS SOLD

A major expense associated with making sales is the cost to the company of the product itself, either to make it or to buy it. For a manufacturer such as XYZ Manufacturing Co. Ltd., included in the cost of goods sold are all costs associated directly with the transformation or production process: raw materials, direct labour, and factory overhead. A manufacturer transforms raw materials into a different final product. The process involves the acquisition of raw materials (the product of another manufacturer) and the placement of the raw materials into process. It also involves the effective combination of labour and machinery to transform the raw materials into the desired product.

In the statement of cost of goods manufactured (Exhibit 3) all the costs directly associated with the manufacturing process are included: raw materials costs, direct labour, and factory overhead items directly associated with the manufacturing process.

**EXHIBIT 3**

XYZ Manufacturing Company Ltd.
Statement of Goods Manufactured
for the Year Ending December 31, 1995

| | | |
|---|---|---|
| Work-in-process inventory, December 31, 1994 | | $ 158,000 |
| Raw materials used: | | |
| Raw materials inventory, December 31, 1994 | $ 290,000 | |
| Raw materials purchases | 1,450,000 | |
| Raw materials available | $1,740,000 | |
| Less: Raw material inventory, December 31, 1995 | 260,000 | |
| Raw materials used | $1,480,000 | |
| Direct labour | | 265,000 |
| Factory overhead: | | |
| Supervision | $ 65,000 | |
| Indirect factory labour | 185,000 | |
| Power | 55,000 | |
| Heat and light | 20,000 | |
| Depreciation | 60,000 | |
| Other | 75,000 | |
| Total factory overhead | | 460,000 |
| Total manufacturing costs | | 2,205,000 |
| Total cost of goods in process, 1995 | | $2,363,000 |
| Less: Work-in-process inventory, December 31, 1995 | | 163,000 |
| Cost of goods manufactured | | $2,200,000 |

In the statement of earnings (Exhibit 2) the cost of goods sold is calculated in two steps. The first step is to determine the cost of goods available for sale, which is the sum of the finished goods inventory, December 31, 1994, and the cost of goods manufactured in 1995 (as per Exhibit 3). The second step in determining the cost of goods sold is to subtract the finished goods inventory as of December 31, 1995 from the cost of goods available for sale.

Cost of goods sold                                         $2,162,000

Determining the cost of goods manufactured (Exhibit 3) requires a five-step process. First, the raw materials used are found by adding beginning raw materials inventory and raw material purchases during 1995, then subtracting the ending raw materials inventory as of December 31, 1995. For step two, add direct labour, $265,000, representing factory labour that is directly involved in the production of the goods.

Step three adds the last component of the manufacturing process, "factory overhead." Included under this heading are the costs of supervision (the salaries paid to supervisors and plant managers), indirect factory labour (the cost of maintenance and clean-up crews), power (the electricity used to run the machines), heat and light (only costs associated with the factory facility), depreciation (the write-down of the useful life of the plant and equipment used directly in the production process), and other expenses (the cost of supplies for maintenance, incidental materials used in the manufacturing process too minor to be costed as raw materials, insurance on the plant and equipment, and so on). The sum of the factory overhead items included in the statement of cost of goods manufactured is $460,000. This means XYZ Manufacturing Co. Ltd. incurred "total manufacturing costs" in 1995 of $2,363,000. Step four determines the "total cost of goods in process in 1995" by adding to "total manufacturing costs" the beginning work-in-process inventory (as at December 31, 1994). The final step in determining the cost of goods manufactured is to deduct the ending work-in-process inventory (as at December 31, 1995) of $163,000 from the total cost of goods in process, 1995.

Understanding the accounting for costs and the different types of inventory for a manufacturer is complex. It may help to remember that there are three basic costs — raw materials, direct labour, and factory overhead — and three types of inventory — raw materials inventory, work-in-process inventory, and finished goods inventory. A diagram of the flow of costs (Figure 1) may aid your understanding.

### Cost of Goods Sold, Nonmanufacturer or Merchandiser

With merchandising or nonmanufacturing enterprises, such as distributors and retailers, there is no transformation process. The economic function of the merchandiser is to bring the goods to a convenient location for resale. Therefore, the merchandising company's cost of goods sold includes purchase cost and freight-

**FIGURE 1**

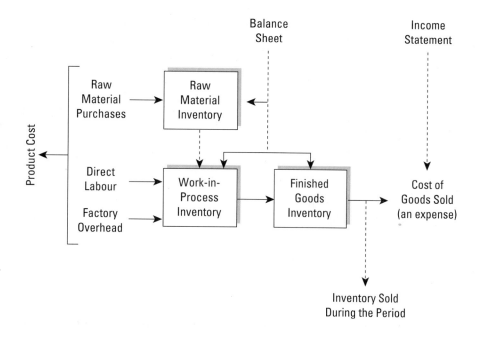

in. Exhibit 4 illustrates the cost of goods sold section for the wholesale subsidiary of XYZ Manufacturing Co. Ltd.

The cost of goods sold section is similar to that reported in Exhibit 2. Note, however, that the number of items listed to get net purchases is far less than required to list the cost of goods manufactured. As a consequence, the normal practice for nonmanufacturing companies is to include the full details within the cost of goods sold of all the activities associated with cost of goods sold. Because the company does not transform or change the goods it sells, there is only one type of inventory: finished goods. The first step is to determine the delivered cost of purchases, which is the purchase cost plus any "freight in." From the delivered cost of purchases, purchase returns and allowances and purchase discounts (reductions for quick payment) are deducted. The sum of "net purchases" and beginning inventory gives "cost of goods available for sale." Finally, "cost of goods sold" is the result of deducting the ending inventory from "cost of goods available for sale." Figure 2 summarizes this process.

*EXHIBIT 4*

### XYZ Wholesale Subsidiary Company Ltd.
### Statement of Cost of Goods Sold
### for the Year ending December 31, 1995

| | | | |
|---|---|---|---|
| Cost of goods sold: | | | |
| Inventory, December 31, 1994 | | | $100,000 |
|     Purchases | | $660,000 | |
|     Freight in | | 24,000 | |
|     Delivered cost of purchases | | $684,000 | |
| | | | |
|     Less: Purchase discounts | $ 6,000 | | |
|         Purchase returns and allowance | 20,000 | 26,000 | |
| Net purchases | | | 658,000 |
| | | | |
| Cost of goods available for sale | | | $758,000 |
|     Less: Inventory, December 31, 1995 | | | 96,000 |
| | | | |
| Cost of goods sold | | | $662,000 |

*FIGURE 2*

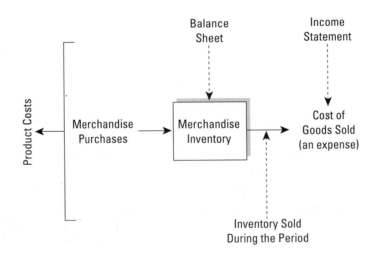

The other subsidiary is a service organization. Because its economic activity is the provision of service, not the manufacture or distribution of goods, it will have no cost of goods sold or gross profit. Instead, after sales or revenues, the direct expenses of generating service revenue, and then selling and administrative expenses, will be deducted to determine operating profit.

## GROSS PROFIT

Gross profit (or gross margin) is determined by subtracting the "cost of goods sold" from "net sales." It represents the markup, or margin, the enterprise charges or earns on its product costs.

| | |
|---|---|
| Gross profit | $738,000 |

## OPERATING EXPENSES

Operating expenses are usually categorized as "general and administrative," or "selling" expenses. The categories are usually listed separately, but this is not always necessary. Executive salaries, office payroll, office expenses, rent, electricity, and the like are the usual items included as general and administrative expenses. Selling expenses include salespeople's salaries and commissions, as well as advertising, promotion, and travel costs.

| | |
|---|---|
| Operating expenses | |
| General and administrative | $145,000 |
| Selling | $225,000 |

## DEPRECIATION EXPENSE

As mentioned earlier, depreciation is the allocation of the cost of an asset over its useful life. The income statement, for a period of time, records all the costs associated with obtaining revenues. Expenditures, such as those made to acquire production equipment or trucks to deliver goods, would, if charged against the revenues generated during the first year of expenditure though the asset had a few more years of use, result in understated profits in the first year and overstated profits in subsequent years. As discussed in the section on accumulated depreciation on the balance sheet, the issue of understating or overstating is handled by spreading the purchase cost of the asset over several statement periods. The income statement records the amount of depreciation expense allocated to the income statement period. (It should be noted that depreciation applied to production-related fixed assets is recorded under manufacturing overhead whereas depreciation on all other fixed assets, such as office furniture, company cars, and so on, is recorded under operating expenses.)

| | |
|---|---|
| Depreciation expense | $ 80,000 |

The operating expenses are totalled and reported.

Operating expenses       $450,000

## OPERATING PROFIT

Operating profit represents the net gain from the enterprise's normal operating activities. It is calculated by subtracting "operating expenses" from "gross profit."

Operating profit       $288,000

## OTHER INCOME AND OTHER EXPENSES

The company may have revenues that are not directly related to its primary business (such as interest earned on investments and sale of land or equipment). To include them under net sales would distort that figure and make comparison of performance over several years unrealistic. Other expenses often include interest the company must pay on money it has borrowed. Other income and other expenses are usually reported after operating profit has been calculated.

Other income       $ 20,000

Other expenses, interest     100,000

## NET PROFIT BEFORE TAX

Net profit before tax represents the company's determination of its income before estimation of its tax liability.

Net profit before tax      $208,000

## ESTIMATED INCOME TAX EXPENSE

Corporations earning profit must pay income tax that is calculated by applying a predetermined tax rate to the net profit before tax. If the net profit before tax is $208,000 and the tax rate is 22 percent, the estimated income tax would be $46,000.

Estimated income tax expense    $ 46,000

## NET EARNINGS

After all revenues have been added and all expenses subtracted, the residual is net earnings. If expenses exceed revenues, the residual is a net loss.

Net earnings       $162,000

## FACTS TO REMEMBER ABOUT THE INCOME STATEMENT

1. The income statement covers a period of time. (The balance sheet shows the financial position of the enterprise at one point in time.)

2. Sales (revenues) made during a period are recorded. This does not necessarily mean that cash was collected.

3. Expenses incurred during the period to make these sales are recorded. This does not necessarily mean that cash was paid out.

4. The formal structure of an income statement is: sales first, then expenses, ending with net earnings (or loss).

5. Above all, remember an income statement matches expenses to revenues, for a specified period of time.

■
**SECTION**
■
**THREE**
■

## THE STATEMENT OF RETAINED EARNINGS

Retained earnings represent the account that forms the connection between the balance sheet and the income statement. The retained earnings are the earnings remaining after dividends on preferred and common stock have been paid; that is, the earnings retained in the company. When an enterprise starts in business, it has no retained earnings. As soon as it has any profits or losses, however, the retained earnings account is affected. (If losses are greater than earnings, the account is listed as "Retained deficit.") For example, assume the following dividends were paid and earnings retained by XYZ Manufacturing Co. Ltd.

| | | |
|---|---:|---:|
| Net earnings for the year 1995 | | $162,000 |
| Less: 1995 dividends paid on preferred shares | $ 7,000 | |
| 1995 dividends paid on common shares | 42,000 | 49,000 |
| 1995 net increase in retained earnings | | $ 113,000 |

The statement of retained earnings for XYZ Manufacturing Co. Ltd. would be as presented in Exhibit 5.

*EXHIBIT 5*

---

### XYZ Manufacturing Co. Ltd.
### Statement of Retained Earnings
### for the Year ended December 31, 1995

| | |
|---|---:|
| Retained earnings: December 31, 1994 | $413,000 |
| Net earnings for the year, 1995 | 162,000 |
| | $575,000 |
| | |
| Less: 1995 dividends paid on | |
| Preferred shares | $ 7,000 |
| Common shares | 42,000 |
| Retained earnings: December 31, 1995 | $526,000 |

---

The statement of retained earnings is straightforward. To the initial opening balance of retained earnings ($413,000 as of December 31, 1994) is added the net earnings for the year as determined from the statement of earnings, $162,000 for 1995. The resulting subtotal is $575,000. From this subtotal the total of dividends paid, $49,000 during 1995, is subtracted, yielding the retained earnings as of December 31, 1995: $526,000.

## THE AUDITOR'S REPORT AND FOOTNOTES

The financial statements of a company are relied upon by management, shareholders, creditors, and potential investors. Shareholders and creditors place more credibility on statements prepared by independent auditors. Also, statutory regulations require an independent auditor for public corporations and for some private companies. Auditors report to the shareholders, not to the management, stating whether, in their opinion, the statements present fairly the financial position of the firm in accordance with generally accepted accounting principles and in a manner consistent with the previous year's report.

Financial reports are condensed and formalized. Footnotes are used where explanation may be necessary, and to provide additional relevant information, such as stock options, details of long-term debt, and the details of unconsolidated subsidiaries. It is essential to read footnotes in addition to the numbers in the balance sheet in order to appreciate fully the implications of the financial statements.

## EXERCISES IN BALANCE SHEET CONSTRUCTION

### Exercise 1
### Paul Webster Retail Florist

| | |
|---|---:|
| Capital, P. Webster | $ 27,900 |
| Accumulated depreciation, store fixtures | 12,000 |
| Accounts payable | 12,300 |
| Goodwill | 6,000 |
| Store fixtures, cost | 22,500 |
| Inventory | 7,500 |
| Bank loan (90-day note) | 6,600 |
| Cash | 11,100 |
| Accrued expenses payable | 900 |
| Accounts receivable | 12,600 |

## Assignment:

Different accounts are listed above, in random order, for the florist business of Paul Webster. The accounts are as at January 31, 1996.

**1.** Determine whether the account is a current asset, fixed asset, intangible asset, current liability, long-term liability, or net worth account.

**2.** Prepare a balance sheet as at January 31, 1996.

### Exercise 2
### Thomas Hardware Store Ltd.

| | |
|---|---:|
| Land | $ 19,500 |
| Prepaid expenses | 12,800 |
| Accrued expenses payable | 10,500 |
| Notes payable, due in 90 days | 34,800 |
| Long-term debt | 54,000 |
| Accumulated depreciation, building and equipment | 57,200 |
| Marketable securities | 18,000 |
| Accounts payable | 73,700 |
| Accounts receivable | 60,000 |
| Common stock (Authorized 2,500 shares; issued 2,052) | 51,300 |
| Organization expenses | 2,500 |
| Building and equipment, cost | 119,000 |
| Retained earnings | 131,500 |
| Taxes payable | 5,200 |
| Cash | 4,400 |
| Inventory | 182,000 |

## Assignment:

Different accounts as at January 31, 1996 are listed above in random order for Thomas Hardware Store Ltd.

**1.** Determine whether each account is a current asset, fixed asset, intangible asset, current liability, long-term liability or an equity item.

**2.** Prepare a formal balance sheet as at January 31, 1996 for Thomas Hardware Store Ltd.

### Exercise 3
### Smith Furniture Manufacturer Inc.

| | |
|---|---|
| Accumulated depreciation, buildings | $ 59,800 |
| Patents | 7,900 |
| Building, cost | 170,100 |
| Accumulated depreciation, equipment | 137,700 |
| Bank loan, short-term | 153,300 |
| Common stock (Authorized and issued 20,000 shares) | 58,500 |
| Equipment, cost | 230,600 |
| Inventory | 299,200 |
| Accrued expenses payable | 16,300 |
| Long-term debt, due within one year | 8,800 |
| Cash | ? |
| Investment in subsidiary* | 52,600 |
| Prepaid expenses | 9,000 |
| Taxes payable | 19,400 |
| Marketable securities | 60,000 |
| Land | 23,100 |
| Mortgage, due in 2008 | 100,500 |
| Goodwill | 16,100 |
| Organization expenses | 3,300 |
| Accounts receivable | 296,300 |
| Preferred stock (Authorized 2,000 shares, $100 par value) | 52,100 |
| Retained earnings | 348,500 |
| Accounts payable | 178,900 |
| Debentures, due 2001 | 44,000 |

*Represents a 50 percent ownership in a major hardwood supplier.

## Assignment:

The above accounts are taken from the records of Smith Furniture Manufacturer Inc. as at December 31, 1995. Prepare a balance sheet for the company and determine the cash position. *Hint: a balance sheet must balance!*

### EXERCISES IN INCOME STATEMENTS

### Exercise 1
### Buckner Department Store Ltd.
### (in 000s of dollars)

| | |
|---|---:|
| Selling expenses | $ 1,104 |
| Net operating profit | 483 |
| Cost of goods sold | 6,670 |
| Other income | 46 |
| Gross margin (profit) | 1,840 |
| Net sales | 8,510 |
| Administrative expenses | 253 |
| Other expenses | 69 |

## Assignment:

Different income statement items for the Buckner Department Store Ltd. are listed above in random order. All refer to the year ending January 31, 1996 and are in thousands of dollars. The tax rate is 45 percent.

**1.** Prepare a formal income statement for the period ending January 31, 1996 for the Buckner Department Store Ltd.

### Exercise 2
### J. Crawford Retail Sales Inc.
### (in 000s of dollars)

| | |
|---|---:|
| Gross profit | $ 543 |
| Net profit before tax | 240 |
| Selling expenses | 160 |
| Ending inventory | 475 |
| Net sales | 2,125 |
| Beginning inventory | 393 |
| General and administrative expenses | 143 |

## Assignment:

Different income statement items of J. Crawford Retail Sales Inc. are listed above in random order for the three-month period ending April 30, 1996. Prepare an income statement for the period ending April 30, 1996 for J. Crawford Retail Sales Inc. Assume the income tax rate is 50 percent. **Note:** to complete this exercise the following items will have to be calculated: (a) cost of goods sold, (b) purchases, and (c) net profit after tax.

### Exercise 3
### Young Textile Mills Inc.
### (in 000s of dollars)

| | |
|---|---:|
| Direct labour | $ 753 |
| Goods in process, December 31, 1995 | 384 |
| Sales discounts | 27 |
| Manufacturing overhead | 579 |
| Other income | 75 |
| Goods in process, December 31, 1994 | 390 |
| Other expense, interest | 84 |
| Raw materials, December 31, 1995 | 489 |
| Administrative expenses | 294 |
| Finished goods, December 31, 1994 | 222 |
| Selling expenses | 147 |
| Sales returns and allowances | 33 |
| Raw materials, December 31, 1994 | 498 |
| Finished goods, December 31, 1995 | 219 |
| Sales | 5,490 |
| General expenses | 255 |
| Indirect labour | 99 |
| Other expense, royalty | 18 |
| Material purchases | 2,958 |

## Assignment:

Income statement items are listed above in random order. All are period accounts for the year ending December 31, 1995, except where noted. Assuming a tax rate of 40 percent, prepare an income statement and statement of cost of goods manufactured for Young Textile Mills Inc. for the year ending December 31, 1995.

*Exercise 4*
*Durham Lumber Ltd.*
*(in 000s of dollars)*

| | |
|---|---:|
| Selling expenses | $ 504 |
| Direct labour | 1,980 |
| Finished goods, December 31, 1994 | 604 |
| Other revenue | 284 |
| Depreciation, manufacturing equipment | 848 |
| Indirect labour | 1,320 |
| Sales returns and allowances | 44 |
| Depreciation, office equipment | 96 |
| Sales discounts | 60 |
| Administrative expenses | 940 |
| Raw materials used | 8,360 |
| Other manufacturing overhead | 324 |
| Net sales | 15,356 |
| Goods in process, December 31, 1994 | 292 |
| Gross profit | 2,520 |
| Estimated income tax expense | 68 |
| Raw materials, December 31, 1995 | 2,160 |
| Cost of goods manufactured | 12,848 |
| General expenses | 628 |
| Net earnings | 116 |
| Other expenses, interest | 452 |
| Raw materials, December 31, 1994 | 2,146 |
| Net operating income | 352 |

## Assignment:

Income statement items for Durham Lumber Ltd. are listed above in random order. All are period accounts for the year ending December 31, 1995, except where noted. Prepare an income statement and statement of cost of goods manufactured for Durham Lumber Ltd. To complete the assignment, sales, material purchases, ending goods in process, and finished goods inventories and cost of goods sold will have to be calculated.

## EXERCISES ON THE RELATIONSHIP OF THE INCOME STATEMENT AND BALANCE SHEET

### Exercise 1
### Bargain Stores Incorporated
### (in 000s of dollars)

| | |
|---|---:|
| Inventory, June 30, 1996 | $ 758 |
| Gross profit | 857 |
| Long-term notes payable | 31 |
| Store fixtures, net | 144 |
| Selling expenses | 341 |
| Accounts payable | 288 |
| Income tax expense | 12 |
| Retained earnings, June 30, 1995 | 540 |
| Cash | 48 |
| General and administrative expenses | 432 |
| Accrued expenses payable | 96 |
| Accounts receivable | 324 |
| Dividends | 12 |
| Notes payable | 252 |
| Inventory, June 30, 1995 | 684 |
| Common stock | 36 |
| Sales | 3,398 |
| Depreciation expense | 36 |
| Income tax payable | 7 |
| Store fixtures, cost | 180 |

## Assignment:

Different balance sheet and income statement accounts are listed above in random order. The balance sheet accounts are as at June 30, 1996, except where noted. The income statement amounts are for the year July 1, 1995 to June 30, 1996, in thousands of dollars.

**1.** Determine whether each account is a balance sheet or income statement item.

**2.** Prepare an income statement for Bargain Stores Incorporated for the year ending June 30, 1996.

**3.** Prepare a statement of retained earnings for the year ended June 30, 1996.

**4.** Prepare a balance sheet as at June 30, 1996 for Bargain Stores Incorporated.

## Exercise 2
## Oliver Wholesalers — Proprietorship
## (in 000s of dollars)

| | |
|---|---:|
| Capital — Oliver, December 31, 1994 | $ 600 |
| Cash | 44 |
| Net sales | 4,326 |
| Accounts receivable | 413 |
| Gross profit | 1,024 |
| Accumulated depreciation, December 31, 1994 | 416 |
| Net earnings | 90 |
| Notes payable — bank | 520 |
| Purchases | 3,502 |
| Long-term bank loan | 26 |
| Prepaid expenses | 29 |
| Depreciation expense | 52 |
| Inventory, December 31, 1994 | 822 |
| Accrued expenses payable | 34 |
| Drawings — Oliver | 56 |
| Selling expenses | 437 |
| Equipment, cost | 520 |
| Inventory, December 31, 1995 | 1,022 |
| Capital — Oliver, December 31, 1995 | 634 |
| Cost of goods sold | 3,302 |
| Accounts payable | 346 |
| General and administrative expenses | 445 |

## Assignment:

Different balance sheet and income statement accounts are listed above in random order, in thousands of dollars. The balance sheet accounts are as at December 31, 1995, except where noted. The income statement amounts are for the year ending December 31, 1995.

**1.** Determine whether each account is a balance sheet or income statement item.

**2.** Prepare an income statement for Oliver Wholesalers — Proprietorship for the year ending December 31, 1995.

**3.** Prepare a statement of retained earnings for the year ended December 31, 1995.

**4.** Prepare a balance sheet as at December 31, 1995 for Oliver Wholesalers — Proprietorship.

### Exercise 3
### Wilson Commercial Printers Limited
### (in 000s of dollars)

| | |
|---|---:|
| Equipment, cost | $ 490 |
| Goodwill | 37 |
| Work-in-process inventory, December 31, 1994 | 53 |
| Accounts receivable, net | 318 |
| Gross profit | 451 |
| Accounts payable | 166 |
| Raw materials used | 611 |
| Accumulated depreciation, building | 98 |
| Net profit before tax | 154 |
| Accumulated depreciation, equipment | 223 |
| Preferred stock | 16 |
| Investment in subsidiary (more than 50 percent ownership) | 154 |
| Estimated income tax expense | 48 |
| Selling expense | 88 |
| Prepayments | 10 |
| Finished goods inventory, December 31, 1994 | 46 |
| Bank loan, due in 90 days | 104 |
| Raw materials inventory, December 31, 1994 | 61 |
| Marketable securities | 38 |
| Long-term debt due within one year | 10 |
| General and administrative expenses (includes depreciation expense) | 239 |
| Land | 12 |
| Material purchases | 625 |
| Taxes payable | 25 |
| Other income | 53 |
| Direct labour | 336 |
| Common stock | 95 |
| Building, cost | 109 |
| Other expenses, interest | 23 |
| Net long-term debt | 226 |
| Cost of goods manufactured | 1,046 |
| Net sales | 1,482 |
| Cash | ? |
| Retained earnings | 328 |
| Accrued expenses payable | 49 |
| Factory overhead (includes depreciation expenses) | 98 |
| Premium on stock | 19 |
| Retained earnings, December 31, 1994 | 222 |

### *Assignment:*

Listed above in random order are balance sheet and income statement accounts as at December 31, 1995, except where otherwise noted, for Wilson Commercial Printers Limited (W.C.P.L.). Prepare an income statement, statement of cost of goods manufactured, and a statement of retained earnings for W.C.P.L. for the year ending December 31, 1995. Also prepare a balance sheet as at December 31, 1995, using cash to balance assets and claims.

### Exercise 4
### Allison Boat Makers Inc.
### (in 000s of dollars)

| | |
|---|---:|
| Long-term bank loan | $    100 |
| Work-in-process inventory, December 31, 1994 | 110 |
| Insurance expense — factory equipment | 22 |
| Net sales | 4,603 |
| Net profit after tax | 278 |
| Factory heat, light, and power | 58 |
| Other expenses, interest | 85 |
| Cost of goods available for sale | 3,420 |
| Accounts receivable | 448 |
| Wages payable | 228 |
| Direct labour | 1,350 |
| Sales returns and discounts | 243 |
| Raw materials inventory, December 31, 1994 | 78 |
| Goodwill | 238 |
| Prepaid expenses | 43 |
| Total manufacturing costs | 3,173 |
| Accumulated depreciation, factory building and equipment, December 31, 1994 | 1,028 |
| Factory supervision | 280 |
| Cost of goods sold | 3,223 |
| Total cost of goods in process, 1995 | 3,283 |
| Organization expenses | 10 |
| Selling expenses | 238 |
| Total current liabilities | 610 |
| Retained earnings, December 31, 1995 | 835 |
| Raw material used | 1,363 |
| Bonds payable, 2001 | 493 |
| Factory building and equipment depreciation expense | 100 |
| Marketable securities | 85 |
| Common stock | 433 |
| General and administrative expenses | 377 |
| Accounts payable | 148 |
| Cost of goods manufactured | 3,193 |
| Taxes payable | 83 |
| Office space rental | 275 |
| Dividends paid on common stock, 1995 | 23 |
| Raw material purchases | 1,355 |
| Factory building and equipment, cost | 2,348 |

| | |
|---|---:|
| Net operating profit | 490 |
| Investment in subsidiary | 388 |
| Other income | 23 |
| Accrued expenses payable | 18 |
| Preferred shares | 358 |
| Estimated income tax | 150 |
| Dividends paid on preferred shares, 1995 | 28 |
| Cash | 40 |
| Bank loan, due March 1996 | ? |

### *Assignment:*

Listed above in random order are balance sheet and income statement accounts for the year ending, or as at December 31, 1995, except where otherwise noted for Allison Boat Makers Inc. (A.B.M.I.). Prepare a statement of cost of goods manufactured, an income statement, and a statement of retained earnings for the year ending December 31, 1995. Also, prepare a balance sheet as of December 31, 1995, using "Bank loan due March 1996" as the balancing figure.

# PART

# AN INTRODUCTION TO
# FINANCIAL MANAGEMENT

The purpose of Part 3 is to introduce the basic techniques used by financial managers and analysts to assess and project the financial performance and position of a business. An understanding of the basic financial statements discussed in Part 2 is essential to an understanding of this part. Several financial analysis tools will be discussed and their application to the financial management cases summarized. Financial analysis and management is not just number pushing; judgment must be exercised in deciding which numbers to look at and how to interpret them. Often, a "qualitative factor," something not expressed in numbers, is more important to the solution of a problem than all the numbers involved.

The topics that will be discussed are:

- Financial goals
- Cash sources and uses statement
- Financial ratio analysis
- Projected financial statements
- Sensitivity analysis
- Forms of ownership
- Bankruptcy
- Credit analysis
- Sources and types of financing

## FINANCIAL GOALS

There are five basic financial goals: profitability, stability, liquidity, efficiency, and growth. To survive, every business must meet each of these goals to some extent, though each must determine for itself the relative emphasis to place on each of the five goals.

*Profitability* refers to the generation of revenues in excess of the expenses associated with obtaining the revenues. This is the "bottom-line" test of how successful a firm's operators have been as shown at the bottom of the income statements.

**EXHIBIT 1**

LMN Retail Co. Ltd.
Income Statement
for the Years Ending January 31
(in 000s of dollars)

|  | 1994 | 1995 | 1996 |
|---|---|---|---|
| Sales | $2,188 | $2,123 | $2,715 |
| Cost of goods sold: | | | |
|     Beginning inventory | $ 380 | $ 383 | $ 388 |
|     Purchases | 1,695 | 1,672 | 2,167 |
|     Cost of goods available for sale | $2,075 | $2,055 | $2,555 |
|     Less: Ending inventory | 383 | 388 | 450 |
|     Cost of goods sold | 1,692 | 1,667 | 2,105 |
| Gross profit | $ 496 | $ 456 | $ 610 |
| Operating expenses: | | | |
|     General and administrative | $ 188 | $ 203 | $ 238 |
|     Selling | 193 | 210 | 282 |
|     Depreciation | 37 | 37 | 35 |
|     Total operating expenses | 418 | 450 | 555 |
| Net operating profit | $ 78 | $ 6 | $ 55 |
| Other expenses — interest | 8 | 6 | 8 |
| Net profit before tax | $ 70 | $ 0 | $ 47 |
| Estimated income tax | 18 | 0 | 12 |
| Net earnings | $ 52 | $ 0 | $ 35 |

**EXHIBIT 2**

LMN Retail Co. Ltd.
Balance Sheet
as at January 31
(in 000s of dollars)

|  | 1994 | 1995 | 1996 |
|---|---|---|---|
| ASSETS | | | |
| Current assets: | | | |
| Cash | $ 5 | $ 12 | $ 15 |
| Net accounts receivable | 200 | 180 | 200 |
| Inventory | 383 | 388 | 450 |
| Total current assets | $588 | $580 | $665 |
| Fixed assets, net | 122 | 85 | 80 |
| TOTAL ASSETS | $710 | $665 | $745 |
| | | | |
| LIABILITIES | | | |
| Current liabilities: | | | |
| Accounts payable | $170 | $160 | $178 |
| Notes payable — bank | 70 | 58 | 108 |
| Taxes payable | 15 | | 12 |
| Accrued expenses | 13 | 30 | 20 |
| Total current liabilities | $268 | $248 | $318 |
| Long-term liabilities | 75 | 50 | 25 |
| | | | |
| Total liabilities | $343 | $298 | $343 |
| | | | |
| EQUITY | | | |
| Common stock | $ 37 | $ 37 | $ 37 |
| Retained earnings | 330 | 330 | 365 |
| Total equity | 367 | 367 | 402 |
| | | | |
| TOTAL LIABILITIES AND EQUITY | $710 | $665 | $745 |

*Stability* refers to a business's overall financial structure. For example, a businessman may wish to invest as little of his own money as possible in his firm and finance his operation mainly through loans. If the debt-equity mix is too far out of balance, the firm could go bankrupt should some of the creditors want their money back at an "inconvenient" time. Many of the spectacular financial disasters reported in the newspapers result from neglecting the goal of stability.

*Liquidity* is a business's ability to meet short-term obligations. For example, a manager may wish to invest as much of her firm's cash in inventory and equipment as possible, but if she does and cannot pay her employees or creditors on time, she can be forced into bankruptcy.

*Efficiency* in business means the efficient use of assets. Efficient use of assets has an impact on profitability, stability, liquidity, and the ability of the enterprise to grow.

*Growth* refers to increasing in size or acquiring more of something. A businesswoman may assess her financial performance by calculating, for example, how much sales or assets have increased this year over last year. While there are many widely held concerns about growth in general (for example, the zero population growth movement) business people and investors remain very interested in financial growth.

There are no clear-cut guidelines on how much or how little financial performance is adequate or on how to trade off performance on one financial goal in favour of another. For example, 10 percent sales growth may be terrible for a firm in one industry but excellent for a firm in another. Similarly, a high level of liquidity may be preferable to growth for a firm at one time and detrimental for the same firm at another.

Financial analysis and projections are used to assess achievement of financial goals. The financial statements of LMN Retail Co. Ltd. will be used to illustrate the development of the cash sources and uses statement and the financial ratios. Exhibit 1 presents the income statements of LMN for 1994, 1995, and 1996; Exhibit 2, the balance sheets as at January 31, 1994, 1995, and 1996.

In addition to discussing the cash sources and uses statement and financial ratio analysis, Part 3 will illustrate an elementary process for developing projected financial statements. It will also examine the forms of business organization, credit evaluation, and sources of short-term and intermediate-term financing for small and medium-sized businesses.

## CASH SOURCES AND USES STATEMENT

**SECTION**

**TWO**

The cash sources and uses statement shows changes between two balance sheets. Over time, as shown in the LMN example, a company will have several balance sheets. There are a number of ways to analyze a set of balance sheets; one is by the cash sources and uses statement. Examine the 1994 and 1995 balance sheets of LMN Retail Company Ltd. The changes in balance sheet accounts, in thousands of dollars, are as follows:

| | |
|---|---|
| Cash, an increase of | $ 7 |
| Net accounts receivable, a decrease of | 20 |
| Inventory, an increase of | 5 |

| | |
|---|---|
| Fixed assets, a decrease of | 37 |
| Accounts payable, a decrease of | 10 |
| Notes payable — bank, a decrease of | 12 |
| Taxes payable, a decrease of | 15 |
| Accrued expenses, an increase of | 17 |
| Long-term liabilities, a decrease of | 25 |
| Common stock, no change | |
| Retained earnings, no change | |

This procedure shows what has happened in each account, but does not give much insight into the way these changes relate to one another to result in a reduction in total assets of $45,000 (or a reduction in total liabilities and equity of $45,000).

Some of these changes represent money coming into the company. For example, the reduction of accounts receivable represents an incremental cash collection of $20,000. In other words, the reduction through collection of accounts receivable is a source of cash to the LMN. Similarly, the reduction of fixed assets, either through sale or depreciation, has an incremental impact on cash (in other words, it is a source of cash).

An increase in a creditor's claim represents the postponement of a cash payment; therefore it is also a source of cash. For example, the $17,000 increase of accrued expenses is a source of cash. Total sources of cash for the year ending January 31, 1995 for the LMN Retail Company Ltd. are:

| Sources | (in 000s of dollars) |
|---|---|
| Net accounts receivable | $20 |
| Fixed assets, net | 37 |
| Accrued expenses | 17 |
| Total sources | $74 |

Inspection of the income statements in Exhibit 1 reveals that in the 1995 fiscal year, LMN charged $37,000 in depreciation expenses. The $37,000 reduction in net fixed assets is caused by this depreciation write off, not by any sale of fixed assets. If LMN were on a cash basis (that is all sales were for cash and all expenses paid as incurred), the impact of the operations in the fiscal year would have been to increase cash $37,000 — the net earnings plus depreciation. The cash was used when the fixed asset was purchased. Depreciation is a noncash allocation of the original expenditure.

Some of the changes represent cash outflows or uses of money. The investment in inventory increased by $5,000. This amount represents a reduction in the cash position of LMN because of the purchase of additional items. Similarly, a reduction in a creditor's claim represents a cash outflow or use of cash. For example, the decrease of accounts payable by $10,000, notes payable — bank by $12,000, taxes payable by $15,000 and long-term liabilities by $25,000 are uses of cash. In summary, for the fiscal year ending January 31, 1995 the uses of cash by LMN Retail Company Ltd. were:

| Uses | (in 000s of dollars) |
|---|---|
| Inventory | $ 5 |
| Accounts payable | 10 |
| Notes payable — bank | 12 |
| Taxes payable | 15 |
| Long-term liabilities | 25 |
| Total sources | $67 |

For the 1995 fiscal year, the sources of cash for the LMN Retail Company Ltd. were $7,000 greater than the uses of cash. In other words, the firm had a net cash inflow of $7,000 as represented by the increase in the cash account. Exhibit 3 presents the cash sources and uses statement of LMN Retail Company Ltd. for the year ending January 31, 1995.

***EXHIBIT 3***

**LMN Retail Co. Ltd.**
**Cash Sources and Uses Statement**
**for the Year Ending January 31, 1995**
**(in 000s of dollars)**

| | |
|---|---|
| Sources of cash: | |
| Net accounts receivable | $20 |
| Fixed assets, net | 37 |
| Accrued expenses | $17 |
| Total sources | $74 |
| Uses of cash: | |
| Inventory | $ 5 |
| Accounts payable | 10 |
| Notes payable — bank | 12 |
| Taxes payable | 15 |
| Long-term liabilities | 25 |
| Total uses | 67 |
| Net cash increase | $ 7 |
| Cash, January 31, 1994 | 5 |
| Cash, January 31, 1995 | $12 |

In summary, sources of cash are decreases in assets, increases in liabilities, and increases in equity. Conversely, uses of cash are increases in assets, decreases in liabilities, and decreases in equity. For the sake of clarification it might be useful to take the viewpoint of an owner of a small enterprise at the cash register. The collection of a sale immediately increases the cash. If customers wish to pay their bills by credit card rather than cash, the impact on the retailer is the foregone cash collection and the increase in accounts receivable. If the retailer subsequently sells the accounts receivable to a bank, the retailer's cash position will increase and accounts receivable will decrease. In contrast, if a supplier on delivery of goods demands immediate payment, the owner must reach into the cash register to make payment. However, if the supplier does not wish payment immediately, the impact is the postponement of a payment and the preservation of, or incremental impact on, cash. Subsequently, when the account payable is paid, there will be a use of cash.

As an analytical tool, cash sources and uses statements can be prepared for any period the analyst desires, providing balance sheets are available. Exhibit 4 presents the cash sources and uses statement for the LMN Retail Company Ltd. for a two-year period ending January 31, 1996.

***Exhibit 4***

### LMN Retail Co. Ltd.
### Cash Sources and Uses Statement
### for Two Years Ending January 31, 1996
### (in 000s of dollars)

| | |
|---|---:|
| Sources of cash: | |
| Fixed assets, net | $ 42 |
| Accounts payable | 8 |
| Notes payable—bank | 38 |
| Accrued expenses | 7 |
| Retained earnings | 35 |
| **Total sources** | $130 |
| Uses of cash: | |
| Inventory | $ 67 |
| Taxes payable | 3 |
| Long-term liabilities | 50 |
| **Total uses** | 120 |
| Net cash increase | $ 10 |
| Cash, January 31, 1994 | 5 |
| Cash, January 31, 1996 | $ 15 |

In analyzing the statements, *first* identify the major changes (Exhibit 4), which are as follows:

| Sources | (in 000s of dollars) |
|---|---|
| Bank loan increase | $38 |
| Fixed assets decrease | 42 |
| Retained earnings (profits) | 35 |
| Uses | |
| Inventory increase | $67 |
| Payment of long-term debt | 50 |

The analyst cannot tell whether the profits were used to increase inventory or whether the bank loan was used to pay off the long-term debt. Instead, a general flow of cash can be observed. Also, without more information, the decrease in fixed assets can be a result either of depreciation or the sale of fixed assets. On this point, the income statement records that the total depreciation expense for 1995 and 1996 was $72,000 ($37,000 + $35,000). If the only change in fixed assets had been an increase is accumulated depreciation on the balance sheet, the decrease in fixed assets would have been $72,000 not $42,000. It appears LMN bought $30,000 worth of fixed assets. In other words, reported changes in financial position would be more accurate if a $72,000 source (increase in accumulated depreciation) and a $30,000 use (increase in cost of fixed assets) were shown. Such as:

Source of cash:

   Depreciation                                $72

Uses of cash:

   Fixed assets                                $30

The second step in analysis is to interpret the desirability of these major changes. Essentially, LMN management has used cash generated from operations (profits and depreciation) to (a) invest in inventory, (b) buy more fixed assets, and (c) pay off some of the company's long-term debt. Because cash from operations was not sufficient for this purpose, LMN management has, in effect, substituted short-term debt (bank loan) for long-term debt (the $50,000 paid off). Were all of these moves appropriate? It depends. For example, it appears that LMN's sales are now beginning to grow (see Exhibit 1). It is possible that the inventory increase was made in anticipation of growth; alternatively, it could be that it made the growth feasible by having a larger variety or quantity of goods available for sale. The relative amount of inventory will be examined in the next section of this chapter to see whether LMN management increased by too much. Because the terms of the long-term debt are not known, it is impossible to comment on the appropriateness of retiring some of the debt. Ordinarily, more information would be available to make better judgments about the desirability of changes. Sound financial practice requires the financing of current assets with combinations of short- and long-term sources, and of long-term assets with long-term financing sources.

The cash source and uses statement is a valuable tool, but clearly it has limitations. For example, the analyst is not able to determine in the LMN example whether the increase in inventory was excessive or not relative to the increase in sales for LMN. Ratio analysis is required to complement the statement of changes in financial position.

**SECTION**

**THREE**

## FINANCIAL RATIO ANALYSIS

As changes occur in the size of a company's various accounts, it is difficult to analyze what is happening by casual inspection of income statements and balance sheets. If only one or two accounts changed, it would be a relatively straightforward task to identify and interpret such developments. However, most of the accounts usually fluctuate. This makes the reasons for the fluctuations hard to determine.

An approach developed to assist in identifying and interpreting changes in financial performance and condition is called ratio analysis. A ratio is simply a fraction: it has two parts, a numerator (the top) and a denominator (the bottom). Using the LMN example, endless possible ratios could be calculated by taking various numbers on the income statements and balance sheets and deriving fractions. Most of the calculations would be meaningless. Financial analysts have agreed, however, upon a common set of 15 to 20 ratios that are useful in assessing financial performance and financial position. Exhibit 5 presents several ratios for the LMN Retail Company Ltd.

Some observations of Exhibit 5 follow:

1. The ratios are grouped into five categories; the headings refer to the five financial goals. In other words, the ratios help analyze the company's progress toward each of these financial objectives.

2. The ratios do not look like fractions! Each fraction has been simplified as much as possible.

3. Some ratios are percentages; others are in days; others are in the form of proportions, and so on. The differences are the result of the varying combinations of numbers used in the fractions.

4. Each ratio has been calculated over three years so that ratios can be compared over time and to identify changes in them. A single ratio does not provide much insight as to the direction in which a firm is heading.

*EXHIBIT 5*

## LMN Retail Co. Ltd.
## Ratio Analysis
### for the Years Ending January 31

|  | 1994 % | 1995 % | 1996 % |
|---|---|---|---|
| Profitability: | | | |
| (i) Vertical analysis[1] | | | |
| Sales | 100.0 | 100.0 | 100.0 |
| Cost of goods sold | 77.3 | 78.5 | 77.5 |
| Gross profit | 22.7 | 21.5 | 22.5 |
| Operating expenses: | | | |
| General and administrative | 8.6 | 9.6 | 8.8 |
| Selling | 8.8 | 9.9 | 10.4 |
| Depreciation | 1.7 | 1.8 | 1.3 |
| Subtotal | 19.1 | 21.3 | 20.5 |
| Net operating income | 3.6 | 0.2 | 2.0 |
| Other expenses — interest | 0.4 | 0.3 | 0.3 |
| Net profit before tax | 3.2 | 0.0 | 1.7 |
| Estimated income tax | 0.8 | 0.0 | 0.5 |
| Net profits | 2.4 | 0.0 | 1.3 |
| (ii) Return on investment[2] | 15.2 | 0.0 | 9.1 |
| | | | |
| Stability: | | | |
| Net worth to total assets | 51.7 | 55.2 | 54.0 |
| Interest coverage (times) | 9.8x | 1.0x | 6.9x |
| | | | |
| Liquidity: | | | |
| Current ratio | 2.2/1 | 2.3/1 | 2.1/1 |
| Acid test | 0.8/1 | 0.8/1 | 0.7/1 |
| Working capital ($000s) | 320 | 332 | 347 |
| | | | |
| Efficiency: | | | |
| Age of receivables[3] | 33.4 days | 30.9 days | 26.9 days |
| Inventory in days cost of goods sold[3] | 82.6 days | 85.0 days | 78.0 days |
| Age of payables in days purchases[3] | 36.6 days | 34.9 days | 30.0 days |
| Fixed assets/sales (%) | 5.6 | 4.0 | 2.9 |
| | | | |
| Growth: (%)[4] | | | |
| Sales | | (3.0) | 27.9 |
| Net earnings | | (100.0) | — |
| Assets | | (6.3) | 12.0 |
| Equity | | 0.0 | 9.5 |

1. Detail may not add to totals because of rounding.
2. Assumes 1993 retained earnings is 1994 retained earnings less 1994 net earnings, i.e., $330,000 – $52,000 = $278,000.
3. A 365-day year is used.
4. Brackets indicate negative amounts.

## INTERPRETATION OF RATIOS

How to interpret ratios will be discussed before we outline their calculation. As an example, the net profit/sales ratio is made up of two numbers from the income statement, net profit after tax, and net sales. The objective is to gain an indication of the change in profit relative to the change in sales. From LMN's income statements (Exhibit 1) net profit after tax declined from $52,000 to $0 and then rose to $35,000. Also, because sales declined from 1994 to 1995, some decrease in profits could be expected. Did profits decline more or less than sales? That is a hard question to answer without preparing the net profit/sales ratio. If both profits and sales had declined together to the same extent, the relationship between them would have remained the same; that is, the ratio of net profit to sales would be constant. From the ratios in Exhibit 5, the analyst can see that the relationship has changed: in 1994 profits were 2.4 percent of sales; in 1995 they are 0 percent of sales. In short, profits declined more than sales. From 1995 to 1996 sales increased as did the ratio of net profit to sales. Seemingly, this increase in the profitability ratio is good. This conclusion might be premature, however. For one thing, other firms in LMN's industry might have performed better. It would be useful to look at a set of industry ratios to check this possibility. For another, maybe LMN was intentionally trading off profitability for some other financial goal, such as growth, in which case the return to profitability at a level below 1994 might be an expected consequence. To verify whether the latter is the case, other ratios must be inspected and the goals of management must be investigated.

Ratios are indicators of change. They simplify relationships between numbers but net profit/sales has shown us that LMN's profitability on one dimension has declined. The ratio does not tell us whether that was good or bad or even why the decline occurred. Clearly, a ratio changes if the numerator changes, the denominator changes, or both change. In order to understand the trend of net profit/sales from 2.4 percent to 0 percent to 1.3 percent, the cause of that change must be found. Why did profits change? Why did sales change? In short, a close look at the components of the ratio is required.

## CALCULATION OF RATIOS

It is suggested that in the following examples the student insert the data from the financial statements (Exhibits 1 and 2) of LMN Retail Company Ltd. to verify the calculations in Exhibit 5.

### Profitability

Vertical analysis is the restatement of the income statement in percentages, using net sales for the year as the base, that is, 100 percent. The term *vertical* arises from the fact that percentages are calculated on a vertical axis within one year, in contrast to growth ratios, such as sales growth, which make a horizontal comparison across several years of statements. The purpose of the analysis is to eliminate the impact of absolute dollar sales on expense amounts.

For example:

$$\text{Cost of goods sold to sales} = \frac{\$ \text{ Cost of goods sold}}{\$ \text{ Net sales}} \times 100 = ?\%$$

This ratio indicates the amount spent to provide the products sold; its complement is as follows:

$$\text{Gross profit to sales} = \frac{\$ \text{ Gross profit}}{\$ \text{ Net sales}} \times 100 = ?\%$$

This ratio measures the percentage of each sales dollar left to pay operating expenses and contribute to profits after paying for cost of goods sold. An increasing gross profit to sales ratio trend may be the result of a reduction in cost of goods sold (better cost control in a manufacturing firm, more astute buying in a retailing firm, etc.) or the result of an increase in selling prices or both. The opposite is true of a declining trend in gross profit to sales. Because cost of goods sold is usually the major expense associated with obtaining sales revenue, financial managers pay close attention to changes in this ratio. For manufacturing concerns, percentages should be calculated for each component of the cost of goods sold.

The next area of study is the level of operating expenses:

$$\text{Operating expenses to sales} = \frac{\$ \text{ Operating expenses}}{\$ \text{ Net sales}} \times 100 = ?\%$$

and the residual after deducting operating expenses from gross profit is

$$\text{Net operating income} = \frac{\$ \text{ Net operating income}}{\$ \text{ Net sales}} \times 100 = ?\%$$

The net operating income ratio indicates what percentage of each sales dollar is left after operating expenses are met. For LMN Retail Company Ltd., despite the increase in net operating profit in dollars from 1995 to 1996, the net operating profit percentage is down from 1994. On review of the operating expense ratios and cost of goods ratio, the factor creating the downward trend is operating expense. Despite the decrease in operating expense ratios between 1995 and 1996, the analyst may wish to investigate the substantial increase in selling expense ratios. A possible explanation may be that LMN management, after suffering a decline in sales in 1995, decided to expand sales volume through increased promotion expenses. Other explanations are feasible. The analyst uses the ratios to decipher management's intent and measure their capabilities.

$$\text{Return on investment} = \frac{\text{\$ Net profit, usually after tax, before dividends}}{\text{\$ Average year's equity}} \times 100 = ?\%$$

$$\text{Average year's equity} = \frac{\text{Last year's ending equity} + \text{This year's ending equity}}{2}$$

Because there are several ways to calculate return on investment (ROI), care should be exercised in using this ratio. There are other methods of calculating these components that are equally good. It is important to use one consistently and to identify the method used. The previous year's equity is found in the previous year's balance sheet.

ROI is a way of measuring how much money was made from operations relative to the shareholders' investment. (A company's equity section includes the original investment of the shareholders plus the profits retained in the company.) For the LMN shareholders, ROI has been declining from 15.2 percent in 1994 to 9.1 percent in 1996.

To assess ROI, look both at the trend (it is downward for LMN) and at alternative investment returns shareholders might make. For example, if a shareholder is comparing LMN to government bonds, he would have to assess the relative returns (returns have been higher for LMN) with the relative risks (risk is much lower with government bonds). If the ROI is the same or less for LMN stock versus government bonds over time, prudent shareholders will invest in the lower-risk bonds.

## Stability Ratios

$$\text{Net worth to total assets} = \frac{\text{\$ Total net worth (i.e., equity)}}{\text{\$ Total assets}} \times 100 = ?\%$$

$$\text{Debt to total assets} = \frac{\text{\$ Total liabilities}}{\text{\$ Total assets}} \times 100 = ?\%$$

$$\text{Net worth to total assets (\%)} + \text{Debt to total assets (\%)} = 100\%$$

The net worth to total assets ratio, expressed as a percentage, indicates the amount of assets that were financed by the owners either through capital stock or reinvested profits (retained earnings). In general, the higher the ratio, the more interested prospective lenders will be in advancing funds. If the ratio is too low, the owners' investment may be so low that irresponsibility results. Also, creditors, in such cases, may have inadequate protection. There are no general rules for evaluating the size of this ratio: look for trends and seek comparative industry data to assess its appropriateness. An unfavourable trend may forebode difficulty in raising additional money, should it be required.

The debt to total assets ratio is another way of expressing the same thing. Because total liabilities plus equity equal total assets, the net worth and debt ratios equal 100 percent. For example, in 1994, LMN's net worth to total assets ratios was 51.7 percent; its debt ratio was 48.3 percent.

$$\text{Interest coverage} = \frac{\text{Period net profit before interest and taxes}}{\text{Interest expense}} = ? \text{ times}$$

The interest coverage calculation indicates how many times the company's profit could pay the interest on the debt it owes. A high coverage ratio indicates minimal risk for lenders, and potential for increasing present loans. Before-tax profit is used because income taxes are calculated after deducting interest expenses. Thus, the ability to pay interest expenses is not affected by income taxes. If a company cannot cover the interest payments from its profit, it will have to delve into its cash and other assets. Failure to meet debt obligations can cause bankruptcy. An unfavourable trend or comparison with the industry average may also give the company a poor credit rating, impairing its ability to obtain additional debt. By taking into account any fixed charges or obligations the company may incur, this ratio can be made more inclusive and therefore more indicative of potential problems in meeting long-term obligations.

### Liquidity Ratios

Liquidity is the capability of a company to meet its short-term obligations. There are a number of ways to assess liquidity for a company. Ratio analysis is used to indicate whether liquidity problems appear to exist and whether more complex analysis is warranted.

$$\text{Current ratio} = \frac{\text{Total current assets}}{\text{Total current liabilities}} = ?/1$$

The current ratio is a measure of a company's short-term liquidity. It reflects the relative balance between short-term assets and short-term liabilities. In the LMN example the 1994 current ratio is 2.2/1 (also expressed as 2.2:1), which can be interpreted as $2.20 in current assets for every $1 in current liabilities. The rationale for using this ratio is that a company must meet its short-term obligations with short-term assets. As long as the company has more current assets than current liabilities, there is a margin of safety, which is necessary in case the company must pay off some of its current liabilities. Every industry has found a different level of current ratio to be appropriate. There are no firm guidelines as to the "right" current ratio for a company.

The current ratio can be too high as well as too low. If too much money is kept in cash or marketable securities, for example, that money may not be being put to work as effectively as it could be. Enterprises usually earn more from investment in improvements than the interest earned from marketable securities.

$$\text{Acid test ratio} = \frac{\text{Cash + Marketable securities + Accounts receivable}}{\text{Current liabilities}} = ?/1$$

The acid test ratio (ATR) is a tougher test of liquidity than the current ratio. Usually, the main difference between the two calculations is the amount of money invested in inventory. Because inventory is often the least liquid current asset (the most difficult to convert into cash in a hurry), its inclusion in a liquidity ratio may overstate a company's immediate liquidity. There is no standard to help decide what is an appropriate ATR.

$$\text{Working capital} = \text{Current assets} - \text{Current liabilities} = \$?$$

Working capital, which is expressed in dollars (not as a percentage), is another way to assess liquidity. The rationale is that after the enterprise has enough current assets available to cover its current liabilities, the money left over — working capital — is available to "work with." With this ratio too, there are no standards, but most managers appear to think that "more is better."

### Efficiency Ratios

Efficiency ratios adjust asset investments for volume levels. For current assets, "interval" ratios are used, and for fixed assets, a percentage based on sales is used. There are three common "interval" ratios: the age of receivables, inventory in day's cost of goods sold, and the age of payables. The intent in each case is to relate the position of the asset with the undertaking of an operating activity. Accounts receivable are generated by credit sales. Inventories are future expected sales at cost, and therefore are related to cost of goods sold. Accounts payable are credit purchases.[1]

$$\text{Age of accounts receivable} = \frac{\$ \text{ Accounts receivable}}{\$ \text{ Average daily sales}} = ? \text{ days}$$

where

$$\text{Average daily sales} = \frac{\text{Total period sales}}{\text{Number of days in period}} = \$ ?/\text{day}$$

The average daily sales term in the denominator of the age of accounts receivable is the total sales for the period, divided by the number of days in the period. For example, the average daily sales for LMN Retail Company Ltd. in 1995 would be calculated as follows:

$$\frac{\$ 2,123,000}{365} = \$ 5,816/\text{day}$$

Age of accounts receivable, expressed in days, shows the average number of days' sales that remain uncollected. In other words, on January 31, 1994 LMN had 33.4 average days' worth of sales for which money had not been received. In 1995 and 1996 sales and receivables changed for LMN. Management was able to reduce the amount of money invested in receivables, relative to sales level, from about 33 days to 31 days to 27 days. An inspection of the balance sheet (Exhibit 2) may not have yielded the extent of this improvement in the receivables position.

Another way to think of the age of receivables is in terms of the length of time a company must wait, on average, after making a credit sale, to collect its money. If the LMN Retail Company Ltd. had credit terms of "due in 10 days," an age of receivables of 30 days indicates poor credit management. The opposite would be true if its terms were "due in 60 days." The longer the age of receivables, the more money it takes to operate the firm because the company's customers have use of the company's money between the time goods are delivered and the time they are paid for. On the other hand, credit terms and procedures that are too stringent may drive customers away.

$$\text{Inventory in days' cost of goods sold} = \frac{\$ \text{ Ending inventory}}{\text{Average daily cost of goods sold}} = \text{? days}$$

where

$$\$ \text{ Average daily cost of goods sold} = \frac{\text{Period cost of goods sold}}{\text{Number of days in period}} = \$ \text{ ?/day}$$

Normally, management plans its inventory to meet sales expectations. The analyst does not have the management's expectation. Consequently, the most recent cost of goods sold is substituted for the sales estimate. Because inventory is valued at cost, cost of goods sold (or number of units sold times unit cost) is used for the calculation, not sales (i.e., number of units sold times selling price).

The inventory interval measure, expressed in days, indicates how fast merchandise moves through the business — from the date received to the date sold. For example, even though LMN substantially increased its investment in inventory between 1995 and 1996, the flow of inventory to sales improved.

A trend of longer interval measures may indicate that the company is carrying excessive inventory for its sales level or that its inventory is becoming obsolete. Higher inventory levels represent larger amounts of money a company has tied up. Reducing inventory will not only release money that may be used more productively elsewhere; usually it will also cut down on storage costs, obsolescence, and so on. However, firms can lose business by not having inventory (known as "stock-outs") when the customer requests goods. Most companies try to balance the costs of running out of inventory and the costs of keeping large stock levels.

Another ratio for examining inventory is "inventory turnover." This ratio measures the number of times inventory turned over, that is, was sold. Inventory turnover is calculated by dividing cost of goods sold by the ending inventory:

$$\text{Inventory turnover} = \frac{\$ \text{ Cost of goods sold}}{\text{Ending inventory}} = \text{? times}$$

The results for LMN Retail Company Ltd. by year are: 4.4 times in 1994, 4.3 times in 1995, and 4.7 times in 1996. The faster goods move through the business, the higher the turnover ratio will be.

$$\text{Age of accounts payable} = \frac{\text{\$ Accounts payable}}{\text{\$ Average daily purchases}} = \text{? days}$$

where

$$\text{\$ Average daily purchases} = \frac{\text{Total period purchases}}{\text{Number of days in period}} = \text{\$ ?/day}$$

Age of payables, expressed in days, shows how long the company takes to pay for what it buys on credit. Compared with industry figures and the terms of credit offered by the company's suppliers, this ratio indicates whether the company is depending too much on its trade credit. If the age of payables is excessive, creditors may demand repayment immediately, causing cash problems for the company, or they may stop supplying the company until it pays for its previous purchases. Even though stretching the age of payables generates funds for a firm, a bad credit reputation may develop and cost the company dearly in the long-term. In contrast, if the age of payables is very low in comparison with industry practice, it may indicate the company is forgoing a potential source of cash.

Good management of payables can save a company money. Many suppliers offer terms such as "1/10, net 30," which means a 1 percent discount if the invoice is paid within 10 days, and the total bill must be paid within 30 days. The savings made possible by paying 1 percent less within ten days works out to an annual interest rate of about 18 percent. Because bank loan rates are usually less than 18 percent, borrowing to take advantage of such discounts can increase profits.

$$\text{Fixed assets as a percent of sales} = \frac{\text{Fixed assets, net}}{\text{sales}} = \text{?\% or \$ per sales dollar}$$

The above ratio represents the investment in fixed assets per dollar of sale. LMN Retail has made increasingly efficient use of fixed assets given the decline in the ratio from 0.056 in 1994 and to 0.029 in 1996.

### Growth Ratios

Growth ratios are easy to calculate and can be done for any financial item. Usually, four growth rates are calculated before any more intensive growth analysis is made. Growth can be calculated over any period of time, one week or one decade. The Exhibit 5 ratios for LMN are for one-year periods. Growth is expressed as a percentage change from one point in time to another, with the first point in time as a base.

$$\text{Sales growth} = \frac{\text{Year 2 sales} - \text{Year 1 sales}}{\text{Year 1 sales}} \times 100 = \text{?\%}$$

$$\text{Profit growth} = \frac{\text{Year 2 profits} - \text{Year 1 profits}}{\text{Year 1 profits}} \times 100 = ?\%$$

Profit growth may be calculated before or after tax. In either case the approach used should be acknowledged.

$$\text{Asset growth} = \frac{\text{Year 2 total assets} - \text{Year 1 total assets}}{\text{Year 1 total assets}} \times 100 = ?\%$$

$$\text{Equity growth} = \frac{\text{Year 2 equity} - \text{Year 1 equity}}{\text{Year 1 equity}} \times 100 = ?\%$$

In calculating growth ratios, special care has to be taken in two instances. In the first, the year 1 position is zero thereby generating a growth ratio of infinity. The other occurs when one or both of the years have negative figures. The best practice is to treat such situations as undefined and not to report any number. For example, a review of the profit growth ratio from Exhibit 5 for 1996 shows that net earnings grew from zero in 1995, to $35,000 in 1996. The profit growth ratio calculation would require the analyst to divide by zero yielding a meaningless number.

### Other Ratios

Many other ratios are useful in certain circumstances. Three ratios often used by investors to assess investment performance are:

$$\text{Dividend yield} = \frac{\text{Annual dividend per share}}{\text{Current market price per share}} \times 100$$

$$\text{Price earning ratio} = \frac{\text{Current market price per common share}}{\text{Earnings per common share}}$$

$$\text{Earnings per common share} = \frac{\text{Net profit after tax less preferred dividends}}{\text{Number of issued common shares}}$$

## PROJECTED FINANCIAL STATEMENTS

**SECTION**

**FOUR**

Every financial statement reviewed so far reflects past performance or position but, in order to plan future operations, anticipation of future performance or position is required. Statements prepared in anticipation of the future are called *projected* or *pro forma* statements. There are three basic reasons for preparing projected statements:

1. To forecast financial performance or position (e.g., what will profit likely be next year?);

2. To examine the interrelationship of financial policies with changes in marketing and production policies (e.g., if sales double, how much more money will be required in inventory investment?); and

3. To forecast cash needs, debt needs, capacity to expand operations, and others (e.g., how big will the bank loan have to be six months from now?).

Projections can be made if enough information is available to prepare meaningful estimates of future performance and position. *However, a projected statement is only as good as the estimates, assumptions, and judgments that went into its preparation.* Three basic types of information can be used to prepare projected statements:

1. Managers' estimates (e.g., a sales forecast);

2. Past financial relationships (e.g., financial ratios of previous years); and

3. Assumptions as to what might occur.

It is important to explain the source of every number on a projected statement, usually with footnotes that outline the basis of the calculations. For example, a footnote for an inventory estimate may be as follows:

> Inventory calculated on the basis of 35 days average daily cost of goods sold. The age of inventory during the previous 5 years ranged between 30 and 40 days.

There are two basic types of projected statements. One is a projection based on the assumption that management will continue to follow past financial policies. The objective of this approach is to show what would happen if this were so. Proponents of change in financial policy often use this technique to show impending disaster unless changes are made. The other type of projection is based on a suggested set of changes. The objective of this approach is to show the impact on likely future performance and position if these changes were followed. These two approaches are often mixed in practice.

### NEED FOR A BALANCING FIGURE

For both the projected balance sheet and the projected income statement, a balancing figure is needed. Seldom can each account on each statement be projected in such a way as to make the statement "work out." For example, it is common when projecting a balance sheet to leave either "cash" or "bank loan payable" to the end and then insert a number that makes the balance sheet balance. For the income statement, the account often used to offset other estimates is "purchases" in the cost of goods sold section. No two projected statements are likely to be identical: individuals tend to use different assumptions about the future and, consequently, to have different balancing figures.

## PROJECTED INCOME STATEMENT

Always begin a set of projected statements with the income statement, followed by the balance sheet and, finally, if desired, the cash sources and uses statement. Inventory, receivables, and payables are based on the income statement. Also, it is pointless to estimate the change in retained earnings on the balance sheet before attempting to project net profit on the income statement.

The following procedure should be used:

1. Estimating a new sales volume is the first and most important step. Use managers' estimates and/or past growth trends as guidelines.

2. Use the profitability ratio analysis to estimate cost of goods sold, gross profit, and operating expenses. Modify these for new information or for a developing trend.

3. Choose the extent of detail in the operating expenses section according to the quality of the information available and the objectives in preparing the projected income statement.

4. Prepare more than one projected income statement whenever appropriate. For example, if sales volume estimates vary significantly, statements based on a high, reasonable, or low projected sales volume may prove useful.

Perhaps it would be useful to develop a projected income statement. Exhibit 6 outlines a projected income statement for 1997 for LMN Retail Company Ltd. Included in the exhibit is the basis of the estimate. Please note that the first step is estimating sales. The general manager of LMN Retail Company Ltd., given his promotion plans, the economic potential in his region, and inflation rates, expected a 20 percent growth rate in sales from 1996. In reviewing the cost of goods sold from his ratio analysis, the general manager believed that he could maintain the 1996 performance; that is, cost of goods sold would be 77.5 percent of sales. The complement, gross profit, would be 22.5 percent of sales. In reviewing his control of expenditures in the past year, the general manager felt that he could maintain general and administrative expenses at 8.7 percent of sales, and he intended to spend a fraction less on promotion, making a total of 10 percent of sales on selling expenses. Because the equipment and store fixtures would be maintained at the same level, the general manager expected no change in the depreciation charges in 1997. With regard to other expenses, such as interest, he was uncertain about how much to set aside, but decided to allow 0.3 percent of sales, which was in line with past trends. The taxes were given to him by his accountant.

The determination of the income statement, after the assumptions have been made, is nothing more than an exercise in arithmetic. The key judgment is whether the analyst agrees with the assumptions and their implications. Students should review the assumptions outlined in Exhibit 6 with the financial ratios to be found in Exhibit 5 and reach their own conclusions as to the reasonableness of the projected income statement.

**EXHIBIT 6**

### LMN Retail Co. Ltd.
### Projected Income Statement
### for the Year Ending January 31, 1997
### (in 000s of dollars)

| Item | Basis of Estimate | Amount |
|------|-------------------|--------|
| Sales | 20% growth from 1996[1] | $3,258 |
| Cost of goods sold | 77.5% of sales[2] | 2,525 |
| | | |
| Gross profit | 22.5% of sales | $ 733 |
| | | |
| Operating expenses | | |
| General and administrative | 8.7% of sales[1] | $ 283 |
| Selling | 10% of sales[1] | 326 |
| Depreciation | same as 1996[1] | 35 |
| | | |
| Subtotal | | 644 |
| | | |
| Net operating income | | $ 89 |
| Other expenses | 0.3% of sales[1] | 10 |
| | | |
| Net profit, before tax | | $ 79 |
| Taxes | 25% of net profit before tax[3] | 20 |
| | | |
| Net earnings | | $ 59 |

1. Manager's estimate.
2. Last year's best estimate.
3. Supplied by accountant.

## PROJECTED BALANCE SHEET

Preparing a projected balance sheet is usually more difficult than preparing a projected income statement. The main reason for this is that there is no one key account — such as sales on the income statement — that helps determine many others on the balance sheet. Generally, each balance sheet account must be calculated separately. Here are a few guidelines:

1. Begin by deciding what the balancing account will be (usually cash or bank loan payable).
2. Fill in all the accounts that will probably remain the same (e.g., land will be the same if none is to be bought or sold).
3. Fill in the accounts already calculated. For example, retained earnings will change in accordance with the estimated profit (from the projected income statement) and in accordance with any plans for dividend payments.
4. Estimate the other accounts. Usually, a good way to begin is by using averages or trends of previous years' ratios and then adjusting these as needed. For example, suppose the estimated sales for next year were $3,258 and, based on previous patterns, the age of accounts receivable was expected to be 30 days. All but one component of the formula used to calculate age of accounts receivable, $ accounts receivable total, is known. Solve the formula to get an estimate of this missing number.

$$\text{Age of accounts receivable} = \frac{\text{Accounts receivable}}{\dfrac{\text{Sales}}{365}}$$

$$\text{Therefore, 30 days} = \frac{\text{Accounts receivable}}{\dfrac{\$3,258}{365 \text{ days}}}$$

$$\text{Accounts receivable} = 30 \text{ days} \times \$8.926/\text{day}$$
$$= \$268$$

Therefore, estimated accounts receivable is $268,000. A similar process using the appropriate formula and estimates can be used to estimate ending inventory and accounts payable.

5. After filling in all but the balancing figure, calculate it.

Exhibit 7 presents a projected balance sheet as of January 31, 1997, based on stated assumptions, for LMN Retail Company Ltd. In this projection, the general manager decided to maintain a minimum cash balance of $ 15,000 and to use the bank loan as the plug or balancing figure. The manager reviewed the ratio analysis and determined the assumptions as set out. With regard to fixed assets, the general manager planned to invest $35,000 in new equipment during the year, thereby incurring no net change in the fixed asset account. Initially, the manager planned to pay off the long-term debt. Again, note the key role that judgment plays in the development of an appropriate assumption. The determination of the amounts for the accompanying balance sheet accounts is a matter of arithmetic calculation. The student should verify the calculation, noting that the calculations have been rounded to the closest $1,000. In determining what the bank loan, that is, the plug figure, should be, the student should use the balance sheet equation that assets must equal the sum of liabilities and equity. In the initial extensions, the assets total $916,000, and equity totals $461,000. This means that total liabilities must equal $455,000. There are no long-term liabilities to be deducted, meaning total current liabilities equals $455,000. From this total of $455,000, the $248,000 in current liabilities, which include accounts payable, taxes payable, and accrued expenses, must be deducted. This means that the only other current liability available, notes payable — bank, must provide the residual amount of $207,000 in order for the balance sheet to balance.

In this case the interpretation of the balancing figure was fairly straightforward. However, if you assume that the cash was used as the balancing figure and the bank loan was set at $80,000, what would the resulting balance showing in the cash account be? You would first determine the liabilities, the sum of current liabilities accounts payable, $216,000; bank loan, $80,000; taxes payable, $12,000; and accrued expenses, $20,000; yielding total current liabilities of $328,000. To this total of $328,000, add long-term liabilities of zero and the total equity of $461,000 giving a total of $789,000. This, then, would be the total for total assets from which would be subtracted net fixed assets of $80,000 to get total current assets of $709,000. However, the current asset section would already include assets worth $821,000, the sum of net accounts receivable and inventory. To balance, cash would have to equal *negative* $112,000. Negative cash is a bank overdraft, so an additional loan of $112,000 must be added to the $80,000 already provided for.

In another illustration, you may find that if you use a bank loan as a plug, it may be negative; say "negative $30,000." How do you interpret this? This is similar to saying that instead of the enterprise owing the bank $30,000, the bank owes the company $30,000; in other words, the company has a deposit of $30,000.

## Projected Cash Sources and Uses Statement

This statement is rarely prepared. After preparing a projected income statement and balance sheet, most analysts do not find much cause to do a projected cash sources and uses statement. It is easy to construct, however, after one or more projected balance sheets have been completed. Follow the same procedures that are outlined for historical cash sources and uses statements.

## Comments on Projected Statements

In the preceding example, the general manager should review the projected statements in terms of whether they make sense and what conclusions can be made. One obvious observation: if he is successful in gaining the $207,000 loan, the provision he has made in his projected income statement for interest of $10,000 will be insufficient. A second concern would be that his plans call for a

*Exhibit 7*

LMN Retail Co. Ltd.
Projected Balance Sheet
as of January 31, 1997
(in 000s of dollars)

| Item | Basis of Estimate | Amount |
|---|---|---|
| **ASSETS** | | |
| Current assets: | | |
| Cash | Minimum equal to 1996 level[1] | $ 15 |
| Net accounts receivable | 30 days sales[2] | 268 |
| Inventory | 80 days cost of goods sold[2] | 553 |
| Total current assets | | $ 836 |
| | | |
| Fixed assets, net | No change[3] | 80 |
| | | |
| TOTAL ASSETS | | $ 916 |
| | | |
| **LIABILITIES** | | |
| Current liabilities: | | |
| Accounts payable | 30 days purchases[4] | $ 216 |
| Notes payable — bank | Plug or balancing figure | 207 |
| Taxes payable | No change[3] | 12 |
| Accrued expenses | No change[3] | 20 |
| Total current liabilities | | $ 455 |
| | | |
| Long-term liabilities | Paid off[3] | 0 |
| | | |
| Total liabilities | | $ 455 |
| | | |
| **EQUITY** | | |
| Common stock | No change[1] | $ 37 |
| Retained earnings | 1996 plus 1997 net earnings | 424 |
| | | |
| Total equity | | $ 461 |
| | | |
| TOTAL LIABILITIES AND EQUITY | | $ 916 |

1. Manager's estimate.
2. Manager's estimate from ratios.
3. Last year's level, best estimate.
4. Projected purchases equal cost of goods sold plus increased inventory ($2,525,000 + ($553,000 − $450,000) = $2,628,000).

92 percent increase of the current bank loan. Finally, while the return on equity is 13 percent, a substantial increase from the 1996 levels can only be accomplished with an increase in the bank's commitment in the business and may not compensate for the risk undertaken.

One thing to remember is that no projected statement is "right." The analysis can, and often should, continue to try new possibilities to see "what would happen if ..." This is often referred to as a sensitivity analysis.

**SECTION**

**FIVE**

## SENSITIVITY ANALYSIS

Sensitivity analysis serves to test key assumptions made in the projected statements. This analysis will indicate which assumptions significantly affect the results of projected statements and, hence, need to be monitored most carefully after a decision is made.

The following guidelines can be used to perform sensitivity analysis:

1. Choose the assumption(s) you plan to vary. These may be internal factors that the company controls or external factors that the company does not control.

2. Revise your assumption(s) making other reasonable assumption(s).

3. Recalculate the appropriate accounts for the projected statements.

4. Reconstruct the projected statements with the new assumption(s) and determine the affect on key accounts (required financing, net income).

5. Use this additional information to supplement your original conclusions.

Consider the projected balance sheets, as of January 31, 1997, for the LMN Retail Company Ltd. Sensitivity analysis, using "what if" questions, allows the manager to explore the results of altering financial, marketing, and/or production policies. For example: "What will happen to the bank loan if credit policy is tightened/relaxed?"

On first iteration, the only accounts affected are the balance sheet accounts of "Accounts receivable" and "Notes payable — bank." The longhand way of assessing the impact of the revised assumption is to redo the projected balance sheet. Exhibit 8 presents a revised projected balance sheet for LMN Retail Company Ltd. assuming receivables of 60 days.

Revising projected balance sheets, especially when done by hand, is burdensome. The test of sensitivity, at least the first iteration, can be done quickly by limiting the focus on the two accounts, recognizing that a change in one requires a similar change in the other. From Exhibit 8, increasing the age of receivables to 60 days (doubling the period) doubled the "Net accounts receivable" account by the amount of $268,000. A similar offsetting increase is required for the "Notes payable — bank," which increased $268,000 to a total of $475,000. By recognizing

*EXHIBIT 8*

## LMN Retail Co. Ltd.
## Revised Projected Balance Sheet
## as at January 31, 1997
## (in 000s of dollars)

| Item | Basis of Estimate | Amount |
|------|-------------------|--------|
| ASSETS | | |
| Current assets: | | |
|     Cash | Minimum equal to 1996 level[1] | $ 15 |
|     Net accounts receivable | 60 days sales[5] | 536 |
|     Inventory | 80 days cost of goods sold[2] | 553 |
|     Total current assets | | $1,104 |
| | | |
| Fixed assets, net | No change[3] | 80 |
| | | |
| TOTAL ASSETS | | $1,184 |
| | | |
| LIABILITIES | | |
| Current liabilities: | | |
|     Accounts payable | 30 days purchases[4] | $ 216 |
|     Notes payable — bank | Plug or balancing figure | 475 |
|     Taxes payable | No change[3] | 12 |
|     Accrued expenses | No change[3] | 20 |
|     Total current liabilities | | $ 723 |
| | | |
| Long-term liabilities | Paid off[3] | 0 |
| | | |
|     Total liabilities | | $ 723 |
| | | |
| EQUITY | | |
|     Common stock | No change[1] | $ 37 |
|     Retained earnings | 1996 plus 1997 net earnings | 424 |
| | | |
|     Total equity | | $ 461 |
| | | |
| TOTAL LIABILITIES AND EQUITY | | $1,184 |

1. Manager's estimate.
2. Manager's estimate from ratios.
3. Last year's level, best estimate.
4. Projected purchases equal cost of goods sold plus increased inventory ($2,525,000 + ($553,000 − $450,000) = $2,628,000).
5. Revised manager's estimate.

the necessity of the "plug" figure to offset any change, sensitivity analysis can be done quickly. The results below show how such an analysis can be done and presented.

| Assumption Age of Accounts Receivable | Amount (000s) | Change in Plug[3] ($000s) | Bank Loan January 31, 1997 (000s) |
|---|---|---|---|
| 30 days | 268[1] | — | 207 |
| 45 days | 402[2] | +134 | 341 |
| 60 days | 536 | +268 | 475 |
| 15 days | 134 | −134 | 73 |

1. See Exhibit 7, original estimate.

2. Accounts receivable $= 45 \text{ days} \times \dfrac{3,258}{365 \text{ days}}$

   $= 45 \text{ days} \times 8.926/\text{day}$

   $= 402$

3. Change in Plug   = Change in Asset assumption from original estimate

   = New estimate − original asset estimate

   For example: $ 134 = 402 − 268.

The above sensitivity analysis shows that if LMN management relaxes its credit policy from 30 days sales to 60 days, the required bank loan for the company as of January 31, 1997 will be $475,000, an increase of $268,000. The increase in the bank loan equals the increase in accounts receivable. A similar format could be used to determine how variations in inventory policy and accounts payable policy would affect the required bank loan.

The impact on the loan varies with whether the analyst is changing a revenue or expenses assumption, or an asset or liability assumption. An increase in revenue will increase net earnings, which will add to the cash position or subtract from the bank loan. Expenses have the reverse effect: a reduction in net earnings yields a reduction in cash or an increase in the bank loan. Increases in assets lead to reductions in cash or increases in the bank loan. Increases in liabilities yield increases in cash or reductions in bank loans.

**SECTION**

**SIX**

## FORMS OF OWNERSHIP

There are three major legal forms of ownership: sole proprietorship, the partnership, and the limited company. It is important to note which form of ownership is involved because the different characteristics of each will have implications for the operation of the firm. The following section explains the various forms of ownership, their advantages, and their disadvantages.

### SOLE PROPRIETORSHIP

A sole proprietorship is a business owned and usually operated by a single individual. Its major characteristic is that the owner and the business are one and the same. In other words, the revenues, expenses, assets, and liabilities of the sole proprietorship are also the revenues, expenses, assets, and liabilities of the owner. A sole proprietorship is also referred to as the proprietorship, single proprietorship, individual proprietorship, and individual enterprise.

A sole proprietorship is the oldest and most common form of ownership. Some examples include small retail stores, doctors' and lawyers' practices, and restaurants.

### Advantages

A sole proprietorship is the easiest form of business to organize. The only legal requirements for starting such a business are a municipal licence to operate a business and a registration licence to ensure that two firms do not use the same name. The organization costs for these licences are minimal.

A sole proprietorship can be dissolved as easily as it can be started. It can terminate on the death of the owner, when a creditor files for bankruptcy, or when the owner ceases doing business.

A sole proprietorship offers the owner freedom and flexibility in making decisions. Major policies can be changed according to the owner's wishes because the firm does not operate under a rigid charter. Because there are no others to consult, the owner has absolute control over the use of the company's resources.

### Disadvantages

As mentioned earlier, the financial condition of the firm is the same as the financial condition of the owner. Because of this situation, the owner is legally liable for all debts of the company. If the assets of the firm cannot cover all the liabilities, the sole proprietor must pay these debts from his or her own pocket. Some proprietors try to protect themselves by selling assets such as their houses and automobiles to their spouses.

A sole proprietorship, dependent on its size and provision for succession, may experience difficulties in obtaining capital because lenders are leery of giving money to only one person who is pledged to repay. As a result, the sole proprietor has often to rely on friends, relatives, and government agencies for funds or loan guarantees.

A proprietorship has a limited life, being terminated on the death, bankruptcy, insanity, or imprisonment of the proprietor. Retirement or the whim of the owner can also end it.

A proprietorship, depending on its size and provision for succession, may also experience difficulties in attracting new employees because there are few opportunities for advancement, minimal fringe benefits, and little employment security.

## PARTNERSHIP

A partnership is an unincorporated enterprise owned by two or more individuals. A partnership agreement, oral or written, expresses the rights and obligations of each partner. For example, one partner may have the financial resources to start the business while the other partner possesses the management skills to operate the firm. There are three types of partnerships: general partnerships, limited partnerships, and joint ventures. The most common form is the general partnership, often used by professional groups that are prohibited from incorporating. Also, limited partnerships have been used in real estate developments in order to transfer tax benefits to investors.

### Advantages

Partnerships, like sole proprietorships, are easy to start up. Registration details vary by province, but usually entail obtaining a licence and registering the company name. Partners' interests can be protected by formulation of an "agreement of partnership." This agreement specifies all the details of the partnership.

Complementary management skills are a major advantage of partnerships. Partnerships are consequently a stronger entity and can attract new employees more easily than proprietorships. A stronger entity also makes it easier for partnerships to raise additional capital. Lenders are often more willing to advance money to partnerships than to proprietorships because all of the general partners are subject to unlimited financial liability.

### Disadvantages

The major disadvantage of partnerships is that partners, like sole proprietors, are legally liable for all debts of the firm. In partnerships, the unlimited liability is both joint and personal. This means that if a partner(s) cannot meet his or her share of the debts, the other partner(s) must pay all debts.

Partners are also legally responsible for actions of other partners. Many partnerships include in their agreements stipulations as to what decisions — financial or otherwise — can be made without the consent of all partners. Even with this agreement, however, partners are still liable to creditors for actions under the firm's name. In these cases, a suit can be brought by the partners against a partner's actions that were not in accord with the agreement.

Partnerships are not as easy to dissolve as sole proprietorships. Partnerships terminate on the death of any one partner or when one of the partners breaks the partnership agreement or gives notice to leave. It is often difficult for firms to find new partners to buy an interest. As a result, partners often take out term insurance on the lives of other partners to purchase the interest of a deceased partner, and sale prices are preset.

## CORPORATIONS

Corporations, unlike proprietorships or partnerships, are created by law and are separate from the people who own and manage them. Corporations are also referred to as limited companies. In corporations, ownership is represented by shares of stock. The owners, at an annual meeting, elect a board of directors that has the responsibility of appointing company officers and setting the enterprise's objectives.

### Advantages

Corporations are the least risky from an owner's point of view. Shareholders of corporations can only lose the amount of money they have invested in company stock. If an incorporated business goes bankrupt, owners do not have to meet the liabilities with their own personal holdings unless they, as individuals, have guaranteed the debts of the corporation. However, banks, before granting loans to smaller enterprises, usually ask for the personal guarantees of the shareholders/managers. Corporations are taxed at lower rates than individuals. This permits a corporation that retains earnings to build its equity base faster than unincorporated enterprises.

Corporations may be able to raise larger amounts of capital than proprietorships or partnerships through the addition of new investors or through better borrowing power.

Limited companies do not end with the death of owners. A limited company can terminate only by bankruptcy, expiry of its charter, or a majority vote of its shareholders. With this continued life and the greater growth possibilities, limited companies usually can attract more diversified managerial talent.

### Disadvantages

It is marginally more expensive and complicated to establish corporations than proprietorships or partnerships. A charter, which requires the services of a lawyer, must be obtained through the provincial or federal government. In addition to legal costs, a firm is charged incorporation fees for its charter by the authorizing government.

Dividends to shareholders from limited companies are taxed twice — on the profits they earn and on the dividends which come out of the profits. In proprietorships and partnerships earnings are only taxed once — as the personal income of the individuals involved. Furthermore, if the enterprise suffers a loss, the shareholders of corporation cannot use the loss to reduce other taxable income.

With diverse ownerships, corporations do not enjoy the secrecy that proprietorships and partnerships have. A company must send each shareholder an annual report detailing the financial condition of the firm.

## BANKRUPTCY

Bankruptcy has been mentioned a number of times in this chapter, but what is it? How do you become bankrupt? What happens when you are bankrupt? What are the implications of bankruptcy?

Bankruptcy proceedings are a court-administered process that supervises the disposition of property of an individual or corporation that is unable to pay its obligations. The process may start with either a voluntary petition to the court by the debtor, or an involuntary petition by a creditor. For an involuntary petition to be granted, the creditor must prove that the debtor committed an act of bankruptcy, which include handing over assets to a trustee for benefit of the creditors, a fraudulent transfer of property, a failure to meet obligations when due, or an admission of insolvency. In both cases, the petition to the court is a request for the appointment of a trustee to oversee the debtor's property, with the ultimate goal of eliminating the outstanding debt through orderly payment, or discharge by the court.

The court in granting a petition will establish a trustee. The trustee will take dominion over the debtor's property. The property will be disposed of, and proceeds distributed in a prescribed order. First to receive proceeds are *deemed trusts*, such as outstanding payroll deductions for workers' compensation, unemployment insurance, Canada Pension, and employees' income taxes. *Secured creditors* are next; these include those creditors who have prior claims to assets that the debtor used as collateral for loans. Third are *preferred creditors*, including the trustee, landlords, employees, and tax collectors. Fourth come *unsecured creditors*, which usually are trade creditors, or secured creditors whose claim was larger than the asset pledged as security. *Preferred shareholders* are fifth, and last are the *common shareholders*. The ranking is important: deemed trusts and secured creditors must be satisfied from the proceeds from the property before any proceeds from assets given as collateral can be used to satisfy the claims of the next strata of creditors — unsecured creditors. Given this order of distribution, deemed trusts and secured creditors fare much better than lower ranked creditors. Usually the bankrupt's property is insufficient to make even nominal payments to unsecured creditors.

Once the court has approved the trustee's disposition of the bankrupt's property, all amounts still outstanding are forgiven or discharged. If the bankrupt is an enterprise, the enterprise ceases to exist. If the bankrupt is an individual, the individual is free to restart unencumbered with debt and possessing minimal, if any, assets.

# CREDIT

When customers can purchase goods or services without paying cash immediately, they are buying "on credit." Credit is a major factor in today's business environment for both the seller and the buyer. Consumers use credit cards; firms purchase from suppliers on credit; banks lend short-term money to help companies or individuals. Attractive credit terms can increase sales by keeping present customers and attracting new ones.

Credit is riskier and more expensive than cash operations. The decision to offer credit means the credit-granting company must also be ready to accept the risk that some customers will not pay their debts. Credit management attempts to differentiate good-risk customers from poor-risk ones. Credit managers look at four characteristics to differentiate these firms. These are called the "four Cs of Credit": business conditions, character, capacity to repay, and collateral. The principles of credit analysis apply to bank loans, supplier credit, applications for charge accounts, and numerous other instances where credit is involved.

## BUSINESS CONDITIONS

Current or pending legislation (which could drastically affect the operation of a firm), economic conditions (such as seasonal and cyclical sales patterns, growth and profit potential, competitive conditions), social trends (such as changes in market and in customer buying behaviour), and technological changes (such as innovations) are important indicators of a firm's likely success within an industry. Credit officers and bankers look at a firm in the context of its industry to determine, "What does the firm have to do in order to operate successfully? Is this possible for this firm?"

## CHARACTER

An important consideration is the character of the borrower. Past credit records are good indications of a firm's (or individual's) chances and inclinations for paying liabilities. The marketing, production, and financial expertise of the management are critical to the success of a corporation. "Character," therefore, involves not only the trustworthiness of the borrower, but also the capacity to achieve operating goals.

## CAPACITY TO REPAY

Projected statements provide useful information about possible future financial performance and position. As stated earlier, in Section Three, ratio analysis helps the analyst make conclusions about a company's past financial policies and present position. Projected statements, as discussed in Section Four, take the analyst beyond the present to predict both the money needs of the company and when repayment may be possible. If repayment seems doubtful in the near term, the analyst will review the projected stability and return on equity ratios to ascertain whether the company can gain longer term debt or equity financing.

Depending on the risk the lender is willing to accept, the ratios and projections may indicate the need for securing a loan against the possibility of default or bankruptcy. Restrictions on future borrowing or further capital investment may also be found necessary. These methods of protection help ensure the lender of a higher likelihood of repayment.

## COLLATERAL

Lenders often seek protection in the event of a default (the credit loan is not repaid in full or in the time specified). This protection is usually in the form of collateral, which refers to assets pledged against the loan. Many terms, such as *secured*, *assigned*, and *mortgaged* have the same meaning but are applied to different assets. *Mortgage* is the term applied to an assignment of immoveable property, while *chattel mortgage* is a pledge against moveable property. For most secured business loans, a *floating charge* is applied. A floating charge is a charge against all assets in a category, whether owned currently or in the future. Normally, the collateral is matched with the term of the loan: receivables and inventory assignments with short-term loans and mortgages with medium-term and long-term debts.

Creditors who are secured recognize they rank ahead of all claimants to the company's assets, with one exception — deemed trusts. (See Section Seven.) However, the creditor's willingness to accept certain assets as collateral varies according to the lender and the loan situation. The realizable value of collateral varies with the selling and collecting skills of the lender, the state of the economy, and the saleability of the asset. While lenders take collateral, their main protection against default is the capability of the borrower's management. As a firm sinks into bankruptcy, the value of the borrower's assets deteriorates significantly. The best security against loan default is a well-run company in a prosperous industry.

## CREDIT ANALYSIS

Every credit situation requires judgment, not just mathematical computation. LMN Retail Company Ltd.'s request for additional bank financing of $99,000, bringing their total to $207,000, provides a useful example for credit analysis.

The bank manager, on receiving the projected statements outlined in Exhibits 6 and 7, would see almost immediately that there was insufficient provision for interest in other expenses. If the banker's current prime rate was 10 percent and was applied to a $207,000 loan, it would mean minimum interest of about $21,000 per year. Adjusting earnings or net profit before tax for added interest would have an additional impact on the bank loan. For example, if interest was believed to be $21,000, this means that the net profit before tax would be $68,000 and the expected income tax expense would be $17,000, leaving $51,000 net earnings. This not only reduces the retained earnings in the projected balance sheet by $8,000, but also implies increasing the bank loan by $8,000. The net return to the owners of LMN Retail would also be reduced.

At least for this one year, the company needs an additional bank loan. If the sales trend continues, by 1998 the company will need still more money. On its first calculation, the bank might not be concerned in 1997, given that its major collateral would be net accounts receivable of $268,000. Banks are usually reluctant to place high values on retail inventory as collateral because of the chance of possible fraud in a quick resale.

There may be some collateral value in the fixed assets, though these assets seem to need replacement often. As a consequence, the collateral position to support a $207,000 loan may be regarded by a commercial bank (ignoring retail inventory) as unreasonable in this instance. If the commercial bank decides to place some reliance on inventory, it may be willing to lend more. The bank, in reviewing the projected balance sheet (Exhibit 7) would likely suggest that LMN Retail Company Ltd. should be looking to its suppliers for more credit. The bank is limited in its net margin, which is the difference between its normal lending rate and what it must pay for funds. (See Exhibit 9 outlining returns in bank prime lending rates, deposit rate, etc.) Supplier creditors, when they supply goods, generally invest substantially less than the dollar amount reported as accounts payable. In a number of cases, the supplier may only invest 75 cents out of pocket for each dollar of his or her sale. This means that the supplier, if he or she collects the sale, would yield contribution to fixed costs and profit of 25 cents for each 75 cents invested, a return of 33.33 percent.[2] Given the high returns for the supplier and the probable marginality of this account for the bank, the bank may set a lower credit line determined almost entirely by the collateral position of the net accounts receivable. If the bank agreed to invest up to 75 percent of accounts receivable, this would mean that it would be willing to lend approximately $200,000.

The owners should carefully inspect the projected statements, too. Their returns are marginal in comparison with the stock market returns listed in Exhibit 9. The stock market is a diversified portfolio of securities encompassing all types of industries. It would seem that LMN Retail, which is subject to the vicissitudes of economic forces in one locality, should, if it is going to compensate itself for the risk undertaken, be demanding a higher return on its equity investment than the average. The owners might ask what things can be done to improve returns. Improving the returns can be accomplished in two general ways, improving the profits, or by reducing the investment required to produce those profits. The information and background of LMN Retail Company Ltd. operations is too sketchy to make other than the general comments found above.

**EXHIBIT 9**

## Annualized Returns as of December 31 for Selected Investments
## (in percentages)

| Year | 3-Month Government of Canada Treasury Bill[1] | Bond Yield Average 10 years and over Govt. of Canada[1] | Chartered 90-day Deposit Receipts[1] | Chartered Prime Business Loan Rate[1] | Toronto Stock Exchange Index[2] |
|------|------|------|------|------|------|
| 1964 | 3.82 | 5.03 | 4.25 | 5.75 | 25.2 |
| 1965 | 4.54 | 5.40 | 4.88 | 6.00 | 6.6 |
| 1966 | 4.96 | 5.76 | 5.13 | 6.00 | (6.9) |
| 1967 | 5.95 | 6.54 | 5.75 | 6.50 | 17.9 |
| 1968 | 6.24 | 7.30 | 6.50 | 6.75 | 22.5 |
| 1969 | 7.81 | 8.33 | 7.50 | 8.50 | (0.9) |
| 1970 | 4.44 | 6.99 | 5.80 | 7.50 | (3.8) |
| 1971 | 3.21 | 6.55 | 4.62 | 6.00 | 7.8 |
| 1972 | 3.65 | 7.12 | 5.13 | 6.00 | 27.1 |
| 1973 | 6.35 | 7.70 | 8.50 | 9.50 | (0.1) |
| 1974 | 7.12 | 8.77 | 9.75 | 11.00 | (25.8) |
| 1975 | 8.64 | 9.49 | 9.46 | 9.75 | 19.8 |
| 1976 | 8.14 | 8.47 | 8.20 | 9.25 | 11.0 |
| 1977 | 7.17 | 8.77 | 7.24 | 8.25 | 9.7 |
| 1978 | 10.46 | 9.68 | 10.40 | 11.50 | 29.1 |
| 1979 | 13.66 | 11.32 | 13.84 | 15.00 | 42.5 |
| 1980 | 17.01 | 12.67 | 17.35 | 18.25 | 28.8 |
| 1981 | 14.41 | 15.27 | 15.70 | 17.25 | (9.4) |
| 1982 | 9.80 | 11.69 | 9.18 | 12.50 | 4.2 |
| 1983 | 9.71 | 12.02 | 8.50 | 11.00 | 33.6 |
| 1984 | 9.84 | 11.66 | 9.50 | 11.25 | (2.3) |
| 1985 | 9.24 | 10.06 | 7.75 | 10.00 | 23.97 |
| 1986 | 8.24 | 9.23 | 7.95 | 9.75 | 8.70 |
| 1987 | 8.41 | 10.34 | 8.40 | 9.75 | 6.14 |
| 1988 | 10.94 | 10.36 | 11.01 | 12.25 | 10.63 |
| 1989 | 12.22 | 9.69 | 12.25 | 13.50 | 20.35 |
| 1990 | 11.47 | 10.51 | 11.58 | 12.75 | (14.1) |
| 1991 | 7.42 | 9.00 | 7.48 | 8.00 | 12.0 |
| 1992 | 7.01 | 8.36 | 7.08 | 7.25 | (1.4) |
| 1993 | 3.87 | 7.28 | 3.91 | 5.50 | 32.6 |
| 1994 | 7.44 | 9.13 | 7.29 | 8.00 | (0.2) |

**1.**  Source: Bank of Canada.

**2.**  Source: Toronto Stock Exchange.

$$\text{Yield} = \frac{\text{Dividends} + \{\text{TSE}(t) - \text{TSE}(t\text{-}1)\}}{\text{TSE } t\text{-}1}$$

t = any year

*Note:* Brackets denote losses.

The cases that follow should enable the student to undertake a more thorough analysis of the risk and return trade-offs from the viewpoint of both the owner and the credit supplier or the lender.

## SOURCES AND TYPES OF FINANCING

There are several sources of financing. The costs, availability, and conditions must be analyzed for each source in order to obtain the right "fit" for the firm. Financing sources can be categorized into three maturities: short-term, medium-term, and long-term. The cost of financing varies directly with the investor's perception of the risk of financing.

### SHORT-TERM FINANCING

Enterprises can obtain short-term financing from trade creditors, chartered banks, factor companies, and the short-term money market. Short-term financing is for a period of less than one year.

Trade credit refers to purchasing goods or services from suppliers on credit. It appears on the balance sheet as accounts payable. The buyer is allowed a period of time, usually 30 or 60 days, in which to pay for the goods or services received. To encourage prompt payments of credit sales, sellers often offer a discount from the invoiced amount if payment is made within 10 days of billing. If the purchaser cannot pay the account within the given period, the creditor will often charge an interest penalty.

The Canadian chartered banks are another important source of short-term financing. Demand loans with a "line of credit" are the most common type of credit given by banks. A line of credit means the bank can arrange for an individual or a company to borrow up to an agreed sum over a certain period of time. This helps companies with seasonal products who may experience cash shortages in the off-season. The borrower is charged a rate of interest for demand notes and a fee for the unused portion of the line of credit. However, a bank can demand repayment of these demand loans at any time.

Another method of short-term financing is "factoring." Instead of pledging accounts receivable for a bank loan, a borrowing company will sell the accounts receivable to a "factoring" company. Thus, except for paying the factoring company a fee, the firm does not have to concern itself with collecting the accounts or the risk of a bad debt. Customers' payments go to the factoring company rather than the seller.

### MEDIUM-TERM FINANCING

Medium-term financing is for a period of over one year but not longer than ten years. Firms often require medium-term financing for growth, either for additional working capital or for new assets such as plant expansion, equipment, or machinery. Medium-term financing in the form of term loans can be obtained from chartered banks, life insurance companies, or pension funds. Interest rates are generally higher for these longer-term loans.

The most common source of this type of financing is through the chartered or commercial banks. Banks usually permit loans of this nature to remain unpaid for reasonable periods of time provided the company has pledged the required collateral, the interest payments are made on time, and the amount of the loan is reduced in an orderly fashion.

Mortgage companies, life insurance companies, and trust companies are other sources for medium-term financing. As with banks, collateral usually is required. If financing is required for equipment purchases, the equipment supplier will often provide financing.

### LONG-TERM FINANCING

Long-term financing takes place over a period of 10 years or longer. The major sources of long-term financing are from equity and long-term debt financing. Equity financing refers to the original money invested by common and preferred shareholders plus new issues of stock as well as all profits retained in the business. This money is seldom repaid. Individuals, investment companies, and pension plans are the major purchasers of preferred and common stocks.

Long-term debt financing refers to bonds or debentures issued by the lender. Insurance companies, trust companies, mortgage loan companies, and pension plans are the major purchasers of long-term debt issues. Fixed interest rates are levied and must be paid with repayments of principal at specified times.

Leasing is used increasingly in Canada. As a financial source, leasing is a surrogate for medium-term and long-term debt. A financial lease is an arrangement whereby the lessee acquires the use of an asset over its useful life. In return, the lessee promises to pay specified amounts, which are sufficient to cover the principal and interest objectives of the lessor. Normally, the lessor looks solely to the contract with the lessee to meet his financial objectives.

Generally, long-term interest rates are higher than medium- and short-term rates, although market conditions will influence this relationship. Interest rates increase with the length of loans because of the premium demanded for forgoing liquidity, plus the increased instability of long-term security prices.

### SUMMARY

The financial analysis and management of an enterprise are complex tasks. This chapter has presented only an elementary framework. In order to be used successfully in the following exercises and cases, the framework requires judgment not just calculations.

The overall objective of the financial manager is to determine the expected return on investment and evaluate the risk incurred to earn the return. Projected results are required to determine the expected return. Quantitative analysis (cash sources and uses statement, ratio analysis, projections, and collateral appraisal) plus evaluation of qualitative factors (character and business conditions) are employed to assess the risk.

## NOTES

1. For those who have calculators and wish to set up the determination of these efficiency ratios quickly, the calculation can be handled by first dividing the numerator by the denominator and then multiplying the resulting fraction by 365.
2. Contribution is explained in greater detail in the marketing management section.

## ⋮ FINANCE EXERCISES

### Exercise 1
### ABC Distribution Company Ltd.
### (Cash Sources and Uses Statement)

#### Balance Sheets
#### as at November 30
#### (in 000s of dollars)

|  | 1988 | 1989 | 1990 |
|---|---|---|---|
| **ASSETS** | | | |
| Current assets: | | | |
|     Cash | $ 12 | $ 40 | $ 16 |
|     Accounts receivable | 3,820 | 4,532 | 6,440 |
|     Inventories | 4,720 | 5,048 | 9,460 |
|     Total current assets | $ 8,552 | $ 9,620 | $15,916 |
| Other investments | 600 | 552 | 712 |
| Net fixed assets | 1,772 | 2,160 | 5,176 |
| Other assets | 368 | 336 | 940 |
| TOTAL ASSETS | $11,292 | $12,668 | $ 22,744 |
| **LIABILITIES** | | | |
| Current liabilities: | | | |
|     Working capital loan | $ 2,688 | $ 1,512 | $ 4,252 |
|     Accounts payable | 912 | 1,752 | 3,856 |
|     Taxes payable | 328 | 952 | 736 |
|     Other current liabilities | 312 | 456 | 252 |
|     Total current liabilities | $ 4,240 | $ 4,672 | $ 9,096 |
| Term bank loan | | | 4,200 |
| Mortgages payable | 752 | 564 | 468 |
|     Total liabilities | $ 4,992 | $ 5,236 | $ 13,764 |
| **SHAREHOLDERS' EQUITY** | | | |
|     Common stock | $ 4,384 | $ 4,384 | $ 4,384 |
|     Retained earnings | 1,916 | 3,048 | 4,596 |
|     Total shareholders' equity | $ 6,300 | $ 7,432 | $ 8,980 |
| TOTAL LIABILITIES AND SHAREHOLDERS' EQUITY | $11,292 | $12,668 | $ 22,744 |

### *Assignment:*

From the balance sheets of ABC Distribution Company Ltd., prepare a statement of changes in financial position for:

**a.** one year ending November 30, 1989,

**b.** one year ending November 30, 1990,

**c.** two years ending November 30, 1990.

### Exercise 2
### ABC Distribution Company Ltd.*
### (Calculation of Ratios)
### Income Statements
### for the Years ending November 30
### (in 000s of dollars)

|  | 1988 | 1989 | 1990 |
|---|---|---|---|
| Net sales | $19,436 | $23,544 | $32,624 |
| Cost of sales | 14,284 | 16,492 | 22,520 |
| Gross profit | $ 5,152 | $ 7,052 | $10,104 |
| Operating expenses: |  |  |  |
| Bad debt expense | $ 264 | $ 20 | $ 108 |
| General and administrative expense | 736 | 828 | 1,012 |
| Interest expense | 248 | 220 | 412 |
| Salaries | 2,776 | 3,280 | 4,420 |
| Selling expense | 752 | 888 | 1,320 |
| Depreciation | 264 | 264 | 416 |
| Total operating expenses | 5,040 | 5,500 | 7,688 |
| Operating profit | $ 112 | $ 1,552 | $ 2,416 |
| Other income | 396 | 552 | 444 |
| Profit before tax | $ 508 | $ 2,104 | $ 2,860 |
| Income taxes | 248 | 972 | 1,312 |
| Net earnings | $ 260 | $ 1,132 | $ 1,548 |

*ABC Distribution Company Ltd. is a Dawson Lumber Company Ltd.

## Assignment:

Listed above are the income statements of the ABC Distribution Company Ltd. and a ratio sheet. Calculate the missing ratios and evaluate the company's performance.

## ABC Distribution Company Ltd.*
### Ratio Sheet
### for Selected Dates and Periods
### (365-day year)

|  | 1988 | 1989 | 1990 |
|---|---|---|---|
| **PROFITABILITY:** | | | |
| (i) Vertical analysis | | | |
| Sales | 100.0% | — | — |
| Cost of goods sold | — | 70.0% | — |
| Gross profit | — | — | 31.0% |
| Operating expenses: | | | |
| Bad debt expense | 1.4% | — | — |
| General and administrative | — | 3.5% | — |
| Interest expense | — | — | 1.3% |
| Salaries | 14.3% | — | — |
| Selling | — | 3.8% | — |
| Depreciation | — | — | 1.3% |
| Operating profit | 0.6% | — | — |
| Other income | — | 2.3% | — |
| Profit before tax | — | — | 8.8% |
| | | | |
| (ii) Return on average equity | — | 16.5% | — |
| | | | |
| **STABILITY:** | | | |
| Net worth to total assets | 55.8% | — | — |
| Interest coverage (times) | — | 10.6X | — |
| | | | |
| **LIQUIDITY:** | | | |
| Current ratio | 2.02:1 | — | — |
| Acid test | — | 0.98:1 | — |
| Working capital ($000) | — | — | 6,820 |
| | | | |
| **EFFICIENCY:** | | | |
| Age of receivables | 71.7 days | — | — |
| Inventory in days cost of goods sold | — | 111.7 days | — |
| Age of payables in days purchases* | — | — | 52.3 days |
| Fixed assets/sales (%) | 9.1% | — | — |

|  | 1988–89 | 1989–90 |
|---|---|---|
| **GROWTH:** | | |
| Sales | 21.1% | — |
| Net earnings | — | 36.7% |
| Assets | 12.2% | — |
| Equity | — | 20.8% |

*Assumes purchases are equal to cost of sales plus ending inventory minus beginning inventory.

## Exercise 3
## DEF Company Ltd.
## (Projected Statements)

### Assignment:

**A.** The following data has been supplied to you by the general manager of DEF Company Ltd., a retailing firm.

   **1.** Prepare a projected income statement for the next year.
   **2.** Prepare a projected balance sheet for the next year.

**B.** The sales manager disagrees with the general manager's sales projection. She believes sales will be $1,000,000. Do another set of projections using the sales manager's sales estimate.

| | |
|---|---:|
| **1.** Sales projection | $750,000 |
| **2.** Gross profit | 20% of sales |
| **3.** Last year's ending inventory | $150,000 |
| **4.** This year's age of ending inventory | 90 days |
| | Cost of goods sold |
| **5.** Other operating expenses | 8% of sales |
| **6.** Income tax | 25% of net profit before tax |
| **7.** Accounts payable | 40 days purchases |
| **8.** Accounts receivable | 10 days sales |
| **9.** Taxes payable | 30% of year's taxes |
| **10.** Land — at cost | $30,000 |
| **11.** Buildings and fixtures — at cost | $90,000 |
| **12.** Accumulated depreciation | |
|    — building and fixtures at end of last year | $21,000 |
| **13.** Depreciation expense for the year | $6,000 |
| **14.** Common stock | $100,000 |
| **15.** Retained earnings at the end of last year | $75,000 |
| **16.** Salary expense | $42,000 |
| **17.** Dividends | 25% of net earnings |
| **18.** Cash or bank loan | Plug |

# ▪▪▪▪ ▪ CASES FOR PART 3 ▪ ▪▪▪▪

# C A S E  3.1  DAVE EVANSON SPORTS

Bob Hansen, manager of the Owen Sound branch of the Royal Canadian Bank, had to make a decision concerning the recent loan request for Dave Evanson Sports. Dave Evanson, owner of an Owen Sound sports store, had requested an increase in a working capital loan to $85,000 to finance an expansion of his business.

It was early February 1985 and Bob had recently been sent the financial statements for Dave Evanson Sports (see Exhibit 1). Bob knew that he must make a decision quickly as Dave wanted to have the changes to his store completed by March 1, 1985 in time for the start of the spring sporting goods season.

## BACKGROUND

Dave Evanson entered the sporting goods business in 1972 when he purchased Wayne's Sport and Camera Shop located on the main street in Owen Sound. At that time, the store carried cameras, guns, ammunition, fishing equipment and, in winter months, hockey equipment. Over the next five years Dave maintained the winter season emphasis on hockey equipment as well as golf clubs and tennis rackets for the summer season. By 1977 he had dropped cameras, guns, and ammunition from his store. Since 1977, Dave had developed the team sport market by offering uniforms and crested clothing as well as trophies. He began to promote the store vigorously in the local sports community through sponsorships of teams and through discounts offered to coaches and minor sports organizations.

Dave faced a significant set-back to the establishment of a clientele in 1980 when a fire destroyed the main street store. However, Dave was able to re-establish his business in 1981 at a new location. He rented part of this new location to Mark's Guns Store for extra income.

## DAVE EVANSON

Dave had always had a keen interest in sports as a player and as a coach. He had an excellent product knowledge that was often sought after by patrons who would wait for his assistance. He was constantly reading about sports merchandising trends in order to purchase the proper quality and selection of merchandise for each season. Dave's strength was in his personality and the customer contacts that he had developed in the local market. His expertise concerning sports equipment was unquestioned.

Dave was excited about the new expansion when Bob had lunch with him recently. Dave believed that the expansion was a critical step to improve the profitability and, as a result, the value of the business. Dave indicated that after 13 years in the business he was considering selling at least part of his interest to reduce the amount of stress he felt from day-to-day operations.

## SPORTING GOODS INDUSTRY

The sporting goods business was extremely competitive. The gross profit achieved from the sale of sports equipment was declining as a result of competitive pricing. Lower quality sporting goods had been sold in department stores, discount stores, and in hardware stores such as Canadian Tire.

The higher quality products were often sold in specialty sports stores such as Evanson's store. In larger cities, specialty stores had acquired special areas of service for a competitive advantage. These specialty stores offered a large selection of merchandise for a few sports, or even a single sport, rather than for a broad range of sports.

The merchandise in the industry was subject to seasonal demand. This put pressure on the purchasing skills of retailers as the inventory for each season had to be sold to obtain enough space and money to allow for the purchase of the new season's inventory. This led to end-of-season price cutting and a further reduction of margins for retailers.

The one bright spot in the industry was the increasing market for higher margin "soft goods" such as sports footwear, clothing, and casual wear put out by such companies as Adidas, Nike, New Balance, and Reebok.

## OWEN SOUND MARKET

Dave faced competition from another large Owen Sound sports store, Rowland Sports, as well as from stores in the area with sports departments, such as Canadian Tire, Pro Hardware, K mart, and Woolworth. Rowland Sports was a direct competitor to Dave's store. It carried similar quality lines of sporting goods but did not carry a large selection of sports wear. Dave had attempted to differentiate himself from the sports department of a discount or hardware store through the sale of high quality products and through excellent service. In spite of this differentiation, price competition was fierce amongst the local stores.

## SOFT GOODS

In order to increase the gross profit of his store, Dave initiated a plan in 1984 to sell brand name soft goods lines of footwear and clothing such as Nike, Brooks, and Adidas. He was convinced that the only way to maintain profitability was to move into the soft goods market (Exhibit 2).

Dave was successful in securing a franchise deal with Athlete's Foot in 1983. Through this arrangement, Dave had received better purchasing discounts and longer terms of payment. The normal terms of purchase were 3 to 4 percent net 30 days. Better terms could only be secured if orders were placed three months in advance. The franchise agreement gave discounts of 5 to 7 percent net 60 days. Dave paid royalties of 3 1/2 percent on all sales of items purchased through the Athlete's Foot buying group.

Dave knew that the soft goods business required a different strategy for success. The soft goods were more fashionable than his sporting goods line. He found that women were frequenting his store more often because of the new merchandise. Dave had begun promotions with local aerobics instructors in order to increase his sales of athletic clothing for women. His store layout for the new spring season would be rather cluttered unless changes were made (Exhibit 3). Dave felt that the store's present layout did not allow him to merchandise the new items properly. He was also concerned that the clientele and merchandise found in Mark's Guns Store might have adverse effects on the success of his efforts to attract the appropriate consumers for his soft goods business.

**EXPANSION PROPOSAL**

Dave's proposal to overcome these problems was to create a separate store for clothing in the space now rented to Mark's Guns (Exhibits 3A and 3B). The store would be connected to the main store by a new entrance to be constructed. However, it would be run by a different staff, headed by his wife. Dave's wife had retail experience both in sporting goods and in a nearby flower shop, but not retail clothing. The new store was to be called "Down Under" in the special spring promotions to be put on the radio. Dave felt that the promotion for Down Under would be the most effective way of advertising the casual wear he carried to potential customers.

In the past, Dave had arranged a $40,000 line of credit to cover his working capital needs to help finance changes in the business and growth. He had further secured a $10,000 bank overdraft to cover seasonal peak purchases of inventory in May and November just prior to the two big sporting seasons. The $10,000 overdraft was required to be paid off each year; however, the outstanding balance of the $40,000 line of credit was reviewed annually and had been permitted to be carried on the books each year. Dave was requesting an increase in his financing from the $50,000 total funds he had available to $85,000. He estimated that renovations and new equipment required for Down Under would cost $25,000.

Bob had requested an indication of the size of Dave's present clothing inventory, as well as the margin Dave had achieved from these items. Unfortunately, Dave's records did not contain this information. However, because clothing was a high margin item, Dave felt that this inventory might not move as quickly, therefore he anticipated that he might have to carry an additional 20 days of inventory.

Dave was extremely optimistic about the possible sales growth from this move. He felt that the new layout would help the merchandising for both the sports equipment and the soft goods. He felt that overall sales growth would be about 10 percent in the first year of operation. He expected sales growth for the second year to range between 10 and 30 percent as the Down Under store became more established. He did not plan to increase the advertising budget significantly for the new store. He felt that he would simply use the same expenditure, but use the message "Visit Down Under next to Dave Evanson Sports."

**THE DECISION**

Bob Hansen had to decide quickly whether he wanted to grant the loan to finance Down Under. Dave's previous financial performance had been hurt by the fire in 1980 and the interest rates and recession in 1981. Furthermore, the decision to open Down Under would cut off the rental income from Mark's Guns Store. This income had been a significant portion of past profits before tax.

Bob worried that much of the loan would be invested in assets that could not be easily converted to cash in the event of a style change.

Bob wondered whether he wanted to risk money in a business in which Dave had limited experience. He also wondered what would happen to the frequent golf games he had enjoyed with Dave in the summers should he reject the proposal.

*Exhibit 1*

| | | | | | |
|---|---|---|---|---|---|
| **Dave Evanson Sports**<br>**Income Statements[1]**<br>**for Years Ending January 31** | | | | | |
| | **1981** | **1982** | **1983** | **1984** | **1985** |
| Sales | $233,870 | $362,655 | 325,962 | $358,390 | $402,373 |
| Cost of sales: | | | | | |
| Beginning inventory | — | 69,847 | 106,648 | 70,000 | 72,000 |
| Purchases | 236,514 | 305,084 | 183,151 | 228,072 | 307,204 |
| Cost of goods available | $236,514 | $374,931 | $289,799 | $298,072 | $379,204 |
| Less: ending inventory | 69,847 | 106,648 | 70,000 | 72,000 | 105,000 |
| Cost of goods sold | 166,667 | 268,283 | 219,799 | 226,072 | 274,204 |
| Gross profit | $ 67,203 | $ 94,372 | $106,163 | $132,318 | $128,169 |
| Expenses: | | | | | |
| Wages and benefits | $ 36,592 | $ 57,383 | $ 46,030 | $ 55,293 | $ 64,153 |
| Advertising | 6,265 | 6,732 | 8,796 | 7,807 | 8,230 |
| Depreciation | 10,086 | 4,682 | 4,233 | 8,342 | 5,473 |
| Vehicle expenses | 6,717 | 9,079 | 5,062 | 7,468 | 7,537 |
| Store overhead | 12,958 | 18,394 | 20,454 | 24,564 | 19,222 |
| Miscellaneous expenses | 3,403 | 3,976 | 3,259 | 2,905 | 5,072 |
| Total expenses | 76,021 | 100,246 | 87,834 | 106,379 | 109,687 |
| Operating profit | ($8,818) | ($ 5,874) | $ 18,329 | $ 25,939 | $ 18,482 |
| Less: Other expenses: | | | | | |
| Interest and bank charges | 16,981 | 19,033 | 14,560 | 11,943 | 13,504 |
| Plus: Other revenue: | | | | | |
| Rent | 7,420 | 7,054 | 8,763 | 7,902 | 5,499 |
| Gain or disposal of assets | 14,175 | | | | |
| Insurance re. fire 1980 | 2,300 | | | | |
| Net income before tax[2] | ($1,904) | ($17,853) | $ 12,532 | $ 21,898 | $ 10,477 |

| | | | | | |
|---|---|---|---|---|---|
| **Statements of Retained Earnings**<br>**for Years Ending January 31** | | | | | |
| | **1981** | **1982** | **1983** | **1984** | **1985** |
| Retained earnings start of year | $49,949 | $48,045 | $30,192 | $42,724 | $64,622 |
| Income retained for year | (1,904) | (17,853) | 12,532 | 21,898 | 10,477 |
| Retained earnings at year end | $48,045 | $30,192 | $42,724 | $64,622 | $75,099 |

1. Consolidated.
2. The income tax expense had not been charged due to the carry forward of previous losses. Dave Evanson expected future profits to be taxed at a rate of 25 percent.

*EXHIBIT 1 (cont'd)*

|  | Balance Sheets as at January 31 | | | | |
|---|---|---|---|---|---|
|  | **1981** | **1982** | **1983** | **1984** | **1985** |
| **ASSETS** | | | | | |
| **Current assets:** | | | | | |
| Cash | $ 831 | $ 1,348 | $ 915 | $ 567 | $ 100 |
| Accounts receivable | 3,265 | 6,710 | 4,158 | 8,066 | 5,490 |
| Inventories | 69,847 | 106,648 | 70,000 | 72,000 | 105,000 |
| Prepaids | 818 | 3,735 | 3,635 | 660 | — |
| Other current assets | 2,149 | | | | |
| Total current assets | $ 76,910 | $118,441 | $ 78,708 | $ 81,293 | $110,590 |
| **Fixed assets:** | | | | | |
| Land | $ 30,525 | $ 30,525 | $ 30,525 | $ 30,525 | $ 30,525 |
| Building and store fixtures | 99,451 | 105,007 | 107,413 | 122,549 | 122,549 |
| Less: Accumulated depreciation | 26,826 | 31,509 | 35,742 | 44,084 | 49,557 |
| Net fixed assets | 103,150 | 104,023 | 102,196 | 108,990 | 103,517 |
| Other assets | 18,761 | 18,761 | 18,761 | 18,761 | 18,761 |
| **TOTAL ASSETS** | $198,821 | $241,225 | $199,665 | $209,044 | $232,868 |
| **LIABILITIES** | | | | | |
| **Current Liabilities:** | | | | | |
| Accounts payable | $ 11,198 | $ 44,782 | $ 34,899 | $ 23,687 | $ 39,698 |
| Bank overdraft | 1,557 | 3,126 | — | — | — |
| Bank demand loan | 40,000 | 80,802 | 30,977 | 44,245 | 35,568 |
| Loan — Victoria Grey | — | 4,687 | — | — | — |
| Current portion long-term debt | 9,824 | 2,000 | 2,000 | — | — |
| Other current liabilities | 1,942 | 1,926 | 4,193 | 11,301 | 9,627 |
| Total current liabilities | $ 64,521 | $137,323 | $ 72,069 | $ 79,233 | $ 84,893 |
| **Long-term liabilities:** | | | | | |
| Mortgage[1] | $ 50,080 | $ 42,000 | $ 40,000 | $ 30,000 | $ 30,000 |
| Shareholder loan[2] | 6,030 | 1,565 | 14,727 | 15,044 | 8,194 |
| Loan payable[3] | 30,000 | 30,000 | 30,000 | 20,000 | 34,537 |
| Total long-term liabilities | 86,110 | 73,565 | 84,727 | 65,044 | 72,731 |
| **SHAREHOLDERS' EQUITY** | | | | | |
| Share capital | $ 145 | $ 145 | $ 145 | $ 145 | $ 145 |
| Retained earnings | 48,045 | 30,192 | 42,724 | 64,622 | 75,099 |
| Total equity | 48,190 | 30,337 | 42,869 | 64,767 | 75,244 |
| **TOTAL LIABILITIES AND EQUITY** | $198,821 | $241,225 | $199,665 | $209,044 | $232,868 |

1. Collateral for the mortgage was the building and store fixtures.
2. Shareholder's loan was from Dave Evanson and was unsecured.
3. Loan payable referred to a long-term loan Dave Evanson had from several family members, on an unsecured basis.

*EXHIBIT 1 (cont'd)*

| Ratio Analysis | | | | | |
|---|---|---|---|---|---|
| | **1981** | **1982** | **1983** | **1984** | **1985** |
| Profitability: | | | | | |
| Sales | 100.0% | 100.0% | 100.0% | 100.0% | 100.0% |
| Cost of goods sold | 71.3 | 74.0 | 67.4 | 63.1 | 68.1 |
| Gross profit | 28.7 | 26.0 | 32.6 | 36.9 | 31.9 |
| Expenses: | | | | | |
| Wages and benefits | 15.6 | 15.8 | 14.1 | 15.4 | 15.9 |
| Advertising | 2.7 | 1.9 | 2.7 | 2.2 | 2.0 |
| Depreciation | 4.3 | 1.3 | 1.3 | 2.3 | 1.4 |
| Vehicle expense | 2.9 | 2.5 | 1.6 | 2.1 | 1.9 |
| Store overhead | 5.5 | 5.0 | 6.3 | 6.9 | 4.8 |
| Miscellaneous expenses | 1.5 | 1.1 | 1.0 | 0.8 | 1.3 |
| Total expenses | 32.5 | 27.6 | 27.0 | 29.7 | 27.3 |
| | | | | | |
| Operating profit | (3.8) | (1.6) | 5.6 | 7.2 | 4.6 |
| Interest expense | (7.3) | (5.2) | (4.5) | (3.3) | (3.4) |
| Rent revenue | 3.1 | 1.9 | 2.7 | 2.2 | 1.4 |
| Other income | 7.0 | | | | |
| Net income before tax | (0.8) | (4.9) | 3.8 | 6.1 | 2.6 |
| | | | | | |
| Return on Investment | (3.9) | (45.5) | 34.3 | 40.7 | 15.0 |
| | | | | | |
| Liquidity: | | | | | |
| Current ratio | 1.19:1 | 0.86:1 | 1.09:1 | 1.03:1 | 1.30:1 |
| Acid test | 0.06:1 | 0.06:1 | 0.07:1 | 0.11:1 | 0.07:1 |
| Working capital | 12,389 | (18,882) | 6,639 | 2,060 | 25,697 |
| | | | | | |
| Efficiency (Based on 365-day year): | | | | | |
| Age of receivables | 5.1 days | 6.8 days | 4.7 days | 8.2 days | 5.0 days |
| Age of inventory | 153 days | 145 days | 116.2 days | 116.2 days | 139.8 days |
| Age of payables | 17.3 days | 53.6 days | 69.5 days | 37.9 days | 47.2 days |
| | | | | | |
| Fixed assets per sales dollar | $0.44 | $0.29 | $0.31 | $0.30 | $0.26 |
| | | | | | |
| Stability: | | | | | |
| Equity to total assets | 24.2% | 12.6% | 21.5% | 31.0% | 32.3% |
| Interest coverage | 0.9X | 0.06X | 1.9X | 2.8X | 1.8X |

| | **81–82** | **82–83** | **83–84** | **84–85** |
|---|---|---|---|---|
| Growth | | | | |
| Sales | 55% | (10.1%) | 9.9% | 12.3% |
| Profit | — | — | 74.7% | (52.2%) |
| Equity | (37%) | 41.3% | 51.1% | 16.2% |
| Assets | 21.3% | (17.2%) | 4.7% | 11.4% |

*Exhibit 2*

| Product | Price Range | Average Price | Average Cost | Margin on Selling Price |
|---|---|---|---|---|
| **Dave Evanson Sports** |  |  |  |  |
| **Random Selection of Products, Prices, and Margins** |  |  |  |  |
| Tennis rackets | $ 40–180 | $ 90 | $ 44 | 51% |
| Squash rackets | $ 15–140 | $ 60 | $ 45 | 25% |
| Bikes | $120–600 | $225 | $150 | 33% |
| Skates | $ 50–200 | $140 | $ 90 | 36% |
| Baseball gloves | $ 30–70 | $ 50 | $ 28 | 44% |
| Golf clubs | $100–300 | $200 | $125 | 38% |
| **Footwear by line** |  |  |  |  |
| Reebok | $ 40–70 | $ 55 | $ 33 | 40% |
| Brooks | $ 30–75 | $ 45 | $ 29 | 36% |
| Adidas | $ 35–150 | $ 40 | $ 25 | 38% |
| Nike | $ 30–85 | $ 40 | $ 30 | 25% |
| Pumas cleats | $ 30–50 | $ 30 | $ 17 | 43% |
| **Soft Goods** |  |  |  |  |
| Slazenger shirts | $ 20–30 | $ 25 | $12.50 | 50% |
| OP shirts | $ 28–42 | $ 35 | $17.50 | 50% |
| Wassaga jogging suits | $ 65–85 | $ 70 | $35.00 | 50% |
| Brooks shorts | $ 18–22 | $ 20 | $10.00 | 50% |
| Kway jackets | $ 30–50 | $ 40 | $20.00 | 50% |
| Slazenger sweaters | $ 28–32 | $ 30 | $15.00 | 50% |

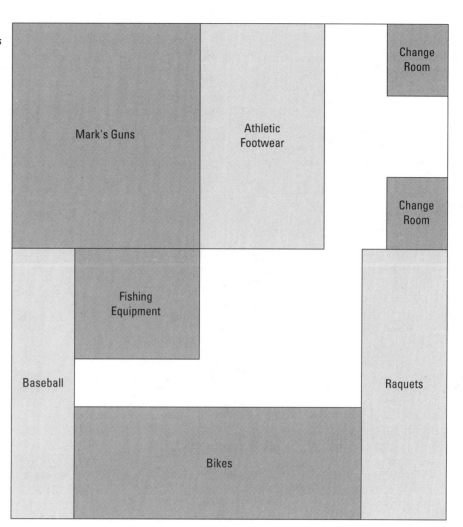

***EXHIBIT 3A***
***Dave Evanson Sports***
***OLD LAYOUT***
***(Summer Season)***

***EXHIBIT 3B***
***Dave Evanson Sports***
***NEW LAYOUT***
*(Summer Season)*

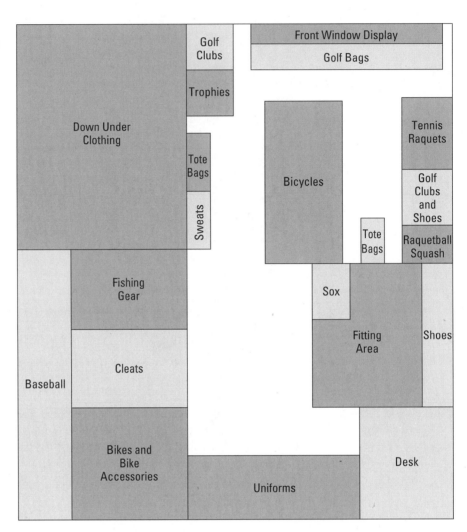

## C A S E **3.2**   DAWSON LUMBER COMPANY LIMITED

In March 1991, Ms. Sheila Spence, the new vice-president of the Eastern Ontario Region of the National Bank of Canada, was reviewing the file of the Dawson Lumber Company, one of the region's biggest borrowers. The following day Mr. Doug Dawson, and Mr. John Manning, the president and controller respectively of the Dawson Lumber Company, would present their request to the bank's loan committee for a line of credit of up to $10 million. The line of credit was in addition to the current term bank loan. The loan committee, consisting of Ms. Spence, the central credit manager, and the assistant central credit manager, would then make a recommendation to the bank's board of directors. This recommendation would be the basis of the bank's decision on Dawson Lumber's request.

**PRE-1988**

The Dawson Lumber Company was founded in the 1870s by the Dawson family to market the lumber on their land. After the original lumber stands near Cornwall, Ontario, had been depleted, the wholesale lumber business was continued and slowly expanded. In 1950, Dawson Lumber owned four small lumber yards in the Cornwall area, each operating as a separate company.

In 1965, Mr. J.H. Dawson became president and amalgamated the four companies into the Dawson Lumber Company. The company acquired seven more lumber yards north and west of Cornwall, Ontario, but further growth was limited by Mr. J.H. Dawson's belief that growth should only be financed by internally generated funds. For over one hundred years, Dawson Lumber had been dealing with the Cornwall branch of the Eastern Bank and, in 1985, borrowed approximately $1.5 million to finance an inventory build-up needed to meet seasonal sales. From April to November, 77 percent of the sales occurred evenly, while 23 percent were evenly distributed from December to March. The company's sales were between $10 and $15 million in the early 1980s, with 90 percent being wholesale sales to local residential contractors. Exhibit 1 presents profit before tax from 1980 to 1990.

In 1986, Mr. J.H. Dawson realized that, because of his health, he would not be able to continue managing the company. His son, Mr. Doug Dawson, agreed to take over as president. Mr. Doug Dawson had taken over the business initially in the summer of 1984 when his father became ill. After his father returned, Mr. Doug Dawson assumed the advertising and budgeting responsibilities for the company.

**1988 AND 1989**    Mr. Doug Dawson had a postgraduate degree in business administration and several years' teaching experience. When he became president of the company, Dawson Lumber had been primarily a wholesale business, subject to the volatility of the demand for housing. The new president felt that, with minimal changes in inventory and yard operations, the company could take advantage of the growing retail market for building products and thereby stabilize its operations.

He approached the company's banker, the Cornwall branch manager of the Eastern Bank, with a request for a loan to finance these changes in the company. However, the Eastern Bank branch manager would support only a seasonal loan to finance inventory and refused to pass the loan application on to his superiors.

Consequently, Mr. Doug Dawson approached the National Bank of Canada with his plans and needs. The National Bank of Canada, in 1988, granted an initial operating line of credit of $3 million, to be used for working capital. The National Bank took accounts receivable and inventory as collateral, and, as a condition of the loan, Dawson Lumber undertook to provide quarterly financial statements and monthly reports of inventory, sales, and receivables.

Mr. Doug Dawson reorganized the company's 11 branches into three regions. The Northern Region served an urban market and consisted of three yards just outside the city of Ottawa. Four lumber yards in the Cornwall area made up the Eastern Region and five lumber yards near Kingston formed the Western Region. The Eastern Region was a rural market while the Western Region was partially a resort and partially an urban area. In an attempt to minimize inventory levels, one branch in each region operated as a depot. A fleet of trucks kept frequent and regular schedules between the lumber yards and the depot to provide rapid delivery to the customer.

Each region was made the responsibility of an area supervisor who had worked for many years in the company's lumber yards. A management committee consisting of the president, controller, and area supervisors met monthly to discuss operational strategy. The committee set budgets for each branch every four months. Exhibits 2 and 3 outline the financial statements from 1988 to 1990.

**1990 PROJECTIONS**    Exhibit 4 outlines the projected capital expenditures for 1990 and 1991. The projected 1990 capital expenditures of $1.8 million were primarily for improvements in the company's showrooms and display areas. Depreciation and profit were expected to cover these capital expenditures. A sales increase of $6.4 million was anticipated for 1990, based on the opinions of contractors, yard managers, and business publications on the outlook for the economy and the housing market. Operating profit was expected to be $2.92 million, assuming a gross margin of 30 percent and expenses of $6.08 million. To finance an increase of $2.52 in receivables and inventory, a total operating line of credit of $3.6 million for working capital was requested and granted by the National Bank.

**1990 ACTUAL**

After spending six months studying the potential of the Ottawa market and discussing the revised capital budget with the bank, Dawson Lumber opened a discount home centre in September 1990. To finance the new outlet, the bank granted a term loan of $4.2 million.

The discount home centre was aimed at the retail market. The concept enabled the consumer to purchase in one store all types of building and household products such as tiles, wallpaper, carpet, lumber, plumbing supplies, and lighting fixtures. Each item in the store had two prices clearly marked so that the customer only paid for the services received. The regular price was the price at which the item could be charged and delivered. The discount price applied if the customer wished to pay cash and take the goods away. A third price was also charged if the customer wished to pay cash and have the purchase delivered. The new store's sales in its first two months of operations were $2.28 million.

Sales in 1990 were $2,680,000 greater than projected, and capital expenditures were $3,600,000 above budget. In addition to granting the term loan, the National Bank increased the company's operating line of credit to $5 million.

**1991 PROJECTIONS**

For 1991, Mr. Doug Dawson projected a 65 percent increase in sales to $54 million and an operating profit of 8 percent of sales. To finance inventory and receivables of up to $24 million in June and July, an operating line of credit of $10.8 million was requested.

**THE NATIONAL BANK**

As she reviewed the file, Ms. Spence looked for anything which suggested that the bank should take steps to increase its protection of the loan. She particularly noted the increase in profits since 1986 and her predecessor's confidence in Dawson's management. However, she closely examined the 1991 projections, questioning their accuracy. It was obvious that, because 65 percent of Dawson Lumber's sales were to contractors, the company was still dependent on the housing market. Total housing starts in Canada were 181,600 in 1990 versus 215,400 in 1989. New housing construction had slowed considerably in January and February of 1991, being about 40 percent of the starts in the same period of 1990. However, five-year mortgage interest rates had declined to 11.5 percent in February 1991 from the high of 14.25 percent in 1990. Also, the value of building permits had rebounded from a three-year low in December 1990. As she examined this information, Ms. Spence wondered whether she should recommend an increase in Dawson Lumber's operating line of credit, and, if so, by how much and under what terms as to collateral and management growth plans.

*Exhibit 1*

| Dawson Lumber Company Limited<br>Profit Before Tax<br>($000s) | |
|---|---|
| 1980 | 40 |
| 1981 | 12 |
| 1982 | (144) |
| 1983 | 440 |
| 1984 | 512 |
| 1985 | 536 |
| 1986 | 644 |
| 1987 | 1,020 |
| 1988 | 508 |
| 1989 | 2,104 |
| 1990 | 2,860 |

*Exhibit 2*

| Dawson Lumber Company Limited<br>Income Statements<br>for the Years Ending November 30<br>(in 000s of dollars) | | | |
|---|---|---|---|
| | **1988** | **1989** | **1990** |
| Net sales | $19,436 | $23,544 | $32,624 |
| Cost of sales | 14,284 | 16,492 | 22,520 |
| Gross profit | $ 5,152 | $ 7,052 | $10,104 |
| Operating expenses: | | | |
| Bad debt expense | $ 264 | $ 20 | $ 108 |
| General and administrative expense | 736 | 828 | 1,012 |
| Interest expense | 248 | 220 | 412 |
| Salaries | 2,776 | 3,280 | 4,420 |
| Selling expense | 752 | 888 | 1,320 |
| Depreciation | 264 | 264 | 416 |
| Total operating expenses | 5,040 | 5,500 | 7,688 |
| Operating profit | $ 112 | $ 1,552 | $ 2,416 |
| Other income | 396 | 552 | 444 |
| Profit before tax | $ 508 | $ 2,104 | $ 2,860 |
| Income taxes | 248 | 972 | 1,312 |
| Net earnings | $ 260 | $ 1,132 | $ 1,548 |

*Exhibit 3*

| Dawson Lumber Company Limited<br>Balance Sheets<br>as at November 30<br>(in 000s of dollars) | | | |
|---|---|---|---|
| | **1988** | **1989** | **1990** |
| **ASSETS** | | | |
| Current assets: | | | |
| Cash | $ 12 | $ 40 | $ 16 |
| Accounts receivable | 3,820 | 4,532 | 6,440 |
| Inventories | 4,720 | 5,048 | 9,460 |
| Total current assets | $ 8,552 | $ 9,620 | $15,916 |
| Other investments | 600 | 552 | 712 |
| Net fixed assets | 1,772 | 2,160 | 5,176 |
| Other assets | 368 | 336 | 940 |
| TOTAL ASSETS | $11,292 | $12,668 | $22,744 |
| **LIABILITIES** | | | |
| Current liabilities: | | | |
| Working capital loan | $ 2,688 | $ 1,512 | $ 4,252 |
| Accounts payable | 912 | 1,752 | 3,856 |
| Taxes payable | 328 | 952 | 736 |
| Other current liabilities | 312 | 456 | 252 |
| Total current liabilities | $ 4,240 | $ 4,672 | $ 9,096 |
| Term bank loan | | | 4,200 |
| Mortgages payable | 752 | 564 | 468 |
| Total liabilities | $ 4,992 | $ 5,236 | $13,764 |
| **SHAREHOLDERS' EQUITY** | | | |
| Common stock | $ 4,384 | $ 4,384 | $ 4,384 |
| Retained earnings | 1,916 | 3,048 | 4,596 |
| Total shareholders' equity | $ 6,300 | $ 7,432 | $ 8,980 |
| TOTAL LIABILITIES AND<br>SHAREHOLDERS' EQUITY | $11,292 | $12,668 | $22,744 |

*EXHIBIT 4*

|  | 1990 | | 1991 |
|---|---|---|---|
| **Dawson Lumber Company Limited**<br>**Capital Expenditures**<br>**1990 and 1991**<br>**($000s)** | | | |
|  | **Projected** | **Actual** | **Projected** |
| Showroom renovations | 140 | 320 | 160 |
| Showroom expansion for<br>  two lumber yards | 320 | 280 | — |
| New showrooms for<br>  two lumber yards | 1,040 | 1,700 | 400 |
| Land for new yard in<br>  Northern Region | 100 | 100 | — |
| Land for new yard in<br>  Western Region | — | — | 60 |
| New vehicles | 200 | 1,400 | 480 |
| New retail outlet in Ottawa | — | 1,600 | — |
| Total | 1,800 | 5,400 | 1,100 |

## C A S E  **3.3**   ELLINGTON INDUSTRIAL SUPPLY INC.

In June 1995 Mr. Ellington was working out the financial details of a tentative plan to build an extension onto his warehouse. He was concerned as to what source of funds he should use in order to raise the $100,000 required for construction costs.

**THE COMPANY**

Ellington Industrial Supply Inc. (EISI) was a distributor of machine tools, maintenance parts, and related equipment in Lakeside. One hundred kilometres north of a metropolitan area and situated on a large lake, Lakeside was the largest and fastest growing industrial centre in its region. Lakeside had a population of 55,000. In addition it served the surrounding farming communities and summer cottage trade. The customers of EISI were mostly industrial maintenance departments, but there was also some high margin retail business, principally from farmers in the surrounding area.

Mr. Ellington purchased the business from its previous owner, Mr. Hodges, in February 1992. As part of the purchase agreement, Mr. Hodges took a note payable from EISI. By 1992 Mr. Ellington had already gained wide experience in a series of jobs. He had worked for a variety of different companies, including one of his current metropolitan-based competitors. During those years, however, he was dominated by a persistent ambition to operate his own business. His first personal venture was a retail hardware store in Riverton, which he sold when he acquired the EISI.

Mr. Ellington felt pleased with the progress his company had made in the three years since he had purchased it. He had enjoyed considerable success in building up sales. His confidence was such that, in August 1994, EISI purchased its rented facilities, when the landlord offered the property to EISI at what Mr. Ellington regarded as "a very attractive price." By June 1995, monthly sales volume averaged more than $100,000. (Exhibit 1 gives income statements for the past three years.) Mr. Ellington was also proud of the company's reputation for dependability and integrity. He believed his success was due largely to the personalized service and engineering advice he offered his customers. He also realized that an important factor in attracting new customers and building lasting customer relationships was his success in obtaining exclusive rights to handle the products of some of the better manufacturers. Maintaining good supplier relations with those manufacturers who granted him exclusives was a key element to future success.

**COMPETITION**

Until late 1994, EISI had been the only distributor of machine tools and parts who was situated in Lakeside. Competition had come from salespeople operating from out-of-town warehouses. In the fall of 1994 another distributor started up an operation in Lakeside. Mr. Ellington believed, however, that the new competitor would not conflict directly with more than a small part of his business because of the exclusive distribution rights he held and his specialized products. This new distributor also did not as yet have the reputation for dependable service that EISI enjoyed.

**THE FUTURE**

Although market information was limited, Mr. Ellington thought that EISI had about 35 percent of the machine tool and equipment market in Lakeside and the surrounding region. Given the existing market potential, he felt that he could not expect to increase his sales beyond $2,000,000 without expanding his geographical market area. For the next two years he projected probable sales to be $1,400,000 for the year ending January 31, 1996, and $1,600,000 for the year ending January 31, 1997. He felt sales could fall as low as $1,300,000 and $1,500,000 for fiscal years 1996 and 1997 respectively, or go as high as $1,600,000 and $1,800,000.

**THE PROBLEM**

In June 1995, one of Mr. Ellington's major concerns was the cramped space in EISI's warehouse. With its present facilities he felt EISI could not handle any significant increases in inventory on hand. In order to maintain the high standard of service and delivery, he wanted to add a warehouse extension as soon as possible. At the same time one of his top priorities was to reduce the age of EISI's accounts payable to 60 days before the end of the fiscal year. If he failed to do so he feared that he would put some of EISI's exclusive distribution agreements in jeopardy. First, Mr. Ellington wanted to determine the amount of money EISI needed to carry out his plans, and then to decide which source of funds to use. Several options were available. His preference was to borrow either from the bank or from a private lender. He did, however, have another alternative, namely selling shares in EISI to a local investor. At the time of his decision, Mr. Ellington was hesitant to use equity financing. He felt he would not get as much now for a share in the company as he could expect in a year when his hard work had paid off in increased profits. He was also wondering about the company's capability to generate its own funds.

*Exhibit 1*

| Ellington Industrial Supply Income Statements for the Years Ending January 31 | | | |
|---|---|---|---|
| | **1993** | **1994** | **1995** |
| Net sales | $465,055 | $799,960 | $1,033,410 |
| Cost of sales: | | | |
| Opening inventory | $113,255 | $154,490 | $171,040 |
| Purchases | 363,330 | 602,430 | 804,695 |
| Cost of goods available for sale | $476,585 | $756,920 | $975,735 |
| Less: closing inventory | 154,490 | 171,040 | 237,315 |
| Cost of sales | 322,095 | 585,880 | 738,420 |
| Gross margin | $142,960 | $214,080 | $294,990 |
| Expenses: | | | |
| Wages and commissions | $ 91,810 | $126,955 | $153,085 |
| Rent[1] | 9,715 | 11,100 | 5,550 |
| Interest expenses | 13,615 | 14,610 | 16,875 |
| Provision for doubtful accounts | 3,355 | — | — |
| General selling expenses | 14,550 | 13,780 | 11,930 |
| General administrative expense | 38,215 | 52,360 | 66,425 |
| Depreciation | — | 5,150 | 12,180 |
| Total expenses | 171,260 | 223,955 | 266,045 |
| Net profit (loss) | $ (28,300) | $ (9,875) | $ 28,945 |

1. With the purchase of the land and building, rent expense had now been eliminated.

*EXHIBIT 2*

|  | 1994 | 1995 | 1996 |
|---|---|---|---|
| **Ellington Industrial Supply Inc.** **Balance Sheets** **as at January 31** | | | |
| **ASSETS** | | | |
| Current assets: | | | |
| Cash | $43,030 | $8,755 | $710 |
| Accounts receivable, net | 64,250 | 100,835 | 169,345 |
| Inventory | 154,490 | 171,040 | 237,315 |
| Prepaid interest | 1,510 | 1,510 | 870 |
| Total current assets | $263,280 | $281,140 | $408,240 |
| Fixed assets | | | |
| Automobiles | $17,175 | $17,175 | $23,925 |
| Land | | | 30,440 |
| Building | | | 61,470 |
| Equipment | | | 1,995 |
| Subtotal | $17,175 | $17,175 | $117,830 |
| Less: accumulated depreciation | | 5,150 | 17,330 |
| Total fixed assets | 17,175 | 12,025 | 100,500 |
| Other Assets | | | |
| Goodwill | 15,000 | 15,000 | 15,000 |
| Deferred charges | 3,285 | 1,925 | 1,375 |
| TOTAL ASSETS | $298,740 | $311,090 | $525,115 |
| | | | |
| **LIABILITIES** | | | |
| Current liabilities | | | |
| Accounts payable | $92,320 | $145,370 | $251,250 |
| Other current liabilities | 7,895 | 5,925 | 17,925 |
| Total current liabilities | $100,215 | $151,295 | $269,175 |
| Long-term liabilities | | | |
| Bank loan[1] | $63,450 | $50,850 | $38,250 |
| GMAC payable[2] | 15,120 | 8,865 | 2,605 |
| Hodges payable[3] | 98,255 | 88,255 | 88,255 |
| Mortgage payable[4] | | | 86,060 |
| Total long-term liabilities | 176,825 | 147,970 | 215,170 |
| TOTAL LIABILITIES | $277,040 | $299,265 | $484,345 |
| | | | |
| **EQUITY** | | | |
| Common stock[5] | $50,000 | $50,000 | $50,000 |
| Retained earnings | (28,300) | (38,175) | (9,230) |
| TOTAL EQUITY | 21,700 | 11,825 | 40,770 |
| TOTAL LIABILITIES AND EQUITY | $298,740 | $311,090 | $525,115 |

1. $75,000 was borrowed in 1992. Principal payments — $1,050 per month; interest — 0.75 percent per month.
2. Balance owing on a truck bought in 1992. It was totally repaid in April 1995.
3. Loan from previous owner of the business, secured by inventory, incurred in February 1992 as part of the purchase agreement. Principal payments of $5,000 due in January 1993 and 1994, with payment of $10,000 due every succeeding January. Interest of 10 percent to be paid half-yearly on the balance of principal owing in January and June.
4. Mortgage loan made in August 1994 when EISI purchased the property and building. Five-year mortgage for $87,500 at 9 percent. Combined interest and principal payments of $880 were due each month.
5. Ellington originally invested $50,000.

*Exhibit 3*

| Ellington Industrial Supply Inc. Long-term Debt Interest and Principal Payments for Selected Fiscal Years Ending January 31 | | | | |
|---|---|---|---|---|
| **Fiscal Year** | **Opening Balance** | **Interest Payment** | **Principal Payment** | **Ending Balance** |
| 1.  Bank loan | | | | |
| January 31, 1996 | 38,250 | 2,875 | 12,600 | 25,650 |
| January 31, 1997 | 25,650 | 1,740 | 12,600 | 13,050 |
| January 31, 1998 | 13,050 | 590 | 13,050 | 0 |
| 2.  GMAC payable | | | | |
| January 31, 1996 | 2,605 | 100 | 2,605 | 0 |
| 3.  Hodges payable | | | | |
| January 31, 1997 | 88,255 | 8,826 | 20,000[1] | 68,255 |
| January 31, 1998 | 68,255 | 6,826 | 10,000 | 58,255 |
| 4.  9% mortgage payable | | | | |
| January 31, 1996 | 86,060 | 7,481 | 3,079 | 82,981 |
| January 31, 1997 | 82,981 | 7,198 | 3,362 | 79,619 |
| January 31, 1998 | 79,619 | 6,889 | 3,671 | 75,948 |

**1.** The $10,000 principal payment due January 31, 1996 was not paid and will have to be added to the January 31, 1997 payment.

C A S E 3.4  GARDINER WHOLESALERS
INCORPORATED (A)

In early February 1983, Kathy Wilson, assistant credit manager of Gardiner Wholesalers Inc., sat at her desk reviewing the financial information she had gathered on two of her company's accounts — S.D. Taylor Jewellers Ltd. and Elegance Jewellers Inc. Gardiner Wholesalers Inc., a jewellery wholesaler located in southwestern Ontario, had for many years followed a policy of thoroughly assessing the credit standing of each of its accounts about one month after Christmas. The assessment, which would be used to determine if changes in credit policy were necessary, had to be submitted to both the credit manager and the sales manager in one week. Ms. Wilson wondered what comments and recommendations concerning the two accounts should be put in her report.

The retail jewellery trade was largely composed of national chain stores such as Birk's, Peoples', and Mappins and smaller independent jewellers like S.D. Taylor Jewellers Ltd. and Elegance Jewellers Inc. Most retail jewellers carried both jewellery lines, such as gold and diamond rings, and giftware items, such as silverplated items and crystal. Most jewellery chains purchased jewellery pieces from jewellery manufacturers, and mounted the finished products in-house. Independent jewellers were supplied by wholesalers, like Gardiner Wholesalers Inc., who received the jewellery and giftware from such manufacturers as Jolyn Jewellery Inc., the French Jewellery Co. of Canada Ltd., Royal Doulton, and Belfleur Crystal. The wholesalers distributed products to regional department stores, small regional jewellery chains, and independent jewellery stores. An independent jeweller would be supplied by at least five jewellery wholesalers.

Jewellery store sales were lowest during the summer months and peaked during the Christmas season. The smaller, often family-owned, independent jewellers were much more affected by the seasonal pattern of jewellery sales than were the national chain-store operations. As a result, the independent jewellers relied heavily on their suppliers for financial support, in the form of extended credit, in order to remain competitive with national chain stores. The competition among suppliers for the retail jewellery trade made credit terms and retailer financing necessary wholesale features. Factors that influenced the consumer purchase decision were style, selection, quality, and customer credit. In 1982, layaway sales accounted for 25 percent of all retail jewellery store sales. Layaway sales were necessary in the jewellery business because people often balked at making large cash expenditures for luxury items. The layaway sales technique was also a powerful tool in influencing customers to purchase more expensive items.

S.D. Taylor Jewellers Ltd., located in London, Ontario, had been purchasing jewellery products from Gardiner Wholesalers for the last 25 years. The store handled a complete line of jewellery and giftware items. Peak periods of sales were traditionally Christmas, Valentine's Day, Mother's Day, and graduation time. Seventy percent of S.D. Taylor's sales were cash, and 30 percent were on 90-day instalment plans. Instalment terms called for a 10 percent deposit and there were no interest charges or carrying costs on the remainder of payments made within 90 days.

S.D. Taylor Jewellers Ltd. had been established in 1953 as a sole proprietorship and was incorporated in 1958. The couple who owned and operated the business were noted for their friendliness and were well respected in the local business community. Mr. Taylor was a member of the Southwestern Ontario Jewellers' Association and had attended numerous courses offered by the Gemological Institute of America. On reviewing the company's file, Ms. Wilson found that payments on account had, for the most part, been prompt.

Elegance Jewellers Inc. was a comparatively new customer of Gardiner Wholesalers Inc., having switched suppliers in early 1981. No reason for the change was given in the files. Elegance Jewellers Inc. was owned by a small group of businessmen who had interests in four other unrelated businesses. The company owned and operated two small-sized jewellery stores, both located in Sarnia, Ontario. The Elegance Jewellers stores carried mostly jewellery lines, and very little giftware. Most of Elegance Jewellers' sales were for cash. Instalment plans were available and called for a 20 percent deposit plus a one-percent-per-month carrying charge on the outstanding balance. Comments in the file indicated that Elegance Jewellers' account had been satisfactory through 1982.

Both accounts were sold on standard terms of 1/10, net 30, and the terms were extended to net 90 during the fall. The sales manager felt that the extension of a fairly liberal credit policy to Gardiner Wholesalers' customers was necessary to remain competitive in a tough market.

Prior to starting her report, Ms. Wilson investigated some pieces of economic information. She was aware that the Canadian economy was doing very poorly and that consumer spending was down in 1982. The Statistics Canada report on retail jewellery store sales confirmed her belief that 1982 had been a poor year (see Exhibit 1). Ms. Wilson also had some 1981 financial information on the jewellery industry published by Dun and Bradstreet. She found that, on average, the age of receivables was 21 days; the current ratio was 1.8:1; the age of inventory was 230 days; and net worth was 44 percent of total assets. Although these statistics were from 1981, Ms. Wilson felt that they were still reasonable today. With that information in mind, Ms. Wilson leafed through the company files (Exhibits 2 through 7) and prepared to write her report.

*EXHIBIT 1*

| Annual Sales Growth of Jewellery Stores in Ontario | | |
|---|---|---|
| Year | Independent Stores | All Stores[1] |
| 1982 | 1.2% | 1.5% |
| 1981 | 10.5% | 7.3% |
| 1980 | 6.3% | 8.3% |
| 1979 | 7.3% | 8.9% |
| 1978 | 25.4% | 21.3% |
| 1977 | 7.8% | 5.9% |

**1.** Includes chain stores.
Source: Statistics Canada Catalogue 63-005, *Retail Trade*.

*EXHIBIT 2*

| Elegance Jewellers Incorporated Income Statements for Years Ending June 30 | | |
|---|---|---|
| | 1981 | 1982 |
| Sales | $860,765 | $991,402 |
| Cost of sales | 387,000 | 472,800 |
| Gross profit | $473,765 | $518,602 |
| Operating expenses: | | |
|    Selling and administrative | $292,058 | $357,103 |
|    Depreciation | 22,295 | 26,868 |
|    Total operating expenses | 314,353 | 383,971 |
| Operating profit | $159,412 | $134,631 |
| Unusual income (loss) | (5,250) | (5,850) |
|    Subtotal | $154,162 | $128,781 |
| Less: interest expense | 17,388 | 76,040 |
| Net profit before tax | $136,774 | $ 52,741 |
| Income taxes | 34,193 | 13,184 |
| Net earnings | $102,581 | $ 39,557 |
| Dividends paid | $ 17,500 | $ 25,000 |

*EXHIBIT 3*

| Elegance Jewellers Incorporated<br>Balance Sheets<br>as at June 30 | | |
| --- | --- | --- |
| | **1981** | **1982** |
| ASSETS | | |
| Current assets: | | |
| Cash | $ 580 | $ 638 |
| Accounts receivable | 4,613 | 21,612 |
| Inventory | 574,097 | 577,718 |
| Prepaid expenses | 2,667 | 2,975 |
| Total current assets | $ 581,957 | $ 602,943 |
| | | |
| Loans to employees | 13,175 | 12,837 |
| Investment in subsidiary | | 343,120 |
| Other investments | 8,805 | 8,992 |
| | | |
| Fixed assets: | | |
| Land | $ 12,758 | $ 12,758 |
| Buildings | 187,018 | 220,535 |
| Furniture and fixtures | 30,938 | 54,255 |
| Fixed assets, cost | $ 230,714 | $ 287,548 |
| Less: accumulated | | |
| depreciation | 83,637 | 110,505 |
| Total fixed assets | 147,077 | 177,043 |
| | | |
| TOTAL ASSETS | $ 751,014 | $1,144,935 |
| | | |
| LIABILITIES | | |
| Current liabilities: | | |
| Working capital loan | $ 66,475 | $ 5,210 |
| Accounts payable | 189,887 | 111,870 |
| Income taxes payable | 61,830 | 1,235 |
| Long-term debt due within one | | |
| year | 4,967 | — |
| Total current liabilities | $ 323,159 | $ 118,315 |
| | | |
| Bank loan (due December 31, 1983) | | 209,208 |
| Long-term notes payable | 76,410 | 451,410 |
| | | |
| TOTAL LIABILITIES | $ 399,569 | $ 778,933 |
| | | |
| EQUITY | | |
| Common stock | $ 55,000 | $ 55,000 |
| Retained earnings | 296,445 | 311,002 |
| TOTAL EQUITY | 351,445 | 366,002 |
| | | |
| TOTAL LIABILITIES AND EQUITY | $ 751,014 | $1,144,935 |

*EXHIBIT 4*

### S.D. Taylor Jewellers Ltd.
### Income Statements
### for Years Ending June 30

|  | 1981 | 1982 |
|---|---|---|
| Sales | $1,029,651 | $1,162,488 |
| Cost of sales | 484,176 | 566,894 |
| Gross profit | $ 545,475 | $ 595,594 |
| Operating expenses: |  |  |
| Salaries and benefits | $ 185,167 | $ 215,360 |
| Overheads | 61,709 | 73,487 |
| Advertising | 36,997 | 46,320 |
| Supplies | 34,978 | 41,750 |
| Depreciation | 17,529 | 19,712 |
| Bad debt | 2,064 | 3,467 |
| Other miscellaneous | 40,226 | 46,690 |
| Total operating expenses | 378,670 | 446,786 |
| Operating profit | $ 166,805 | $ 148,808 |
| Plus: other income | 16,424 | 18,700 |
| Subtotal | $ 183,229 | $ 167,508 |
| Less: interest expense | 18,484 | 26,837 |
| Net profit before tax | $ 164,745 | $ 140,671 |
| Income taxes | 41,186 | 35,168 |
| Net earnings | $ 123,559 | $ 105,503 |
| Dividends paid | $ 49,500 | $ 42,000 |

*EXHIBIT 5*

### S.D. Taylor Jewellers Ltd.
### Statement of Retained Earnings
### for Years Ending June 30

|  | 1981 | 1982 |
|---|---|---|
| Beginning retained earnings | $ 326,107 | $ 400,166 |
| Net earnings for the year | 123,559 | 105,503 |
| Subtotal | $ 449,666 | $ 505,669 |
| Less: dividends | 49,500 | 42,000 |
| Ending retained earnings | $ 400,166 | $ 463,669 |

***EXHIBIT 6***

|  | S.D. Taylor Jewellers Ltd.<br>Balance Sheets<br>as of June 30 | |
|---|---|---|
|  | **1981** | **1982** |
| ASSETS | | |
| Current assets: | | |
| Cash | $    4,860 | $    4,983 |
| Accounts receivable | 52,640 | 63,267 |
| Inventories | 442,756 | 538,337 |
| Prepaid expenses | 8,308 | 11,628 |
| Total current assets | $508,564 | $618,215 |
| | | |
| Loans to employees | 14,151 | 14,145 |
| Investment in subsidiary | 60,355 | 39,616 |
| Other investments | 8,715 | 9,093 |
| | | |
| Fixed assets: | | |
| Land | $  14,913 | $  14,913 |
| Buildings and fixtures | 221,017 | 256,317 |
| Less: accumulated | | |
| depreciation | 140,076 | 159,788 |
| Total fixed assets | 95,854 | 111,442 |
| | | |
| TOTAL ASSETS | $687,639 | $792,511 |
| | | |
| LIABILITIES | | |
| Current liabilities: | | |
| Working capital loan | $  15,110 | $  34,733 |
| Notes payable (bank) | 106,142 | 164,429 |
| Accounts payable | 91,512 | 92,430 |
| Income taxes payable | 42,064 | 10,709 |
| Total current liabilities | $254,828 | $302,301 |
| | | |
| Long-term debt | 12,209 | 6,105 |
| | | |
| TOTAL LIABILITIES | $267,037 | $308,406 |
| | | |
| EQUITY | | |
| Capital stock | $  20,436 | $  20,436 |
| Retained earnings | 400,166 | 463,669 |
| | | |
| TOTAL EQUITY | $420,602 | $484,105 |
| | | |
| TOTAL LIABILITIES AND EQUITY | $687,639 | $792,511 |

***EXHIBIT 7***

| Gardiner Wholesalers Incorporated<br>Aging of Accounts Receivable as at December 31, 1982 | | | | | | |
|---|---|---|---|---|---|---|
| **Due From** | **Prior** | **Sept.** | **Oct.** | **Nov.** | **Dec.** | **Totals** |
| S.D. Taylor Jewellers Ltd. | | $15,423 | $ 2,426 | $ 9,366 | $ 2,732 | $29,947 |
| Elegance Jewellers Inc. | $1,320 | 16,916 | 3,554 | 15,073 | 31,601 | 68,464 |

# C A S E 3.5 GARDINER WHOLESALERS INCORPORATED (B)

Two days had passed since Ms. Kathy Wilson, assistant credit manager for Gardiner Wholesalers Inc., had begun her report[1] on two of the company's accounts — S.D. Taylor Jewellers Ltd. and Elegance Jewellers Inc. Her analysis of the past financial performance of the two companies was complete and Ms. Wilson felt she was ready to make some recommendations. However, lunch with Jim Ferraro changed her mind. Mr. Ferraro was the assistant manager in charge of loans at a downtown bank, and a personal friend of Ms. Wilson. He suggested that a credit appraisal report should include projected statements, so that the future financing needs of the two jewellery retailers could be estimated. This additional information would then help Ms. Wilson to determine if these accounts would need to extend their payables in order to finance operations.

The next day, Ms. Wilson proceeded to have a meeting with Laurine Breen and Bert Haase, the managers of the two Elegance Jewellery Stores. Mr. Haase discussed operations for the past few months, describing them as "a little slow." He mentioned that, because of the slowdown in sales volume, Elegance Jewellers had reduced prices on some items, which "squeezed our margins a little more." Mrs. Breen added that the company was dropping its one-percent-per-month carrying charge on layaway sales, "in order to stimulate sales." Mr. Haase thought that the overall sales growth for the fiscal year would be between 5 and 10 percent and that, even though operating expenses had increased substantially last year, this year they would increase at about the same rate as sales. Mr. Haase also thought that inventory would be reduced because of closer scrutiny of inventory levels in the past few months, and that capital expenditures for renovations to the building were expected to equal depreciation expenses. Mrs. Breen concluded the meeting with a remark that she hoped Ms. Wilson would acknowledge in her report: "I hope you noticed that we've been paying our accounts more quickly than last year!"

In a meeting with Mr. Stan Taylor, manager and owner of S.D. Taylor Jewellers Ltd., Ms. Wilson again discussed recent retail performance. Mr. Taylor said that he experienced a "negligible" reduction in margins. He felt the expected sales growth for the coming year would be between 5 and 10 percent, with operating expenses expected to increase at the same rate. Mr. Taylor had no plans for changes in the credit policy of his company. Mr. Taylor noted that S.D. Taylor Jewellers Ltd. had been paying its accounts at comparatively the same rate as last year, and that he had been watching inventory levels more carefully. Mr. Taylor also told Ms. Wilson that the increase in buildings and fixtures was expected to equal depreciation, so the net book value would remain the same.

With this additional information from the two retailers in mind, Ms. Wilson set out to complete her report.

### NOTES

1. For details on the nature of this report see "Gardiner Wholesalers Incorporated (A)."

# C A S E 3.6   LAWSONS

"I think I have all the information needed for your request, Mr. Mackay. Give me a couple of days to come up with a decision and I'll contact you one way or another — good day!" So said Jackie Patrick, a newly appointed loans officer for the Commercial Bank of Ontario. She was addressing Mr. Paul Mackay, sole proprietor of Lawsons, a general merchandising retailer in Riverdale, Ontario. He had just requested a $97,000 bank loan to reduce his trade debt, as well as a $13,000 line of credit to service his tight months of cash shortage. Jackie felt she was fully prepared to scrutinize all relevant information in order to make an appropriate decision. Her appointment as loans officer, effective today, February 18, 1987, was an exciting opportunity for her as she had been preparing for this position for some time.

## LAWSONS

Lawsons had been operating in Riverdale for nearly five years. Mr. Mackay felt that his store stressed value at competitive prices, targeting low to middle income families. The store offered a wide range of products in various categories such as:

- infants', children's, and youths' wear
- ladies' wear
- men's wear
- accessories (footwear, panty hose, jewellery, etc.)
- home needs (domestics, housewares, notions, yarn, stationery)
- toys, health and beauty aids
- seasonal items (Christmas giftwrap, candy)

To help finance the start up of the business in 1982, Mr. Mackay secured a $50,000 long-term loan from the Commercial Bank of Ontario at the prime lending rate plus 1 1/2 percent. As Mr. Mackay's personal assets were insufficient for security, the bank loan had been secured by a pledge against all company assets, and by a guarantee from Lawsons' major supplier, Forsyth Wholesale Ltd. (FWL).

Mr. Mackay's store, with the exception of its first partial year, had always generated net income. However, after drawings, Mr. Mackay's equity in the firm decreased each year to its present level of (9,257). Exhibits 1, 2, and 3 present Lawsons' income statements, balance sheets, and selected financial ratios.

**PURCHASING PROCEDURES**

Mr. Mackay purchased most of his inventory from FWL, a wholesaler who dealt in the product categories and merchandise that Mr. Mackay stocked in his store. Other stock, not supplied through FWL was purchased directly from local suppliers. Through an arrangement with FWL, Mr. Mackay made his merchandising decisions at two annual trade shows in May and October. At the May show, Mr. Mackay decided on back-to-school supplies, Christmas merchandise, and fall and winter clothing. Spring and summer merchandise was decided upon at the October show. FWL's purchasing agents accumulated all of the orders from the various retailers it dealt with and, as a large buying group, executed the orders and negotiated prices with the manufacturers. The merchandise was sent to FWL from the individual manufacturers and then was distributed to the respective retail outlets, such as Lawsons. FWL required partial payment for this merchandise before the start of the particular selling season. The remainder was due in scheduled repayments throughout the selling season. Mr. Mackay was pleased with the arrangement that he had secured with FWL. He was convinced that his product costs were lower as a result.

**PAUL MACKAY**

Paul Mackay was 40 years old. He immigrated to Canada in 1982 from his native England, where he had been employed by an insurance company as an accountant. Educationally, Mr. Mackay had completed a Business Economics degree at a military academy. When Mr. Mackay came to Canada, he admitted that he was unsure about what recognition he would receive for his previous labours, both corporate and educational. Consequently, Mr. Mackay embarked upon an entrepreneurial career. Candidly, Mr. Mackay expressed this attitude: "I knew I wouldn't be satisfied in some corporate hierarchy — I knew I needed to be in business for myself." In May 1982, a retail vacancy became available in Riverdale. Mr. Mackay seized this opportunity to turn his dream of independence into a reality, and opened Lawsons with the financial backing of FWL.

Mr. Mackay was an active resident of Riverdale, often involving himself in community activities. He worked long hours at his store, performing both managerial and clerical duties. Frequently, Mr. Mackay could be seen in his store with price gun in hand, pricing and stocking goods, or bagging merchandise at the cash register.

**THE PROBLEM**

Low earnings and necessary owner withdrawals had contributed to Mr. Mackay's increasing trade debt. Past due amounts on trade debt were charged a penalty of 17 1/2 percent interest. Mr. Mackay indicated that of the present $108,618 in trade debt, he was paying penalty interest on $96,834. All of the overdue trade debt was owed to FWL; it was this overdue debt that had prompted his loan request. Mr. Mackay knew that, if he could transfer this trade debt to some other form of debt with lower interest charges, profitability could be increased. Mr. Mackay indicated that the current portion of the trade debt would be an acceptable amount to carry for this time of year.

The total trade debt had increased to its present level in fiscal 1987 when Mr. Mackay decided that additional retail space would increase sales volume. Mr. Mackay felt that his present store size was too small to effectively display product lines and, therefore, decided that expansion was a necessary step to the store's turnaround. Additional furniture, fixtures, and leasehold improvements totalled $18,000, which was financed by FWL and added to Mr. Mackay's trade debt. Mr. Mackay explained that FWL financed the improvements at Lawsons because they were interested in Mr. Mackay improving to the point where he could start paying off the trade debt owed to them. At the time of the expansion, FWL's financial director stated, "If this expansion is a means towards debt repayment, and I believe it is, FWL is committed to financing the expansion." To go along with this capital expenditure, a greater investment in inventory was needed. Sales results in 1987 indicated to Mr. Mackay that the expansion was helping to improve sales volume.

Mr. Mackay believed that with his purchasing arrangements with FWL a seasonal line of credit was necessary, so that he could manage the months with tight cash positions. February through June were months of cash outflows, with the total cumulative cash outflows peaking at about 4 percent of sales. Exhibit 4 presents monthly sales percentages as well as the cash flows, whether cumulative net inflows or outflows.

## PROJECTIONS

Mr. Mackay did not anticipate any additional capital expenditures for some time, given the just completed expansion. Sales growth of 10 percent in each of the next two years was projected. With respect to interest charges, Mr. Mackay calculated that if less expensive debt could be found, Lawson's interest expense for all debt, including the proposed line of credit, would be $13,750 and $13,460 for 1988 and 1989, respectively. Store salaries would remain constant as a dollar amount because of improved employee productivity. Mr. Mackay realized he had a great deal of money tied up in inventory, but he hoped that, as he gained greater experience in handling the added sales volume, inventory could be reduced to pre-1987 levels. With respect to drawings, Mr. Mackay explained that, due to his depleted savings, future withdrawals from the firm would be at the 1987 level.

## JACKIE PATRICK

Ms. Patrick had hoped that her first loan request in her new position would be straightforward. However, a closer look indicated that this request would certainly require careful attention and scrutiny. She suspected her superiors would be reviewing her first series of recommendations carefully, given her newness in the position.

**EXHIBIT 1**

| | Income Statements for the Years Ending January 31 | | | |
| --- | --- | --- | --- | --- |
| | **1984** | **1985** | **1986** | **1987** |
| Sales | $212,699 | $253,889 | $263,166 | $325,105 |
| Cost of goods sold | 152,874 | 184,178 | 191,974 | 233,755 |
| Gross profit | $ 59,825 | $ 69,711 | $ 71,192 | $ 91,350 |
| Operating expenses: | | | | |
| Store salaries | $ 14,909 | $ 19,077 | $ 20,617 | $ 22,289 |
| Heat and utilities | 3,662 | 3,511 | 4,262 | 4,444 |
| Building maintenance and repairs | 169 | 203 | 254 | 181 |
| Rent and property tax | 14,182 | 14,182 | 12,355 | 11,996 |
| Insurance and taxes | 2,967 | 2,354 | 1,727 | 3,461 |
| Depreciation: | | | | |
| furniture and fixtures | 3,187 | 1,785 | 1,476 | 3,914 |
| leaseholds | — | 80 | 242 | 1,588 |
| Interest: | | | | |
| long-term debt | 5,709 | 5,666 | 4,640 | 4,209 |
| trade debt | 2,362 | 2,977 | 5,738 | 14,785 |
| Other operating expenses | 7,008 | 11,920 | 13,056 | 13,846 |
| Total operating expenses | 54,155 | 61,755 | 64,367 | 80,713 |
| Net income | $ 5,670 | $ 7,956 | $ 6,825 | $ 10,637 |

*EXHIBIT 2*

|  | Balance Sheets as at January 31 | | | |
|---|---|---|---|---|
|  | **1984** | **1985** | **1986** | **1987** |
| **ASSETS** | | | | |
| Current assets: | | | | |
| Cash | $ 1,298 | $ 1,399 | $ 1,980 | $ 4,832 |
| Accounts receivable | 1,139 | 1,172 | 2,412 | 6,014 |
| Inventory | 60,609 | 70,396 | 76,814 | 99,850 |
| Prepaids | 1,393 | 1,581 | 1,501 | 1,880 |
| Total current assets | $ 64,439 | $ 74,548 | $ 82,707 | $112,576 |
| **Fixed assets:** | | | | |
| Furniture and fixtures, cost | $ 16,082 | $ 16,082 | $ 17,396 | $ 30,600 |
| Less: accumulated depreciation | 7,157 | 8,942 | 10,418 | 14,331 |
| Net book value | $ 8,925 | $ 7,140 | $ 6,978 | $ 16,269 |
| Leaseholds, cost |  | $ 600 | $ 3,399 | $ 8,087 |
| Less: accumulated depreciation |  | 80 | 322 | 1,910 |
| Total fixed assets | 8,925 | 7,660 | 10,055 | 22,446 |
| Intangibles | 42 | — | — | — |
| **TOTAL ASSETS** | $ 73,406 | $ 82,208 | $ 92,762 | $135,022 |
| **LIABILITIES** | | | | |
| Current liabilities: | | | | |
| Accounts payable | $ 21,696 | $ 35,643 | $ 53,247 | $108,618 |
| Other current liabilities | — | 467 | 135 | 1,225 |
| Total current liabilities | $ 21,696 | $ 36,110 | $ 53,382 | $109,843 |
| Long-term bank loan | 44,918 | 41,732 | 38,084 | 34,436 |
| **TOTAL LIABILITIES** | $ 66,614 | $ 77,842 | $ 91,466 | $144,279 |
| **PROPRIETOR'S CAPITAL** | | | | |
| Balance, beginning of year | $ 10,576 | $ 6,792 | $ 4,366 | $ 1,296 |
| Add: net income | 5,670 | 7,956 | 6,825 | 10,637 |
| Subtotal | $ 16,246 | $ 14,748 | $ 11,191 | $ 11,933 |
| Less: drawings | 9,454 | 10,382 | 9,895 | 21,190 |
| Balance, end of year | 6,792 | 4,366 | 1,296 | (9,257) |
| **TOTAL LIABILITIES and PROPRIETOR'S CAPITAL** | $ 73,406 | $ 82,208 | $ 92,762 | $135,022 |

*EXHIBIT 3*

| Ratio Analysis | | | | |
|---|---|---|---|---|
| | **1984** | **1985** | **1986** | **1987** |
| PROFITABILITY | | | | |
| (A) Vertical analysis: | | | | |
| Sales | 100.0% | 100.0% | 100.0% | 100.0% |
| Cost of goods sold | 71.9% | 72.5% | 72.9% | 71.9% |
| Gross profit | 28.1% | 27.5% | 27.1% | 28.1% |
| Operating Expenses: | | | | |
| Store salaries | 7.0% | 7.5% | 7.8% | 6.9% |
| Heat and utilities | 1.7% | 1.4% | 1.6% | 1.4% |
| Building maintenance and repairs | 0.1% | 0.1% | 0.1% | 0.1% |
| Rent and property tax | 6.7% | 5.6% | 4.7% | 3.7% |
| Insurance and taxes | 1.4% | 0.9% | 0.7% | 1.1% |
| Depreciation: | | | | |
| furniture and fixtures | 1.5% | 0.7% | 0.6% | 1.2% |
| leaseholds | — | — | 0.1% | 0.5% |
| Interest: | | | | |
| long-term debt | 2.7% | 2.2% | 1.8% | 1.3% |
| trade debt | 1.1% | 1.2% | 2.2% | 4.6% |
| Other operating expenses | 3.3% | 4.7% | 5.0% | 4.3% |
| Total operating expenses | 25.5% | 24.3% | 24.6% | 25.1% |
| Net income | 2.6% | 3.2% | 2.6% | 3.3% |
| (B) Return on investment | 65.3% | 142.6% | 241.1% | N/A |
| LIQUIDITY | | | | |
| Current ratio | 2.97:1 | 2.06:1 | 1.55:1 | 1.02:1 |
| Acid test ratio | 0.11:1 | 0.07:1 | 0.08:1 | 0.10:1 |
| Working capital | $ 42,743 | $ 38,438 | $ 29,325 | $ 2,733 |
| EFFICIENCY (Based on 365-day year) | | | | |
| Age of receivables | 2 days | 2 days | 3 days | 7 days |
| Age of inventory | 145 days | 140 days | 146 days | 156 days |
| Age of payables[1] | 55 days | 67 days | 98 days | 154 days |
| Net fixed assets/sales | $ 0.04 | $ 0.03 | $ 0.04 | $ 0.07 |
| STABILITY | | | | |
| Net worth/total assets | 9.3% | 5.3% | 1.4% | N/A |
| Interest coverage | 1.7X | 1.9X | 1.7X | 1.6X |

| | **1984–85** | **1985–86** | **1986–87** |
|---|---|---|---|
| GROWTH | | | |
| Sales | 19.4% | 3.7% | 23.5% |
| Net profit | 40.3% | (14.2%) | 55.9% |
| Total assets | 12.0% | 12.8% | 45.6% |
| Net worth | (35.7%) | (70.3%) | N/A |

**1.** Aging is based on purchases, which are equal to cost of goods sold, plus ending inventory, less beginning inventory.

*EXHIBIT 4*

| Sales and Cumulative Net Cash Outflow by Month | | |
|---|---|---|
| **MONTH** | **% OF SALES** | **CUMULATIVE NET CASH OUTFLOW** |
| February | 3.5 | Yes |
| March | 5.4 | Yes |
| April | 7.5 | Yes |
| May | 8.3 | Yes |
| June | 11.1 | Yes |
| July | 12.9 | No |
| August | 12.4 | No |
| September | 9.3 | No |
| October | 5.8 | No |
| November | 6.2 | No |
| December | 13.6 | No |
| January | 4.0 | No |

# C A S E **3.7**   MAPLE LEAF HARDWARE LTD.

On May 29, 1981, Mr. Stuart Foreman, assistant manager of the London, Ontario branch of the Central Canadian Bank, was reviewing information he had received from Maple Leaf Hardware Ltd. Mr. Robert Patrick, president and manager of Maple Leaf Hardware Ltd., had requested an increase in his line of credit with the bank to cover seasonal working capital needs. Mr. Foreman, who had just received a transfer and promotion to the London branch, realized he would have to evaluate this request carefully.

**COMPANY BACKGROUND**

Mr. Patrick was 32 years of age. His father had established his own hardware business in Nova Scotia in 1951. Robert had worked in his father's store since the age of 16, gaining valuable sales and management experience. In 1973, Mr. Patrick accepted a job offer from a large retail department chain. Two years later he was transferred to London, Ontario, and eventually became manager of one of the branch stores. In 1978, he decided to leave the department chain in order to become his own boss. He opened his own retail hardware store with a personal investment of $60,000 and $40,000 from a close friend, Mr. Les Harrison, and incorporated the company on September 1, 1978. Mr. Patrick was able to arrange a long-term loan of $120,000 and a line of credit of $30,000 with the Central Canadian Bank through Mr. Terry Woods (Mr. Foreman's predecessor, who had recently left the bank). After a detailed analysis, Mr. Patrick decided to locate his business on Maple Leaf Street in a growing area of the city. He was able to rent a recently vacated building with 6,500 square feet of space and adequate parking facilities. The nearest store was located several kilometres away. Initially, only two full-time and three part-time employees were hired to assist Mr. Patrick. As the business grew additional part-time employees were hired. Sales increased steadily during the first few years, and in 1980, Maple Leaf Hardware Ltd. realized its first profit.

**THE INDUSTRY**

During the 1950s, home and garden supplies, or hardware, were distributed primarily through small, independently owned stores. The major alternative distributor was the hardware department of the major department stores. Since that decade, many large scale retailers have begun to sell hardware. Statistics Canada reported that of the estimated $6.4 billion total retail hardware sales in 1980, only 12 percent of that total was realized in traditional hardware stores.

The increased competition has resulted in much consolidation within the industry. Chain store hardware organizations in Canada included Bannister and Jenkins Ltd., Cochrane-Dunlop's Dominion Hardware Stores Ltd., Merit Stores Ltd., and J. Pascal Ltd. There were also cooperative groups such as Pro Hardware (317 stores) and Home Hardware (625 stores). Buying for these large organizations was mainly done on a central basis. Another major outlet for hardware items was building supply stores.

There were over 20 stores in London in the retail hardware business, including independently owned, chain, and department stores. Hardware stores offered a wide variety of goods including tools, plumbing and electrical supplies, appliances, cookware, lawn and garden equipment and, in some cases, sporting goods and toys. The major determinant of a hardware store's success was its location, as it was important to have a large area from which to draw customers. This was especially true for independent stores.

Hardware sales were traditionally highest around Christmas. January to April were slow months, while sales were much stronger from May to August. Because of this seasonality, and since a company had to order inventory well in advance, a hardware store's greatest need for working capital financing usually occurred in February or March. The strongest cash position was in December. In February or March, a hardware store the size of Maple Leaf Hardware Ltd. would require from $40,000 to $60,000 more working capital than was required in December.

In difficult economic times, with increasing inflation and interest rates, many industries were hit hard financially; however, this was not the case with the hardware industry. During economic recessions, consumers' emphasis shifted from purchasing new goods to repairing and rebuilding old goods. Statistics Canada estimated that residential repair expenditures would reach $3,113.1 million in 1981, an increase of 10.1 percent. This high level of repair expenditures was expected to be a source of increased sales for hardware stores. In recent months housing starts had also picked up. Statistics Canada estimated that the value of new residential construction would reach $12,304.2 million in 1981, an increase of 12.4 percent over 1980's preliminary total of $10,949.4 million.

## PRESENT SITUATION

Mr. Patrick presented his proposal for an increase in the short-term line of credit from $50,000 (the line of credit which had been granted last year) to $80,000. Mr. Patrick included in his report specific information which Mr. Foreman had requested, including financial statements for the years the company had been in operation (see Exhibits 1 and 2). Exhibit 3 provides financial ratios for the company and also includes available industry information. Mr. Patrick stated that sales for the year ending December 31, 1981, were expected to be close to $850,000. A further increase in sales of 10 to 20 percent was anticipated in 1982. There were no anticipated purchases of fixed assets in the next few years. Mr. Patrick planned to pay a common stock dividend of $10,000 each year starting on December 31, 1981. The rent was expected to increase by $1,200 per month commencing in September with the signing of a new two-year lease. Mr. Patrick was planning to introduce a new inventory control system which he hoped would eventually reduce the age of inventory to the industry average of the past few years; however, he was not sure if he would be able to accomplish this within the next year.

Mr. Foreman set out to decide whether or not to increase the size of the line of credit for Maple Leaf Hardware Ltd. He noted in his file that on one occasion in the past the company had been slow in sending financial data the bank had requested, but when Mr. Foreman mentioned the incident, Mr. Patrick dismissed it as a misunderstanding with Mr. Woods. In further conversation, Mr. Foreman learned that Mr. Patrick and Mr. Harrison (who owned 40 percent of the common shares) had recently had some disagreements as to how Mr. Patrick should be running the business. According to Mr. Patrick, "Les and I go 'way back. We've had our differences throughout the years, but things always get straightened out. I'm the major shareholder in this business, and I know how to run a hardware store profitably. I think sometimes Les forgets that."

Since this was Mr. Foreman's first evaluation of a loan request in his new position, he wanted to proceed cautiously and perform a thorough analysis. He realized he would have to present his decision within the week.

*EXHIBIT 1*

|  | Maple Leaf Hardware Ltd.<br>Income Statements<br>for Selected Periods<br>($000s) | | |
|---|---|---|---|
|  | **4 months to<br>Dec. 31, 1978** | **Year ended<br>Dec. 31, 1979** | **Year ended<br>Dec. 31, 1980** |
| Sales | $200 | $609 | $709 |
| Cost of goods sold | 135 | 406 | 468 |
| Gross profit | $ 65 | 203 | 241 |
| Operating expenses: | | | |
| Wages[1] | $ 26 | $ 86 | $ 91 |
| Rent | 18 | 57 | 60 |
| Property tax | 3 | 10 | 12 |
| Utilities | 2 | 7 | 8 |
| Depreciation | 3 | 9 | 9 |
| Advertising | 3 | 11 | 12 |
| Other | 15 | 15 | 9 |
| Interest | 6 | 18 | 16 |
| Total operating expenses | 76 | 213 | 217 |
| Net profit before tax | ($ 11) | ($ 10) | $ 24 |
| Income tax[2] | — | — | 1 |
| Net profit after tax | ($ 11) | ($ 10) | $ 23 |

1. Includes manager's salary of $12,000 in 1979 and $15,000 in 1980.
2. Tax laws allow the company to offset the $24,000 profit of 1980 with the combined $21,000 loss of the previous two years. Thus in 1980, the company only pays tax on the $3,000 difference at the rate of 25 percent.

*Exhibit 2*

| | | | |
|---|---|---|---|
| **Maple Leaf Hardware Ltd.** **Balance Sheets** **as at December 31** **($000s)** | | | |
| | **1978** | **1979** | **1980** |
| ASSETS | | | |
| Current assets: | | | |
| Cash | $ 17 | $ 6 | $ 5 |
| Accounts receivable | 10 | 15 | 16 |
| Inventory | 147 | 160 | 208 |
| Total current assets | $174 | $181 | $229 |
| Fixed assets: | | | |
| Leasehold improvements (net) | $ 39 | $ 36 | $ 33 |
| Fixtures (net) | 48 | 42 | 36 |
| Total fixed assets | 87 | 78 | 69 |
| TOTAL ASSETS | $261 | $259 | $298 |
| LIABILITIES | | | |
| Current liabilities: | | | |
| Accounts payable | $ 55 | $ 62 | $ 85 |
| Working capital loan | — | 9 | 10 |
| Current portion of long-term debt | 8 | 8 | 8 |
| Total current liabilities | $ 63 | $ 79 | $103 |
| Long-term debt[1] | $109 | $101 | $ 93 |
| TOTAL LIABILITIES | $172 | $180 | $196 |
| EQUITY | | | |
| Common stock | | | |
| R. Patrick | $ 60 | $ 60 | $ 60 |
| L. Harrison | 40 | 40 | 40 |
| Retained earnings | (11) | (21) | 2 |
| TOTAL EQUITY | 89 | 79 | 102 |
| TOTAL LIABILITIES AND EQUITY | $261 | $259 | $298 |

**1.** Principal payments of $667 were due each month. The interest rate was 15 percent. The loan was secured by personal assets of the owners.

*Exhibit 3*

| | Canadian Hardware Stores Industry Ratios[1] | | Maple Leaf Hardware Ltd. Ratios | | |
|---|---|---|---|---|---|
| **Maple Leaf Hardware Ltd.** **Financial Ratios** | 1978 | 1979 | 1978 | 1979 | 1980 |
| **PROFITABILITY** | | | | | |
| (A) Vertical analysis | | | | | |
| Sales | 100.0% | 100.0% | 100.0% | 100.0% | 100.0% |
| Cost of goods sold | 68.9% | 67.8% | 67.5% | 66.7% | 66.0% |
| Gross profit | 31.1% | 32.2% | 32.5% | 33.3% | 34.0% |
| Expenses: | | | | | |
| Wages | | | 13.0% | 14.1% | 12.8% |
| Rent | | | 9.0% | 9.4% | 8.5% |
| Property tax | | | 1.5% | 1.6% | 1.7% |
| Utilities | | | 1.0% | 1.1% | 1.1% |
| Depreciation | | | 1.5% | 1.5% | 1.3% |
| Advertising | | | 1.5% | 1.8% | 1.7% |
| Other | | | 7.5% | 2.5% | 1.3% |
| Interest | | | 3.0% | 3.0% | 2.3% |
| Total expenses | 27.2% | 27.8% | 38.0% | 35.0% | 30.6% |
| Net profit before tax | 3.8% | 4.3% | (5.5%) | (1.6%) | 3.4% |
| Income tax | 1.1% | 1.2% | — | — | 0.1% |
| Net profit after tax | 2.7% | 3.1% | (5.5%) | (1.6%) | 3.2% |
| (B) Return on Investment | 14.9% | 18.7% | (34.9%) | (11.9%) | 25.4% |
| **LIQUIDITY** | | | | | |
| Current ratio | 1.87:1 | 1.85:1 | 2.76:1 | 2.29:1 | 2.21:1 |
| Acid test | 0.53:1 | 0.45:1 | 0.43:1 | 0.27:1 | 0.20:1 |
| Working capital ($000s) | 64 | 73 | 111 | 102 | 126 |
| **EFFICIENCY** (Based on 365 days, except 1978, which is based on one-third of a year.) | | | | | |
| Age of accounts receivable in days sales | 26.0 | 21.8 | 6 | 9 | 8 |
| Inventory in days C.G.S. | 137.4 | 143.1 | 132.5 | 143.8 | 162.2 |
| Age of accounts payable in days cost of goods sold | 48.12 | 44.3 | 49.5 | 55.7 | 66.3 |
| **STABILITY** | | | | | |
| Net worth/Total assets | 37.5% | 36.0% | 34.1% | 30.5% | 34.2% |
| Interest coverage | | | 0.00X | 0.44X | 2.50X |

| | 1978–79 | 1979–80 |
|---|---|---|
| **GROWTH** (percentages) | | |
| Sales | 18.6% | 16.4% |
| Net profit | 38.7% | — |
| Total assets | 18.6% | 15.1% |
| Equity | 14.2% | 29.1% |

1. Compiled from Statistics Canada Information, Catalogue 61-207.

# C A S E **3.8**   MATERIAUX BOISVERT LTÉE.

In January 1992, Yvan Martinault, commercial account manager at the main branch of the Crown Bank of Canada in Chicoutimi, Quebec, stared at his computer wondering how to approach his most recent loan request. François Lachapelle, new owner and president of Materiaux Boisvert Ltée., had just requested an increase in the company's line of credit from $1.6 million to $2.2 million. Although Yvan was expecting a request for additional funds to cover working capital needs, previous financial forecasts had indicated a need of only $1.8 million. Yvan was somewhat surprised by the amount requested, but knew the application had to be processed quickly for head office approval in Montreal.

**COMPANY BACKGROUND**

Materiaux Boisvert sold hardware and building materials to retail customers as well as industrial contractors. The business was founded in 1982 in Chicoutimi by five partners who established a loyal customer base through reliable customer service and the establishment of a family-oriented atmosphere. The company operated two retail and distribution outlets in Chicoutimi. A large hardware store and lumber yard were located near the centre of the city while a smaller outlet was situated in the suburbs. The business was very successful, with sales reaching an all-time high of $20 million in 1985, which resulted in profits of $500,000 for the same year.

In 1986, the firm was purchased by Produits Forestier Saguenay (PFS), a large company whose core business was the manufacture of hardwood materials for export. The owners of PFS wished to invest extra money in a cash-producing business and thus purchased Materiaux Boisvert for its cash potential. Although Materiaux Boisvert became a separate operating division of PFS, management goals focused solely on the desire to make money. This new style of management created constant friction between managers and employees, which resulted in the unionization of employees in 1987. Management neglect and employee tensions began to affect many aspects of business operations, especially the company's reputation for customer service. By late 1989, the economic climate also began to deteriorate. A deepening recession worsened the firm's sales and receivables position and the company suffered three consecutive years of losses before being purchased by the Lachapelle family in September 1991.

At the time of the purchase, the Lachapelles already owned a major hardware and building supply outlet in Chicoutimi and were looking to penetrate further into the market. Thus, they took advantage of the opportunity to buy out their competitors. The rights to the company name as well as to the physical assets of Materiaux Boisvert were purchased with the exception of the land and buildings, which were rented for $200,000 per year with an option to purchase them within five years.

Mr. Lachapelle, François's father, was a well-respected client of the Crown Bank of Canada, which was financing a line of credit for his first company. Since Mr. Lachapelle eventually wanted his son to take over the family business, he placed François in charge of Materiaux Boisvert's operations. François Lachapelle was 27 years of age and was in the process of completing a Master's degree in Business Administration in Toronto. François was very familiar with all aspects of the hardware industry, having worked in the family business in various positions for many years. For François, the opportunity to run his own business was a personal goal. He had many ideas for turning Materiaux Boisvert into a thriving business and was eager to devote all his attention to the firm's operations.

## THE HARDWARE AND BUILDING MATERIALS INDUSTRY

The majority of hardware and building materials firms in Chicoutimi serviced both the retail and industrial markets. Hardware products consisted of tools, plumbing, paint, and electrical and garden supplies, while building materials included all supplies required for external and internal home or building construction. Building materials products were numerous and ranged from lumber and dry wall to shower moulds, windows, and doors.

The retail and industrial markets for hardware and building supplies were highly seasonal. Retail sales were slowest during the winter months, particularly in January and February. Peak periods occurred in May and June, with highest sales in May. Retail sales were not adversely affected by economic swings since customers delayed the purchase of new goods by repairing existing goods during difficult economic times. Although industrial sales also peaked in May and June, the industrial market remained strong during the period May to November. Unlike the retail market, the industrial market's close ties with the construction industry had a greater impact on sales during difficult economic periods.

## THE COMPETITION

The Chicoutimi market was served by two types of competitors: pure hardware and building supply outlets (the independents) and mass merchandisers (the chain stores). Canadian Tire was the only mass merchandiser in Chicoutimi with two locations in the area. Canadian Tire was a national chain that competed mainly in the retail hardware market, with a product mix that ranged from traditional hardware goods sold in most hardware stores to sporting goods and electrical appliances. Canadian Tire promoted its products using an aggressive advertising and promotion strategy; however, once in the store, customers received minimal service.

Independent hardware and building supply outlets sold a wide range of products necessary for the complete construction of homes or buildings. Advertising was more localized and achieved mainly through the use of pamphlets, flyers, newspapers, or radio. Customer service was an extremely important differentiating factor for most independents and many stores catered to their own loyal clientele.

Hardware and building materials companies in Chicoutimi faced intense competition due to the numerous competitors in the area. Seven local hardware and building supply companies competed through intense price wars, especially on most traditional materials and big ticket items.

**MATERIAUX BOISVERT**

Materiaux Boisvert operated in both the retail and industrial markets with the majority of sales (70 percent) in the industrial contract market. The company's retail margins traditionally ranged from 26 to 29 percent while contract margins ranged from 18 to 20 percent, compared to margins of approximately 32 percent and 23 percent for the industry. As margins were higher for retail sales, François hoped eventually to penetrate further into this market.

Materiaux Boisvert offered a 3 percent discount to its best customers for accounts paid before the 15th of the following month with the remaining balance due in 60 days. Other customers were offered net 60 days for debt payments while less stable customers were offered payment terms of net 30 days. François would have preferred to reduce all receivables to net 30 days; however, industry standards of 60 days restricted tight credit control.

The company relied on several hardware suppliers for the purchase of its hardware and building materials. Building materials prices, with the exception of lumber, were negotiated by a buying group consisting of 15 buyers from different geographic regions. Materials were then purchased by Materiaux Boisvert separately based on the negotiated price. Although many of the company's competitors also purchased materials from the same suppliers, none of the company's competitors participated in the buying group process.

The volatility of the lumber industry demanded good insight into the lumber market and required sharp purchasing skills. Materiaux Boisvert had its own purchaser who bought wood and lumber materials based on market dynamics and prices.

Industry terms for the majority of supplies were traditionally 2 percent in 10 days, net 30 days. François hoped to take advantage of the 2 percent discount as much as possible. The company's working capital needs were traditionally highest in June and François estimated that he would need approximately $150,000 more in June than in September.

**EVENTS LEADING UP TO THE LINE OF CREDIT REQUEST**

Before the purchase, Materiaux Boisvert was given a liberal maximum line of credit of $3.2 million because of the size and equity position of Produits Forestier Saguenay. Unfortunately, the Lachapelles did not have similar equity to place in the business and the loan was subsequently renegotiated to $1.6 million. The loan was secured by the company's accounts receivable and inventories as well as $250,000 of the Lachapelles' personal assets.

Both the Lachapelles and the bank realized that the new line of credit would likely be insufficient for peak period operations. Therefore, Yvan agreed to re-examine the company's loan requirements after several months of operations under new management. Yvan estimated that the new loan requirements would likely be close to $1.8 million; however, François requested $2.2 million.

## PRESENT SITUATION

The purchase of Materiaux Boisvert caused significant changes to the financial position of the company under new management. First, the company's fiscal year automatically changed from ending May 31 to ending September 30 since the firm was purchased in September. Second, Materiaux Boisvert was no longer a division of PFS and, therefore, investments and interdivisional accounts related to PFS would no longer be relevant.

Third, the purchase of Materiaux Boisvert resulted in the creation of a new business entity for the Lachapelles. Therefore, 1992 opening retained earnings would be equal to zero.

Finally, François's plans for turning the business around required a different set of operating assumptions than under previous management. François provided Yvan with three sales scenarios for the new fiscal year: most likely, optimistic, and least likely. Under the most likely scenario, 1992 sales were estimated to be close to 1991 sales with a 5 percent increase for 1993.

François planned to reduce wages and salaries to 10.2 percent of sales, while better account management would reduce bad debts to no more than 0.5 percent of sales. Accounting and lawyer's fees would return to pre-1991 levels of approximately $40,000 per year. François also estimated that tight control of travelling expenses, advertising, office supplies, and vehicle rentals would result in yearly expenditures of $24,000, $53,000, $60,000, and $5,000, respectively. Maintenance and repairs would likely remain the same in dollars as in 1991. Materiaux Boisvert also rented a small portion of a nearby parking lot. The parking lot lease had expired and would not be renewed in the future.

The Lachapelles purchased the company for $1.1 million of which $600,000 was paid in cash, resulting in an inflow of owner's capital for 1992. The remaining $500,000 would be owed to PFS as long-term debt of the company; previous long-term debt owed to the bank by PFS would not be assumed by the Lachapelles. Changes in the company's debt position would reduce interest expenses to approximately $300,000 per year.

## THE MEETING

A meeting was scheduled between the Lachapelles and Yvan to discuss the new request. As Yvan began to arrange for the meeting, he reflected that although the Lachapelles were long-standing customers of the bank, he had never dealt with François before. He knew he would have to perform a more thorough analysis of Materiaux Boisvert's operations and statements to prepare for the session.

**EXHIBIT 1**

| Materiaux Boisvert Ltée.<br>Income Statement<br>For the Years Ending May 31<br>($000s) | | | |
| --- | --- | --- | --- |
| | **1989** | **1990** | **1991** |
| Net Sales | $16,222 | $15,093 | $13,807 |
| Cost of Goods Sold | | | |
| Beginning inventory | 3,765 | 3,553 | 3,369 |
| Purchases[1] | 12,766 | 11,915 | 9,882 |
| Cost of goods available for sale | 16,531 | 15,468 | 13,251 |
| Ending inventory | 3,553 | 3,369 | 2,538 |
| Cost of goods sold | 12,978 | 12,099 | 10,713 |
| Gross Profit | 3,244 | 2,994 | 3,094 |
| Operating Expenses | | | |
| Wages and salaries | 1,655 | 1,521 | 1,488 |
| Insurance | 32 | 36 | 15 |
| Utilities | 81 | 70 | 76 |
| Maintenance and repairs | 260 | 262 | 199 |
| Office equipment rental and maintenance | 16 | 20 | 20 |
| Travelling expenses | 32 | 31 | 31 |
| Vehicle rental | 41 | 46 | 9 |
| Parking lot rental | 8 | 8 | 9 |
| Advertising | 49 | 58 | 72 |
| Property tax | 49 | 44 | 47 |
| Office supplies | 65 | 68 | 77 |
| Bad debt expense | 97 | 104 | 316 |
| Accounting and lawyer's fees | 65 | 52 | 124 |
| Corporate expenses paid to PFS | 32 | 35 | 88 |
| Depreciation: buildings | 49 | 42 | 46 |
|       other fixed assets | 227 | 206 | 225 |
| Other operating expenses | 32 | 31 | 32 |
| Total operating expenses | 2,790 | 2,634 | 2,874 |
| Operating Profit | 454 | 360 | 220 |
| Other Expenses | | | |
| Interest | 443 | 441 | 442 |
| Other | 13 | 308 | 19 |
| Total other expenses | 456 | 749 | 461 |
| Net profit before tax | (2) | (389) | (241) |
| Income tax expenses (Credit)[2] | 0 | 33 | 0 |
| Net profit after tax | $ (2) | $ (356) | $ (241) |

1. Purchases include any purchase discounts taken.
2. Tax laws allow the company an income tax credit of $33,000 to offset previous profits. The company's tax rate is 15 percent on income of $200,000 and 45 percent on all income above $200,000. Therefore, if profit were $500,000, tax would be calculated at 15 percent of $200,000 and 45 percent of $300,000.

*Exhibit 2*

| | Materiaux Boisvert Ltée.<br>Statement of Retained Earnings<br>For the Years Ending May 31<br>($000s) | | |
|---|---|---|---|
| | **1989** | **1990** | **1991** |
| Retained Earnings at Beginning of the Year | $3,574 | $3,572 | $3,216 |
| Net Profit | (2) | (356) | (241) |
| Retained Earnings at End of the Year | $3,572 | $3,216 | $2,975 |

*Exhibit 3*

|  | Materiaux Boisvert Ltée. Balance Sheets as at May 31 ($000s) | | |
| --- | --- | --- | --- |
|  | 1989 | 1990 | 1991 |
| **ASSETS** | | | |
| Current Assets: | | | |
| Cash | $ 0 | $ 0 | $ 29 |
| Accounts receivable | 2,727 | 2,678 | 2,124 |
| Due from Produits Forestier | 9 | 741 | 228 |
| Inventory | 3,553 | 3,369 | 2,538 |
| Prepaid expenses | 71 | 61 | 49 |
| Other current assets | 125 | 34 | 0 |
| Total current assets | 6,485 | 6,883 | 4,968 |
| Investments | 665 | 676 | 914 |
| Fixed Assets: | | | |
| Land | 527 | 527 | 527 |
| Buildings (net) | 1,299 | 1,257 | 1,252 |
| Other fixed assets (net) | 1,329 | 1,123 | 898 |
| Total fixed assets | 3,155 | 2,907 | 2,677 |
| TOTAL ASSETS | $10,305 | $10,466 | $8,559 |
| **LIABILITIES** | | | |
| Current Liabilities: | | | |
| Working capital loan | $2,660 | $2,811 | $1,354 |
| Accounts payable | 2,195 | 2,576 | 2,513 |
| Owed to Produits Forestier | 46 | 18 | 65 |
| Current portion of long-term debt | 193 | 212 | 253 |
| Total current liabilities | 5,094 | 5,617 | 4,185 |
| Long-term debt | 1,634 | 1,422 | 1,188 |
| TOTAL LIABILITIES | 6,728 | 7,039 | 5,373 |
| **OWNER'S EQUITY** | | | |
| Common stock | 5 | 5 | 5 |
| Contributed capital | 0 | 206 | 206 |
| Retained earnings | 3,572 | 3,216 | 2,975 |
| TOTAL LIABILITIES AND EQUITY | $10,305 | $10,466 | $8,559 |

*Exhibit 4*

|  | Materiaux Boisvert Ltée.<br>Balance Sheets<br>as at May 31<br>($000s) | | |
|---|---|---|---|
|  | **1989** | **1990** | **1991** |
| PROFITABILITY | | | |
| (A) Vertical Analysis | | | |
| Net sales | 100.0% | 100.0% | 100.0% |
| Cost of goods sold | 80.0% | 80.2% | 77.6% |
| Gross profit | 20.0% | 19.8% | 22.4% |
|  | | | |
| Operating expenses: | | | |
| Wages and salaries | 10.2% | 10.1% | 10.8% |
| Insurance | 0.2% | 0.2% | 0.1% |
| Utilities | 0.5% | 0.5% | 0.6% |
| Maintenance and repairs | 1.6% | 1.7% | 1.4% |
| Office equipment rental and<br>    maintenance | 0.1% | 0.1% | 0.1% |
| Travelling expenses | 0.2% | 0.2% | 0.2% |
| Vehicle rental | 0.3% | 0.3% | 0.1% |
| Parking lot rental | 0.0% | 0.1% | 0.1% |
| Advertising | 0.3% | 0.4% | 0.5% |
| Property tax | 0.3% | 0.3% | 0.3% |
| Office supplies | 0.4% | 0.5% | 0.6% |
| Bad debt expense | 0.6% | 0.7% | 2.3% |
| Accounting and lawyer's fees | 0.4% | 0.3% | 0.9% |
| Corporate expenses paid to<br>    PFS | 0.2% | 0.2% | 0.6% |
| Depreciation: Buildings | 0.3% | 0.3% | 0.3% |
|             Other fixed assets | 1.4% | 1.4% | 1.5% |
| Other operating expenses | 0.2% | 0.2% | 0.2% |
| Total operating expenses | 17.2% | 17.5% | 20.8% |
|  | | | |
| Operating profit | 2.8% | 2.4% | 1.6% |
|  | | | |
| Other expenses | | | |
| Interest | 2.7% | 2.9% | 3.2% |
| Other | 0.1% | 2.0% | 0.1% |
| Total other expenses | 2.8% | 5.0% | 3.3% |
|  | | | |
| Net profit before tax | 0.0% | -2.6% | -1.7% |
| Income tax expense (credit) | 0.0% | 0.2% | 0.0% |
| Net profit after tax | 0.0% | -2.4% | -1.7% |
|  | | | |
| (B) Return on Investment | -0.1% | -10.2% | -7.3% |

***Exhibit* 4 *(cont'd)***

|  | 1989 | 1990 | 1991 |
|---|---|---|---|
| **LIQUIDITY** | | | |
| Current ratio | 1.27:1 | 1.23:1 | 1.19:1 |
| Acid test | 0.54:1 | 0.61:1 | 0.57:1 |
| Working capital ($000s) | 1,391 | 1,266 | 783 |
| **EFFICIENCY** | | | |
| Age of receivables | 61 days | 65 days | 56 days |
| Age of inventory | 100 days | 102 days | 86 days |
| Age of payables | 63 days | 79 days | 93 days |
| **STABILITY** | | | |
| Net worth/Total assets | 34.7% | 32.7% | 37.2% |
| Interest coverage | 1.0X | 0.1X | 0.5X |
| **GROWTH** | | **1989–90** | **1990–91** |
| Sales | | –7.0% | –8.5% |
| Net profit | | | |
| Total assets | | 1.6% | –18.2% |
| Equity | | –4.2% | –7.0% |

### C A S E 3.9   SIMCOE COUNTY STAMPINGS LIMITED

Early in April 1987, John Elgie, the commercial lending manager at the Barrie office of Provincial Trust, had just concluded a meeting with George Emery, the general manager of Simcoe County Stampings Limited (SCS). Acting on a forecasted increase in business volume, Mr. Emery had requested financing of $125,000 to buy a new metal stamping press plus an increase in their line of credit to cover seasonal working capital needs. The current line of credit was for a maximum of $150,000.

**THE METAL STAMPING INDUSTRY**

The metal stamping industry is involved in the process of taking flat sheets of metal that are two dimensional (having width and length), and through the use of a stamping press and a three dimensional pattern known as a die, the metal is transformed into a uniquely shaped product having width, length, and height.

The industry manufactured a profuse number of products that individuals come into contact with on a daily basis. Common examples would include bottlecaps, metal bakeware, pots and pans; the metal bodies of household appliances such as toasters, microwave ovens, and washing machines; and on a larger scale, the metal body parts of an automobile.

The Canadian industry was comprised of approximately 600 companies (see Exhibit 1). Half of the companies were located in Ontario and 52 percent of the companies had less than 10 employees.

Although the industry was very competitive, it was also quite supportive. The Precision Metal Association (PMA) provided a forum for its members to share concerns and ideas on how to make their individual operations more efficient. The PMA was comprised of approximately 50 Canadian members and 1,000 members in the United States.

Two recent trends had become apparent in the industry. Some of the larger manufacturing companies, who at one time had a metal stamping department as part of their manufacturing operation, were contracting out the business in an attempt to reduce their labour costs. The second trend involved a movement away from metal stampings to plastic molded parts resulting in decreased weight and lower costs.

Companies within the industry could be separated into two segments based on their clientele and the volume of business. The segments were commonly referred to as automotive and nonautomotive.

**The Automotive Segment**

A stamping company supplying to the automotive segment produced a limited variety of products at a very high volume, often producing several hundred thousand units of the same item. The segment was extremely price competitive and it was not unusual for a company to lose an order with a large customer if a competitor underbid the existing manufacturer by one or two cents per unit. Contracts were typically tendered on a yearly basis.

Due to the large volume of metal purchased for these contracts, the purchasing agents could order directly from the steel manufacturers. The steel companies offered 30-day credit terms and provided customers with price discounts and reduced delivery times on orders.

During economic slumps in the auto industry, the companies supplying this segment would aggressively seek to take lower volume business away from the nonautomotive segment producers by cutting prices in an effort to keep their facilities operating.

**The Nonautomotive Segment**

Stamping companies supplying to the nonautomotive segment relied heavily on a wide variety of small volume orders, ranging from several dozen units up to several thousand. Each time a different product was produced, setup time was required to change the dies used to form the part, adding to increased labour costs.

Due to the lower volumes steel could not be sourced directly from the mill. Instead, small orders were placed through warehousing companies and, due to production schedules at the mill, delivery often took between 14 and 16 weeks. The warehouses allowed 60-day terms and did not offer any discounts.

The duration of contracts with nonautomotive customers could range from two or three days (essentially until the completion of the order), or up to one year. Customers awarded contracts based on a combination of service, price, and quality.

**COMPANY BACKGROUND**

SCS was founded in the early 1900s and operated as a family business for over 60 years. By 1968 sales had reached $78,000 and the family decided to sell the business. George Emery and two other individuals purchased the business from the family.

All three partners shared equally in the ownership of the business, but only two participated actively in its daily activities. Mr. Emery managed the operation while the other active partner provided engineering services. The third shareholder considered SCS as an investment and felt as long as he received his minimum dividend of $2,000 per year, he would leave the management of SCS up to Mr. Emery.

The company's objective was to maintain a client base that would allow the business to generate a 20 percent gross profit and a 5 percent net profit. SCS had approximately 50 customers and during the 1970s and early 1980s no one customer represented more than 3 percent of the sales volume. As a result, SCS produced a wide variety of products with limited volumes providing steady monthly sales. Steel was ordered from warehouse agents.

It was the company's policy to provide price quotes to the customer on any item they were capable of producing. Often the customer would be quoted a lower price elsewhere, but later return to SCS dissatisfied with the quality of the lower-priced product. Over the years, SCS had developed a reputation for producing a level of quality that other competitors could not duplicate.

Recently SCS had lost an important account that represented 17 percent of fiscal[1] 1986 sales. This customer had been quoted a lower price by a competitive firm and had given all of its 1987 business to this company.

Last year a newly formed company, Arctic Sun Heaters, approached SCS to produce the shell for a kerosene heater. The product had an innovative design and was more efficient than any other kerosene heater on the market. SCS produced 30,000 shells for Arctic Sun, which generated $120,000 in sales. The shells were produced from early May through to November and delivered in equal monthly amounts.

Normally SCS offered 60-day credit terms to their customers. However, Mr. Emery felt Arctic Sun had a cash management problem since they abused the 60-day limit. As a result, SCS put them on COD terms for the balance of the year.

## PRESENT SITUATION

Mr. Emery expected 10 to 20 percent growth in sales from SCS's regular client base, plus a phenomenal surge in business from Arctic Sun.

Due to the superiority of their product and the response from the retailers, Arctic Sun was predicting sales of 150,000 units for the upcoming season. The manager of Arctic Sun had offered the contract to Mr. Emery if he could produce the shells at the same price per unit as SCS had charged last year and allow them 90-day credit terms.

Mr. Emery knew from experience that the current presses, some of which were up to 40 years old, would be able to produce the shells, but they would also produce a higher level of scrap than normal since they were not designed for such a large-size stamping.

He felt the new press would result in reduced material wastage and also increase the productivity of the labour working on this particular machine up to 20 percent. The new press would also provide the capacity to produce larger size stampings for other clients, representing a new business opportunity for the company. The press would cost $125,000 installed and would be depreciated over 10 years. Overall, Mr. Emery felt that if he took the Arctic Sun contract for 1988 his cost of goods sold (COGS) would work out to approximately 80.6 percent of sales due to the decrease in labour and scrap. If, however, he did not take the contract, he would still probably buy the new press, but his COGS for 1988 would be about 83.2 percent of sales. Similarly, purchases, including the Arctic Sun contract, would be $1,076,000 or $844,000 without the Arctic Sun contract for 1988. If the cost savings did not materialize, however, the COGS might rise to as high as 87 percent of sales for 1988.

As John Elgie walked to his car, he thought about how different the surrounding landscape looked two years ago when he first approached SCS seeking their lending business. At that time he was fresh out of university and Provincial Trust had just opened their branch office in Barrie. The company had been very aggressive in seeking business, and in most cases had to entice clients away from other financial institutions.

Initially, Mr. Elgie experienced difficulty in reaching Mr. Emery. Mr. Emery spent most of his weekends in the summer racing high speed boats or attending meetings of the PMA, of which he had been a member of the board of directors at the time. During the week, it was not at all unusual to call for an appointment and be informed he was involved in a meeting concerning a local industrial training program, funded by the government.

When Mr. Elgie finally did get to meet with Mr. Emery, SCS was locked into a high interest, long-term loan. Provincial Trust was able to offer a financing arrangement at a lower interest rate that allowed SCS to save $5,000 per year in interest on their long-term debt, although it had cost SCS $17,000 to complete the refinancing.

Two years ago SCS had been considered "out in the country"; now there were new housing developments all through the area. As Mr. Elgie drove back to the office, he knew he would need to inform Mr. Emery of his decision as soon as possible if Mr. Emery was to commit to Arctic Sun and the new press.

Mr. Emery had been excited about the opportunity with Arctic Sun, but Mr. Elgie was wondering what the result would be if those sales did not materialize. Mr. Elgie wondered when the line of credit would reach its peak next year. Would the Arctic Sun contract affect the seasonality of the loan in any way? Mr. Elgie had SCS's financial statements (see Exhibits 2, 3, 4, and 5) and felt he had all the necessary information to make the decision.

## Notes

1. Fiscal year: any 12-month accounting period adopted by a business (i.e., "fiscal 1986" would refer to the period from April 1, 1985, to March 31, 1986).

*Exhibit 1*

---

### Canadian Metal Stamping Industry[1]
### 1986
### Industry Composition by Geographical Location

| Province | Number of Establishments |
|---|---|
| Newfoundland | 4 |
| Prince Edward Island | 1 |
| Nova Scotia | 8 |
| New Brunswick | 9 |
| Quebec | 122 |
| Ontario | 300 |
| Manitoba | 24 |
| Saskatchewan | 15 |
| Alberta | 45 |
| British Columbia | 72 |
| Yukon/Northwest Territories | 0 |

### Industry Composition by Average Number Employed

| Average Number Employed | Number of Establishments |
|---|---|
| 0–4 | 181 |
| 5–9 | 128 |
| 10–19 | 98 |
| 20–49 | 119 |
| 50–99 | 38 |
| 100–199 | 29 |
| 200–499 | 7 |
| 500–999 | 0 |
| 1,000 or over | 0 |

**1.** Statistics Canada Catalogue 41-251B, ISSN 0835-0124.

*EXHIBIT 2*

|  | Income Statements for the Years Ending March 31 ($000s) | | | | |
|---|---|---|---|---|---|
|  | **1983** | **1984** | **1985** | **1986** | **1987** |
| Net sales | $1,180 | $1,609 | $1,502 | $2,011 | $1,826 |
| Cost of goods sold: | | | | | |
|    Beginning inventory | $ 133 | $ 142 | $ 146 | $ 141 | $ 130 |
|    Purchases | 561 | 750 | 648 | 878 | 856 |
|    Freight | 17 | 16 | 11 | 14 | 13 |
|    Direct labour | 232 | 366 | 366 | 472 | 460 |
|    Manufacturing overhead | 150 | 189 | 203 | 244 | 207 |
|    Depreciation | 36 | 36 | 37 | 40 | 54 |
|    Cost of goods available for sale | $1,129 | $1,499 | $1,411 | $1,789 | $1,720 |
|    Ending inventory | 142 | 146 | 141 | 130 | 141 |
|    Cost of goods sold | $ 987 | $1,353 | $1,270 | $1,659 | 1,579 |
| Gross profit | $ 193 | $ 256 | $ 232 | $ 352 | $ 247 |
| Selling and administrative expenses: | | | | | |
|    Management and office salaries | $ 51 | $ 70 | $ 81 | $ 90 | $ 96 |
|    Interest on long-term debt | 35 | 43 | 39 | 43 | 36 |
|    Interest on bank loan | 26 | 11 | 12 | 11 | 8 |
|    Automobile and travel expenses | 29 | 28 | 27 | 27 | 31 |
|    Office expenses | 5 | 8 | 8 | 10 | 8 |
|    Advertising | 1 | 1 | 1 | 2 | 4 |
|    Bad debts | 1 | 6 | 0 | 2 | 0 |
|    Miscellaneous | 31 | 26 | 25 | 28 | 28 |
|    Total selling and administrative expenses | 179 | 193 | 193 | 213 | 211 |
| Operating profit | $ 14 | $ 63 | $ 39 | $ 139 | $ 36 |
| Other income | 0 | 5 | 2 | 1 | 2 |
|    Subtotal | $ 14 | $ 68 | $ 41 | $ 140 | $ 38 |
| Other expenses: | | | | | |
|    Employee profit sharing | 0 | 2 | 2 | 18 | 3 |
|    Refinancing charges | 0 | 0 | 0 | 17 | 0 |
| Income before taxes | $ 14 | $ 66 | $ 39 | $ 105 | $ 35 |
| Income taxes | 4 | 16 | 10 | 26 | 9 |
| Net income after tax | $ 10 | $ 50 | $ 29 | $ 79 | $ 26 |

*Exhibit 3*

| | Statement of Retained Earnings<br>for the Years Ending March 31<br>($000s) | | | | |
|---|---|---|---|---|---|
| | **1983** | **1984** | **1985** | **1986** | **1987** |
| Retained earnings at beginning<br>of the year (deficit) | $ (9) | $(19) | $ 28 | $ 51 | $123 |
| Net income | 10 | 50 | 29 | 79 | 26 |
| Subtotal | $ 1 | $ 31 | $ 57 | $130 | $149 |
| Dividends paid | 20 | 3 | 6 | 7 | 7 |
| Retained earnings at end<br>of the year (deficit) | $(19) | $ 28 | $ 51 | $123 | $142 |

*EXHIBIT 4*

| | Balance Sheets As of March 31 ($000s) | | | | |
|---|---|---|---|---|---|
| | **1983** | **1984** | **1985** | **1986** | **1987** |
| **ASSETS** | | | | | |
| Current assets: | | | | | |
| Cash | $ 0 | $ 0 | $ 0 | $ 0 | $ 0 |
| Accounts receivable (net) | 184 | 231 | 197 | 310 | 312 |
| Inventories[1] | 142 | 146 | 141 | 130 | 141 |
| Prepaid expenses | 3 | 4 | 4 | 3 | 3 |
| Other current assets | 0 | 0 | 0 | 3 | 2 |
| Total current assets | $329 | $381 | $342 | $446 | $458 |
| Fixed assets: | | | | | |
| Land | $ 5 | $ 5 | $ 5 | $ 5 | $ 5 |
| Building and equipment, cost[2] | 435 | 457 | 474 | 664 | 681 |
| Less: accumulated depreciation | 205 | 241 | 278 | 311 | 365 |
| Building and equipment, net | 230 | 216 | 196 | 353 | 316 |
| Total net fixed assets | 235 | 221 | 201 | 358 | 321 |
| **TOTAL ASSETS** | $564 | $602 | $543 | $804 | $779 |
| **LIABILITIES** | | | | | |
| Cuurent liabilities: | | | | | |
| Bank loan[3] | $108 | $108 | $127 | $113 | $115 |
| Ontario Development Corporation loan | 31 | 5 | 0 | 20 | 0 |
| Accounts payable | 167 | 219 | 168 | 195 | 240 |
| Profit-sharing payable | 0 | 0 | 0 | 12 | 2 |
| Due to shareholders | 3 | 0 | 0 | 7 | 7 |
| Taxes payable | 4 | 15 | 5 | 14 | 3 |
| Current portion of long-term debt | 43 | 35 | 35 | 50 | 42 |
| Total current liabilities | $356 | $382 | $335 | $411 | $409 |
| Long-term debt[4] | 221 | 186 | 151 | 264 | 222 |
| Total liabilities | $577 | $568 | $486 | $675 | $631 |
| **SHAREHOLDER'S EQUITY (DEFICIENCY)** | | | | | |
| Preferred stock | $ 5 | $ 5 | $ 5 | $ 5 | $ 5 |
| Common stock | 1 | 1 | 1 | 1 | 1 |
| Retained earnings (deficit) | (19) | 28 | 51 | 123 | 142 |
| Total shareholders' equity | (13) | 34 | 57 | 129 | 148 |
| **TOTAL LIABILITIES AND SHAREHOLDERS' EQUITY** | $564 | $602 | $543 | $804 | $779 |

1. Inventories consisted of 50 percent raw materials, 25 percent work-in-process, and 25 percent finished goods.
2. The building at cost represented $100,000 and had accumulated depreciation of $48,000.
3. Provincial Trust, secured by accounts receivable and inventory.
4. Provincial Trust, prime plus 2.75 percent, payable $3,500 monthly plus interest, secured by all property, plant, and equipment.

*Exhibit 5*

| Ratio Analysis | | | | | |
|---|---|---|---|---|---|
| | **1983** | **1984** | **1985** | **1986** | **1987** |
| PROFITABILITY | | | | | |
| Sales | 100.0% | 100.0% | 100.0% | 100.0% | 100.0% |
| Cost of goods sold: | | | | | |
|     Purchases | 47.5% | 46.6% | 43.1% | 43.7% | 46.9% |
|     Freight | 1.4% | 1.0% | 0.7% | 0.7% | 0.7% |
|     Direct labour | 19.7% | 22.7% | 24.4% | 23.5% | 25.2% |
|     Manufacturing overhead | 12.7% | 11.7% | 13.5% | 12.1% | 11.3% |
|     Depreciation | 3.1% | 2.2% | 2.5% | 2.0% | 3.0% |
|     Cost of goods sold | 83.6% | 84.1% | 84.6% | 82.5% | 86.5% |
| Gross profit | 16.4% | 15.9% | 15.4% | 17.5% | 13.5% |
| Selling and administrative expenses: | | | | | |
|     Management and office salaries | 4.3% | 4.4% | 5.4% | 4.5% | 5.3% |
|     Interest on long-term debt | 3.0% | 2.7% | 2.6% | 2.1% | 2.0% |
|     Interest on bank loan | 2.2% | 0.7% | 0.8% | 0.5% | 0.4% |
|     Automobile and travel expense | 2.5% | 1.7% | 1.8% | 1.3% | 1.7% |
|     Office expense | 0.4% | 0.5% | 0.5% | 0.5% | 0.4% |
|     Advertising | 0.1% | 0.1% | 0.1% | 0.1% | 0.2% |
|     Bad debts | 0.1% | 0.4% | 0.0% | 0.1% | 0.0% |
|     Miscellaneous | 2.6% | 1.6% | 1.7% | 1.4% | 1.5% |
|     Total selling and administrative expenses | 15.2% | 12.0% | 12.8% | 10.6% | 11.6% |
| Income before tax | 1.2% | 4.1% | 2.6% | 5.2% | 1.9% |
| Net income after tax | 0.8% | 3.1% | 1.9% | 3.9% | 1.4% |
| Return on average equity | | 476.2% | 63.7% | 84.9% | 18.8% |
| STABILITY | | | | | |
| Net worth to total assets | (2.3%) | 5.6% | 10.5% | 16.0% | 19.0% |
| Interest coverage (times) | 1.2X | 2.2X | 1.8X | 2.9X | 1.8X |
| LIQUIDITY | | | | | |
| Current ratio | 0.92:1 | 1.00:1 | 1.02:1 | 1.09:1 | 1.12:1 |
| Acid test ratio | 0.52:1 | 0.60:1 | 0.59:1 | 0.75:1 | 0.76:1 |
| Working capital ($000s) | ($27) | ($1) | $7 | $35 | $49 |
| EFFICIENCY | | | | | |
| Age of receivables | 56.9 days | 52.4 days | 47.9 days | 56.3 days | 62.4 days |
| Age of inventory | 52.5 days | 39.4 days | 40.5 days | 28.6 days | 32.6 days |
| Age of payables | 108.7 days | 106.6 days | 94.6 days | 81.1 days | 102.3 days |
| Fixed assets/sales | 19.9% | 13.7% | 13.4% | 17.8% | 17.6% |
| | | **1983–84** | **1984–85** | **1985–86** | **1986–87** |
| GROWTH | | | | | |
| Sales | | 36.4% | (6.7%) | 33.9% | (9.2%) |
| Net profit | | 400.0% | (42.0%) | 172.4% | (67.1%) |
| Assets | | 6.7% | (9.8%) | 48.1% | (3.1%) |
| Equity | | | 67.7% | 126.3% | 14.7% |

# C A S E  **3.10**   SMITH AND HAYWOOD DRILLING

In mid-June 1986, Don Jackson, regional vice-president at the Canadian Bank of Commercial Enterprises (CBCE) in Toronto, began to consider his most recent loan proposal. Senior management and several other investors had just presented him with their plan for a management buyout of Smith and Haywood Drilling (S&H) from the parent company, Charger Resource Services Ltd. (Charger). They had asked for $1,250,000 to help finance the purchase and provide some working capital. Closing date for the deal with Charger had been set for August 1.

**COMPANY HISTORY**   S&H was located in a mid-sized mining town in Northeastern Ontario. The company, which began operations in 1927, originally consisted of a diamond drilling division and a mining equipment manufacturing division. In 1951, J.R. Beam purchased the drilling division from the original owners, retaining the original S&H name. Then, in 1964, the manufacturing division was sold to Al Menard and Fred Allick. The two companies had no legal ties, and continued to operate as separate entities.

Charger entered the picture in 1977 when S&H was purchased by Turbine Resources Ltd. (Turbine) of Calgary. Charger, a division of Turbine, was given management responsibility for S&H. Charger also owned an oil and gas drilling company, oil workover companies, an oil field rental company, a heavy equipment sales company, and several other companies.

S&H sold drilling services to senior and junior mining companies exploring for mineral deposits. The process was called diamond drilling because a diamond drill bit was used to cut and remove a sample core from the earth. This circular rock core, ranging from one to three inches in diameter, was then examined by mining company geologists to determine if it contained sufficient quantities of the desired mineral to warrant further mining development. By examining core from several different drill holes, geologists could map out the position, size, and consistency of the ore body under the surface of the earth. Exhibits 1 and 2 illustrate typical diamond drills.

S&H was one of the five largest drilling companies in Canada, with drills operating in Ontario, Quebec, Saskatchewan, the Yukon, and the Northwest Territories. It was also a major player in international drilling circles, having drilled in countries such as Chile, Brazil, Morocco, France, Kenya, and New Zealand. Partnerships with overseas drilling contractors helped ensure the company access to foreign markets. S&H did exploration work in search of gold, uranium, nickel, iron ore, and a host of other minerals on behalf of its customers. Although it mainly drilled holes ranging from 150 to 2,000 feet in depth, the company had also developed new technology which allowed it to drill up to depths of 15,000 feet. S&H used three different drilling techniques: surface, underground, and reverse circulation. During the exploration boom of the late 1960s, S&H operated approximately 56 drills (half underground and half surface), and employed over 150 people. By 1986, the fleet had been cut to 25 surface drills and three underground drills, with a work force of about 100.

## EXPLORATION INDUSTRY AND ECONOMY

Price and reputation were key success factors in the exploration industry. Jobs were won through a competitive bidding process based on cost per foot drilled. If all drilling companies tendered similar bids, the company with a proven reputation would usually be awarded the contract. News travelled quickly in mining circles. Word of mouth could be a powerful promotional tool for a company that provided quality drilling service, but it could also jeopardize the future of one which continually performed poorly.

Longyear, Morrisette, Bradley, Midwest, and S&H were the major players in the Canadian diamond drilling industry. There were also many small regional companies operating two or three drills and specializing in small contracts that the large companies could not complete profitably.

In 1986, there was a substantial amount of mining exploration being done in Canada. S&H was winning its fair share of contracts, but according to Tim Sampson, general manager of S&H, the company was performing poorly. Despite this knowledge, management was unable to convince Charger that changes were necessary. S&H was quickly developing a poor reputation because its equipment was old and frequently broke down. Charger was unwilling to provide S&H with the necessary funding for capital improvements.

Flow-through shares, introduced by the federal and Quebec governments in 1983, had been the reason for the revitalization of the exploration industry. Investors were able to buy shares in a mining company and write off 133.3 percent of the cost of the shares against personal income. Therefore, for every dollar invested in a mining company, investors were able to deduct $1.333 from their taxable incomes that year. Not only was there an immediate tax shelter for investors, there was also the possibility of future profits should the exploration pay off and the company's stock price rise. Flow-through shares especially benefitted the junior mining companies that did not own producing metal mines, and that had no continuous revenue source. They relied on equity financing to support their exploration activities, and flow-through shares provided them with a tremendous new source of exploration funds. This in turn translated into a boost in the demand for drilling. See Exhibit 3 for Canadian exploration expenditure statistics.

The state of the economy had a large impact on the exploration industry because these programs were always among the first to be cut back during economic downturns. This situation is highlighted by the sharp drop in expenditures during the 1981–82 recession (Exhibit 3). Much of the exploration done in Canada was initiated by junior mining companies that did not have the resources to sustain drilling programs during a recession. These junior companies represented a substantial portion of S&H sales.

Another factor that made S&H more susceptible to economic downturns was Charger's decision not to have S&H pursue underground drilling. Most underground drilling was done by senior mining companies that had metal-producing mines operating (i.e., Inco, Noranda, Lac Minerals, etc.). Due to their size, many of these companies had the financial resources to continue drilling throughout a recession.

## THE MANAGEMENT BUYOUT

Jackson had just finished meeting with four of the people involved in the proposed buyout. Tim Sampson and Jack Hartley, general manager and chief accountant of S&H respectively, represented the employee group of six men who had initiated the buyout proposal. Collectively, the employee group had over 100 years of combined experience in the diamond drilling business at S&H. All were deeply committed to the company and thought that it could be run more effectively under their control than under Charger's. Exhibit 4 contains a profile of the employee group.

S&H had very little experience with the CBCE. In the past, all financing had been done through Charger. However, this lack of a relationship was remedied by the presence of the other two investors: Al Menard and Fred Allick. Jackson and the CBCE had done business with them since they had purchased the manufacturing division of S&H in 1964. Menard, a chartered accountant who had acted as controller for the two divisions long ago when they had operated as one company, was well-acquainted with the diamond drilling business. Allick, his business partner since 1964, was a metallurgical engineer primarily responsible for sales with the manufacturing company. Both men would become major shareholders, and act as directors of the new S&H if the bank granted the loan and the deal closed. Jackson was impressed by the past track record and experience of both men. Their heavy investment and presence at this meeting showed they had a great deal of confidence in the employee group that would continue to run S&H.

Charger had agreed to sell the assets of S&H to the employee group for $2 million. It had also agreed to a vendor take-back of $400,000. This offer meant that the new S&H would owe Charger $400,000, to be paid back $50,000 per year. This condition left the employee group to raise the remaining $1.6 million. The two new investors and the employee group had been able to raise $850,000 through the sale of common shares. The breakdown was as follows:

| | |
|---|---|
| Allick Investments Ltd. | $250,000 |
| Menard Investments Ltd. | 250,000 |
| Swiss Investor | 200,000 |
| Employee Group | 150,000 |
| Total Equity | $850,000 |

The remaining $750,000 they hoped to secure with a long-term loan from the bank. The additional $500,000 requested was needed for working capital, because S&H would no longer have the financial support of Charger for day-to-day activities.

## FUTURE OPERATIONS

The employee group had some major changes in mind for the operation of S&H. Sampson explained that the past income statements were misleading for a number of reasons. Hidden in the general and administrative expenses were cost allocations from Charger's head office. S&H had no control over these costs, yet was expected to generate sufficient profits to cover them. Another problem was the manner in which revenue was recorded. S&H occasionally performed drilling for customers who dealt directly with Charger. Since S&H was under Charger's control, Charger often retained revenue received for work performed by S&H. Therefore, S&H incurred all the expenses to complete a project but did not receive appropriate credit for the revenue generated. All of these factors helped contribute to the poor financial performance seen in Exhibits 5, 6, and 7.

Due to some uncertainty surrounding the future of flow-through shares, the six members of the employee group had agreed that a conservative sales growth estimate of 10 percent a year for the next two years was appropriate. They also planned to move back into underground drilling again and expected some growth and stability from this area. Tighter cost controls and the elimination of the corporate overhead charges would lead to some dramatic expense improvements. Job costs were expected to drop to 81 percent, and general and administrative to 9.8 percent of sales in 1987 and 1988. Interest expenses, if the loan were granted, would be $180,000 in 1987 and $158,000 in 1988. Rather than continue to sell off assets as they had been forced to do under Charger, management planned to spend $150,000 per year on new drilling equipment. In order to improve performance and rebuild the solid reputation of S&H, management had determined that this was the minimum capital expenditure necessary. Income taxes would be 25 percent on the first $200,000 of income, and 50 percent on any income above that.

The balance sheet of S&H would bear little resemblance to that found in Exhibit 5, which provides figures for 1983–85. The employee group was buying only the inventory and fixed assets. The only remaining liability to Charger would be the $400,000 vendor take-back. All accounts receivable and payable would be transferred to Charger and become its responsibility. The new level of payables and receivables would both be based on an average of 45 days. Hartley and Sampson indicated that they would like to maintain 30 days' worth of operating expenses in cash. Prepaid insurance would average $50,000 in each of the next two years.

Major changes were also planned for the inventory system at S&H. The current use of many different types of equipment required S&H to carry hundreds of different parts because, for example, each motor required a different type of oil filter. Standardization should result in tighter control being maintained over inventory. The ending inventory of the new S&H had been revalued at $690,000. Although this dollar value might not shrink drastically, the new system would make it easier to monitor inventory levels and reduce confusion in the warehouse. The new cost base for property, plant, and equipment would be $1,350,000. The increased value reflected acquisitions made during the negotiation period. The low equity position would be replaced with the new investment plus any retained earnings.

**THE DECISION**

Jackson had to carefully weigh the risks involved with this management buyout and the request for funds against the possible positive outcomes for the bank before rendering his decision.

*EXHIBIT 1*
*A Smith and Haywood*
*Diamond Drill*[1]

**1.** Company brochure.

**EXHIBIT 2**
**Diagram of a Typical**
**Diamond Drill[1]**

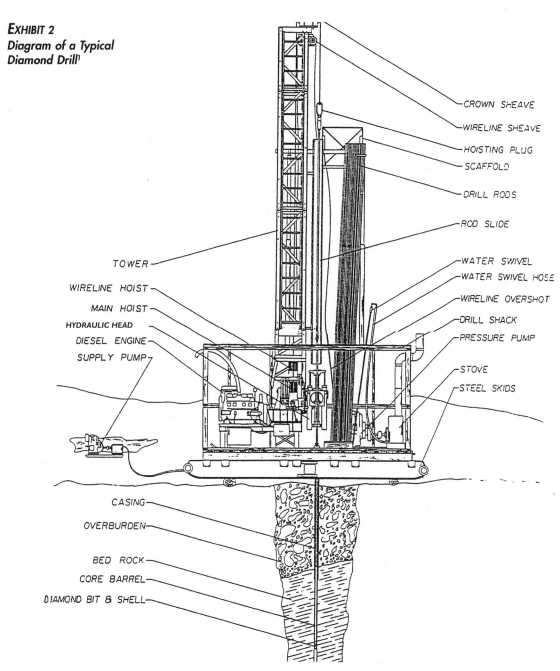

CROWN SHEAVE

WIRELINE SHEAVE

HOISTING PLUG

SCAFFOLD

DRILL RODS

ROD SLIDE

WATER SWIVEL

WATER SWIVEL HOSE

WIRELINE OVERSHOT

DRILL SHACK

PRESSURE PUMP

STOVE

STEEL SKIDS

TOWER

WIRELINE HOIST

MAIN HOIST

HYDRAULIC HEAD

DIESEL ENGINE

SUPPLY PUMP

CASING

OVERBURDEN

BED ROCK

CORE BARREL

DIAMOND BIT & SHELL

**1.** Company brochure.

**EXHIBIT 3**
*Mining Exploration
Expenditures in
Canada*[1]

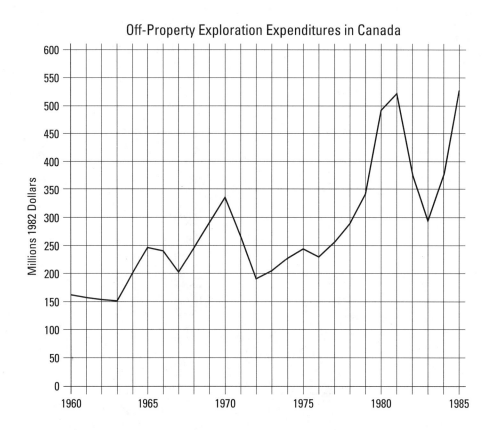

Off-Property Exploration Expenditures in Canada

1. *The Northern Miner Magazine,* November 1986.

*Exhibit 4*

---

### Employee Group Profiles

---

**Tim Sampson, Professional Engineer
General Manager**

---

- Graduated Mechanical Technologist in 1963
- Professional engineer in 1970
- Spent five years with Timberjack Machines in R&D
- 18 years at S&H
- Held positions of equipment coordinator, assistant branch manager, assistant general manager, and general manager
- Married with two children
- Age 46

---

**Gord Watson
Equipment Supervisor**

---

- 26 years' experience with S&H
- Held positions of mechanic, shop foreman, branch superintendent, and equipment supervisor
- Holds Class "A" Interprovincial Mechanic's Licence
- Married with three children
- Age 44

---

**Al Fisher
Manager of Operations**

---

- 24 years' experience with S&H
- Worked up through all field positions: helper, runner, runner-foreman, foreman, fieldman, and manager of operations
- Married with two children
- Age 42

---

**Jack Hartley
Chief Accountant**

---

- Graduated in Business Administration (Accounting)
- Presently enrolled in CGA (Certified General Accountant) course
- Nine years at S&H as a junior accountant, purchasing agent, office manager, and chief accountant
- Married with two children
- Age 33

*EXHIBIT 4 (cont'd)*

---

**Blaine Peters**
**Shop Foreman**

---

- 13 years with S&H
- Held positions of apprentice mechanic, junior mechanic, journeyman Class "A" mechanic, and shop foreman
- Married with two children
- Age 28

---

**Bob Peters**
**Senior Mechanic**

---

- 23 years with S&H
- Held positions of apprentice mechanic, journeyman, and senior field mechanic
- Divorced with two children
- Age 41

---

*EXHIBIT 5*

| | 1983 | 1984 | 1985 |
|---|---|---|---|
| **Income Statement and Retained Earnings[1]** **For the Years Ending December 31** **(in $000s)** | | | |
| Revenue | $4,424 | $5,752 | $6,253 |
| Job costs[2] | 3,854 | 5,162 | 5,416 |
| Gross profit | 570 | 590 | 837 |
| | | | |
| Operating expenses: | | | |
| General and administrative[3] | 938 | 1,345 | 966 |
| Depreciation | 587 | 356 | 200 |
| | | | |
| Total operating expenses | 1,525 | 1,701 | 1,166 |
| | | | |
| Operating profit | (955) | (1,111) | (329) |
| Gain on sale of assets | 40 | 470 | 290 |
| | | | |
| Net income before taxes | (915) | (641) | (39) |
| Income taxes | 0 | 0 | 0 |
| Net income (loss) | $ (915) | $ (641) | $ (39) |
| | | | |
| Beginning retained earnings | $2,414 | $1,499 | $ 858 |
| Net income (loss) | (915) | (641) | (39) |
| Ending retained earnings | $1,499 | $ 858 | $ 819 |

**1.** Source: Company records.
**2.** Purchases are equal to 40 percent of job costs.
**3.** Composed of expenses such as office salaries, legal fees, insurance, utilities, advertising, employee training, etc.

*EXHIBIT 6*

|  | Balance Sheet[1] (in $000s) | | |
|---|---|---|---|
|  | **1983** | **1984** | **1985** |
| **ASSETS** | | | |
| **Current Assets** | | | |
| Cash | $ 216 | $ 139 | $ 558 |
| Accounts receivable | 554 | 475 | 966 |
| Due from Charger | 21 | 110 | 7 |
| Inventory[2] | 480 | 556 | 607 |
| Prepaid expenses | 9 | 9 | 2 |
| Other | 120 | 104 | 86 |
| Total current assets | 1,400 | 1,393 | 2,226 |
| | | | |
| Plant, property, and equipment, Cost | 5,143 | 4,221 | 1,191 |
| Accumulated depreciation[3] | 3,881 | 2,861 | 214 |
| Plant, property and equipment, Net | 1,262 | 1,360 | 977 |
| Goodwill | 107 | 0 | 0 |
| **TOTAL ASSETS** | $2,769 | $2,753 | $3,203 |
| **LIABILITIES** | | | |
| **Current liabilities** | | | |
| Accounts payable | 630 | 611 | 1,336 |
| Due to charger | 639 | 1,283 | 1,047 |
| **TOTAL LIABILITIES** | 1,269 | 1,894 | 2,383 |
| **SHAREHOLDERS' EQUITY** | | | |
| Common stock | 1 | 1 | 1 |
| Retained earnings | 1,499 | 858 | 819 |
| **TOTAL LIABILITIES AND AND SHAREHOLDERS' EQUITY** | $2,769 | $2,753 | $3,203 |

1. Source: Company records.
2. Inventory consisted of diamond drill bits, spare parts, casing, and consumables.
3. Depreciation schedule for plant, property, and equipment is as follows:

| Drilling equipment and tractors | -10 years straight line |
|---|---|
| Vehicles | -5 years straight line |
| Buildings | -20 years straight line |

**EXHIBIT 7**

| | Ratio Analysis | | |
|---|---|---|---|
| | **1983** | **1984** | **1985** |
| PROFITABILITY ANALYSIS | | | |
| (i) Vertical analysis | | | |
| Sales | 1.000 | 1.000 | 1.000 |
| Job costs | .871 | .897 | .866 |
| Gross margin | .129 | .103 | .134 |
| Expenses: | | | |
| General and administrative | .212 | .234 | .154 |
| Depreciation | .133 | .062 | .032 |
| Total expenses | .345 | .296 | .186 |
| Operating income | –.216 | –.193 | –.052 |
| Gain on sale of assets | .009 | .082 | .046 |
| Net income before tax | –.207 | –.111 | –.006 |
| | | | |
| (ii) Return on investment | N/A | N/A | N/A |
| | | | |
| STABILITY | | | |
| Net worth to total assets | 54% | 31% | 26% |
| | | | |
| LIQUIDITY | | | |
| Current ratio | 1.1 | .7 | .9 |
| Acid test | .6 | .3 | .6 |
| Working capital ($000s) | 131 | –501 | –157 |
| | | | |
| EFFICIENCY | | | |
| Age of receivables (365 days) | 45.7 | 30.1 | 56.4 |
| Age of inventory (365 days) | 45.5 | 39.3 | 40.9 |
| Age of payables (180 days)[1] | 73.6 | 53.3 | 111.0 |
| | | **1983–84** | **1984–85** |
| GROWTH | | | |
| Revenue | | 30% | 8.7% |
| Net earnings | | N/A | N/A |
| Assets | | –.6% | 16.3% |
| Equity | | –42.7% | –4.5% |

**1.**   180 days was used as the base because the majority of purchases were made during a six-month period.

# C A S E 3.11   STUDIO TESSIER LTÉE.

On the morning of August 8, 1986, Monique Lavoie took another sip of coffee as she leafed through the loan request on her desk. As manager of the Quebec city branch of the Atlantic Bank of Canada, Monique had to make a decision concerning an extension on a working capital loan. The clients, Paul and Nicole Tessier, owned and managed Studio Tessier, a woman's clothing shop and an interior design studio. Armed with their most recent financial statements and a detailed set of floor plans, the Tessiers had requested a $38,000 increase in their working capital loan, in order to finance an expansion of the design business. Monique knew she would have to respond as soon as possible, as Paul and Nicole were anxious to complete the expansion for the Christmas season.

The Tessiers had been clients of the bank since their business began in 1980. They were an energetic couple who felt that the opportunity for creativity and the chance to pursue their interests in a career context outweighed the difficulties of running a small business. Paul was well known in the community, and served on the boards of several community service organizations. He was currently the president of the Quebec City Executives Club and served on the board of directors for the city's Business Improvement Association. Nicole coordinated several major fashion shows a year to raise funds for local charities such as the hospital and art gallery. The couple were also very involved in their church and worked on many parish projects.

***STUDIO TESSIER***

Studio Tessier was located on the outskirts of Quebec City, in an 18th century home that once belonged to Nicole's grandmother. The main floor, of the house was home to Salon Tessier, an upscale women's clothing boutique. The interior design business operated out of the second floor, which consisted of two show rooms of furnishings and artwork, Paul's office, and a second smaller office that Nicole shared with the office manager of the two businesses. Nicole managed the boutique and Paul ran the interior design business. Their small support staff included a full-time seamstress, a shipper, an office manager who handled the accounts for both businesses, and an assistant who alternated between the sales floor and the design studio.

Paul and Nicole had been in business together for approximately seven years, and their management styles were as different as their personalities.

Nicole kept detailed records of her business. A perpetual inventory count was kept, and with each sale, client files and sales records were adjusted. Nicole also kept a close watch on her payables and receivables.

In contrast, Paul's approach was more tactical, and he was less committed to record keeping. Paul enjoyed the people-interaction of the business, the thrill of a sale, and the details of negotiating a contract. He did not keep up to date inventory records, and was somewhat lax in recording sales and collections. At one point in the year, the office manager approached Paul with a severe cash flow problem. After making several phone calls, Paul calmly collected $44,000 in billings he had not yet recorded. Recently, Paul had been very flexible with customer deposits, usually required as down payment before work began. Despite Paul's relaxed approach to paperwork, much of the growth for Studio Tessier over the past few years had come from the design business.

## SALON TESSIER

Nicole's boutique carried lines by designers such as Albert Nipon, Alfred Sung, Ellen Tracey, and Louis Guy Giroux, as well as a selection of fine jewellery and leather goods. Over the years, Salon Tessier had developed a reputation as a fashion boutique that provided excellent service and offered exclusive lines in the Quebec City area. Two main aspects of Nicole's marketing plan were her client files and fashion shows. Detailed records on each customer were kept to enhance the personalized service the boutique provided. Fashion shows also helped reinforce the high fashion image Nicole wanted to project. In-store shows were held once a month and major shows occurred 10 times a year.

Nicole did all the buying for the boutique, and made frequent trips to Montreal, Toronto, and New York. Because orders were placed six to eight months before each season, there was little flexibility in the fashion business. Overall, Nicole aimed for margins of 40 percent of selling price.

## PAUL TESSIER, INTERIOR DESIGN

Paul ran the design business with the help of an assistant who sold in the boutique during slow periods. Paul worked on both residential and institutional projects. The latter category was very price sensitive and contracts were awarded through a bidding process. While he aimed for gross margins of 30 percent overall, competition in the institutional market made this goal difficult to achieve. Residential clients were more attractive because jobs were personal in nature and cost was not the principal concern with each decorating decision. As a result, margins were closer to his 30 percent target with this segment. Over the past year, Paul had handled many institutional projects, but wanted to increase his effort with the residential sector in the future.

## HISTORY

The Tessiers opened Salon Tessier in April 1980. Nicole worked full time in the boutique, while Paul continued working with a local manufacturing firm and accepted design projects on a part-time basis. During the first two years, Salon Tessier experienced strong sales growth and solid profits.

In 1982, based on the advice of a management consultant, the Tessiers decided to expand the clothing business. The second storey of the house was redecorated and the boutique's sales area was doubled along with inventories. At this time, Paul left his job to commit full time to the interior design business. But by Christmas 1982, it was apparent that the boutique's expansion was premature. Sales did not materialize to the degree anticipated, and merchandise had to be discounted drastically. The sales area was reduced to its original size by the spring of 1983, and a loss of $30,823 was incurred that year.

A new accounting/consulting firm was contracted for 1984. During this year, Studio Tessier incorporated and the land and building were transferred to the Tessiers' personal holdings. In 1984, a profit was once again realized.

A mild recession in 1985 caused layoffs with local manufacturers and affected sales at Studio Tessier, resulting in a net loss. Yet 1986 was a record year with a net income of $40,483.

Over the last two years, sales in the boutique appeared to have levelled off due to increased competition in the area. Much of the growth anticipated for fiscal 1987 would come from the decorating business. Sales for Paul Tessier, Interior Design would constitute approximately 65 percent of total sales for Studio Tessier in the coming year. Income tax expense was projected at 25 percent of profit for 1987.

## INVENTORIES

The inventories of Studio Tessier could be divided into three main categories: 1) garments and jewellery, 2) wallpaper, draperies, and carpeting, and 3) furnishings and art work. Given the five distinct seasons in the women's clothing business (summer, fall, winter, "holiday," and spring), each approximately two to four months in length, turnover of inventory was very important. Despite the seasonality, working capital requirements stayed relatively consistent throughout the year. Unpopular items were discounted in order to move them and make room for the next season's line. Accounts with clothing suppliers were payable every 30 days, or 60 days. For wallpaper and carpeting, orders were placed and inventory was held a very short period of time before installation. Manufacturers gave 30 to 45 days to pay and were not especially strict. Furnishings and art work caused more of a cash shortage and pieces were carried an average of one year. Suppliers expected payment in 30 days. A large inventory for furniture and art work was essential in the design business.

## EXPANSION PROPOSAL

"If the expansion is completed by November 1986, I believe sales should reach $925,000 in fiscal 1987. At the very least I anticipate 10 percent growth over current sales levels," Paul had said to Monique.

The expansion proposal consisted of adding three boutiques to the existing house. The idea was to create an exclusive shopping area, increasing the benefits of travelling the distance to Studio Tessier. The Tessiers already had clients who were interested in renting space, among them a shoe store, a beauty salon, and a jewellery shop. The second floor of the expansion would provide floor space needed to expand Paul's business and give Nicole a better office. The rental income from the three outlets would cover the mortgage payments on the addition. In this way, Paul could increase the floor space for his business without major additions to fixed costs. However, Paul felt that $5,000 in fixtures would be required in the new showroom and office.

The Tessiers planned to keep the ownership of the building in their name, and would finance the addition with a mortgage. A working capital loan of $100,000 was requested to finance the inventories and accounts receivable. At present, the Tessiers had a working capital loan of $63,000, which was secured by inventories, and other personal assets with a realizable value of $12,500.

**THE DECISION**

Monique Lavoie recalled the excitement in Paul Tessier's voice as he described the expansion and presented the blue prints. She knew she would have to work fast, as her clients were anxious to hear her decision.

*EXHIBIT 1*

| | Consolidated Income Statements for the Years Ending July 31 | | |
|---|---|---|---|
| | **1984** | **1985** | **1986** |
| Net sales | $660,155 | $561,540 | $720,106 |
| Cost of goods sold | 348,320 | 388,750 | 473,763 |
| Gross profit | $311,835 | $172,790 | $246,343 |
| Operating expenses: | | | |
| Subcontracting[1] | $ 97,825 | $ | $ |
| Executive salaries | 51,500 | 58,213 | 68,813 |
| Wages | 47,356 | 49,743 | 37,033 |
| Auto travel | 14,420 | 8,145 | 18,767 |
| Rent | 9,426 | 9,845 | 9,680 |
| Local accounting | 7,026 | 5,691 | 5,229 |
| Advertising and promotion | 17,676 | 18,320 | 20,370 |
| Telephone | 3,399 | 3,623 | 4,078 |
| Insurance | 3,168 | 4,103 | 4,560 |
| Bank interest and charges | 8,595 | 7,686 | 7,346 |
| Employee benefits, etc. | 1,259 | 1,343 | 3,788 |
| Utilities | 2,393 | 3,255 | 2,833 |
| Supplies, office and store | 8,948 | 4,196 | 4,660 |
| Miscellaneous expenses | 5,499 | 4,068 | 4,663 |
| Credit card charges | 3,960 | 2,953 | 2,939 |
| Depreciation | 1,811 | 1,449 | 1,601 |
| Total expenses | 284,261 | 182,633 | 196,360 |
| Net income before tax | $ 27,574 | ($9,843) | $ 49,983 |
| Income tax | 2,500 | | 9,500 |
| Net profit after tax | $ 25,074 | ($9,843) | $ 40,483 |

**1.** In 1984, the accountant recorded subcontracting as a separate expense. In the following years, subcontracting expense was included in cost of goods sold.

*EXHIBIT 2*

| | Statement of Retained Earnings for the Years Ending July 31 | | |
|---|---|---|---|
| | **1984** | **1985** | **1986** |
| Retained earnings, beginning of year | $ | $23,824 | $11,618 |
| Net income after tax | 25,074 | (9,843) | 40,483 |
| Subtotal | $25,074 | $13,981 | $52,101 |
| Less: dividends | 1,250 | 2,363 | 2,500 |
| Retained earnings, end of year | $23,824 | $11,618 | $49,601 |

*Exhibit 3*

| | Balance Sheets as at July 31 | | |
|---|---|---|---|
| | **1984** | **1985** | **1986** |
| **ASSETS** | | | |
| Current assets: | | | |
| Cash | $ 1,562 | $ | $ |
| Accounts receivable | 12,273 | 6,154 | 28,706 |
| Notes receivable | 24,473 | | |
| Inventory | 90,705 | 108,473 | 149,044 |
| Income tax recoverable | | 1,387 | |
| Prepaid expenses | 2,393 | 2,524 | 3,087 |
| Total current assets | $131,406 | $118,538 | $180,837 |
| | | | |
| Fixed assets: | | | |
| Furniture and fixtures, cost | $ 9,054 | $ 9,054 | $ 13,479 |
| Less: accumulated depreciation | 1,811 | 3,260 | 4,861 |
| Total fixed assets | 7,243 | 5,794 | 8,618 |
| | | | |
| Goodwill | 3 | 3 | 3 |
| | | | |
| TOTAL ASSETS | $138,652 | $124,335 | $189,458 |
| | | | |
| **LIABILITIES** | | | |
| Current liabilities: | | | |
| Accounts payable | $ 32,281 | $ 43,306 | $ 46,731 |
| Bank loan | 47,500 | 53,064 | 62,905 |
| Loan payable | 12,500 | | |
| Customer deposits | 13,253 | 13,625 | 110 |
| Taxes payable | 8,435 | 2,578 | 17,238 |
| Bonus payable | | | 10,625 |
| Due to shareholders | 854 | 139 | 2,243 |
| Total current liabilities | $114,823 | $112,712 | $139,852 |
| | | | |
| **SHAREHOLDERS' EQUITY** | | | |
| Common stock authorized 5 million shares, issued 5 | $ 5 | $ 5 | $ 5 |
| Retained earnings | 23,824 | 11,618 | 49,601 |
| | | | |
| TOTAL LIABILITIES AND SHAREHOLDERS' EQUITY | $138,652 | $124,335 | $189,458 |

*EXHIBIT 4*

| | Ratio Analysis | | |
|---|---|---|---|
| | **1984** | **1985** | **1986** |
| PROFITABILITY | | | |
| (A) Vertical analysis: | | | |
| Sales | 100.0% | 100.0% | 100.0% |
| Cost of goods sold[1] | 52.8% | 69.2% | 65.8% |
| Gross Profit | 47.2% | 30.8% | 34.2% |
| Operating expenses: | | | |
| Subcontracting | 14.8% | | |
| Executive salaries | 7.8% | 10.4% | 9.6% |
| Wages | 7.2% | 8.9% | 5.1% |
| Auto travel | 2.2% | 1.5% | 2.6% |
| Rent | 1.4% | 1.8% | 1.3% |
| Local accounting | 1.1% | 1.0% | 0.7% |
| Advertising and promotion | 2.7% | 3.3% | 2.8% |
| Telephone | 0.5% | 0.6% | 0.6% |
| Insurance | 0.5% | 0.7% | 0.6% |
| Bank interest and charges | 1.3% | 1.4% | 1.0% |
| Employee benefits | 0.2% | 0.2% | 0.5% |
| Utilities | 0.4% | 0.6% | 0.4% |
| Supplies | 1.4% | 0.7% | 0.6% |
| Miscellaneous | 0.8% | 0.7% | 0.6% |
| Credit card charges | 0.6% | 0.5% | 0.4% |
| Depreciation | 0.3% | 0.3% | 0.2% |
| Total operating expenses | 43.1% | 32.5% | 27.3% |
| Net income | 4.2% | (1.8%) | 6.9% |
| (B) Return on equity | 210.4% | (55.5%) | 132.2% |
| STABILITY | | | |
| Net worth/total assets | 17.2% | 9.3% | 26.2% |
| Interest coverage | 4.2X | nil | 7.8X |
| LIQUIDITY | | | |
| Current ratio | 1.14:1 | 1.05:1 | 1.29:1 |
| Acid test ratio | 0.33:1 | 0.07:1 | 0.21:1 |
| Working capital | $16,583 | $5,826 | $40,985 |
| EFFICIENCY (Based on 365-day year) | | | |
| Age of receivables | 7 days | 4 days | 15 days |
| Age of inventory | 95 days | 102 days | 115 days |
| Age of payables | 34 days | 41 days | 36 days |
| Fixed assets/sales | .01 | .01 | .01 |
| | | **1984–85** | **1985–86** |
| GROWTH | | | |
| Sales | | (15%) | 28% |
| Net profit | | (139%) | NA |
| Total assets | | (10.3%) | 52.4% |
| Equity | | (51%) | 327% |

**1.** For 1985 and 1986 included cost of subcontracting.

# C A S E **3.12**   TALICH FABRICATING INC.

Ted Heath, manager of the downtown branch of the Dominion of Canada Bank in London, Ontario, had to make a decision regarding a loan proposal in time for a meeting Monday morning. It was now late Friday afternoon. Mr. Talich, president of Talich Fabricating Inc. (TFI) and a long-standing customer of the bank, had visited Mr. Heath the previous week with a plan for an expansion of TFI's facilities. Mr. Talich needed money for working capital and for the construction of the plant addition. He had gone to the mortgage division of a life insurance company, which had agreed to lend him the money needed for the plant addition. He was asking Mr. Heath to increase TFI's line of credit to cover his increasing need for working capital. Mr. Heath knew as he reviewed the TFI file that he would have to evaluate the proposal as objectively as possible, especially in view of a recent memo received from the bank's head office (Exhibit 1).

**COMPANY HISTORY**

Mr. Talich was 52 years of age. He and his wife immigrated to Canada from Europe in 1980. For several months he worked in Toronto as a labourer, then moved to London in response to an advertisement for trained machinists. Since Mr. Talich had both excellent qualifications and experience he was given a position in a newly formed division of a large Canadian metal-fabricating company. The division produced metal furniture, metal partitions, and lockers for educational institutions, hospitals, and other customers.

The division grew rapidly. Mr. Talich advanced within the company on the basis of his own skill and determined nature. Eventually he was made plant superintendent of the division, and his responsibilities included meeting production requirements, maintaining plant efficiency through a system of standards, and supervising a staff of over 100 workers, most of whom were highly trained. Mr. Talich was expected to select, train, and supervise foremen. As well, he participated in the industrial relations procedures in the plant. As plant superintendent he earned a reputation for his product knowledge, his ability to solve problems, and the exacting standards he set for himself. These attributes resulted in Mr. Talich's increasing participation in the design of new products and the capital budgeting for the plant.

Late in 1985, Mr. Talich's company merged with another large company and he learned that the new management had decided to phase out the metal furniture division. But he wanted to remain in the metal furniture industry, and the company's decision prompted him to enter into business for himself.

In 1986, Mr. Talich started TFI. The company's financing was provided primarily by Mr. Talich's own savings and a bank loan secured by his personal assets. The first years were extremely difficult ones. Mr. Talich worked long hours with little help and with limited facilities. During this period he withdrew only $15,000 to $25,000 a year from the company for the support of his family. Gradually, however, the company began to grow, producing a quality product at a price which made TFI highly competitive. Mr. Talich maintained that high product quality and guaranteed service combined with a fair price would be a successful combination for the metal furniture market.

Producing metal furniture, partitions, and lockers exclusively for educational institutions in the years 1986 to 1990 created certain problems for TFI. Most of TFI's orders were gained by tendering a bid. Skilful bidding is required as contracts missed due to noncompetive bids could not easily be replaced. Nor could contract estimates be adjusted to offset rising costs. In addition, government funded agencies, who were TFI's principal clients, were traditionally slow in settling their accounts. In most instances these customers took from 60 to 120 days after delivery to complete payment.

In 1993, Mr. Talich purchased the Pioneer Co. Ltd. in order to help offset the government business. Pioneer was a small, specialized operation that produced a high-quality line of metal office furniture. A drafting table that Pioneer had manufactured and marketed as a licensee was redesigned by Mr. Talich and became a very profitable product for TFI.

In 1994, TFI moved from its rented quarters in an old building to a more modern plant in an industrial area of the city. At that time, Mr. Talich's lawyer and accountant advised him that, for estate and tax management purposes, TFI should not purchase the new building. They advised Mr. Talich to form a property company called Talich Property Inc. (TPI), which would buy the plant and then rent it to TFI. Acting on behalf of TPI, Mr. Talich convinced the mortgage division of a life insurance company to loan TPI $1.0 million to finance the building. The loan was secured by a mortgage on the property. TFI paid a monthly rental for the use of the facility. The rent had been established by an appraiser at fair market value.

**INDUSTRY SITUATION**

At the start of the 1990s, government financed institutions faced continued pressure to reduce costs in view of rising government deficits. Pressure was felt among the suppliers as competition for contracts increased. Some metal furniture manufacturers, particularly those with other related product lines or those that were divisions of large established companies, began to cut prices. Industry participants viewed this as a move to force small and inefficient operators out of the industry. The price-cutting policy intensified through 1992, 1993, and 1994. TFI was able to compete in these years due to its low overhead, company reputation, and contacts already developed by Mr. Talich through his years in the industry. In early 1995, with the sharp increase in material costs and continued price competition, the outlook looked bleak for industry participants. From the half dozen or more Ontario manufacturers who had been in the industry in 1985 only four major competitors remained. Midway through 1995, a year which promised to be difficult for TFI, two major manufacturers announced their withdrawal from the market. Each of these Ontario-based operations was a division of a large company and each cited inadequate returns as the major reason for quitting the metal furniture industry.

**EXPANSION PROPOSAL**

Mr. Talich assessed this turn of events in 1994 as an opportunity for the makers of metal furniture to pass increased raw material costs, previously absorbed by the manufacturers, on to customers. There was also the chance for enterprising companies to increase their market share significantly.

In order to compete during the lean years of the early nineties, TFI had been forced to restrict capital expansion. Lack of plant facilities now posed a severe impediment to any expansion plans. Even at present levels of production, raw materials and finished goods were stacked in aisles on the production floor. The blocked aisles restricted the workers' ability to perform their jobs, limited productive capacity, and increased costs.

In early 1995, Mr. Talich purchased the manufacturing rights to a new line of metal shelving for institutional and commercial use from Trans World Manufacturers. This product's earnings potential, based upon market response to date, was limited by the lack of plant capacity. Mr. Talich wished to build a 651 square metre addition to the present plant, which would increase the plant area by approximately one-third and provide ample storage for finished goods and raw materials. Mr. Talich, acting on behalf of TPI, had asked TPI's mortgagee to finance the addition to the plant. The mortgagee agreed to provide the $750,000 needed to finance the plant extension. The cost of the addition would be reflected in increased rent charged TFI by TPI.

In presenting his request for the bank to extend TFI's current line of credit of $1.9 million to handle the expected increase in working capital needs, Mr. Talich had indicated that, effective immediately, prices on existing products would be raised by 5 percent. The price increase would reflect the high cost of materials and labour. Most customers to whom he had spoken did not object to price increases reflecting increased costs. These individuals had indicated that they were more concerned that quality and service remain the same. Mr. Talich felt that the price increase would do much to improve his profitability (Exhibits 2, 3, and 4).

In addition to the price increase, Mr. Talich projected TFI's future total sales volume to increase by 25 percent in 1996 and by a further 20 percent in 1997 if the expansion could be financed. Purchases were expected to be 75 percent of cost of goods sold. He also felt that working capital requirements would increase in direct proportion to sales increases but that expenses would remain constant as a percentage of the new dollar sales figure. Income taxes were expected to rise to a 42 percent rate. With regard to capacity, Mr. Talich projected that current equipment would be adequate to handle the proposed increases in sales and that any further capital expansion could be put off until late in 1997.

*EXHIBIT 1*

---

**MEMO**:        DOMINION BANK OF CANADA

**DATE**:        August 16, 1995

**TO**:          Branch Managers

**FROM**:        Vice-President,
                 Commercial Services

---

In view of the recent forecasts by our economists on the movement of interest rates, the shortage of raw materials, the tightening of the money supply, and the general business outlook for the upcoming quarter, I would like to remind all managers that in periods of economic uncertainty our standards for quality and risk factor should be weighed even more heavily in investigating alternative commercial placements.

The growth of loans outstanding at the branch level should not exceed 2 percent. Similarly, as loans are repaid, every effort should be made to place available funds with the proposals offering the highest return and least risk.

***EXHIBIT 2***

|  | Talich Fabricating Inc. Income Statements for the Years Ending September 30 (in 000s of dollars) | | | |
|---|---|---|---|---|
|  | **1992** | **1993** | **1994** | **1995** |
| Sales[1] | $9,230 | $7,913 | $7,728 | $11,420 |
| Cost of goods sold[2] | 7,075 | 6,305 | 6,163 | 9,332 |
| Gross profit | $2,155 | $1,608 | $1,565 | $2,088 |
| Operating expenses: | | | | |
|    Selling expenses | $ 323 | $ 294 | $298 | $419 |
|    Administrative expenses | 280 | 293 | 324 | 487 |
|    General expenses | 405 | 374 | 359 | 518 |
|    Management bonus | 725 | 184 | | |
|    Depreciation | 47 | 93 | 70 | 174 |
|    Total | 1,780 | 1,238 | 1,051 | 1,598 |
| Net operating profit | $375 | $370 | $514 | $490 |
| Interest | 27 | 21 | 47 | 101 |
| Less: extraordinary expenses[3] | | | 119 | |
| Net profit before tax | $348 | $349 | $348 | $389 |
| Income tax | 146 | 147 | 146 | 164 |
| Net earnings | $202 | $202 | $202 | $225 |
| Initial retained earnings | 381 | 583 | 785 | 987 |
| Ending retained earnings | $583 | $785 | $987 | $1,212 |

1. Sales and profit ($000s) for the years 1989 through 1991 were as follows:

|  | **1989** | **1990** | **1991** |
|---|---|---|---|
| Sales | $2,336 | $5,014 | $6,252 |
| Net earnings | 15 | 140 | 211 |

2. Cost of goods included raw materials, rent, direct labour, indirect labour, depreciation, and plant overhead. Purchases of materials for the years 1992 to 1995, respectively, were:

|  | **1992** | **1993** | **1994** | **1995** |
|---|---|---|---|---|
| Purchases | $5,329 | $3,126 | $5,605 | $7,152 |

3. In 1994, TFI experienced nonrecurring expenses as part of its relocation to a new plant site.

*EXHIBIT 3*

| | **Talich Fabricating Inc.**<br>**Balance Sheet**<br>**as at September 30**<br>**(in 000s of dollars)** | | | |
|---|---|---|---|---|
| | **1992** | **1993** | **1994** | **1995** |
| ASSETS | | | | |
| Current assets: | | | | |
| Cash | $ 13 | $8 | $3 | $3 |
| Accounts receivable | 2,179 | 1,804 | 1,760 | 2,173 |
| Inventory | 456 | 794 | 834 | 1,547 |
| Prepaid expenses | 17 | 19 | 31 | 28 |
| Total current assets | $2,665 | $2,625 | $2,628 | $3,751 |
| | | | | |
| Due from Talich Properties | | | 367 | 174 |
| | | | | |
| Fixed assets: | | | | |
| Plant Equipment | $381 | $489 | $867 | $1,140 |
| Vehicles | 168 | 168 | 274 | 303 |
| Tooling[1] | | | | 295 |
| Subtotal | $549 | $657 | $1,141 | $1,738 |
| Less: accumulated<br>   depreciation | 249 | 341 | 411 | 585 |
| Total fixed assets | 300 | 316 | 730 | 1,153 |
| | | | | |
| Other assets: | | | | |
| Goodwill | 104 | 104 | 104 | 104 |
| TOTAL ASSETS | $3,069 | $3,045 | $3,829 | $5,182 |

**1.** In previous years tooling had been expensed in the year purchased. TFI's accountant recommended that tooling be capitalized and depreciated. Mr. Talich felt purchases of tooling would be sufficient to maintain the 1995 level for the next two years. Mr. Talich intended to depreciate all tooling at the rate of one-third per year.

*EXHIBIT 3 (cont'd)*

|  | 1992 | 1993 | 1994 | 1995 |
|---|---|---|---|---|
| LIABILITIES | | | | |
| Current liabilities: | | | | |
| Bank loan | $440 | $752 | $993 | $1,815 |
| Accounts payable | 853 | 542 | 1,061 | 1,237 |
| Other payable | 957 | 404 | 313 | 276 |
| Total current liabilities | $2,250 | $1,698 | $2,367 | $3,328 |
| | | | | |
| Long-term liabilities: | | | | |
| Lien notes payable[1] | | $69 | $172 | $127 |
| Due to shareholders[2] | 135 | 306 | 170 | 124 |
| Notes payable Pioneer | | 86 | 17 | |
| Notes payable Trans World | | | | 269 |
| Deferred income tax | — | — | 15 | 21 |
| Total long-term liabilities | 135 | 461 | 374 | 541 |
| TOTAL LIABILITIES | $2,385 | $2,159 | $2,741 | $3,869 |
| | | | | |
| SHAREHOLDERS' EQUITY | | | | |
| Authorized: | | | | |
| 10,000 common, no par value | | | | |
| Issued: | | | | |
| Common | $101 | $101 | $101 | $101 |
| Retained earnings | 583 | 785 | 987 | 1,212 |
| TOTAL EQUITY | 684 | 886 | 1,088 | 1,313 |
| TOTAL LIABILITIES AND SHAREHOLDERS' EQUITY | $3,069 | $3,045 | $3,829 | $5,182 |

1. Purchases of tooling and equipment were financed through suppliers and finance companies using lien instruments. Mr. Talich felt that the lien notes would remain relatively constant over the next two years.
2. For tax purposes this money was considered to be distributed to the shareholders (principally Mr. Talich). However, to accommodate TFI's working capital requirements, the account was set up as a liability.

*Exhibit 4*

|  | TFI | Pioneer | Trans World | Total |
|---|---|---|---|---|
| **Talich Fabricating Inc.** | | | | |
| **Sales and Manufacturing Cost Breakdown** | | | | |
| **by Product Line in 1995** | | | | |
| **(in 000s of dollars and percentages)** | | | | |
| Sales | $9,011 | $1,299 | $1,110 | $11,420 |
| Manufacturing costs: | | | | |
| Material | $5,135 | $533 | $467 | $ 6,135 |
| Labour | 986 | 234 | 241 | 1,460 |
| Overhead | 1,117 | 285 | 336 | 1,737 |
| Total | 7,237 | 1,051 | 1,044 | 9,332 |
| Gross profit | $1,774 | $248 | $66 | $2,088 |
| Sales | 100.0% | 100.0% | 100.0% | 100.0% |
| Manufacturing costs: | | | | |
| Material | 57.0% | 41.0% | 42.1% | 53.7% |
| Labour | 10.9% | 18.0% | 21.7% | 12.8% |
| Overhead | 12.4% | 21.9% | 30.3% | 15.2% |
| Total | 80.3% | 80.9% | 94.1% | 81.7% |
| Gross profit | 19.7% | 19.1% | 5.9% | 18.3% |

# PART

# AN INTRODUCTION TO HUMAN RESOURCES

This chapter is about people who accomplish tasks through other people; people who are resourceful, mobilized, and inspired in a team effort to make an organization purr from the factory floor to the boardroom door, and beyond. People operate machines, put together financial statements, and meet customers. Very few flourish in a human resources department, and that is why the cases in this chapter were framed in diversified back drops, with decision makers from every functional department *except* human resources. The scope of decisions discussed ranges from determining a training policy for a national corporation with 50,000 employees to reprimanding one individual who works at a local branch office with only 100 other people.

This introduction's discussion barely scratches the surface of an abundance of research and ongoing study into human behaviour. Its vocabulary is simple because an intense examination of social and psychological jargon is well beyond the scope of this book.

## THE ART OF WORKING WITH PEOPLE

■

**SECTION**

■

**ONE**

■

Effective people management takes greater skill than is needed to put together financial statements or to decide a marketing plan. Theorems for financial analysis can be learned; however, working with people requires more than education. It takes practice, unfaltering dedication, and continual introspection.

Valuable people managers, like works of fine art, are composed of 95 percent style and communication. Some managers were born with people skills. Others work hard to measure up to the demands of the 1990s era of human resources. Regardless, there is only one formula for being or becoming an effective manager. Yours!

## ONE FORMULA

Given that our global population exceeds one billion uniquely designed souls, it follows that there are in excess of one billion ways to deal with this population. Add to this formula a component that takes into consideration the implications of an interpersonal relationship. Each party to an alliance brings unique perceptions, personality, and attitudes to the bargaining table, sometimes prompting the other party to act in ways they otherwise would not. Add to the equation an element that takes into consideration the rapid pace of change in business and society that affects every single member of the population. Finally, place parentheses around the equation and multiply it by the numbers of permutations of human behaviour that can occur among a group of people.

## A SEVEN-STEP DECISION-MAKING PROCESS

Despite its complexities, decision making can be reduced to a few steps that provide a starting point, a checklist that may later be refined into a personal system.

## STEP ONE: SIZE-UP AND PRIORITIZE

### Size-Up

Historically, decision making has been viewed as problem based, a curiosity that has contributed a dubious approach to decision making where behavioural issues are concerned. Rather than viewing all decision making as problem based, effective people managers perceive issues differently. They:

> *Identify the concerns, predicaments, and disagreements within the organization and deal with them as though they were challenges, not problems; identify all the stakeholders in the organization, not just the ones who are immediately associated with the issue.*

Everyone who demonstrates a vested interest in the activities of an organization is a stakeholder. Stakeholders may be categorized into: stockholders, managers, employees, customers, contractors, creditors, the local community, and the members of the broader public bargaining arena.

Consider the challenge of dismissing several employees in response to lowered profitability. At first blush, severance appears to affect only those employees who will be cut and their immediate families. Not so! Other community retail and manufacturing concerns will be affected by reduced buying power in their consumer base. As well, remaining employees will necessarily take on greater work loads, larger responsibilities, and anxieties over the possibility that they, too, may be dismissed.

### Prioritize

*Once the challenges have been identified, we need to critically evaluate their order of urgency: How quickly must each issue be confronted?*

If a valued employee has just resigned, the decision maker may need to act swiftly, with restricted opportunity to gather or analyze information. For instance, the case in this chapter entitled *Ottawa Valley Food Products* presents decision makers with a 20-minute time frame in which to act, if action is germane to the issue.

All problems cannot be resolved adequately in the short-term. Once the most urgent challenges have been cleaned from the slate, managers analyze secondary factors, and root causes that culminated in catastrophe. Neglecting underlying or longer-term elements of a decision-making process will lead to recurrence of similar problems. Repeatedly *reacting* to persistent scrapes leaves decision makers with no time to devise solutions for larger challenges in the organization. After a while, they become ineffective "firefighters."

### STEP 2: DETERMINE A PROCESS

*Develop an appropriate list of questions to answer. These questions will be unique to every human resources challenge.*

Try to decide on the most important aspects of behaviour that have contributed to the current challenge. Then, set up a conscientious list of questions. To compile your list of questions consider all of the topics covered in this introduction, especially the topics pertaining to guiding changes in the organization, in its groups, and in its individuals.

No matter how hard they try, managers never achieve perfect information and frequently face the frustrating task of making decisions based on flawed or incomplete facts. No one person can expect to have impeccable knowledge of a situation, especially where people are concerned. In a real world scenario decision makers attempt to narrow broad fields of information by selecting only pertinent facts, and by exchanging feedback with key players. An astute manager knows when it is time to quit asking questions and to start taking action. This cutoff point may be influenced by finances (what is the marginal benefit of pursuing more information?), or it may be governed by time constraints (what will happen if I wait longer before I take action to resolve this issue?).

### STEP 3: ANALYZE

Very simply, in this part of an approach to decision making:

> *Answer the list of questions established in Step 2.*

Like questions, answers are never perfect; however, managers can strive for optimal, if not ideal.

### STEP 4: SET OBJECTIVES

Having gained a clear mastery of the facts, the obstacles, and the possible root causes of the challenges:

> *Establish an optimal objective, the best possible outcome under the circumstances; then, set a realistic second objective for a minimally acceptable outcome.*

### STEP 5: ESTABLISH ALTERNATIVES FOR ACTION

> *In the range between the ideal and the minimal objectives, devise a range of alternatives for action.*

Alternative courses of action consist of distinct and reasonable avenues to follow during the process of dealing with group or individual stakeholders. Organizations take a dim view of absurd or impractical alternatives, generated simply to impress an audience with rampant creativity. Effective alternatives can be as few as two: the ideal course of action, and a contingency plan that can be pulled into play in the event that the ideal strategy fails.

### STEP 6: ACTION PLAN OR IMPLEMENTATION

Here, decision makers present vital and specific components of their optimal alternative, paying close attention to details like the location of discussions, the atmosphere created, the vocabulary used, and even the body language employed to convey a consistent message.

An effective action plan deals with the short, medium, and longer term. It tackles challenges head-on.

### STEP 7: EVALUATION

> *Every plan needs follow-up, an assessment of results that provides some measure of success. Some managers choose to administer questionnaires to stakeholders. Others set simple objectives that are measurable in monetary terms, like profitability or increased sales. Still others attempt to set objectives that are measurable in behavioural terms, a daunting task for nonprofessionals.*

Regardless of the evaluation method, it is important to set a time frame on the evaluation process. It is critical to weigh the impact of external factors, like changes in the market, which may thwart the behaviours of the key players. Because business environments are dynamic, evaluation is an ongoing and dynamic process.

**SECTION**

**TWO**

## MANAGEMENT OF CHANGE

Today's environment demands attention to rapid economic and social change. For instance, *downsizing*, a term that has become synonymous with the 1990s, is a phenomenon that has altered corporate climate forever. Downsizing is characterized by widespread tendencies for business to pare back human resources in order to bolster the bottom line. Downsized companies have minimal numbers of employees who individually must take on more tasks, more subordinates, or more responsibilities. Downsized companies aim to survive *leaner, meaner* corporate climates. Some firms testify that downsizing is integral to a sharply competitive international economy.

### DEMOGRAPHIC SHIFTS

One trend that resulted in vast change to North American business was the aging of its population. This phenomenon has been attributed to a post-World War II baby boom. Returning soldiers and new immigrants contributed significantly to a population explosion in North America.

"Baby boomers" exercise considerable influence on business and government organizations by virtue of their sheer numbers. The boomers cause sweeping trends in consumer spending when they move through each stage of their lives. By these shifts in spending, an aging population forces economic transformations. Over the next 20 years, the boomers will force business to refocus on contemporary and futuristic growth sectors like health care, retirement banking, and leisure activities. Human resources will need to continually adjust to this constantly changing focus.

An aging population has also brought about a so-called generation "X." This entire age group following the boomers feels that it is impossible to accomplish a better lifestyle than that achieved by the previous generation. They also believe that boomers will continue to occupy middle and upper management positions well past contemporary retirement age, diminishing job and promotion opportunities for the "Xers" during the next quarter century.

### VALUE CHANGES

Changing social values, like moves to legislate equality for women and visible minorities, have brought pressure to bear on organizations. Affirmative action has resulted in considerable controversy. Most recently, there has been a backlash by administrators who believe that equity policies dilute the effectiveness of an organization.

Heightened awareness of social responsibilities, the increasing role of the media, and the inclination of the population as a whole to be better educated cause organizations to be cautious about their actions, more defensive in their strategic plans, particularly when they will be subjected to intense public scrutiny.

### INTERNATIONAL FORCES

The end of the Cold War and the lowering of global trade barriers have brought pressure to bear on organizations to survive greater competition from an international market place. Companies who want to sell parts, end products, or services internationally are expected to meet certain standards for quality. Businesses in 90 countries have ISO9000 registration (International Organization for Standardization based in Geneva, Switzerland). In some companies, the drive to meet world class standards is a prognosticator of compromised human resources standards.

While we are quick to criticize the impact of economic and social change, we also need to acknowledge its value. We need to refocus on teaching and guiding rather than directing. We need to encourage team work and responsiveness rather than one-sided decision making to meet the challenges of change.

■
**SECTION**
■
**THREE**
■

## GUIDING THE ORGANIZATION THROUGH CHANGE: MACRO-ORGANIZATIONAL ISSUES

Macro-organizational issues have to do with the organization itself, its formal and informal structures, its merit and punishment systems, and the effect of those systems on the success or failure of organizational decisions.

### GOAL SETTING

First, organizations set overall objectives for the entire company. Then they establish individual goals for unique units or subdivisions. When the organization's people, from the mail room to the boardroom, contribute to the formulation of objectives, they become more committed to those goals.

Misapplied or blanket goals work against an organization's overall effectiveness. For example, a manager in charge of introducing a new product to a new market will incur escalated expenses and reduced profitability. Compare this manager's task to that of a manager charged with selling an existing product in a mature market. If the success of each of the two managers is measured on their division's respective profitabilities, then the manager with the new product may be inclined to skimp on expenses. Skimping may jeopardize the longer-term success of the division.

## EVALUATION

Setting goals requires recording the objectives of the organization and its subgroups. Then the objectives are reviewed after an appropriate period of time to see how well they worked. An organization needs to decide appropriate sensors so that it can get early warning about problems. Long-term goals are subject to many changes in a complex environment. For example, an organization introduces a new product that fails; now management must isolate its actions and responsibilities from external effects like new legislation, then re-assess the viability of the venture.

## FEEDBACK

Frequent feedback is necessary for goal setting to work. The leaders and the followers, the managers and the team, need to exchange ideas regularly and honestly. The more rapid and accurate the feedback the more quickly people learn and the more opportunity they have to adjust.

Contrast the performance of a precision figure skating team with the performance of a hockey team. After the skaters have *completed* their presentation, they submit to feedback from judges. The skaters have no opportunity to adjust the execution of their act during the performance. If the judges were unimpressed with the earlier aspects of the drill, the skaters receive no interim feedback. They are left with no opportunity to alter their presentation. Hockey players receive frequent and sometimes strongly negative feedback from referees and from the other team's members *continuously and throughout* their performance. They have plenty of opportunity to adjust their actions during the game. Regardless of the tenor of the feedback, a successful team will adjust.

The precision team may have practised its presentation intensively, and as a result, mistakenly believes that it is executing a perfect performance. Without feedback during the performance, the skaters will retain a distorted view until the end of the presentation. The hockey team may also have practised extensively, but immediate and accurate feedback corrects its perception of its performance *at the time that correction is required.*

## ORGANIZATIONAL STRUCTURE

Organizations are divided into subgroups. Subgroups are designed around the functions of the subunits, and the needs for divisions to communicate effectively with each other. An organization needs to be structured for appropriate authority, control, and evaluation of decisions. A corporation's structure is more than a diagram of lines and boxes. It represents a natural synergy that matches the challenges of its environment. Griener and Metzger[1] proposed several organizational structures. When placed on a continuum, these structures range from an *elevated* pyramidal design to a *flat* team structure (Exhibit 1).

***Exhibit 1***
***Organizational***
***Structures***

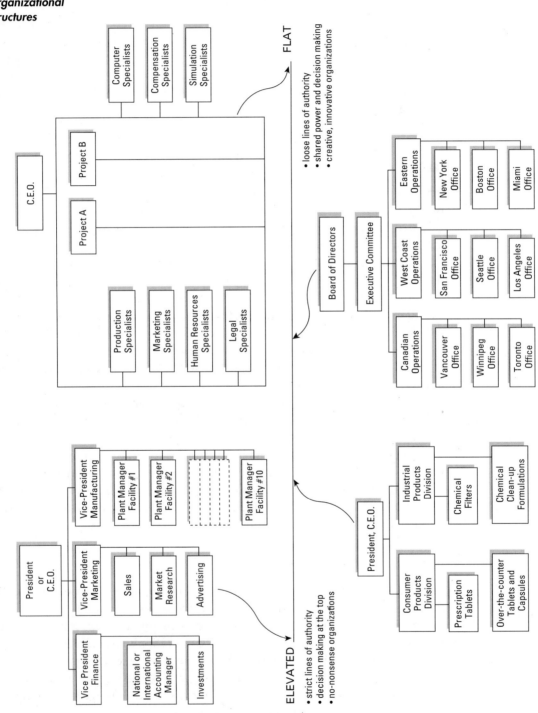

FLAT

- loose lines of authority
- shared power and decision making
- creative, innovative organizations

ELEVATED

- strict lines of authority
- decision making at the top
- no-nonsense organizations

Historically, we have become accustomed to a pyramidal organizational structure where there is strong authority at the apex issuing directives *downward* to subordinates. At the top of this structure's clear chain of command are a few administrators who perform all of the planning and decision making. This design is the *elevated* structure depicted in Exhibit 1. At the other end of a continuum of organizational structures shown in Exhibit 1 is a structure where charts are frowned upon. It is a *flat* design, composed of overlapping teams where *authority* is delegated *downward*. Top management devotes its attention to strategic planning. An elevated structure allows for plenty of feedback, for better or worse. A flat structure yields less feedback from within its fluid lines and flexible chain of command.

## EFFECTIVE ELEVATED STRUCTURES

The various elevations in a pyramidal structure create differences in rank and status. Authority comes from position. Usually, the corporation is divided into departments. Each department has a specialized function like marketing or production or research. Companies with effective elevated structures specialize in selling a single product that holds no promise of innovation in either its marketing or its production. Usually, the product has been marketed in an existing consumer base for many years. The company competes largely on price for market share. A manufacturer of laundry detergent is a good example of a company that will function well with an elevated structure. It will thrive only as long as the company forecasts environmental changes, and introduces appropriate but small innovations when the market requires it.

## MIXED STRUCTURES

Between the poles of the continuum in Exhibit 1, there are other organizational structures. One of those typically manufactures more than one product or line of products, targeted at different consumers. This enterprise is divided into departments or subunits according to the product (line) manufactured or marketed. Each division manager enjoys considerable autonomy in decision making. He or she is charged with the profitability of the unit. There may be a layer of management between the divisions and the chief executive officers. This layer of management is charged with strategic planning for the whole organization and evaluation of performance of the divisions.

Next on the continuum of Exhibit 1 is a chart representing an organization that needs to be near its end consumers for frequent contact, usually delineated by geography. A chain of fast food outlets is the best example. Each district office is located in a market with a large consumer base. Each district manager is responsible for profitability in a saturated market or for market development in a new consumer base.

### FLAT STRUCTURES

At the opposite end of the continuum in Exhibit 1 is a flat structure. It is appropriate for a company requiring great flexibility, a company involved in many projects simultaneously. Groups of employees with specialized skills or functions are assigned and re-assigned to various projects at appropriate times. Employees work for many superiors at once and are usually highly skilled. Decisions are made by consensus of the team on any one project and everyone shares responsibility for evaluation of results.

These models for organizational design have been presented as distinct points on a continuum stretching from an elevated to a flat structure. This presentation is misleading. The continuum should portray a third dimension that allows the organization to employ various combinations and permutations of the structure at the same time within different departments. For instance, it may be possible for a company that manufactures breakfast cereal to employ an elevated, no-nonsense structure for most of its organization; however, within substructures, like the maintenance department, it may be better to utilize a flat structure, a team approach to solving complex electronic problems in machinery and equipment.

Similarly, a company that manufactures and markets diverse product lines may require an elevated structure for older products, ones at the end of their life cycle. However, it would be counterproductive to employ an elevated structure within those divisions charged with marketing new products to new markets. At these introductory stages, a flat structure will foster creativity and innovation.

Finally, the organizational structure, the corporate backbone, may require modification from time to time. The organization's structure may be at the root of counterproductivity, detracting from the effectiveness of communication among the organization's human resources. Modification will meet the challenges of a changing environment, re-align effective communication, and provide appropriate and timely feedback to the people who comprise the essence of the organization.

**SECTION**

**FOUR**

## GUIDING GROUPS THROUGH CHANGE

Within an organization there are formal groups like the accounting department, the marketing division, the consumer products group, or the industrial products division. Formal groups are easy to identify because members are brought together to accomplish an economic task. Formal groups have distinct reporting structures, merit systems, and chain of command. The members of a formal group do not have to like each other — they just have to work together to get a job done.

Informal groups have a tendency to spring up within organizations in response to social or emotional needs of potential members. For instance, extracurricular clubs bring together people with common interests like sports or the arts and other cultural pursuits. Still other informal groups band together because the members want to feel some fellowship, prestige, protection, or safety. These kinds of informal groups have standards, shared values, and attitudes that members are expected to reflect. Sometimes the standards are well-publicized and verbalized, but most times these values are tacitly *understood* by all of those who come in contact with these informal groups.

For better or worse, attitude changes are accomplished in groups. Otherwise, the individual who has been isolated for an attitude change will resist the change in favour of maintaining the norms of the group. This "group think" phenomenon is particularly true for groups where individual members have become united by emotional bonds, rather than economic ties. Consider the example of a group of people who have banded together in response to a *common enemy*. Its members have been drawn together by powerful human emotions like hate, and by powerful human needs like safety and self-preservation. Street gangs constitute a contemporary example of a group united by strong emotional bonds in response to a common enemy.

Managers who purposefully or inadvertently become a common enemy within an organization encounter solid emotional ties binding the individuals in the group opposing them, usually a group that has banded together for protection and commiseration. Often, groups that have evolved in response to a common enemy cross economic, hierarchial, and departmental boundaries. They seldom or never hold formal meetings, except when one of their members needs support, or when there is a bargaining issue like management-union negotiations for wages.

Consider the example of a dictatorial manager, one who rides rough shod over everyone in his wake, claiming that every one of his or her colleagues and peers is too sensitive. This managerial behaviour results in many personality conflicts, overt and covert. Everyone from the mail room to the boardroom prefers to avoid this manager's tongue-lashings; however, an occasional brave soul will openly confront him or her. In organizations where this kind of managerial behaviour has been allowed to continue unchecked, the odds of winning a confrontation with this manager ride with the manager. Despite the fact that he or she is prone to winning, there is still an informal group of people (out there) united emotionally against this manager. This informal group is covertly waiting and hoping to support any individual who will become sufficiently brave or reckless to openly confront the boss.

Marketing managers are acutely aware that persuasive communication can change a consumer group's attitude toward a product or service. Similarly, persuasive communication can change a group's attitudes toward the boss or the job. Persuasive communication has four basic elements: a target, a communicator, a message, and a setting.

*Target*

The target, similar to a marketing target, is the group whose attitude we want to change.

*Communicator*

The communicator is the person who wants to persuade the group (the target) to adopt a specific attitude. Targets respond better to communicators who are respected, persons with higher social or economic status, persons who have proven themselves trustworthy, or have proven themselves to be credible and not self-serving. If a target admires the communicator, the target will perceive himself or herself to have similar characteristics and will be inclined to modify attitudes to be consistent with those of the persuasive, respected communicator. For this reason, celebrities are sometimes used to endorse products or services.

*Message*

An effective message presents an incongruity between the position held by the communicator and the target's attitude. This inconsistency leads to stress. The larger the discrepancy, the greater the stress. The greater the stress, the greater the chance of achieving a change in attitude, *up to a certain level of stress*. For example, telling inebriated drivers that their actions are antisocial (and in fact could cause death) is too incredible a message. Instead, telling these drivers that their actions may result in loss of their driver's licence is more believable. This latter message holds immediate and tangible consequences for the target. If the stress of the message is too intense or obscure, the target may reject the message and maintain the initial attitude.

Inviting the target to ask questions and to gather information reduces the target's stress. By asking questions, sharing information, and expressing opinions to the communicator and/or within the group the target is able to decrease or alleviate stress to reasonable levels. This lower degree of discomfort will lead to a change of attitude. In other words, the communicator (employer or supervisor) will be wise to be receptive to exchanges (confrontational or otherwise). This kind of openness is integral to shared power or empowerment, a topic that will be discussed later in this introduction.

*Setting*

The setting is the environment in which the message is delivered. The communicator should preview the value of formal versus informal settings, the people who should be present and those who should not, the use of positive body language (smiling or nodding approval) at appropriate junctures, and the use of negative body language (frowning).

It is important to remember that people differ in the way they learn, in the way they acquire attitudes, and in the way they change them. Attitudes that are more central to the target are less likely to change. Targets who exhibit high self-esteem are more likely to believe their attitudes are correct, and therefore may present bigger challenges in terms of changing. Such targets may have more confidence in their values because they respect the initial influencer of their values, specifically the people with whom they have close and emotional relationships. Managers cannot treat groups solely as a collection of rational, reasoning beings who can be argued intellectually into a change.

### SHARED VALUES

Almost all organizations have group cultures, meaning that their members share certain attitudes and values. Contemporary groups work hard to mould a set of common attitudes, organizational "creeds" or mission statements that publicize their values, front and centre.

Uniformity and like-mindedness provide the internal glue of stability, while diversity among group members drives adaptiveness and innovation. Informal groups, much like volunteer organizations, constitute themselves from like-minded individuals who stick together through thick and thin because of beliefs and emotional bonds, sometimes compromising the creativity and innovation of the group. Striking the right balance between promoting like-mindedness and diversity requires an extraordinary juggling act on the part of the group leader.

**SECTION**

**FIVE**

### GUIDING INDIVIDUALS THROUGH CHANGE

Change in an individual's environment, even the smallest shift, can be frightening because change threatens economic safety, social well-being, and/or emotional stability. Individuals usually demonstrate evidence of distress when they are asked to modify their behaviour to meet climactic changes in business. If they showed no signs of disturbance, it would be unlikely that change would be forthcoming. People make changes in their lives out of love, loyalty, or commitment, not because intellect compelled them to action.

### EMOTION VERSUS INTELLECT

Influencing behaviour modification to meet the challenges of an altered business climate is a complex and demanding process for managers. It doesn't happen overnight, and it doesn't happen without discomfort. Managers need to constantly remind themselves that influencing individuals to make changes is a much more emotional task than an intellectual one.

### MOTIVATION FOR CHANGE

Managers need to understand their personal motivations for change in order to avoid confusion about their reasons for requesting behavioural shifts in subordinates. Because managers are under pressure from superiors, their objectives may be designed (consciously or subconsciously) to satisfy their own needs rather than to modify operations under their span of responsibility. Sometimes when they are unclear of their own motives, managers trade off the longer term for short-term advantages that augment their image in the eyes of superiors; frequently damaging their long-term relationship with subordinates.

### RESPONSIBILITY FOR CHANGE

The drive to change behaviour can come from the top or the bottom of the organization with varying degrees of success. In some circumstances, employees may accept no responsibility, believing that the "boss" has an obligation by virtue of his or her position to "make" them change. A failure to accept responsibility may have complex origins; however, it generally accompanies a feeling of powerlessness on the part of employees, a belief that they have an external locus of control. We will discuss methods for empowering employees and getting them to accept responsibility later in this chapter. For now, it is sufficient to understand that responsibility for behavioural change needs to be shared between or among all of the people seeking change.

### CONTROL OF CHANGE

Managers cannot forget that the target, the person(s) whose behaviour managers want to modify, controls the final decision to change his or her behaviour. No matter how much a manager desires to modify employees' conduct, and no matter how much power the manager holds, it is the employee who ultimately controls the final decision to change. No one can *make* another person do things they don't *want* to do.

Cultivating an internal locus in employees, enticing them to take control of changing their own behaviour, leads to better and more lasting results. Thus, it is important for subordinates to understand the challenge, the need for change. The process of empowering employees, getting them to take an active role, is more demanding, emotion-laden, and frustrating for managers than is simply *dictating* behavioural changes to subordinates.

### PROCESS FOR CHANGE

The best way to help people deal with change is to help them understand its sources and to anticipate its possible outcomes so that every member of the organization feels part of planning for the future. Effective managers become mentors to their stakeholders in an adaptation process by using the following guidelines:

1. Ask everyone to participate in the decision-making process; explain the reasons for pending changes, and invite feedback.

2. Be supportive when it is appropriate. Be prepared to acknowledge individual and group concerns. Be clear and honest.

3. Provide appropriate help, training, advice, and assistance to stakeholders on modifications to personal career plans that may become imminent in light of environmental changes.

4. Look deeper; be prepared to abandon the safety of management status in the group in order to persuade rather than direct a decision-making process.

## ORGANIZATIONAL BEHAVIOUR: TOPICS

### LEAVITT'S CAUSE/MOTIVATION/BEHAVIOUR MODEL

**SECTION**

**SIX**

A useful starting place to understand behaviour is offered by H.J. Leavitt in *Managerial Psychology*.[2] He states that behaviourial analysis begins with three basic assumptions:

1. All behaviour is caused (by conditions outside the individual).
2. All behaviour is motivated (by forces that are internal to the individual).
3. All behaviour is goal-directed (toward that which will neutralize the prior cause and motivation).

Leavitt proposed that behaviour was the overt or observable response to an external stimulus (cause) and to internal needs (motivation). Behaviour may consist of activities, expressed feelings, expressed expectations, and/or expressed perceptions. An individual operates in an environment that conditions him or her into having certain beliefs, values, customs, and factual information that in turn cause or stimulate certain behaviours. These *external* forces are coloured by the individual's perception of them.

### MOTIVATION

According to *Webster's*,[3] a motive is "something (as a need or desire) that causes a person to act" and further it "implies emotion or desire operating on the will and causing it to act." Motivation originates from needs, discomforts, or stresses that cause people to take action.

Intrinsic motivation, which comes from inside the self, leads people to take action because they *want* to take action. Extrinsic motivation means doing something to win a reward from outside the self, like money. Extrinsic motivation will, in many instances, override intrinsic motivation. In other words, someone will begin to do something because he or she gets paid for it, not for the fun of it. The trick is to get that person to do the job for fun and, almost as a by-product, to get paid for it.

Most theories of motivation are similar in that they are all based on needs. The thing that distinguishes one theory from another is the kinds of needs underlying someone's decision to take action on those needs.

### Maslow's Hierarchy of Needs[4]

One of the best known models attempting to explain motivation is *Maslow's Theory*. Maslow proposed a hierarchy of needs that was based on the following three assumptions:

1. Behaviour is based on attempts to satisfy needs.
2. Needs are arranged in a succession of five tiers, like ascending stair steps, with the lowest level needs at the bottom tier.
3. A satisfied need is not a motivator.

**EXHIBIT 2**
**Maslow's Hierarchy of Needs**

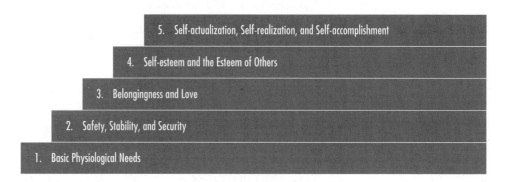

5. Self-actualization, Self-realization, and Self-accomplishment
4. Self-esteem and the Esteem of Others
3. Belongingness and Love
2. Safety, Stability, and Security
1. Basic Physiological Needs

Maslow proposed that people advance from the lowest level toward the highest, after each successive need level has been totally satisfied. He also argued that people lose their desire for self-actualization when they are not allowed to progress normally up the rungs of the ladder The four levels of needs shown in Exhibit 2 are self-explanatory; however, the level of self-actualization is sometimes misunderstood. People who operate at the level of self-actualization exhibit the following characteristics:

1. Clear (versus unclear) perception,
2. Openness to different experiences (versus closed),
3. Spontaneity (versus guardedness),
4. Autonomy (versus dependency),
5. Objectivity (versus subjectivity),
6. More creativity (versus less creativity),
7. Democratic tendencies (versus autocratic ones), and
8. Great ability (versus a limited ability) to love others.

Despite its historical value, Maslow's model presents limited opportunity for application in North American business where employees' lower-level needs are normally satisfied. As well, Maslow's model is considered to be of limited value to understanding behaviour because it is based on deficiencies, human needs, or tensions that result from lack or want. The model's worth comes from understanding the top two or three echelons of needs.

### Herzberg's Hygiene/Motivators

Frederick Herzberg[5] provided another model for understanding motivation. He proposed a two-tiered approach to factors affecting job satisfaction. The first continuum, which he called *hygiene* or *maintenance* factors, stretches from one pole, called "job dissatisfaction" to "no job dissatisfaction" at the opposite pole. (see Exhibit 3). These external or environmental factors will *not* lead to job satisfaction; however, when they are fulfilled, these factors can serve to *reduce job dissatisfaction*. In Exhibit 3, the point marked "X" on the hygiene continuum demonstrates that the individual in question is very high on this *maintenance* scale.

**EXHIBIT 3**
*Herzberg's Hygiene/ Motivators*

Herzberg's Hygiene Factors
- policy and administration of the organization
- supervision/leadership
- working conditions
- interpersonal relationships in the organization
- the individual's status within the organization
- salary
- job security
- satisfying personal life

Herzberg's Motivators
- achievement
- recognition
- advancement
- opportunity to growth

Herzberg termed the second continuum *motivators,* because he believed that these factors were important to the individual's job satisfaction and thus central to job productivity and performance.

Herzberg's motivators are shown on the second continuum in Exhibit 3. The point marked "X" indicates that the individual in question is very low on this continuum that leads to job satisfaction. Thus, individual "X" has a good work environment, but very little job satisfaction. Conversely, the individual indicated by the point marked "Y" in the exhibit has a bad job environment, but all of the motivators are present. Thus, individual "Y" shows both job satisfaction and dissatisfaction. It is possible for a person to work in abysmal physical or external conditions and yet to be very satisfied with his or her job, to be productive. The job, however hot, dirty, cold, or wet, may allow the individual freedom to act, an atmosphere of approval, an opportunity for promotion and/or education, the chance to set goals and to do some planning, and the reasonable possibility of accessing information.

### McClelland's Acquired Needs Theory[6]

McClelland, a Harvard psychology professor, proposed that people are motivated by growth needs. Growth needs are *acquired* over time as a result of life experiences. Growth motivation presents the view that human needs are self-generated. It is only human nature, this theory argues, to reach out for something more no matter what our state of satisfaction. People who are well fed and comfortable do not languish, rather they develop needs for greater achievements in terms of their personal potential. Growth models view human potential as open-ended.

McClelland described three acquired needs:

1. **Need for Achievement**. The desire for doing better, for reaching desirable goals, to solve complex problems, to be more productive.
2. **Need for Affiliation.** The desire for positive relationships, to maintain friendly and warm relations with others.
3. **Need for Power.** The desire to control others, to influence others' behaviour.

He studied achievement-needy people extensively and found that they set objectives for themselves, worked hard to reach those objectives, and then set their objectives a little higher.

McClelland believed that achievement need could be taught and learned by:

1. Teaching people to think, talk, and act like high achievers,
2. Stimulating people to set higher, well-planned goals,
3. Helping people to become more aware of themselves, and
4. Creating a group spirit with shared hopes, fears, and successes.

Effective upper level managers have a low need for affiliation, and a high need for power. Power is an effective motivator when it is used to accomplish group objectives, but not when it is used to glorify the self. Sometimes individuals with excellent leadership skills misuse their need for power. Such individuals never reach the top because they abuse their need for power, and inevitably are sabotaged by people they exploited on their journey.

Whatever model managers favour, motives can be divided into at least two major groups: those arising from clear-cut, unambiguous basic needs and those originating from "psychological" (achievement or belongingness) needs that are much more difficult to validate.

## PERSONALITY

### Perception

We all interpret people and situations differently. Our attitudes, values, social norms, needs, religious beliefs, education, and experiences create personal bias. How do you see the world? In Figure 1[7] do you see a young woman or an older one?

Most of us acknowledge that we have selective perception. We filter out some messages and pay more attention to others. Similarly, we selectively perceive the behaviour of people in our environment. If we *expect* people to act in a certain way, then we will concentrate on those expected behaviours and ignore other behaviours. In a phenomenon called projection, we demonstrate a tendency to attribute our feelings to others, blaming them for predicaments that we actually control.

### Perception Distortion

An individual's image is in the perception of his or her beholders. Each of us creates for ourselves an image that we present to the world in an effort to have other people see us as the kind of person we value. Despite the fact that a created image may be functional, it contributes to an abundance of mixed messages.

**FIGURE 1**
*Old Woman or Young Woman*

Source: Harold J. Leavitt, *Managerial Psychology*, 4th ed. (Chicago: University of Chicago Press, 1978).

When two or more people practise an image, a polished, creative conduct, over a long period of time, they develop astute ways of persuading each other that the image is real. Then, when the chips are down, people *act* on how they *feel*. Their action (or performance) may be worlds apart from the messages they send, thereby delivering mixed and sometimes conflicting signals.

Sometimes, people are said to be "acting out of character." They may be, in fact, acting totally within their real personality, which may be quite different from their "practiced and polished" image. It is important for everyone to be in touch with those emotions beneath the facade, to closely examine their own feelings and those of individuals who appear to have demonstrated unusual or unexpected behaviours.

Open communication, which involves active listening and honest feedback, can reduce repercussions from mixed messages. Two or more people need to be careful to check and double-check that the message received was the intended one (the one the sender planned to deliver). The use of feedback to reduce perception distortions was discussed at some length earlier in this chapter under the heading *Goal Setting*.

### Perception or Prejudice?

People are intuitive. It is impossible for them to become completely objective. Rather than striving for objectivity, it is better to acknowledge the characteristics of personal filters and then understand the limitations on whatever information permeates this private bias.

Have you ever heard someone claim to have acted more from intuition than intellect? That person has learned that self-doubt in reasonable doses is warranted; however, he or she does not always discard personal perceptions and judgments. He or she understands personal biases and uses those filters wisely.

## USING PERCEPTION IN PERSONALITY ISSUES

Job performance is influenced by personality, an individual's most striking or dominant characteristics. Personalities are described in various ways: shy, happy, introverted, extroverted, assertive. Everyone develops likes or dislikes for certain personality traits, avoiding people who do not complement their preferences. While it is possible to avoid disliked personalities in a social setting, in an economic setting (an organization) it is almost impossible to escape personality conflicts. In organizations people are brought together from many social, economic, and cultural backgrounds. Understanding the way in which personality (practiced or real) can catalyze interpersonal conflict is a first step to dealing with friction where personality traits have triggered the conflict.

The most familiar example of a disliked personality is the nonconformist. This nonconformist is often isolated or fired because his or her daily work gathers dust. This employee is an eccentric who develops unusual ideas rather than addressing the assigned work load, a nuisance who raises aggravating questions. While nonconformists are disliked for their inability to get the day-to-day work done, an organization can benefit from their presence because they continually offer new perspectives, for better or worse. It falls to the group who must work with the nonconformist to decide the worth of this maverick's recommendations; however, the group rarely gets to this advanced judgment point in a decision-making process before the nonconformist is isolated or terminated from the group.

### Personality Formation

Research demonstrates that personality is influenced by an individual's basic physiological nature, by the groups with whom he or she interacts, and by his or her individual learning process. Some personality characteristics are inherited from biological parents. Others are learned reactions to people in an individual's environment. For example, if individuals expect negative reactions from friends or family, and if they do not like negative reactions, they will tailor their behaviours in order to glean approval. Thus, the groups with whom people *want* to associate will affect personalities, or at least, the external manifestation of personality characteristics; therefore, groups can be used to mould suitable personality traits in new members.

A person's learning process, in and of itself, helps to determine personality. Everyone learns in a unique manner, demonstrating unique responses to the same stimulus. Needs govern learned characteristics. For instance, if an employee has a strong need for acceptance, he or she exhibits tendencies that garner acceptance, in their perception. With time, tendencies to certain behaviours become one aspect of personality.

People exhibit different personalities within different groups. If one's family accepts or encourages aggressiveness, then the individual exhibits this personality trait when they are with family. If, however, friends have different expectations or unpleasant reactions to aggressiveness, the individual curtails this characteristic when they are with friends.

### Personality Typing

Researchers have proposed scores of measures and classifications of personalities. Inevitably, investigators caution that personality is dynamic over time and over different circumstances. Katherine Briggs and Isabel Meyers[8] developed a series of questions in order to measure and categorize personalities. They devised four preference scales that, when tallied, resulted in 16 personality types. Perhaps the greatest benefit from their work lies not in typing personalities, but in conveying the need to accept and appreciate differences in others, even disliked personalities.

Differences in personality and personal preferences may lead us to like or dislike working with certain people, based solely on *our* judgments of *them*. Meyers and Briggs encourage us to look beyond personal preferences to the underlying value in communicating with different personality types. People who look deeper than personality conflicts, specifically addressing the fact that perception has coloured their judgment, can arrive at better and fresher organizational decisions.

There are many widely used tests that help to assess personality and thereby attempt to predict in advance how an employee will behave. However, assessing personality is a tough task because there are too many external factors that can affect predictions. The biggest problem in forecasting behaviour from tests is that the tests themselves are highly culture and gender bound. Day-to-day assessment of personality is probably the best predictor of human behaviour, for those employers who regularly deal with people they know well.

### Using Personality Concepts in Business

Understanding personality's influence on behaviour may provide a starting point to resolve personality conflicts, or to influence personality changes. Distinct personalities handle situations differently. A secure, confident person will take disappointments in stride, directing anger or frustration outward, at the disturbing individual or object. Such an individual will want to fight. A less confident personality, an individual who has less belief in his or her own abilities, will direct anger and hostility inward, toward himself or herself. This individual tends to criticize himself or herself unduly for stupidity or inadequacy. With support and guidance from an employer, this self-doubting individual can learn to trust his or her own ability. Similarly, the more confident individual may be encouraged to look inward and to draw on reasonable doses of self-doubt.

Interpersonal conflict can often be attributed to distorted perception of personality (between two people or among a group). Managers can resolve interpersonal and intergroup conflict by inviting the parties to the conflict to look deeper than appearances, into the underlying factors that affect personality and self-concept. As well, managers can promote open, honest communication in a supportive setting so that distortions may be minimized. An effective methodology for communication is to invite the "speaker" to recapitulate what he or she "thinks" the speaker who preceded him or her said. By using this methodology for interpersonal or group communication, the previous speaker is afforded an opportunity to clarify wrong or mixed signals, messages that may have been misinterpreted.

### ATTITUDES

Earlier we discussed persuasive communication, a mechanism for changing group attitudes. Understanding an individual's attitudes can lead managers to select the right ones in employees and to influence changes in attitudes thought to be counterproductive.

Attitudes are inclinations to feel or behave in a certain way toward an object, person, or idea. People reflect attitudes in their behaviour, functioning in ways that are consistent with their attitudes. Therefore, one way to change behaviour is to change attitudes, using peer group pressure, persuasion, or reward.

## Attitude Formation

Like personality, attitudes are learned responses to outcomes. If an attitude is rewarded, whatever that reward may be, an individual tends to adopt that attitude. For example, if a child is rewarded (intrinsically or extrinsically) for gaining high grades, and if the child perceives the benefits of those rewards, then they will have a positive attitude toward studying and acquiring knowledge. If, however, the child perceives punishment for academic achievement such as ridicule from peers, criticism, or ostracism from a group, he or she will develop tendencies to dislike academics, and to neglect studies.

Similarly, if an employee experiences outcomes that are personally disliked, that employee will develop a negative attitude toward the job, the organization, or the boss. The case entitled *Anna* in this chapter is an example of rampant bad attitudes throughout an organization. This case study will test decision makers' abilities to unscramble the "chicken versus the egg" puzzle that goes something like this: some researchers argue that bad attitudes result in poor productivity, absenteeism, and high employee turnover rates. Conversely, other investigators argue the opposite: poor productivity causes bad attitudes, and jobs in which employees perform poorly may become disliked jobs.

## Changing Attitudes

People prefer their many attitudes to be consistent with each other and with their behaviour. Once people retain definite attitudes toward a person, object, or idea, they tend to construct similar attitudes toward related objects, ideas, or persons. Nonetheless, it is possible to induce individuals to change their behaviour so that their actions appear to be *inconsistent* with their attitudes.

When an inconsistency is introduced, people experience discomfort. Enough discomfort will cause people to undertake action to reduce the dissonance between their attitudes and their behaviours. They might attempt to change the attitudes, or they might attempt to change the behaviours, or they may develop new ways of rationalizing the inconsistencies. For example, when it became obvious that society disapproved of the act of driving a vehicle under the influence of alcohol, some people decided to change their attitudes. They changed from believing that they were capable of inebriated driving to adopting society's attitudes toward drunk driving. It changed their behaviour. Others convinced themselves that they were capable of continuing the unacceptable habit. They rationalized their behaviour, and most often isolated themselves from society's norms (and from friends and family).

Managers can influence attitude changes in people by introducing a dissonance between their behaviour and their attitudes. Take for example an employee who is frequently absent because he or she harbours negative attitudes toward their work. Managers can take action to cause the employee to change their behaviour so that it is inconsistent with their attitude. An attitude change will follow. If managers motivate the employee with recognition or praise or money (in small amounts) and if the employee then begins to reduce absenteeism, their behaviour will become inconsistent with their attitudes. Once their behaviour has changed and they have reduced their days of absenteeism, a natural thought process ensues. The thought process goes something like this: "If I dislike this job, then why do I show up to work every day?"

Conversely, if the reward is too large, and if the employee engages in the earlier described thought process, the answer is different. The answer now becomes: "I show up to work everyday because the pay is so high." This undesirable response amounts to a justification or rationalization of the behaviour, rather than a reason for the employee to change an attitude.

## VALUES

Values are abstract principles that are more generalized than attitudes. Values underlie large groups of attitudes. Values form as individuals mature. During value formation, people are influenced by individuals they respect. A target may have thousands of attitudes but only a dozen or so values. Values are *not* directed toward an object, idea, or person; they are statements of goodness or badness. They influence a target to believe he or she *should* have certain attitudes. It is difficult to get a handle on someone's values. A target can strongly believe in a work ethic and still exhibit a bad attitude toward his or her current job.

Employers need to be careful to not misinterpret a subordinate's values. An individual may dislike his or her current job; however, it is unfair to characterize that employee as disliking work altogether. The employee may dislike only certain aspects of his current job. When that employee takes on a different job, or when the job is changed to diminish disliked aspects, the employee will exhibit a more positive attitude toward it.

## POWER

Researchers have described three kinds of power:

1. **Personal Power:** an ability or faculty to control or to feel in control of our environment.
2. **Interpersonal Power:** an ability to influence others.
3. **Organizational Power:** an ability to mobilize others in an organization (not to be confused with one's position in the organization's chain of command).

Investigators describe two loci of control in personal power, internal and external. Locus of control influences perception; it colours the way people view causation in their lives. "Internals" are characterized as individuals who believe they are in control of their own destiny. "Externals" believe they are controlled by luck, by chance, or by more powerful people. It is important for managers to understand the loci (internal or external) of employees and how they view causation because managers can attempt to alter employees views to ones that will make them feel more control.

Internals — people who are high in personal power — tend to be high in interpersonal and organizational power. They are better negotiators who are less likely to resort to coercion. They possess stronger leadership characteristics and are more comfortable and effective at mobilizing others. Their work groups tend to be more productive and their workers more satisfied.

### Shared Power: Empowerment

Most people, whether externals or internals, prefer to have power and control in every aspect of their lives. When employees are given directions and required to simply respond to those directions, they have no control over their jobs. Earlier in this chapter, we discussed power and achievement, the higher needs that are motivators. Similarly, shared power, getting employees to perceive themselves as more powerful (more in control), can be motivational. By delegating decision making downward, thereby sharing power, managers increase feelings of ownership in subordinates. Job satisfaction becomes greater and employees are more productive. The following checklist represents situations where shared power is appropriate.

1. When managers and subordinates can work *together* to establish goals for the tasks that they undertake mutually, exchanging information, and using a participatory decision-making approach.

2. When managers and subordinates can indulge in *two-way communication and utilize active listening techniques*. One way to effect two-way communication is to hold regular meetings. Managers need to give suitable feedback but, more importantly, they need to listen to the feedback that is given to them, and to double check that they have heard exactly what the employees intended to say, even if it makes the manager feel uncomfortable.

3. When groups of employees can be developed *together* to tackle cohesive decision making: if we believe what we have just read about attitudes, we acknowledge that individuals become obliged to change their attitudes and become more committed to their tasks and goals when the entire group of employees is supportive of changes.

4. When employees can be given responsibility to take action on policies that administration has decided. For example, when a company guarantees to exchange or refund defective products, allowing front-line employees to fol-

low through on this policy will create a positive atmosphere for both employees and customers. If the same company is prone to criticize employees, to force them to engage an extensive line of authorization for refunds, or to chastise them for making independent decisions to exchange defective products, employees become frustrated and feel powerless. To the dissatisfied customer the employee appears uncooperative when, indeed, it is the employee's superiors who have been inconsistent, forcing the employee into disputing the customer's claim, despite a policy to the contrary. An annoyed customer will be less likely to repurchase from a corporation that sends mixed messages to its employees. Many firms make the mistake of immobilizing their front lines, the employees who meet the customer.

## POWER TECHNIQUES

### Positional Power or Authority

When an organization or an individual relies on the *power of position,* their thinking goes something like this: "I am the boss, I am in authority, therefore you should and will do what I say." This leadership technique works well in the short-term; however, over the longer term, reliance on formal power alone will result in low credibility for the manager and low compliance from subordinates.

Positional power is "worn on the shoulder" and depends on the availability of reward and punishment resources. Managers, where they are able to, use money, promotions, compliments, or other kinds of rewards to gain control over employees. Conversely, managers can punish employees, in order to control them, by withholding pay, reprimanding, dismissing, or suspending them. These latter techniques are clear, overt forms of punishment.

The problem with positional power is that it has been delegated by a third party, an individual's superiors. When that individual is no longer in the position (having been removed for one reason or another) he or she no longer holds power. The good thing about positional power is that it works to restrict behaviour, to get people to arrive at work on time, to spend their time working rather than dawdling, and to carry out policies that lead the organization to its goals.

Positional power is an "effortless" technique. Anybody can do it. A manager does not have to be particularly inspired to understand that demoting, cutting pay, or firing an employee will constitute a big blow to that subordinate's vital needs.

On a subordinate level, if the employee knows that the boss can and will punish, he or she is likely to act, at least in the boss's presence, respectfully and submissively. On the other hand, if the boss is a supportive person, open to honest feedback, the employee will give him what he or she asks for, even if the feedback is not pleasant. A supportive boss, one who does not rely on positional power, may have to tolerate emotional upset from people relating feedback he or she doesn't want to hear.

There are disadvantageous outcomes of positional power. When employees really don't like an authoritarian boss, they can pool their collective subordinate power formally (in a union organization) or informally (in response to a common enemy) in order to retaliate.

## Coercive Power

Coercive power is the use of blackmail and pressure tactics to influence people to change their behaviour. It is the only power technique not sanctioned by society, yet the one most widely used. Coercive power depends on threats or promises, real or perceived, in order to get subordinates to comply.

Coercive power also relies on a system of rules, real or perceived, to which everyone agrees and in which everyone believes. Someone may unexpectedly breach the rules of the relationship. For instance, someone may fabricate a lie about the other party, flustering them, thereby placing them in a weaker position. This tactic is often employed on both sides of a power struggle, by the underdog and by the person in power.

One source of coercive power is ownership: "I own the company, and you don't, so I can coerce you," which is similar to "I have the baseball bat, and you don't, so I can threaten to play the game without you." Coercive power can also have its source in numbers. Unions can quickly rally to change the balance of power, to alter the behaviour of a superior.

Finally, coercive power can be sourced in anonymity, covert discussions or actions. A manager can dispense distasteful work assignments and anonymously sabotage a merit system, always acting outside the knowledge of the subordinate.

## Manipulative Power

This kind of power is based on the recognition that people have complex emotional needs, like affection, dependency, support, approval, and recognition. Machiavelli was probably the first manipulator to describe this power technique. In modern times, many organizations use manipulation models in sales training.

Manipulation works best when we enter into a relationship with someone who is not a subordinate. It is difficult to use positional power and so we use the relationship as a tool, buying gifts or sharing tidbits of personal information. Then, we use the relationship, with its implications of loyalty and friendship, to get what we want. A good manipulator never exposes himself or herself completely, never gets so involved in the relationship that he or she cannot abandon it. He or she works secretly, taking very small steps at a time, exploiting people's needs for approval, support, recognition, and participation. Sometimes the manipulator exploits an entire group of people, developing cohesiveness and rapport so that he or she can use group pressure to influence an individual.

### Persuasive Power

Managers who are in a position to exercise power within economic organizations have access to the tools of reward and punishment if they need them. In volunteer organizations, however, these tools are completely unavailable, and so the volunteer leader must draw on persuasive power techniques.

Persuasive or personal power was discussed earlier under *Persuasive Communicators*. A leader with personal power is able to articulate the norms, values, and goals of individuals, groups, and an organization in a way that is easily accepted and understood by all. He or she is an effective leader who is perceived as credible. His or her power is independent of position and he or she is able to influence others because they respect and want to be like their leader. If you refer back to the section on attitudes you will see that this leader is an ideal communicator.

### Charismatic Power

Charismatic power is a rare, almost undefinable, kind of power that is probably some unique mix of personality, physical appearance, and an ability to inspire others. Whether we are born with it or whether we are able to acquire it through experience, the source of charismatic power continues to be the subject of much debate.

### LEADERSHIP

Many organizations have begun to hold regular training programs in order to reinvent a stronger corporate culture with which to influence people to meet the challenges of the turn of the century. Some corporations have even established permanent training facilities to bolster self-development techniques. One of the most well investigated areas in contemporary corporate training programs is leadership style.

Leadership style is the pattern of behaviours we use to influence others. Over the years, researchers have attempted to describe leadership style by application of various models.

### Theory X and Theory Y[9]

Douglas McGregor classified managers according to different sets of managerial beliefs. Exhibit 4 demonstrates McGregor's Theory X and Theory Y classifications. According to McGregor, a *Theory X* manager assumes that people dislike work and will avoid it if at all possible. He also assumes that people prefer to be directed, and are motivated by money, threats, and security. A *Theory Y* manager believes that people enjoy work to which they are committed and are able to exercise self-control and self-direction. Theory Y managers believe that people are motivated by the achievement of objectives.

**EXHIBIT 4**
**McGregor's**
**Theory X and**
**Theory Y**

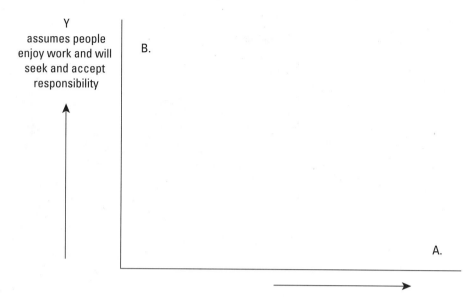

Y
assumes people
enjoy work and will
seek and accept
responsibility

B.

A.

X assumes people dislike work and need to be
controlled and coerced — most people lack
responsibility and ambition and prefer to be led

In Exhibit 4, the point marked "A" demonstrates appropriate leadership style, according to McGregor, in situations where people need high direction or are unwilling to accept responsibility. The point marked "B" demonstrates appropriate management style when it is fitting for managers to share power.

### The Managerial Grid

Robert Blake and Jane Mouton[10] put a new spin on McGregor's theory by labelling the vertical and horizontal axes as *concern for people* and *concern for production,* respectively. Their model is shown in Exhibit 5.

### Situational Leadership

Paul Hersey and Kenneth Blanchard[11] propose that there is no optimal leadership style, that various styles are appropriate in different situations. Furthermore, these authors contend that leadership style is not static. It should be fluid and adaptive to each new situation in time, even where the same employee or group is involved. *The Hersey Blanchard Model* is shown in Exhibit 6. In this model, the axes are labelled "supportive behaviour" and "directive behaviour." These descriptives refer to leadership conduct.

Hersey and Blanchard defined directive behaviour, the horizontal axis, as the extent to which a leader engages in one-way communication, where the leader spells out the job (role) of the followers, tells them what to do and how to do it, and then closely supervises the followers' behaviour.

*EXHIBIT 5*
*Blake and*
*Mouton's*
*Managerial Grid*

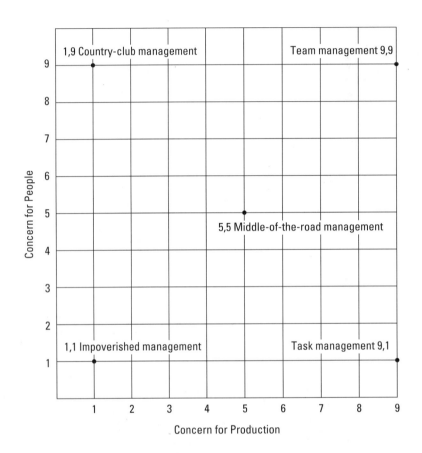

They defined supportive behaviour, the vertical axis, as the extent to which a leader engages in two-way communication, listens, provides support and encouragement, facilitates interaction, and involves followers in decision making (that is, praising, listening, and facilitating).

Hersey and Blanchard have shown that four leadership styles depicted in Exhibit 6 represent different combinations of directive and supportive behaviour that vary on three dimensions: 1) the amount of direction the leader provides, 2) the amount of support and encouragement the leader provides, and 3) the amount of follower involvement in decision making, the readiness or willingness of the follower.

S1 leadership style is high on direction and low on support, called "directing." An S2 leadership style is high on both direction and support, and referred to as "coaching." An S3 leadership style is called "supporting." S4 leadership turns over decisions and responsibility for implementation to the followers, and is called "delegating."

To understand this model it is important to remember that others perceive us in whatever way they choose. In order to influence someone's behaviour, to exercise leadership, we need to ensure that *our* perception of our behaviour, *how*

**EXHIBIT 6**
*Hersey and
Blanchard's
Situational
Leadership*

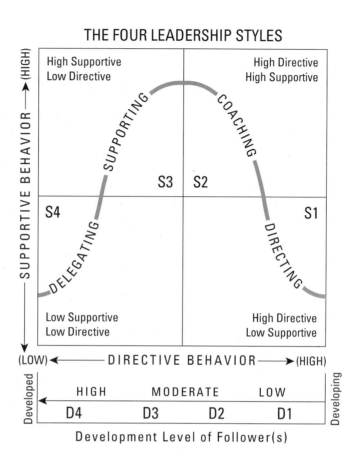

THE FOUR LEADERSHIP STYLES

High Supportive
Low Directive

High Directive
High Supportive

SUPPORTING

COACHING

S3   S2

S4                              S1

DELEGATING

DIRECTING

Low Supportive
Low Directive

High Directive
Low Supportive

SUPPORTIVE BEHAVIOR ——▶ (HIGH)

(LOW) ◀—— DIRECTIVE BEHAVIOR ——▶ (HIGH)

Developed

HIGH        MODERATE        LOW

D4          D3          D2          D1

Developing

Development Level of Follower(s)

*we intend to act,* matches the perception of the individuals we attempt to influence. If the two perceptions do not match, it is likely that the audience, the person(s) we try to influence, will act on their own perception.

Hersey and Blanchard defined the **development level** of their model as the competence and commitment of follower(s) to perform a particular task without supervision. Competence can be taught through training (direction) and learned through experience. Commitment is a combination of confidence and motivation. Exhibit 5 shows four development levels, which can change for the same follower(s) with direction and support.

An effective leader shifts his or her style back and forth according to the development levels of groups and individuals. To understand the shifts in leadership style, depicted by the thick black line curved through and above the mid axis in Exhibit 5, imagine a follower learning a new task. Then plot the behaviour of the leader (the thick line) as the follower becomes more competent and committed to the task.

## ETHICS

In a study of ethics, it is important to remember the earlier discussion of perception and to understand that individuals use their own perception and invest their own moral convictions in their judgments of others. We will study case characters in this chapter, and colleagues in the real world, who bring a unique perception and an original set of moral convictions to the bargaining table. If, in a situation, our moral conviction or our perception conflicts with someone else's, who is right? Who will concede?

The Centre of Business Ethics at Bentley College[12] has reduced the complex topic of ethics into six simple questions to ask yourself when you are making a decision:

1. Is it right?
2. Is it fair?
3. Who gets hurt?
4. Would you be comfortable if the details of your decision were reported on the front page of your local newspaper?
5. What would you tell your child to do?
6. How does it "smell"?

When you analyze the case entitled *Hibbs's Web*, work in your study group and have every member of the group communicate his or her answers to these six questions about the issues in the case. In order to decide which issues are ethical ones, it is important to remember that every issue and every decision involves moral judgments. Ethics is *not* a peripheral theme.

In the short-term, decisions that the majority view as unethical may sometimes pay off for an individual or an organization. However, it is more important to focus on the longer haul and to recognize that history will judge the entire life of a venture, not just the short-term.

### One Corporation's Response to an Ethical Issue

Corporations, like individuals, who protect public image at all costs, and who believe in and follow through on their image, have enjoyed success over the longer term. Take for example, Johnson & Johnson, the corporation that manufactures the Tylenol brand.

In 1982, Johnson & Johnson exhibited an exemplary response to cyanide deaths in Chicago, deaths that were connected to its product. At that time, the Tylenol brand held 35 percent of the over-the-counter analgesic market. When catastrophe struck, the company recalled batches and advised consumers not to take Tylenol capsules until the mystery had been solved. It was found that someone unconnected with the manufacturer inserted the cyanide and replaced the capsules onto retail shelves.

Although the company was completely cleared of any wrongdoing, all Tylenol capsules were recalled, 31 million bottles with a retail value of $100 million. Although Johnson & Johnson experienced immediate and massive losses, they set about to rebuild the brand. The company offered to replace capsules with safer (tamper-proof) tablets and set up a toll-free number for consumers to call. Finally, they developed a tamper-resistant package.

Johnson & Johnson's Tylenol brand fell below 7 percent market share in 1982. By May 1983, Tylenol had regained almost all the lost market share and continued to hold a 35 percent share of market until 1986, when another woman died from cyanide-laced Tylenol. At that juncture, the company decided to manufacture tamper proof caplets only. By July 1986, the revised Tylenol brand had regained a 32 percent share of the market.

### Proacting an Ethical Image

The impact of media on corporate public image is undeniable. Media can work to hurt images by fanning a problem or triggering a herd instinct to public criticism of the subject of scrutiny. Johnson & Johnson used media in a positive way. They ran television advertisements informing the public about the disaster. They suspended regular advertising and provided a powerful media interest with the most accurate and up-to-date information.

Above all, Johnson & Johnson demonstrated an exemplary response, confronting the issue head on, promoting and presenting an ethically understandable stance through the media rather than ignoring the problem or adopting a "wait and see" attitude. By their action Johnson & Johnson avoided allowing the media to run amok, putting its own spin on events. The corporation took responsibility early on and acted in the best interests of its consumers.

## CONCLUSION

While you work through the cases in this chapter, try to apply each of the concepts discussed in this introduction. Try to develop a mobilized, resourceful, inspired style that will serve you well in every aspect of your decision-making process. Learn to tailor your decision-making skills to the challenges of each different set of circumstances. Effective management of human resources in the final analysis is a creative approach to people and circumstances. Creativity in leadership and managing human resources means thoughtful action by a concerned person who has an understanding of the whole situation.

### NOTES

1. Larry E. Griener and Robert O. Metzger, *Consulting to Management* (Englewood Cliffs, NJ: Prentice-Hall, 1983).

2. Harold J. Leavitt, *Managerial Psychology,* 4th ed. (Chicago: University of Chicago Press, 1978).

3. *Webster's New World Dictionary,* 2nd college ed. (Toronto: Nelson, 1970).

4. A.H. Maslow, "A Theory of Human Motivation," *Psychological Review* 50 (1943): 370–96. See also A.H. Maslow, *Motivation and Personality,* 2nd ed. (New York: Harper and Row, 1970).

5. F. Herzberg, *Work and the Nature of Man* (Cleveland: World Publishing, 1966).

6. D.C. McClelland, *The Achieving Society* (Princeton N.J.: Van Nostrand, 1961).

7. Figure 1 is from a German psychology laboratory and was drawn before 1900.

8. Sandra Krebs Hirsh and Jean M. Kummerow, *Introduction to Type in Organizational Settings* (Van Nuys, CA: Consulting Psychologists Press, 1987).

9. Douglas McGregor, *The Human Side of Enterprise* (New York: McGraw-Hill Book Company, 1960).

10. Robert Blake and Jane S. Mouton, *The Management Grid III* (Houston: Gulf Publishing Co., 1985).

11. Paul Hersey and Kenneth Blanchard, *Management of Organizational Behaviour: Utilizing Human Resources,* 5th ed. (Englewood Cliffs, NJ: Prentice-Hall Inc., 1988).

12. W.M. Hoffman and E.S. Petry, Jr., "Business Ethics at Bentley College," *Moral Education Forum 16* (Fall 1991).

# ■■■■ CASES FOR PART 4 ■■■■

**CASE 4.1** Anna

■

**CASE 4.2** Bell Canada

■

**CASE 4.3** Big Brothers (BB)

■

**CASE 4.4** Carl Jones (A)

■

**CASE 4.5** Consulting for George Lancia

■

**CASE 4.6** Johnson & Johnson Company (A)

■

**CASE 4.7** The Food Terminal (A)

■

**CASE 4.8** Hibbs's Web

■

**CASE 4.9** Medictest Laboratories (A)

■

**CASE 4.10** Ottawa Valley Food Products

■

**CASE 4.11** Royal Hardware

# CASE 4.1    ANNA

At 7 o'clock on a warm spring night, an unsuspecting Morris Secord prepared to step through the door of the Grand Boardroom and into the path of Anna Head's fury.

Anna's exasperation was the culmination of a series of incidents that began when she was first hired. She had been waiting two hours to confront Morris, mentally reviewing the events that had led to tonight's crisis.

**REPORTING STRUCTURES**

Morris Secord was a senior middle manager in a prestigious public relations firm, headquartered in New York. Branch offices were located in most major cities on the eastern seaboard. The company had recently established a new division, Executive Placement Services (EPS). Anna Head was one of four consultants who comprised the new EPS group. Ray Harris was Anna's direct supervisor. Harris reported to Secord.

**THE FIRST EPISODES**

Ray Harris and Anna Head had been hired five years ago, within two weeks of each other. Both reported to Jim Hunt, assistant vice-president of client development, when they first joined the company. Hunt spoke about Anna:

> I tried to take her "under my wing," to show her the ropes. But Anna was too independent. I could tell she thought me persnickety. I am the kind of manager who wants all of the bases covered. I don't like surprises. She had no time for the details.
>
> One time, she told me to quit pointing my finger at her and then stalked out of my office. I gave her a few minutes to cool down and then I went to her office. I had just started talking when her husband walked into the room. He wouldn't leave us alone until he was convinced that she was all right. Anna had telephoned her husband, upset, after she left my office.
>
> Anna thought she knew it all. She had every angle worked out in her mind and only presented me with alternatives from which to choose. Whenever I questioned the technicalities that led to her options, she implied that I was finicky, that I was wasting her time on trivia.
>
> She told me that I acted like her father and that she didn't need a second father. Granted, I may have been a little soft. My wife was sick at the

time and I may have projected my wife's fragility onto Anna. You would think that Anna would have appreciated my indulgent attitude toward her, but no, she wanted to be treated objectively, like she was "one of the guys."

During my last performance appraisal of her, I asked her to outline a five-year career plan. She responded that she wanted to be in middle management within five years. I told her she would never make it because she had no "people" sense, no savvy. As a minor example of her naiveté, I characterized her deportment. I told her that she walked like a monomaniac with a mission. In fact, I could hear her stomping her way to my office long before she appeared at my door.

I also told her that she smiled and giggled too much. Only an idiot smiles all of the time. Her laugh disclosed her insecurity and immaturity. Her demeanour grated on my nerves.

When the EPS group was formed, I was one of a panel of three managers who interviewed the candidates for four new consulting jobs. Anna scored very high with the other two managers on the panel. In fact, and despite my reservations, I ranked her second in the whole group of applicants. Nevertheless, I wanted to test her mettle. So I called her into my office after all of the interviews were finished and I told her that she had scored fifth. In other words, there were four candidates who ranked above her. She would not get one of the jobs. My purpose was to test her commitment. For all I knew, Anna might have applied for the job on a whim.

Anna called in sick the next day. Since she had been upset about not getting one of the new jobs, I telephoned her home. I asked her if she wanted me to "pull some strings" in order to get a fifth position created for her in the new group. She declined, but then she went out of her way to go to the personnel office the next day, where she reviewed her employee file. Through that file, she discovered that she had been ranked first by the other two managers. Then she came to my office and confronted me.

Just to get her out of my office, I conceded that she had earned one of the new jobs and I bade her good riddance. She was a thorn in my side, and I was glad when she was gone.

| | |
|---|---|
| **RAY HARRIS'S VIEWPOINT** | About seven months ago, I went to work on Monday morning and discovered that Anna was no longer working out of the New York office. She had moved to Boston and was servicing her clients from an office there. |

When I questioned Morris Secord about the secrecy surrounding Anna's transfer, he told me that he, too, had just found out about the transfer. One of the vice-presidents told him, nonchalantly, in a shared taxi from the airport. Morris was as surprised as I was. I was Anna's supervisor; Morris was my immediate superior, and neither of us knew about Anna's move until afterward. Apparently she sold the idea, privately, to the vice-president. We were expected to just go along with it.

About three weeks after Anna's move, I went to see the vice-president on an unrelated issue. I took the opportunity to ask how things had happened so easily for Anna. The vice-president explained that Anna's accounts were all near Boston, and she felt that Anna had successfully commuted to New York headquarters for every administrative meeting.

**ANNA'S VIEWPOINT**

Ray Harris and I worked together when I first started at this company. In order to achieve my new consultant's position, I went through a rigorous screening process. I was quite surprised when Ray just showed up as my boss without having to go through the same interview mechanism. However, I had begun to accept anomalies in this company as standard fare.

I first met the vice-president when she visited some of my clients with me on a preliminary check of my effectiveness in the community. Within a few hours, she befriended me. She was like a kindred spirit. I told her about some of my problems at work, and I told her that my husband was starting the MBA program at Harvard that autumn. I felt that she understood when I explained how much I wanted to be with my husband. Despite the fact that I had personal reasons for wanting to move to Boston, I justified a transfer on the basis of its feasibility to the company, not solely on the basis of private reasons. She spoke to the president on my behalf and my transfer to Boston was approved. The vice-president was thrilled, actually, because my move represented a tangible link, a beginning of an effort at regional consolidation.

My communication problems with Ray began in earnest about three weeks after I moved to Boston. I was on that damned train, commuting to New York, sometimes five days a week. Some days, Ray would call a meeting and then cancel it after I arrived in New York. Other times, I would arrive in New York with the files that Ray had requested, and he would claim to have asked for totally different files, files that were still in Boston. I spent 60 percent of my time on the train and in New York. I felt like I was neglecting my clients.

I requested a private meeting with Ray to clear the air. We held the meeting, but it did nothing to resolve the situation. Ray concluded that I was threatened by him. After that meeting, Ray went on a "faxing" campaign. He faxed so much information to me that I thought the machine would burn up. Then, he started calling my clients and visiting them without my prior knowledge. My clients began to realize that there was a problem, that there were differences between Ray and me.

I went to see the vice-president several times while the situation continued to degenerate. I wanted advice. I wrote three or four letters to her. Her response was, "Hang in there. You will learn to grow with people like Ray." Things got worse.

A month ago, I wrote a letter to Morris Secord and requested a meeting with him to discuss the apparent problems between Ray and me. I never heard back from him.

Today, I commuted to my regular meeting with Ray and the other three consultants. During the meeting, Ray announced with an authoritative tone in his voice that he wanted to see me in his office after the meeting. We met in his office about 4 o'clock, whereupon he told me that my behaviour lately was unacceptable and that the letter I wrote a month ago to Morris was inexcusable. I couldn't believe that Morris had shown my letter to Ray. I felt violated. I was furious.

I found out that Morris was in another meeting.

I have been waiting outside the Grand Boardroom for two hours, all the time thinking about how my health and my home life have disintegrated over the past few months, and feeling like I am obsessed by my work, but just too driven to quit ...

**THE SHOWDOWN**

The door to the Grand Boardroom opened and Morris Secord stepped out. "Don't you like my work?" Anna snapped at him. "Are you trying to *force* me to quit?" Despite her determination to maintain a professional presence, Anna began to sob. "Why don't you *do* something?"

Morris knew he would have to do something soon.

**C A S E**   **4.2**   BELL CANADA: THE PROFIT
ORIENTATION SEMINAR

In August 1991, Fiona Crossling, manager of professional development at
the Bell Institute for Professional Development in Montreal, Quebec,
reviewed her files and thought about the week that lay ahead of her. By the
end of it she and her colleague, Joyce Dowdall, would begin to introduce
the newly developed *Profit Orientation ... it's your business* seminar to the 400
seminar facilitators who would deliver it to over 50,000 Bell employees in
Ontario and Quebec.

The objective of this seminar was to provide each participant with a
good understanding of Bell's financial picture, and to show them how they
could all play a role in the company's financial performance (increasing revenues and decreasing costs).

Fiona's final task was to put together a plan for evaluating the effectiveness of the seminar.

**COMPANY
BACKGROUND**

Bell Canada, a subsidiary of Bell Canada Enterprises (BCE) Inc., was Canada's largest supplier of telecommunications services providing advanced
voice, data, image, radio, and television transmission to nearly seven million customers in Ontario, Quebec, and the Northwest Territories.

Since its beginning in 1880, Bell Canada has been an international
leader in ascertaining customer needs, developing services to meet those
needs, advancing technological innovations to build and manage networks
to support those services, and managing the entire process to ensure superb
customer service. A recent national survey rated Bell Canada as Canada's
best corporate citizen due to quality goods and services. Total operating revenues in 1991 amounted to $7.7 billion, as outlined in Exhibit 1. Local and
long-distance telephone service were Bell's two major revenue streams.
Local services revenues were earned mainly by providing network access
services to business and residence customer markets. Together these revenue streams accounted for 82 percent of Bell Canada's consolidated total
operating revenues in 1991. Bell Canada was subject to the jurisdiction of
the Canadian Radio-television and Telecommunications Commission
(CRTC) in various respects, including its rates, costing, and accounting procedures.

Bell Canada had five subsidiaries and associated companies (see Exhibit 2). The chief executive officer of Bell Canada headed an extensive executive hierarchy: one chief operating officer, three executive vice-presidents, 15 vice-presidents, and over 70 assistant vice-presidents. There were four levels of management below the assistant vice-president (a fifth-level manager). Fiona Crossling was a first-level manager in the Bell Institute for Professional Development.

## THE TELE-COMMUNICATIONS INDUSTRY

The beginning of the 1990s was tense and full of rapid changes for the major players in the $13 billion national long-distance market. The monopoly that Bell Canada and other regulated phone companies in Canada (B.C. Telephone Co., Alberta Government Telephones Ltd., and Maritime Telegraph and Telephone Co.) enjoyed for so long seemed threatened. In May 1990, Unitel Communications Inc., a partnership between Canadian Pacific Ltd. and Rogers Communications Inc., reapplied to the CRTC to enter the long-distance market. Shortly after, B.C. Rail Telecommunications (BCRL) followed suit. Unitel maintained that competition was necessary in this industry to lower costs and increase innovation. It stated that Canadian businesses were at a severe disadvantage when it came to telephone expenses, and would certainly benefit from reduced rates. It also alleged that competition would increase long-distance business by over 2 percent. Both companies wanted to interconnect their own network with the Bell network to send and receive calls.

The CRTC had to decide if it was in the best interest of Canadians to allow these companies into the market. The CRTC decision would be an important and historic one. If competition in the Canadian long-distance market became a reality, other companies would enter the market. If approved, Unitel services and services from other competitors could be available as early as 1993. Unitel planned to focus its efforts on the entire nation, and BCRL had planned to concentrate in selected Ontario, Quebec, and B.C. markets. Unitel predicted that it could capture 10 percent of the market by 1998, and another 10 percent by the year 2007.

Bell Canada, who controlled over half the national long-distance market, was vehemently opposed to competition. It claimed that it could offer lower long-distance rates, maintain lower costs, and be more productive without competition. Bell felt that with its monopoly, it could increase productivity and efficiency 6 percent annually through new technology for the next five years. More importantly, regional telephone companies such as Bell relied on the long-distance profits to cover the costs of local service. Bell incurred almost two dollars in long-distance revenues for every one dollar it collected in local revenue. This subsidy allowed it to control the price of local services. Bell's strategy to hold onto the long-distance market was called VISION 2000. Under the plan, long-distance rates for large volume users would be reduced by more than $900 million over five years. Large rate reductions would also benefit most long-distance users. Bell stated that it would not be able to achieve this goal under the proposals of Unitel and BCRL.

Industry observers predicted that the intense competition and jostling for business that was so prevalent in the United States could occur in Canada. More than 200 companies contended for business in the States, although many were small operations reselling long-distance time purchased from the majors. The three largest (AT&T, MCI, and US Sprint) fought fiercely for big corporate clients but most visibly for ordinary residential customers.

## CHANGES AT BELL CANADA

In early 1991, Bell began scrutinizing its operation. Jean Monty, chairman of Bell Canada, stated that Bell must cut costs and raise productivity. In March 1991, Bell planned to reduce its work force from 54,964 to 50,100 through an extensive voluntary retirement incentive plan. The company began striving toward the lowest costs and lowest price offerings in North America. After results that showed a slow down in revenue growth, the chief executive officer ordered management to cut $40 million more from expenses. Long-term projections for Bell's long-distance business, which accounted for half of the company's revenues and most of its profit, were substantially reduced. Bell forecasted sales of $6.75 billion in the year 2002, down 47 percent from the original estimate of $12.33 billion. These projections were downsized due to heavy competition and the company's announcement of price cuts in 1992.

## THE BELL INSTITUTE FOR PROFESSIONAL DEVELOPMENT

Training and development was formerly a departmental responsibility. In September 1990, Bell moved to a more centralized form of training and development, and the Bell Institute for Professional Development (BIPD) was created. All management and nonmanagement training was thus brought together under one roof. Through course development, training, and education, 350 BIPD managers strove to increase the professionalism and skill levels at Bell. Roughly 1,500 courses were available to employees, and these courses were run on demand.

Fiona Crossling was hired by the BIPD after spending 18 months in a revenue journals position. Her experience in accounting at Bell was utilized when developing the Profit Orientation Seminar and an earlier seminar entitled *Profit Orientation ... making sense of the dollars*. This seminar outlined the implications of spending capital dollars and was delivered to 7,000 employees in Ontario and Quebec.

## PROFIT ORIENTATION ... IT'S YOUR BUSINESS

The Profit Orientation Seminar evolved as a response to an internal survey done in 1989. The survey questioned employees about the six mission values at Bell Canada. Bell's six mission values were and still are:

1. Customer satisfaction
2. Excellence
3. Innovative and action-oriented behaviour

4. Team spirit

5. Profit orientation

6. Market leadership

It was found that most people in the organization did not understand the profit orientation mandate, and thus did not understand how they could play a role in financial matters within the company. It was decided by the BIPD, and a team of executives from Ontario and Quebec regions, that a company-wide seminar dealing with this mandate would be developed. The overall objective of the seminar was to provide participants with a good understanding of the corporate financial picture, and to encourage them to take an active, informed role in making financial decisions on their jobs. This came at an important time given the changes taking place in the industry. With the inevitability of reduced future revenue, cost control appeared to be a significant way to improve profitability at Bell.

*Seminar Development*   Fiona Crossling and Joyce Dowdall were responsible for creating this corporate seminar. With the direction and support of the assistant vice-president within the Professional Development Institute and their regional client representatives, they initiated the seminar development. They interviewed experts from different fields within the company (capital, expenses, business units, budgets, and results). It was through this process of data collection that they discovered areas that employees needed to understand. Pilot sessions were given in Montreal and Toronto during the summer of 1991. Feedback from these sessions helped Fiona and Joyce focus the seminar on areas that really mattered to employees.

Fiona reflected on the mindset of the employees: "The original seminar focused not only on profit orientation but on business units — something that Bell is moving toward quickly. However, people are currently not being measured on this. After the pilot sessions we discovered that people's priorities were mostly centred around their jobs and their departments rather than the company's future direction. Our objective was to create an atmosphere at the seminar where people could bring out their own objectives for improving the company within their department, so that each employee would understand what role he/she played."

The Profit Orientation Seminar was designed to last one half-day at local Bell offices and institutions. Videotaped modules were added to the seminar to teach financial education information. Group discussions and activities, conducted by the facilitator, were incorporated to relate the information received into action the participants could take on their jobs. The seminar was designed to train between 12 and 30 people at a time. In most cases, these people would all be from the same department within a Bell Centre. This small group size ensured that participants benefited from interacting with people from all levels of management and nonmanagement.

***The Role of the
Facilitator***

The facilitator's role was crucial to the success of this seminar. The facilitator was trained to lead the overall program, guide participants through discussions and activities, and provide clarification on instructions when necessary. Most importantly, the facilitator used local examples of success stories to relate the content of the seminar to the participants' daily jobs. This helped illustrate the action they could take as a result of the information they received. Facilitators were also responsible for the logistics surrounding the rollout of the seminar within the organization. This included such items as arranging presentation facilities, inviting participants, and ensuring that a sufficient quantity of participant materials were available at each session. (See Exhibit 3 for a sample invitation letter sent to employees.) The half-day seminar was broken up into the following 12 phases:

1. Welcome and Introductions (20 minutes)

   The first segment of the seminar focused the individuals on the seminar's objective, and made them feel comfortable. The facilitator outlined the activities for the day, and allowed the participants to introduce themselves. During an activity called the icebreaker, participants worked together in groups. Their task was to determine Bell's total operating expenses for 1990. The facilitator ended this phase with a small discussion on operating expenses.

2. Introduction to Profit Orientation (5 minutes)

   This video segment introduced the basic financial terms such as profit, revenue, and expenses that would be discussed during the seminar. It described the need for and benefits of making a profit, and the opportunity for individual impact. This video module ended with a brief interview with Robert Kearney, Bell's chief operating officer.

3. Profit Orientation Trivia (25 minutes)

   The facilitator engaged the groups in an activity related to finances that was fun, and not intimidating. The groups answered the following questions:

   (a) How many employees work at Bell?

   (b) How much does Bell pay in salaries and wages?

   (c) How much does Bell contribute to pensions and benefits?

   (d) How much does Bell spend on travel expenses?

   (e) What was the amount of the depreciation expenses?

   (f) How much does Bell pay for stationery supplies?

   All the group answers were put up on a board and discussed.

4. A Closer Look at Profitability (8 minutes)

   The financial lesson introduced in phase two was continued. Participants were shown how Bell makes a profit. This segment was very important as it illustrated how immense the operating expenses at Bell were ($5.4 billion in 1990). This segment also highlighted the impact that individuals could have on the overall performance of the company.

5. Jeopardy ... Round 1 (20 minutes)

Much like the popular television game show, this phase facilitated discussion on the major themes discussed so far, and encouraged teamwork as groups came up with answers. The groups were questioned on topics such as equity, retained earnings, the six mission values, the role of the CRTC, depreciation expense, and a host of other concepts. More importantly, the groups generated ideas about Bell's profitability and how they could have an impact. These action-items were updated throughout the seminar.

6. Intermission (20 minutes)

7. A Closer Look at Expense (10 minutes)

The exorbitant operating expenses at Bell were examined in this sobering video module. The module stressed the importance of generating $7.3 billion in revenue to cover expenses. The costs of employing individuals outside of their salaries was an important theme. It was at this point in the seminar that participants realized that they could affect the expenses and revenues at Bell.

8. Jeopardy ... Round 2 (20 minutes)

As in round 1 of Jeopardy, the participants built upon the ideas they had covered up to this point. A key part of this game was the opportunity it gave the facilitator to move around the room and encourage discussion. The groups added to the action-item lists they developed in the first round of Jeopardy.

9. Expense Budget Process (10 minutes)

This video module reinforced the need for individual and local attention to expenses. Employees were acquainted with business units, a company structure that was smaller, more manageable, and enabled decision making at lower levels.

10. Final Jeopardy (20 minutes)

The final questions of the quiz were asked and the winning team was congratulated.

11. Group Action Planning (30 minutes)

This was the crux of the entire seminar. Groups were given 30 minutes to review the lists they had generated and develop a profitability action plan that could be implemented locally. The groups were instructed to determine the people at the local Bell office who should be responsible for carrying out the steps of the plan, and how the plan should be communicated throughout the district. A group spokesperson was chosen to deliver the plan to the audience.

12. Closing Remarks and Feedback Questionnaire

Participants were asked to fill out a questionnaire that gauged how they enjoyed the seminar. The questionnaire focused on how the participants liked the seminar, how useful it was, whether or not they would recommend it to colleagues, how the videos enhanced the course, and how they would rate the facilitator. They were asked if they could be phoned to follow up on some of their responses.

**FIONA CROSSLING'S CONCERNS**

Although the pilot session had gone well, Fiona had concerns about the use of local facilitators and about the seminar itself: "The facilitators are critical to the success of this seminar. We strongly recommended to the executive team members that in selecting their candidates, they choose individuals who are not necessarily financial experts, but rather those people who have demonstrated good interpersonal skills. We also asked that people be chosen from all levels of management or nonmanagement in an attempt to break down some of the traditional barriers and level-consciousness that, unfortunately, still exist. It is critical that facilitators share the same message with all participants, regardless of the resistance they may encounter along the way. I know that the training session I have with the facilitators is of the utmost importance. If a facilitator leaves our training with a poor understanding of what profit orientation is, the participants will also have that perception."

Fiona knew that other problems could arise during the implementation of this seminar throughout Bell's territory. One of the main problems would be the varying levels of interest of the facilitators. Some facilitators would be prohibited by their managers from taking a half-day to run the seminar, due to the time that it took from daily activities. Others might have to wait to deliver it until other issues at the local facility had been addressed. Most often, the attitudes of the facilitators toward cost control and the usefulness of the Profit Orientation Seminar would reflect that of their bosses. In many cases, managers were either not impressed with the training programs, or felt that they added no value to "their" facility. Fiona commented: "Many of the managers and nonmanagers have seen mission statements and similar seminars come and go. They could view this initiative as the latest flavour of the month, and not see its relevance to Bell."

**EVALUATION**

Fiona wanted to devise a plan for gauging the effectiveness of the Profit Orientation Seminar. Bell would need to know: a) if the seminar influenced people to make more informed decisions, and b) where positive results would be visible. Fiona prepared a questionnaire to be filled out by randomly selected seminar participants three to six months after the seminar (Exhibit 4). Would this questionnaire be enough to measure the impact that the seminar had on the employees of Bell Canada?

Fiona knew that changes in the environment were putting extreme pressure on Bell. The Profit Orientation Seminar could play a large part in empowering Bell's employees to make wise decisions on their job, to become committed to the future effectiveness, efficiency, and profitability of the organization.

*EXHIBIT 1*

| Consolidated Statement of Income for the Years Ending December 31 (millions of dollars) | 1991 | 1990 | 1989 |
|---|---|---|---|
| OPERATING REVENUES | | | |
| Local and access services | 2575.3 | 2428.1 | 2259.4 |
| Toll and network services | 3738.4 | 3778.9 | 3606.0 |
| Terminal, directory advertising | 1415.3 | 1447.7 | 1407.5 |
| Total operating revenues | 7729.0 | 7654.7 | 7272.9 |
| | | | |
| OPERATING EXPENSES | 5555.7 | 5610.5 | 5381.4 |
| Net revenues | 2173.3 | 2044.2 | 1891.5 |
| OTHER INCOME | 20.0 | 45.2 | 38.9 |
| INTEREST CHARGES | 544.5 | 517.0 | 460.8 |
| Income before interest and taxes | 1648.8 | 1572.4 | 1469.6 |
| INCOME TAXES | 662.8 | 606.7 | 594.5 |
| Net income | 986.0 | 965.7 | 875.1 |
| | | | |
| DIVIDEND ON PREFERRED SHARES | 73.6 | 67.0 | 61.4 |
| NET INCOME APPLICABLE TO COMMON SHARES | $912.4 | $898.7 | $813.7 |

*EXHIBIT 2*

---

## Subsidiaries and Associated Companies
## as at December 31, 1991

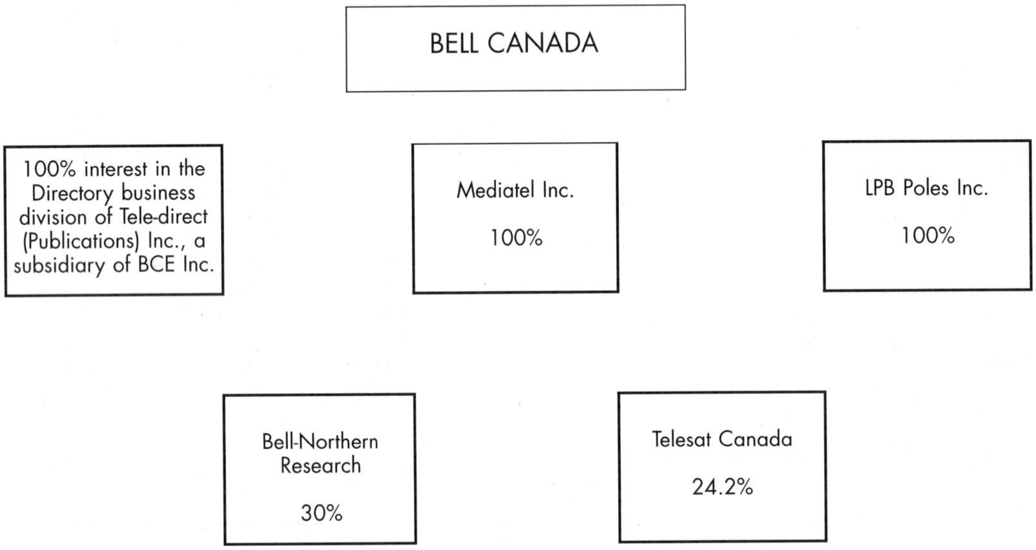

---

| | BELL CANADA | |
|---|---|---|

| 100% interest in the Directory business division of Tele-direct (Publications) Inc., a subsidiary of BCE Inc. | Mediatel Inc.<br><br>100% | LPB Poles Inc.<br><br>100% |
|---|---|---|

| | Bell-Northern Research<br><br>30% | Telesat Canada<br><br>24.2% |
|---|---|---|

---

*EXHIBIT 3*
*Sample Invitational Letter*

*Profit Orientation Seminar ... it's your business*

---

**"My hope is that through this seminar everyone will have the opportunity to see how they can affect the profitability of the company."**

*Wes Scott, EVP Ontario Region*

Each one of us makes an impact on our profitability every day by the way we do our jobs and the decisions we make. Our rapidly changing technological, competitive, and economic environments demand that we build on our past successes ... and seize every opportunity to make a positive impact on our bottom line.

BSS Operations (Insert name of YOUR organization here), in partnership with the Bell Institute for Professional Development, invite you to attend a seminar designed to help you make the most of those opportunities. While at the seminar, you'll gain insight into Bell Canada's financial picture, and ways that you can influence our future profitability.

Your opportunity to participate in the seminar has been scheduled for:

Date:        October 10, 1991
Time:        8:30 am to 11:45 am
Location:    (Insert: address, Room, any special access info)

I'm looking forward to seeing you there!

Seminar Facilitator

---

*Exhibit 4*
*Profit Orientation*
*Seminar Survey*

Over the last year, thousands of employees in the Ontario/Quebec region have participated in the local *Profit Orientation Seminars*. This short survey is designed to gauge your reactions to the seminar you attended.

Most questions can be answered by circling the number(s) that correspond to your response. Please read each question carefully and answer all questions in order.

Participants for this survey have been randomly selected by organization code. All your responses are strictly confidential. Do not put your name on the questionnaire. When you have completed the questionnaire please staple it in half and return through company mail.

Thank you for your participation in this survey. Your input is very important to the effective monitoring and improvement of educational programs such as *Profit Orientation*.

1. The information received at this seminar has given me a general understanding of Bell's financial picture.

    1-Strongly agree
    2-Agree
    3-Neither agree nor disagree
    4-Disagree
    5-Strongly disagree

2. The knowledge gained in this seminar has been useful to me on my job.

    1-YES        2-NO

3. If you answered Yes to question 2, please provide examples: (otherwise leave the space below blank).

4. Since the *Profit Orientation Seminar,* I have acted on the ideas generated during the session I attended.

    1-Strongly agree
    2-Agree
    3-Neither agree nor disagree
    4-Disagree
    5-Strongly disagree

**EXHIBIT 4 (cont'd)**

5. In my job, I can influence the company's overall profitability in the following way(s):

   1-revenue generation
   2-cost reduction
   3-optimizing capital investments
   4-effective customer service
   5-none of the above

6. Conditions in my job that allow me to be involved in matters that affect the company's profitability are:
   1-participative decision making
   2-understanding of company finances
   3-having necessary tools and support
   4-empowerment
   5-none of the above

7. Overall, how satisfied are you with this seminar?

   1-Very satisfied
   2-Satisfied
   3-Neither satisfied nor dissatisfied
   4-Dissatisfied
   5-Very dissatisfied

8. Would you recommend this seminar to colleagues?

   1-YES      2-NO      3-DON'T KNOW

## C A S E  **4.3**  BIG BROTHERS (BB)

Glen Mitchell, executive director of Big Brothers of London Inc., reviewed 1994's annual report and knew changes would have to be made. Volunteers were so scarce that total matches between big and little brothers had dropped by 40 percent over the past two years, to 119 paired companions. At the same time, 110 boys marked time on a waiting list, anticipating matches with big brothers, a wait that sometimes consumed two years.

Recruitment and retention of volunteer big brothers were now crucial issues for the organization. As well, Big Brothers of London relied heavily on funding from The United Way Campaign,[1] a funding agency that distributed monies based on results achieved by recipient organizations. In order to increase donations from The United Way, Glen needed to improve the number of matches and to demonstrate the organization's effectiveness in meeting its objectives.

**THE CONCEPT**

BB was part of a national nonprofit agency that attempted to provide boys aged 6 to 16 from father-absent homes with consistent adult male companionship. Because of a paucity of volunteers willing to become big brothers, the London organization concentrated its efforts on the age group from 7 to 13 years.

For the most part, the boys had shared only negative experiences with adult males. Although some boys had never known a dad, many others had witnessed family violence. Many boys carried "emotional scars" resulting in poor attitudes toward men in general. When they were matched with a big brother, the boys were able to see that "there were men (out there) who didn't drink excessively, didn't hit women, and who provided an adult male influence they could hold in high esteem."[2]

**HISTORY**

In 1903, Irvin Westheimer, a Cincinnati businessman, found a young boy rummaging through trash in an alley. He befriended the boy and found out that the boy was fatherless. Mr. Westheimer's friends and associates agreed that boys like this could benefit from interested men who would act as a big brother to them.

Big Brothers originated in 1909 in New York City when 40 men agreed to each initiate a relationship with a boy who had been in trouble with the law. This original group believed that many boys who ran afoul of the law came from father-absent homes and they concluded that a male influence might help to redirect these boys toward a better path in life.

Big Brothers began in Toronto, Canada, in 1913. The Canadian operation focused its efforts on fatherless boys who had appeared in juvenile court. Over the years, the original concept was altered. In 1950, the agency widened its mandate to *any* boy lacking consistent adult male identification, not just those who had encountered trouble with the law. Championed by a provincial court judge, Big Brothers of London incorporated in 1971. By the late 1980s, the number of London boys who were matched with big brothers had increased to 200 per year from an initial 50 per year. There was an overabundance of volunteers willing to make a two-year commitment to a father-absent boy, and as many as 90 matches were made annually.

In 1994, 213 men inquired about becoming a big brother; however, the number of volunteers who applied plummeted to 41. Despite the fact that a stipulated commitment for volunteers was reduced from two years to one, the number of matches dropped to 32; Glen expected there would be less than 25 matches made in 1995.

**CURRENT SOCIOECONOMIC CLIMATE**

The city of London, like many other cities, had not fully recovered from a recession early in the decade. This economic slowdown displaced many white and blue collar workers to other occupations or to the ranks of the unemployed. The remaining employees who survived widespread corporate downsizing experienced additional pressures with added responsibilities becoming part of their workload; therefore, it was not surprising to find that market research on existing and potential volunteers indicated that a "lack of time" was the single most frequently cited reason for refraining from becoming volunteer big brothers.

To counter a broad-based fear of having to create extra time in an already overloaded week, Glen tried the following tactic in print promotions and information sessions: *"In reality, most volunteer Big Brothers involve little brothers in their routine activities (e.g., auto repairs, biking, mall trips, etc.) much the way a parent will spend time with their own children."* Despite this message, the number of volunteers continued to plunge. Glen speculated that there were other reasons for the decline. Some potential volunteers claimed that unemployment left them with little time for activities other than job searches. Newly unemployed men faced the likelihood of relocation to another city, presenting the possibility that they would be unable to fulfil the year's obligation to a boy.

A portion of London's population was transient. Thirty thousand students attended the University of Western Ontario from September through April. As well, the city was home to many service-oriented corporations that frequently relocated adult male employees in their 20s and early 30s, the prime age for volunteering to be a big brother. Glen found that more established men in the community were usually married and preoccupied with young families of their own.

The fear of being accused of sexual abuse was more prevalent in society in general and, in particular, in the city of London. Local law enforcement officials recently garnered intense publicity over an investigation into a child pornography ring. Media attention to allegations of abuse, whether true or false, threatened careers and families, making many men hypersensitive to the risk of associations with unrelated children.

Big Brothers of London attempted to confront the issue of false allegations of sexual abuse at its information sessions, providing strict rules of conduct. The process to become a big brother was so rigorous that the possibility of truth to allegations of sexual abuse was negligible. Nevertheless, fear prevailed.

Universally, the number of single parent households headed by women had grown significantly in the past few years. Many social service agencies, like the Children's Aid and CPRI[3], weathered cutbacks that led to reduced programs. Many organizations had pared back to minimal numbers of legally mandated policies. Problems that did not fit their core agenda were sometimes referred to volunteer agencies like Big Brothers. This trend to downsizing, increasingly evident throughout the public sector, put ever-increasing pressure on volunteer social service organizations.

Consequently, while there was a glut of existing and potential little brothers, and an unprecedented need for agencies like Big Brothers, there was a dearth of volunteers willing to become adult companions.

## FUNDING

In 1995, close to 58 percent of the London agency's receipts came from the United Way's annual fund raising drive. The balance of funding came from private donations and other Big Brothers activities like the annual "Bowl for Big Brothers" event, which brought in over $37,000, slightly short of the committee's $45,000 goal. See Exhibit 1 for the agency's schedule of receipts and disbursements for fiscal 1995.

London Big Brothers paid 2.75 percent of their annual receipts to the national parent organization to support national advertising, workshops, conventions, and public relations. Otherwise, in most operating and policy matters, London Big Brothers Inc. was autonomous.

The extent of funding and the continued commitment of donors and donor agencies was dependent on the viability of the organization. Many organizations competed for dwindling donor dollars. An increase in the number of matches would improve Big Brothers' image and its chances of benefiting from larger donations and United Way allocations. In turn, greater revenues would allow the organization to hire additional staff to support existing case workers.

## ORGANIZATIONAL STRUCTURE

Exhibit 2 shows an organization chart for the London agency, including a list of committees to which a cross-section of board and staff members and other volunteers belonged. A volunteer board of directors formed committees to direct and oversee Big Brothers functions. Each committee established its own goals and objectives.

In addition to their screening and matching functions, the two caseworkers currently employed by Big Brothers functioned as expert sources for longer-term big brothers who needed to further explore problems in their match or to discuss other issues related to their role. The only prerequisite for the caseworker's job was education and experience in social services. Both caseworkers held a Bachelor of Science in Social Work (B.S.W.) and one had worked with a Children's Aid Society before joining Big Brothers.

Periodically, the London agency accepted placements of social work students from local post-secondary institutions to assist their caseworkers. Other volunteer aids helped caseworkers on an as needed basis, usually keeping contact by telephone with the big and little brother matches and reporting any problems to the caseworkers.

## LITTLE BROTHER PROFILE

Little brothers were boys aged 7 to 13 who had little or no male companionship. They had been often disappointed by broken promises from "unreliable" fathers or other adult males. They came from homes in which contact with a father or other adult male was once a month or less. The majority of the agency's contacts were mothers of these boys. It was not uncommon that when the agency blitzed for volunteers or sponsored a major fund raising event, the numbers of boys on the waiting list grew because single mothers contacted the agency during these promotional efforts.

A 1994 study[4] investigated the long-term impact of Big Brothers of Ontario on little brothers who had been matched as of December 31, 1980. Statistics showed that in 1980, children from families headed by women were economically disadvantaged. In fact, 32 percent of the little brothers came from homes in which the sole source of income was social assistance. The employment earnings of the remaining mothers was estimated at 38 percent of the average income of two parent families with children. The poverty rate for Ontario's female-led single parent families was 55 percent compared with less than 9 percent for two parent families.

The study showed, with statistical significance, that former little brothers had fared quite well in a comparison to the rest of the population. Over 80 percent of them attained at least a secondary school diploma, compared to 60 percent of the other people in their age group. In addition, there was an observable advantage for those little brothers who were matched the longest with a big brother.

With regard to social psychological attitudes, it was found that an "excellent" relationship with a big brother disproportionately tended to result in higher educational attainment for the little brothers; in turn, these higher levels of education disproportionately resulted in higher self-esteem. With regard to other attitudinal variables, former little brothers who felt that they would personally make good parents disproportionately tended to highly respect authority and had acquired a heightened sense of right and wrong.

Lately, more boys presented the agency with multiple problems: school troubles, hyperactivity, emotional problems, and difficulty in relationships with peers and adults. Many of these boys were referred by social service agencies that were under financial pressure.

## BIG BROTHER PROFILE

Any male over the age of 18 was eligible to become a big brother. In 1995, market research on London's big brother volunteers indicated that 27 percent were in the age group 20 to 29. Another 27 percent were aged 30 to 34 with the balance split equally among the 35 to 39, 40 to 44, and 45 to 49 age groups. Approximately half of the volunteers had children of their own. The primary reason for becoming a volunteer was to "help people." The majority chose Big Brothers because they knew an existing big brother, or discovered by "word of mouth" that volunteers were needed. London's matches had historically averaged two and a half years in length.

Most big brothers took between two months and three years before reaching the decision to become a volunteer. Thirty-six percent took between one and three years to make their decision. Close to half of the surveyed big brothers indicated that they lacked confidence in making the decision to get involved or were unclear of their expected role as a big brother. Only 4 percent were previous little brothers.

## ONE BIG BROTHER'S EXPERIENCE

One volunteer who had been a big brother for four years offered to be interviewed. When living in Toronto, Gerrard (not his real name) had volunteered weekly in an institution for the physically and mentally challenged. When he began his job in London, four years previously, Gerrard approached BB on his own and explained that he wanted to "live a balanced life" and, by volunteering, he would be able to "give something back to society." He reported that, over the years, he had procured at least two other successful big brothers for the London agency through his own work and social contacts.

When he had a new baby, his first child, Gerrard's little brother came to his home and blended with family activities every second week. In the intervening weeks, Gerrard and his little brother pursued one-on-one activities like attending sports events, going to a movie theatre, fishing, or attending an agency-sponsored event. Gerrard had discussed this revised visiting plan with his little brother before the new baby arrived. He offered to see his little brother every second week at an activity of the little brother's choice, or to visit in the intervening weeks at Gerrard's home. His little brother chose weekly contact, and so far, the little brother had adjusted well to this new schedule. He was enthusiastic about helping Gerrard with the baby, the household chores, and minor repairs.

When asked hypothetically if he would become a big brother to a boy with more challenges like hyperactivity or emotional complexities, Gerrard was not interested, adding that if he were younger and without a family of his own, he would consider a more challenging little brother.

Gerrard was a white-collar executive. He held a university degree, enjoyed a good lifestyle, and presented himself as a thoughtful, sensitive, composed individual in his mid-thirties. Like many big brothers, he had very little contact with other BB volunteers. Despite his financial comfort, Gerrard understood how economics could discourage some volunteers from becoming big brothers. His suggestion for overcoming this problem was that the agency create and staff a general purpose room in its headquarters. Gerrard thought that a staffed and renovated room at the house, or in another central location, could function as a general meeting place to hold games like dominoes or cards, or to show videos. One or several matches could use the facility simultaneously. With this general purpose room in place, most big brothers would be able to utilize public transportation and they would be able to reduce the cost of activities with little brothers to almost nothing, eliminating much of the out-of-pocket cost of movies, sports activities, and meals or snacks. Big Brothers of London wholly owned a renovated house located centrally in the city. At present, the small house, stationed on a tract of land that provided limited parking, was almost totally consumed by offices and a small reception area.

One concern for the agency was the budget constraint of hiring additional staff and security. Big Brothers could access outside facilities like the Boys' and Girls' Club for the sole use of Big Brothers for special events.

## THE PROCESS OF BECOMING A BIG BROTHER

Once a volunteer made a decision to become a big brother, the process (Exhibit 3) took three to four months. Each candidate completed an application form with references, and each was submitted to a police check to assure they had a clear police record for the past five years. As well, the agency discussed the application with the volunteer's partner, if appropriate.

A caseworker then conducted a lengthy interview with the volunteer. This meeting covered the volunteer's family background, education, employment, social life, interests, and activities. During this same interview, the case worker initiated discussions of sexual orientation, drugs, and alcohol usage. They also reviewed Big Brothers' Sexual Abuse Prevention Program with the potential candidate.

If the applicant were recommended for a second interview, he met at a later date with the agency's executive director, Glen.

Once the applicant was matched with a little brother, he was expected to keep regular contact with his caseworker in order to discuss his experiences, for better or worse. The big brother was required to visit his little brother regularly for three or four hours a week. Volunteers were asked to stick to a one-on-one format during visits, to limit the involvement of their family or friends, and to keep their visits as active as possible, like throwing a ball around a park rather than watching television together. No overnight trips were allowed for the first three months of the relationship and after that, big brothers were to contact the caseworker if an overnight trip were planned.

### THE MARKET FOR VOLUNTEERS

Big Brothers of London competed for volunteers with many nonprofit organizations, all of whom had recently experienced a decline in numbers. Statistics Canada reported that half of all volunteers were in the 25 to 44 age group. The participation rate of volunteers tended to increase with age (to peak at the 35 to 44 age group) and with education (those with a university degree were most likely to volunteer). Surprisingly, Statistics Canada also reported that 60 percent of volunteers enjoyed an annual income of greater than $60,000, and that half of all volunteers became involved with an organization when someone within the organization approached them. Only 17 percent sought out the organization, on their own initiative.

Market research in London indicated that many community members were willing to help the agency in many ways, but extremely few wanted to become big brothers. Even when told that they would spend only three to four hours per week, 70 percent said that they would still *not* become a big brother, nor would they become a big brother for just the months of July and August with no future obligations. Justification varied from specific problems, like a lack of transportation, to general issues like family and time constraints.

### THE BIG BUNCH PROGRAM

The agency's Program Committee decided to pursue a new concept during the upcoming year, the Big Bunch program, designed for boys on the waiting list. Each month, BB would host one agency activity, assigning several (a bunch of) boys from the waiting list to two or three volunteers for the monthly special event. There would be no one-to-one contact; however, the plan would support the interests and the hopes of the boys on the waiting list. Volunteers would be asked to make a six-month commitment to the program.

Volunteers for this program would still be required to go through the same intensive screening process as big brothers, except for the last few steps involved in matching. Glen hoped to target the student population at Western, encouraging them to apply in the spring (March/April) and then to join the Big Bunch program when they returned in the autumn. During the students' summer vacation, the agency could process applications, check references, and be ready to accept the volunteer when he returned in September for his education.

### THE FUTURE

The 1995 market research group recommended an aggressive marketing plan that involved hiring a marketing coordinator to implement an augmented recruiting effort. They suggested a direct mailing campaign and telephone follow-up. A colour photograph of a man and a boy "having fun together" would be sent to a list of prospective males, procured through a marketing firm's database.

The plan was costly and Glen wondered if the "fun" message, also depicted in BB's logo (Exhibit 4), was the most appropriate appeal that could be made to potential volunteers. The first step in his action plan would be to motivate existing committees and volunteers to raise more funds for the marketing campaign, which would ultimately render an increased number of matches, which, in turn, would generate more funds for the purpose of hiring another caseworker.

Recently, the national Big Brothers organization had contracted Angus Reid to conduct a survey of matches before, during, and after closure. Glen wondered what sorts of questions would be appropriate to help measure the many positive benefits for little brothers and big brothers resulting from a match. Statistics from evaluations like this held potential to bolster his ability to point to positive outcome from matches in promotional efforts.

With all of this in mind, Glen sat down to prepare a plan for the organization, including a strategy for augmenting recruitment and for the retention of volunteer big brothers.

### Notes

1. United Way was an agency that solicited corporate and individual donations on behalf of several volunteer organizations. Membership in the group of United Way agencies precluded these recipient organizations from soliciting corporate donations for operations. Corporate donations could be directed to assets or special projects.
2. Quote from a Big Brother's caseworker.
3. The Child & Parent Resource Institute (CPRI) formerly ran many support programs such as anger counselling.
4. Project Impact: A Program Evaluation of Big Brothers of Ontario, April 1994, the Social Planning & Research Council of Hamilton & District.

*EXHIBIT 1*

## Statement of Changes in Fund Balances
## for the Year Ending March 31, 1995

### REVENUE

| | |
|---|---:|
| United Way donations | $138,000 |
| Bowling for Big Brothers campaign | 24,329 |
| General | 8,381 |
| Hole-in-One | 3,943 |
| Net Bingo proceeds | 11,939 |
| City of London grant | 8,550 |
| Nevada income | 3,567 |
| Interest | 1,808 |
| | $200,517 |

### EXPENDITURES

| | |
|---|---:|
| Salaries | $136,612 |
| Employee benefits | 17,450 |
| Recruitment and education | 9,484 |
| Stationery and office expenses | 7,241 |
| Affiliation fees | 5,788 |
| Property taxes | 4,756 |
| Telephone | 3,434 |
| Promotion | 3,294 |
| Postage | 3,196 |
| Insurance | 3,021 |
| Travel allowance | 2,743 |
| Audit and legal | 1,700 |
| Utilities | 1,500 |
| General expenses | 1,328 |
| Repairs and maintenance | 923 |
| Recreation | 338 |
| | $203,808 |
| Net increase (decrease) in fund balances | ($3,291) |
| Opening fund balance | $ 71,083 |
| Fund Balance — March 31, 1995 | $67,792 |

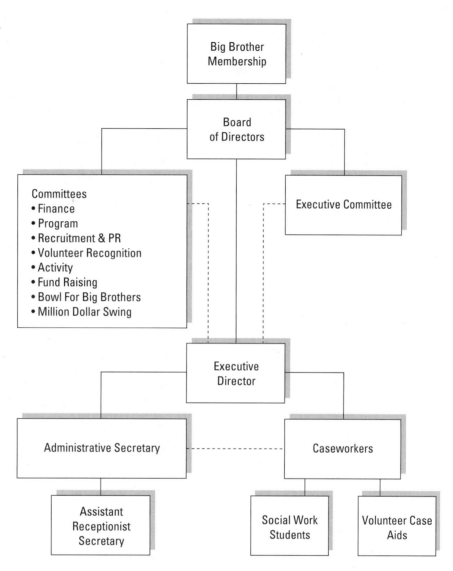

*EXHIBIT 2*
*Big Brother*
*Organizational*
*Structure*

*EXHIBIT 3*
*Application*
*Process*

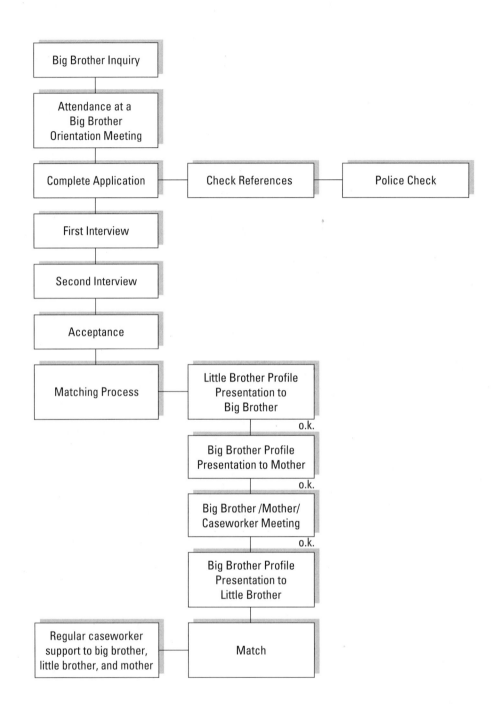

**EXHIBIT 4**
**The Agency Logo**

# C A S E  **4.4**   CARL JONES (A)

It was 5:00 p.m. on January 28, 1994, when Carl Jones, maintenance supervisor for the day shift at McLaughlin Pharmaceutical in Calgary, Alberta, wondered whether to discipline an employee for inappropriate behaviour on the job. In his first month as supervisor, Carl had observed one employee, Joe Podivinski, failing to do his assigned work, taking too long to complete scheduled work, and performing maintenance procedures in an unsafe manner. Carl wanted to take appropriate action to resolve the problem, but was concerned with acting in accordance with the collective agreement between the Energy and Chemical Workers Union and the management of the plant.

**BACKGROUND**

McLaughlin Pharmaceutical (est. 1955) was an international manufacturer of brand name ethical pharmaceuticals. With just under 100 plant employees, McLaughlin had supported an established union, a local branch of the National Energy and Chemical Workers Union, since 1962. "Satisfactory" relations between the management and the plant workers continued from 1962 to 1994. In 15 separate negotiations, collective agreements had been reached successfully with the exception of two short strikes in 1972 and 1982. Management-labour relations continued to improve since the last strike, when union negotiations became the responsibility of the Canadian management. Until 1982, employees resented the American parent (company management) negotiating collective agreements for a "very different and unique" Canadian operation.

The collective agreement divided the plant into three different wage groups for defining wage rates, layoff procedures, and number of union stewards. These wage groups were: production (60 employees), plant engineering (25 employees), and warehousing (12 employees). (See Exhibit 1 for a description of classifications.)

The grievance procedure within McLaughlin's collective agreement was standard to most manufacturing plants (see Exhibit 2). Fifteen grievances had been filed since 1962. In 10 of these cases, complaints stemmed from the plant engineering/mechanics department and ranged from supervisory harassment to equipment safety concerns.

**CARL JONES**

Carl Jones, 35, had been employed at McLaughlin for 15 years, starting as a janitor on the evening shift. Married with three children, he was known by fellow workers as an intelligent man with a good sense of humour, who occasionally could be quite "bull-headed" if he did not get his way. Although Carl never attended college or trade school, he was considered to be extremely mechanically adept, a "self-taught" mechanic.

Eventually, Carl worked his way to a position on the day shift as a mechanic (semi-skilled) and, after attending some management courses at night school, was offered a supervisory position in December 1993. This new position placed him in charge of managing and directing 16 fellow employees and reporting directly to the engineering department manager, Patrick O'Shea. (For a partial plant and union organizational chart, see Exhibit 3.) Carl had this to say about his promotion:

> I'm up to the challenge of the supervisor's position in the engineering department. I consider myself very lucky to have been promoted considering the stiff competition within the department. Quite frankly, people around here, including myself, were very surprised about my promotion.

Management appointed Carl with a few reservations. According to John Corso, plant manager:

> When O'Shea, Spaxman, and I discussed Carl's promotion, we agreed that there was no one else as qualified for the position. We were concerned about his ability to make decisions and manage the older "characters" within the maintenance department.

**JOE PODIVINSKI**

Joe Podivinski began working on the day shift at McLaughlin in 1963 at the age of 20. Joe obtained his mechanical tradesman papers while working at the plant in 1970. Originally from Great Britain, he was an active member in the labour movement during his youth. Joe, a widower, was a friendly, boisterous man who was well-liked by fellow employees, so much so that he had been acting union steward for the maintenance department since 1982, when he ran in the plant union elections. He enjoyed and took great pride in his position in the plant's union.

Since his election, Joe had personally filed two grievances against McLaughlin's management: one was against a supervisor for harassment and the other was for another supervisor's "improper procedure" in dealing with a problem within the maintenance department. He had often bragged to other maintenance employees about his ability to "bring down any person in management." Carl remembered Joe's remarks while once working with him:

> There are so many ways to get even with management through the union. I enjoy seeing those "white shirts" squirm when they deal with me. I enjoy tripping them up in their lies and showing them they can't pull the wool over my eyes!

Joe and Carl were on good terms at the time of Carl's appointment; however, the two men had been known, previously, to have some "rather loud and heated" disagreements concerning ways to fix machinery and other maintenance matters.

**RECENT INCIDENTS**    On January 6, 1994, after just one week in his new supervisory role Carl designated Joe to a high priority job that entailed removing a collar from a shaft on a motor. On his morning rounds, Carl found Joe helping another mechanic on a different project, rather than completing his assigned job. When Carl asked him about the motor, Joe responded that the plant's two-arm pullers were not capable of tackling the job. He would need a three-arm puller. Carl believed that a two-arm puller would suffice and, in order to check his conviction, asked another mechanic, Bethel Johnson, to look at the motor the next day. Within five minutes, Bethel had the collar removed using the same equipment that had been accessible to Joe.

Another problem occurred the following week. On January 13, Carl assigned Joe to make some pipe brackets for one of the factory's finishing rooms. He asked Joe to make these fittings from existing materials within the room. In Carl's estimation, the job should have taken approximately four hours. Joe finished the job in a day and a half. Carl was bothered about this situation because his instructions were disobeyed when Joe built the new fittings from new and very expensive material.

Carl also witnessed Joe abusing his 15-minute break and half-an-hour lunch times and leaving his assigned work area during the day to socialize with other mechanics.

Carl's concerns over Joe's behaviour became heightened on January 28, when he received a memo from the plant's nurse, Clare Underwood, concerning Joe Podivinski's recent eye flash burns and his past history of accidents within the plant (see Exhibit 4). The news of the eye burns came as a complete surprise to Carl. Joe had not reported the incident to him. According to company procedure, employees were responsible for notifying their supervisor of any accident within the workplace. Clare had mentioned Joe's accidents to previous supervisors, but nothing had been done. Carl was concerned because he knew that the cost of WCB[1] fees were related to the number of WCB claims.

When questioned about Ms. Underwood's concerns, especially the welding flashes, Joe indicated that when he lit the arc of the welding tool his safety mask did not fall into place. After investigating the incident himself, Joe commented that the screws were too tight.

Joe was an experienced welder and responsible for all necessary safety precautions and the preventive maintenance of his equipment. Therefore, Carl believed Joe was negligent. He should have checked the equipment before starting to weld, in order to make sure his mask fit properly.

**CARL'S DECISIONS**    Carl wondered what to do about these incidents concerning Joe. According to McLaughlin's rules for disciplinary action, if he decided to reprimand Joe, he would have to justify the offences according to the agreement (see

Exhibit 5). Carl was concerned about the repercussions of any action he might take in this matter, and wanted to pursue suitable action in handling his difficulties with Joe.

## NOTES

1. Worker's Compensation Board.

**EXHIBIT 1**

| McLAUGHLIN PLANT CLASSIFICATIONS | | | |
|---|---|---|---|
| **Wage Group** | **Department** | **Classification** | **# of Stewards** |
| Plant Engineering | Production Engineering | Mechanic, Skilled<br>Electrician<br>Painter | |
| | Packaging Equipment Services<br>Sanitation (First Shift) | Mechanical, Semi-skilled<br>Serviceman<br>Janitor | 1 |
| | Sanitation (Second Shift) | Serviceman<br>Janitor | 1 |
| Production | Solid Dosage | Senior Compounder<br>Operator, Packaging<br>Line Leader<br>Processor | 1 |
| | Liquids, Creams, and Ointments | Senior Compounder<br>Line Leader<br>Operator, Packaging | 1 |
| | Sterile Products (First Shift) | Senior Compounder<br>Operator, Sterile Mfg. | 1 |
| | Sterile Products (Second Shift) | Senior Compounder<br>Operator, Sterile Mfg. | 1 |
| Warehousing | Receiving | Receiver<br>Return Goods Checker | 1 |
| | Shipping | Shipper<br>Warehousing Checker | 1 |

*EXHIBIT 2*
*Article 16 — Grievance*
*Procedure*
*McLaughlin*
*Pharmaceutical Collective*
*Agreement*

16:01    Should any grievance arise between the Company and the Union, or an individual worker during the term of this Agreement, it is agreed there will be no suspension of work on account of any dispute arising therefrom, but an earnest effort shall be made to settle such dispute according to the following procedure:

**Step 1.**    An aggrieved worker with the Steward shall present all details of the grievance to the appropriate immediate supervisor who shall render a decision within two (2) working days.

**Step 2.**    If the immediate supervisor's decision is not satisfactory or if the time limit has expired, the Steward shall within two (2) working days present the grievance in writing to the appropriate Department Manager or his representative, who shall render his decision in writing within two (2) working days.

**Step 3.**    If the decision of the Department Manager or his representative is not satisfactory or if the time limit has expired, the Steward along with the Chief Steward or the Deputy Chief Steward shall present the grievance to the Plant Manager, or his representative within two (2) working days. The Plant Manager, or his representative shall render a written decision within three (3) working days after the meeting.

**Step 4.**    If the decision of the Plant Manager or his representative is not satisfactory or if the time limit has expired, the Grievance Committee may within three (3) working days request a meeting with the President of the company or his representative. This meeting shall be held within four (4) working days after the receipt of the request. The President or his representative shall render his decision in writing within five (5) working days after the meeting.

16:02    When the Company takes disciplinary action under its rules and regulations with a worker who has completed his probationary period, his Departmental Steward shall be notified in writing of such discipline within 24 hours. If such a worker is discharged while at work, he may have an opportunity to discuss the matter with his Department Steward before leaving the Company premises in a place designated by his Foreman, and he may initiate a written grievance in Step 3 within fourteen (14) calendar days following the sending of notification by registered Mail by the Company to the last address on record with the Company.

16:03    The time limits set forth above may be extended by mutual agreement.

16:04    Any grievance which is not registered in writing at Step 2 within ten (10) working days of the alleged occurrence shall not be recognized.

***EXHIBIT 3***
***Partial Plant***
***Organization***
***Chart at***
***McLaughlin***
***Pharmaceutical***

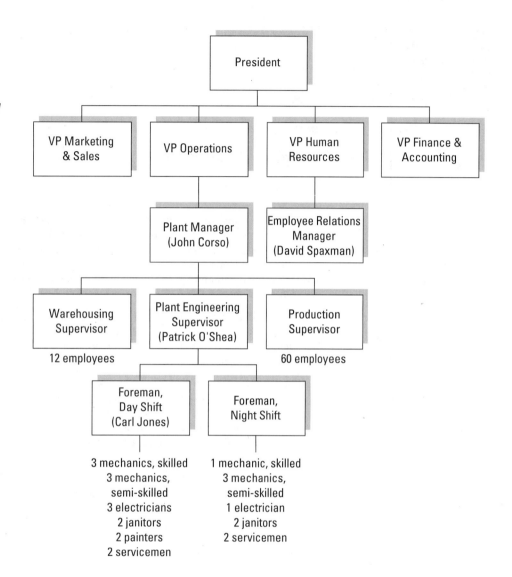

*EXHIBIT 4*
*Interdepartmental*
*Memo from Clare*
*Underwood to*
*Carl Jones*

**TO:** Carl Jones

**FROM:** C. Underwood

**DATE:** January 28, 1995

**SUBJECT:** JOE PODIVINSKI

---

As you know, Joe suffered flash burns on December 20, 1993, and January 19, 1994. Two things concern me about these incidents. First, they appear to be due to carelessness, because this type of accident should not occur to a qualified tradesman. Second, Joe did not report the accidents until the following day on both occasions.

Since joining McLaughlin, Joe has had eight accidents involving his eyes, two of which were WCB (Worker's Compensation Board claims), plus 58 minor accidents, six other WCB claims, one of which was lost time (see attached).

Although the incidence of minor accidents has lessened over the years, the number of serious injuries has not. I have some concern that it is a matter of time before Joe has a very serious accident. I do not want to discourage him from reporting accidents, but I feel that he should exercise more caution on the job.

I have not received an injury report from you for this current accident and I would appreciate it if you would take the above into consideration when making your recommendations.

CU:mm

cc: David Spaxman, Employee Relations Manager

*EXHIBIT 4 (cont'd)*

## JOE PODIVINSKI — ACCIDENTS

**1986**
12 minor accidents, including:   July 9 — laceration to hand — WCB
Aug 19 — foreign body in eye

**1987**
13 minor accidents, including:   July 16 — burn to arm from
welder — WCB
Dec 12 — foreign body in eye

**1988**
8 minor accidents, including:   May 27 — foreign body in eye
Aug 10 — burn to eyelid
Dec 4 — bruised hand — WCB, lost
time

**1989**
5 minor accidents, including:   Dec 9 — bruised elbow — WCB

**1990**
5 minor accidents

**1991**
8 minor accidents, including:   Nov 8 — injury to hand — WCB
Nov 23 — foreign body in eye

**1992**
3 minor accidents, including:   May 25 — foreign body in eye — WCB
Dec 6 — back strain — WCB

**1993**
3 minor accidents, including:   February 28 — foreign body in
eye — WCB
Dec 20 — flash burn to eye

**1994**
1 minor accident, including:   January 19 — flash burn to eye

*EXHIBIT 5*
*McLaughlin*
*Pharmaceutical's Rules for*
*Disciplinary Action*

## GROUP A OFFENCES  STANDARD DISCIPLINE

1st offence — Written Warning
2nd offence — Final Warning
3rd offence — Dismissal

1. Habitual lateness in punching time clocks or habitual violation of time clock rules.

2. Violation or disregard of Plant or Departmental safety rules or common safety practices including:
   a) carelessness in regard to accidents and the safety of others,
   b) failure to report a work injury to Supervisor when first able,
   c) horseplay, scuffling, running or throwing things,
   d) smoking or striking lights in prohibited areas,
   e) wearing rings, watches, loose jewellery, or loose clothing.

3. Absence from work without prior permission from Supervisor, except in cases of personal illness or emergency where it was impossible to obtain such prior permission.

4. Soliciting or collecting contributions for any purpose on Company premises without prior approval of the Plant Manager.

5. Bookmaking, gambling, or similar activities of a serious nature.

6. Being on Company premises when off duty without proper authority.

7. Failure to start work at the beginning of the shift, leaving work station before the end of the shift, or leaving assigned place of work during work hours without authorization of Supervisor.

8. Use of profane or abusive language toward fellow employees.

9. Disregarding supervisory instruction on good manufacturing practices or standard operating procedures.

10. Failure to notify immediate supervisor of absence due to emergency or personal illness when first able or giving false reason for absence.

*EXHIBIT 5 (cont'd)*

## GROUP B OFFENCES    STANDARD DISCIPLINE
1st offence — Final Warning
2nd offence — Dismissal

11. Reporting for work while under the influence of intoxicants or drinking intoxicants on Company property.

12. Entering restricted areas or admitting employees or visitors to Company property without proper authorization.

13. Unauthorized removal or defacing of Company notices posted in the plant.

14. Deliberately punching another employee's time card.

15. Sleeping during working hours.

16. Wanton or wilful neglect in the performance of assigned duties or in care of Company property.

17. Fighting or attempting injury to another employee on Company property.

18. Petty theft or misuse or removal of confidential information such as blueprints, lists, manufacturing data, etc.

19. Offering or receiving money or other valuable consideration in exchange for obtaining employment with the Company, or promotion or any change of working conditions therein.

20. Refusing to give information or giving false information when accidents are being investigated, or falsifying or assisting iin falsifying Company records.

*Exhibit 5 (cont'd)*

---

**GROUP C OFFENCES**     **STANDARD DISCIPLINE**
1st offence — Dismissal
2nd offence — Dismissal

21. Insubordination by refusal to perform work assigned.

22. Making false claims or misrepresentations in an attempt to obtain sickness or accident insurance benefits, workmen's compensation or other similar payments.

23. Conduct violating common decency or morality.

24. The unauthorized use, introduction, sale, or possession of narcotics on Company premises.

25. Possession of firearms or unlawful weapons on Company property.

26. Conviction in any court of law of a crime considered by the Company to be of a serious nature.

27. Malicious mischief or conduct resulting in:

    a) the injury of other employees,

    b) the damage or destruction of property of other employees or of the Company or its products.

28. Theft that is considered by the company to be of a serious nature.

---

# C A S E  **4.4**  CARL JONES (A)—APPENDIX

## A GLOSSARY OF INDUSTRIAL RELATIONS TERMINOLOGY

According to most authors, the term *industrial relations* is an all-encompassing expression that includes every form of interaction between employers and employees: relations between unions and management, unions themselves, management and the government, and between unions and the government. Ergo, the study of industrial relations is a complex field, one that many researchers have spent years investigating and characterizing.

Our current survey of this theme will be limited to an introduction to some of the jargon, and a few of the concepts.

### INDUSTRIAL RELATIONS TERMINOLOGY[1]

#### Labour Relations/Union–Management Relations

This term refers to the interaction that takes place between employee organizations (unions) and employers (management/owners). You may have heard the relationship described as "strained," or alternately positive, depending on the particular organization under review and the specific period of time under study.

#### Unions

A labour union or a trade union is an association of workers, usually employed in the same company or industry or practising a similar trade that is recognized under the terms of a Labour Relations Act. In some circumstances, powerful national or international unions like the Canadian Auto Workers' Union will make attempts to organize dissatisfied employees in smaller nonrelated industries. Generally, the more powerful unions are more persuasive with managers and employers. They can bring their collectively greater membership and greater expertise to bear in any negotiations between labour and management. When a company's employees threaten to join one of the larger unions, management will normally make sincere efforts to avert the unionization.

Despite the negative image that management sometimes paints of unions, the primary purpose of a union is to improve the conditions of the workplace for its members by addressing issues such as wage rates, job security, and working environment. As well, the union provides support and guidance for employees who may feel that they have been treated unfairly by management or the hierarchy.

Workers join unions because:

- The collective power of employees is exerted.
- It increases an employee's sense of economic security.
- An official certification of the union as bargaining representative has already occurred (no choice).
- People enjoy membership in groups.

### Types of Unions

#### Craft

Members carry on the same craft or trade, i.e., International Association of Firefighters.

#### Industrial

Members usually include most of the workers eligible for union membership in a particular organization or industry, i.e., International Chemical Workers' Union.

#### Local Union

Unions are also differentiated according to their jurisdiction (international, national, or local).

The local union is the lowest level of a union. Most activities are centred at the local level; that is, workers join the local union and pay dues to the local union, and interact with members of the local union more often than they would with the larger body. All members are allowed to vote on union matters. The membership elects representatives who handle the administration of the union.

#### Functions of Local Unions

- Local union members elect delegates to represent all of the unionized workers in "collective" bargaining talks with management.
- The local union administers the "collective" agreement that is reached with management, ensuring that the company abides by the provisions in the agreement.

#### Parent Unions

The Parent Union is the final authority over the actions of the local union. The parent union can be regional, national (like CUPE, or the Canadian Auto Workers), or international (like the Steelworkers, or the Longshoremen).

## Functions of Parent Unions

- There is an executive that sets major union policies
- They aid locals in: legal strikes[2] by sending strikers to the picket lines,[3] strike fund control, research, collective bargaining.
- They lobby[4] government to promote the interests of labour.

## Collective Bargaining

Collective bargaining is the process by which employees negotiate the terms of their employment with their employer. Before negotiations for an agreement can commence, the company and the union establish their respective bargaining committees. The company negotiating committee usually includes: the industrial relations manager, a plant/operations manager or representative, and other specialists needed for negotiations like wage negotiation specialists.

The union negotiating committee usually consists of a select group of union representatives such as the president of the local, the vice-president, and the chief steward. Once a written agreement has been accepted, each party must honour it. Deadline procedures are put in the document to prevent either party from stalling to fulfil its commitments to the collective agreement.

## Collective Agreement

A collective agreement is an contract in writing between an employer and the union representing the employees. The agreement usually contains provisions respecting conditions of employment, rates of pay, hours of work, rest periods, safety and health standards, and the rights or duties of the parties to the agreement. Ordinarily, the agreement is for a definite period such as one to three years.

## Shop Steward/Union Committee Person

A steward is the union person, usually elected, who represents workers in a particular shop or department. He/she collects dues, solicits new members, announces meetings, and receives, investigates, and attempts the adjustment of grievances.

## Grievance

An employee/employer can file a grievance for a disagreement respecting the interpretation, application, administration or alleged violation of the collective agreement. In every collective agreement, the grievance procedure outlines clearly the steps which must be followed to settle an alleged violation of the agreement The initial steps usually involve the employees' supervisor and possibly the shop steward.

### Arbitration

Arbitration is the procedure by which an arbitrator (board/single person), acting under the authority of both parties to a dispute, hears both sides of the controversy and issues a written decision, which may also include a compensatory award. The decision is, ordinarily, binding on both parties. Arbitrators are usually appointed by the parties concerned, but under special circumstances they are appointed by the Minister of Labour (elected official who heads the federal labour).

There are two main types of arbitration: "interest disputes" and "rights disputes." Interest disputes arise between an employer and union when a fundamental disagreement occurs during the negotiation of a new collective agreement. A rights dispute is one that occurs between an employee and a union. A rights dispute involves the interpretation, application, or administration of the collective agreement that governs the employer/employee relationship.

Compulsory arbitration can occur as a last step in the grievance procedure set out in a collective agreement. Only a small percentage of grievances result in this last step.

### NOTES

1. Definitions from *Glossary of Industrial Relations Terms* (Ottawa: Ministry of Labour, 1992).

2. A strike is defined by *Webster's Dictionary* as the act of stopping work in order to put pressure on an employer. Additionally, a "strike-breaker" is defined as a person who is engaged to do a striker's work, or a company who supplies workers to an employee during a strike.

3. Picket line is defined by *Webster's Dictionary* as a group of workers posted to dissuade other workers or clients from entering their place of work during a strike.

4. A "lobby" is a group of people who bring pressure to bear on legislators to pursue policies favourable to their interests. " Lobby" is also a verb, meaning to influence in favour of a certain policy by constantly seeking interviews, writing letters, bringing external pressures to bear. A "lobbyist" is one person engaged in bringing pressure to bear.

# C A S E **4.5**  CONSULTING FOR GEORGE LANCIA

Cam Matthews shook his head as he looked over the financial statements in front of him. It was June 1993, and he had been hired as a consultant to bring George Lancia's organization under control. George, who wanted a break from the management of his various businesses, was concerned about the successes of his investments. Cam, a 24-year-old recent business graduate, knew upon reading the statements that the financial position was worse than George realized. Cam's foremost concern was how to manage and to relate to George. Cam believed significant changes would have to be made. He wondered what problems he should anticipate.

**GEORGE LANCIA**

George Lancia was the 45-year-old owner of the organization. He had worked on his own in order to support himself through high school. Upon graduation, he worked as a surveyor's assistant for two years, after which he sold securities for five years. At various times during these years he had owned a movie theatre, a drive-in theatre, and a restaurant. He had also begun to buy and sell real estate, including rental properties, and had created a substantial amount of wealth through these dealings.

In 1985, George was approached by Kevin Gibson with the idea of leading a syndicate to invest in several fast food restaurants in Eastern Ontario. George agreed to invest in this venture. By 1988, the restaurants' performances had failed to improve and George was forced to buy out the other investors.

Three years later, George was approached with another investment opportunity, a nursing home and retirement lodge in the small town of Sterling, Ontario. George responded with an offer that was accepted in principle; however, the actual agreement was still being completed by the lawyers.

George built a new house in 1991. By this time, all of his cash was tied up in six restaurants, the retirement home, the rental properties, and the new house.

**MANAGEMENT STRUCTURE**

George's investments were set up as individual, numbered corporations. In theory, this structure was intended to protect him from personal liability and to save the structure from problems in a single unit. However, two sources of exposure could not be avoided. Both George's reputation and his borrowing ability within this very small town would be hindered if any of the individual corporations were to go bankrupt. The banks and creditors had recently begun to ask for personal guarantees on any new debt requested by George.

In general, George made all decisions and approved all spending. His primary source of control was monthly financial statements, which he often viewed several months late and did not trust their accuracy. He seldom had direct contact with his front-line employees.

George's secretary, Sharon, was 23 years old and had received a college diploma in bookkeeping. Sharon had been named the "controller" of the company. She prepared financial statements, managed the payroll, and handled supplier relationships. Her assistant, Caroline, who was 24 years old with a commerce degree from Brock University, helped Sharon prepare the financial statements. Both women had a difficult time remaining productive during the day; statements were occasionally late or inaccurate. George was aware of this situation but wondered how the office computers would be run and the filing and banking handled without Sharon and Caroline. Because George wished to avoid any conflict, Sharon had an effective veto on the decisions in her area.

*Restaurants*   Kevin Gibson was the general manager of the restaurant operations. He was 22 years old when he started working for George. Kevin had no formal management education but had managed fast food restaurants since the age of 18. George had given him full control over decisions at first, claiming that he "would totally step aside and let Kevin do his thing." When commenting on his own management approach, George said he "preferred to sell an idea rather than tell people what to do." George would review the monthly financial statements and then hold "grilling sessions" during which he would ask Kevin for explanations of any apparent poor results. Kevin would then be asked to project the next month's results. George would write down these projections and file them to be pulled out and pointed to during next month's "grilling session." George received other information informally from time to time, in the form of phone calls from banks, suppliers, employees, or the franchiser, whenever there were problems.

For various reasons, Kevin was unable to provide positive results over time, causing George to lose patience and to take back the formal authority. Currently, Kevin had no authority to make any decisions without George's approval; however, he did anyway. Most of the restaurant staff and suppliers had never heard of George and assumed Kevin was the owner. George wondered who would manage the restaurants if Kevin left and therefore did not want to create any friction between himself and Kevin. Additionally, George hoped Kevin would repay the money he had loaned him on a handshake to finance Kevin's house.

Jeff Cranney, a 35-year-old with no management education or former management experience, managed the restaurant in Cobourg. He had invested a substantial amount of cash to build the store in 1991 and currently held 49 percent of the shares. However, this restaurant was not managed effectively and had significant operating problems. George was worried that he would be forced to buy Jeff out if these concerns were addressed.

John and Lucy Wilson approached George in September 1992 and asked him to sell them the restaurant in Peterborough. They provided two houses as a down payment and intended to pay the rest over time. From the perspectives of the bank, the employees, and the landlord, George remained responsible for the asset. John and Lucy were middle-aged with no management education or supervisory experience. John worked as a linesman for a power company; Lucy was a health care aide. George wanted to avoid any conflict here as well to prevent "being left with a real mess."

*The Sterling Manor*  The Sterling Manor was a nursing home and retirement lodge that housed 62 residents and employed close to 50 employees. The negotiations between George and the retirement home's initial owners, the Vaughans, were intense. The Vaughans, the Ministry of Health, and the bank had expressed considerable doubt about George's ability to run the home successfully. It was expected that any additional conflicts or problems would further hinder their perception of him.

At the same time, major changes in the industry were pending. The government had developed stricter regulations to increase the level of quality and service in the industry. These regulations stipulated how the funding should be allocated among nursing, food services, and housekeeping. These changes would reduce net profit considerably, and management would face a much greater challenge than before, when financing was plentiful and regulations minimal.

Linda Baxter was the administrator of the Sterling Manor. She had been a nursing assistant for 25 years and had a diploma in long-term care management. Linda was very personable and concerned about doing a good job. However, she lacked several important technical skills regarding computers, time management, and supervising. She had been hired by the Vaughans and continued to report to them on a regular basis. Whenever she and George disagreed, Linda stated that she still worked for the Vaughans and threatened to seek their decisions. The administration of the home was very disorganized. Phones went unanswered, and Linda's desk was piled with paperwork and mail dating back to 1989. Linda lacked focus or direction and felt that she was accomplishing very little. With the pending regulations, Linda was worried that others would question her competence; therefore, she reacted defensively when anyone attempted to get involved in her work.

Heather Irvin was the director of nursing at the Manor. She was a registered nurse with 30 years' experience. Heather found it difficult to organize and run a staff while dealing with all the conflict and confusion among George, Linda, and the Vaughans. She recognized the importance of management control in a nursing organization, where health and lives are at stake. It was her opinion that Linda did not understood how to operate a health business. So, in order to protect her own position, Heather refused to listen to Linda. Instead, she complained constantly to George about Linda. Because George knew very little about nursing, he could not effectively evaluate Heather's work. He worried about what would happen if she quit. He had not heard any negative comments from anyone else about her work, so he basically gave her complete freedom.

**Real Estate**

Margaret Dennett managed the apartment building in Belleville. She had been given authority to make decisions about the tenants and daily operations but continuously called George about problems she encountered. George did not have the time to find a replacement for her and therefore, to prevent upsetting Margaret, did not attempt to change the situation.

**PERFORMANCE**
**Restaurants**

The restaurant operation had performed poorly for the past three years. The stores had reached their overdraft limit several times, and George had been forced to inject $70,000 from his personal line of credit. Labour productivity was low, quality and service were substandard, current marketing activities were expensive and ineffective, and relations with banks, suppliers, and the franchisers were very poor. In the spring of 1993, Kevin had diverted $70,000 cash from the restaurants to secure equipment and working capital for an ice cream store, a venture that had lost $3,000 per month since its inception.

**The Sterling Manor**

The Sterling Manor had been barely breaking even for the past several months and was near its overdraft limit. The new union was in the midst of contract arbitration that, when completed in late 1993, would likely expose the home to a retroactive wage settlement of between $200,000 and $500,000. Whenever George accumulated money in the business, the Vaughans withdrew it as advance payment on the Manor's purchase price. George did not want to jeopardize the sale and was therefore reluctant to approach the Vaughans about this.

George did not understand the Ministry of Health's new funding model and did not know whether the home would be a good purchase, or even if it would survive, under the new system. George did not seem aware of the severity of the Manor's financial position.

George had almost reached the limit of his personal credit line and could not count on significant cash flows from his businesses in the short-term. He had pledged to limit his drawings from the Manor; there were minimal funds coming from the restaurant operations; and recent vacancies had eliminated any positive cash flow from his rental properties.

**GEORGE AND CAM**

George and Cam had met several times during the spring of 1993. By this time, George was tired and wanted nothing more than to hand over the reins of his business to someone else and step back for awhile. He wanted to remove himself from day-to-day management of all assets and to remain merely as a hands-off investor. In June, George hired Cam as a consultant, asking him to prepare a plan to bring the organization under control, specifically, to "find a way to clean up all the junk on my plate."

Cam had graduated in 1992 with a degree in business administration from Wilfrid Laurier University and had started working as a consultant to medium-sized businesses. His experience consisted of co-op positions[1] with large companies, part-time restaurant management during school, and research and consulting since his final year of school.

During their initial meetings together, George repeatedly said to Cam:

> I've promoted myself to the level of my own incompetence. I know that now, and so from here on, I'm going to be like Henry Ford — I'm going to hire the expertise that I lack myself. That's where you come in — you have the education that I missed out on. I'll give you the benefit of my 25 years' experience in business, and you give me the benefit of your education.

Cam knew from the start that it would be a grave mistake to underestimate the value of George's "school of hard knocks" education, but felt that he, too, had several significant contributions to make. Cam wondered where to start. He wanted to make sure he had a good understanding of the organization and its problems before he made recommendations or attempted any changes. Cam also wondered if he should expect any problems in dealing with George.

### NOTES

1. The university offered a business program that combined regular course work with work terms at various companies.

## **C A S E** 4.6   A JOHNSON & JOHNSON COMPANY (A)

On Wednesday January 4, 1989, Mark Simpson, manager of human resources for a Johnson & Johnson Company (J & J), was deeply concerned. He had just spoken with Doug Bishop, the supervisor of the maintenance department, and learned that an employee had physically assaulted another employee eight days earlier during the Christmas shutdown. Doug had just learned of the incident from the victim. This J & J Company had never before had an incident of violence in the work place. Mark now faced one of the toughest problems he had encountered in his first six months with J & J. He knew it was imperative that he act quickly.

Johnson & Johnson Worldwide was the world's largest health care company. It had three divisions: Consumer, Pharmaceutical and Professional. By 1988, Johnson & Johnson Worldwide was operating in 47 countries, had approximately 81,000 employees, sales of $9 billion and net earnings of $974 million. This J & J company was one of the 13 members of the Johnson & Johnson family of companies in Canada.

**THE COMPANY**    J & J's facilities included offices and a plant, in total employing about 400 nonunionized, salaried employees in 1989. J & J produced and sold various consumer products.

J & J's management believed that the company's success was due to the attention it paid to four key groups: 1) the trade and, ultimately, the end consumer, 2) its employees, 3) the community, and 4) its shareholders. The company's credo articulated J & J's responsibilities to these groups (see Exhibit 1).

Management believed that employee productivity was dependent on both physical and mental health. Therefore, management believed its role was to commit to the well-being of its employees. Studies have indicated that employee health is a major productivity issue for companies. The annual costs to businesses for absenteeism, lateness, substandard work performance, negligence and other actions resulting from poor employee health, either emotional or physical, are staggering (see Exhibit 2).

J & J took its responsibility to its employees seriously. It initiated a comprehensive "LIVE FOR LIFE" wellness program which included an on-site exercise facility with fitness classes, an extensive health and safety program, and an Employee Assistance Program (EAP). The EAP offered confidential counselling for all employees. It had various programs for problems including physical or emotional illness, financial, marital or family distress, alcohol or drug abuse, legal or other concerns. Employees were also encouraged to use the EAP if they were concerned about a fellow employee and wanted advice. Exhibit 3 outlines the EAP. In addition, there was a health services supervisor on staff.

J & J tried to hire individuals who would fit into its corporate culture. In the words of Mr. Perry, the vice-president human resources, "We try to hire people who care about people, because it is difficult to teach someone to care." Mr. Perry was well-liked and respected by J & J's employees, because it was obvious that he cared. The staff in the human resources department enjoyed working for Mr. Perry. Mark described Mr. Perry in the following manner: he is progressive, he is a strong believer in empowering people (delegation), he has a strong commitment to the company's credo, and he is an outstanding leader in his functional area and in the community at large. One of management's practices was to give perks, such as tickets for sporting, arts and cultural events, to provide spontaneous recognition to employees for outstanding performance.

J & J had progressive hiring policies. The company met its responsibility to the community by hiring people with special needs, such as the mentally challenged. In order to follow this policy, J & J used Adult Rehabilitation Centre (ARC) Industries. ARC was a nonprofit organization that trained approximately 200 handicapped adults. The centre had two objectives: to provide training and extended-term work programs for those who were not currently able to compete for community employment and to provide training and vocational guidance for those who were preparing for competitive employment in the community. ARC sponsored three programs: Community Contract Placement, Work Experience Placement, and Employment Placement.

ARC's six-week "Work Experience Placement Program" allowed an individual and a prospective company to determine whether further employment would be mutually beneficial. The work experience placement provided a worker with the opportunity to test out his or her capabilities.

In April 1985, J & J participated in the "Work Experience Program." ARC supplied a candidate, Cheryl McNeil, to work in the labs. ARC also provided a community placement services supervisor to J & J to initially help get the work-term in action. As a result of a successful six weeks, Cheryl was hired as a permanent part-time worker (27.5 hours/week) in July 1985. The placement services supervisor remained involved for a three-month follow-up period. In addition, after Cheryl was hired, ARC Industries supplied personnel to augment the previous training provided to the lab employees. The training was used to address the employees' questions about Cheryl's abilities, needs and behaviour patterns.

Furthermore, the trainer focused on the employees' fears and discomfort associated with working with a mentally challenged individual. This process was necessary because the company wanted to ensure that the integration of Cheryl would not interfere with the existing operations. Initially, some problems were encountered, but, through coaching and counselling, Cheryl became a productive employee.

In late 1985 another opportunity to use ARC surfaced. The human resources group approached the cafeteria company, which was contracted to provide J & J's cafeteria food services, and suggested it sponsor a candidate for the "Work Experience Program." J & J's arrangement with the cafeteria company required this company to manage the food staff; however, J & J ultimately paid the wages of the staff. The cafeteria company decided to participate and, once again, ARC Industries was asked to supply a candidate.

The candidate ARC sent to the cafeteria company was Tom Phillips. The six-week trial period was successful and, in December 1985, the cafeteria company offered Tom a full-time position as a dishwasher in the cafeteria. Tom's job resulted in daily contact with most employees and, consequently, he became well known within the organization. Employee attitudes toward Tom were positive; people wanted him to succeed.

After working for the cafeteria company for one year, Tom applied to a job posting for a maintenance position on the second shift at J & J. His application was accepted, because Tom was considered capable of performing the same work as the existing employees. He was hired in December 1986. It was decided that the maintenance staff did not require the training provided by ARC to facilitate Tom's integration, because they all knew him.

## MAINTENANCE DEPARTMENT

The maintenance staff consisted of the supervisor, Doug Bishop; the second shift lead technician, Frank Cromwell; Dave Thompson; Tim Hudson; Bob Clark; and now Tom Phillips. Doug and Dave worked the first shift from 7:30 a.m. to 3:30 p.m. When conflicts arose in the department, Doug's approach to problem-solving was to tell employees "work this out or you will all be in trouble." Doug reported to Jason Sommers, manager engineering.

The other four men worked the second shift from 4:30 p.m. to 12:30 a.m. During the second shift, Frank, the lead technician on that shift, had been responsible for supervision and job assignment. On a daily basis he monitored and redirected activities in line with priorities and manpower availability. See Exhibit 4 for a work history of Doug and the second shift workers.

As the men on the second shift had gotten to know each other better, they had started to pull pranks on each other. Unknown to Doug, they jumped out of lockers, threw water at each other and put salt in each other's pop. Tom, being a newcomer, had not taken part in the pranks when he first started working with the group

## TOM PHILLIPS

Shortly after being hired full-time by J & J, Tom decided that he did not need to maintain contact with ARC; subsequently, he severed his ties with ARC. His work performance was satisfactory, although, unknown to management, he also participated in the horseplay. Tom was not always able to distinguish the serious from the silly. His mood swings would lead him to withdraw and he would go for several days without talking to a particular individual, in response to a comment or a prank. His fellow workers would try to coax him out of his "moods," but, if they were unsuccessful, they would then choose to ignore him.

His co-workers were always supportive and concerned about his welfare: they provided him with a ride to work; they would speak to management if they were concerned about his well-being; they monitored his eating habits and sometimes supplied him with lunch if he was short of money.

**THE INCIDENT**

On Wednesday, December 28, 1988, during the Christmas plant shutdown, Tom had thought that Bob was playing a joke on him by asking Frank to assign Tom to a different job than the one Tom wanted to do. Tom had wanted to vacuum the carpet in the eating area; this task had not been assigned by Frank and was not a priority, given the holiday. Tom apparently wanted to perform this task, because he wanted to be near the people who were watering plants in the cafeteria. He had been chatting with them earlier and they had been very friendly.

When Frank insisted that Tom do the job he had been assigned, Tom lost his temper and assaulted Bob, punching him in the chest and mouth. Tom's actions thoroughly surprised his co-workers, because he had never done anything violent before nor had he ever threatened to do anything. As he was considerably stronger than Bob, Frank and Tim had to intervene to pull Tom off Bob. Bob, who was upset and angered, demanded to know what had provoked Tom. The misunderstanding was quickly resolved; Tom apologized, and the four men decided not to report the incident because Bob said he was not hurt.

Eight days later, on January 5, 1989, when all employees had returned to work following the Christmas holidays, Bob visited the company's health services because he was concerned about the bruise which had developed on his chest. Upon discovering the source of the bruise, the nurse convinced Bob to report the incident to his supervisor. The following day Bob informed Doug; Doug then spoke to his boss, Jason Sommers. Subsequently, Mark Simpson was called, because of the seriousness of the incident.

Mark wanted to recommend a solid course of action to Mr. Perry. As he had only worked at J & J for six months, he wanted to demonstrate his human resources skills through the careful management of this problem. His previous work experience included employee relations responsibilities for a large multi-plant automotive operation.

Mark knew that he faced a very complex problem. This was a difficult situation to handle, especially because there had never been anything like it before at J & J. He wondered what criteria he should consider before making recommendations to Mr. Perry. He thought of a few potential alternatives: 1) follow the performance improvement procedures (see Exhibit 5); 2) use the company's EAP services; 3) get ARC Industries involved; 4) suspend Tom with or without pay for an appropriate period of time (Mark considered a four-week suspension without pay to be the minimum industry practice for this type of incident); or 5) fire him in accordance with the company's position on violent behaviour (see Exhibit 6). As Mark sat down to formulate an action plan he wondered if there were any other alternatives he should consider.

*EXHIBIT 1*

---

### *Our Credo*

We believe our first responsibility is to the doctors, nurses and patients,
to mothers and fathers and all others who use our products and services.
In meeting their needs everything we do must be of high quality.
We must constantly strive to reduce our costs
in order to maintain reasonable prices.
Customers' orders must be serviced promptly and accurately.
Our suppliers and distributors must have an opportunity
to make a fair profit.

We are responsible to our employees,
the men and women who work with us throughout the world.
Everyone must be considered as an individual.
We must respect their dignity and recognize their merit.
They must have a sense of security in their jobs.
Compensation must be fair and adequate,
and working conditions clean, orderly and safe.
We must be mindful of ways to help our employees fulfill
their family responsibilities.
Employees must feel free to make suggestions and complaints.
There must be equal opportunity for employment, development
and advancement for those qualified.
We must provide competent management,
and their actions must be just and ethical.

We are responsible to the communities in which we live and work
and to the world community as well.
We must be good citizens—support good works and charities
and bear our fair share of taxes.
We must maintain in good order
the property we are privileged to use,
protecting the environment and natural resources.

Our final responsibility is to our stockholders.
Business must make a sound profit.
We must experiment with new ideas.
Research must be carried on, innovative programs developed
and mistakes paid for.
New equipment must be purchased, new facilities provided
and new products launched.
Reserves must be created to provide for adverse times.
When we operate according to these principles,
the stockholders should realize a fair return.

### *Johnson & Johnson*

---

*EXHIBIT 2*
*Our Personal Problems*
*Do Affect Our Work*
*Lives*

**The Canadian Mental Health Association reports:***

- 1/3 of the population will struggle with a serious emotional problem
- 2/5 will be hospitalized to treat illness resulting from emotional problems
- 50% of marriages will end in divorce
- 60% of women and 10% of men will be victims of sexual assault by the time they reach the age of 19
- 22% of adults suffer from alcohol or drug problems.
- Personal problems don't play favourites
- Recognition of the overlap between our personal and work lives
- 33% of employees in one London organization reported personal family problems that had adversely affected their work performance in the previous year
- 65–80% of employee terminations are due to personal or interpersonal factors rather than technical factors.

*Statistics as of October 1989.

*EXHIBIT 3*
*Employee Assistance*
*Program*

Johnson & Johnson recognizes that a wide range of personal problems can have an adverse effect on job performance. In most instances, the employee will overcome such personal problems independently. In other instances, good management techniques will serve either as guidance or motivation to resolve the problems so that the employee's job performance can return to an acceptable level. In some cases, however, the efforts of the employee and the supervisor fail to have the desired effect, and unsatisfactory performance persists over a period of time.

We believe it is in the interest of both our employees and the Company to provide an Employee Assistance Program (EAP) to help with these lingering problems.

The Employee Assistance Program is designed to retain employees with personal problems by assisting them in arresting the further advance of those problems. If left unattended, they might otherwise render the employee unemployable.

**EAP POLICY GUIDELINES**

**1.** Johnson & Johnson recognizes many human problems can be successfully treated, provided they are identified in the early stages and appropriate referral is made. This applies whether the problem is physical or emotional illness, financial, marital or family distress, alcohol or drug abuse, legal or other general concerns.

**2.** Johnson & Johnson recognizes alcoholism as an illness which can be treated.

*EXHIBIT 3 (cont'd)*

3. Employees with personal problems will be given the same opportunity for treatment as employees with any physical illness. It must be recognized, however, that successful resolution of such problems requires a high degree of personal motivation on the part of the employee.

4. This program is preventative and is intended to correct job performance difficulties at the earliest possible time. It is in no way meant to interfere with the private life of the employee. The concern of the Company with alcoholism and personal problems is strictly limited to their effects on the employee's job performance.

5. Where indicated, sick leave will be granted for treatment or rehabilitation on the same basis as is granted for other health problems.

6. Since family problems can impair job performance, referrals can also be made for a family member. An eligible family member is a spouse or a dependent child. An employee's parents, brothers and sisters are also included if they are members of the employee's household.

### Confidentiality

Employees are assured that their job security and future promotional opportunities will not be jeopardized by utilizing the Employee Assistance Program. All records with respect to personal problems are completely confidential.

### Types of Referral

1. Self Referral
   Employees or family members who feel they have a problem are encouraged to seek help on a voluntary basis through the EAP Administrator. A decision on the part of an employee to seek help voluntarily will not be reported to management or entered into personal records.

2. Management Referral
   This is to be based on documented, persistent deteriorating job performance as noted by the immediate supervisor. The employee will be referred by the supervisor to the EAP Administrator, who will make an evaluation and, where appropriate, either provide treatment or suggest referral for treatment or assistance.

### Employee Responsibility

1. The employee is expected to maintain job performance and attendance at an acceptable level.

2. Where there is a problem detrimentally affecting work performance and appropriate treatment is obtained, the employee is to continue with the treatment program to completion.

**EXHIBIT 3** *(cont'd)*

3. If the employee refuses the help that is offered and his job performance and attendance do not improve, or continue to deteriorate, the employee is subject to normal disciplinary procedures.

4. Where the employee cooperates with assistance and/or treatment, but, after a reasonable period of time, is still unable to bring work performance up to an acceptable level, normal disciplinary procedures will also apply.

**Employer Responsibility**

1. To maintain, wherever possible, full job benefit protection for the employee undergoing treatment.

2. To make every possible effort to provide time, where necessary, for the employee to receive treatment by appointment.

3. To provide the time for periodic EAP educational seminars for all employees.

4. To ensure full confidentiality of all EAP records.

---

**EXHIBIT 4**
*Work History*

**Doug Bishop**—Supervisor

| | |
|---|---|
| June 1985 | lead technician |
| March 1988 | supervisor, maintenance |

**Frank Cromwell**—Lead Technician

| | |
|---|---|
| December 1986 | technician |
| May 1987 | lead technician, second shift |

**Bob Clark**—Technician

| | |
|---|---|
| July 1987 | technician |

**Tom Phillips**—Technician

| | |
|---|---|
| December 1986 | technician |

**Tim Hudson**—Technician

| | |
|---|---|
| October 1988 | temporary technician (1-year contract) |
| December 1988 | permanent technician |

*EXHIBIT 5*

---
### E M P L O Y E E   H A N D B O O K
---

## Performance Improvement Procedures
Performance improvement includes the following three stages:

### 1. Verbal Discussion

At least one verbal discussion with the employee outlining the aspects of performance which are below standard. Your Supervisor may choose to record this discussion, depending on the severity of the incident.

Employees are encouraged to discuss differences, including contributing circumstances, with their supervisor.

### 2. Performance Improvement Plan

The second stage is to provide the employee a written Performance Improvement Plan. This plan must outline specific improvements which you will be expected to attain within a specified period of time, and an outline of the probable consequences if improvement is not demonstrated.

### 3. Suspension/Dismissal

If an employee has not achieved the improvements outlined by the Performance Improvement Plan, suspension or termination may result.

---

*EXHIBIT 6*

---
### E M P L O Y E E   H A N D B O O K
---

## Actions Subject to Termination
The following actions may result in the immediate termination of an employee:

- Possession of a dangerous weapon on Company property.
- Refusal to follow job responsibilities or duties other than when safety is a factor.
- Falsification of records.
- Illegal purchase, manufacture, transfer, use, sales, consumption or possession of non-prescribed chemical substances on Company property or while on Company business.
- Violent or threatening behavior.
- Harassment of any kind.
- Behavior that threatens another individual's character or reputation.
- Unauthorized disclosure of Company or confidential information.
- Misappropriation of Company funds.
- Theft, unauthorized use of or negligence of Company property or products.
- Conviction for careless or impaired driving if assigned a fleet vehicle.

---

# C A S E **4.7**   THE FOOD TERMINAL (A)

In July 1991, three months after graduating from the Western Business School, 23-year-old Mike Bellafacia knew that he was in for a rough ride.

> When I arrived at the store, the staff morale was terrible. The previous manager had made a mess of things, the recession was hitting home, sales were spiralling downward quickly, and my store was losing $10,000 per week. To make matters worse, most of the key people in the company felt that I didn't deserve the store manager's position.

As the recently appointed store manager of the newest Foodco location in St. Catharines, Ontario, Mike knew that he had to turn the store around by improving its financial performance and the employee morale. He also knew that something had to be done immediately because the losses at this store were seriously affecting the entire company.

**FOODCO LTD.**     Foodco Ltd. (FC), with its head office located in St. Catharines, Ontario, was a large player in the Niagara Peninsula grocery retailing industry. FC, a retailer in this market since 1962, was currently made up of seven stores: three St. Catharines locations, one Welland location, one Port Colborne location, and two Lincoln locations. Most of the ownership and key management positions were held by Frank Bellafacia, Tony Bellafacia, and Rocco Bellafacia, as shown in Exhibit 1. Selected financial ratios for FC are shown in Exhibit 2.

FC had created a powerful presence in this industry by developing and refining a strategy that worked. Their product offering was that of any typical supermarket: groceries, meats, bakery and dairy items, packaged foods, and nonfood items. Each store carried eight to ten thousand different items. FC planned to widen the selection available by adding more lines, and to follow a general trend in consumer preferences toward an increased percentage of nonfood items in the product mix. Central to FC's strategy was a well-managed marketing effort. Weekly flyers were distributed that highlighted five or six items. FC priced these items below cost to draw customers. The rest of the flyer's products were representative of all the product groups. FC's ability to differentiate itself from the other competitors centred around its corporate vision: low food prices and fast, friendly service.

Central to the FC competitive strategy was the mandate to be the low-price leader among conventional supermarkets, during good and bad economic times. Mike Bellafacia stated: "This is a no frills and low price store for a no frills and low price clientele. Most markets are shifting in this direction." FC had developed aggressive expansion plans with six stores being considered for development.

## THE RETAIL GROCERY INDUSTRY

The job of managing the store and the staff became crucial to the overall success of FC, given the demanding challenges in the industry. The industry was shifting from a simple mass market to a spectrum of distinct, serviceable segments. A recent statistic stated that 30 percent of consumers switch stores every year. Moreover, a new Food Marketing Institute study found that consumers buy on the basis of the following criteria (ranked in decreasing priority): service, quality products, variety, and low prices. Thus, there was now more opportunity for competitive differentiation based on service and on quality than on price alone.

There were tremendous opportunities for niche players to enter the market, and such entrants had been observed. Health and organic food stores, fruit markets, and independent single-commodity stores (i.e., pet food stores) emerged and were servicing their target segments more effectively than the supermarkets were willing or able to do. Consumer demands varied from region to region, and many small independent retail grocers emerged to meet these demands both in the Niagara Peninsula and across all of Ontario. These independents managed not only to survive, but to take sizable portions of market share from the major chains. This shift toward niche marketing and catering to the local market outlined the need to employ store managers who understood how to please and retain the local customer.

## THE ROLE OF THE STORE MANAGER

The success of FC depended upon each of the seven store managers operating his/her store consistently with the corporate strategy. Traditionally, the road to store manager (SM) began within one of the stores at a lower management position. The family culture within each food terminal location was very important to FC management. Thus, store managers were selected from within the company to ensure a leader who understood the FC vision and values. Five managers reported directly to the SM, as shown in Exhibit 3, and their development was an important job for the SM. The SM position became increasingly more important at FC. Many of the current SM functions that used to be handled by the head office were delegated downward to the store level to allow head office to focus on overall company strategy. The stores were now more attuned to the local market they serve. An SM was responsible for the following:

1. Ensuring that merchandising skills were strong among all department managers

2. Monitoring local market information

3. Focusing staff on organizational goals (such as sales, gross margin, and profit goals)
4. Organizing weekly staff meetings
5. Developing all employees and encouraging staff training
6. Generating and producing sales, gross margin, and profit objectives
7. Meeting cost objectives (motivating the staff to be cost conscious)
8. Analyzing the performance of each interstore department
9. Attending FC "Top Management Meetings" (TMMs)

## MIKE BELLAFACIA'S BACKGROUND

Mike Bellafacia graduated from the University of Western Ontario with an Honours Business Administration degree (HBA). During his summers at university, he was assigned special projects from his father that focused on a variety of company problems. Mike would combine the analytical skills developed in the business school with his knowledge of the family business to address these issues. In his last year in the HBA program, Mike and a team of student consultants spent the year focusing on the long-term strategy and competitive advantage of FC. They examined every aspect of the company and developed many strategic recommendations for the top management at FC.

Upon graduation, Mike decided to work for FC. He planned to start off working in some of the various departments (i.e., the produce department) at different stores within FC, and work his way up in order to get the experience he needed to manage a store. This would have allowed him the opportunity to work under some of the most knowledgeable managers in the company. He didn't expect to be store manager so soon.

## THE SCOTT AND VINE LOCATION: THE FIRST MONTH

Mike's career at FC was supposed to begin in one of the departments in the company. Both Mike and FC management felt strongly about that. However, while Mike was on vacation in May, FC management made a chancy decision. As of June 1, 1991, Mike Bellafacia would take over the SM position at the Scott and Vine location from the existing SM. The store's performance was deteriorating, and Mike was expected to change things. Mike reflected on the first week at the three-month old location:

> When I first started I was extremely nervous. The district supervisor brought me to the store to have a meeting with the department managers, and I could see the look of disappointment in their eyes. Most of these managers had been forced to move to this new store from other locations. The staff morale was definitely low to begin with. Combined with the fact that I am the boss's son, they probably assumed that I was sent to check on them.

After getting settled in, Mike began to realize that something was terribly wrong at the Scott and Vine food terminal. The store was not producing a bottom line, and many of the 95 employees were not performing well. Mike commented:

> This building used to be a Food City that was on the verge of closing down. We acquired it, and picked up where they left off. The task I had was to get above average performance from an average staff. They were just not driven to succeed, were poorly trained, and many of them, especially the managers, didn't want to be there.

> The previous manager had performed poorly by FC standards. Although he had been an SM at other grocery stores, he was unable to create a productive atmosphere at this one. When this location opened, the sales level was $160,000 per week, but by Mike's first month it had dropped by 17 percent. FC management expected this location to be operating at over $200,000 per week. The other St. Catharines stores were operating at over $350,000 per week. They had a long way to go.

> What took place at the Scott and Vine location was a symptom of a more serious problem: the performance of FC as a whole. Mike explained the situation:

> Some of what was happening here can be attributed to FC. They became fat cats and, in the process, they lost touch with the customers. Pricing had gone way out of line, cross-border shopping was cutting into our bottom line, and our marketing efforts were poor. The weekly ads that are developed by head office for all the stores were not drawing in customers like they used to. As a result, we had no word-of-mouth advertising, which is so essential to a retail outlet. When our sales across the board went down, we had only ourselves to blame.

***SORTING THROUGH***
***THE DISORDER***

The job of managing the food terminal was overwhelming, and the problems were endless. Some of the more prevalent problems are listed below:

1. Product rotation (a job monitored by department managers and very important for customer satisfaction) was handled improperly.
2. It was not uncommon to find empty counters and shelves.
3. The staff paid very little attention to cleanliness. (Customers complained about this.)
4. Customers were not treated with respect by those employees who had frequent contact with them.
5. Department managers were doing a poor job of managing and motivating the employees in their departments.
6. Department sales and gross profit results were poor. (See Exhibit 4 for a breakdown of departmental sales and gross profit figures.)

Difficulties arose within the staff that made the SM job even more strenuous. Mike described the situation:

There were a lot of people problems that I had to face. The weekly staff meetings we had together were a joke. Instead of a time to interact and solve problems together, it was just a waste of time. As well, the entire staff was demoralized due to the continual failure to meet monthly performance goals since the store opened. We had the worst performance in the FC organization. The controller of the company told me that the Scott and Vine location was hurting the entire company. I felt as though head office was blaming me for the store's poor performance and I knew that I had to set some goals that we could all rally behind.

For the first month I was very autocratic. I had to be! I replaced all the cashiers that month, because of the numerous customer complaints about their attitude, but that was just the beginning of my problems. The part-time staff were continually standing around doing nothing. The receiver was not handling the deliveries very well. I found it tough to get along with the department managers. My worst employee problems came from the produce and meat managers. They just were not doing their jobs well. I tried going over the product orders with them, developing schedules, and assisting with their product display plans. I even brought in some of FC's department experts to go over things with them. They would not listen to any of my suggestions. Even though I had some problems with my grocery manager, I began to see that he had real potential for managing. There was some resentment toward me for being a family member and getting the SM position so young, and as a result, people would not open up to me. I also knew that some of the other SMs at other locations didn't want me to succeed, and I found myself conveniently left out of important SM meetings. To make matters worse, after two months here, the general manager of FC made it known that I should be pulled out of this job.

**FACING THE FUTURE**   It was a tough season to compete in the retail grocery business. Mike Bellafacia found this out after only two months at the food terminal and the situation was now grave. The Scott and Vine location was losing over $10,000 per week, and the sales level was stagnant. The staff morale had changed very little. Customers were not responding to advertisement efforts, and things looked as if they were going to worsen. Mike reflected on what had happened during these last two months and where things were going. He wondered if he was responsible for the mess the store was in — had he mismanaged his managers, thereby making the situation worse? Had FC made a big mistake putting him in the position of SM. Thinking back on his education, Mike commented:

> The business school helped me understand the decision-making process. I'm not afraid to make decisions, do analysis, and pin-point problem areas. But it didn't teach me how to get the job done, the execution of a decision. More importantly, I was not prepared to deal with people who didn't have the training I did, or the desire to succeed as I did.

Although he was unsure about these issues, he focused on what he should do to get the Scott and Vine food terminal operating profitably, with good management and with a growing customer base. As he looked over the financial data, he wondered if he should lay off some employees to bring the wages expense down. Mike reflected on this: "We didn't have the sales to support the exorbitant number of employees we had at the store." He was concerned about how he would handle these lay-offs. He also thought about the serious morale problem. Many of the employees were lazy and demotivated, and customers complained regularly about cleanliness and service. He wondered if there was a way to use the weekly meetings to his advantage. Things seemed just as complicated as they did in June.

***EXHIBIT 1***
***Personnel***
***Organization***
***Chart***

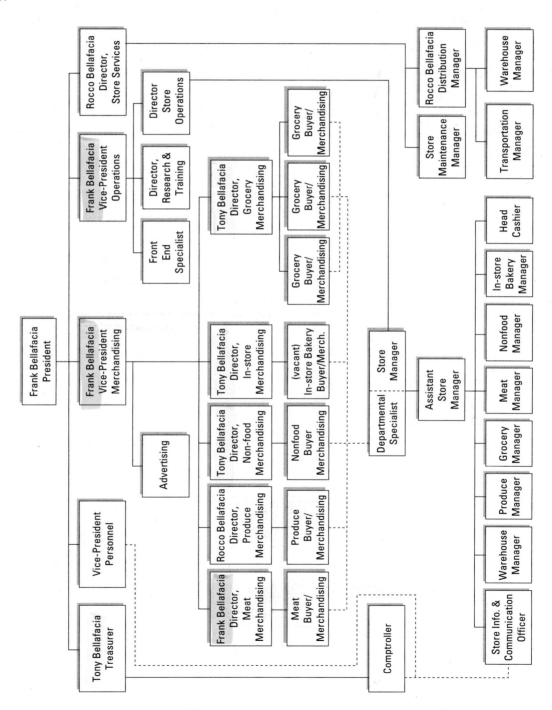

*EXHIBIT 2*

| Selected Financial Ratios | | | | | |
|---|---|---|---|---|---|
| | 1986 | 1987 | 1988 | 1989 | 1990 |
| PROFITABILITY | | | | | |
| Cost of goods sold | 81.2% | 80.2% | 79.7% | 78.7% | 78.3% |
| Operating expenses | 19.4% | 18.7% | 19.1% | 19.6% | 19.8% |
| Net income before tax | –1.1% | 0.5% | 0.3% | 0.7% | 0.7% |
| RETURN | | | | | |
| After-tax return on equity | 0.0% | 715.0% | N/A | 725.0% | 94.2% |
| STABILITY | | | | | |
| Interest coverage[1] | 1.28X | 1.36X | 1.05X | 1.19X | 2.37X |
| LIQUIDITY | | | | | |
| Net working capital ($000)[1] | –1,447 | –2,051 | –13 | –316 | –243 |
| GROWTH | | | | | |
| Sales | | 26.0% | 10.7% | 14.1% | 15.5% |
| Assets[1] | | 16.7% | 3.8% | 11.2% | 9.6% |
| Equity[1] | | -0.3% | 1.2% | 4.9% | 19.5% |

**1.** Denotes a ratio calculated from the statements of Bellafacia's Consolidated Holdings Inc.

***EXHIBIT 3***
***Scott and Vine***
***Organizational***
***Chart***

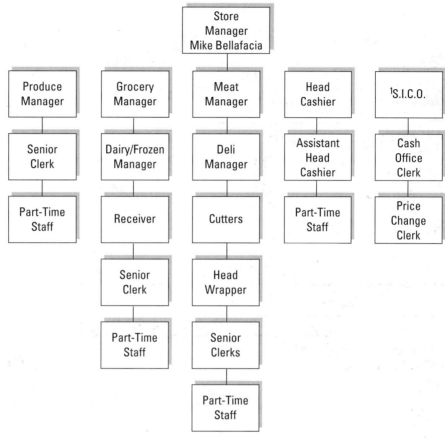

1.   Store Information & Communications Officer. Responsible for maintaining the lines of communication between the store and head office.

*Exhibit 4*

---

**Selected Financial Indicators
Scott and Vine Location
for the Week Ending June 9, 1991**

---

**DEPARTMENTAL PERFORMANCE**

| DEPARTMENT | SALES($) | GROSS PROFIT($) | % OF SALES |
|---|---|---|---|
| Produce | 22,677 | 4,602 | 20.3 |
| Grocery | 77,363 | 12,467 | 16.1 |
| Meat | 32,963 | 7,629 | 23.1 |
| Nonfood | 4,784 | 1,228 | 25.7 |
| IS-Bakery | 2,337 | 934 | 40.0 |
| TOTAL | 140,124 | 28,860 | 19.2 |

---

**OVERALL STORE PERFORMANCE (ONE WEEK)**

| WEEKLY INDICATORS | BUDGET ($) | ACTUAL ($) |
|---|---|---|
| SALES | 155,000 | 140,124 |
| GROSS PROFIT | 33,683 | 26,860 |
| EXPENSES: | | |
| Wages | 16,483 | 19,600 |
| Supplies | 1,895 | 1,410 |
| Other Expenses | 17,091 | 16,257 |
| TOTAL EXPENSES | 35,469 | 37,267 |
| NET INCOME | (1,786) | (10,407) |
| # OF CUSTOMERS | 7,723 / WEEK | |

# C A S E 4.8   HIBBS'S WEB

Frederick Fontaine, west coast division manager for the Uvex Corporation, knew he needed to take action before nine o'clock the next morning. Otherwise, it was highly probable that Alex Fuhrman would commence a law suit against one of his division's employees, Christopher Hibbs, and against the Uvex Corporation itself. A law suit risked press coverage and conjecture that could diminish the success of Uvex's next public stock offering, due to be underwritten early in the new year.

**THE COMPANY**

The Uvex Corporation started as a small family-owned medical centre on the southwest coast. The original owners were a father and son team of physicians who seized an opportunity to develop a private medical health-care facility. Over the years, the two men recruited only the best physicians in their fields to expand the enterprise across the nation. Last year, this strategy paid off in revenues of $750 million. Uvex specialized in pioneering treatments for cancers and ancillary surgical procedures for cosmetic recovery. The company's research labs were at the leading edge of cancer research in North America.

**ALEX FUHRMAN**

Immediately after graduating from an MBA program, Alex Fuhrman had joined the Uvex Corporation as its director of accounting and finance. At that time, nine years ago, the corporation was still a small family-owned business with centres primarily on the west coast. The business flourished, increasing revenues almost exponentially after Alex became involved in restructuring for expansion.

**ORGANIZATIONAL STRUCTURE**

Nine years ago, Uvex was organized along geographical lines. Each of its medical centres engaged in all types of treatments and undertook to collect and receive all payments from patients. Payroll and accounting were handled by Alex's staff at head office in San Francisco. The original organizational structure is depicted in Exhibit 1.

Five years after Alex joined Uvex, the company went public[1] in order to fund a monumental expansion into cancer research and treatment. At that time, Uvex rationalized all of its cancer procedures to the San Francisco location. The company built a state-of-the-art facility for cancer treatment and research in the foothills of San Rafael, 25 km from the existing facility. The old San Francisco site was renovated into executive suites for vice-presidents and their staff.

The new San Rafael facility was highly capitalized with sophisticated radiation therapy units. The close proximity of research talent to treatment devices effected rapid and creative exchange of innovative techniques. Cancer patients from all other Uvex centres were transported to San Rafael for treatment. The company's reputation flourished.

In order to better service its patients from the central part of the country, Uvex looked forward to installing state-of-the-art radiation therapy units in Salt Lake City. The Salt Lake centre currently administered chemotherapies only. In order to fund this new equipment, Uvex would issue another public stock offering early next year.

Uvex's newest organizational design is shown in Exhibit 2. Vice-presidents for marketing, human resources, and financial planning were now located at the company's head office in San Francisco. There were regional managers in charge of specific geographies, and all cancer facilities and treatment planning were managed through the San Rafael facility.

## THE SAN RAFAEL GROUP

The final aspect to be formulated at San Rafael was the research facility. Uvex was considered to be the vanguard of cancer research because its staff was the best and the brightest in the country. The research group consisted of a core of leading scientists with doctoral degrees in biochemistry. These supervisory investigators were assisted by lab technicians, nutritionists, and mental health professionals with varied backgrounds. Most of the treatment centre's medical doctors were involved in part-time clinical studies in conjunction with the full-time scientists. Pay scales at San Rafael were commensurate with experience and were the highest in the industry.

The San Rafael centre enjoyed abundant donations from grateful patients and their families. As well, many private and public groups and businesses contributed significant funds to specific researchers or research endeavour.

Despite their accomplishments, the staff in the cancer centre were prone to mental fatigue and stress. Managing this group's creativity and intensity required extensive people skills, empathy, and attention to team spirit. Alex Fuhrman was the ideal choice to head the administration of the cancer research and treatment division. Alex was a competent, sensitive "people" manager and a talented financial administrator, who chose to maintain an office in the San Rafael centre in order to be close to the staff.

As was the case with the reorganization of Uvex's other divisions, an accounting manager was hired for the west coast division. The accounting manager was to compile monthly expense statements for each department, and to handle simple receivables, payables, and payroll functions with a staff of two or three clerks. Alex was involved in the initial screening process of the candidates The final decision to hire Christopher Hibbs was made by Frederick Fontaine. Hibbs had previously worked as a bookkeeper for the city of Sacramento. His former boss offered high praise of Hibbs in his letter of recommendation.

Alex's last act within the accounting division was to set up systems for reporting expenses to the various department heads within the San Rafael centre. After that, department heads would set their own budgets for operating funds and capital expenditures. To aid their estimates, each department head now received monthly statements from the accounting manager.

In order to foster a smooth transition to responsibility centres in the cancer facility, Alex conducted seminars for the department heads who were, primarily, long-term employees, and usually the only doctoral degrees in their departments. As a general rule, the scientists viewed budgeting as secondary to research. Consequently, the first seminar was lightly attended even though Alex ordered pizza for the lunch-hour meeting. After Alex's first seminar, there was widespread shock in the research centre. The next seminar was highly enlisted and the budgeting process was hotly debated. Department heads did not want to take responsibility for budgeting and controlling expenses. Alex persisted and, after about a month's lapse in time, the department heads appeared to mellow.

**THE MEMO**

Frederick Fontaine harboured some early reservations about Hibbs because the new accounting manager seemed to want to make numerous changes to the accounting system that Alex installed. Frederick was not convinced that Hibbs was adequately qualified to alter the process; however, as time passed and the department heads appeared placated, Frederick forgot his worries. Besides, finance and accounting were not particular strengths of Frederick's, and he preferred to avoid dealing with them. Hibbs sent his financial reports directly to the executive controller of Uvex.

One Friday night when he was working late, Frederick requested security to give him entry into the accounting manager's office so that he could retrieve a requisition for a specialized piece of equipment. While he was in Hibbs's office, Frederick noticed a memo that sat in the middle of Hibbs's desk. The memo was addressed to the controller and dated the week previous. It read in part:

> ... In the general and research accounts, I have found several thousands of dollars discrepancy. It may be that there are funds missing. I thought you should know that Alex Fuhrman was the only person who had access to the accounts prior to my arrival at the centre.

The next morning, Frederick called the controller's office and asked about the memo. The controller admitted to receiving the memo from Hibbs, and expressed some mystification about it. He explained that after nine months with the company, Hibbs's first fiscal year end report was due within the next two weeks. The controller expressed a belief that Hibbs had encountered problems trying to reconcile accounts when he began to compile results for the centre's fiscal year end. So far, the controller had not taken time to challenge Hibbs about the memo.

Frederick then drove to the research centre and stopped by Alex's office, without announcing his arrival. He brought with him a photocopy of the memo. After reading the note, Alex was outraged and insisted on an immediate meeting with Hibbs, the controller, and Frederick.

**THE MEETING**

A meeting was hastily organized for that afternoon. During the confrontation, it became apparent that the centre's department heads had become alarmed when they received their first monthly statements from Hibbs. Subsequently, they plied considerable pressure on Hibbs to do something to relieve their fears about budget cuts. Hibbs had succumbed to the pressure and decided to alter the centre's methods for depreciation in order to understate the expenses. As well, Hibbs decided to defer some expenses to future periods and to recognize revenues when treatment services were rendered rather than when the cash was received from the patients. These modifications amounted to acceptable accounting practices when they were disclosed; however, the net result was that the centre reported a much higher profitability than in previous years. Hibbs had become confused when he was unable to reconcile the statements at year end with the systems that Alex had instituted.

The controller asked:

So, you put together fraudulent statements and then sent them to me?

Hibbs responded haughtily:

With a broad stretch of the imagination, you could call the statements fraudulent, but I don't like that term.

Alex spoke to Hibbs heatedly:

And then you wrote a letter to the controller at the executive suites, and you implicated me in what you termed "missing funds."

Hibbs was remorseless:

Well, you didn't do such a hot job, Alex.

He paused to pick up a departmental budget and waved it under Alex's nose:

The department heads were devastated by the budgeting process. They didn't understand it all.

Alex shot back:

Did you try to explain it to them?

Hibbs looked smug:

That was your job, Alex, and you did not do it well.

Alex insisted that Hibbs submit a written retraction to the staff at the executive offices, an explanation to the department heads, and an apology.

Hibbs flatly refused, and launched into a tirade of righteous indignation.

Frederick suddenly stood up and left the room. He was exasperated by the situation. The controller mopped his brow and stared silently at the ceiling while Hibbs mercilessly elaborated his resentment at being asked to apologize.

Before Hibbs could finish his speech, Alex left the room abruptly and without further comment.

At six o'clock that night, Frederick received a telephone call from Alex's lawyer:

> Mr. Fontaine, my client and I believe that Christopher Hibbs's memo is slanderous toward Alex Fuhrman. Unless you dismiss him and put into writing a retraction of the allegations that he has made, we will file a libel suit against him and the Uvex Corporation. We will be in court when it opens tomorrow morning at 10 o'clock.

## Notes

1. To "go public" means to sell shares of the company to outside investors on the public stock exchange.

**EXHIBIT 1**
**Former Organizational Structure**

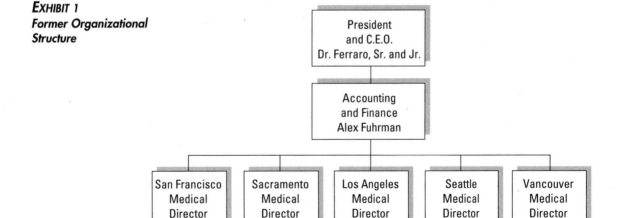

*EXHIBIT 2*
*New Organizational*
*Structure*

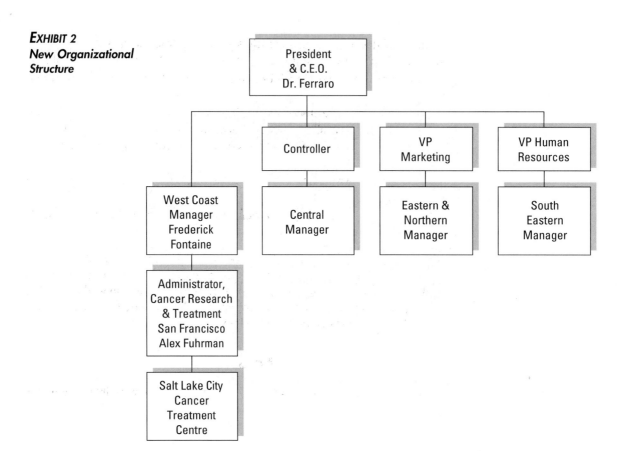

### C A S E **4.9**   MEDICTEST LABORATORIES (A)

In April 1994, Jean Kelly, manager of the Southwestern Ontario region of Medictest Laboratories, faced a tough situation in Sarnia, Ontario. The Ontario government had imposed funding cutbacks to the Ontario Health Insurance Plan (OHIP) for all testing centres in the province, creating a severe need for cost cutting. Over the past two years, Medictest Laboratories had reduced costs by improving work-flow efficiency. However, further cost reduction was necessary and required a review of the supervisory structure. Jean had designed a new organizational structure that streamlined management and furthered the company's objectives for augmenting employee decision-making power, but this structure would require the dismissal of five long-term supervisors. Jean wondered how to implement these changes without a negative impact on morale, productivity, and motivation.

**THE INDUSTRY**

The technology-based health care industry was rapidly changing. In particular, the testing laboratories industry was experiencing significant streamlining due to funding cutbacks and the impacts of new technology and automation.

Labs received testing orders from doctors, hospitals, and medical centres. Upon filling each order, the labs would bill OHIP[1], which paid a specified amount for each type of test. Labs were responsible for controlling their costs in order to achieve a profit. As the Ontario Government attempted to decrease its expenses, funding for health care came under severe pressure. The compensation provided by OHIP for testing was significantly reduced. The laboratories were faced with a 17 percent decrease in funding for completion of the same work; this placed tremendous pressure on the profit margins. Many testing laboratories attempted to adapt by restructuring, downsizing, and streamlining. Further funding reduction was expected over the next two years. The Ontario Ministry of Health offered a restructuring credit, based on market share, for those testing centres that reduced their costs beyond industry standards and invested significantly in new technology.

Each medical laboratory was required by law to have a medical doctor on the Board of Directors to be accountable for medical care. Although usually not directly involved in the operation of the lab, this person approved all major decisions before they were implemented and facilitated the relationship between the for-profit labs and the public hospitals.

## MEDICTEST LABORATORIES

Medictest Laboratories' head office was based in London, Ontario, and operated a chain of private medical laboratories in Canada. It was comprised of labs and specimen collection centres throughout Canada. These centres determined the most appropriate tests to be performed and then executed the tests.

As stated in the 1993 annual report, the company's commitment was "to seize the opportunity to serve the needs of the health care marketplace, to persevere in innovation, to achieve the defined objectives and to realize the shared vision of leadership in health care." Medictest's future objective was to become more automated through the integration of state-of-the-art technology. In general, Medictest had a reputation for its ability to make excellent decisions. It was also known as a nonunionized, people-oriented company that truly cared for its employees and believed in its values (see Exhibit 1). Upon hiring dedicated and hard-working employees, Medictest was considerate and thoughtful toward them, recognizing them as a valuable resource. The company placed high priority on enabling employees to develop to their full potential and to advance within the organization. The employees were very close and tight-knit among the Ontario labs, often remaining with the company for long employment periods.

Medictest had begun to establish goals to augment empowerment, teamwork, and shared responsibility. These concepts were gradually being implemented by restructuring leadership teams and by choosing leaders who fit with these objectives. Former pyramid-style systems of authority were being replaced with new structures for decision making. A self-directed team approach was designed to empower employees to make decisions. The intent of the restructuring program was to re-align resources in order to operate more effectively and efficiently.

Because of funding changes and the company's goals for empowerment, head office began to review the leadership and support staff structure across Ontario. Recent changes had been made to the upper management structure, including consolidating four regional management positions into one. Medictest Sarnia was a target of consideration for restructuring because of the large size of its management team. Discussion about these changes had begun two years ago.

## MEDICTEST SARNIA

The Sarnia location was a large laboratory, processing thousands of specimens daily, operating on a 24-hour basis. This testing facility served physicians, patient centres, hospitals, and other Medictest locations, handling one-third of Medictest's testing in Ontario. Most of this testing was for Southwestern Ontario, although some tests were also completed for clients in other regions. Because of the high volume of work done at this location, the Sarnia lab had a great impact on the perceived quality of service provided by Medictest in general; therefore, there was significant pressure on the management at Medictest Sarnia.

Medictest Sarnia currently operated with 12 supervisors and 234 employees, many of whom had been with the subsidiary since its origin 20 years ago (see Exhibit 2). Most of the testing was completed at one main location, but there were also several smaller nearby sites that were part of the same operation.

Within the past two years, measures had been taken to improve work-flow efficiency. Six months ago, it had become evident that, although costs needed further reduction, no additional improvements were possible within the current structure.

Jean Kelly had worked for Medictest for two years. In her former position as operations manager, she had been responsible for all operations done by this laboratory. Recently, her position had expanded to manager of Southwestern Ontario, which also gave her the responsibility of market share and revenue generation within this region. Upon graduating from Leeds University in England with a post-graduate degree in medical microbiology, Jean had worked for six years as a laboratory manager at Toronto East General Hospital. Over the past few years, she had taken business courses through continuing education. Jean was asked by head office to review the current supervisory structure and develop a revised one that would cut down on costs and facilitate the goals of empowerment. Jean found the ensuing changes exciting and challenging. She had been given a few months to report the structural changes to the regional manager.

Jean's objectives for redesigning the current structure were to reduce costs, to ensure profitability, and to build a new organizational team that would support empowerment through responsibility and leadership. Although there was some teamwork already in place, the supervisory structure was so large that there was no need to be interdependent or even to meet regularly. Jean thought that a leaner management team, with different responsibilities than the existing team, would be better equipped to carry out these new interdependent roles. The revised structure had to "make sense" by providing a logical connection among the departments. Jean also hoped to better integrate the testing facilities with client services and improve relationships with other Medictest locations. In developing a different supervisory team, Jean had to choose leaders who possessed the core technical competency and, more importantly, displayed the appropriate leadership skills to fit the new objectives.

**Effects on Management**

Before Jean made any changes, she gave the supervisors the option to take part in designing a new structure, either directly or indirectly. They were given three options: to be directly involved in the design; to fine-tune the structure after it had been designed; or to be told after the decisions were made. They chose to have no active involvement, reasoning that they were too close as a group, and preferred to be told about the changes once they were decided upon by upper management. Jean had expected this because the individuals would have felt that they were negotiating for each others' jobs. Although this eliminated some valuable input, Jean believed it would be less painful for the supervisors.

While Jean analyzed the current structure, some interesting dynamics began to take place among the supervisors. Each supervisor was competent and hard-working, having worked for Medictest for an average of 18 years, with minimal movement or change in responsibility or position. They knew each other well and were comfortable with their roles and work environment. They had known for the past two years that changes were going to be made. Six months ago, they became aware that these changes would be structural and would affect their positions. Anxiety levels escalated. They wanted to hear about the changes as soon as possible and were uncomfortable with the delay. Although productivity was unaffected by the anxiety, some supervisors began to protect their turf by emphasizing the size and importance of their particular unit at every opportunity.

The supervisors realized that there would be a smaller leadership team and thus began inwardly to assess their own strengths and weaknesses, reasoning whether their style of leadership would be one of those desired for the new roles. Each supervisor's individual level of anxiety depended on his or her personal situation; most of them could determine from their own intuitive comfort level whether they would be chosen to stay.

Jean held one-on-one discussions with the supervisors. The two supervisors of specimen collection began increasingly to inquire about the severance package, alternate careers, and retirement options. It appeared to Jean that they were prepared to leave Medictest.

Even those supervisors who felt strong in their role experienced high anxiety. Resumés were prepared and other job opportunities were considered. While work performance continued normally, the supervisors behaved differently. They were quieter than before and vigilant for signals of what changes would be made. Jean had to be extremely careful of her actions. For example, she occasionally had to delegate meetings to supervisors if she could not attend; her choice of supervisor now took on new meaning for the supervisors. Another time, when Jean discussed the severance packages with the group of supervisors, she had to be careful with whom she made eye-contact.

*Effects on the Staff*    Great lengths had been taken by management to prevent the staff members in Sarnia from knowing about the pending structural changes, in order to keep the situation manageable for the supervisors. Within the past few weeks, the staff members had found out that a review of the supervisory structure was taking place. They were anxious about the effect these changes would have on them and were concerned that the "right" supervisors be chosen to stay. Several employees who were fond of their supervisors discreetly approached Jean, encouraging her to "bear in mind the right person for the job."

Additionally, the staff were aware that the largest laboratory, located in London, was expanding due to automation. This knowledge created the fear that the lab in Sarnia would be closed, because of its proximity to London.

*DEVELOPING*
*REVISED*
*STRUCTURE*

Jean saw several opportunities for effective change to the current structure at Medictest Sarnia.

The lab service representative was basically responsible for new business, while the client service representative was in charge of keeping current business. Jean decided that these positions could be consolidated due to market place changes.

The courier supervisor had taken early retirement in January 1994 with a separation package. His position had not been filled since his departure, and this had not created any problems. There was some apparent overlap and excess supervision of the specimen collection centres and courier operations. Jean concluded that the courier and collection centres staff could be streamlined under one supervisor, instead of the previous four. However, this would require a strong, energetic supervisor who was capable of handling the increased responsibility.

The supervisors of Testing Centres 1 and 2 currently shared the same staff; Jean decided their positions could be merged into one with few problems.

Testing Centre 3 was highly complex and completed 80 percent of the tests. It currently had a strong supervisor with potential for interregional liaison with other Medictest locations.

Testing Centre 5 was of low complexity but high importance and was highly interdependent with Testing Centre 4. These centres could logically be merged.

The customer service department dealt with customer requests and communicated testing solutions to customers. This department operated within a vacuum, separate from testing. The lack of communication regarding customer requests negatively affected the level of service provided to the customers. Jean saw the opportunity to address this concern by linking it with Testing Centres 1 and 2, under one supervisor.

Billing was closely audited by OHIP every two years. OHIP subtracted a percentage from revenue for each minor error found. Each billing form had to contain specific and correct information (e.g., the ordering doctor's name) in order to prevent this direct loss of revenue. Because of the high cost of error, it was important that this department be well managed. The current supervisor had high expertise in this function, which could be utilized throughout the region. By separating billing from customer service, this supervisor could focus externally on the reduction of error rates throughout the specimen collection centres in various locations.

Based on the above observations, Jean developed a new structure that reduced the number of supervisory positions by five (see Exhibit 3). Working closely with Helen Hoi, the head office director of human resources, Jean now had to evaluate the current supervisors. Helen had previously been a manager at Medictest Sarnia and had worked with these supervisors several years ago.

The best candidates had to be chosen for these new positions. Jean would need leaders who would be willing and able to move forward with twice as many staff members as before. Because of the closeness of the group, it was difficult to evaluate the supervisors without disclosing any information. After a thorough evaluation of the current supervisors, their skills, assurance, and ability to take on increased responsibility, Jean and Helen developed a list of six supervisors to form the revised leadership team.

**THE NEXT CHALLENGE**

Head office and the medical director agreed to the structural changes. The next challenge Jean faced was the communication of the decisions and the logistics involved in that process. How should the changes be conveyed to the supervisors leaving, to those supervisors staying, and to the staff? Where should the discussions be held? Who should communicate the decisions? In what sequence? What should the physical set-up be? How should head office be involved? There were many questions that would have to be thoroughly addressed before the plan was implemented. Jean wanted to develop a clear, specific plan that would maintain employee morale, enable the operations to continue, maintain self-confidence in those chosen to stay, and redirect those not chosen in such a way that their dignity would be preserved. Jean wondered what reactions to expect from the supervisors and the staff. She wanted to effect the changes within the next month. It was important for this process to be recognized in the future as a natural change effect, instead of a "Black Day."

## NOTES

1. OHIP is a program run by the Ontario government that provides free basic health services to Canadian citizens and landed immigrants living in Ontario.

EXHIBIT 1
*The Values of Medictest*

**QUALITY**
Doing the right things the right way.

**COMPETENCE**
Having the appropriate attitudes and abilities.

**CARING**
Showing genuine concern for others.

**RESPECT FOR THE INDIVIDUAL**
Treating people as individuals, with the same understanding and appreciation we seek for ourselves.

**MUTUAL TRUST AND OPENNESS**
Having confidence enough to rely on others and to be open to new and different people and ideas.

**INTEGRITY**
Being reliable and accountable in word and behaviour.

**TEAMWORK**
Accepting a "hierarchy of roles with equality of persons" willing to work together as "we."

**COMMUNICATION**
Listening is the key.

**BALANCE**
Keeping home and work in perspective, recognizing that one helps the other.

**SIMPLICITY**
Maintaining humility, humour, and a common-sense approach to work and life.

*What is expected of all individuals can be summarized as Competence and Mutual Trust.*

***EXHIBIT 2***
***Current Structure —***
***Sarnia***

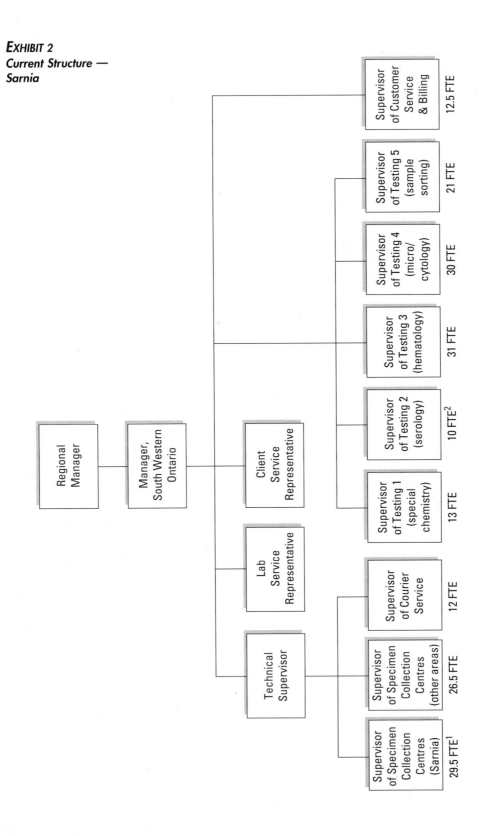

|  |  |
|---|---|
| Regional Manager | |
| Manager, South Western Ontario | |
| Lab Service Representative | |
| Client Service Representative | |
| Technical Supervisor | |
| Supervisor of Specimen Collection Centres (Sarnia) | 29.5 FTE[1] |
| Supervisor of Specimen Collection Centres (other areas) | 26.5 FTE |
| Supervisor of Courier Service | 12 FTE |
| Supervisor of Testing 1 (special chemistry) | 13 FTE |
| Supervisor of Testing 2 (serology) | 10 FTE[2] |
| Supervisor of Testing 3 (hematology) | 31 FTE |
| Supervisor of Testing 4 (micro/cytology) | 30 FTE |
| Supervisor of Testing 5 (sample sorting) | 21 FTE |
| Supervisor of Customer Service & Billing | 12.5 FTE |

1. FTE = full-time equivalent
2. Note: Testing centres 1 and 2 share the same staff

***EXHIBIT 3***
***Proposed Structure —***
***Sarnia***

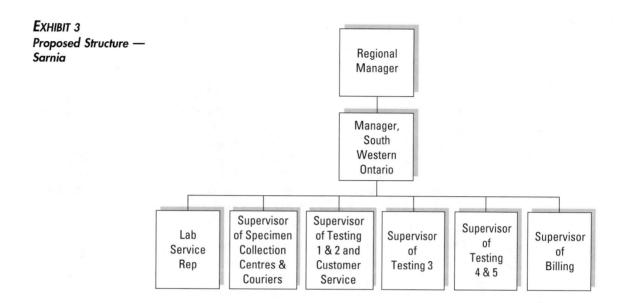

## C A S E 4.10    OTTAWA VALLEY FOOD PRODUCTS

At 2:30 on the afternoon of February 13, R.J. Jennings received a hand delivered note from Karen Russell, a highly respected and well-liked administrative assistant. The note explained that all of the executive assistants in the company had vacated their respective posts in support of Mary Gregory, and were gathered in the employees' lounge. Earlier that day, Jennings had told Gregory that her employment would not be continued at the end of her six-week probationary period because she was unable to handle the duties necessary to be his administrative assistant.

**THE COMPANY**

Ottawa Valley Food Products (OVFP) manufactured and distributed a line of low calorie and diet food products to national grocery chains. The company was located in Arnprior, a small town about 65 km southwest of the nation's capital. OVFP employed 100 production workers and 18 management and support staff.

**R.J. JENNINGS**

Jennings had worked for OVFP for 31 years, beginning as a production line worker at the age of 23. He was ever-respected by his contemporaries for his plant management expertise. Administration at OVFP felt that much of the company's success could be attributed to Jennings's dedication to operating the most efficient production process in the Ottawa Valley.

Jennings's high expectations for all employees were surpassed only by his own personal standards. It was common to find him working at his cluttered desk past 8 p.m., and on weekends.

Although Jennings was eligible for early retirement in one year, he had indicated no desire to exercise that option. When approached by the personnel department on the issue of retirement, Jennings had quipped that he was too busy to retire.

**ELLA ARNOLD**

After 10 years as Jennings's assistant, Ella Arnold had taken early retirement at the beginning of January. Her eyesight had deteriorated and, at 58 years of age, Ella felt she could afford to take life easier. Over the years, Ella and Jennings had become close friends. Ella was willing to work overtime, often without pay, frequently breaking previous personal commitments. In Jennings's opinion, his long-time assistant had a sixth sense for her job. She knew when things were building up for Jennings and would go out of her way to shield him from distractions to his work. Ella often ran errands for Jennings, even on her lunch hours. When Ella retired, the personnel department replaced her with Mary Gregory.

**MARY GREGORY**

Mary started to work as Jennings's assistant on January 16. She had graduated the previous spring with a bachelor's degree in administrative studies from a well-known Canadian university. For the next few months, Mary had travelled extensively throughout Europe and the Far East before returning to her family home in Arnprior to start her job at OVFP. She was 24 years old.

The initial episode in a series of events leading to today's predicament occurred on her first day. About an hour into the morning's work, Jennings called Mary on her interoffice line and asked her to bring him coffee and the morning newspaper on her way back from her break in the staff lounge. This request was a morning routine he had practised for almost 10 years. Mary refused, claiming that she was quite busy. However, Jennings had purposely given Mary a light work load on her first day. Nonetheless, he fetched the coffee and newspaper himself and dismissed the incident as first-day jitters.

The second incident was more disturbing to Jennings. For several months, OVFP had pursued an order from a national chain that did not previously carry OVFP's products. The chain's purchasing agent had requested a meeting with Jennings to discuss production and shipping schedules prior to signing a contract with OVFP.

On the day of the meeting with the purchasing agent, Jennings walked into his office late and found Mary chatting to the agent about her previous weekend's activities. Jennings, surprised to find her in his office and shocked by her chatty attitude toward this important client, bluntly asked Mary to leave the office. Within hearing range of the purchasing agent, Mary not only refused Jennings's request, she elaborated that she had not been drafted into the armed services, finished her anecdotal dissertation to the purchasing agent, and only then left the office, slamming the door behind her.

Jennings was humiliated and sensed the embarrassment of the agent. When the purchasing agent left, Jennings called Mary into his office and demanded an explanation.

Mary simply repeated her earlier comments:

> I wasn't drafted into the army. You're not my drill sergeant. I was having a pleasant conversation with a very friendly client, and you were very rude to ask me to leave like you did. That's all there is to it.

This morning, Mary refused to file the previous day's production reports in a filing cabinet that was inside Jennings's office, far away from her desk. He had called her away from her work, into his office, to ask that she file the reports.

"No bloody way," she snapped and stomped out of his office.

Jennings believed he had worked too long and too hard to achieve his current level of respect, and he was not about to hand over control to a "green" college kid. He was a senior manager at OVFP and he felt that his time was better spent on pressing company problems. Ella Arnold had never refused a request, even on her own time.

**THE NOTE**

Jennings turned his attention to the note he had been handed by Karen Russell. He read it three times before the message hit home. Either he backed down and reversed his decision to release Mary at the end of her probationary period, or all 10 of OVFP's administrative assistants would travel to Ottawa to publicize their grievances on the Canadian Broadcast Corporation's (CBC) six o'clock newscast. The producer of the evening news had promised to air the women's complaint if it was not resolved by show time.

It was now 2:40 p.m. The women had threatened to leave the lounge for the trip to Ottawa by 3 o'clock. Jennings had less than 20 minutes to take action, if he felt action was necessary.

# C A S E 4.11 ROYAL HARDWARE

John Kurtis, president and majority shareholder of Royal Hardware Company Limited, decided it was time for action. His company was in the midst of an internal reorganization, but Ernie Lamb, one of his oldest friends, was thwarting the success of the transition. Every day, John received more complaints about Ernie's lack of cooperation.

**THE COMPANY**

Royal Hardware was located in Hartsville, 80 km from a major industrial and commercial centre. The company manufactured and distributed doorknobs, shelving, miscellaneous hardware products, and gaskets for industrial use. Royal also distributed a line of small consumer appliances.

Industrial and wholesale buyers could choose from 520 hardware items, some with up to 10 colour and material variations. Royal was widely known in the industry for its custom work. The company could copy any competitor's product or manufacture any product to a customer's specifications. John Kurtis summarized Royal's production strategy:

> We will produce anything, in any amount, as long as we have an order for it.

**GROWTH AND STRATEGIC PLANNING ISSUES**

Royal's hardware line had grown vigorously in the past decade; however, it was not expected to grow as rapidly in the future. Trends in the industry indicated that cost cutting and price competition would become greater factors in the home and industrial hardware markets.

To date at Royal Hardware,, there were many inefficiencies. Salespeople sometimes brought in orders for delivery of discontinued lines. Inventories became obsolete. In the past year, $192,000 of inventory had to be written off. Production workers often complained of poor quality parts, which led to constant adjustments of assembly tasks. Because of scheduling problems, parts for orders were often not available, and work-in-process inventories built to very high levels. Employees consumed too much time searching for parts.

Royal produced and assembled most of its own parts. Its competitors were dependent on separate suppliers for unassembled parts. Recently, and consistent with prevailing trends to Just In Time (JIT) inventories, Royal's competitors had begun to carry smaller amounts of raw materials and work-in-process inventories, sometimes holding only an hour's worth of materials on hand.

Mr. Kurtis believed it was crucial for Royal to reorganize, to develop better operating information and systems, and to institute better controls over inventories. He appointed Stan Burns to the production supervisor's role and gave him the task of developing a production system for Royal. He hired Will Hilton to develop a materials requisition system. Kurtis asked Ernie Lamb to help coordinate the various activities required for the reorganization.

## PERSONNEL

In the Hartsville plant and head office, Royal employed 72 people. Fifty-seven were hourly-rated production workers, eight were salaried office staff, and seven were members of the management team. On the shop floor, 41 people were employed in the control of inventory, shipping, receiving, stamping, degreasing, plating, and painting. Sixteen people were employed on design, component manufacturing, and assembly.

The average age of the workers was 44 and there was a four-to-one ratio of women to men in the plant. Key plant jobs were held by senior employees. There were no back-up personnel to replace them if they left or if they were absent.

In general, worker management relations were satisfactory. Royal had very low absenteeism (and turnover), which employees attributed to an "acceptable" wage, the infrequency of layoffs in the plant, and the fact that jobs were neither too difficult nor too demanding. Employees attributed high morale to the fact that the union had recently agreed on a new contract with higher wages, wages that were slightly above the standards of other Hartsville plants. As well, they felt that purchase of new equipment had made some jobs easier, and the recent hiring of more women increased the seniority and security of many workers.

Stan Burns believed that the workers, especially the older ones, felt that there was no reason to do above-average work, since there was no pay or other incentive for doing so. Management wanted to develop an incentive program, but one could not be introduced until proper work standards had been established. At one time, management did try to introduce a piece-work plan, but the labourers rejected the offer due, primarily, to an inadequate inventory system that caused them to spend excessive amounts of time searching for parts.

## REORGANIZATION ISSUES

Will Hilton summarized his frustrations:

> Ernie says he is always too busy in the plant (where Stan is supposed to be in control) to help me out. This is the same story everyone else gets. Most of the production workers still go to Ernie for advice and help. Old customers keep asking for Ernie, and that doesn't help either.

Previously, Ernie Lamb had been responsible for inventory, production, scheduling, and shipping, as well as general plant upkeep. Overall, Lamb was to make sure that the plant could produce what was demanded by the sales force and to get the products out to meet delivery deadlines. With reorganization, two new positions — scheduling and controlling — were created, and the old position of plant supervisor was eliminated. Instead, there was now a production supervisor, Stan Burns. The scheduling and control functions were given to Will Hilton and Keith Holland, respectively.

Lamb was assigned the task of comparing theoretical standards against actual labour standards and making appropriate recommendations to Ned Learner, the costing coordinator. As well, Lamb was asked to work with designer Stew Morris and Ned Learner in developing accurate material lists for costing purposes, to work with Keith Holland and Will Hilton to develop a requisition system for purchasing, and to be available to Stan in an advisery capacity related to production problems.

Ernie had not been carrying out these tasks. He acknowledged the extent of the problems associated with reorganization; however, he said:

> I can't see the relevance of these jobs they want me to do. I'm a people person, not a paper person.

About Stan Burns, Ernie said:

> What's the use of going to Stan when he doesn't have the answers? Stan will have to learn it the same way I learned it ... he will have to make his own decisions.

About his lack of attention to his new tasks:

> I can't concentrate on my new job since daily problems take up too much time.

Ernie's lack of cooperation had divided the plant into two factions. An older worker summed up the sentiments of the more senior workers:

> Stan's been trying hard to get things running the way he thinks they should, by using all his new ideas, but Ernie's the only one here who knows how this place really works. We make this place run and Ernie knows that.

Another employee summarized the feelings of the younger labourers:

> It's good at last to have someone at the controls who's got some new ideas in his head. You've got to change with the times — Stan can, but Ernie's been here too long.

**THE DILEMMA**   Management agreed that Royal's systems problems needed to be addressed. But, before the bigger issues could be solved, John Kurtis had to do something about Ernie Lamb. Ernie had indicated an interest in retiring within two years, but there had been questions raised about his value to the company if his behaviour continued to hinder the reorganization.

*EXHIBIT 1*

---

### Management Personnel Data

---

**STAN BURNS**

---

| | |
|---|---|
| Position: | Production Supervisor |
| Age: | 43 |
| Years with company: | 1 |
| Background: | Design and metal works foreman |
| Responsibilities: | Maintain and improve production, handle personnel function for plant |
| Education: | Engineering diploma from U.K. |

---

**WILL HILTON**

---

| | |
|---|---|
| Position: | Production Coordinator (Scheduling) |
| Age: | 37 |
| Years with company: | 2 |
| Background: | Production planning supervisor in clothing industry |
| Responsibilities: | Scheduling, inventory control, purchasing for some parts |
| Education: | Grade 12 and production planning courses |

---

**KEITH HOLLAND**

---

| | |
|---|---|
| Position: | Controller |
| Age: | 34 |
| Years with company: | 1.5 |
| Background: | Sales management and office administration in drug industry |
| Responsibilities: | Office management, development and operation of control systems |
| Education: | Attended university for three and a half years, Certified Management Accountant |

---

*EXHIBIT 1 (cont'd)*

---

### NED LEARNER

| | |
|---|---|
| Position: | Costing Coordinator |
| Age: | 47 |
| Years with company: | 21 |
| Responsibilities: | Costing and standards development, maintaining and updating material and labour standards, costing and production |
| Education: | Grade 12 |

---

### ERNIE LAMB

| | |
|---|---|
| Position | Plant Manager |
| Age: | 68 |
| Years with company: | 40 |
| Background: | Worked his way up through the plant |
| Responsibilities: | Developing purchasing controls, pricing, updating standards, establishing information flows |
| Education: | Grade 10 |

---

### GORD PULDING

| | |
|---|---|
| Position: | Vice-President and Sales Manager |
| Age: | 69 |
| Years with company: | 31 |
| Background: | Selling and administration |
| Responsibilities: | Development and sales territories, account administration, sales force management, pricing |
| Education: | Attended university for three years |

---

### JOHN KURTIS

| | |
|---|---|
| Position: | President and majority shareholder |
| Age: | 53 |
| Years with company: | 31 |
| Background: | Commissioned officer in the RCAF, purchasing of some parts, personnel administration, public relations |

# PART

# AN INTRODUCTION TO MARKETING MANAGEMENT

The crux of marketing has never changed. A good marketer sets out to give the customer what he or she wants or needs. However, the pace of product changes, competitive reactions, and governmental impacts have accelerated significantly in the last 10 years. No longer can we launch a new product and hope to stand alone for 18 months. Competition can copy and often better the product quickly, and then possibly produce it off-shore at a better price. The marketing arena has "upped the ante" for advertising, promotion, and personal selling, requiring large sums of money to be wagered on any new product or new positioning stance. Because the stakes have never been higher, the importance of a good market analysis and a thorough marketing plan is crucial. The new global playing field offers problems and opportunities that did not exist prior to this time. Knowing the consumers and competition in these other markets will be critical to any success in the marketplace.

Not-for-profit businesses have also caught on to marketing lessons and are applying them to hospitals, social work agencies, and government departments. A thorough evaluation of relevant marketing factors, with or without a profit objective, has improved the operations of many not-for-profit establishments.

*JUST WHAT IS A MARKETING ANALYSIS*

*AND*

*WHAT IS A MARKETING PLAN?*

These terms are simple in theory, but comprehensive, complex, and multifaceted in their implementation.

*The marketing analysis* investigates the consumer, trade, competition, corporate capabilities, research, and external factors that must be examined in making good decisions.

*The marketing plan or marketing program* describes the:

- Product or service to be introduced or revitalized
- Price that should be set
- Distribution channels to be used
- Promotion that will be presented

This textbook provides many good examples of actual marketing case scenarios that require an in-depth analysis before alternatives can be weighed and reasonable decisions made and implemented. A skeletal outline of this process might look like this:

ROLE

ISSUES

OBJECTIVES

MARKETING ANALYSIS

- Consumer
- Trade
- Competition
- Corporate capabilities
- Research
- STEP analysis (social, technological, economic, political)

ALTERNATIVES

DECISION/PLAN OF ACTION

- Product
- Price
- Distribution
- Promotion

MONITORING PLAN

Let us examine each of these pieces of the process in more depth. It is important to state your role as vice-president marketing or owner/manager, and so on, so that you can examine any constraints or considerations, such as time or money, that may have an impact on your analysis and/or decision. A clear statement of issues, in order of priority, will ensure that you do not get off track during the analysis and that you address all the major problems with your alternatives and decision/plan of action. It would be wise to highlight any corporate objectives that are set out (e.g., capture 15 percent share of the market, have a minimum 12 percent return on investment, or find a good Big Brothers match for 200 boys this year), as most people perform better when they have certain specific objectives that they should meet. If there are no corporate objectives, it is advisable to note that the standard for assessing the feasibility of the potential alternatives might be difficult to establish. Any personal objectives of the person in the role should also be noted early, as they may have some impact on the weighting of the alternatives and ultimate decision. For example, if the owner is known to be a risk-taker, that should be factored in when evaluating the advantages and disadvantages of each alternative marketing plan.

Once the stage has been set, the marketing analysis may now begin.

## MARKETING ANALYSIS

**SECTION**

**ONE**

### *CONSUMER ANALYSIS AND TRADE ANALYSIS*

Understanding the consumer[1] is the most important task of a good marketer. If you know nothing about how a consumer buys or might buy your product, then you have substantially reduced your chance of success. You are depending on luck in simply hoping that a segment of the population will be interested enough in your product to buy it. Luck is an important ingredient of success, but it should not be asked to work on its own.

The consumer analysis should address six areas:

- *Who* are the existing and potential customers of your product or service?
- *What* do these consumers want from the product or service?
- *How* do they make their purchasing decisions?
- *Where* do they go to shop for the product or service?
- *When* do they shop?
- *Why* do they behave as they do?

The results of these questions will probably separate the different consumers into distinct groups or segments, based upon major differences in the way they purchase and the types of purchases they make.

Examination of these segments will fall into six categories, as outlined in Table 1.

From this examination, ideal marketing plans for each segment can be developed. Note that these plans take into account what we know about the consumers, but they are not our finished plans as we have not taken into account the

*TABLE 1*

| Consumer Analysis | | | |
|---|---|---|---|
| | Segment 1 (Size) | Segment 2 (Size) | Segment 3 (Size) |
| Who | | | |
| What | | | |
| How | | | |
| When | | | |
| Where | | | |
| Why | | | |

| Implications from the Consumer Analysis | Ideal Mktg Plan 1 | Ideal Mktg Plan 2 | Ideal Mktg Plan 3 |
|---|---|---|---|
| Product/Service | | | |
| Price | | | |
| Distribution | | | |
| Promotion | | | |

implications of trade, competition, corporate capabilities, research, and STEP analysis. Notice, again, that if you do not have good consumer information, your plan will be based on your own experience, hunches, and educational guesses. These components, while important, should be used in tandem with good information from research (done either internally or externally), examination of prior years' experiences, and future trends in the relevant industry.

## Who

In Canada and the United States, almost all products and services are purchased in a different way or for different reasons by different consumer segments. These segments used to be described solely demographically according to age, sex, income, or location. Today's consumer groups are more often separated by socio-economic factors such as lifestyles, values, occupations, etc. For example, "baby boomers"[2] have become "yuppies,"[3] who are evolving into "woofs."[4] "Generation X"[5] has given researchers a whole new segment to research and study in depth to understand its buying patterns and help companies to use these results. It is important, from a marketing sense, to describe the relevant market segment so that you can actually "see" them and have enough information (size, location, lifestyle, etc.) to be able to reach them through the appropriate media. You must also calculate what percentage of them you will need to convince to buy the product or service so that the corporate objectives may be reached. It is essential to recognize that most products or services will not suit all segments of consumers. Often, it is critical to define the market segments, analyze them, and then pick a target market that best suits the company's product and skills.

We must also be aware that the person who actually pays for the product is sometimes not the most important "consumer." Anyone who has wandered down the cereal aisle of a grocery store with a six-year-old has experienced the "influence" factor. The adult may end up purchasing chocolate-flavoured marshmallows when he or she had intended to buy Corn Flakes or Shredded Wheat. Attention to possible influence segments has proved to be important for many companies. Even more have encountered failures at the cash register due to a lack of analysis in this area. Over 60 percent of car purchases are now decided upon by women. This fact has automobile companies designing cars, features, and promotion for these women and their natural segments. According to the Bureau of Labour Statistics, single working fathers are one of the fastest growing segments in the U.S. workforce, increasing to more than one million in 1992. There are products and services that this group needs and to whom it will be worth marketing. An appropriate outcome of the "Who" category analysis should be a good description of each significant segment and its size. Implications for the future marketing plan may then be drawn.

### What

What the consumer wants when he or she purchases a particular product or service results in some interesting discoveries. We all probably feel that we are quite rational shoppers, but when we examine what we have bought in the last week, we see that it is more complex than toothpaste to prevent cavities, clothes to keep us warm, and a car to transport us from point A to point B. We are, in fact, purchasing a "package of benefits" that may include such things as sex appeal, status, image, etc. The "Grunge look"[6] is not only comfortable but lends a particular "I don't care" image that many young people want to project. People often define themselves, or are defined by others, according to the type of clothes, cars, or houses that they own. The functional importance of many products and services is not always the crucial factor in the "package of benefits" that a consumer purchases. Identifying these "benefits" is critical to a good consumer analysis.

## Where

Where do existing or potential consumers want to go to buy a particular product or service? This is an important piece of analysis for retail businesses and restaurants. Retailers will tell you that there are three important factors in retailing: *location, location, location*. Malls can often command a much higher rent than a free standing building in a poor area of the city because the mall brings traffic, traffic, and more traffic.

It is no accident that the major fast food chains have sprung up around each other. Their site selection analysis has shown that it is worthwhile to be stationed among their competition. Other factors, such as proximity to major highways or waterways for shipping, residential closeness for convenience stores, or a store that "fits" the product's image, may all be key ingredients, depending upon the needs or perceived needs of the consumer segment.

Putting the right product in the wrong location could result in the marketing failure of a perfectly good product. For example, people who purchase Paris originals do not want to see their clothes in K mart. A new hybrid concept has, however, captured a growing percentage of the U.S. and Canadian market. People who wish to pay less for their clothes, home accessories, furniture, etc., but still want high quality products, are flocking to the highly successful upscale discount malls. "Big box" retailers are taking a higher and higher percentage of our purchases. Some examples of these "big box" retailers include Wal-Mart, Home Depot, Winners, the Price Club, and many more to follow. They offer value, a wide variety of products and, in some, superior service. They are often located on the city's perimeter for cheaper building costs, and large parking opportunities.

## When

When is it that potential or existing consumer segments purchase the product or service? Daily? Weekly? Monthly? Yearly? Seasonally? In the morning, afternoon, or evening? Holidays? For instance, it has been found that fast food restaurants take in 75 percent of their income between 11:00 a.m. and 3:00 p.m.

Sunday shopping has changed the buying behaviour of many of us. Individual businesses, however, are now examining how well it suits their customers and, ultimately, their profits.

The customer life cycle stages are also important to consider. The traditional marriage cycle from engagement ring to retirement home has drastically changed to a current cycle that leads from engagement ring→ first home or apartment→ children→ divorce→ "blended"[7] family→ new home→ retirement condominium. Each of these stages and numerous variations brings new and different needs that the smart marketer will identify and incorporate into his or her plans. Companies also have different stages of growth, retrenchment, or downsizing that affect their purchasing behaviour. Occasionally, special discounts and bargains can entice consumers to buy when they would not normally do so, but this is unusual. Marketers had better adapt to the consumer's wants, needs, and desires if they want to be successful.

## How

How do consumers choose the products and services that they purchase? There are myriad devious and hidden, conscious and subconscious factors at work during the buying process of many purchases. Consumers go through various stages during this process, including:

- Awareness of the product or service
- Knowledge of the product's or service's characteristics
- Favourable attitude toward the product or service
- Purchase
- Post-purchase (often reinforcement) experience and feelings
- Repeat purchase

It is not mandatory that consumers go through all these steps or that they go through them at the same speed. It is important, for marketing purposes, that relevant steps be identified so that the appropriate promotion package highlighting the key points can be designed. For instance, some companies use billboards with catchy slogans to arouse interest in the product even before it is brought to market. For example, billboards used sequentially over four months, that read:

**FIGURE 1**

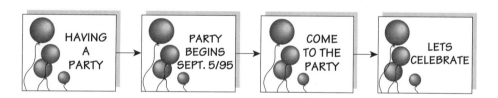

were used for a new mall. No one knew what was coming and what this party was to be became a popular topic of conversation. Awareness and interest were the key points. After the mall opened, a new promotion targeted to induce shopping and continue shopping was employed.

It is also important to determine whether each consumer segment might prefer to shop by cash, credit card, layaway, instalments, or cash debit cards. Clearly, these considerations will change according to the cost of the product or service and the type of consumer segment. It is necessary to note, however, that anomalies do exist. For instance, while students' yearly income is usually low, they do have a large portion of their disposable income available for their own personal use. Hence, the popularity of expensive designer shirts and jeans and the proliferation of leather jackets among university students.

## Why

Why do consumers purchase the products and services that they do? This is another multifaceted area for consideration.

People are driven by:

- Price
- Quality
- Salesperson advice and assistance
- Style and design
- Image that the product or service gives to them
- Other people's opinions, often word-of-mouth
- Advertising
- Warranty and service, etc.
- A variety of other factors

Some purchases are planned, whereas others are impulse-generated. Consider the major factors that caused you to buy your last pair of shoes, shirt, appliances, haircut, and bicycle. Did you progress through the buying stages? What were the key factors influencing your ultimate choice of product or service? Notice that your answers will change for each product and that the features attracting people will differ from person to person. It is critical for the company to design and promote its products or services in ways that fill the target consumers' priorities.

## TRADE ANALYSIS

Consumers often do not purchase their products directly from the manufacturer. There is usually some kind of chain that may include a middleman (a wholesaler and/or distributor manufacturer's agent) and/or a retailer.

**FIGURE 2**

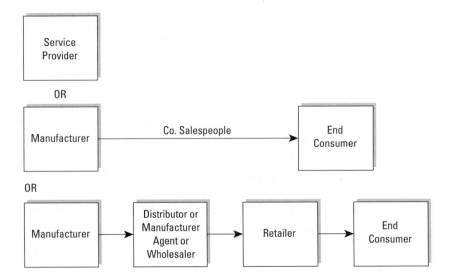

The needs and concerns of these middle people must be attended to or the product may never make it to the end consumer. Distributors and retailers are often concerned with the reputation of the product, the size of their margins, supportive corporate advertising, depth of product line, and other factors. These "middle" consumers are just as important to satisfy as the end consumer and must not be neglected in the marketing analysis.

## SUMMARY

In summary, the consumer and trade analysis are critical starting points for all marketing analyses. A product that is designed, positioned, priced, and promoted to suit a specific target market will be on the path to success. Only a thorough analysis of the consumer and trade groups or great luck will assure this. The pieces of the consumer analysis connect up with the marketing plan in the following manner:

***FIGURE 3***

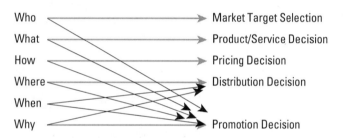

## COMPETITION

A realistic understanding of the competition's strengths and weaknesses is a critical aspect of a good marketing analysis. Too often we believe so strongly in our product's superior characteristics that we downplay the qualities and significance of the competition's strategies. We must ask ourselves:

1. Who is or might be the competition?
   - direct
   - indirect
2. How effective is their marketing plan?
   - product
   - price
   - distribution
   - promotions

3. Can and will they react to our new or revised entry into the marketplace?

4. What will their reaction be? A drop in price, increased advertising and promotion, increased incentives to wholesalers, or nothing?

Too often we ignore the importance of an established reputation and existing distribution. Most new products fail, often due to a lack of attention to the competition. Healthy respect for and attention to the competition are essential to a successful marketing plan that will "position" itself well within the marketplace with utmost consideration of its competitors' plans.

One way of characterizing competition in product/service categories is the *product life cycle*. It refers to the pattern that all products/services seem to follow at varying speed from birth (introduction), through adolescence (growth) and adulthood (maturity), to death (decline and withdrawal). In general, the concept is diagrammed as follows:

*FIGURE 4*

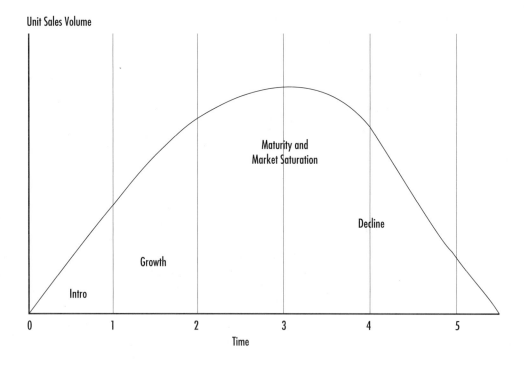

This curve can be designed for any product, service, product line, or even a product category. It varies in shape according to the product type. For example, the product life cycle of a fad such as "Earth Buddies" would be steep, whereas a mature product line such as aircraft would be stretched out along the top.

This concept is useful in many respects. The overall shape gives us clues to an approximate time horizon for the product or service. For example, a short product life cycle means we must recoup and exceed our investment in a short

*FIGURE 5*

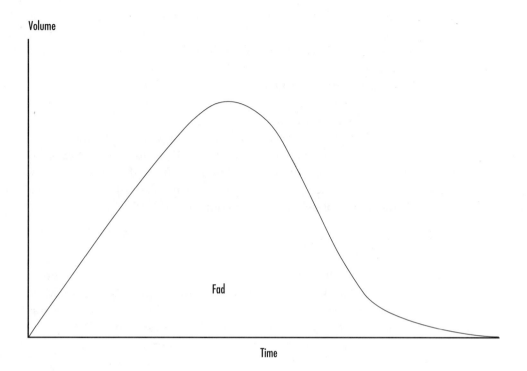

Fad

*FIGURE 6*

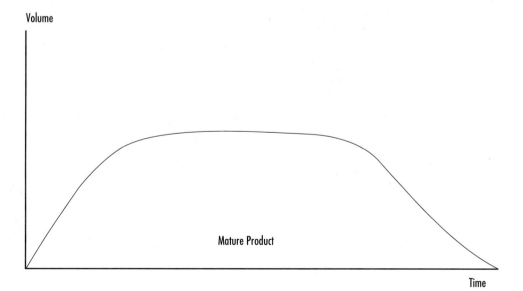

Mature Product

time period. This often results in high initial prices and more aggressive marketing. Fashion and fad products are an example of this. Trendy clothing, such as plaids, will have a short life cycle. Other products are often more difficult to predict. For example, will roller blades have the short life cycle of a fad or will they enter the longer, more traditional realm of rollerskates, bicycles, skis, skates, and even skateboards. It is much easier to examine a product's life cycle in retrospect than it is to predict it.

The process of prediction, however, will draw out some useful implications for pricing, advertising, and other parts of the future marketing plan as well as production/operations and finance. Although we do not have a crystal ball, thoughtful estimates will go a long way in assisting the design of an appropriate marketing plan to baffle our competition.

## CORPORATE CAPABILITIES

The ultimate success of a product or service may not begin and end with the product itself, but rather hinge on the overall strengths and weaknesses of the company. For example, Procter and Gamble may be successful in introducing a new razor with superior cutting ability. A smaller company with less money for advertising, no existing drug store/supermarket distribution, and no established reputation in the razor field may try to introduce the same product and fail miserably. These smaller companies have shown the strongest success in "niche" marketing, where they target a relatively small unserviced segment of the market. If they do it well, they may expand to larger chunks of the market. Computer software companies that design custom programs or programs for particular industries are proving to be highly successful at fulfilling the "needs" of particular smaller segments or niches that are not well served by the larger, more generic types of software.

Often, it is not enough to have a superior product or service. Corporate capabilities in the relevant areas of finance, production/operations, management skills and depth, and existing market reputation may be critical. Major marketing successes have been made by small unknown companies with few corporate strengths, but, given the existence of fierce competition and often unknowledgeable consumers, this proves to be the exception rather than the rule. It is wise to assess the functional strengths and weaknesses of the company that is being analyzed and assess if they "fit" the marketing plan that is developing. If certain requisite strengths are missing, consider what impact that is likely to have on the launch of the product or service. Can the weaknesses be shored up?

Other questions to consider are:

- What supportive resources are needed?
- Are they available?
- Can they be purchased? At what cost?

- Can the existing distribution channel handle the new product?
- Do we need new salespeople? At what cost?
- Do we have the necessary equipment? Management? Reputation? Money? Communication Skills?
- Can we provide the backup service, guarantee, warrantee that the consumer wants/needs?

This sampling of questions is incomplete, but it will start the process of corporate evaluation.

## MARKET RESEARCH

Market research is a vast area of information collection, analysis, and dissemination. Some companies do their own research, while others hire independent market research firms to conduct the necessary studies. For instance, the Leo Burnett ad agency in 1993 found out that for Americans:

- Women and older people are most likely to floss their teeth.
- 80 percent of people between 18 and 34 say they will usually give up their bus or subway seat to an elderly or pregnant passenger.
- 6 percent of men in rural America use nail polish or gloss.
- 15 percent of Americans sleep in the nude.

This may be interesting information for all of us but it will be valuable to only certain companies.

Whatever the approach, certain objectives must be clearly outlined at the start and adhered to throughout or a costly array of unnecessary information may result. These objectives include:

1. What specific information is needed? (i.e., how often do people buy new refrigerators? What factors are most important to them in the buying process?)
2. How will that information be used? (i.e., to design or redesign the features of the refrigerator, to develop the promotion package, etc.)

Paying close attention to these benchmarks should reduce unnecessary time and expense during the research process. Initial research may take the form of telephone surveys, sales reports, trade magazines, government statistics, observation of competitors, or personal interviews. Choices will depend on the type of information that is sought and the budget available. When considering a new product or service, groups of potential consumers are sometimes brought together, introduced to the product or service, and questioned about their interest in it and whether they would purchase or not if it was available. These *focus groups* are less expensive than test marketing the product or service and often give good results on how potential consumers will react to the product, or to design or name changes. They can also offer input into problems they foresee in the distribution or promotion plans.

Some companies may decide to proceed from focus groups to a test market on a small scale introduction before they invest in a costly national or international launch.

Market research, if well done, can enhance the possibility of a market success or save the company a large investment in a product that consumers will not ultimately support. Care must be taken, however, in the type and design of the appropriate research. You must know what it is that you want the research to find out for you, what you will do with the information, and how much it is worth to you in both time and money.

Some common sources of market research include:

1. Experience
   - Examine the competition
   - Study the suppliers in the industry
   - Collect, where available, industry information from trade organizations such as the Milk Marketing Board and the Chamber of Commerce in your area

2. Secondary material. Look in the library for:
   - *Statistics Canada* — watch the results as they may or may not directly reflect your size, type of company within the general, average industry statistics that are collected
   - Industry statistics — often collected and expanded upon by trade magazines and other interested parties (e.g., marketing research companies that specialize in certain areas such as restaurants, computers, etc.)
   - Periodical articles (e.g., the *Business Quarterly, Harvard Business Review,* etc.)

3. Surveys. Be careful here as to of whom, how, and where the questions are asked. A survey is only as good as its design, implementation, and interpretation. For example:
   - The Personal Interview. The interviewer may influence the respondent by how he or she asks the question and, possibly, the respondent's desire to help/please the interviewer.
   - A Mail Survey. Accuracy is increased due to the time and thought that the respondent can take. Unfortunately, it usually has the lowest response rate (often about 2 percent of those contacted).
   - A Phone Survey. Offers the opportunity for a large variety among people sampled. However, there is a growing trend that people do not wish to be invaded by this type of questioning, especially at dinner time!

The area of market research is vast and growing rapidly. We have only opened the door to some ways and means in this introduction.

## STEP ANALYSIS

The STEP analysis is completely external to the company and its products or services. It involves the examination of the noncontrollable: social, technological, economic, and political issues that may have an impact on the viability of the specific product or service under analysis.

### Social

The social patterns in North America will continue to change in the next decade. Some of these factors include:

- an increasing divorce rate and, therefore, more single parent units;
- reduced frequency of smoking and continued fitness involvement;
- AIDS, and its impact on sex education and advertising; and
- further "cocooning" of the "yuppie" generation, as they become more centred on their own families and basic values.

The International Mass Retail Association has a message for store operators, "Wake up and smell the Geritol!" Age Wave Inc., a San Francisco market research firm, found that majorities of older consumers spend money on themselves, make impulse purchases, prefer established brands over generic goods, and spend extra for quality merchandise. Safety is still an unbelievable issue to seniors and those approaching that designation.

It is important that marketers identify the relevant social trends and whether they offer opportunities or problems for their plans.

### Technological

The product life cycle may need to be adjusted as the speed of technological changes accelerates. Home computers may become as common as televisions or telephones as they become cheaper and more user friendly. The Internet may connect us all through electronic mail and expose increased amounts of information to those who choose to access it. Many similar products will be introduced and die before their time as they are replaced by more advanced technological competitors. Large investments in research and development will be needed to stay in the forefront. Some companies will choose to lag behind a little and copy the pioneers. Marketers must examine their own products and services to see if technology will have a positive or negative effect on them in the marketplace.

### Economic

The recession of the late 1980s and the one of the early 1990s have had a drastic effect on retailing, housing, travel, and much more. Products and services that thrived during healthy economic periods may be ruined with a downturn. Other products and services, such as used car sales, are more active during tough times. Exposure to shifts in the economy should be identified by the marketer. None of us can accurately predict the future, but flexibility to adapt to changes in the economy is critical to success. Some experts are predicting another recession for the late 1990s and the possibility of entire countries going bankrupt. Each industry would be affected differently by such changes, particularly as we become a more global economy.

### Political

Political problems and opportunities should always be considered as they relate to the product or service being analyzed. Laws regarding labelling, truth in advertising, price controls, interest rates, etc., may have an impact on the product a marketer is examining. The Surgeon General's warning about cigarettes and the restrictions on their advertising have had a dramatic effect on sales of cigarettes in the United States and Canada. In Europe and Third World countries that do not have the same political intervention, sales of cigarettes are booming. Will they follow the North American trends? If so, what should the tobacco companies do to survive?

### Summary

It is important to emphasize that although the marketer has little or no control over these STEP factors, he or she must understand and be able to adapt to them. Early analysis in this area will often enable the successful marketer to proact rather than react to major trends and changes.

**SECTION**

**TWO**

## MARKETING PLANS

When the market analysis and a study of its implications are completed, it is useful to re-examine the original issues and objectives so that relevant marketing plans may be designed. There are often several alternative marketing plans that appear to be appropriate. Each will contain certain product, price, distribution, and promotion strategies and decisions.

The marketing program or plan should contain just the right "mix" to entice the consumer to buy. It should be consistent with the results from the consumer, trade, competition, corporate capabilities, market research, and STEP analyses.

## PRODUCT POLICY DECISIONS

The consumer and competition analyses should help to define the final product or service. Its "package of benefits" will offer what the consumer is looking for from the product/service. Some considerations will include the depth and breadth of the product line. For example, how many styles, sizes, colours, and types of food should a restaurant's menu contain?

In a highly developed country with a proliferation of products and services available to the population, nonfunctional aspects of the product, such as packaging, shape, and design are important. For example, the colour, labelling, shape, and style of perfume containers, shampoo bottles, and beer bottles have contributed greatly to the products' success or failure in the marketplace. Currently, environmental concerns have focused attention on the ability of the product and its packaging to be recycled and/or to biodegrade. Future trends will probably lean toward less packaging, and product differentiation may revert to the features of the product itself.

Emphasis, again, should be on what benefits, functional and psychosocial, that the consumer wants in the design of the final product or service. For example, in Japan, some childcare facilities are expanding their hours of operation to 24 hours a day to accommodate the long working hours of their consumers.

## Pricing Decisions

It is in the area of pricing that break-even and profit objectives may be examined and variations evaluated. With some products or services a high price (low volume) skimming strategy is appropriate. In other instances, a low price market penetration will result in many people (high volume) buying at a cheap price. The easiest, most flexible calculation to use during this evaluation is a break-even calculation:

$$\text{Break-even volume (in units)} = \frac{\$ \text{ Fixed Costs}}{\$ \text{ Unit Contribution}}$$

$$\$\text{Unit Contribution} = \$ \text{ Selling Price per unit} - \$ \text{ Variable Cost per unit}$$

or

$$\text{Break-even volume (in sales dollars)} = \frac{\$ \text{ Fixed costs}}{\% \text{ margin made on each sale}}$$

To translate the break-even sales dollars to units needed to break even, divide the sales dollars by the selling price of one unit:

$$\frac{\text{Sales \$ volume to break even}}{\text{Selling price per unit}} = \text{units needed to break even}$$

Break-even volume will show what number of units or dollar sales it will be necessary to achieve so that no profit or loss is made.

Suppose a company has designed a new line of sweatshirts and the marketing person is considering two pricing options:

## Option 1

Under option 1 the sweatshirts will sell for $40. The cost to produce the sweatshirt is $15 for labour and materials and $2.50 for delivery. Fixed overhead for the factory is $10,000 per annum. Administrative and office expenses are $20,000 per year. Commission to the company sales people is 10 percent of selling price per shirt. Salaries will be $50,000 per year. Projected advertising for the first year is $30,000. Is the company likely to see a profit in the first year of selling its new sweatshirts? The break-even calculation would necessitate that costs be separated into fixed (those that do not vary directly with the sales volume) and variable (those that occur as each unit is made and/or sold).

Therefore, total fixed costs, in this example, include:

| $ 10,000 | fixed overhead |
| $ 20,000 | administrative and office expenses |
| $ 50,000 | salaries |
| $ 30,000 | advertising |
| $110,000 | Total Fixed Costs |

Variable costs include:

| $15.00 | labour and materials |
| $ 2.50 | delivery |
| $ 4.00 | sales commission (10 percent of selling price) |
| $21.50 | Total Variable Costs |

Therefore, unit contribution is:

Selling price − Variable cost

i.e., $40 − $21.50 = $18.50 per unit

Therefore, break-even volume in units is:

$$\text{B/E} = \frac{\$110,000}{\$18.50/\text{unit}}$$

$$= 5,946 \text{ units}$$

Thus, the company will have to sell 5,946 sweatshirts in the first year to break even. If they wanted to make a $30,000 profit, then 7,568 sweatshirts would have to be sold ($110,000 + $30,000 ÷ $18.50).

## Option 2

What if the company decided to sell the sweatshirts for $50 each? A quick new calculation would show that only 3,860 ($110,000 ÷ $28.50) sweatshirts would have to be sold to ensure break-even and 4,913 sweatshirts ($140,000 ÷ $28.50) to make the required $30,000 in profit. It would seem, at first glance, that the $50 price is more feasible, but other considerations need to be examined. For example:

- What are similar competitive sweatshirts selling for at this time?
- How price sensitive are the consumers?
- Would a $35 selling price result in substantially more volume?
- What percentage of the total sweatshirt market does each of these options represent if the market is 100,000 sweatshirts?
- What percentage of the relevant (i.e., mid-price) sweatshirt market does each of these options represent, if the mid-price sweatshirt market is 50,000 sweatshirts?
- Can any of the other costs be changed with higher volume, subcontracting, new machines, etc.

It is not difficult to make the numbers "work" for any plan, but that is not the objective. Numbers that make sense and are consistent with the analysis are the appropriate ones to use.

There are numerous other costs for manufacturing, distributing, and promotion that will occur in various marketing situations and the marketing cases to follow. If there is a chain of manufacturer, wholesaler, distributor, retailer to end consumer you must ensure that all the appropriate margins or markups are calculated and that the relevant selling price is used for the company under analysis. A margin refers to the difference between cost price per unit and selling price per unit. Some people like to express margin as a percentage of selling price and others as a percentage of cost. For example, suppose an item cost the seller $1 and it sold for $2:

$$\text{Margin as a percentage of selling price } = \frac{\$2-1}{\$2} \times 100 = 50\%$$

$$\text{Margin as a percentage of cost (markup) } = \frac{\$2-\$1}{\$1} \times 100 = 100\%$$

Look to see if the method is specified in each circumstance. When it is unspecified, we suggest you use the margin-as-a-percentage-of-selling-price method. Markdown is usually expressed as a percentage of selling price. For example, if our sweatshirt were marked down to $36, it would be a 10 percent markdown in price:

$$\frac{\$40-36}{\$40} \times 100 = 10\%$$

Follow the margin descriptions closely in each case, remain flexible, and always state your assumptions.

It is evident that there are many possible variables to explore. Choose the ones that seem most appropriate and are consistent with the consumer and competitive analyses. Look for:

- the number of units or sales dollars necessary to break even
- the number of units or sales dollars necessary to achieve the corporate profit objective
- the percentage that each of these is of the total market for the product or service
- the percentage that each of these is of the relevant market segment for the product or service
- the percentage of production capacity that each of these will require

The ultimate price that is chosen should take into account the consumer's needs, competitive reaction, and overall financial feasibility given the size of the relevant market and the competition within it.

## DISTRIBUTION DECISIONS

Decisions regarding distribution are made at the outset, and thereafter infrequently changed. Promotion and pricing decisions are made and changed often, but the first distribution decision usually needs to be the right one as changes are difficult to manoeuvre and costly to implement. Each manufacturer needs to decide how to get its product to the end consumer. Often, there are middle people who take on services for their clients. These services may include:

- holding inventory
- delivering
- making sales pitches
- invoicing and billing

Often, distributors carry many noncompeting lines that are in the same industry. For instance, a sporting goods distributor usually takes on lines of noncompeting sports equipment and accessories, then stores and sells them to the independent sporting goods retailers and chains. Other common distribution channels are shown in Figure 7.

Sometimes the distribution is already determined. For instance, in Ontario, all beer and liquor, with a few exceptions, must be sold through government retail outlets, although this distribution may change under Mike Harris's government. Usually, however, there are a variety of options to consider that involve issues such as:

- Who performs what tasks (e.g., stocks the retail shelves, does warranty work)?
- Who bears what costs (e.g., has to hold the inventory)?

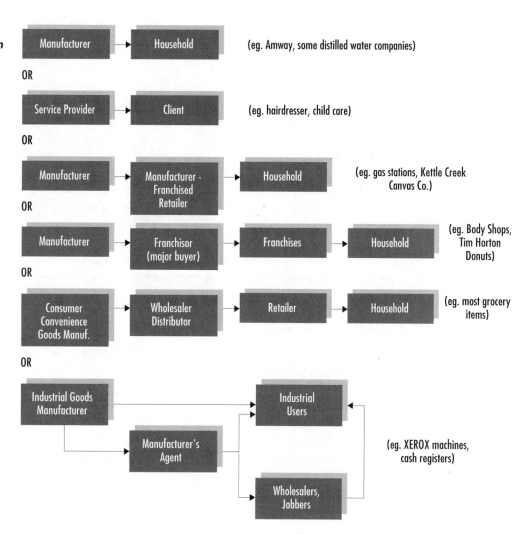

**FIGURE 7**
*Distribution Channels*

Manufacturer → Household    (eg. Amway, some distilled water companies)

OR

Service Provider → Client    (eg. hairdresser, child care)

OR

Manufacturer → Manufacturer - Franchised Retailer → Household    (eg. gas stations, Kettle Creek Canvas Co.)

OR

Manufacturer → Franchisor (major buyer) → Franchises → Household    (eg. Body Shops, Tim Horton Donuts)

OR

Consumer Convenience Goods Manuf. → Wholesaler Distributor → Retailer → Household    (eg. most grocery items)

OR

Industrial Goods Manufacturer → Industrial Users
Industrial Goods Manufacturer → Manufacturer's Agent → Industrial Users
Manufacturer's Agent → Wholesalers, Jobbers → Industrial Users    (eg. XEROX machines, cash registers)

- Who makes decisions on selling methods, advertising, amount of stock to carry, etc.?
- Who gets what share of the final sales dollar?

  Some relatively new forms of retail distribution include:

- discount, off-price malls
- designer's own stores (e.g., Esprit and Levi's stores)
- electronic shopping
- catalogue shopping

- specialty stores
- strip malls (small, 4 to 10 stores all in a line or "strip")
- hypermarketing[8]
- home shopping network on television

Hypermarketing involves huge stores that offer food and nonfood items at everyday low prices. They cater to the so-called "new collars." These "new collars" are usually young, well-educated people with combined incomes of $25,000 to $50,000. They are semiprofessionals such as paramedics or hygienists as opposed to doctors, etc. They want quality merchandise, but do not want to pay top price for it. This market is growing and there are many retailers now targeting it.

Consumer needs and buying trends will create new forms of distribution and lop off others. Research and/or competitive analysis may help to decide what the original distribution for the product should be. Changes to this channel will seldom occur unless significant advantages are found.

## PROMOTION DECISIONS

Some people equate promotion with advertising, but that definition is too narrow. Promotion includes:

- advertising (newspapers, magazines, billboards, radio, trade journals, television, Internet, infomercials, etc.)
- personal selling (door-to-door, telephone, salesforce)
- sales promotion (coupons, premiums, contests, samples, direct mail, point-of-purchase displays, endorsements, and the wearing of brand name clothes by celebrities)
- packaging

The marketer must decide, based upon results from the consumer, trade, research, competitive, and STEP analyses, what form of promotion will get the desired results of awareness, interest, knowledge, purchase, or repeat purchase. Occasionally, the government may decide to restrict certain advertising. For instance, 10 years ago, cigarettes were advertised on television! Currently, some consumer groups are trying to "persuade" newspapers and magazines not to carry cigarette advertising at all. Beer and liquor advertising is already restricted and may become more so in the future. Overall, the marketer must decide:

- What media (TV, radio, magazine, billboard, videos, etc.)?
- What message (i.e., what are the most important factors to communicate? Price, location, brand, hours, etc.)?
- What frequency (repetitive, seasonal, annual, etc.)?

- How much money should be spent (budget)?
- How will the results of the communications campaign be evaluated (effectiveness)?

If these questions cannot be positively answered, then a great amount of money may be wasted. More and more money is being spent by businesses on various forms of promotion. The effectiveness of each piece is often difficult to determine. Successful marketers will, however, attempt to evaluate their promotion policy decisions following any major changes, or at least yearly.

## SUMMARY

From the various *alternative marketing plans*, the most feasible one should be chosen as the decision and a plan of action should be devised. The *plan of action* will outline:

- What is to be done
  - Product
  - Price
  - Distribution
  - Promotion
- Who is to do it
- When it is to be done
- Why it is being done (support)

With the plan of action completed, it may appear that the marketing position is complete. However, the marketplace is constantly changing. New competitors and new trends emerge and it is important to monitor the results of the marketing plan that is ultimately implemented. The process should be a loop:

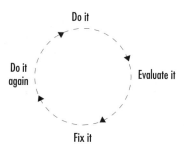

The marketing process will then become circular, reducing the chance of leaving failing products out in the marketplace when appropriate changes could have been made to improve them or decisions made to pull them out of the market.

Overall, it is evident that marketing is more of an art than a science. There is no one equation for success. There are no guarantees given. It is, however, an

***FIGURE 8
Marketing
Frameworks***

A. ROLE/PROBLEM/OBJECTIVES

B. MARKETING ANALYSIS

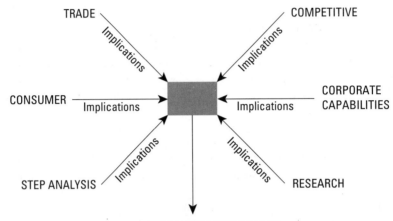

C. ALTERNATIVE MARKETING PLANS
(Product, Price, Distribution, Promotion) of each
** Financial feasibility of each

D. DECISION
- the "best" alternative
- describe/support

E. PLAN OF ACTION
- Who will do what?
- When? How?

F. MONITORING PLAN
- Do it ... fix it ... Do it again
- How will you measure performance?
- How will you react to the results?

Back to the Beginning

(Annual Marketing Audit)

G. REVOLVING PROCESS
- re-examination throughout the life of the product
  or service

arena wherein a thorough analysis, consumer satisfaction, creativity, and luck may combine to spell **SUCCESS**.

As Peter Drucker said, "the way to grow a business is through marketing, because its purpose is to create a customer, the business enterprise has two, and only two, basic functions: marketing and innovation. Marketing and innovation produce results, all the rest are 'costs'."[9]

## NOTES

1. The terms *consumer* and *customer* will be used interchangeably.
2. Postwar babies described demographically by their age.
3. Yuppies — young, urban professionals.
4. Woofs — well-off older folks.
5. Name coined by Canadian author, Douglas Coupland, to describe the generation born in the 1960s and 1970s following the baby boom.
6. Grunge refers to oversize, untidy jeans, T-shirts, etc.
7. Two divorced families blending together as a new family.
8. For more information on hypermarketing, see Michael Pearce, *Retail Marketing Management, Text and Cases* (Scarborough, ON: Nelson Canada, 1992).
9. Peter F. Drucker, *The Practice of Management* (New York: Harper & Row, 1982), p. 37.

# ■■■■ Cases for Part 5 ■■■■

# C A S E 5.1   MARKETING ARITHMETIC EXERCISES

### *MARKETING ARITHMETIC EXERCISES*

## Exercise 1

A ballpoint pen manufacturer had the following information:

| | |
|---|---|
| Plastic tubes: top and tip | .06/pen |
| Ink | .01/pen |
| Direct Labour | .01/pen |
| Selling price | .20/pen |
| Advertising | $ 40,000 |
| Managerial and secretarial salaries | $100,000 |
| Salespeople's commissions | 10% of selling price |
| Factory overhead | $ 60,000 |

Total ballpoint pen market is 10 million pens
Total inexpensive ballpoint pen market is 8 million pens

Calculate:

**a.** unit contribution
**b.** break-even volume in units
**c.** share of total market to break even
**d.** share of *relevant* total market to break even
**e.** total profit for the company if 3 million pens are sold

## Exercise 2

A large shampoo and toiletries manufacturer was trying to decide whether to introduce a new product onto the market — Product X. Sarah Jones, the branch manager, was responsible for the final decision. She had the following information on Product X:

| | |
|---|---|
| Cost of product/unit | $.73 |
| Freight and delivery/unit | $.03 |
| Selling and other head office expenses/unit | $.08 |

There were other somewhat similar products on the market but they were cheaper in quality and cost to produce. Retail margins were expected to be equal to the competition at 25 percent of the selling price to consumers. In this case, Sarah's company would sell directly to the retailers. The drugstores would also expect a cooperative advertising allowance of 5 percent of their selling price. In similar situations, the manufacturer usually offered price-reducing allowances to the drugstores (at least 5 times per year) so that they could pass this savings on to their consumers. These deals were in the order of 10 percent of retail selling price and accounted for approximately 65 percent of the annual volume.

Sarah knew that $450,000 of equipment would have to be purchased to manufacture Product X. Other fixed costs allocated to the product would reach $100,000 before advertising plans were included. These advertising program options would range from a high of $1,000,000, to a mid-range of $500,000, to a modest program launch of $150,000. In future years advertising programs would probably level out at $300,000.

Sarah needed to decide on the approximate retail selling price. Three options seemed available:

| | |
|---|---|
| $1.95/unit | Selling price to reflect the superior quality of the product |
| $1.65/unit | Selling price to stay on target with the competition |
| $1.25/unit | Selling price to underbid the competition in an attempt to gain increased volume. |

She knew that management expected a break-even position on new products in the first year and a 10 percent return on total investments in each of the following years. Sarah had projected that the total market for Product X would be 18,560,000 units but that the relevant market in which it would be positioned would be approximately 6,750,000 units. These markets were expected to grow at approximately 8 percent per year.

**a.** What price should Product X be? Why?

**b.** What level of advertising should be used in the first year? Why? Is there other information you would like to know? What information?

**c.** What share of the total market will Product X have to attain to meet the corporate objectives?

**d.** What share of the *relevant* market will Product X have to attain to meet the corporate objectives?

### Exercise 3

Richard Miller was preparing a new product analysis for Brand A. Based on his market research, his decision was to sell at $10 retail. Retailers customarily expected a 40 percent margin and wholesalers a 20 percent margin (both expressed as a percentage of their selling price). Brand A's variable costs were $2/unit and estimated total fixed costs were $28,000. At an anticipated sales volume of 9,000 units, would Richard's Brand A make a profit?

## Exercise 4

For a summer job, Joe wanted to work independently. Acme Vacuum Company had agreed to hire him to sell its vacuum cleaners on a door-to-door basis. The company estimated that Joe's variable costs per actual sale would amount to approximately 60 percent of the selling price of the cleaners. Joe's fixed costs for the summer, including room, board, and spending money, would amount to $2,500. Joe figured that he needed $4,500 to finance his second year at university comfortably. Acme estimated that a keen salesperson could sell $15,000 worth of vacuum cleaners in a four-month period. Joe knew that he could return to his old summer job in a factory. Although his salary would be assured at this factory job, Joe would be able to save only $3,500 for his schooling. Which job should Joe take?

# C A S E 5.2   APEX LIFE

Mark Silver, president and chief executive officer of Apex Life Canada, smiled as he sipped his morning coffee and read the headline of an August 24, 1993, article in the *Toronto Star*: "Universities tell provincial gov't ... HIKE TUITION 30% ... and students are outraged." In fact, over the last few months, Mark had encountered several articles regarding this issue, and with each one he read, his excitement had grown. Apex Life was about to introduce the Seed Endowment, a new form of educational savings plan. While the finishing touches on the product had almost been completed, several key aspects of the marketing plan had yet to be finalized.

While other educational savings plans already existed in the market, the insurance industry had not introduced a product similar to the Seed Endowment. Mark was excited about the potential of his product and the opportunity it created for Apex Life to enter a new segment of the industry. Mr. Silver did not want to waste any time bringing this new innovation to market. It would not be long before Apex Life's competitors recognized the same potential in this segment of the industry.

**BACKGROUND**

Post-secondary institutions have had no choice but to increase the cost to students in order to compensate for reductions in government funding. A report by the Council of Ontario Universities concerning tuition fee reform was mentioned in the August 24, 1993, article in the *Toronto Star* and included comments such as, "The proposals in this paper require university students to assume a greater share of the cost of providing for their own higher education." Over a six-year period, through the late 1980s and early 1990s, university students witnessed an alarming rise in tuition fees from less than $1,000 to over $2,000 per year. With these fees expected to increase at twice the rate of inflation over the following 20 years, it was easy to understand the increasing difficulties in funding a post-secondary education.

In the early 1990s, three major demographic trends had developed:

1. A large portion of the population had moved into retirement years and this group would continue to grow as medical advances increased life expectancy.

2. The baby-boomer generation continued to dominate financial and cultural aspects of society. Because they were now moving toward middle age, insurance needs were changing from protection to protection and accumulation.

3. An increase in the birth rate occurred. As baby-boomers matured and continued to have children, they created an *echo-boom*. Older members of the echo-boom were also moving into their child-bearing years.

Coupled with projected cutbacks in government spending, this new echo-boom had created an opportunity to sell educational savings products to parents of this new generation, who were increasingly concerned about their ability to pay for their children's future education.

## THE LIFE INSURANCE INDUSTRY

Like many industries, the Canadian Life and Health Insurance industry suffered from overcapacity. While the bulk of the market was held by a small number of companies, there were over 200 licensed insurers pursuing 28 million Canadians. In fact, the top 10 companies controlled over 80 percent of the market, while the remaining players competed fiercely to increase their portion of what was left.

The competitive situation was further aggravated by the federal government's recent removal of restrictions on the ownership of companies offering life insurance products. As a result of these changes to the Insurance Companies Act and the Bank Act, heavy competition from large banks and trust companies developed. These organizations already had very large distribution networks through which to sell products. Considering all financial institutions, the six Canadian-owned chartered banks represented over 56 percent of all assets in the market. The largest life insurance company ranked tenth in terms of total assets. These massive new players would only accelerate the already excessive competition in the insurance market.

When questioned about the competitive environment, Mark suggested that:

In the long run, competition in the market place will continue to drive prices down and depress earnings. It will become increasingly important to carefully target areas that have conditions that offer the opportunity to develop profitable business. Our biggest challenge is being able to create products with features and benefits that enable one to escape the commodity pricing trap — in either current or new segments of the industry.

## APEX LIFE

Mark stated:

Our business objective is to provide quality insurance products and services to meet the evolving financial security of individuals and businesses, allowing us to prosper, attain long-term growth, and provide a fair return to our stockholders.

On the basis of pure fundamentals, Apex Life was in an excellent competitive position. The company was founded in 1964 and purchased in 1966 by a large multinational corporation. Apex Life found a niche in the life insurance market and grew to offer the highest return to shareholders in the industry. Ranked as twenty-ninth in the industry in terms of premiums collected last year, and sixtieth in total assets, Apex Life had still boasted the highest average return on equity in the industry in the previous four years. In addition, the company had reported a profit for 15 consecutive years, a feat virtually unheard of for a smaller insurance company.

Apex Life's affiliation with its multinational parent and consistent profitability translated into a strong capital base and provided secure funding for future growth. It also suggested stability to potential shareholders and customers. This was an important asset considering the changes that were taking place in the market.

As a result of fierce competition over the last decade, many shareholders were leaving the industry. Years of below average returns had prompted the beginning of a major restructuring in the life insurance industry. Mark saw Apex Life as one of the few companies whose balance sheet was of "uniform high quality." With virtually no debt and the possession of a large pool of capital for investment, the company was well positioned to take advantage of others' misfortunes. It was able to obtain portfolios of insurance companies who were undergoing their own internal restructuring or leaving the business altogether. This enabled Apex Life to grow at a rate far exceeding that which was available through new business activities alone.

While Apex Life was one of the few successful companies in the industry, its size did create some challenges. One such challenge was achieving economies of scale. While its base of operations was small and low-cost compared to competitors, Mark indicated that Apex Life was not willing to sacrifice profitability by writing large volumes of new business in a market suffering from "over-capacity, under-performance, and excessive price-cutting." Mark realized that the key to success under these conditions was to develop exclusive distribution systems that would enable Apex Life to charge slightly more for its products. As a result, Apex Life turned its efforts toward niche marketing and focused on "aggressive, managed, profitable growth" by taking advantage of these smaller opportunities and pushing its distribution systems to maximum capacity. Currently, Apex Life was sufficiently staffed to handle significant growth in its existing market segments and to add complementary lines over the next few years. Its modest size and focus on niche markets enabled Apex Life to find opportunities to produce profitable business in segments of the market that would be considered too small by many of its major competitors. By following this strategy, Apex Life had achieved tremendous success (refer to Exhibit 1 for selected financial data).

**CONSUMER ANALYSIS**

With this in mind, Mark spent considerable time deciding who to target with Apex Life's Seed Endowment. In Canada, there were more than

400,000 babies born each year in the early 1990s. Educational savings plans had penetrated only 10 percent of this market. Mark had broken down the potential consumer into parents and grandparents. This market grew with the population over the years.

Parents could be further subdivided into baby-boomers, who had delayed having children, and echo-boomers, who were now entering their child-bearing years. Mark was considering two types of parents in these segments. The first were individuals who had attended university themselves. They knew how important university was to them and wanted to make sure that their children would have the same opportunity. The second type of parents were thought to be immigrant families. They had come to Canada with nothing and had worked very hard to be successful. They wanted their children to have more advantages than they had. More than likely lacking any formal education themselves, these parents recognized its value and wanted to make sure that their children had the best opportunities possible.

Regardless of their background, Mark felt that these families would require a reasonable income, at least $50,000 a year, in order to afford the annual premiums of an educational savings plan. As costs continued to grow, many parents were worried that they would not be able to afford their children's education when the time came. An educational savings plan forced parents to save now, so that the financial burden down the road would be tremendously reduced.

The second major segment Mark considered was grandparents, between the ages of 55 and 70. They were expected to have the largest disposable income of any segment as they had accumulated a significant amount of capital over the years. This was especially true for the parents of baby-boomers. Generally affluent, with large disposable incomes, they paid a considerable amount of taxes. No longer looking for opportunities to help their adult children, grandparents instead looked to their grandchildren. They wanted to make sure that their grandchildren had every opportunity possible. According to Mark, what better gift to give your grandchild than a paid for education? Mark expected this segment to represent between 25 to 30 percent of the market, but he also felt there was a great opportunity here and grandparents could reach as high as 50 percent of his sales.

There was another issue affecting the educational savings plan industry. This was the idea of "*socially responsible giving*," which had become an important issue for both parents and grandparents. As opposed to gifts that would be wasted, broken, or even stolen within a short period of time, educational savings plans provided them with a gift that could only help the child's future.

**EDUCATIONAL SAVINGS PLANS**

Unlike traditional life insurance products that were bought in response to the fear of loss through personal life changes or crisis, the purchasers of educational planning products were motivated instead by parents' hopes and dreams for their children. Yet Mark noted, "a family's financial plan that does not specifically include educational planning as one of the overall objectives can have future catastrophic financial and personal effects for all concerned."

In addition to the enormous costs for a young family with children, the career costs for a child without a post-secondary education were equally frightening. The relationship between education and unemployment was quite clear (refer to Exhibit 2 for statistics). For these reasons, and others mentioned earlier, specialist companies had been formed to offer educational savings plans.

Educational savings plans were designed to allow a "subscriber" (normally a parent or grandparent) to accumulate funds, over a limited period of time, to help finance the post-secondary education of a designated "beneficiary" (the child). The subscriber would normally contribute to the plan from the time the child was born, until he or she was ready to begin a post-secondary education. Most plans included a limited lifetime. Generally, subscribers could only make contributions to the plan for 18 consecutive years. When the beneficiary began his or her post-secondary education, he or she received the proceeds from the plan in the amount agreed upon by the subscriber and the insurance company when the plan was initiated. As a result, the financial burden was tremendously reduced at the time the individual entered a post-secondary educational institution.

Although not seasonal, economic fluctuations did affect the educational savings plan market. During recessionary times, more people worried about being able to afford a post-secondary education for their children. In addition, rising interest rates improved the marketability of these plans. As interest rates rose, insurance companies could offer better returns on educational savings plans, since it was easier for them to earn a higher return on their pool of invested funds. Recovering from a lengthy recession, the government had focused heavily on economic issues in the past year. This had resulted in cutbacks in all areas, including education.

## COMPETITIVE PRODUCTS

While new to Apex Life's portfolio of products, educational savings plans had been on the market for years. Although many companies offered different products, all plans on the market could be grouped into one of two general categories: a "Registered Education Savings Plan" or a "Universal Life" product.

## Registered Education Savings Plans (RESP)

RESPs were known as "pooled" funds, since all plans eligible to be cashed in the same year were pooled together. In the first year of post-secondary education, the beneficiary received back almost all of the contributions made by the subscriber during the life of the plan. The amount of money that a beneficiary was entitled to in the second, third, and fourth year was determined by the amount of interest that had accumulated in the pool up to that point. If a subscriber stopped contributing to the fund before the life of the plan was up, or if the beneficiary decided not to continue an academic career, they could collect all contributions made up to that point. However, the interest they had earned stayed in the pool and was divided among the remaining beneficiaries.

Besides the requirement that a child attend an approved post-secondary institution in order to receive his or her fair share of the fund, other restrictions also applied. The child had to attend a school by a certain age (usually 19), and once he or she had started, that individual was not allowed to take a break (such as a year off to travel in Europe) until he or she had completed the term of the policy, normally four years. The only way a beneficiary could break these two rules and remain eligible was to obtain special permission from the company managing the fund. This pardon could be difficult to obtain.

Due to their legislation by the federal government, RESPs had some other notable restrictions. For tax shelter purposes, the federal government limited the amount the subscriber could contribute to the plan ($1,500 annually or $31,500 lifetime). The fund's manager was also restricted as to where the contributions could be invested. This generally resulted in a much more conservative portfolio and, as a result, a smaller return to the beneficiary.

The main attraction of RESP products was the interest income shielding. Through government legislation, subscribers did not have to pay taxes on interest earned during the life of the plan. The interest was taxed only when the plan was cashed in, and the tax was paid by the child, rather than the subscriber. Keeping in mind that the beneficiary would more than likely be in a much lower tax bracket, taxes paid would be much smaller.

**Universal Life Products**

Universal Life products were similar to RESPs in that they were also "pooled" funds. However this pool worked differently in terms of its restrictions and penalties. If subscribers cancelled their policy within the first seven years they would lose everything, including their contributions. After that, there was something called a surrender clause. Between years 7 and 15 of the policy, the amount of contributions and interest the subscriber would lose, if they forfeited, would decrease from everything to nothing. After the fifteenth year of the policy, the subscriber could pull out and receive everything contributed up to that point, including the interest those contributions had earned. While it seemed like a larger risk, if one stayed in the program he or she was likely to benefit more from the pool, since those that pulled out early lost either all or most of both their contributions and interest. This left a larger pool to be divided among the remaining eligible beneficiaries. There was also greater potential in the Universal Life products, since there were no restrictions on where the contributions could be invested. The funds could be better diversified and, as a result, earn a better return.

Although not registered with the government, the interest earned on these policies was also tax-sheltered. This was only made possible because the subscriber had to buy life insurance on the beneficiary and contribute to the educational savings plan. Keeping in mind that the focus of the customer was not life insurance but rather forced savings for the beneficiary's future education, the insurance portion didn't really make a lot of sense as far as Mark was concerned. As Mark put it, "you can get what you want out of it, but you have to take on some extra baggage." Similar to the RESP, the beneficiary rather than the subscriber was taxed on the interest, provided the policy was gifted to the beneficiary.

**The Seed Endowment**

When considering what was available, Mark believed that there was a significant opportunity for his company. In his words, there were "no products out there sufficiently satisfying the needs of consumers." As a result, Apex Life developed the "Seed Endowment."

Similar to the Universal Life products, there were no restrictions on how much one could contribute to the plan or where the contributions were invested. Upon maturity the endowment could be utilized for either a "traditional" education or for a "life" experience as Mark indicated. For example, the beneficiary might decide that touring the museums in Europe or opening a small business was the route to pursue. The Seed Endowment allowed for alternative "life" choices without penalizing the subscriber.

With the Seed Endowment, only a small portion of life insurance was involved. This was minimal compared to the Universal Life products. It was just enough that if the child were to die before the policy matured (18 years), the subscriber was insured for the maturity value of the policy. Unlike the other products on the market, the beneficiary was guaranteed a certain portion of the expected payout each year (maturity value). The beneficiary was not guaranteed everything because of the uncertainty of the return Apex Life would earn on the contributions. However, it was still much better than the pooled funds where nothing was guaranteed.

There was also no forfeiture of interest if the subscriber decided to stop the policy. Only a small surrender clause existed, so that a high proportion of the contributions and interest earned would be returned to the subscriber in the event that he or she decided to cancel the policy. This penalty was considerably smaller than that involved with either the Universal Life products or the RESPs. Unfortunately, up to this point, Apex Life had not found a way to shield the interest earned from being taxed immediately (the life insurance portion of the premium was too small). However, once the product was gifted to a child, the interest would be taxable on the child's earnings rather than the subscriber's. (For a comparison of the benefits provided by each of the products on the market, refer to Exhibit 3.)

**DISTRIBUTION ANALYSIS**

One of the most important decisions was how to get the product into the hands of the consumer. At the time, Mark was considering two different ways to distribute the Seed Endowment.

**Managing General Agency**

The first option was to distribute the product through a Managing General Agency (MGA). This was the traditional approach for companies in this market. While the primary role of this company would be to act as a national sales arm, it would also assist Apex Life with further development of the product. This assistance would provide Mark with an understanding of what the agents would sell and what the market needed. As Apex Life's national distributor, the MGA would assume most of the responsibilities in bringing the Seed Endowment to market.

The MGA would recruit regional sales management organizations (or general agents as they are called in the industry), who in turn would hire individual agents to distribute the product to the end consumer. The MGA, responsible for the management of the entire chain, would have to train, motivate, and offer support to the general agents. It would have to monitor the completion of application forms, maintain all relationships, and respond to all inquiries from both Apex Life and the agents selling the product to the end consumer. This would allow Apex Life to concentrate on the administration and actual marketing of the product.

Due to the MGA's involvement, Apex Life's marketing costs would be greatly reduced. No direct mail package or significant marketing campaign would be needed since the agents themselves would establish credibility with the end consumer. Aside from the cost of developing the product, Apex Life would also have to assist in training seminars for general agents regarding both Apex Life and the Seed Endowment, and cover all relative printing costs. Mark estimated that he would have to spend close to $40,000 to cover everything under this distribution option.

This alternative did have its drawbacks. While the Seed Endowment would be the only educational product sold by the MGA, this was not the case for the agents they recruited to sell the product to the end consumer. Both general agents and the individual agents would carry a variety of life insurance products from several different companies, including other competitive educational savings plans. It was really out of Apex Life's hands when it came to how, and if, the product would actually be presented to the end consumer. It all depended upon the products that the agents felt would best meet the needs of the consumers they were dealing with, their compensation, and the products' projected returns. This placed tremendous importance on not just the seminars, but also on the competitiveness of Apex Life's product.

Like other companies in the industry offering educational savings plans, Mark was concerned about the high commission fees demanded by this distribution alternative. Commissions could run as high as 116 percent in the first year and then drop down to 5 percent in the following years. This additional cost would be reflected in the benefits the customer received when cashing in the policy. Apex Life could not adjust the annual premium to compensate for this if it was to remain competitive on price and meet the company's policy of no less than a 17 percent return on any product sold. While it was not perfect, Mark realized that on the whole this distribution route provided the opportunity for wider exposure and the greatest potential for rapid sales growth.

**Direct Mail**

The second option was "direct mail." This required that Apex Life be responsible for all aspects of the marketing plan, including development costs, printing, mailing, advertising, and support staff to handle the end consumer. Rather than dealing with an agent, interested consumers would now phone Apex Life directly to inquire and purchase the product.

One of Mark's questions with this route was to whom he should mail his packages. He knew who the end consumers would likely be, but how could he find them? One option available was to purchase lists of people from different companies, such as publishers or market research organizations. At the time, Mark was considering nine different lists, yet he was unsure which ones would be the most effective in reaching his end consumer. Two different groups of lists were being considered. The first included magazines and national surveys aimed at young parents, while the second contained similar lists targeting seniors (refer to Exhibit 4 for a description of each list). Unfortunately, these lists did not cover everyone Mark wished to target. He was having difficulty in deciding how to reach both lower income parents and families with a strong ethnic background.

Compared to dealing directly with an agent, Mark felt that direct mail involved less pressure from the consumer's perspective. However, with no direct contact between the agent and the end consumer, Apex Life would have to establish its credibility in other ways. This would require a very strong marketing campaign. Mark considered a variety of media channels, including local television, daily newspapers, radio, and consumer magazines, as well as some cooperative advertising opportunities (refer to Exhibit 5 for potential magazines and relevant costs). There were an unlimited number of companies that could be approached for co-operative activity. However, Mark suggested that "only companies with educational value, commitment to customer service and the environment, and an untarnished reputation should be considered" (refer to Exhibit 6 for potential co-operative partners). Although this option looked solid from a financial and exposure standpoint Mark felt there were some risks. Mark was also concerned about the cost and timing of the direct mail campaign and advertising.

Mark estimated that he would mail approximately 200,000 packages to households across Canada, with an expected net response rate of about 1 percent. Estimating that the average size of a policy would be around $500, this meant total premiums for the first year would come in around $1,000,000.

In terms of marketing costs, this option was considerably more expensive. Mark estimated that his total budget for marketing this product via the direct mail route would be close to $270,000. This included all printing, mailing, creative development, lists, lettershop, postage, public relations, and about $50,000 for advertising. While these fixed costs would be significantly higher, Mark knew that he would benefit a great deal since there were no commissions to be paid under this distribution route. Although heavily lopsided in the first year, Mark estimated that if he averaged this over the 18 years of the policy, he would be saving about 20.8 percent of the premium each year. A large portion of these savings would be passed on to the end consumer in terms of a larger payback when the policy was cashed in.

Other costs Mark had to consider under either distribution option included a $36 annual administration fee per policy, a 2 percent tax on premiums, and guaranteed fund insurance estimated at .5 percent per policy. In addition, there was a benefit cost to every policy. This was the portion of the annual premium that would have to be paid to the beneficiary when the policy was cashed in, 18 years down the road. (For a breakdown of variable costs under both distribution alternatives, refer to Exhibit 7.)[1]

**CONCLUSION**

Before Apex Life could launch the Seed Endowment, Mark Silver knew there were several decisions to be made. Although he was unsure when to introduce his product into the market, he realized that a solid marketing plan was an absolute necessity if the Seed Endowment was going to have the impact that he felt was possible.

## NOTES

1. Because of the economic reality that a dollar today is more valuable than a dollar a year from now, it is necessary to adjust the future cash flows of Apex Life to reflect this. Subscribers of Apex Life's Seed Endowment will be contributing to the plan for up to 18 years. In order to compare these contributions and the related costs to the marketing expenses incurred in the first year of the plan, the future cash flows must be adjusted in order to reflect their value in today's dollars. This adjustment process is referred to as *present valuing*.

*EXHIBIT 1*

|  | 1992 | 1993 | Est. 1994 |
|---|---|---|---|
| **Selected Financial Data for Apex Life[1]** (in million of $) | | | |
| **Revenue from Premiums:** | | | |
| New business[2] | 1.2 | 12.4 | 12.0 |
| Old business[3] | 14.6 | 14.8 | 27.0 |
| Acquisitions[4] | 0.0 | 1.8 | 2.5 |
| *Total* | 15.8 | 29.0 | 41.5 |
| **Investment Income Revenue** | 4.9 | 7.0 | 12.0 |
| *Total Revenue* | **20.7** | **36.0** | **53.5** |
| Net Income | .2 | 4.3 | 5.0 |
| Total Assets | 69.0 | 120.0 | 150.0 |

1. From company reports.

2. Premiums generated through the development of new products.

3. Premiums generated through existing products.

4. Premiums generated through portfolios acquired from other companies.

*EXHIBIT 2*

| **Statistics Canada** **1986 Unemployment Figures** | |
|---|---|
| **Level of Education** | **Unemployment Rate (%)** |
| Public School | 13.6 |
| High School | 12.2 |
| Post-Secondary Diploma | 7.2 |
| University Degree | 4.3 |

*Exhibit 3*

| Benefit Comparison of Competitive Products at Different Premium Levels[1] | | | |
|---|---|---|---|
| Product | 1st Year Payout | Payout for Next 3 Years | Total Payout |
| @ $250 per year for 18 years[2] | | | |
| RESP | $4,300 | $1,456/year | $8,668 |
| Universal Life | 3,000 | 1,540/year | 7,620 |
| **Seed Endowment — Direct Mail** | **3,255** | **2,440/year** | **10,575** |
| **— MGA** | **2,120** | **1,590/year** | **6,890** |
| @ $500 per year for 18 years | | | |
| RESP | $8,800 | $2,912/year | $17,536 |
| Universal Life | 6,000 | 3,080/year | 15,240 |
| **Seed Endowment — Direct Mail** | **6,510** | **4,880/year** | **21,150** |
| **— MGA** | **4,420** | **3,180/year** | **13,780** |
| @ $1,000 per year for 18 years | | | |
| RESP | $17,800 | $5,824/year | $35,272 |
| Universal Life | 12,000 | 6,160/year | 30,480 |
| **Seed Endowment — Direct Mail** | **13,020** | **9,760/year** | **42,300** |
| **— MGA** | **8,480** | **6,360/year** | **27,560** |

1.   Numbers based on an estimated return of 6 percent on all contributions invested in the fund.
2.   Life insurance portion of the premium included.

EXHIBIT 4
*Potential Lists for Direct Mail Distribution*[1]

**Parents**

*New Parents — Family Communication*
This is a list of respondents to bind-ins in *Expecting* and *Best Wishes* magazines. These direct-responsive new mothers are highly targetable through the selections offered, and want the best of everything for their children (birth to four years). 73 percent are female; 99.4 percent at home address.

*Target Families*
This is a list of responders to a national survey that promises high-value coupons for completed questionnaires. Survey responders have requested further mailings of interest that match their behaviours, interests, and demographics.

*Prospects Unlimited — Kids Base*
This is a list of consumers who have recently purchased children's goods, from newborn to teenage items. Information is gathered from subscription files, survey, retail purchases, and warranty cards.

*Parenting Magazine*
This is a list of active subscribers to a publication written especially for contemporary parents. The magazine features articles on health and fitness, education, personal appearance, and fashion as well as travel, investments and home design. Subscribers are upscale, well-educated professionals, with average income in excess of $50,000.

*Parents Magazine*
This is a list of subscribers to *Parents Magazine*. It is edited for young women aged 18 to 34 with growing children. Editorial coverage emphasizes family formation and growth, focusing on day-to-day needs and concerns of today's woman as a mother and a woman. 82 percent are female; 62 percent of these women are employed; their median age is 31.

*Sesame Street Magazine*
This is a list of children aged 2 to 6 whose parents have subscribed to *Sesame Street*, one of America's leading educational magazines. 88 percent of the parents are between the ages of 25 and 39. 72 percent of mothers attended/graduated from college or completed post-graduate work.

*Highlights for Children*
This is a list of subscribers to *Highlights for Children*. These subscribers are young Canadian families with an above average interest in their children's education and development. They are discriminating parents who demand quality for their children.
Issue: Small quantity (12,000 only) of the total is sold directly to the parents. The majority is sold at schools and delivered to the home.

*Wonders Catalogue Buyers*
This is a list of buyers and inquirers of clothing from an upscale catalogue. Products are colourful, contemporary clothing for today's best-dressed children and parents.

**Grandparents**

*Target Mail — Seniors*
This is a list of responders to a national survey that promises high-value coupons for completed questionnaires. Survey responders have requested further mailings of interest that match their behaviours, interests, and demographics.

1. Information obtained from report submitted by Flair Communications for Apex Life.

**EXHIBIT 5**

| Circulation and Cost of Potential Magazines[1] | | | | | | |
|---|---|---|---|---|---|---|
| | CIRCULATION | | NATIONAL COSTS | | ONTARIO COSTS | |
| | **National** | **Ontario** | **1 p / 4 c** | **½ p / 4 c** | **1 p / 4 c** | **½ p / 4 c** |
| Today's Parent | 132,732 | 72,753 | $8,680 | $6,570 | $6,085 | – |
| Chatelaine | 904,454 | 489,667 | $30,530 | $19,845 | $18,015 | $11,710 |
| Canadian Living | 592,570 | 319,929 | $23,155 | $15,050 | $14,790 | $10,385 |
| Homemakers | 1,289,000 | 675,000 | $24,800 | – | $16,690 | – |

1.   Information obtained from report submitted by Flair Communications for Apex Life.

**EXHIBIT 6**
*Potential Cooperative Partners*

**Packaged Goods**
- General Mills — Cheerios
- Kraft/General Foods
- Thomas J. Lipton
- Gerber
- Popsicle
- Campbell's soup
- Nestlé Enterprises
- Kellogg's
- Johnson & Johnson
- Quaker Oats

**Travel**
- Club Med
- American Express Travel
- Sheraton
- Air Canada

**Leisure**
- Collegiate Sports
- Jumbo Video
- Toys "R" Us
- W.H. Smith
- Moyers
- Double Day
- Pizza Hut
- Gap
- Grolier
- Sesame Street Magazine

**Manufacturers**
- Reebok
- IBM
- Sony
- Crayola
- Lego
- Roots
- V-tech
- Little Tikes
- Kodak
- Avon

*Exhibit 7*

| | Cost Structure Under Different Distribution Alternatives[1] | | | | | |
|---|---|---|---|---|---|---|
| **Seed Endowment — Direct Mail** | | | | **Seed Endowment — MGA** | | |
| **Annual Cash Flows** | **Total Cash Flows for 18 Years** | **18 Years of Cash Flows Present Valued[2]** | | **Annual Cash Flows** | **Total Cash Flows for 18 Years** | **18 Years of Cash Flows Present Valued[1]** |
| $250 | $4,500 | $1,812 | **Premiums** | $250 | $4,500 | $1,812 |
| | | | Costs: | | | |
| $36 | $ 648 | $ 261 | • Admin. and Overhead | $ 46 | $ 828 | $ 333 |
| 5 | 90 | 36 | • Premium tax (2%) | 5 | 90 | 36 |
| 1 | 18 | 7 | • Guaranteed Fund (.5%) Insurance | 1 | 18 | 7 |
| 0 | 0 | 0 | • Commission (20.8%) | 52 | 936 | 377 |
| 171 | 3,078 | 1,240 | • Benefit Cost[3] | 112 | 2,016 | 812 |

1. Figures reflect the cash flows of one unit.

2. These figures have been actuarially adjusted to reflect the notion that $1 a year for 18 consecutive years is actually worth much less than $18 today, due to present valuing. For example, $1 a year from now, discounted at a rate of 8 percent is really worth only $.92 today. Similarly $1 two years from now is worth only $.85 today.

3. Refers to portion of premium paid to beneficiary when plan cashed in.

# C A S E **5.3**   ASHBROOKS (A)

In August 1986, Mr. John Ross, then vice-president operations for F.W. Woolworth Co. (FWW), had been given the task of launching a new specialty store concept called Ashbrooks in Canada. He had six months to develop a complete marketing plan and launch the first three stores. As of August 1987, after the first six months of operation, sales and profitability levels were 30 to 35 percent below initial projections. As general manager for Ashbrooks, Mr. Ross sat back to review the process and to decide what to do next. Ashbrooks was considered in a test for its first 12 months, after which senior FWW management would decide whether to continue it in the specialty group or discontinue it.

**COMPANY BACKGROUND**

F.W. Woolworth Co. was a large American retailing organization with sales of $6.5 billion in 1986. Headquartered in New York, FWW had several key divisions including: U.S. Woolworth, Woolworth Canada, Woolworth Overseas Corp., Woolworth Germany, Richman Brothers, and Little Folk Shop. Divisional information regarding sales and income are shown in Exhibit 1. Exhibit 2 provides Woolworth Canada results.

Originally a variety store operation known as a "five and dime" in the early part of the 1980s, FWW underwent a dramatic transformation from a traditional general merchandise retailer to one of the world's largest specialty store operators. With 30 specialty retail formats in 1986, including 17 launched within the past four years, FWW reputedly operated more specialty units than any other retailer in the world. All but five of the 656 new stores opened in 1986 were specialty stores. FWW management seemed determined to play a dominant role in specialty retailing throughout the world.

The decision to rapidly expand existing specialty store formats and acquire new ones was motivated by management's recognition that specialty stores had been producing higher sales per square foot, faster rates of sales gains, higher operating profit margin, and higher returns of investment than general merchandise operations. In addition, FWW management had at its disposal significant funds from the profits of its large, but more mature, general merchandise and family footwear business (Kinney).

Management forecast that a major share of FWW's future sales and profit growth — and virtually all of FWW's unit expansion — would come from specialty stores. By 1991 specialty stores were expected to account for 46 percent of total sales, versus 35 percent in 1986 and 28 percent in 1982. Specialty operating income was anticipated to represent 65 percent of total operating income by 1991 versus 52 percent in 1986 and 39 percent in 1982. Exhibit 3 presents financial statements for F.W. Woolworth Co. for 1984–86.

**THE ASHBROOKS IDEA**

In early 1986, Woolworth's Canadian corporate research team was handed the task of finding high potential markets for future retail growth. They knew that any new concept should have a potential for large volume and strong margins; that is, they were looking for new merchandising concepts that would be profitable for FWW and widely accepted by the Canadian consumer.

The first market that was examined was the women's fashion apparel market. However, that market was deemed to be oversaturated and very competitive. An examination of trends in the U.S. market revealed the emerging kitchen, bathroom, and bedroom accessory market as an area of high retail growth and excitement.

FWW management felt that a U.S. firm, R.G. Branden's, had the best new strategy for targeting this home accessories market. It was a "colour driven" concept that focused on a wide spectrum of 20 to 30 colours and their various shades. It allowed the consumer to coordinate all aspects of her bathroom (e.g., towels, shower curtain, vase, flowers, and other accessories), kitchen and/or bedroom.

R.G. Branden's opened its pilot store in Kendall, Florida in 1985 and announced it expected to have a total of nine stores in Dade, Broward, and Palm Beach counties by 1990. By early 1988 there would be six stores. Branden's specialized in selling brand name housewares, linens, and accessories at competitive prices. The store was approximately 50,000 square feet of selling space with an upscale warehouse atmosphere. The visual impact of the store was based on large colour-blocked displays: hundreds of towels in different hues covering entire walls, a plate display in 30 different colours, one lamp style in 15 to 20 colours, and so on.

"Generally, we fill a void in the marketplace," claimed Jack Chadsey, Branden's president and chief operating officer. "We have positioned ourselves between the mass merchandisers and the department stores. We consider ourselves the Toys 'R' Us or The Limited of the home furnishings business."

Branden's was owned by Dayton-Hudson Corporation, a major Minneapolis-based general merchandise retailer. Dayton-Hudson would not disclose financial information about Branden's and as of 1987 maintained that it was still "in test."

Branden's located as anchor stores in large strip centres near, but not adjacent to, major shopping centres. The prototype store was opened in the Kendall area, just south of Miami, largely because of the area's large number of new homes under construction and its relatively affluent customer base.

Branden's concept research indicated that customers were unhappy that department stores had repositioned themselves in apparel at the expense of home accessories at a time when customers were spending more money on the home. Branden's was targeted at the well-educated, married woman aged 25 to 45 whose family income was $35,000 or above who used to shop for home accessories at department stores.

"Our concept is proving successful," asserted Mr. Chadsey in 1986. "We're very pleased with our Kendall store, and sales at the Plantation store have exceeded our first year goals. We consider ourselves lifestyle oriented. We offer everything for the home except furniture and major appliances. In addition to housewares and linens, we have products like cookware, cutlery, lamps, and file cabinets."

Mr. Ross was enthusiastic but cautious about the Branden's concept. One of the reasons for his caution was that he had been taught and exposed to using only two to three colour spectrum of merchandise, as opposed to the multitude of colours that Branden's carried. He felt a carefully researched and planned marketing program would be needed to introduce such a new and untried strategy to the Canadian consumer.

The research team had given Mr. Ross a picture of the customer they might target in Canada. She would be female (very few male customers were expected), between the age of 25 and 55, and decorating her second home. She would belong to a $20,000 to $80,000 income family. She might be a "pink collar worker," a housewife, or a young professional. She would use credit over half the time, as her purchases would be substantial when coordinating entire rooms. The average purchase would be three times larger than what an average general merchandise buyer would spend on home accessories in other general merchandise stores. It was estimated that 70 percent of these consumers would not know how to decorate or colour coordinate well. Store image would be important to them.

**THE NAME**

Mr. Ross reasoned that the name of the store would be an important factor in its success, especially in its early states. He felt that any association with the Woolworth's/Woolco image would not appeal to his targeted consumers. As he pondered possibilities for a name for the new store, Mr. Ross tried several approaches. For example, he went through English novels to find names that might be appealing to his intended customers.

In time, 12 names were selected for careful consideration: Ashbrooks, Jordan Malone, Creighton Harris, Caulfield's, Stephanie Powers, Hunter Dalton, Home Gallery, Russel Holmes, Creighton Powers, Ashley Holmes, Russell Powers, Creative Colours, and L.B. Ashbrooks.

A marketing expert was retained to conduct two focus groups, varying in respondent income level. The respondents were presented with the store concept, layout, and the 12 names. All of them picked the same name: Ashbrooks. They said that it gave them a feel of "traditional family history," and that "the Ashbrooks family would stand behind their merchandise." It was not regarded as a "stuffy" or "snobbish" name, and the respondents felt that they could wear casual dress to the store. The name also did not have a stereotyped image in terms of merchandise that would be carried (i.e., not furniture, men's wear, or paint). Apparently, everyone felt comfortable with the name and thought that it was not unusual but easy to remember.

Mr. Ross and FWW management chose Ashbrooks as the store name and envisioned 100 stores across Canada. He knew what he wanted to do: "I want to do this store right, which means we'll have to be the best in everything we do, especially merchandising, customer service, and presentation. There won't be second chances." He decided to bring in outside specialists in every functional area rather than depend on the traditional Woolworth's/ Woolco resource base and way of thinking.

## PLANNING THE ASSORTMENT

One of Mr. Ross's first moves was to bring in John Guerin as manager, merchandising and sales. As a FWW sales manager for the fashion apparel market, Mr. Guerin was already experienced in a colour dominated market. the next step was to gather a set of expert buyers already in the home accessories marketplace. Mr. Ross and Mr. Guerin went to the trade shows, found, and hired individuals they considered to be "the best buyer of housewares in Canada, the best bedding buyer in Canada, and the best bathroom buyer in Canada." These individuals, experienced in large department stores and specialty stores, were creative, professional buyers who apparently knew their markets and were excited about the Ashbrooks concept.

These buyers were sent to R.G. Branden's for a week to examine, in depth, the merchandising mix, colour assortments, SKUs, price points, etc. The manager of R.G. Branden's was extremely cooperative with them as he did not view the Canadian company as any threat. He spent time explaining how the market worked, only asking that they not take any pictures of the operation. The buyers returned to Canada very excited about all the possibilities that this new avenue seemed to offer.

Despite his buyers' experiences with colour, Mr. Ross was uneasy. He asked himself, "What do I really know about colours?" and concluded not enough. He then asked his buyers, "If I told you to pick 12 colours of dinnerware, which colours would you pick? and "How would these few colours be coordinated across rooms?" He felt the answers he got were not sufficient knowing how critical colour would be to Ashbrooks' success.

Mr. Ross then hired a colour consultant, Lynn Darby, who was an expert in a field that he had never heard of prior to the last few months. Lynn Darby followed the colour fashions in North America and Europe. She taught the Ashbrooks merchandising group about colours: which to have, how many, and how to display them. She helped them put their assortments together, choose the colours that were in vogue, and tie it all together. They were taught how to bring a colour swatch through at least one line of merchandise. For example, the mauve of a vase should be available in artificial flowers and a toss cushion. The Ashbrooks team felt it was a tremendous education process.

Lynn Darby put together a Colour Manual (Exhibit 4) that was used as part of the staff training program. It was also used by the buyers working with the manufacturers to develop Ashbrooks "colour driven" concept. Ms. Darby worked with Ashbrooks for six months. Mr. Ross felt that no other retailer in Canada would be able to offer such an interior decorating service to its customers via a well-trained sales staff. Staff were expected to take customers through the store, across departmental lines, to find coordinated items. The staff were also trained how to "dress for success" by a certified image consultant.

The next step was to tell manufacturers the colours that Ashbrooks wanted. There were approximately 150 Canadian manufacturers who made the products they wanted to carry and about 50 percent of them dealt not with Woolworth's or Woolco, but rather the specialty boutique shops. However, these suppliers did not seem to have the necessary colour depth. For example, a supplier might carry the primary colours and one fashion colour in towels but not the 18 or so colours that Mr. Ross was looking for to satisfy the Ashbrooks "colour driven" concept.

The Ashbrooks merchandise group debated the question: "Should we change the concept because our suppliers can only supply us with two, three, or four colours?" They decided to stick with the concept, which meant that they would have to convince some suppliers to radically change their business.

Mr. Ross decided to bring the CEOs, owners, chief executives, and sales managers of each major manufacturer into FWW headquarters in Toronto to sell each company individually. They gave each management group a full presentation of the Ashbrooks plan, including slides from R.G. Branden's. The manufacturers were reminded of Woolworth's financial strength and commitment, and asked to "come on stream and join this exciting time or Woolworth's will do it without you by going to U.S. suppliers." Mr. Ross remembered this time as an exhausting process, but necessary and extremely successful. Most but not all manufacturers agreed to supply Ashbrooks.

The suppliers seemed very excited about being a part of this new approach in Canadian retailing. Although regular supplier terms were negotiated, emphasis was placed in three areas. Suppliers would have to carry backup inventory, fast delivery turnaround would have to be met in order to keep their colour assortment in stock at all times, and the original concept would not be changed to accommodate supplier merchandise that would not fit the Ashbrooks store layout.

The specific merchandising concept was to develop a top of the mind position for home textiles, houseware, table top, and home accessories by having assortment dominance within these four categories of merchandise. The longer term aim was to become a destination store in this market. Assortment dominance was to be achieved by having all sizes and colours in depth within a limited range of stock-keeping units (SKUs). The SKU assortment would be narrow and deep.

The merchandise dominance concept would be enhanced through the utilization of floor to ceiling wall displays that would clearly indicate to the customer what business Ashbrooks was in. These displays would approximate Branden's "wall of plates," its "wall of throw pillows," and its "wall of toilet seats."

The merchandise team decided to merchandise medium quality, current season, recognizable national brands. They would not sell top department store merchandise lines or discounters' private label-type merchandise. They would only carry merchandise that would fit the self-selection concept and that would not require knowledgeable sales help. Ideally, Ashbrooks would have a merchandise mix of 80 percent well-known brands and 20 percent private or house brands.

## LOCATION

Management decided locations for Ashbrooks should be sought that provided 25,000 to 30,000 square feet selling space at low rent where possible in high traffic, visible locations in trading areas with 80,000 to 120,000 people. Management was targeting a broad-based customer group: the middle 70 percent of customers, not the lower nor the upper 15 percent in terms of household incomes. Extensive research was conducted by the Ashbrooks marketing department on potential locations across Canada. Abandoned conventionally sized supermarkets seemed to offer exactly what was being sought. Several sites were becoming available as grocery chains moved to larger-sized formats and as new competition from grocery super stores and wholesale clubs were closing down some conventional supermarkets. These locations were being taken over by specialty mass merchandisers, such as Toys 'R' Us and super drug store operations like Herbies. Eighteen empty Dominion store sites were examined in particular. Potential locations were analyzed for potential market size, trading area population, and potential growth expected for the next five years.

Three sites were selected: a large regional mall in Toronto, a small regional mall in Sarnia, Ontario, and a mega-mall in Edmonton. Square One in Toronto was thought to have an estimated trade area size of 120,000 people in a bedroom community and estimated trade area potential sales of $15,600,000. Approximately 70 30,000 square foot stores competed in the Square One trade area. Mr. Ross estimated that a 30,000 square foot store in this area would achieve $4,328,000 in annual sales. The West Edmonton Mall was located in a trade area size of 80,000 people and was estimated to have trade area potential sales of $10,400,000. Mr. Ross estimated that a 30,000 square foot store in this area would gain $4,210,000 in sales. The Lambton Mall, in Sarnia, was chosen as a test market for the viability of smaller regional area locations.

## LAYOUT AND VISUAL MERCHANDISING

Each store was planned to have 25,000 to 30,000 square feet of selling area and would be divided into four sections by main aisles that would run from front to back and side to side. A race track around the perimeter of the store was intended to ensure efficient customer traffic flow. The counters in the interior of the store were five feet high so that customers could see around the whole store from the perimeter aisle. The walls were used to display merchandise right up to the ceiling to emphasize dominant assortment impact.

The main aisle contained fashion or fad merchandise, while promotional merchandise was on the lateral aisles. Core programs were on the aisles. Basic merchandise was displayed on gondolas between the merchandise on the lateral aisle and the wall. At the end of the main aisle was a seasonal swing department, which was the only place in the store that a strict classification of merchandising was not used. The impression of overwhelming selection was intended through the use of high impact mass displays. Wherever possible, colour blocking was used to visually brighten the merchandising impact. Most floor displays were five-foot gondolas at eye level. Eye level signs indicated brand name, product description, product features, and price. The back of the sign indicated corporate pricing, service, and guarantee policies. The merchandise was stocked in depth on the sales floor behind or adjacent to sample presentations that were available for the customer to handle. The fashion aisle was frequently changed to provide new exciting merchandise to attract the customers attention and reinforce the image or fashionability in the store. See Exhibit 5 for photographs for the Ashbrooks image, merchandising, and layouts.

At the outset, Mr. Ross was determined to find Ashbrooks' own style rather than doing everything "the Woolco way." After the stores had been open and results were not as projected, the Square One store became "John's lab" because various layouts, display techniques, and other changes were frequently made over the next few months at that store in an attempt to find the winning formula.

## STAFFING

Mr. Ross did not want to use the personnel supervisor who hired the staff for Woolworth's and Woolco. He personally interviewed several new people to do the hiring for Ashbrooks. He chose Maureen Sheridan for this position even though she had no experience in the personnel field. She was in a management training program at Simpson's, but, most importantly to Mr. Ross, she was a "nice" person and presented herself well. He reasoned that "a nice person would hire other nice people who would treat the customers nicely."

The new Ashbrooks stores were to be open organizations of six or seven key people and Mr. Ross "didn't really care if they knew what a towel was" at the moment of hiring. Between 200 to 300 people were interviewed for each store. All sales staff were paid a base salary plus a percentage on the dollar gross profit realized in their respective areas of the store. A major part of the sales associates' training was a program on colour coordination, not all aspects of interior decorating, that was headed by Lynn Darby. This training was intended to give Ashbrooks a unique service offering for Canadian consumers.

The original organization chart is shown as Exhibit 6.

## PRICING

Price was not expected to be a major factor for customers when choosing products. The merchandise group felt all merchandise was priced competitively with Ashbrooks' core competition: that is, they priced against traditional and promotional department stores. Generally price points for comparable merchandise was thought to be under the department stores and higher than the promotional department stores. High-priced merchandise was not carried as staff feared this could create the impression of a high-priced store. Towels, for instance, started at $16.99 and went as high as $39.

The value image was not to be conveyed by low prices, but through the convenience of the shopping trip, the fashionability of the merchandise, service, and quality merchandise at reasonable prices.

## ADVERTISING AND PROMOTION

Mr. Ross and his team interviewed several advertising agencies to see how they would promote the opening and the initial states of market entry for Ashbrooks. The basic idea was a strong "colour" statement to the consumer, but not in a "hard sell" format. Glowinsky and Gee, Vickers and Benson won the contract. They designed and recommended colour flyers to feature the complete colour range available in each individual item being advertised. All advertising employed the positioning statement: "We've got your colour." The copy highlighted one's ability to colour coordinate fashion accessories for the bedroom, bathroom, and kitchen.

In February 1987, the promotional effort began. The first flyer was a "teaser" to arouse interest, followed by a colour flyer aimed at attracting the target market to the store. Exhibit 7 shows excerpts from the second flyer. Both pieces were controversial within the company. The intent was to sell the concept and the flyer won an advertising award. [However, it was not very successful in bringing people into the stores.] Some managers felt that Ashbrooks stayed too long with the flyers. Soon, Ashbrooks advertising was moved to print ad inserts in the newspaper, then radio to support the print, then just radio. About $600,000 in advertising was budgeted for the three stores for launch in the first year, about 8 percent of sales expected. Management planned to budget advertising at about 4 percent of sales in the second year.

## FINANCIAL PROJECTIONS

Ashbrooks' financial projections were based on several key figures. Average estimated Ontario per capita expenditures on home textiles housewares, table top, and home accessories were expected to be $130. The gross profit was targeted at 43 percent of sales and costs-to-sell were estimated at 26 percent of sales. Expected store sales were to average $4,000,000. The targeted return on investment was 16.2 percent

## THE FIRST SIX MONTHS

On February 25, 1987, right on schedule six months after the basic concept was established, the first Ashbrooks store opened at Square One in Mississauga. In March 1987, Mr. Ross's team opened the Sarnia store and in April they opened the West Edmonton Mall store.

At the end of six months the results were tallied. Positive results included average sales per customer of over $50, favourable comments by customers, 56 percent of business on credit, 8,000 "preferred customers" on a mailing list, and a bridal registry of over 200 names. However, Ashbrooks was between 30 and 35 percent below projections in both profits and sales. Gross margins were only 38 percent.

Mr. Ross and his team were under pressure to perform. Senior FWW executives began making suggestions for change, which caused Ross and his management team to worry about losing their concept all together. He knew that he had to review the results, analyze his own feelings, and decide what to do. Senior management in Toronto was pressuring them to change the concept. And, apparently, R.G. Branden's was also struggling.

*EXHIBIT 1*

| | F.W. Woolworth Co. Divisional Results (U.S. $Million) | | | |
|---|---|---|---|---|
| | 1986 | | 1982 | |
| | Sales | Net Income | Sales | Net Income |
| **General Merchandise** | | | | |
| Woolworth U.S. | 1,954 | 96 | 1,707 | 66 |
| Woolworth Canada | 1,436 | 70 | 1,350 | 52 |
| Woolworth Germany | 907 | 52 | 717 | 40 |
| **Specialty** | | | | |
| Kinney: U.S. | 1,500 | 195 | 910 | 88 |
| Kinney: Canada and Australia | 317 | 35 | 222 | 12 |
| Richman | 261 | 17 | 198 | 4 |
| Other | 197 | (9) | 85 | (5) |

Source: 1986 Annual Report.

*Exhibit 2*

| | F.W. Woolworth Co. Canadian Results (Canadian $Millions) | | | | | |
|---|---|---|---|---|---|---|
| | **1986** | **1985** | **1984** | **1983** | **1982** | **# Stores at Jan. 31, 1987** |
| **Total Woolworth Canada** (in Canadian dollars) | | | | | | |
| Sales (millions) | 2,036 | 1,986 | 1,876 | 1,739 | 1,670[1] | |
| Income before unallocated items (millions) | 97 | 95 | 84 | 74 | 64[1] | |
| **Woolworth Stores** | | | | | | |
| Sales (millions) | 395 | 396 | 384 | 354 | 330 | |
| Selling area in sq. ft. at year end (thousands) | 3,323 | 3,415 | 3,452 | 3,473 | 3,435 | 173 |
| Sales per average sq. ft. | 117 | 115 | 111 | 102 | 96 | |
| **Woolco Stores** | | | | | | |
| Sales (millions) | 1,593 | 1,556 | 1,487 | 1,385 | 1,320 | |
| Selling area in sq. ft. at year end (thousands) | 11,322 | 11,366 | 11,360 | 11,388 | 11,322 | 119 |
| Sales per average sq. ft. | 140 | 137 | 131 | 122 | 117 | |
| **Specialty Stores[2]** | | | | | | |
| Sales (millions) | 48 | 34 | 5 | — | — | |
| Selling area in sq. ft. at year end (thousands) | 568 | 543 | 43 | — | — | 155 |
| **Kinney Shoe Corporation Canada[3]** (in Canadian dollars) | | | | | | |
| Sales (millions) | 380 | 321 | 282 | 259 | 229 | |
| Selling area in sq. ft. at year end (thousands) | 1,251 | 1,211 | 1,157 | 1,109 | 1,110 | |
| Sales per average sq. ft. | 309 | 271 | 249 | 233 | 223 | |

1. Includes catalogue stores, which were closed in 1982.
2. Includes Robinsons, Activeworld, Kids Mart, Afterthoughts.
3. Includes Kinney, Footlocker, Lady Foot Locker, Fredelle, Lewis, Sportelle, Randy River, Raglans.

Source: 1988 Annual Report.

*EXHIBIT 3*

| F.W. Woolworth Co.<br>1986 Annual Report | | | |
|---|---|---|---|

**Consolidated Income Statement**
For the fiscal years ended January 31, 1987, 1986, and 1985
(in millions except per share amounts)

| | **1986** | **1985** | **1984** |
|---|---|---|---|
| **Revenues** | | | |
| Sales, including sales from leased departments of $257, $253, and $252 | $6,501 | $5,958 | $5,737 |
| Other income | 30 | 32 | 26 |
| | 6,531 | 5,990 | 5,763 |
| **Costs and expenses** | | | |
| Costs of sales | 4,287 | 3,952 | 3,853 |
| Selling, general, and administrative expenses | 1,689 | 1,545 | 1,472 |
| Depreciation and amortization | 125 | 111 | 105 |
| Interest expense | 56 | 68 | 82 |
| | 6,157 | 5,676 | 5,512 |
| **Income before income taxes** | 374 | 314 | 251 |
| Income Taxes | 160 | 137 | 110 |
| **Net income** | $214 | $177 | $141 |
| **Net income per common share** | $3.25 | $2.75 | $2.22 |

**Consolidated Balance Sheet**
January 31, 1987, 1986, and 1985 (in millions)

| | **1986** | **1985** | **1984** |
|---|---|---|---|
| ASSETS | | | |
| **Current assets** | | | |
| Cash, and short-term investments of $193, $115, and $95 | $239 | $143 | $119 |
| Merchandise inventories | 1,327 | 1,264 | 1,108 |
| Other current assets | 118 | 114 | 108 |
| | 1,684 | 1,521 | 1,335 |
| Owned properties, less depreciation and amortization | 978 | 838 | 767 |
| Leased properties under capital leases, less amortization | 91 | 90 | 100 |
| Deferred charges and other assets | 97 | 86 | 109 |
| | $2,850 | $2,535 | $2,311 |

***EXHIBIT 3*** *(cont'd)*

|  | 1986 | 1985 | 1984 |
|---|---|---|---|
| **LIABILITIES AND SHAREHOLDERS' EQUITY** | | | |
| **Current liabilities** | | | |
| Accounts payable | $455 | $454 | $375 |
| Accrued liabilities | 293 | 262 | 235 |
| Income taxes | 77 | 59 | 24 |
| Current portion of reserve for discontinued operations | 20 | 26 | 33 |
| Dividends payable | 18 | 16 | 15 |
| Current portion of long-term debt and obligations under capital leases | 18 | 14 | 50 |
|  | 881 | 831 | 732 |
| Long-term debt | 248 | 245 | 250 |
| Long-term obligations under capital leases | 110 | 111 | 122 |
| Other liabilities | 90 | 74 | 69 |
| Deferred taxes | 37 | 30 | 30 |
| Reserve for discontinued operations | — | 21 | 57 |
| Shareholders' equity | 1,484 | 1,233 | 1,051 |
|  | $2,850 | $2,535 | $2,311 |

**EXHIBIT 4**
**Excerpts from**
**Ashbrooks: The Colour**
**Book**

To a scientist, colour is simply the brain's response to stimulus of light; while that is true on a strictly "visual" level, we know from our own experience that colour can also affect our moods and our sense of well-being.

We know, for example, that certain colours warm us, excite us, may even increase our respiration rate, heart beat, and blood pressure, while other colours make us feel calm, serene, sad, or depressed.

\* \* \* \* \*

Yellow:

- Increases heart beat, respiration, and blood pressure, but in a pleasantly stimulating way, as opposed to red's intensity.
- Expresses cheerfulness, happiness, intellectual stimulation, and optimism when light or medium shades are selected. Dark or muddy tones can be used to suggest fear, cowardice, and, in some cases, greed.
- Most frequently selected by "optimistic" people who are striving toward future goals, or who seek change in their lives.

\* \* \* \* \*

In order to understand how colour "works," it is necessary to analyse and categorize it in three distinctive ways: hue, value, and intensity.

\* \* \* \* \*

In bathrooms containing a tub, we use the shower curtain as a focal point; in powder rooms, the area around the basin should be highlighted with colour.

\* \* \* \* \*

Because the eye reads from left to right, colours are arranged in vertical sections across a wall or shelf unit. Ideally, one vertical section is assigned to each shade in the assortment.

\* \* \* \* \*

What would you do?
A customer has asked you to help coordinate her bedroom. She would like to use a new Ashbrooks sheeting pattern that is a combination of pink, peach, grey, and white. Her carpet is pale blue. What would you recommend to help "dress" her bed? What colour lamps would you select? What other accessories would you suggest?

*EXHIBIT 5*

(a) Ashbrooks initial logo.

(b) Original store concept for Ashbrooks.

(c) Feb. 25, 1987, the first Ashbrooks store at Square One Shopping Centre in Mississauga, Ontario.

(d) April 1987, the third Ashbrooks is opened at the West Edmonton Mall in Edmonton, Alberta. (March 1987, second Ashbrooks in the Lambton Mall in Sarnia, Ontario).

(e) As you enter an Ashbrooks, a giant "lifestyle wall" emphasizes Canadian Lifestyle living, and the colour characteristics of the store.

(f) Ashbrooks customer guarantee policy is well displayed in the front entrance.

(g) Ashbrooks "towel wall" displays the largest colour selection of towels in Canada.

(h) Ashbrooks "wall of plates" shows in-depth sizes and colours within a limited range of styles.

(i) Ashbrooks new employees were trained to: (1) present themselves to customers (2) how to dress for success (3) product knowledge. The day before opening they were presented with their diplomas.

***EXHIBIT 6***
***Organization***
***Chart***

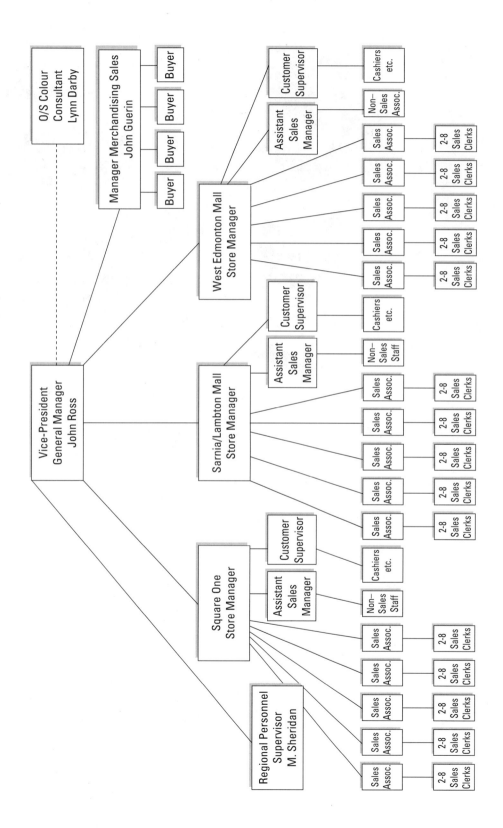

# C A S E **5.4**    ASHBROOKS (B)

Mr. John Ross, general manager for Ashbrooks, was deeply concerned about the poor performance of the new chain (see Ashbrooks (A) for background). While he continued to experiment with changes, he also commissioned some consumer research. Two hundred respondents were interviewed in mall intercepts at Square One in Toronto. Respondents were qualified as "females, aged 30 to 45, with total annual household incomes of at least $30,000 who shop as Square One at least once every two months."

The objectives for the study were as follows:

1. To measure the level of awareness of Ashbrooks, specifically as a provider of home accessories and fashion items for the bedroom, bathroom, and kitchen.

2. To determine the shopping behaviour in the store of those aware of Ashbrooks.

3. To rate the relative importance of selected home accessory store attributes to store choice and Ashbrooks' performance on these attributes.

4. To solicit the specific likes and dislikes of Ashbrooks among shoppers.

The results provided to Mr. Ross are shown as Exhibits 1 to 11. He wondered what these results meant for Ashbrooks and what to do next.

*EXHIBIT 1*

| Ashbrooks Awareness Study<br>Awareness of Ashbrooks | |
| --- | --- |
| | **Total %** |
| Unaided | 42 |
| Aided | 48 |
| Total | 90 |
| Not aware | 10 |

**EXHIBIT 1** (cont'd)

| | Home Accessories % | Bathroom Accessories % | Bedroom Accessories % | Kitchenware and Housewares % |
|---|---|---|---|---|
| Comes to mind | 25 | 32 | 20 | 18 |
| Shopped in last 3 months | 9 | 12 | 4 | 8 |
| Shopped most often (if shopped in last 3 months) | 3 | 10 | 5 | 5 |

**EXHIBIT 2**

| | Ashbrooks Awareness Study Awareness/Use | | | |
|---|---|---|---|---|
| | Home Accessories % | Bathroom Accessories % | Bedroom Accessories % | Kitchenware and Housewares % |
| **Comes to Mind** | | | | |
| The Bay | 77 | 50 | 62 | 65 |
| Sears | 72 | 60 | 72 | 55 |
| Woolco | 45 | 32 | 24 | 31 |
| Eaton's | 39 | 28 | 38 | 33 |
| Simpson's | 31 | 29 | 32 | 34 |
| Ashbrooks | 25 | 32 | 20 | 18 |
| Top Specialty Store | 10 | 6 | 3 | 9 |
| **Shopped in Last 3 Months** | | | | |
| Sears | 33 | 23 | 23 | 14 |
| The Bay | 28 | 13 | 14 | 17 |
| Woolco | 21 | 9 | 5 | 13 |
| Eaton's | 12 | 5 | 9 | 6 |
| Ashbrooks | 9 | 12 | 4 | 8 |
| Top Specialty Store | 4 | 2 | 3 | 5 |
| None | 26 | 38 | 45 | 29 |
| **Shopped Most Often (if Shopped Last 3 Months)** | | | | |
| Sears | 30 | 30 | 38 | 20 |
| The Bay | 23 | 14 | 21 | 24 |
| Eaton's | 15 | 10 | 15 | 6 |
| Woolco | 11 | 11 | 4 | 13 |
| Simpson's | 3 | 6 | 4 | 13 |
| Ashbrooks | 3 | 10 | 5 | 5 |
| Top Specialty Store | 2 | 2 | 4 | 3 |

*EXHIBIT 3*

| Ashbrooks Awareness Study Advertising | |
|---|---|
| | **Total Aware %** |
| **Source of Awareness** | |
| Saw store in mall | 58 |
| Radio ads | 16 |
| Word of mouth | 11 |
| Newspaper ads | 8 |
| Flyers | 8 |
| Other | 4 |
| **Shopped at Ashbrooks Because of Ad** | **Shoppers %** |
| | 19% |
| **Type of Ad Which Brought People in** | **Shopped Because of Ad[1] %** |
| Radio ads | 50 |
| Newspaper ads | 42 |
| Flyers | 29 |

1.  Interpret with caution due to small sample size.

*EXHIBIT 4*

| Ashbrooks Awareness Study Adoption | |
|---|---|
| | **Total %** |
| Shopped | 63 |
| Aware/Not shopped | 22 |
| Shopped/Not purchased | 30 |
| Purchased | 34 |
| Purchased only once | 15 |
| Repeat purchase | 19 |
| Committed shoppers | 10 |

*EXHIBIT 5*

| | Ashbrooks Awareness Study Awareness/Shopping/Purchase Conversion Matrix | | | | |
|---|---|---|---|---|---|
| Total sample | (200) | | | | |
| | % | | | | |
| Total awareness | 90 | 100% | | | |
| Total shopped | 63 | 70 | 100% | | |
| Total purchased | 34 | 38 | 54 | 100% | |
| Total repeat purchase | 19 | 21 | 30 | 56 | 100% |
| Total committed | 10 | 11 | 16 | 30 | 54 |

*EXHIBIT 6*

| | Ashbrooks Awareness Study Shopping Behaviour | | | | | | | |
|---|---|---|---|---|---|---|---|---|
| | Total Aware % | Unaided Aware % | Shopped % | Shopped/ Not Purchased % | Purchased % | Purchase/ Not Repeat[1] % | Repeat Purchaser[1] % | Committed[1] % |
| **Times Shopped Past 6 Months** | | | | | | | | |
| Once | 22 | 17 | 29 | 49 | 12 | 23 | 3 | 0 |
| 2–5 times | 41 | 50 | 56 | 49 | 59 | 70 | 53 | 37 |
| 6+ times | 14 | 21 | 18 | 2 | 25 | 7 | 48 | 62 |
| Never | 25 | 10 | — | — | — | — | — | — |
| Average # of times shopped (if shopped) | 3.9 | 5.3 | 3.9 | 1.9 | 5.7 | 2.5 | 8.4 | 7.6 |
| **Times Purchased Past 6 Months** | | | | | | | | |
| Once | | 30 | 43 | | 45 | 100 | 0 | 5 |
| 2–3 times | | 52 | 42 | | 43 | | 78 | 63 |
| 4+ times | | 16 | 12 | | 12 | | 21 | 32 |
| Never | | 2 | 4 | | — | | — | — |
| Average # of times purchased (if purchased) | | 2.5 | 2.1 | | 2.1 | 1.0 | 3.1 | 3.5 |

1. Interpret with caution due to low sample sizes.

*Exhibit 7*

| | Shoppers % | Repeat Purchases % | Committed % |
|---|---|---|---|
| **Ashbrooks Awareness Study** <br> **Shopping Behaviour** | | | |
| **Last Time Shopped** | | | |
| Last week | 13 | 16 | 26 |
| Last 2 weeks | 7 | 14 | 11 |
| Last month | 40 | 46 | 37 |
| Last 2–3 months | 25 | 19 | 21 |
| More than 3 months ago | 14 | 5 | 5 |
| **Purpose for Buying at Ashbrooks** | | | |
| Gift | 45 | 49 | 42 |
| Single item for home | 36 | 30 | 32 |
| Several items for redecorating room | 27 | 41 | 58 |
| Bought on impulse | 6 | 5 | 0 |

*Exhibit 8*

| | Importance for Store Choice[1] # | Most Important Attributes[2] % | Performance of Ashbrooks[3] # |
|---|---|---|---|
| **Ashbrooks Awareness Study** <br> **Attribute Ratings** | | | |
| Good value for money | 2.7 | 69 | 3.0 |
| High quality products | 2.6 | 48 | 3.9 |
| Good service | 2.5 | 20 | 3.3 |
| Low prices | 2.3 | 17 | 2.2 |
| Wide range of colours | 2.3 | 7 | 4.3 |
| Variety of sizes | 2.3 | 6 | 3.8 |
| Convenient location | 2.2 | 17 | 3.7 |
| Wide range of brands | 2.2 | 7 | 3.6 |
| Attractive presentation | 2.1 | 5 | 4.4 |
| Well-known brands | 1.9 | 7 | 3.5 |

1. Rated on a 3-point scale (1 = Not Important, 3 = Essential).
2. Two choices allowed.
3. Rated on 5-point scale (1 = Poor, 5 = Excellent).

*EXHIBIT 9*

|  | Ashbrooks Awareness Study Likes | | | | | |
|---|---|---|---|---|---|---|
|  | Shopped % | Shopped/ Not Purchased % | Purchased % | Purchase/ Not Repeat[1] % | Repeat Purchaser[1] % | Committed[1] % |
| Good selection/variety | 37 | 27 | 46 | 47 | 46 | 47 |
| Attractive display | 26 | 24 | 28 | 30 | 27 | 26 |
| Wide range of colours | 25 | 20 | 30 | 33 | 27 | 32 |
| Spacious store | 17 | 17 | 18 | 17 | 19 | 32 |
| Quality products | 13 | 8 | 16 | 13 | 19 | 21 |
| Well laid out | 13 | 15 | 10 | 10 | 11 | 11 |
| Clean store | 11 | 8 | 13 | 13 | 14 | 5 |
| Staff friendly/helpful | 10 | 3 | 15 | 3 | 24 | 26 |
| Nothing liked | 2 | 3 | 0 | 0 | 0 | 0 |

1. Interpret with caution due to low sample sizes.

*EXHIBIT 10*

|  | Ashbrooks Awareness Study Dislikes | | | | | |
|---|---|---|---|---|---|---|
|  | Shopped % | Shopped/ Not Purchased % | Purchased % | Purchase/ Not Repeat[1] % | Repeat Purchaser[1] % | Committed[1] % |
| Too expensive/High priced | 29 | 37 | 21 | 30 | 14 | 11 |
| Service not good/Not enough clerks | 10 | 7 | 12 | 10 | 14 | 21 |
| Nothing disliked | 48 | 39 | 55 | 47 | 62 | 58 |

1. Interpret with caution due to low sample sizes.

*EXHIBIT 11*

| | Total % | Total Aware % | Not Aware[1] % | Aware/ Not Shopped[1] % | Shopped % | Shopped/ Not Purchased % | Purchased % | Purchase/ Not Repeat[1] % | Repeat Purchaser[1] % | Committed[1] % |
|---|---|---|---|---|---|---|---|---|---|---|
| | | | | | | | | | | |
| **Age** | | | | | | | | | | |
| 30–34 yrs. | 44 | 46 | 29 | 26 | 52 | 47 | 55 | 60 | 51 | 47 |
| 35–39 yrs. | 31 | 29 | 48 | 37 | 25 | 20 | 30 | 27 | 32 | 32 |
| 40–45 yrs. | 25 | 25 | 24 | 37 | 33 | 32 | 15 | 13 | 16 | 21 |
| **Income** | | | | | | | | | | |
| $30K–$40K | 29 | 26 | 48 | 16 | 29 | 32 | 25 | 20 | 30 | 21 |
| $40K–50K | 30 | 30 | 24 | 33 | 31 | 32 | 30 | 40 | 22 | 26 |
| $50K+ | 42 | 44 | 29 | 51 | 40 | 36 | 45 | 40 | 49 | 53 |
| **Employment** | | | | | | | | | | |
| Full-time | 50 | 48 | 67 | 44 | 49 | 42 | 55 | 57 | 54 | 53 |
| Part-time | 20 | 21 | 14 | 33 | 17 | 19 | 15 | 10 | 19 | 21 |
| Not at all | 30 | 31 | 19 | 23 | 34 | 39 | 30 | 33 | 27 | 26 |
| **Type of Dwelling** | | | | | | | | | | |
| House | 73 | 73 | 71 | 84 | 72 | 69 | 75 | 77 | 73 | 74 |
| Apt./Condo | 27 | 27 | 29 | 16 | 28 | 31 | 25 | 23 | 27 | 26 |
| **Tenure** | | | | | | | | | | |
| Own | 75 | 77 | 57 | 79 | 77 | 76 | 78 | 83 | 73 | 74 |
| Rent | 25 | 23 | 43 | 21 | 23 | 24 | 22 | 17 | 27 | 26 |
| **Household Size** | | | | | | | | | | |
| 1–2 | 24 | 24 | 19 | 9 | 28 | 31 | 25 | 30 | 21 | 22 |
| 3+ | 76 | 76 | 81 | 91 | 72 | 69 | 75 | 70 | 79 | 78 |
| **Interest in Decorating** | | | | | | | | | | |
| Active Decorator | 44 | 44 | 43 | 33 | 48 | 49 | 46 | 50 | 43 | 47 |
| Only when needed | 51 | 51 | 43 | 63 | 48 | 46 | 49 | 43 | 54 | 53 |
| Tedious chore | 6 | 4 | 14 | 5 | 5 | 5 | 4 | 7 | 3 | 0 |

Table title: Ashbrooks Awareness Study[1] — Demographics

1. Interpret with caution due to low sample sizes.

# CASE 5.5 ASHBROOKS (C)

In early April 1989, John Ross, general manager of Ashbrooks, was reviewing the latest results and consumer research for the home accessories chain. Results were still disappointing and time was running out. (See Ashbrooks (A) and (B) for background.) The stores still had not made a profit and senior F.W. Woolworth management were becoming disillusioned with the whole concept. While Mr. Ross knew it often took two or three years for a new retail format to become profitable, he was concerned and wondered what changes if any he might make and what to say to his superiors.

*THE NEW STRATEGY*

In late 1987, Ashbrooks management tried a great number of initiatives to find the winning formula for Ashbrooks. Jeff Burley, the store manager for Ashbrooks Square One, recalled the time as "a new concept a week as we changed layouts, product assortments, advertising, etc. Everyone seemed to have ideas for change."

The new strategy involved some major changes. Some excerpts from that plan follow.

1. Presentation — Ashbrooks will move toward a mass merchandise store concept without losing sight of the specialty store concept. There will be a substantial increase in space given to promotional items throughout the entire store. For example, there will be promotional towels (now $9.99 instead of $19.99), sheets, blankets, comforters, pillows, bathmats, dinnerware, and table cloths. This new approach will bring together the best of a mass merchandise store with the best of a specialty store.

2. Assortment — Ashbrooks will improve assortment in all core departments in order to achieve headquarters store status in these departments. For example, Bath Shop will be increased 30 percent, Towels 30 percent, Tabletop Textiles 35 percent. All assortments will be increased.

3. Value — Value prices will be featured in every department. We will become known for value items, such as ironing boards for $24.99, bathroom scales for $29.99, dinnerware for $29.99, which will be featured on end caps, promotional bunks, and tables in each department. New items with lower price points will be purchased.

4. Promotion — Ashbrooks will become more promotional with store signage and advertising heralding our new slogan "Canada's Largest Home Fashion Accessories Store." We will use flyers and radio advertising.

Maria Purser, Ashbrooks' buyer for Home Textiles, summarized these changes as moving Ashbrooks into lower priced lines, predominantly American, with a narrowed colour breadth (from more than 20 colours to approximately 8 to 12 colours). Maria and Susan Gillis, the Kitchen and Tabletop buyer, agreed they faced difficulties dealing with suppliers. Unlike when they were with their previous employers (Eaton's and Woolco), these buyers were now treated as they put it "as small potatoes in the eyes of the suppliers." This resulted in late deliveries and lack of influence regarding suppliers product decisions.

Susan described her department as changing from an upscale brand name dinnerware boutique to more "casual living" 20 piece dinner sets. As a result, her sales doubled. Originally placemats had been stocked primarily in solid colours, but prints and patterns were now the best sellers. Susan organized her displays into "colour stories" minutely detailed on blueprints for each store. While this took a lot of her time, she felt this seemed to be a successful approach.

The high fashion nature of the assortment led management to expect the need for markdowns, but they were unsure as to the level or timing of these. They decided to have two annual clearance sales, in July and January, to reduce inventories of slow sellers and to avoid an image of being on sale the rest of the year.

Some Ashbrooks staff members at the time reported feeling "they were riding a roller coaster with all these changes."

**F.W. WOOLWORTH 1988**

FWW set new records in revenues, earnings, and store openings in 1988. Revenues jumped 13 percent, net income 17 percent, and an unprecedented 1,154 stores were opened or acquired worldwide moving the total to 7,739 stores. The emphasis was on specialty stores, which were providing $290 per square foot in revenues and $26 per square foot in operating profit compared to $134 and $7 for general merchandise stores in 1988. FWW was moving toward its goal of achieving an average annual net profit of 12 to 14 percent.

**BRANDEN'S**

By late 1987, Branden's had grown to a nine-store home accessories store in Atlanta, Georgia, and Florida. Several competitive imitations had also started. Branden's kept maintaining they were still in the testing stage, despite their three-year life. In 1988, Branden's was still undergoing changes in its product mix, fixtures, and ceiling heights.

In April 1989 Branden's suddenly closed. Ann Barkelew-O'Hagan of Branden's parent Dayton-Hudson said of the closure: "The potential for growth in sales and profit was not as strong as some of the more established divisions of our company, such as Target, Mervyn's, and Lechmere."

In May 1989 another consumer research study was complete. The objectives of this study were as follows:

1. To measure the level of awareness of Ashbrooks, specifically as a provider of accessories and fashion items for the bedroom, bathroom, and kitchen.

2. To determine the shopping behaviour of those aware of Ashbrooks.

3. To rate the relative importance to store choice of selected home accessory store attributes and Ashbrooks' performance on those attributes.

4. To solicit the specific likes and dislikes of Ashbrooks among shoppers.

5. To compare the results of the previous studies to new results.

The study was conducted at Square One in March 1989 using a mall intercept methodology. Two hundred respondents were interviewed who met the following qualifications: females, aged 25 to 49 years, with total annual household incomes of at least $30,000 who shop at Square One at least once every two months.

The results presented to Mr. Ross are shown as Exhibits 1 to 13.

*EXHIBIT 1*

| | Ashbrooks Awareness Study Awareness of Ashbrooks | |
|---|---|---|
| | 1988 % | 1989 % |
| Unaided | 42 | 45 |
| Aided | 48 | 47 |
| Total | 90 | 92 |
| Not aware | 10 | 8 |

| | Home Accessories 1988 % | 1989 % | Bathroom Accessories 1988 % | 1989 % |
|---|---|---|---|---|
| Comes to mind | 25 | 29 | 32 | 36 |
| Shopped in last 3 months | 9 | 12 | 12 | 14 |
| Shopped most often (if shopped in last 3 months) | 3 | 4 | 10 | 11 |

***EXHIBIT* 1** *(cont'd)*

|  | Bedroom Accessories 1988 % | 1989 % | Kitchenware Housewares 1988 % | 1989 % |
|---|---|---|---|---|
| Comes to mind | 20 | 28 | 18 | 22 |
| Shopped in last 3 months | 4 | 5 | 8 | 7 |
| Shopped most often (if shopped in last 3 months) | 5 | 5 | 5 | 3 |

***EXHIBIT* 2**

| Ashbrooks Awareness Study Awareness/Use | | | | |
|---|---|---|---|---|
|  | Home Accessories % | Bathroom Accessories % | Bedroom Accessories % | Kitchenware and Housewares % |
| **Comes to Mind** | | | | |
| The Bay | 72 | 56 | 60 | 61 |
| Sears | 67 | 54 | 60 | 53 |
| Woolco | 62 | 56 | 51 | 58 |
| Eaton's | 53 | 40 | 54 | 44 |
| Ashbrooks | 29 | 32 | 28 | 22 |
| Simpson's | 12 | 12 | 17 | 14 |
| Top Specialty  Store | 9 | 9 | 4 | 19 |
| **Shopped in Last 3 Months** | | | | |
| Woolco | 38 | 20 | 17 | 25 |
| Sears | 35 | 18 | 17 | 14 |
| The Bay | 28 | 12 | 17 | 21 |
| Eaton's | 20 | 12 | 12 | 11 |
| Ashbrooks | 12 | 14 | 5 | 7 |
| Top Specialty Store | 4 | 3 | 2 | 9 |
| None | 19 | 34 | 46 | 31 |
| **Shopped Most Often (if Shopped Last 3 Months)** | | | | |
| Sears | 27 | 18 | 24 | 14 |
| Woolco | 24 | 24 | 19 | 24 |
| The Bay | 10 | 11 | 14 | 15 |
| Eaton's | 9 | 10 | 18 | 14 |
| Ashbrooks | 4 | 11 | 5 | 3 |
| Top Specialty Store | 1 | 4 | 2 | 7 |

*EXHIBIT 3*

| | Total Aware | |
|---|---|---|
| **Ashbrooks Awareness Study**<br>**Advertising** | **1988**<br>% | **1989**<br>% |
| **Source of Awareness** | | |
| Saw store in mall | 58 | 64 |
| Radio ads | 16 | 11 |
| Word of mouth | 11 | 12 |
| Newspaper ads | 8 | 7 |
| Flyers | 8 | 7 |
| Other | 4 | 2 |

| | Shoppers | |
|---|---|---|
| | **1988**<br>% | **1989**<br>% |
| **Shopped at Ashbrooks Because of Ad** | 19 | 25 |

| | Shopped Because of Ad[1] | |
|---|---|---|
| | **1988**<br>% | **1989**<br>% |
| **Type of Ad Which Brought People In** | | |
| Flyers | 29 | 60 |
| Radio | 50 | 30 |
| Newspaper | 42 | 20 |

1. Interpret with caution due to small sample size.

*EXHIBIT 4*

| | 1988 % | 1989 % |
|---|---|---|
| | **Ashbrooks Awareness Study** **Adoption** | |
| Shopped | 63 | 65 |
| Aware/Not shopped | 22 | 21 |
| Shopped/Not purchased | 30 | 25 |
| Purchased | 34 | 40 |
| Purchased only once | 15 | 10 |
| Repeat purchase | 19 | 31 |
| Committed shoppers | 10 | 10 |

*EXHIBIT 5*

| | Ashbrooks Awareness Study Awareness/Shopping/Purchase Conversion Matrix | | | | |
|---|---|---|---|---|---|
| Total sample | (200) | | | | |
| | % | | | | |
| Total aware | 92 | 100% | | | |
| Total shopped | 65 | 70 | 100% | | |
| Total purchased | 40 | 43 | 62 | 100% | |
| Total repeat purchased | 31 | 33 | 47 | 76 | 100% |
| Total committed | 10 | 11 | 16 | 25 | 33 |

*EXHIBIT 6*

| | Total Aware % | Unaided Aware % | Shopped % | Shopped/ Not Purchased % | Purchased % | Purchase/ Not Repeat[1] % | Repeat Purchaser[1] % | Committed[1] % |
|---|---|---|---|---|---|---|---|---|
| **Ashbrooks Awareness Study** **Shopping Behaviour** | | | | | | | | |
| **Average Times Shopped Past 6 Months (If Shopped)** | | | | | | | | |
| 1989 | 5.5 | 6.9 | 5.5 | 2.0 | 7.6 | 2.4 | 9.2 | 12.0 |
| 1988 | 3.9 | 5.3 | 3.9 | 1.9 | 5.7 | 2.5 | 8.4 | 7.6 |
| **Average Times Purchased Past 6 Months (If Purchased)** | | | | | | | | |
| 1989 | 4.0 | 3.7 | | | 3.7 | 1.0 | 4.6 | 5.5 |
| 1988 | 2.5 | 2.1 | | | 2.1 | 1.0 | 3.1 | 3.5 |

1. Interpret with caution due to low sample sizes.

*EXHIBIT 7*

**Ashbrooks Awareness Study**
**Shopping Behaviour**

| | Shoppers | | Repeat Purchasers | | Committed[1] | |
|---|---|---|---|---|---|---|
| | 1988 | 1989 | 1988 | 1989 | 1988 | 1989 |
| **Last Time Shopped** | | | | | | |
| Last week | 13 | 21 | 16 | 31 | 26 | 45 |
| Last 2 weeks | 7 | 9 | 14 | 13 | 11 | 25 |
| Last month | 40 | 21 | 46 | 21 | 37 | 25 |
| Last 2–3 months | 25 | 29 | 19 | 26 | 21 | 5 |
| More than 3 months ago | 14 | 19 | 5 | 7 | 5 | 0 |
| **Purpose for Buying at Ashbrooks** | | | | | | |
| Gift | 45 | 45 | 49 | 44 | 42 | 30 |
| Single item for home | 36 | 38 | 30 | 38 | 32 | 50 |
| Several items for redecorating room | 27 | 31 | 42 | 39 | 58 | 50 |
| Bought on impulse | 6 | 5 | 5 | 5 | 0 | 10 |

1. Interpret with caution due to low sample sizes.

*EXHIBIT 8*

| | Ashbrooks Awareness Study Attribute Ratings | | | | | |
|---|---|---|---|---|---|---|
| | Importance for Store Choice[1] | | Most Important Attributes[2] | | Performance of Ashbrooks[3] | |
| | 1988 # | 1989 # | 1988 % | 1989 % | 1988 # | 1989 # |
| Good value for money | 2.7 | 2.6 | 69 | 61 | 3.0 | 3.2 |
| High quality products | 2.6 | 2.5 | 48 | 37 | 3.9 | 4.0 |
| Good service | 2.5 | 2.5 | 20 | 22 | 3.3 | 3.4 |
| Low prices | 2.3 | 2.4 | 17 | 28 | 2.2 | 2.4 |
| Wide range of colours | 2.3 | 2.3 | 7 | 7 | 4.3 | 4.5 |
| Variety of sizes | 2.3 | 2.2 | 6 | 2 | 3.8 | 4.0 |
| Convenient location | 2.2 | 2.2 | 17 | 14 | 3.7 | 3.7 |
| Range of brands | 2.2 | 2.1 | 7 | 9 | 3.6 | 3.8 |
| Pleasant atmosphere | N/A | 2.1 | N/A | 4 | N/A | 3.9 |
| Attractive presentation | 2.1 | 2.0 | 5 | 2 | 4.4 | 4.5 |
| Well-known brands | 1.9 | 1.8 | 7 | 5 | 3.5 | 3.7 |

1. Rated on a 3-point scale (1 = Not Important, 3 = Essential).
2. Two choices allowed.
3. Rated on 5-point scale (1 = Poor, 5 = Excellent).

*EXHIBIT 9*

| | Shopped % | Shopped/ Not Purchased % | Purchased % | Purchase/ Not Repeat[1] % | Repeat Purchaser[1] % | Committed[1] % |
|---|---|---|---|---|---|---|
| **Ashbrooks Awareness Study Likes** | | | | | | |
| Good selection/Variety | 45 | 49 | 43 | 32 | 46 | 45 |
| Attractive displays | 33 | 20 | 40 | 74 | 30 | 30 |
| Wide range of colours | 29 | 24 | 31 | 16 | 36 | 50 |
| Quality products | 25 | 20 | 28 | 21 | 30 | 30 |
| Spacious store | 17 | 17 | 17 | 11 | 20 | 20 |
| Good prices | 12 | 2 | 16 | 11 | 18 | 15 |
| Well laid out | 12 | 7 | 14 | 11 | 15 | 25 |
| Helpful staff | 10 | 7 | 11 | 5 | 13 | 20 |
| Nothing liked | 0 | 0 | 0 | 0 | 0 | 0 |

1. Interpret with caution due to low sample sizes.

*EXHIBIT 10*

| | Shopped % | Shopped/ Not Purchased % | Purchased % | Purchase/ Not Repeat[1] % | Repeat Purchaser[1] % | Committed[1] % |
|---|---|---|---|---|---|---|
| **Ashbrooks Awareness Study Dislikes** | | | | | | |
| High priced | 40 | 51 | 35 | 58 | 28 | 30 |
| Poor service/Not enough clerks | 4 | 2 | 5 | 5 | 5 | 10 |
| Nothing disliked | 46 | 34 | 52 | 42 | 56 | 55 |

1. Interpret with caution due to low sample sizes.

*EXHIBIT 11*

| | Ashbrooks Awareness Study Ashbrooks Bridal Registry | | | | | |
|---|---|---|---|---|---|---|
| | Aware of Ashbrooks % | Shoppers % | Shopped/ Not Purchased[1] % | Purchasers[1] % | Repeat Purchaser[1] % | Committed[1] % |
| Aware of Ashbrooks Bridal Registry | 22 | 27 | 22 | 30 | 30 | 35 |
| **Likelihood of Registering at Ashbrooks** | | | | | | |
| Very/Somewhat | 45 | 53 | 47 | 57 | 62 | 60 |
| Not very/Not at all | 55 | 47 | 54 | 43 | 38 | 40 |
| **If "Not Very/Not At All," Why Not** | | | | | | |
| Don't like bridal registries/ Don't use them | 33 | 34 | 17 | 47 | 59 | 33 |
| Would register elsewhere | 22 | 30 | 21 | 36 | 26 | 51 |
| Not familiar with ashbrooks | 19 | 8 | 13 | 4 | 5 | 0 |
| Too expensive | 10 | 14 | 17 | 11 | 5 | 0 |
| Would rather buy on own | 10 | 12 | 9 | 14 | 11 | 33 |

1. Interpret with caution due to low sample sizes.

*EXHIBIT 12*

| | Ashbrooks Awareness Study New Door | | | | |
|---|---|---|---|---|---|
| | Aware of Ashbrooks % | Shoppers % | Purchasers % | Repeat Purchasers % | Committed[1] % |
| Aware of new door | 45 | 45 | 50 | 54 | 60 |
| Use door, if aware | 74 | 74 | 82 | 85 | 92 |
| Used door first, time in store, if used | 9 | 9 | 9 | 7 | 0 |

1. Interpret with caution due to low sample sizes.

*EXHIBIT 13*

| | Total % | Unaided Aware % | Not Aware[1] % | Aware/ Not Shopped[1] % | Shopped % | Shopped/ Not Purchased % | Purchased % | Purchase/ Not Repeat % | Repeat Purchaser % | Committed[1] % |
|---|---|---|---|---|---|---|---|---|---|---|
| | | | | **Ashbrooks Awareness Study[1]** **Demographics** | | | | | | |
| **Age** | | | | | | | | | | |
| 25–29 years | 34 | 37 | 31 | 40 | 33 | 37 | 30 | 21 | 33 | 30 |
| 30–34 years | 23 | 21 | 12 | 29 | 24 | 24 | 24 | 32 | 21 | 20 |
| 35–39 years | 20 | 18 | 25 | 7 | 21 | 20 | 21 | 16 | 23 | 20 |
| 40–45 years | 17 | 18 | 25 | 17 | 18 | 10 | 22 | 26 | 21 | 30 |
| 46–49 years | 5 | 7 | 6 | 7 | 5 | 8 | 3 | 5 | 2 | 0 |
| **Income** | | | | | | | | | | |
| $30K–$40K | 22 | 20 | 19 | 21 | 22 | 27 | 20 | 11 | 23 | 10 |
| $40K–50K | 27 | 17 | 38 | 29 | 26 | 31 | 22 | 37 | 18 | 10 |
| $50K+ | 50 | 63 | 44 | 50 | 52 | 43 | 57 | 53 | 59 | 80 |
| **Employment** | | | | | | | | | | |
| Full-time | 60 | 62 | 50 | 52 | 61 | 57 | 64 | 53 | 67 | 70 |
| Part-time | 19 | 17 | 25 | 24 | 17 | 18 | 16 | 16 | 16 | 10 |
| Not at all | 22 | 21 | 25 | 24 | 22 | 24 | 20 | 32 | 16 | 20 |
| **Type of Dwelling** | | | | | | | | | | |
| House | 61 | 67 | 44 | 60 | 65 | 65 | 65 | 79 | 61 | 70 |
| Apt./Condo. | 31 | 28 | 38 | 26 | 29 | 29 | 29 | 16 | 33 | 20 |
| Townhouse | 9 | 4 | 19 | 14 | 5 | 6 | 5 | 5 | 5 | 5 |
| **Tenure** | | | | | | | | | | |
| Own | 62 | 69 | 56 | 60 | 67 | 63 | 69 | 68 | 69 | 80 |
| Rent | 38 | 31 | 44 | 40 | 33 | 37 | 31 | 32 | 31 | 20 |
| **Household Size** | | | | | | | | | | |
| 1–2 | 30 | 32 | 37 | 28 | 31 | 27 | 33 | 26 | 34 | 35 |
| 3+ | 70 | 68 | 63 | 72 | 69 | 73 | 67 | 74 | 66 | 65 |
| **Interest in Decorating** | | | | | | | | | | |
| Active Decorator | 48 | 51 | 50 | 50 | 48 | 37 | 55 | 47 | 57 | 65 |
| Only when needed | 43 | 41 | 44 | 36 | 45 | 57 | 38 | 42 | 36 | 30 |
| Tedious chore | 9 | 8 | 6 | 14 | 7 | 6 | 8 | 11 | 7 | 5 |

1. Interpret with caution due to low sample sizes.

## C A S E  **5.6**   FLEETWAY BOWLING CENTRE

In early March 1994, Harvey Katz, member of the ESAM Group and manager of Fleetway Bowling Centre in London, Ontario, was approached by his bowling alley software supplier about a new program that could combine bowling with the game of Bingo. Harvey wondered if "Bingo-Bowling" would be a good move for Fleetway, considering the negative public perception toward bingo. If he chose to go ahead with supplying the program for his 12 five-pin lanes, many decisions regarding the marketing plan would have to be resolved, including whom to target, what media to choose, and whether this opportunity would be financially attractive for Fleetway.

**GENERAL BACKGROUND**

The ESAM Group, a commercial development firm, was established in the late 1950s by Sam Katz and a partner. ESAM took over Fleetway Bowling Lanes in 1959, when the previous owners could not cover rental payments. During the next 30 years, Fleetway encountered financial problems as bowling continuously declined in popularity from the mid-1970s. Little was done in the way of marketing and improvements to the operation. Fleetway was perceived as an unclean, old, and "boring" place to go. Sam continued to support the lanes because of his interest in the game and his desire to provide a recreational facility for ESAM's many tenants in the surrounding area.

In 1976, Sam moved Fleetway from its strip mall location to an area just west of ESAM's housing developments. The new and much larger facility, Fleetway 40 Bowling Centre (Fleetway), offered 40 five-pin lanes. With increased marketing efforts, Fleetway eventually showed small profits in 1989. Prices reached an all-time high in 1994 of $2.75 per game (adult), $2.00 per game (children) for five-pin and $3.00 per game (adult), $2.00 per game (children) for ten-pin. In addition to this cost, bowling shoes could be rented for $1.75 (adult) and $1.00 (children). These costs were comparable to Fleetway's competitors' prices.

**HARVEY KATZ**

After graduating from the administrative and commercial studies program in finance at the University of Western Ontario, Harvey Katz briefly worked as a life insurance salesman. Persuaded by his father to join the family business, Harvey soon took over as manager of ESAM's many properties. In 1990, he became responsible for Fleetway's operations.

Harvey looked forward to the challenge of changing Fleetway's image. He wanted to create a recreational facility that was fun for the whole family and for all age groups. He believed that, with the right marketing mix, there was no reason why the facility could not become very profitable.

Upon assuming his new position, Harvey discovered three things: the importance of a clean and updated facility, the consumer's expectations for computerized automatic scoring, and the growing demand for ten-pin bowling in Canada. To address these needs at Fleetway, Harvey hired an interior designer to redecorate and create a more "family" type of atmosphere. He constantly changed and improved Fleetway's surroundings with bi-annual renovations and new decor. The highest standards of cleanliness were demanded from Fleetway's employees inside and outside the building. Computerized scoring was introduced to each lane, making Fleetway the second bowling alley in London with such technology. Lastly, Harvey switched over 12 lanes from five-pin bowling to ten-pin bowling.

More changes followed with the introduction of billiard tables, a profitable snack bar (with 40 percent margins on the average selling price), monthly draws for Blue Jay tickets or weekend vacations, free giveaways, Halloween and New Year's Eve parties and "Midnight Madness" bowling — in which bowlers competed for prizes by making designated shots. These changes accompanied a new focus on customer satisfaction and service that led Harvey and Fleetway to win the "Best Quest Gold Award" in 1993, a local award granted for exceptional customer service. Profits increased in the early 1990s, reaching an all-time high in 1992.

**THE BOWLING INDUSTRY: 1950s–PRESENT**

Typically known as a blue collar sport, bowling achieved its peak popularity in the late 1950s/early 1960s. During this period, bowling alley construction flourished in North America. The sport became a favourite social event for North American families, both through leagues and through recreational activity. Its popularity was the result of its appeal to all age groups and its relatively inexpensive price. Additionally, bowling was one of only a few alternatives available for social recreation at this time.

Participation in bowling declined and many alleys were forced to close throughout the following decade. The sport was considered "uncool" and "boring," especially by the younger generation. As alleys were forced to increase their prices to cover higher fixed costs, bowling quickly became too expensive for the average worker and his or her family.

Consumer appeal increased slightly in the mid-1970s when "automatic pin set-up" technology was introduced. Demand eventually levelled off and weakened in the 1980s and early 1990s. Bowling was now competing with many other pursuits for the recreational dollar in a declining economy.

**THE CONSUMER**

Bowlers spanned all ages with the majority occupying the 35 to 59 age group. This adult category was the largest, comprising approximately two-thirds of all bowlers. The golden age group (65 years or older) was the second largest adult category representing 18 percent of all bowlers. (See Exhibit 1 for a consumer profile of bowlers in Canada.)

There were two types of participants: league players and recreational/open play bowlers. In 1993, there were approximately 130,000 five- and ten-pin league bowlers and 1.9 million recreational bowlers in Canada. Both groups shared similar demographics. The main differentiation distinguishing these groups was frequency of play. While league players played on average 1.2 times per week, recreational/open play bowlers bowled as infrequently as once per year, often in groups as part of a social event organized by a church, high school, university, club, etc. Canadian league play had been steadily declining in popularity since the mid-1970s, whereas recreational bowling had been rising.

Leagues consisted of both five- and ten-pin games. A typical league season consisted of 32 weeks from September to April. While the standard ten-pin game was the preferred league sport around the world, Canadians favoured the five-pin game. Invented in 1905 by Canadian businessmen, five-pin bowling was a faster-paced game that could be played over the lunch hour. It was also an easier game for women as the ball size was significantly smaller. In 1994, 70 percent of all league bowlers in Canada were five-pin bowlers. Accordingly, the ratio of 10:5-pin lanes across Canada was a 30:70 split.[1]

## COMPETITION

In 1994, competition for the London bowling dollar was intense. Of the eight competitors, three offered ten-pin bowling exclusively, three offered only five-pin, leaving just two to offer both games. (For competitors' geographical locations, see Exhibit 2.)

Fleetway's major competitor was Southland Bowling Alleys. As part of a large American chain that also manufactured bowling equipment, Southland had the financial support and marketing expertise of its head office. An extremely large facility with 32 ten-pin lanes, Southland was the first fully computer-automated bowling facility in London. Its management was staffed with professional bowlers who had a solid understanding of market trends. Southland housed many strong leagues and open bowling. It also offered a bar and pinball facilities.

Fleetway's other ten-pin competitors — Huron Bowl, Centre Bowlarama, and Royal Bowl — had various advantages and disadvantages. Huron, third to fully computer automate its facilities, had strong league play, affiliation with a large parent company, 32 ten-pin lanes, a bar, and pinball facilities. It did very little marketing and the building had not been updated for many years. Centre Bowlarama had 12 computer-automated ten-pin lanes, and 12 standard five-pin lanes, good management, chain affiliation, a liquor licence, and excellent merchandising and marketing skills. Royal Bowl, with 32 ten-pin lanes, was the newest competitor, having been only a year in operation. It was a fully computerized and modernized licensed facility with a great location. Each ten-pin competitor had unique weaknesses ranging from poor marketing, stale; outdated facilities; or upstairs facilities in poor locations (economically depressed areas of London); and poor management.

Fleetway's competitors in the five-pin game were Fairmont, Eastown Lanes, and the London Bowl-A-Rama. Fleetway and its competitors appeared to be suffering from the decline in popularity of the five-pin game. Fleetway's competitors were fully licensed and had pinball facilities with manual scoring. Fairmont was a friendly, family-operated business with a good location in the basement of a plaza with strong league play. Eastown, with 16 lanes, was also located in a plaza. The last competitor with 24 lanes, London Bowl-A-Rama, was well managed and appeared to be holding its own in five-pin play. Recently, another exclusive five-pin competitor, Plaza Lanes and Billiards, had gone out of business. Fleetway's five-pin competitors faced some disadvantages, including old furnishings and outdated decor, poor locations (customers had to climb stairs), and outdated equipment.

## BINGO-BOWLING

The game of "Bingo-Bowling" was a computerized team sport played across two or more bowling lanes. Unlike regular bowling in which an individual tried to achieve the highest score, Bingo-Bowling required participants to block out their lane's bingo card faster than their competitors (see Exhibit 3 for a sample card and rules). Each lane's team consisted of one to six players. Whenever a certain point combination was achieved (strike, spare, 13 points, etc.), the required element was erased automatically on the electronic bingo card. Bingo-Bowling was a much faster paced game than regular bowling, since it was a race to beat your competitor in blocking out your card. The amount of time spent per game depended on the bingo card selected, as they ranged in the level of difficulty.

Harvey believed that Bingo-Bowling could help solve some of his current problems. A growing consumer preference for ten-pin was leaving five-pin lanes unused, especially on weeknights after 9:00 p.m. when league play finished. Fleetway was also having problems attracting young adults to the facility. Harvey saw a great opportunity to tap the university market, as the University of Western Ontario serviced 28,000 full- and part-time students and was only kilometres from Fleetway. According to a survey of this market conducted for Fleetway, students were not recurrent bowlers (see Exhibit 4). Most participants in the survey characterised bowling as an "uncool way" to spend an evening. However, when asked to rate their enjoyment after a bowling experience, students described it as "fun," "entertaining," and "a completely different experience from a regular night out." Although Harvey believed it would be very difficult to change this group's general attitude toward bowling, he thought the more competitive game of Bingo-Bowling might entice them to become more frequent patrons of Fleetway.

In order to measure student reaction to the game, Harvey initiated a focus group study with six groups of university students. After being invited in for a free trial of Bingo-Bowling, they filled out a questionnaire (see Exhibit 5 for their responses). Overall, the feedback was favourable. In particular, the participants enjoyed competing against their friends and acquaintances.

**THE DECISION**

Harvey wondered if Bingo-Bowling should be introduced at Fleetway. He was concerned about the image that Bingo portrayed: "When I think of Bingo halls, I think of smoky, unclean, shady establishments full of people playing a game they can't afford." As Harvey believed many others agreed with his perception of Bingo, he didn't want to introduce a game whose name could jeopardize the family image he had tried to develop at Fleetway.

Harvey stated: "I'm scared of doing things without a thoroughly thought-out plan. Public perception is so important in this business as word-of-mouth spreads so quickly. If we introduce this game in a hard-sell campaign with lots of advertising and promotion and there are still kinks in the game, we may never be able to recover. However, I don't know if a slow and soft sell approach will get people in to try it."

Other decisions included developing some type of schedule for the lanes: should Bingo-Bowling be offered nightly or on designated days/nights? Should prizes be awarded to the winners? Harvey wondered what pricing strategy to pursue for this new game. Although regular bowling was priced by the game, this might not be appropriate for Bingo-Bowling. A game of Bingo-Bowling, depending on the card, could take anywhere from 20 minutes to 1 1/2 hours. In addition, if Harvey decided to take on a more aggressive approach in targeting university students, he would need to formulate a marketing scheme attractive to these students. One possibility Harvey was considering was using the London Transit Commission to bus students to and from the university to Fleetway at a cost of $100 an evening. It sounded like a good idea, but he didn't know if it would work. Harvey believed he didn't currently have the connections on U.W.O. campus to do an effective job marketing to student groups. He thought hiring a student coordinator might provide Fleetway with a closer relationship with U.W.O. clubs, residences, and faculties. He had no idea what to pay this person or what this position would entail.

The cost of supplying Fleetway's 12 lanes with the Bingo-Bowling software program would be $50/lane. The lanes could still be used for five-pin bowling at any time. Harvey spent $30,000 on advertising last year and had no idea how much to allocate to Bingo-Bowling. Other costs would include promotion, advertising, prizes, etc. (See Exhibit 6 for a list of options.)

Decisions needed to be made soon if Fleetway was to proceed. Harvey would have to decide on a price, determine whether the product should be aimed at league or recreational bowlers, plan a promotional campaign, and formulate a successful implementation plan. He wondered what would be the most effective plan to introduce Bingo-Bowling to the London market. He wanted to have the plan in place by September for the university market.

## NOTES

1. Canadian Five-Pin Association and Ontario Five-Pin Association.

**EXHIBIT 1**
*Canadian Bowling Demographics (League and Recreational)*[1]

**Age**

| Group | % |
|---|---|
| 3–24 | 7 |
| 25–34 | 10 |
| 35–59 | 65 |
| 60 + | 18 |

**Income Groups**

| Income | % |
|---|---|
| under $20,000 | 6 |
| $20,000–40,000 | 36 |
| $40,000–50,000 | 4 |
| +$50,000 | 27 |
| No response | 25 |

**Occupation**

| Type | % |
|---|---|
| Sales | 8 |
| Homemakers | 18 |
| Administration | 14 |
| Trades | 22 |
| Farming | 2 |
| Service | 4 |
| Executives | 6 |
| Retired | 10 |
| No response | 10 |

**Gender**

| Sex | % |
|---|---|
| Female | 50 |
| Male | 50 |

**Marital Status**

| Status | % |
|---|---|
| Single | 29 |
| Married | 71 |

**Education Level**

| Level | % |
|---|---|
| Attended highschool | 33 |
| Finished highschool | 33 |
| Attended post-secondary | 16 |
| Finished post-secondary | 8 |
| No response | 10 |

1. Canadian Five-Pin Association.

***EXHIBIT 2***
***Competition in the London Bowling Market***

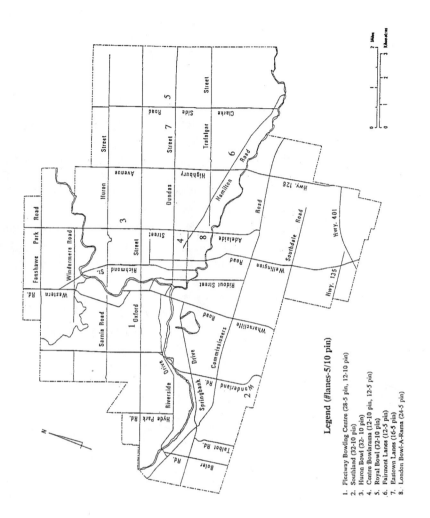

**Legend (#lanes-5/10 pin)**

1. Fleetway Bowling Centre (28-5 pin, 12-10 pin)
2. Southland (32-10 pin)
3. Huron Bowl (32- 10 pin)
4. Centre Bowlarama (12-10 pin, 12-5 pin)
5. Royal Bowl (32-10 pin)
6. Fairmont Lanes (12-5 pin)
7. Eastown Lanes (16-5 pin)
8. London Bowl-A-Rama (24-5 pin)

*EXHIBIT 3*
***Bingo-Bowling Sample Card and Rules***

Object:    The object of "Bingo-Bowling" is to clear your lane's bingo card faster than any other competing lane.

## RULES

1. Divide yourselves into teams of equal size.

2. Player one shall attempt to score one of the point combinations on his/her bingo card with up to three balls.

3. If the score is a strike or a spare, the square will be deleted from the card automatically. However, if the score is one of the other possible point combinations, and the player wishes to delete this square, he/she must press the reset button firmly for 2–3 seconds.

4. The next player follows the same procedure bowling up to three balls.

5. This continues until one lane clears their entire card. When this is achieved, they must shout "Bingo" and they are the winners.

# BINGO–BOWLING
## SCORE CARD

| X | A | / | C | 2 |
|---|---|---|---|---|
| 3 | 4 | 6 | 9 | A |
| S | R | L | 10 | H |
| 15 | 5 | 13 | X | 12 |
| 11 | 7 | 8 | L | 2 |

Sample Score Card

```
        2                    2

            3          3

                  5
```

Value of Pins and their Position

The Meaning of the symbols:

X _____ STRIKE

/ _____ SPARE

A _____ Only both corner pins standing after first ball

H _____ HEAD pin (5 pin) only knocked down by first ball

C _____ CHOP (5, 3, and 2 pins down on first ball)

R _____ RIGHT PIN left standing after first ball

L _____ LEFT PIN left standing after first ball

S _____ SPLIT (2, 3, and 2 pins left standing after first ball)

**EXHIBIT 4**
**U.W.O. Student**
**Bowling Questionnaire**[1]

1. How often do you bowl?

| Never | Few times/year | Once/month | Once/week |
|-------|----------------|------------|-----------|
| **31%** | **63%** | **6%** | **0%** |

2. Do you prefer five- or ten-pin bowling?

| 5-pin | 10-pin |
|-------|--------|
| **33%** | **67%** |

3. How many games do you bowl in one visit to a bowling alley?

| One | Two | Three | >Than Three |
|-----|-----|-------|-------------|
| **6%** | **29%** | **47%** | **18%** |

4. How much do you budget to spend when you bowl?

| <$5 | $5>X>$6.50 | $6.50>X>$8.00 | $8.00>X>$9.50 | More than $9.50 |
|-----|------------|---------------|---------------|-----------------|
| **18%** | **29%** | **50%** | **3%** | **3%** |

5. Do you purchase any food or drinks when you bowl?

| Yes | No |
|-----|-----|
| **69%** | **31%** |

6. How much do you spend?

**Avg. $3.00**

7. How large is your group when you go bowling?

| 1 | 2 | 3 | 4 | 5 | 6 | 7 | 8 | 10 | >15 |
|---|---|---|---|---|---|---|---|----|-----|
| **0%** | **6%** | **12%** | **60%** | **19%** | **3%** | **0%** | **0%** | **0%** | **0%** |

8. What night(s) of the week do you bowl?

| Mon | Tues | Wed | Thur | Fri | Sat | Sun |
|-----|------|-----|------|-----|-----|-----|
| **6%** | **4%** | **31%** | **0%** | **50%** | **0%** | **9%** |

1. Study completed by Benjamin Katchen and Robert Stoller.

**EXHIBIT 5**
**Student Bingo-Bowling**
**Questionnaire[1]**

1. Would you consider yourself a competitive person?

   | Yes | No |
   |-----|-----|
   | **88%** | **12%** |

2. Do you prefer to compete on an individual basis or as part of a team?

   | individual | | | | team |
   |---|---|---|---|---|
   | 1 | 2 | 3 | 4 | 5 |
   | **25%** | **6%** | **0%** | **31%** | **38%** |

3. Do you prefer Bingo-Bowling to regular 5-pin or 10-pin bowling?

   | Bingo-Bowling | | | | Regular Bowling |
   |---|---|---|---|---|
   | 1 | 2 | 3 | 4 | 5 |
   | **44%** | **12%** | **19%** | **12%** | **13%** |

4. How hard was the game?

   | Easy | | | | Hard |
   |---|---|---|---|---|
   | 1 | 2 | 3 | 4 | 5 |
   | **4%** | **20%** | **44%** | **32%** | **0%** |

5. Would you prefer to design your own bingo card?

   | | Yes | No |
   |---|---|---|
   | | **19%** | **81%** |

6. What would be the ideal number of teams to compete against?

   | 1 | 2 | 3 | 4 | 5 | 6 | 6<X<10 | >10 |
   |---|---|---|---|---|---|---|---|
   | **0%** | **12%** | **0%** | **44%** | **12%** | **0%** | **19%** | **12%** |

7. Would you pay more to play Bingo-Bowling than normal bowling?

   | Less | | | | More |
   |---|---|---|---|---|
   | 1 | 2 | 3 | 4 | 5 |
   | **0%** | **3%** | **88%** | **3%** | **6%** |

8. Would you prefer to play by the hour, or by the game for Bingo-Bowling?

   | Hour | Game |
   |---|---|
   | **52%** | **48%** |

9. Would you prefer to play Bingo-Bowling against others in you group, or would you rather play against strangers?

   | Friends and Acquaintances | Strangers |
   |---|---|
   | **81%** | **19%** |

1. Study completed by Benjamin Katchen and Robert Stoller.

**EXHIBIT 5** *(cont'd)*

10. Do you need some sort of prize to motivate your team to win?

| Yes | No |
|-----|-----|
| **56%** | **44%** |

11. What sort of prizes would you suggest?

**Cash, Recognition (Picture), Free Bowling, Gifts, Drinks, Gift Certificates**

12. Would you pay proportionately higher to cover the cost of this prize?

| Yes | No |
|-----|-----|
| **43%** | **57%** |

13. Would you rather bring you own prizes than pay a little more?

| Yes | No |
|-----|-----|
| **37%** | **63%** |

14. Now that you are aware of Bingo-Bowling, will you bowl more often?

| Yes | No |
|-----|-----|
| **40%** | **60%** |

15. What would be the best ways to inform U.W.O. students to the existence of Bingo-Bowling?

(Scale of 1 to 5)

| Flyer | Coupons | Poster Advertising | Gazette | By Faculty | Student Council |
|-------|---------|--------------------|---------|------------|-----------------|
| **2** | **4** | **1** | **5** | **2** | **4** |

16. Give a 3–4 line overview of your experience this evening.

**"Fun, exciting, I like being competitive and be with friends at the same time."**

**"This was a fun experience. I don't bowl, but anything that must be stressed here is that the machinery be maintained more carefully (i.e., the reset button). The game requires speed and the button put some teams at a disadvantage."**

**"Good entertainment for UWO students."**

**"Fun, but at first it is hard to understand."**

**"It took a while to learn the meanings of the letters, but we had fun doing it."**

**"The more people the better, I've never heard of Bingo Bowling so advertising is going to be vital."**

**"It would be nice to have a board that the winning team could have their picture taken and placed on."**

**"Well done, a fun new innovative way to bowl."**

EXHIBIT 6
*Various Promotion/
Advertising Options*

## NEWSPAPER

| Paper (copies/week) | 1/8 page | 1/4 page | 1/2 page | 3/4 page |
|---|---|---|---|---|
| The Gazette (4 times/week) | $212/ad | $375/ad | $718/ad | $1,054/ad |
| Western News (once/week) | $91/ad | $170/ad | $365/ad | $550/ad |
| London Free Press (Daily) | $820/ad | $1,657/ad | $2,485/ad | |

## RADIO

| Breakfast | AAA | Mon – Sat | 6 a.m. – 10 a.m. |
|---|---|---|---|
| Drive | AA | Mon – Fri | 3 p.m. – 7 p.m. |
| Midday | A | Mon – Fri | 10 a.m. – 3 p.m. |
| Weekend | A | Sat | 10 a.m. – 6 p.m. |
| Evening | B | Mon – Fri, Sun | 7 p.m. – Mid. |

| Station/30 sec spots | AAA | AA | A | B |
|---|---|---|---|---|
| **CFPL** (adults) | | | | |
| **CJBK** (youth/teenagers) | $245 | $227 | $210 | $194 |
| **CKSL** (youth/teenagers) | $207 | $175 | $170 | $160 |
| **CHRW & 106.9 FM** (university & college) | $14 | | | |

| PRIZES | Cost to Fleetway | | OTHERS | |
|---|---|---|---|---|
| Hats | $2.00 | | Billboard | $1,000/artwork |
| T-shirts | $3.50 | | Flyers | $.02 + mailing |
| Coupons, printing | $ .02 | | Bus Rental | $100/evening |
| Drinks | $ .10 | | | |

# C A S E 5.7 THE McINTOSH GALLERY

In the early 1990s, in London, Ontario, the McIntosh Gallery was experiencing a problem in inspiring attendance and interest; Kevin Kung, volunteer promotion director, was handed the task of improving the situation as quickly as possible.

**BACKGROUND**

The McIntosh Gallery is a public, nonprofit art gallery situated on the campus of The University of Western Ontario, London, Canada. It serves the university and surrounding community. Built in 1942 with a bequest from the Estate of Wilhelmina Morris McIntosh, it is the oldest university art gallery in Canada. From 1960 to 1969 the programs were administered by artists-in-residence. Since 1969, the university has provided the principal financial support for the operation of the gallery and the program of exhibitions, films, videos on art, lectures, and other events. Additional funding is provided by the government of Ontario through the Ontario Arts Council, The Canada Council, the William Abbott Fund, the McIntosh Estate, and the McIntosh Gallery membership.

The mission of the gallery is to collect, exhibit, research, and interpret exemplary visual art with an emphasis on contemporary Canadian art. Its expressed aims are:

- to collect and preserve our visual artistic heritage in public trust now and for future generations
- to cultivate the appreciation of art
- to make art part of the everyday life on campus
- to encourage visual literacy and critical visual awareness
- to make our visual heritage accessible to all

**COMMUNITY**

The City of London, population 316,000, is part of the densely populated region of Southwestern Ontario. Over five million people reside within a 200-mile radius. London is also mid-way on a direct well-used corridor from the U.S.A. to Toronto. McIntosh Gallery audiences include: the university community of 26,000 students, faculty and staff; the broader London area community of 350,000; a general audience that is increasingly exposed to images of the contemporary art world through the mass media and may seek access, analysis, and understanding; and the more specialized community of artists, art and museum professionals, critics, writers, dealers, collectors, and teachers who also support and contribute to the dialogue.

**GOVERNING AUTHORITY**

The director is the secretary of the McIntosh Gallery Committee, the governing body, which is a standing committee of the University Board of Governors. The director is also accountable to the vice-president (external) for operations as a budget unit head, with other external colleagues in advancement and development, alumni affairs, university relations and information and Foundation Western. Institutional decisions regarding policy and acquisitions are made by the McIntosh Gallery committee and the acquisitions committee, as approved by the University Board of Governors. Operational decisions are made by the director under the authority of the vice-president (external). Three full-time staff report to the director — a curator, installations officer/registrar, and secretary — as well as two part-time gallery attendants and 25 to 30 volunteers.

Responsible for gallery operations, programs, collections, budget and planning, the director's primary ongoing task is to maintain institutional identity and self-determination as a public art gallery within the university context (which often perceives the gallery as a service and less than central to the academic mission). This is becoming a bigger and bigger task as the university is constrained by tightening resources, forcing every department and facility to "do more with *less*." The university is also undergoing a shift to "total quality service" at this time, and this will bring even more responsibilities to the director, Arlene Kennedy, and the curator, Catherine Elliot Shaw.

A volunteer force was formally initiated in September 1990. Over 17 individuals, primarily students, volunteered as tour guides, gallery attendants, researchers, and public relations and general assistants. Most commitments are tied to terms of study and seasonal student workload; however, two nonstudent volunteers continue to give generously of their time on an ongoing weekly basis. An abundance of special projects are accumulated on file for volunteers as an opportunity for direct participation and public gallery experience. Governing committee members are also volunteers, some of whom are faculty.

Volunteer contributions for 1992/93 were:

| | |
|---|---:|
| 8 volunteer gallery attendants | 406 hours |
| 5 research volunteers | 396 hours |
| 3 special events/planning assistants | 378 hours |
| 2 miscellaneous volunteer tasks | 80 hours |
| volunteer committee members | 135 hours |
| | 1,395 hours |

There are also 108 members of the gallery.[1]

The gallery is open 12 months a year and regular weekly hours are:

Mon. closed
Tues. 12 – 7 p.m.
Wed. 12 – 7 p.m.
Thurs. 12 – 7 p.m.

Fri. 12 – 4 p.m.
Sat. 12 – 4 p.m.
Sun. 12 – 4 p.m.

**COLLECTION**

There are approximately 1,700 objects in the McIntosh Gallery's permanent collection. About 25 percent of the permanent collection (valued at $10 million +) is on display throughout the campus and in public outdoor sites. An average of 25 works are donated annually. At least one exhibition is curated from the collection each year and provides a historical context/counterpoint to concurrent exhibitions of contemporary works. The collection, records, and reference library are also a resource for artists, collectors, educators, students, curators, and researchers.

To enhance the visitor's movement from familiar to more challenging work, the gallery provides a constellation of educational vehicles: exhibitions, educational/interpretive activities, and original research and documentation. Information packages, which include such reference materials as biographies, reviews, and bibliographies are available for casual consultation. Gallery Notes, often including artists' statements, offer ideas, insights, and open-ended questions as an approach to the exhibitions. "Meet-the-artist" videotaped interviews provide additional primary information in an informal and nonthreatening manner. Informal walking tours, called "Walkabouts," facilitate a more personal forum for discussion of the work and, where possible, first-hand experience of the artist. Tours for adult and school groups are requested and scheduled on a regular basis. The gallery promotes scholarship relating to visual art practice and, when limited resources allow, produces more extensive publications as a contribution to the existing body of knowledge.

**CONSUMERS**

The McIntosh Gallery conducted annual in-depth consumer/audience surveys of those who visited the gallery from 1989 to 1993. These surveys were broken down into categories of age, residence, and frequency of visit. Exhibit 1 is a synopsis of significant results from the 1993 audience survey. The overall responses from this survey are highlighted in Exhibit 2. Exhibit 3 shows additional visitors' comments that were also collected. Kevin hoped that this information would help him to better understand his "consumer," and therefore ensure that his promotion recommendations would reach them.

A small focus group was also conducted with an introductory business class, the curator, Catherine Elliot Shaw, Kevin, and the instructor. The students revealed many interesting thoughts and opinions. Overall, there was a widespread awareness of the McIntosh Gallery, but only four out of approximately 60 students had actually been in it. Interestingly, the reason many of the students knew of the gallery, they said, was because of its red front door (the only red door on campus). Many students said that they passed by on their way to class but did not have time to enter, or that the door was closed and they did not know if it was open, even though the hours are posted outside the gallery. Kevin knew that there was a long way to go to lead these potential consumers through the traditional marketing steps of AWARENESS > TRIAL > PURCHASE > REPURCHASE, and he was wondering what would be the best way to encourage this process for the gallery.

After the focus group concluded, Catherine Elliot Shaw shared some of her insight from research that she had done surrounding the type of people that a gallery attracts and maintains. (See "Museum Codes and Intentionality: Reconsidering the Temple/Forum Debate" by Catherine Elliot Shaw, April 1992). Some of the highlights of this study show that galleries are often assumed to be the domain of the elite and frequent visitors, who appreciate quiet time to be alone and absorb the artistic work. Less frequent visitors equated museums to a "monument to the dead," while frequent and regular visitors likened it to a library.[2] Catherine believes that a more sports-focused group is less likely to visit a gallery frequently than a quiet, more contemplative group of people.

## PROMOTION

The McIntosh Gallery has two advertising accounts. The operating advertising account pays for promotion of the gallery in general: $2,500 for 1993. The program account pays for advertising specific to gallery programming: $1,600 for 1993. Paid advertising is placed in art specialist periodicals and campus publications with a broad distribution, e.g., the campus phone directory. This is supplemented with a host of free promotional opportunities: public service announcements in the *London Free Press* (the gallery cannot afford to advertise in it), electronic media, news releases distributed through the university's media channels, and appearances on cable television. The *Western News* (campus newspaper directed at faculty, administration, and students) has been a consistent supporter in listing its activities, and the students' *Gazette* does cover it from time to time, but this seemed dependent upon the availability of someone interested in the topic. The Gallery Bulletin is deposited at various pickup points around the campus and throughout London (libraries, galleries, etc.) and included with letters sent on other gallery business as a point of interest and information.

## CURRENT SITUATION

Kevin was enthusiastic about the many possibilities to increase the exposure, knowledge, and attendance of the McIntosh Gallery. He saw a potential for greater exposure through the newspapers and wondered about the possibility of having gallery volunteers write reviews on pieces of the permanent collection. Thus the permanent collection would become better known and the gallery name would appear in the papers more frequently. Other promotional ideas included placing tent[3] cards at residence dining rooms and at campus food outlets. Use of internal campus memos as invitations to openings and as a reminder of new exhibitions was also considered.

Kevin realized that the most responsive segment in the university community would be the students in the art faculty and he wondered if an in-class promotion of the gallery and its facilities (i.e., research, art pieces, etc.) would make it more accessible to them. Kevin also considered involving the gallery in the coming campus arts festival. He had considered that the gallery might provide the hall for musicians and rooms for poetry readings. He saw these opportunities as ways to revamp and broaden the perceived atmosphere of the gallery and to present the gallery more as a building and less as an institution. One of Kevin's early ideas was to have a huge student-designed gallery banner placed on one of the campus's most visible walls as a way to make a big splash for the gallery. The idea was met with great enthusiasm but, unfortunately, was shelved due to the tight promotional budget. The banner would have cost $500. Similarly, gallery posters were met with disapproval because the gallery wanted to set itself apart from the barrage of posters from clubs and fraternities around the campus. In addition, posters required a campus approved seal, which also entailed a significant fee. Above all, the curator felt that any action regarding the gallery should maintain respect for the art and the artists it represents.

Kevin knew that he had a formidable challenge ahead. He must design a promotional strategy that considered his audience, budget, and the aims of the McIntosh Gallery. He must be clear on the objectives that he planned to meet with every dollar, and the timing of each plan was important. His strategy must meet with the approval of the director and the curator. Kevin also had to consider that he was a volunteer and that attaining his university degree while assuming this responsibility was critical. Last year's attendance (1993/94) was 10,400 visitors. Catherine Elliot Shaw would like this figure increase to 15,000 visitors and was challenged as to the best means to do this.

## NOTES

1. The segmented results are available from the McIntosh Gallery for further study.
2. Nick Merriman, "Museum Visiting as a Cultural Phenomenon" in *The New Museology*, 1989.
3. See Exhibit 5 for an example of a tent card.

*EXHIBIT 1*
*Synopsis of Significant*
*Results From Audience*
*Surveys*

---

## 1993

### Age and Population Spreads:

78.8% of all gallery visitors were 15 to 45 years of age.

54.8% of once-a-month visitors were age 15 to 25.

42.2% of all gallery visitors were students.

45.2% of once-a-month visitors were students.

### Residence:

41.0% of London visitors were from the north end of the city.

30.1% of all gallery visitors were from off-campus.

41.5% of first time visitors were from off-campus.

44.0% of off-campus visitors came with the sole purpose of visiting the gallery.

40.0% of first time gallery visitors came to see an exhibition.

72.8% of all visitors indicated that they were supportive of the expansion of the gallery.

---

*EXHIBIT 2*
*McIntosh Gallery*
*Audience Survey —*
*1993[1]*

**Responses**

All responses are listed in descending order. The total number of audience surveys is 166. This is the second survey tabulated under the new hours.

1. *Visit Frequency*

| | | |
|---|---|---|
| first time visitor | 39.2% | (65) |
| once a month | 18.7% | (31) |
| 2–3 times per year | 15.1% | (25) |
| every 2–3 months | 14.5% | (24) |
| less than twice/year | 10.8% | (18) |
| other | 1.8% | (3) |

2. *Visit Pattern*

| | | |
|---|---|---|
| no response | 53.0% | (88) |
| Tues–Fri 1–4 | 16.3% | (27) |
| Tues–Fri 12–1 | 12.0% | (20) |
| Sat–Sun 12–4 | 10.8% | (18) |
| Tues–Thurs 4–7 | 10.2% | (17) |
| other (various) | 4.2% | (7) |

3. *Reason for Visit*

| | | |
|---|---|---|
| exhibition | 53.6% | (89) |
| other | 22.3% | (37) |
| habit | 15.1% | (25) |
| public event at gallery | 9.0% | (15) |
| visit to library | 9.0% | (15) |
| no response | 7.8% | (13) |

4. *Publicity Effectiveness*

| | | |
|---|---|---|
| word of mouth | 29.5% | (49) |
| Western News | 25.9% | (43) |
| The Gazette | 23.5% | (39) |
| gallery light box | 18.7% | (31) |
| no response | 15.7% | (26) |
| Visual Arts dept. | 13.9% | (23) |
| posters | 13.9% | (23) |
| gallery bulletin | 13.3% | (22) |
| other sources | 7.8% | (13) |
| London Free Press listing | 6.6% | (11) |
| London Free Press review | 4.8% | (8) |
| membership mailing | 3.0% | (5) |
| TV London | 1.2% | (2) |
| tourism brochure | 0.6% | (1) |
| Cable 13 | 0.0% | (0) |

5a. *Comparison of Population*

| | | |
|---|---|---|
| student | 42.2% | (70) |
| visitor | 30.1% | (50) |
| visual arts student | 11.4% | (19) |
| faculty | 8.4% | (14) |
| staff | 7.2% | (12) |
| no response | 1.2% | (2) |

**1.** Percentages do not add to 100 percent due to multiple responses.

*EXHIBIT 2 (cont'd)*

5b. *Visitors: Purpose to visit gallery?*

| | | |
|---|---|---|
| no | 56.0% | (28) |
| yes | 44.0% | (22) |

6. *Age Ranges*

| | | | | | |
|---|---|---|---|---|---|
| 15–25 | male: 21.1% (35) | female: | 29.5% (49) | (/84) |
| 26–35 | male: 9.0% (15) | female: | 9.0% (15) | (/30) |
| 36–45 | male: 4.2% (7) | female: | 6.0% (10) | (/17) |
| 46–55 | male: 6.0% (10) | female: | 4.8% (8) | (/18) |
| 56–65 | male: 3.6% (6) | female: | 2.4% (4) | (/10) |
| Over 65 | male: 1.8% (3) | female: | 2.4% (4) | (/7) |

7a. *London Resident*

| | | |
|---|---|---|
| permanent | 42.2% | (70) |
| temporary | 36.7% | (61) |
| other (i.e., outside London) | 12.7% | (21) |
| no response | 8.4% | (14) |

7b. *Area of Residence*
(Calculated only for London residents)

| | | |
|---|---|---|
| northwest | 17.6% | (23) |
| north | 16.8% | (22) |
| no response | 16.8% | (22) |
| central | 14.5% | (19) |
| campus | 6.9% | (9) |
| old north | 6.1% | (8) |
| west | 5.3% | (7) |
| northeast | 4.6% | (6) |
| southwest | 3.8% | (5) |
| east | 3.1% | (4) |
| south | 2.3% | (3) |
| old south | 2.3% | (3) |

8. *Transportation*

| | | |
|---|---|---|
| foot | 57.8% | (96) |
| car | 27.1% | (45) |
| bus | 12.0% | (20) |
| bike | 7.8% | (13) |
| no response | 4.8% | (8) |
| taxi | 0.0% | (0) |

9. *Support for Expansion Plans*

| | | |
|---|---|---|
| very supportive | 36.7% | (61) |
| somewhat supportive | 36.1% | (60) |
| indifferent | 16.3% | (27) |
| no response | 7.8% | (13) |
| other | 3.0% | (5) |
| opposed | 0.0% | (0) |

**EXHIBIT 3**
**Appendix: Visitor Comments[1]**

I am a first time visitor to the gallery. I have heard a lot about it in the last year. As an alumna, I hope I will be back to visit. Thanks.

A fine little gallery! The exhibit was wonderful!

A good idea (to tie the exhibitions together, presenting more challenging, unusual, and interdisciplinary exhibitions, and provoking more thought and discussion), but I haven't paid much attention until recently. I will do so in the future.

Less tripe and more thought, please.

I haven't been around to notice the changes, but I feel that the gallery I saw today accomplished these goals.

I like to follow the work of Ontario artists, particularly those of the '50s and '60s, some of whom I knew.

I have noticed how thought-provoking your exhibits are, although I've never had the opportunity of participating in a discussion of the exhibition except for those offered in my art classes. Advertise about your lectures/discussions more!

(I have noticed these changes) but the period of rotation has greatly decreased and therefore so has exposure to this type of art!

I miss the talks and films.

I see no reason to tie all exhibitions together.

The quality of exhibitions is somewhat less appealing than in the past.

Please show real art, NOT the productions of the Faculty of Visual Arts.

I am somewhat disappointed with the parking situation on the weekends. I would rather have my money go to the gallery than to the university for parking.

Keep up the good work! Thank you.

I am not a serious art enthusiast, I just like to see what happens here every so often. I am in physics and often I go to the UCC, so usually I stop by when I have the time.

I enjoy visiting the gallery on a regular basis. Good work!

I have only been here for three years, but in these three years I have often been disappointed with the shows. I would be more supportive if the criteria for show selection was modified some of the time. Art accessible to a wider cross-section of the public is what I would like to see. The gallery should be satisfying for more than just university art students. I'm sure this would generate more support with a wider base to draw from. Art both intellectually challenging and accessible on a level of the "average" interested person does exist. Finding it may benefit both the gallery and the London population.

All exhibits are interesting and thought-provoking.

It's great! I hope the people who hand out the cash figure this out soon!

1. Survey tabulated by Janette Cousins, August 1993.

**EXHIBIT 3** *(cont'd)*

---

(Have you) ever thought of renting art works to corporations or special functions to raise money? Perhaps the insurance coverage would be too much. The McIntosh does a pleasurable job!

I find the taste in art I see here is frequently tacky and cliché in its attempt to be contemporary and modern. I think a stronger blending of traditional and historical elements in our artistic culture would be advisable. Usually I don't like the exhibits. Their quality is significantly less than the beauty of this little building deserves.

I would like to see more of your permanent collection on display.

Keep up the good work. I liked some of the talks given here last year as well. I would like to see more contemporary works by Canadian artists. The old stuff from the permanent collection I didn't care for too much.

I am in third year science. I do enjoy, however, a bit of *culture*!

I've always found the exhibitions thought-provoking.

I am not very pleased that I have to pay $2 just to park here on the weekends. It doesn't make sense to have to pay when it is the least busy.

I feel the exhibitions could be more challenging. I realize it is necessary to mount student and faculty shows and show the permanent collection, but this takes up space that could be used better, I think.

(I) appreciate the stimulation — mental — generated by the works.

Greater clarity and more information needed in some presentations.

Impressive as is. Keep it simple.

I have generally thought your exhibitions to be amongst the best in the area for a good number of years. Though this past year has not been as interesting as previous years, perhaps because of the political context (words) that would be on the whole better to read sitting down than to stand reading material that because of the limitations of the medium does not allow for much development of thought. Generally I prefer works that stimulate visually not literally.

I would say so (i.e., noticed the changes in programming), although I find I usually learn from most displays at the McIntosh. I like to look at new and different art, but sometimes I wish it were a bit more accessible.

The McIntosh is a lovely, quiet haven for peaceful afternoon visits. Have you considered using parts of the space for music or theatrical performance?

I very much enjoy the various displays you present. However, I am not steeped in art history and wouldn't mind seeing some earlier works as well as current creations.

I always enjoy the exhibitions of graduating classes, including Fanshawe. How about an exhibition similar to the annual Art Mart?

Those who visit and know the gallery have noticed the changes; those who don't come haven't and probably never will unless they break out and become visitors. Anyway, keep up the good work!

---

**EXHIBIT 3 (cont'd)**

I prefer Renaissance paintings, which are very seldom displayed at the McIntosh.

I have enjoyed your exhibits!

I certainly appreciate a challenge to my frighteningly ethnocentric views on art. Provoke! Provoke!

I belong to the Faculty of Engineering Science; the engineering art exhibition is an excellent idea.

I have only visited the gallery twice, as I am a new student. I feel it is a great asset to have a gallery on campus.

This exhibit is interesting but appears to be more documentation of an event that should have been seen at the time. I felt some of the presentation unprofessionally presented, but it did intrigue me!

The display space is well laid out presenting the exhibitions to the viewer.

No free parking??

*EXHIBIT 4*

# EXHIBITIONS

**McIntosh Gallery**

The University
of Western Ontario
London, Ontario
Canada N6A 3K7

Tel: (519) 661-3181
Fax: 661-3292

January 7 – February 6, 1994

## EXHIBITING CULTURE
Western society has entrusted to its museums the task of collecting, preserving and interpreting its cultural history. Over the centuries of a treasure-house tradition, these institutions have developed a codified "museum experience", the combined effect of architectural environment and exhibition design on the individual objects displayed. In an age of specialist institutions, museums are also moving from encyclopaedic collecting to more focussed acquisitions. This month's exhibitions examine the museum/art gallery experience, its collecting function, and its influence upon our understanding of material culture.

## TWO PAVILIONS: MUSEUM AND A TENT FOR THE EXPLORATION OF A DARK CONTINENT
This installation by Regina artist Lorne Beug presents two environments in which we are invited to consider the ambiguous relationship between architectural atmosphere and the objects placed within them. The installation is divided into two sections or "pavilions". The first simulates a Eurocentric museum complete with imitation stone and marble walls and filled with an assortment of pseudo-relics from ancient civilizations. The second, a nylon structure reminiscent in part of medieval European tents, is covered in images collaged from an orientalized view of "exotic cultures". The resulting juxtaposition questions the depiction of non-Western cultures within the prescripted Western perception of the museum environment.

WEST
WING

## GETTING TO THE OBJECT
Despite fundamental changes in the philosophical frame-work of exhibition design, the concept of placing an object within a specially designated space continues to define our understanding of that museum object. From traditional floor-to-ceiling hanging to the "white cube" of contemporary gallery spaces, the lighting, spatial proximity, and other incidental details all influence the assimilation of the visual information. This exhibition features some of the presentation practices used in today's museums but in a skewed manner that emphasizes how the viewer's perceptions of the objects are altered by the display.

EAST
WING

## VALUING ART
Public art galleries collect art as a record of our cultural heritage in the visual arts. Since 1942, the McIntosh Gallery has been devoted to collecting and exhibiting the artwork of our time, a collection which has grown to over 1,700 objects. The value of a public art collection, however, lies in its use as a resource to its community. It is a public trust which demands accountability in the efficient and effective use of limited resources. Selections from the McIntosh Gallery Collection will illustrate some of the motivations for collecting and the costs associated with this universal activity.

LOWER
FLOOR

Gallery Hours

Tuesday-Thursday 12-7 pm

Friday-Sunday 12-4 pm

Closed Mondays

Free Admission

**EXHIBIT 5**

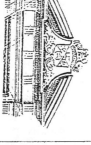

Discover the
McIntosh Gallery
**EXHIBITIONS**

March 24 - April 10, 1994

**THE UNIVERSITY OF WESTERN ONTARIO DEPARTMENT OF VISUAL ARTS GRADUATION EXHIBITION**

This annual exhibition presents work of students who leave in the past 3 or 4 years studied visual communications through the traditions of art making and critical inquiry.

**Opening:Thursday,March24,7:30p.m. Free Public Walking Tour of the Exhibition:** Friday, March 25, 12:15 - 12:50 p.m.

**Gallery Hours**
Tuesday-Thursday 12-7 pm
Friday-Sunday 12-4pm
Closed Mondays
Free Admission

---

Discover the
McIntosh Gallery
**EXHIBITIONS**

March 24 - April 10, 1994

**THE UNIVERSITY OF WESTERN ONTARIO DEPARTMENT OF VISUAL ARTS GRADUATION EXHIBITION**

This annual exhibition presents work of students who have in the past 3 or 4 years studied visual communications through the traditions of art making and critical inquiry.

**Opening:Thursday,March24,7:30p.m. Free Public Walking Tour of the Exhibition:** Friday, March 25, 12:15 - 12:50 p.m.

**Gallery Hours**
Tuesday-Thursday 12-7 pm
Friday-Sunday 12-4pm
Closed Mondays
Free Admission

---

The University of Western Ontario

**Gallery Hours**
Tuesday-Thursday 12-7 pm
Friday-Sunday 12-4pm
Closed Mondays
Free Admission

### C A S E 5.8 MOLLY BLOOM PERFUMES (B)

In October of 1983, Sandra Gibson was attempting to complete the necessary arrangements for the opening of a generic perfume store in the Toronto area. Decisions would have to be made soon on several key aspects of the marketing plan including product mix, pricing policies, promotional strategy, and location. She would have to move quickly in order to be prepared in time for the Christmas rush.

**THE FRAGRANCE INDUSTRY**

Elaborate packaging and heavy expenditures on image-oriented advertising characterized the North American fragrance industry. Though Oscar de la Renta of New York was the best-selling fragrance in North America, many fragrance products were European, with the offerings of French fashion designers capturing a large portion of the market. Fragrances were primarily sold in department stores, drug stores, variety stores, and small cosmetic "boutiques." In addition, direct selling and mail order companies accounted for a portion of total market sales.

Originally, perfumes were made from "absolutes": oils extracted from flowers, together with natural spices (e.g., cinnamon, nutmeg, rosemary) and animal materials (e.g., musk from musk deer). Floral absolutes and other natural ingredients are still used, but most modern fragrances also contain various complex synthetic substances, known as "aroma chemicals."

Fragrance products, which include perfumes, toilet waters, and colognes, are manufactured by mixing the oils of various scents, and can be grouped into six families based on the predominant components: floral, aldehydic, oriental, spicy, tabac, and chypre. Hundreds of specific ingredients, many in minute quantities, are often required in the blending of a single fragrance. Factories in France produce most of the essential oils for fragrances. The oils are mixed together and diluted with alcohol to produce a particular fragrance. A "Perfume" consists of a 25 to 30 percent concentration of essential oils, while a "Cologne" (for women or men) is diluted to approximately 12 percent oils.

**Market Size and Growth**

Toilet preparations and cosmetics accounted for 9.9 percent of total consumer spending in Canada during 1979. Between 1970 to 1979, expenditures by Canadian consumers on toilet preparations and cosmetics grew by an average of 7.8 percent annually in real terms.

|                                                 |                                                                                                                                                                                                                                                                                                                                                                                                             |
| ----------------------------------------------- | ----------------------------------------------------------------------------------------------------------------------------------------------------------------------------------------------------------------------------------------------------------------------------------------------------------------------------------------------------------------------------------------------------------- |
| **Manufacturers of Toilet Preparations and Cosmetics** | Over 40 firms were involved in the manufacture of toilet preparations and cosmetics in Canada, with total factory shipments exceeding half a billion dollars. The value of selected fragrance products manufactured in Canada during the period 1978 to 1982 is summarized in Exhibit 1. |

Most of the companies producing and marketing fragrance products in Canada were subsidiaries of foreign firms or domestic distribution agents for European fragrance lines as trends for fragrance products were almost always set in the United States or Europe before coming to Canada.

The majority of these firms, whether low, medium, or high priced at the retail level, were large companies with sales in the millions and large budgets for advertising (in some cases, up to 10 percent of the sales) used to create an "image" for that product. These firms were also involved in co-op advertising with many retail chains in Canada.

**Retail Sales of Fragrance Products**

Retail sales of domestically manufactured and imported fragrance products continued to increase in the early 1980s despite the impact of a severe economic recession. Exhibit 2 itemizes retail sales trends for various toilet preparations and cosmetics from 1980 to 1982.

The value of imports into Canada of selected toilet preparations and cosmetics during 1981 and 1982 can be seen in Exhibit 3. Most imports were subject to tariffs depending upon the country and origin, with 15 percent being the most common level. France and the United States were the two most important foreign suppliers of perfumes, colognes, and toilet waters.

**Consumer Buying Behaviour**

Toronto families earned and spent more on personal-care products than those in other cities and regions across the country. Of the estimated 1,061,730 households in Toronto, an average of $21 per household per year was spent on perfumes, toilet waters, and colognes. The level of family expenditures on personal care products (including perfumes, toilet waters, and colognes) was generally dependent on family income levels (see Exhibit 4).

The continued growth in expenditures on fragrance products during the early 1980s came despite a severe economic recession. Over 90 percent of Canadian women indicated that they now used perfumes, toilet water, and/or cologne according to industry reports.

The fragrance market had a heavy seasonal peak with approximately 60 percent of sales occurring during the Christmas buying period. There appeared to be four consumer groups in the fragrance product market. Surprisingly enough, men were the largest purchasers of women's fragrance products (estimated at 50 percent of the total market). Men would typically buy these products for their girlfriend or wife as a gift, usually in specialty shops. The majority of these purchases were of expensive designer names as the man would want to impress that special someone with his purchase.

The remainder of the fragrance market belonged to female consumers and was split into three groups. The first group might be called women with "Super-Style." These women were professionals (mid to upper income), usually working in the arts, publishing, radio, and TV, and were considered the trend-setters of the fashion industry. "Super-Style" women were deemed to be self-oriented, pampering themselves and living beyond their means. Fragrance products were important to them and were used every day. They were interested in the packaging, scent, and the type of "lifestyle" that the fragrance portrayed. They were keenly interested in new scents, and once they became "hooked" on a scent, they were very brand loyal. The majority of their purchases were made in specialty shops in the downtown core of a city. This group, representing about 10 percent of women, was responsible for about 15 percent of all fragrance sales.

The second group was labelled the "Style" woman. These women were considered to be lower to middle income and usually worked in areas such as banking or retail. This group also included a high percentage of home-makers who were naturally more family-oriented than the "Super-Style" group. These women were not as interested in spending money on themselves and were consistent, but not overly frequent, users of fragrance products. Low-to-medium price fragrance products were usually bought by this group who did most of their shopping in suburban malls. This group, which appeared less brand loyal than the first, was composed of 70 percent of all women, but only 25 percent of all fragrance sales.

The last female consumer group was called the "Trendy" group. This group contained the real experimenters of the fashion world who loved to be outrageous and attract attention. The women in this group were typically single and in the 17 to 25 year old age category. This group followed whatever trend was "hot" and were heavy purchasers of fragrance products, but not particularly brand loyal. This group was small (only 10 percent of women), but purchased 10 percent of all fragrance products, usually in the urban areas of a city in specialty shops and department stores.

**GENERIC PRODUCTS**

Beginning in the late 1970s, Canadians witnessed the emergence of many types of generic products, usually retailing significantly below the prices of comparable branded products. Generic products lacked the prestige and reputation of established brands in the marketplace, even though in many cases name brands and generics were manufactured in the same factory from the same materials. The generics were able to sell at lower prices because they used inexpensive, functional packaging and did not require the level of advertising support given to branded products. Generic products had been particularly successful in the food and pharmaceutical industries, appealing to a large percentage of the population.

Sceptics insisted that perfume was not a product that could be successfully marketed as a generic. Yvon Lafreniere, vice-president of marketing at Herdt & Charton Inc. (the Montreal-based Canadian marketer of Yves St.

Laurent's Opium fragrance) stated that generics lack the "magic" or "love" associated with the real product.[1]

In 1981, Mark Laracy, a former senior executive with two major designer-name fragrance manufacturers, founded his own company called Parfums de Coeur and rocked the fragrance industry by introducing Ninja, a low-priced perfume similar to Opium and Cinnabar, two famous designer-name oriental fragrances. At $5 for half an ounce (well under half the price of the two competing fragrances), Ninja became an instant success and proved that inexpensive fragrances could sell.

Sales of Ninja in 1984 were forecast to exceed $20 million, with distribution in over 20,000 North American retail outlets. Several other copies of men's and women's designer-name fragrances were also being introduced.

**THE CONCEPT**

Sandra Gibson perceived an opportunity to sell lower-priced comparable generic quality fragrances for two reasons. First of all, high prices and high margins were associated with designer-name products and, secondly, most consumers could not tell the difference between a generic and a popular designer-name product. Gibson, an English graduate from the University of British Columbia, decided to develop a line of generic fragrance products and name them "Molly Bloom," after the heroine in James Joyce's novel *Ulysses* who loved flowers and fragrances and "epitomized sensuality and femininity."

Canadian laws prevented any direct assertion or suggestion that a generic was identical to a particular brand-name counterpart. Gibson's lawyer had advised her, however, that as long as a descriptor like "in the same family as …" was applied, there should be no difficulties. As a result, she felt it would be feasible to create and sell generic fragrances in the Canadian marketplace.

Toronto was the largest metropolitan centre in Canada and had acquired a somewhat cosmopolitan image. Gibson, therefore, felt that it would be the most logical city to support a novel product concept such as generic perfume. The Metropolitan Toronto region consisted of two cities, Toronto and North York, plus four surrounding boroughs: Scarborough, East York, Etobicoke, and York. In addition, the areas surrounding Metropolitan Toronto on the east, north, and west sides had become heavily urbanized and contained many commuters who worked in the Metro area. Four large regional municipalities bordered Metropolitan Toronto: Peel and Halton on the west side, York on the north, and Durham on the east. The suburban areas of the region continued to grow rapidly, while the population of the inner core of Toronto had actually been declining in size in recent years.

Exhibit 5 provides population size and growth data for Metropolitan Toronto and the surrounding regional municipalities, along with comparative data for Ontario and Canada, from the 1976 and 1981 censuses. As shown, the population of the Toronto vicinity was approaching 3.5 million people.

Gibson wanted to move quickly to set up shop as she felt that any delays would impair a start-up time for the Christmas season and provide others with an opportunity to beat her into the marketplace.

Gibson knew that the eventual success or failure of the venture would hinge on how the concept was marketed. Many strategic and operational decisions would have to be made in order to launch the venture, including precise specification of the product line, selection of a location, pricing, and promotional media and messages.

## PRODUCT POLICY
### Fragrances

The main product line would be a set of generic perfumes cloning many of the most successful fragrances currently on the market. The first priority would be to decide how many fragrances to offer, which brand names to copy, and how to name or label the various generic copies. Over 100 widely available fragrances were marketed in Canada. Some of the most popular included Chanel No. 5, L'Air du Temps, Opium, Halston, Oscar de la Renta, and Joy. Chanel No. 5, an aldehydic, was one of the longest established fragrances, having been introduced in 1922. L'Air du Temps, a spicy fragrance, had been introduced by Nina Ricci in 1947. Joy was categorized as a floral, and had been on the market since 1938. Oscar de la Renta belonged to the same grouping and had reached prominent market position since its introduction in 1981. Yves St. Laurent's oriental fragrance Opium was another recent product, developed in 1978, as was Halston, a chypre launched in 1975. Gibson wanted to get established in women's fragrances first and then consider men's fragrances in the future.

The essential oil concentrates were packed in 25 lb. (400 oz.) drums. Prices varied substantially depending on the fragrance. The average total delivered cost to Toronto would be $65 per pound (480 ml) of oils. The large investment required to purchase a single drum of the oil concentrate for one fragrance would clearly constrain Gibson in the number of brand names for which she could provide similar fragrances, particularly at the outset. She envisioned between 10 and 30 offerings initially, with gradual expansion as funds permitted. Fortunately, the shelf life of the oils in concentrated form was lengthy, since each drum would be sufficient when diluted with alcohol to manufacture many bottles of fragrance. Alcohol could be purchased for $30 per 180 oz. (5,400 ml) pail for this purpose.

Two main labelling strategies had been considered. The first dealt with creating specific names for the fragrances similar to what Mark Laracy had done with Ninja in the U.S. Alternatively, the product offerings could be labelled Molly Bloom No. 1, Molly Bloom No. 2, etc., to enhance the simplicity and generic concept of the product.

### Sizes

Perfume was sold in a variety of package sizes. The most common were 7 ml (1/4 oz.), 15 ml (1/2 oz.), and 30 ml (1 oz.) bottles, with the smaller sizes accounting for the bulk of purchases. Typical packagings for women's colognes were 30 ml, 60 ml (2 oz.), and 120 ml (4 oz.) sizes, with the larger bottles being most in demand. Eau de parfum and eau de toilette were packaged in a variety of sizes. Some of the more common were 15 ml, 30 ml, 45 ml (1 1/2 oz.), 60 ml, 100 ml (3 oz.), and 120 ml. It would be necessary to decide whether the Molly Bloom line of products should be packaged in standard quantities or in bottle sizes that were less common and hence less easily compared to their designer-name counterparts. As well, Gibson would have to decide how many and which size options should be offered.

**Atomizers**

Crystal and glass atomizers and bottles represented a complementary product line that could be sold when a customer purchased perfume. Some customers might prefer a more ornate, decorative container than the plain glass bottle offered with each purchase. Retail prices could range from $5 for a small bottle to over $100 for an antique atomizer, and average gross margins in the range of 60 percent could be expected.

**LOCATION**

The choice of a location would have to balance various goals including accessibility, image, traffic flow, and cost. One possibility was a vacancy on the lower level of a small building on Yorkville Avenue. The store contained an area of 1,000 square feet, which could be leased for six years at an annual rate of $19.00 per square foot including utilities.

The Yorkville area of Toronto, located slightly northwest of the major Yonge Street–Bloor Street intersection in the heart of the city had developed into a fashionable and trendy shopping and dining district. The area had become a popular summer shopping area that attracted many tourists as well as local residents.

Alternative locations included downtown Toronto or a suburban site, perhaps in a major shopping mall. The advantage of a downtown location, perhaps in or near the Eaton Centre, was the extremely high traffic flow that would result. Rents in the Eaton Centre, however, could amount to $90 per square foot or more and the store space might be tiny. Rents in other less prominent malls varied according to the location and traffic flow of the mall (see Exhibit 6).

**PROMOTION**

Given the nature of the product, promotion would be critically important to the success of the venture. Gibson had already contacted Anna Spencer, a friend who was a successful creative designer, to help develop an overall concept and suggest specific ideas.

**Point-of-Purchase**

The first area of concern was point-of-purchase material. Spencer designed a two-colour logo in an attractive floral pattern (see Exhibit 7) that could be used on bottle labels, price lists, "dipping paddles" (for sampling fragrances), business cards, brochures, etc. It was decided that the carpeting, wallpaper, furnishings, and fixtures in the store should complement this soft floral pink and gold colour scheme. The interior design of the store had not yet been decided.

***Media Advertising²***

Three major daily newspapers co-existed in the Toronto market: the conservative *Globe and Mail,* the main-line *Toronto Star,* and the up-start *Toronto Sun.* Approximate Toronto area circulation figures were 200,000, 400,000, and 225,000, respectively. The cost of a single, small (e.g., 3 x 4) weekday advertisement in the *Globe and Mail* Ontario edition or the *Toronto Star* would be approximately $300 to $400, compared to about $200 in the *Toronto Sun.* A host of regional community newspapers also existed, usually publishing on a weekly basis. Exhibit 8 summarizes the circulation levels and advertising rates for several of the most prominent community papers.

Possible consumer magazine vehicles for advertising in the Toronto area included *Toronto Life, Avenue,* and *Key to Toronto. Toronto Life* magazine had a monthly paid circulation of over 90,000 copies, primarily in Toronto. A 1/6 page black and white ad in a single issue would cost about $1,100. *Avenue* magazine, on the other hand, focused on the Yorkville area. About 84,000 copies were distributed to selected homes, 5,000 to hotels for distribution to guests, and 16,000 to magazine stands. Rates for 1/6 page were about $800 for one black and white ad with colour costing an additional $400. *Key to Toronto* was a monthly complimentary guide for tourists that was distributed free in the rooms of 66 Metro Toronto hotels and had total circulation exceeding 75,000. The cost of a 1/6 page black and white advertisement would be approximately $650.

Several television and radio stations served the Toronto market. For example, a 30-second spot aired once on CFTO, the CTV affiliate, would cost $450 during the afternoon or $1,300 during evening prime time, in addition to the cost of creating the advertisement. CHUM, one of the more prominent local radio stations, charged $130 for a 30-second commercial on the breakfast program, $70 during mid-morning or early afternoon, and $90 during the late afternoon or early evening.

***Other Promotional Tactics***

Sandra was outgoing and enthusiastic about the product and hoped to obtain free publicity through speaking engagements or media interviews.

Samplers were also being considered. At a total cost of $.40, a tiny vial could be filled with perfume and enclosed in a cardboard covering slightly larger than a box of matches. The cardboard would be printed with the Molly Bloom logo and the address of the store.

Gibson also considered setting up a booth at the annual Women's Show at the Metro Convention Centre. The show attracted 40,000 visitors and would cost Sandra $1,500 for the booth.

The total budget for promotional activities would depend upon a number of factors including the progress of the company during the initial months, the ability of word-of-mouth advertising to generate traffic, and the firm's overall financial resources.

***PRICING***

There were a few key pricing issues that Sandra would have to consider. First of all, since there were enormous variances in the prices of different designer-name products, Gibson wondered whether she should reflect these differences by pricing each fragrance proportionately below its designer-name counterpart. The second major issue was the relationship between price and bottle size purchased. Should she simply charge twice as much for a 30 ml bottle vs. a 15 ml bottle? She also wondered whether she should offer a slight "discount" to encourage customers to purchase larger quantities. Finally, her last pricing concern was how inexpensively she should price vs. a designer-name product. Should moderate, medium, or large discounts be offered to entice customers away from the image-oriented designer products? What constituted "value" to the purchaser of a fragrance product? To obtain a frame of reference, Sandra obtained prices of designer-name products while browsing in local shops (see Exhibits 9 to 11). Whatever price(s) she charged, she wanted to maintain an image of reasonable quality, offer a large enough price incentive to customers, and generate a healthy profit for the store. Gibson expected that an average cost for standard glass bottles would be about $.30 with the labels costing approximately $.05.

## START-UP COSTS

Furnishings, fixtures, and various equipment would likely amount to $15,000 to $20,000. Depending on the breadth and depth of the product lines offered, Gibson estimated that $25,000 to $40,000 in inventory would be required.

## OPERATIONS

Store hours would depend on the location selected. In the Yorkville area, for example, local convention was Monday to Saturday from 10:00 a.m. to 6:00 p.m., while most shopping malls in the Toronto area were open from 9:30 a.m. to 9:30 p.m. daily except for Saturday when the closing was 6:00 p.m. Gibson expected that one full-time employee at an approximate salary of $14,000 including taxes and benefits would be needed to staff the store. Part-time staff could be used as a supplement during busy periods, at roughly $5.00 per hour. Gibson would devote a significant portion of her own time to sell in the store, particularly during busy periods, but time would also be allocated for promotional activities and all necessary administration. Sandra estimated that expenses other than wages to operate the store would cost about $15,000 per year (including insurance, legal, telephone, etc.).

## FINANCING

Gibson was prepared to commit up to $75,000 in personal resources to the business. Any additional financial requirements would have to be obtained through bank loans or from other external sources.

## THE FINAL DECISION

Despite the scepticism of bankers, lawyers, accountants, and many of her friends, Sandra Gibson believed that the Molly Bloom concept was fundamentally sound. With proper marketing, she felt that a retail generic perfume store could turn a profit in its first year of operations. In the long-term, her ambition was to achieve expansion into other markets across North America, perhaps through franchising.

## NOTES

1. Yvon Lafreniere, quoted in *Canadian Business Magazine.*
2. All rates from *Canadian Advertising Rates and Data*, 1983.

*EXHIBIT 1*

| | | | | | |
|---|---|---|---|---|---|
| **Value of Selected Toilet Preparations and Cosmetics Shipped by Canadian Manufacturers in Thousands of Dollars** | | | | | |
| | **1978** | **1979** | **1980** | **1981** | **1982** |
| Perfumes | $ 7,098 | $9,122 | $8,049 | $7,038 | $9,553 |
| Women's colognes and toilet waters | N/A | N/A | 37,544 | 36,800 | 38,528 |
| Men's colognes | N/A | N/A | 6,022 | 5,470 | 7,416 |
| Powders | 6,728 | 6,605 | 6,844 | 7,058 | 8,751 |
| Creams | 21,916 | 23,874 | 26,204 | 26,669 | 32,787 |
| Bath oils, salts, and bubble bath | 10,581 | 11,705 | 10,877 | 12,522 | 11,948 |
| Soaps | 8,574 | 10,156 | 12,606 | 12,496 | 14,766 |
| Shampoos | 29,336 | 32,647 | 38,058 | 42,479 | 48,517 |
| Total of all toilet preparation and cosmetics | 365,477 | 418,467 | 503,832 | 587,825 | 652,444 |

Sources: Statistics Canada, "Pharmaceuticals, Cleaning Compounds and Toilet Preparations," 1982; and "Manufacturers of Toilet Preparations," 1979–80.

*EXHIBIT 2*

| Retail Sales of Selected Toilet Preparation and Cosmetics in Canada in Thousands of Dollars | | | |
| --- | --- | --- | --- |
| | **1980** | **1981** | **1982** |
| Perfumes | $ 20,411 | $ 20,537 | $ 25,588 |
| Women's colognes and toilet waters | 85,889 | 90,152 | 114,149 |
| Men's colognes | 20,610 | 17,705 | 24,386 |
| Powders | 17,663 | 25,059 | 30,255 |
| Creams | 93,763 | 108,470 | 120,436 |
| Bath oils, salts and bubble baths | 35,525 | 34,306 | 40,029 |
| Shampoos | 134,496 | 140,038 | 159,589 |

Source: Statistics Canada, "Sales of Toilet Preparations in Canada," 1981 and 1982.

*EXHIBIT 3*

| Imports of Selected Toilet Preparations and Cosmetics | | | |
| --- | --- | --- | --- |
| | **1981** | **1982** | **Percentage Change** |
| Perfumes | $ 6,230 | $ 5,338 | (14.3) |
| Toilet waters | 1,654 | 3,109 | 88.0 |
| Colognes (men's and women's) | 2,836 | 2,576 | ( 9.2) |
| Creams | 5,218 | 6,711 | 28.6 |
| Bath oils, salts and bubble baths | 1,524 | 1,176 | (22.8) |
| Soaps | 7,938 | 8,193 | 3.2 |
| Shampoos | 10,699 | 14,779 | 38.1 |

Source: Statistics Canada, "Imports," 1982.

*EXHIBIT 4*

| | | **CANADA** | | | **ONTARIO** | |
|---|---|---|---|---|---|---|
| Family Income Range | Total Family Expenditures | Personal Care Expenditures | Percent of Total | Total Family Expenditures | Personal Care Expenditures | Percent of Total |
| Under $10,000 | $ 7,797 | $ 194 | 2.5 | $ 8,055 | $ 218 | 2.7 |
| $10,000–$14,999 | 12,994 | 287 | 2.2 | 12,866 | 283 | 2.2 |
| $15,000–$19,999 | 17,976 | 401 | 2.2 | 18,467 | 420 | 2.3 |
| $20,000–$24,999 | 22,139 | 434 | 2.0 | 22,157 | 427 | 1.9 |
| $25,000–$29,999 | 26,399 | 499 | 1.9 | 25,766 | 491 | 1.9 |
| $30,000–$34,999 | 30,715 | 556 | 1.8 | 31,237 | 579 | 1.9 |
| $35,000–$39,999 | 34,447 | 615 | 1.8 | 33,900 | 627 | 1.8 |
| $40,000–$49,999 | 40,311 | 699 | 1.7 | 40,212 | 709 | 1.8 |
| Over $50,000 | 57,116 | 843 | 1.5 | 56,689 | 838 | 1.5 |
| Weighted average of all income levels | 27,062 | 491 | 1.8 | 28,087 | 514 | 1.8 |

**Average Annual Expenditures of Canadian and Ontario Families on Personal Care During 1982 by Family Income Level in Dollars**

Source: Statistics Canada, "Family Expenditure in Canada," 1982.

*EXHIBIT 5*

| | Population Size and Growth of Selected Areas | | |
| --- | --- | --- | --- |
| | **1976** | **1981** | **Percentage Change** |
| City of Toronto | 633,318 | 599,217 | (5.4) |
| City of North York | 558,398 | 559,521 | 0.2 |
| Borough of Scarborough | 387,149 | 443,353 | 14.5 |
| Borough of East York | 106,950 | 101,974 | (4.7) |
| Borough of Etobicoke | 297,109 | 298,713 | 0.5 |
| Borough of York | 141,367 | 134,617 | (4.8) |
| METROPOLITAN TORONTO | 2,124,291 | 2,137,395 | 0.6 |
| Peel Regional Municipality[1] | 375,910 | 490,731 | 30.5 |
| Halton Regional Municipality[2] | 228,497 | 253,883 | 11.1 |
| York Regional Municipality[3] | 203,915 | 252,053 | 23.6 |
| Durham Regional Municipality[4] | 247,473 | 283,639 | 14.6 |
| METRO and SURROUNDING VICINITY | 3,180,086 | 3,417,701 | 7.5 |
| ONTARIO | 8,264,465 | 8,625,107 | 4.4 |
| CANADA | 22,992,604 | 24,343,181 | 5.9 |

**1.** Includes Mississauga, Brampton, and Caledon.
**2.** Includes Halton Hills, Milton, Burlington, Oakville, and surrounding areas.
**3.** Includes Markham, Newmarket, Richmond Hill, and surrounding areas.
**4.** Includes Oshawa, Pickering, Ajax, Whitby, and surrounding areas.

Source: Statistics Canada, "1981 Census–Provincial Series."

*EXHIBIT 6*

| Mall | Square Footage (000s) | Stores | Weekly Traffic Flow (000s) | Approximate Rental Charges[1] | |
|------|----------------------|--------|---------------------------|-------------------------------|---|
| | | | | Square Foot | Percentage of Sales |
| EATON CENTRE<br>Toronto | 1,575 | 302 | 1,400 | $80–$115 | 8 |
| YORKDALE<br>North York | 1,364 | 200 | 194 | $40–$45 | 4–7 |
| FAIRVIEW MALL<br>North York | 560 | 125 | 300 | $50 | VARIES |
| HAZELTON LANES<br>Toronto | 56 | 40 | N/A | $30 | 9 |
| HUDSON'S BAY CENTRE<br>Toronto | 426 | 75 | N/A | $32 | 7 |
| SHERWAY GARDENS<br>Etobicoke | 920 | 200 | 225 | $20 | VARIES |
| SCARBOROUGH TOWN CENTRE<br>Scarborough | 1,400 | 220 | 200 | N/A | N/A |
| OSHAWA CENTRE<br>Oshawa | 1,002 | 160 | 100 | N/A | N/A |
| MARKVILLE MALL<br>Markham | 500 | 150 | N/A | $35 | 6 |
| HILLCREST MALL<br>Richmond Hill | 550 | 135 | 100 | $25–$50 | 5–8 |
| BRAMALEA CITY CENTRE<br>Brampton | 925 | 250 | 150 | $30–$45 | 6–10 |
| SQUARE ONE<br>Mississauga | 985 | 175 | 250 | VARIES | 6 |
| OAKVILLE PLACE<br>Oakville | 430 | 110 | 125 | $30–$45 | 4–6 |

**Rental Costs and Traffic Flows of Selected Toronto Area Malls**

1. Shopping centres normally charged rent based on the higher of a minimum annual charge per square foot and a percentage of annual gross sales.

Sources: Directory of Canadian Shopping Centres and various shopping malls.

**EXHIBIT 7**
**Logo Design**

*EXHIBIT 8*

| Newspaper | Circulation | Advertising Line Rate[1] | |
|---|---|---|---|
| | | B&W | 1 Colour |
| Brampton Guardian | 25,000 | $0.92 | $2.10 |
| Etobicoke Advertiser-Guardian | 45,000 | 1.02 | 2.10 |
| Markham Economist | 21,000 | 0.92 | 2.10 |
| Mississauga News | 70,000 | 1.18 | 2.10 |
| North York Mirror | 52,000 | 1.07 | 2.10 |
| Oakville Beaver | 25,000 | 0.91 | 2.10 |
| Scarborough Mirror | 55,000 | 1.08 | 2.10 |

**Selected Community Newspaper Circulation Levels and Advertising Rates**

1. A small advertisement of about 3" x 4" would contain approximately 50 lines.

Source: Canadian Advertising Rates and Data, 1983.

*EXHIBIT 9*

**Selected Designer-Name Perfume Prices**

| | 7ml | 15ml | 30ml |
|---|---|---|---|
| Oscar De La Renta | $64.00 | $105.00 | $175.00 |
| Joy | $80.00 | $135.00 | $245.00 |
| Lauren | $80.00 | $105.00 | — |
| Opium | $75.00 | $120.00 | $200.00 |
| Bal a Versailles | $75.00 | $110.00 | $190.00 |
| Chloe | $55.00 | $ 90.00 | — |
| Halston | $42.00 | $ 75.00 | $130.00 |
| Chanel No. 5 | $42.00 | $ 75.00 | — |
| L'Air du Temps | — | $ 70.00 | $120.00 |
| Je Reviens | — | $ 58.00 | $ 90.00 |
| Anais Anais | — | $ 52.00 | — |
| Shalimar | $38.00 | $ 65.00 | — |

**EXHIBIT 10**

| | 30ml | 36ml | 45ml | 50ml | 60ml | 69ml | 100ml | 120ml |
|---|---|---|---|---|---|---|---|---|
| **Selected Designer-Name Eau de Parfum and Eau de Toilette Prices** | | | | | | | | |
| Joy | — | — | $69.00 | — | — | — | — | — |
| Opium | — | $40.00 | — | — | — | $60.00 | — | — |
| Chloe | $30.00 | — | — | — | — | — | — | — |
| Anais Anais | $24.00 | — | — | — | — | — | — | — |
| Oscar de la Renta | — | — | — | — | $34.00 | — | — | $56.00 |
| L'Air du Temps | — | — | — | $23.00 | — | — | $33.00 | — |

**EXHIBIT 11**

| | 30ml | 45ml | 60ml | 70ml | 100ml | 120ml |
|---|---|---|---|---|---|---|
| **Selected Women's Designer-Name Cologne Prices** | | | | | | |
| Bal a Versailles | — | — | $35.00 | — | $60.00 | — |
| Lauren | — | — | $30.00 | — | — | $40.00 |
| Chanel No. 5 | — | $18.00 | $22.50 | — | $37.50 | — |
| Je Reviens | $15.00 | — | $20.00 | — | $27.50 | — |
| Halston | — | $18.50 | — | — | — | $40.00 |

# C A S E **5.9** UNIQUE SENIOR SERVICES

If there is a demand for a service that will benefit society, Carol Parnall will fill this demand. So, in May 1991, Carol hired a consultant to perform a feasibility study on her idea to develop a company that would cater to the elderly. She realized the need of seniors to have someone coordinate daily chores, household matters, and medical requirements. It was now June 25, 1991, and Unique Senior Services (U.S.S.) was nearly a reality. With the feasibility study complete, Carol was faced with several decisions.

## THE SERVICE

Unique Senior Services (U.S.S.) will not perform the actual "hands-on" work; it will act as a coordinator between seniors, business, family members, and public groups. The service will be provided in a manner similar to the head-hunting industry in that the client will deal with one person (the case manager) who will, in turn, deal with business on the client's behalf. Services that U.S.S. will coordinate for the elderly include the following: housekeeping, laundry, meal preparation, shopping, lawn service, seasonal cleaning, snow removal, transportation, banking assistance, and travel arrangements. Constant contact with the senior will be maintained and, upon request, services will be arranged and contracted out (see Exhibit 1 for a diagram of the process flow).

This service is expected to benefit the senior and his or her family by removing the worry of everyday responsibility. At the same time, it allows seniors to retain independence and control of their lives while remaining in their own homes.

## PROCESS

Establishing Unique Senior Services will require a lot of selling and recruiting in the start-up months to secure both clients and services. The first step will be to secure commitment from the various companies that perform the services needed by U.S.S. clients. For instance, a reliable lawn care company will be "hired" on an "as needed" basis. If a senior requests "lawn care" as one of his or her required services, U.S.S. will arrange with the hired lawn care company to service the senior's needs. This method will be used to secure a variety of businesses, developing a list of reliable, trustworthy companies who will provide immediate service for U.S.S. clients.

While contacts with businesses are being made, selling the idea to potential clients will also begin. Sales leads will be generated by making presentations to the end-consumers as well as to institutions who could refer potential clients. When a senior becomes interested in or is referred to U.S.S., Carol will go to the client's home to perform an evaluation of the physical and mental health of the client. This evaluation will determine whether or not the service will be of benefit to the senior. All evaluations will be performed in the home of the client to promote the in-home nature of the service. Once initial sales have been made, Carol will develop a portfolio of clients and spend time managing and coordinating the required services and following up to ensure that the client's needs have been met. Time will still be devoted to the ongoing process of selling and recruiting.

## THE CONSUMERS

Two consumer groups were identified as potential targets: the seniors themselves or their primary caregivers.

The seniors' group will be over the age of 65, but still physically able to perform daily tasks. Statistics Canada data suggest that functional independence begins to decline after the age of 75. In Canada, the percentage of the population over the age of 65 has increased steadily. Since 1981, the number of people aged sixty-five and over has increased at an annual rate of 2 to 4 percent, so that this group currently makes up about 12 percent of the Canadian population. Most of this explosion in the senior citizen population can be attributed to advances in the medical profession, as evidenced by the fact that 4 percent of Canada's population is over 75 years of age. Canada has approximately three million people aged 65 and older with one million over the age of 75.

London's elderly population is undergoing a number of changes, although the rate of growth in the senior population is slower than the national average. Similar to Canadian averages, women in London tend to outnumber men once they are past the age of 65, so that there are 35 percent more senior women than men.

Within London, the heaviest concentration of seniors is found in West London, North London, and Southcrest where, not coincidentally, some of London's community senior residential facilities are found. Within these areas it has been found that 64 percent of the "over 55" age group in London own their own homes and most of these people are either younger than 65 or older than 75. For some reason, seniors between the ages 65 and 75 tend to rent their housing. Over half of the seniors over the age of 75 rent housing, and of those who own almost all are male. There are approximately 35,000 persons over the age of 65, and 13,000 of these are single and living alone.

Convincing the seniors' group to buy the service will be difficult for two reasons. First, they see a service like this as something that will take away their independence and force them to lose control of their lives. This problem will be heightened if the seniors perceive that they cannot trust the individuals providing the care. Seniors as a group tend to have less disposable income than any other age group largely because they live on fixed incomes. Of families headed by seniors, 45 percent live on incomes of less than $20,000 and 50 percent of single individuals live on less than $10,000 annually. Among unmarried seniors, females' income levels tend to be substantially lower than males.

The seniors' primary caregiver is often their son or daughter. To avoid placing their parents in an institution, offspring are caring for their aging parents at home, often sacrificing careers to do so. The increase of women pursuing full-time careers makes this a growing problem. The service that U.S.S. is proposing will remove the burden of caring for a parent and allow the caregiver some flexibility to pursue his or her own interests. It will relieve family members of those time-consuming responsibilities of caring for a parent while, at the same time, allowing seniors to live independent home lives. This service would be particularly attractive to family members who live out of town.

The caregiver that Unique Senior Services projects as its ideal consumer is married, between the ages of 30 and 50, with children and/or a career, and with the responsibility of caring for a single parent either in his or her own home or elsewhere. Three thousand elderly people in London are single and living with a family member.

**BILLING**

Two possible methods of billing the consumer were recommended in the feasibility report. One of those methods involves charging the consumer a monthly fee for the privilege of using the services supplied by U.S.S. The monthly fee would be based on $60 per hour of time that U.S.S. spends managing the senior's personal needs and affairs. Carol did not expect the monthly charge to exceed the 2.5 hour minimum for each client. A retainer of $500 would also be charged at the initial assessment that would be used toward the first eight hours of services provided. The retainer would serve to eliminate bad debts, and to cover some of the cost involved with performing the initial assessment. Beyond the monthly charge, the client would also be expected to cover any cost involved with the contracted services. For example, if a housekeeping service were hired at $8 per hour, U.S.S. would bill the client $8 for the house-cleaning service in addition to the monthly charge. A markup on the cost of the contracted service would not be included.

"Agency billing" was the second alternative method of billing. No monthly fee is charged. Agency billing involves recovering a markup on the cost of services contracted. For example, if U.S.S. hired a house-cleaning company at $8 per hour, it would bill the customer $12. Revenue to U.S.S. is the margin on the actual cost of the service. A retainer of $500 would again be required and used toward the first $500 worth of billings.

Carol expected to coordinate 20 hours of service on average to each client. The average cost of the services to U.S.S. would be $20 per hour. The consumer would be charged a 50 percent markup on the cost of the services.

Each client would be charged a minimum of 2.5 hours per month no matter which method of billing was used.

It was still undecided which method of billing was most appropriate for each target group, and which would prove to be most profitable for Carol.

**COMPETITION**

Currently, there is no company in London providing the same service that Unique Senior Services is proposing; however, there are several organizations that provide care for the elderly.

*Direct Competitors*

London Home Care (LHC) is a publicly funded organization. It arranges home care and integrated home-making services for elderly individuals who have a sustained or periodic physical and/or mental impairment, are not able to provide themselves with care, do not have access to a caregiver, and wish to avoid admission to a care institution. These patients must be referred by their doctor.

If patients qualify for this program their stay will be subsidized as long as they continue to fulfil the ministry requirements. Once these patients no longer qualify for LHC, they can be transferred to a program called Integrated Homemaking Program. This program is also subsidized, but due to the limitations on funding there are restrictions on the number of people allowed to use the service.

*Indirect Competitors*

McCormick Home and Dearness Home in London provide daycare services for seniors. Three days a week volunteers will go to seniors' homes, pick them up, and bring them to the facility. While the senior is at Dearness or McCormick, he or she can visit with others, have a bath, get a haircut, play cards, or get involved in any number of activities. While at the home, a hot lunch is served to all the seniors and at the end of the day they are returned to their homes. The cost of this service is $11 and $12 a day. The homes also offer short-term to long-term care so that the seniors can stay there while they recover from surgery, or so that their caregiver can take time for a vacation.

Nursing homes provide an alternative to living at home. They provide the senior with potentially full-time care in a supervised environment. The growth in this segment of the population is outpacing the growth of facilities to care for them, resulting in a lack of available space.

*Potential Competitors*

Com-Care Ltd., Upjohn, and Para-Med Health Services are all associated with a national organization that provides in-home nursing care and home care. Their business is not targeted to the elderly but this area has become one of their largest consumer groups. They provide both nursing and home care involving light housekeeping, meal preparation, laundry, and shopping. They also send medical persons to the home if necessary. Com-Care Ltd. finds it is contacted 50 percent of the time by the seniors themselves and the other 50 percent by the adult children who are requesting the service for a parent. It receives a great number of jobs on a referral basis.

A big portion of Upjohn's business comes from providing in-home care for seniors who are recovering from an operation and want to be at home but can't look after themselves. These are short-term contracts. Upjohn uses an Ontario news magazine called *Today's Seniors* as its means of advertising, with most other business being generated on a referral basis through London Home Care.

Para-Med is the most aggressive and comprehensive in-home provider in the London market. It not only provides all the services that the other two companies do, but also offers private duty and visiting nurses as well as occupational and physiotherapists.

There are several similar services elsewhere in Canada. Complete Geriatric Care (CGC) have been operating successfully in Toronto since 1981. CGC offers three basic services including institutional placement coordination, case management, and advocacy. To engage the services of CGC it will cost the client and/or family member a retainer of $600 (plus $42 G.S.T.) and an ongoing fee of $90 per hour (plus G.S.T.) for consulting services.

Victoria Elder Care (VEC) is located in Victoria, British Columbia. They charge $75 for the initial assessment and $17 per hour of service thereafter. VEC is a very new company having been in business only a few months. Knowledge of this company was gained through an advertisement placed by VEC in the *Globe and Mail,* which offered to care for elderly people who live in Victoria.

**ENVIRONMENT**

All levels of government have realized the need for improved services for the elderly and many new programs have been awarded government grants to further this goal. There are currently two federally sponsored programs that are designed to improve the services available to seniors. The problem with these programs is that the services must be run by seniors and must be nonprofit in order to qualify for the grant. The extensive administrative detail that has to be performed in order to qualify for financing has proved to be a hindrance, so that few seniors are likely to make use of the opportunity. Further reducing the use of these programs is the fact that they are not advertised, so that awareness is restricted to individuals associated with the government.

At the provincial level Ontario was well on its way to improving its senior support systems, having produced a document entitled "Strategies for Change" that outlines the needs for long-term care in Ontario. This report also outlines the areas in which government money should be invested and which ones would be given priority. These plans have been cancelled since the NDP government took over and a new priority of spending on senior care is being developed. Carol was concerned about the future for institutional funding when the federal budget agenda for 1992 was presented.

Although there were no stated plans for increased senior facilities in London, a new nursing home with senior daycare is already under construction in northwest London that will complement the existing and popular senior facilities.

**CORPORATE CAPABILITIES**

Unique Senior Services will require a bank loan of $3,000. This amount is in addition to the $1,000 contributed by Carol. The money will be used primarily to cover the cost of advertising and promotion but some will also be used to cover office expenses until clients are secured. The amount of funding is quite low because the business will be operated from her home for the first few years. Carol Parnall will serve as the director of the company. Carol has had eight years' experience as a human resources specialist and is currently working for Prime Management Group, a management recruiting firm.

At Prime, Carol's work covers two aspects — selling and recruiting. She has completed the Registered Nursing Assistants (RNA) program at Fanshawe College, and performed the "practical" training portion of her RNA in a nursing home.

Recognizing that she does not possess all the appropriate skills to handle every type of senior need, Carol has decided to have a voluntary advisory board with whom she can meet several times a year to find ways to improve the services provided. This advisory board will be composed of a psychiatrist, a therapist, a gerontologist, someone from a nursing home, someone from business, and a couple of senior citizens.

Costs to run the business will include the advertising budget, phone charges of $50 per month, rent of $1,200 for the year, $30 per month for office supplies, $40 per month in travel costs (mainly gas mileage), interest of 10 percent on the loan, other miscellaneous supplies at $150 for one year and, finally, insurance charges of $30 per month.

**ADVERTISING AND PROMOTION**

An advertising budget of $1,000 has been set for the first year of operation. Carol hoped to stick to this budget, but realized that more might be needed. The objective for the advertising at the start will be to generate referrals. Seniors who are being released from institutional care will hear about this service through nurses and social workers who were caring for them in the institution. Word of mouth will also be an important part of advertising as many seniors live alone in large seniors' apartment building complexes. Seniors will trust each other's judgment and if one of them has had a good experience with U.S.S., more will be willing to try the service.

Carol thought she could give sales presentations to groups such as the McCormick Day Centre staff and Third Age Outreach staff. It will cost $75 to have a printing shop prepare overheads for the presentation. It will cost $495 to print 500 pamphlets to distribute after the presentation. Carol hoped the success of gaining referrals from institutions and word of mouth would all but eliminate the need for active advertising in the future. As a means of attracting the primary caregiver market, Carol wanted to contact some large corporations and sell the idea as part of the benefit package they offer employees.

Newspaper ads could also be taken out in area newspapers. It will cost $1,554 (plus G.S.T.) to run two 1/16″ by 3 3/8″ ads (where 1/8 of a page ad is made up of 2 1/16″ by 4″) in the *Globe and Mail* for six days (for a larger ad double dimension and price). Submission in the *London Free Press* will cost $967 per day. A commercial spot on CFPL London costs $605 for a prime time 30-second spot. An 1/8 of a page ad in *Today's Seniors*, a monthly news magazine that has a circulation of 30,000 in the London area, will cost $225 per month.

Carol thought that having an article written about the company would serve as free promotion and she wondered how to encourage the media to help out with this.

**CONSIDERATIONS**     Carol would like to make Unique Senior Services her full-time career within the next three to five years. For this to be possible she requires that the business provide her with an annual net income of $50,000.

***EXHIBIT 1***
***Purchase Flow***
***Diagram***

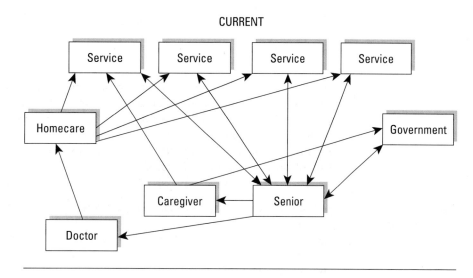

CURRENT

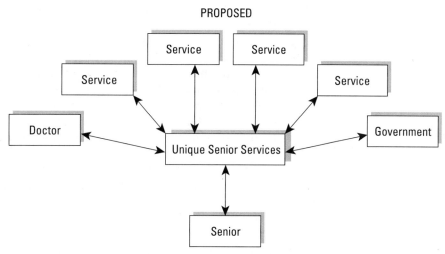

PROPOSED

## C A S E 5.10   VEHICLE INFORMATION PRODUCTS

In June 1993, Tom Brunette, president of Vehicle Information Products (VIP) in Hamilton, Ontario, considered the future of the Auto Pricer, a software product that was in the developmental stage. Tom expected to introduce the Auto Pricer by early 1994, but was undecided on a marketing plan to successfully launch the product, which was the most recent addition to VIP's line of car information software.

**VEHICLE INFORMATION PRODUCTS**

Vehicle Information Products was founded in November 1990, with the objective of providing innovative and creative marketing solutions to the automotive industry. Initial product development focused on the creation of a comprehensive database for all new cars and light trucks available for sale in Canada. The database was kept up-to-date, with information from manufacturers, VIP's dealer affiliates, and VIP's customers.

VIP focused on increasing its product offerings to take advantage of its large database. Currently, there were 13 products in development and 12 staff working for VIP. The company was privately owned; most employees held shares in the business. The largest proportion of funds was provided by a local venture capitalist.

Tom Brunette brought a variety of experience to VIP. He had worked in his family's distribution business for 11 years and obtained a degree in business administration in 1984. After graduation, Brunette became chief financial officer in a car dealership, where his task was to automate the dealership's information. Eventually, Tom began a software business, specializing in dealership automation. In 1992, Tom Brunette was approached by the venture capitalist to consult for Vehicle Information Products. After three months, he became VIP's president.

Tom enjoyed operating VIP. He wanted to provide value-added to the car buyer, wherever possible, such as by supplying the consumer with easier access to car information. Also, Tom hoped VIP could help to improve the relationship between car consumers and car dealers.

**THE AUTO PRICER**

Unlike VIP's current software products, which were sold to leasing and fleet management companies, the Auto Pricer was designed for the end consumer for use on a home computer. With data drawn from VIP's database, the Auto Pricer would contain information, on floppy disks, on the more than 1,000 cars and light trucks available for sale in Canada. The information would also include the following:

- standard equipment (e.g., two doors or four doors)
- specifications (e.g., engine size)
- warranties
- incentives (e.g., cash rebates)
- Manufacturer's Suggested Retail Price

To use the Auto Pricer, a user might select, for example, "cars priced between $25,000 and $30,000" or "trucks available with automatic transmission." The software would then produce a list of the vehicles conforming to these parameters. The user could select a specific model in order to view descriptive text and financial data, including total price, monthly costs, and interest charges. With the Auto Pricer, a user could essentially build a car by adding options (e.g., air-conditioning, four-wheel drive) to a standard vehicle. With each increment, the user would be shown, on screen, the increase in price.

To date, almost $16,000 had been sunk into research and development costs. A new programmer was needed to make the product more consumer-friendly; he or she would be paid a $30,000 to $35,000 salary.

**POTENTIAL USERS**

Tom foresaw three potential users of the Auto Pricer: car buyers, car enthusiasts, and software collectors.

**Car Buyers**

It was difficult for a car buyer to become an overnight car expert, when he or she was only in the market every two to ten years. In a 1992 interview with *Business & Finance* magazine, Tom Brunette stated:

> Two decades ago there were only three automobile manufacturers selling products in Canada. Now there are 30, making it nearly impossible to keep track of all the models available, let alone acquire copies of all the various catalogues and brochures pertaining to those vehicles.

The typical consumer began his or her car search three weeks to a month before buying. Consumers found information through word-of-mouth, car-related literature, and car dealerships, and by bartering with different salespeople before selecting a vehicle and negotiating its price. Salespeople often provided sketchy information, to avoid overloading the customer with information. The dealerships supplied manufacturers' brochures also containing only superficial information.

Comfort and utility were the most important selling points; dealer service was also significant. Car consumers of the 1990s were becoming more sophisticated. They were showing a greater concern for the environment, placing less emphasis on cars as status symbols, and more emphasis on practicality and value, with a trend toward replenishment rather than acquisition. As many as one-quarter of car buyers maintained loyalty to one manufacturer, while the remainder were willing to shop around.

**Car Enthusiasts**

The car enthusiast was the person who followed cars as a hobby, watching for news, facts, and trends. Enthusiasts might talk to friends about their hobby, visit car shows, or read the automotive section of the newspaper and car magazines. Exhibit 1 shows the results of an October 1992 survey of *Carguide* magazine readers. *Carguide* was a Canadian publication available on newsstands and as a souvenir program at the annual Toronto, Ottawa, Edmonton, Winnipeg, and Quebec City car shows.

**Software Collectors**

Tom predicted that the Auto Pricer might appeal to the software collector. This person purchased or copied software for his or her personal computer. Tom wondered whether a driving simulator would make the Auto Pricer more attractive to this consumer. The creation of a simulator could be contracted out at a variable cost of $15 to $20 per software package.

**ALTERNATIVE SOURCES OF INFORMATION**

Currently, there was no comprehensive software data package available to Canadian consumers. Consumers could obtain car information from books, magazines, manufacturers' catalogues and diskettes, and through several small services.

**Books and Magazines**

The Canadian Automobile Association (CAA) published new car list prices in *Autopinion*. Well-known books such as *Lemon-Aid* reviewed used cars, dealerships, and garages. *Auto Trader* was a regional publication that advertised used cars for sale. Numerous American magazines such as *MotorTrend* and *Car and Driver* provided information on new cars, with American prices and data. In 1992, *MotorTrend* had over 26,000 Canadian subscribers while *Car and Driver* had almost 75,000 subscribers in Canada.[1] One such car magazine claimed that as many as 60 percent of new car buyers were magazine users who used up to nine issues in their car search.

**Catalogues and Diskettes**

Automobile manufacturers provided catalogues, but with information changing constantly, these were known in the trade to be out-of-date. Manufacturers' diskettes, which included American pricing data, were available free-of-charge through the mail, to individual customers. The Ford Motor Company was rumoured to have sent out 200,000 of its diskettes to North American consumers in one year.

**Competitors**

Several independently run companies had been developed recently to assist car buyers in their search. Toronto-based Car$mart recommended car makes and models to serve its customers' needs; it then showed its customers a step-by-step overview of how to negotiate a purchase. This company had been successful in attracting professionals who lacked time or simply detested the entire car search process, but were willing to pay the $100 consulting fee.

Another company located in Toronto's outskirts, Consumer Automotive Research Services (CARS), offered free two-hour seminars to aid the car-buying public and a vehicle search for a $54 fee. CARS acted much like a broker, working with a network of 30 Ontario dealers, from whom it received a handling fee.

In the United States, a nonprofit consumer information service, Automotive Experts, advised buyers of dealer invoice costs, unpublished manufacturer-to-dealer rebates, and negotiation strategies through a 24-hour voice mail system that cost $1.95 per minute. AutoVantage OnLine of Texas offered a computer-based service at a cost of $49 U.S. a year. The AutoVantage service provided members with five new car and three used car valuations yearly.

**TRENDS IN THE MARKETPLACE**

According to Statistics Canada, the 1992 new car and truck sales were at their lowest level since 1985.[2] Automobile manufacturers had been hit hard by the recession, with many consumers either putting off new car purchases or switching to used vehicles. During tough economic times, as many as 60 percent of purchases were used cars. When the economy improved, however, the split between new and used vehicle sales might be 50/50. Exhibit 2 provides information on new car and light truck sales in Canada. Cars were seen, more and more, as an investment as car prices rose.

Recently, Canadians spent less time "pleasure shopping" and more time around the house. Comparison shopping was often seen as too time-consuming. More and more Canadian households were investing in personal computers. In 1990, only 16.3 percent of Canadian households owned home computers, while in 1992, that figure had risen to 20.0 percent.[3]

Car dealers have traditionally been somewhat aggressive, but as consumers become more demanding and value-conscious, dealers have been forced to be more consumer-friendly. Innovations include "no dicker" sales lots and "salesperson free" car shows.

A February 23, 1993 *Financial Post* article suggested that many women were unhappy car buying:

> ... A survey of women and the auto industry shows ... (that) while more women are buying cars and taking responsibility for maintenance of the family car, many still feel they aren't given enough consideration in the showroom. More than two-thirds of the respondents were still unhappy with their treatment on buying trips.

While women were taking a more active role in the car purchase, the automotive industry had not yet fully responded.

Tom believed that computer technology, because it was changing so quickly and becoming affordable, would have a huge impact on the way cars were bought and sold. Eventually, VIP could upgrade to CD-ROM technology, which would produce a high quality picture on screen. VIP could also introduce the Auto Pricer on video, which would allow it to include car commercials.

**DISTRIBUTING THE AUTO PRICER**
**Direct Mail**

Tom identified several possibilities for distributing The Auto Pricer.

VIP could advertise the Auto Pricer in newspapers and magazines to develop a mail order business. Responses outside the Hamilton area might require a toll-free phone number. A toll-free telephone line would cost an additional $25 per month, plus $0.31 to $0.48 per minute of calls. Selected advertising costs are listed in Exhibits 3A and 3B.

**Software Retailers**

The second option was to sell the Auto Pricer through a software retailer. The software market was quite fragmented, with thousands of retailers across North America. VIP could sell directly to a few retailers, but a distributor was required for mass retailing. Most distributors were geographically based, so that five or six distributors would be required to cover all of Canada.

The distributor needed to be convinced that the product would sell. While it was often possible to get a foot in the door, the distributor would decide within minutes whether the product was acceptable.

The distributor expected a 10 to 20 percent margin on wholesale price. Distributors demanded a six-month supply of the product and would pay for the product after it had sold. The distributor also desired a hassle-free return policy, in the event that the product did not sell. Each distributor might carry software for 500 different vendors. Some distributors could be convinced to push a product more after receiving free product samples. Usually, the manufacturer led the product's promotion and print advertising in local and daily newspapers and magazines. If the distributor did advertise the product, it expected full cost reimbursement. Only the very large companies like MicroSoft carried out in-store promotions.

The retailer only accepted software products with mass appeal. With so many browsers visiting the retailer, packaging was the "make or break" criterion. Software packaging had to be professional, done by a graphics designer, and not a simple label. The retailer commanded from a 30 to a 100 percent mark-up on wholesale price, depending on price and volume. For example, on a $25 MSP, the retailer expected 100 percent mark-up.

**The Packaging Option**

A third option was to sell VIP's software to a large packager that would then package and label the product as its own. In return, VIP would receive a royalty on all sales of the product.

**PRICING THE AUTO PRICER**

Tom surmised that the Auto Pricer could be priced in the $49.99 to $79.99 range, but was uncertain of the way consumers would respond to such a new product.

**PRODUCING THE AUTO PRICER**

The KAO company in Toronto would copy the Auto Pricer, in bulk, on IBM-compatible diskettes, at a cost of $6.90 per package. An instructions manual could be produced at a cost of $2; minimum order size was 500. Legal envelopes, detailing VIP's copyright on the Auto Pricer, could be produced for

$0.25 each. For the retail option, a glossy plastic cover for the Auto Pricer could be produced at $5 per package. For the mail order option, mailing envelopes that protected the diskettes were available at $1.25 each; the manufacturer required three weeks' notice. The entire package could be assembled at a cost of $0.08 and mailed at a cost of $1.35.

While the VIP database was updated, manually, on a daily basis, the Auto Pricer owners would not have access to these updates. Tom considered the possibility of including a card in the software package with which a consumer could send away for a data upgrade, at a cost of $10 to $20.

## CONCLUSION

Tom Brunette was anxious to commence production and sales of the Auto Pricer by March or April of 1994, but he realized that many questions needed answers. Pricing, distribution, and advertising issues were not resolved. Tom was confident that VIP could offer the consumer an innovative, informational software product, but was uncertain how to effectively market the Auto Pricer.

### NOTES

1. Source: Consumer Magazine and Agri-Medi Notes and Data, July 1993.
2. Source: Statistics Canada, "New Motor Vehicle Sales," Catalogue 63-007.

*EXHIBIT 1*
*Carguide Magazine*
*Reader Survey: Selected*
*Results*
*October 1992*

- Gender:

    91.5% of *Carguide* readers are male

- Age:

    4.8% are 18–24

    24% are 25–34

    35% are 35–49

    24% are 50–64

    5.9% are 65+

- Yearly household income:

    4.5% are <$20,000

    4.5% are $20,000 to 24,999

    10%  are $25,000 to 34,999

    19.4% are $35,000 to 49,999

    29.5% are $50,000 to 74,999

    16.4% are $75,000 to 99,999

    15.7% are $100,000+

- Occupation:

    55.2% are white collar, senior managers, or professionals

    6.5% are in sales

    2.9% are unskilled labourers

    15.8% are skilled labourers

    16.7% are students

    12.6% are retired

- Average time spent reading an issue of *Carguide*: 3 hours, 42 minutes

- Of those who plan to purchase a vehicle,

    89.9% say in the next 12 months

    29.9% say in the next 6 months

    10.2% say in the next 3 months

Source: Carguide magazine.

*EXHIBIT 2*

| | Passenger Car[1] Sales in Canada (In Units of Vehicles) | |
| --- | --- | --- |
| | **1991** | **1992** |
| Newfoundland | 646 | 617 |
| P.E.I. | 121 | 128 |
| Nova Scotia | 1,492 | 1,563 |
| New Brunswick | 1,539 | 1,289 |
| Quebec | 14,086 | 13,818 |
| Ontario | 24,343 | 20,318 |
| Manitoba | 1,606 | 1,360 |
| Saskatchewan | 1,290 | 1,038 |
| Alberta | 6,196 | 4,700 |
| B.C. and Territories | 6,482 | 6,860 |
| TOTAL | 57,801 | 51,691 |

**1.**  All vehicles whose primary function is to carry passengers, including commercial vehicles (taxis, fleets, auto rentals).

Source: Statistics Canada, "New Motor Vehicle Sales," Catalogue 63-007.

EXHIBIT 3A
Selected Advertising
Costs Newspaper
Advertising

**Costs for a 2" x 4" ad:**

| | |
|---|---|
| VANCOUVER SUN | $602.00/day (Friday's Wheels Section) |
| LONDON FREE PRESS | $205.00/day (Saturday's Wheels Section) |
| THE HAMILTON SPECTATOR | $135.00/day (Spectator's Auto Section) |
| TORONTO STAR | $861.00/day (Saturday's Wheels Section)<br>$438.00/day (weekday's High-Tech Section) |
| GLOBE and MAIL | $278.10/day (near car classified ads) |
| FINANCIAL POST | $529.10/2 days (Wed. & Sat.'s Computer Network Section) |
| MONTREAL GAZETTE | $230.00/day (weekday's Automotive Section)<br>$300.00/day (Saturday's Automotive Section) |

EXHIBIT 3B
Selected Advertising
Costs Magazine
Advertising

ALMANACH DE L'AUTO — a French-Canadian new car guide

| (Black & White) | | (4-colour) | |
|---|---|---|---|
| 1 page: | $1,715 | 1 page: | $2,215 |
| 1/2 page: | $1,200 | 1/2 p.: | $1,550 |
| 1/4 page: | $860 | | |

AUTOPINION — a CAA yearly publication

| (4-colour) | |
|---|---|
| 1 page: | $4,150 |
| 1/2 page: | $2,960 |
| 1/4 page: | $1,650 |

WORLD OF WHEELS — a Canadian bi-monthly new car guide (English and French)

(4-colour)
| | |
|---|---|
| 1 page: | $8,390 |
| 1/2 page: | $5,105 |
| 1/3 page: | $3,275 |

*CARGUIDE* — a quarterly Canadian new car guide (English and French)

October/April/July editions

| (Black & White) | | (4-Colour) |
|---|---|---|
| 1 page: | $4,250 | $5,000 |
| 1/2 page: | $2,550 | $3,300 |
| 1/3 page: | $1,910 | $2,660 |

January edition

| (Black & White) | | (4-Colour) |
|---|---|---|
| 1 page: | $7,825 | $8,925 |
| 1/2 page: | $4,700 | $5,800 |
| 1/3 page: | $3,520 | $4,620 |

*CAR AND DRIVER* — an American monthly magazine

(Black & white)
| | |
|---|---|
| 1 page: | $42,690 |
| 1/4 page: | $14,935 |
| 1/6 page: | $10,680 |

*MOTOR TREND* — an American monthly magazine

(Black & White)
| | |
|---|---|
| 1 page: | $34,485 |
| 1/4 page: | $12,070 |
| 1/6 page: | $8,620 |
| 1/12 page: | $4,655 |

*ROAD & TRACK* — an American monthly magazine

(Black & White)
| | |
|---|---|
| 1 page: | $31,055 |
| 1/4 page: | $10,930 |
| 1/6 page: | $7,785 |

# C A S E  **5.11**  VENTURE CARPETS (ONTARIO) LTD.

Would people put garbage on their floor? Grant Heggie, vice-president, sales and marketing at Venture Carpets (Ontario) Ltd. in Mississauga, Ontario, had asked himself this question several times in the last few days. He wondered whether people would, if it had the fine texture and durability of quality broadloom. Grant had to decide whether Venture (Ontario) should distribute a unique brand of carpeting made from recycled plastic pop and ketchup bottles. The product, known as the Enviro-Tech Collection and produced in the United States by Image Carpets Inc., had yet to be introduced into Canada under its own label. It was late 1992, and Venture (Ontario) was offered exclusive distribution rights to the Enviro-Tech name if they decided to add the collection to their product range. Earlier efforts by Venture (Ontario) to introduce the product under their own label, the Royalist Collection, had failed due to erratic fluctuations in federal duties on imported goods of this nature. Two years later, following the stabilization of duties, Grant wanted to reconsider the potential in the Ontario market of this unique brand of carpeting.

**THE CARPET INDUSTRY**

Across Canada, approximately $8 million worth of carpeting was sold through retail each year, and about a third of this was sold in Ontario. The entire market was divided into three main segments: commercial, residential contract, and residential retail. Carpeting required for business purposes represented the commercial side, while home builders made up the residential contract business. These two segments represented about 50 percent of the carpeting industry. The other half was sold through retail outlets to end consumers who were buying carpet for their own home. This was the segment that Venture (Ontario) was considering targeting with the Enviro-Tech Collection. Consumers in this segment fell into one of three categories: price sensitive, value conscious, or quality conscious.

Price was the key purchasing criteria for the price sensitive consumer, which represented about a third of the residential retail segment. Whether it was because of budget constraints or the perception that all carpets were virtually the same, these consumers shopped around for the colour they wanted at the cheapest price. With value conscious consumers, the buying process became a little more complicated. The quality of the product became more important. Features such as warranty, fibre strength, lustrous colourations, and resistance to sun fading were qualities just as important as price. Most consumers fell into this category, which represented over half of the retail segment. The remaining consumers were those that felt price had very little influence in their purchasing decision. They were primarily concerned with the quality of the carpet and were willing to pay for it. Although, on the whole, consumers were becoming much smarter in terms of shopping around for the right carpet to fit their needs, the sales staff at the retail outlets still played a key role in the purchasing decision.

**DISTRIBUTION TO THE RETAIL SEGMENT**

Carpet manufactured at the mill was either sold directly to the retailer or through a distributor. Mills that went directly to the retailer employed their own sales force that was exclusive to that particular mill. While they could offer better prices than the distributor, mills were unable to compete on service. This included such things as product assortment, good credit availability, and the handling of problems and complaints.

Distributors, on the other hand, relied heavily on the service aspect of the business. A key advantage they had over the individual mills was that they were not exclusive to any one mill. They often carried a variety of lines from several different mills, providing the retailer with an assortment of products from which to choose. Due to the number of lines and colour variations in each one of them, the investment in inventory was very high. Distributors would normally spend over $100,000 per line, and considering that most carried close to 50 lines, the financial risk was immense. In addition, most distributors offered other flooring alternatives such as vinyl and ceramic tile. While they could not compete with the mills on price alone, it was important that the distributors offer competitive prices in addition to the service, if they were to be successful. Another important feature critical to the success of the distributor was its sales staff.

Retailers were similar to the distributors in that they too offered several different lines of carpeting. However, not only did they offer products from a variety of mills, but they also purchased from an assortment of distributors. There was no loyalty as far as distributors were concerned. While price was a major factor, it was important for the retailer to offer a wide assortment of products, in terms of colour and quality, since most consumers spent a considerable amount of time shopping around before they made their decision. Retailers commanded a 50 percent mark-up on their cost. The sales staff played a critical role in the success of a carpet. When most consumers entered the showroom, the only thing they had decided upon was the colour. After that, they relied heavily on the sales staff for information regarding quality and price before they made their decision on which product to buy. In fact, due to the nature of the buying process, very little advertising was geared toward the end consumer. A few of the larger mills had developed their own limited advertising campaigns, which benefited both the distributors and retailers. However, as one retailer indicated, "my business is built on referrals." A satisfied customer would not only spread the word, but was also likely to return next time. Advertising, traditionally, had very little impact on the consumer's decision.

## THE COMPETITIVE ENVIRONMENT

At the time, there were about 20 companies competing in the Ontario market. Fifteen of these were either distributors or Canadian mills that had set up a sales staff in Ontario. While the Canadian mills strictly sold their own products, the distributors also carried lines from mills in the United States. The other five organizations were American mills. Similar to those in Canada, they had set up their own sales staff to push their own product lines. It was estimated by Grant that about 60 percent of the market was held by the top four or five companies, which were primarily mills.

There were three categories of carpet sold in the market. Low-end broadloom, primarily made of a substance known as Olefin, sold for between $4 and $17 per square yard. Medium quality carpet, normally made from cheaper nylon and polyester, ranged from $10 to $30 per square yard. And, finally, there were the high-end products. These were made of good quality nylon, polyester, and even wool in the highest quality products. The average retail price per square yard for these products started at about $25 and could run over $130.

Unfortunately for the Canadian mills, there was an increasing trend in the market toward American carpets. Not only were these products far less expensive (up to 30 percent lower), but American mills were much larger, enabling them to offer a much broader selection of products. While a mill in Canada produced 20 to 30 lines, some American mills produced upward of 200. Their colour selection was also more impressive. In 1986, only 6 percent of the market was consumed by American products. In 1991, following the Free Trade Agreement, Grant estimated that this figure had risen to as high as 50 percent and the trend was expected to continue.

## ENVIRONMENTAL ANALYSIS

The Free Trade Agreement had been a very important issue in the carpeting industry over the previous two years. When the agreement passed in January 1990, and all duties were virtually eliminated, U.S. mills began selling in Canada at prices of up to 30 percent less than those that domestic mills could afford to offer. Caught by surprise, several Canadian mills were forced out of business. About a year later, after noticing the dumping that was taking place, the government imposed large duties on American mills trying to export into Canada. These duties ran as high as 26 percent in some cases and allowed the Canadian mills to be competitive once again. As time passed and domestic mills adjusted, the government, by November 1992, once again reduced the duties, to as low as 3 percent. By this time, however, companies such as Venture, which had tried to introduce American products into the Canadian market, had suffered severely. For Venture, the Royalist Collection, its original entry of U.S. products into the market, had basically been ruined.

Another major concern for Canadian distributors importing products from across the border was the value of the Canadian dollar. In the case of the Enviro-Tech Collection, margins could fluctuate anywhere from 9 to 25 percent. Since the price to the retailer had to remain competitive, it was the distributor who had to stomach the squeeze on their margins when the dollar deteriorated.

The carpeting industry was also very sensitive to fluctuations in the economy. In weak economic times, the residential business could essentially "stop overnight," as consumers almost immediately cut back most capital expenditures of this nature; however, the commercial side of the business was slower to react to these economic downturns. When upturns in the economy occurred, the reverse was true; that is, the residential business picked up a lot quicker than the commercial business.

## VENTURE CARPETS LTD.

Venture Carpets began as a Canadian mill in Quebec in 1974 and catered specifically to the commercial sector of the industry. Under new ownership in 1985, the mill used independent distributors to carry their products throughout Canada. Exclusive rights were given to one distributor in each of Venture's five marketing areas including the Maritimes, Newfoundland, Quebec, Ontario, and the West Coast.

Early in 1990, the distributor for Ontario, Cross-Can Agencies (CCA), found itself in trouble. Due to CCA's inability to finance the further growth of their business and the fact that Venture represented about 90 percent of their sales, Venture was becoming an involuntary financial partner with the distributor. After a short period of time, Venture decided to buy out CCA entirely and to enter the distribution side of the business full scale. Although maintaining a solid reputation in the commercial sector and representing close to 2.5 percent of the overall Ontario market, with 27 different lines, Grant felt there was still considerable room to grow. As a result, Grant started to look for new lines to complement their own Venture products. While some of this growth could come from the commercial side of the business, Grant made a decision to consider the residential arena. This was also important considering the poor outlook of the economy. It would be very hard to survive on construction business alone.

Grant began by looking for products that would fit into the traditional Venture philosophy. As he indicated, "We wanted to find a product with a niche ticket but this was hard to find in residential." While keeping price, product range, quality of mill, and uniqueness in mind, Grant found himself looking across the border to American mills. This occurred when Image Carpets Inc. of Armuchee, Georgia, came into the picture. Grant felt the Enviro-Tech Collection was ideal. However, he was very concerned about the way the traditionally conservative Canadian consumer would respond to such a unique product.

## THE ENVIRO-TECH COLLECTION

If you were to throw 650 empty pop bottles on the average living room floor, you would have a serious problem. But if you washed them out, cut them up, melted them down, and spun them into fibres, you would have an effective solution.

Although virtually new to the Canadian market, Image had been making carpet from recycled polyethylene terephthalate (PET) for over 10 years. They had sold over 100 million square yards of carpet made with PET fibres all over the world. Because of its versatility, the usage of PET fibres also extended far beyond the carpet industry. PET was durable enough to be used by the Goodyear Tire Company in their toughest line of Eagle Tires. Auto manufacturers were also using seat belts made with strong PET fibres to withstand sudden shocks and repeated stresses.

By manufacturing all of their own PET fibre, Image had complete control over the quality of its PET carpet products through every stage of the manufacturing process. It also allowed for the production of a consistently high quality product since fibre qualities such as elongation, tenacity, bulk, and lustre were monitored continuously on the production line. In fact, Image was the only carpet mill in the world who extruded their own PET fibre (refer to Exhibit 1 for a complete description of the conversion of plastic containers to carpet).

As Grant perused some literature on the Image products he mentioned:

The Enviro-Tech Collection contributed to the reduction of over 50 million lbs. of plastic containers from landfill sites each year. While PET containers constituted about 6.5 percent of landfill waste by weight, they actually took up eight times the space (per lb.) of paper and glass because of their shape and volume. As well, to produce over 50 million pounds of any popular carpet fibre would, if not made from recycled materials, consume several million barrels of imported crude oil. By purchasing a product from the Enviro-Tech Collection, you are also reducing the depletion of finite reserves of fossil fuel.

For the *"Canadian-made"* conscious consumer, 25 percent of the mill's plastic container requirements came from Canada. Yet not only were consumers doing their part for the environment, they were also investing in exceptional broadloom. The quality, durability, stain resistance, and overall performance of the Enviro-Tech products were far superior to other polyester or nylon products on the market. This was due to the stringent federal controls placed on food-grade PET containers. "Have you ever seen a Coke or Heinz ketchup bottle stained?" Grant asked.

**ISSUE AT HAND**  Following the events of the last two years, Grant was still very interested in carrying the Enviro-Tech Collection. Yet, he was unsure whether he should continue to offer the product under his own label, or to introduce it under the "Enviro-Tech Collection." If Grant decided on the latter, Image had offered Venture exclusive distribution rights to the name in Ontario. While the line would be sold to other distributors under their own label, using the Enviro-Tech name did have its advantages. Grant was also considering offering the same exclusive rights to retailers. This would mean about 400 of the dealers they planned to distribute to would potentially carry the Collection.

From the standpoint of Image, it was a good deal because it was hard to get a distributor to carry the complete line of products. Most distributors already carried a full line of residential carpets. However, in doing so, Image also became responsible for the majority of the marketing costs. Under their own label, Venture would have to invest in a sample stock for the warehouse, costing between $80,000 and $100,000. This was just for samples, not inventory for resale. Under the Enviro-Tech name, Venture's marketing costs would fall to between $20,000 and $30,000.

Image was also offering Venture a unique deal in that they could order the product as they needed it. Venture would not be required to carry inventory, which was very uncommon in the industry. This was a substantial savings since Venture was considering carrying 15 different lines with about 35 colours in each line. This would mean an investment of about $60,000 to $120,000 per line for inventory. By ordering direct, Venture would only be carrying about $40,000 to $50,000 worth of floating inventory (products waiting to be delivered and paid for) in total. There was also the problem of wastage, if they decided to carry inventory. About 5 to 6 percent of each roll of carpet could not be used in the end. After cutting off the exact amount for every order, the end of the roll was often unusable due to its irregular size. By carrying inventory, Venture would absorb this cost.

One drawback with ordering direct, however, was that Image would charge Venture more per square yard. By carrying inventory, they were able to purchase the Collection at a cheaper price and to obtain margins of 28 to 30 percent when selling to dealers. By ordering direct, margins were expected to fall to an average of about 20 percent. It was also estimated by Grant that Venture would lose out on up to 10 percent of potential sales by ordering direct and by having the consumer wait up to five to ten days for delivery, compared to a couple of days if Venture had the product in stock.

The only other incremental costs associated with carrying the Enviro-Tech Collection was the cost of in-store displays for the retailers and the commissions paid to the sales staff. The actual display would cost Venture (Ontario) around $750. However, in order to entice the dealer into carrying the product, Venture (Ontario) covered some of the cost itself and charged the retailer about $500. This was a substantial investment considering the distributor sold their products through about 500 dealers all across the province. Traditionally, salespeople were compensated with a package made up of both a salary and commission. However, since no new sales people would have to be hired to carry the Collection, the only incremental cost that Venture (Ontario) had to cover was the commission component, which worked out to about 2.5 percent of their sales.

**CONCLUSION**

Sitting at his desk, Grant reflected:

> Many people chucked their acceptable garbage into blue boxes and felt good about doing their part. But they rarely got the opportunity to know

what happened to their garbage once it left the curb. Buying products made of recycled materials allowed people to be part of the next step in the program.

While this could be true, Grant was also concerned whether people would really care about this when it came to one of the largest expenditures of their life, next to their home and car.

If he decided that Venture should carry the Collection, what label should he distribute it under? Did it make sense for Venture to carry any inventory? One option Grant considered was eventually carrying inventory in the more popular lines, once these were determined.

Another major issue that troubled the vice-president was how to sell the lines — PET fibres were a form of polyester and, when the first polyester products initially hit the market in the early 1970s, they were of inferior quality. Many changes had occurred since then; however, most people were still resistant to the material as an acceptable product. What would his message be to the dealers? How much should he emphasize the *"environmentally friendly"* aspect of the product? Or should he focus on its quality? One dealer was quoted as saying:

> Once customers see the velvety thickness, richness of colour, competitive price and discover its tough, stain resistant qualities, whatever reservations they may have about laying garbage in their home will vanish.

Grant wondered just how much of this optimism could actually become a reality if he decided to carry the Collection.

*EXHIBIT 1*
**From Ketchup Bottle to
Carpet[1]**

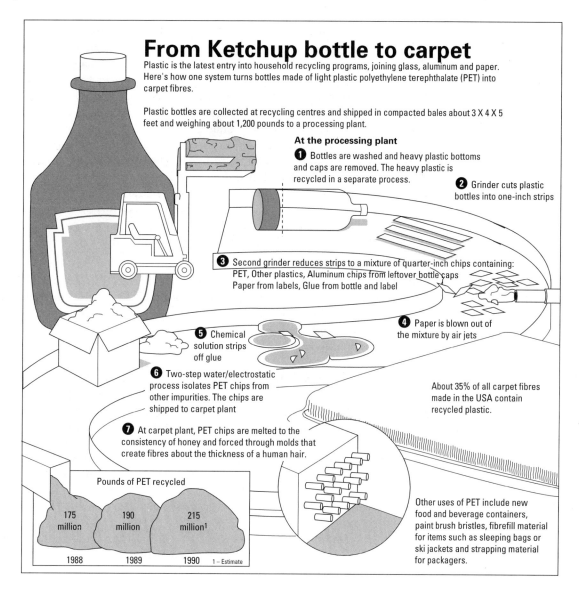

# From Ketchup bottle to carpet

Plastic is the latest entry into household recycling programs, joining glass, aluminum and paper. Here's how one system turns bottles made of light plastic polyethylene terephthalate (PET) into carpet fibres.

Plastic bottles are collected at recycling centres and shipped in compacted bales about 3 X 4 X 5 feet and weighing about 1,200 pounds to a processing plant.

**At the processing plant**

**1** Bottles are washed and heavy plastic bottoms and caps are removed. The heavy plastic is recycled in a separate process.

**2** Grinder cuts plastic bottles into one-inch strips

**3** Second grinder reduces strips to a mixture of quarter-inch chips containing: PET, Other plastics, Aluminum chips from leftover bottle caps Paper from labels, Glue from bottle and label

**4** Paper is blown out of the mixture by air jets

**5** Chemical solution strips off glue

**6** Two-step water/electrostatic process isolates PET chips from other impurities. The chips are shipped to carpet plant

About 35% of all carpet fibres made in the USA contain recycled plastic.

**7** At carpet plant, PET chips are melted to the consistency of honey and forced through molds that create fibres about the thickness of a human hair.

Other uses of PET include new food and beverage containers, paint brush bristles, fibrefill material for items such as sleeping bags or ski jackets and strapping material for packagers.

Pounds of PET recycled

| 175 million | 190 million | 215 million[1] |
|---|---|---|
| 1988 | 1989 | 1990 |

1 – Estimate

**1.**   Copyright, USA Today. Reprinted with permission.

## C A S E 5.12    YESTERDAY'S NEWS (A)

Early in 1985, Gordon Fischel, president of Celltech International, sat in his Moncton, New Brunswick office pondering his latest management decision. The firm's only product — Yesterday's News Cat Litter — had been successfully introduced in Canada's Maritime provinces almost two years earlier and now controlled a significant portion of that market. Also, in the last year, the product had been introduced in the Eastern United States, but had not gained any significant market share.

Because of the high fixed costs associated with the product, a loss of $297,000 was recorded on total sales of $551,000 in 1984. Fischel now felt that the product had reached its potential in Eastern Canada and considered whether he should perhaps exploit different markets in order to increase volume and achieve profitability. Fischel felt confident about the product but knew that the remainder of the marketing decisions must be made before this product could become a success in a new market.

**THE MARKET FOR CAT LITTER**

Cat litter was a product that pet owners usually placed in an area of their home, into which their trained pets deposited their feces and urine (usually in a "litter box"). Cat litter was also used less frequently for garden mulch and for cleaning up small oil spills. Most brands of the product were in pellet form made from clay or alfalfa and could be found in package sizes ranging from 4 lbs. to 25 lbs.

There were essentially four types of cat litter on the market. The first type would mask the smell of the cat box with a perfumed aroma. The second type of litter was essentially the same as the first, except that the scent was time-released when the cat stepped upon the litter. The third type of litter claimed to kill the odor on contact, leaving no foul smell in the air. The fourth type was merely a plain (regular) litter with no perfume.

Cat litter was typically replaced in the litter box when the smell of the cat's feces and urine in the box became unbearable. The task of changing cat litter could be a dreaded job, not just because of the smell, but also because it could be quite messy.

The cat market was now thought to be larger than the dog market for the first time. With the increase in apartment living and the evolution of women in the workforce, many people simply did not have the time or space to walk or care for a dog.

Cat litter sales in North America were increasing by 8 to 12 percent annually and currently stood at CDN $400 million ($370 million in the United States and $30 million in Canada). This growth in sales was a function of the growth in the domestic cat population, which currently stood at 60 million in the United States[1] and 6.5 million in Canada.[2] Based on cat food sales, the cat population appeared to be growing at 8 percent per year.[3] Approximately 25 percent of all sales occurred in the four summer months (May to August).

## CONSUMERS OF CAT LITTER

Consumers of cat litter were mostly cat owners, but a certain percentage of the market was for caged animals (hamsters, gerbils, etc.). According to extensive research commissioned by Fischel, there were essentially two classes of cat litter consumers. The largest group of consumers, called the "nonserious" consumer (estimated at 75 percent of the market), felt that cat litter was a homogeneous product and that all brands were the same. These consumers could note no difference in performance between brands and would often place their litter box in the basement of their home or in a closet, away from where odor could be determined.

These consumers could be further subdivided into two groups. The larger of these two groups (approximately two-thirds of this consumer group) could be considered the "ignorant" consumer. These people purchased a generic or branded product without any thought. They did care about the odor and mess associated with changing a litter box, but believed that all litters currently on the market performed identically. Products offering convenient sizes (easy to carry) and "flashy" packaging might attract this consumer. The second group of this "nonserious" consumer segment could be called the "price-conscious" consumers as they were stubborn in their belief that all cat litters were the same and, therefore, almost always bought generic product (usually in bulk) because of its lower price (15 to 20 percent below national or regional brands). It was thought that this consumer group was not overly bothered by the odor of a cat box and, therefore, bought on the basis of price alone.

The second class of cat litter purchasers were the "serious" consumers who actually compared cat litters and found a desired product through trial and error. They desired a product that controlled the odor of the feces and urine in order to avoid offending guests with the smell of their cat box. In order to satisfy these consumers, a product must be absorbent and not stick to the tray or fur of the animal. Also, the product should have a longer tray life and be easy to clean up.

Both consumer groups would usually purchase their litter in a supermarket, as the majority of sales of the product were found there.

## COMPETITION

In Canada, Lowes "Kitty Litter" was the dominant force with an estimated market share of 25 percent of the Canadian market. In North America Lowes made an estimated $100 million in cat litter sales alone.[4] "Kitty Litter" was a clay-based product that came in two varieties — plain and "New and Improved." The "New and Improved" product had a perfume aroma designed to mask odor. Lowes had not recently spent a great deal on advertising in Canada as the product had been well established for many years. Overall, very little advertising was carried out by cat litter manufacturers in Canada.

Chlorox, a large U.S.-based detergent manufacturer, was the other force in the cat litter industry. Chlorox moved into the Canadian market in 1983 after holding a 15 percent share of the United States market. Chlorox currently had two "time-released" cat litter products — "Litter Green" and the newly launched "Fresh Step."

Chlorox appeared to be having difficulty breaking into Canada and was rumored to be preparing to pull out to concentrate on the United States market.

The remaining Canadian market share was split among generic products, many small companies, and some larger manufacturers who dabbled in cat litter. A rationalization of the smaller companies was predicted as their share was absorbed by the larger, more dominant firms.

**COMPANY HISTORY**
After a successful 20-year career in the Toronto investment business, Mr. Fischel decided that the level of challenge and satisfaction in his current profession was diminishing and it was now time to attempt running his own business. Armed with his business experience and a marketing degree from McGill University, he established a home-insulation firm in Moncton in 1977. After sales peaked at $1.5 million, the withdrawal of federal grants for insulation combined with a large amount of uncontrolled receivables forced him to look for other business ventures. Fischel wanted to ensure that his next product could be produced at a high volume and have a low level of accounts receivable. The product should also be of high quality and perform as claimed.

On the suggestion of a friend, Fischel began to look seriously at the cat litter market. During the summer of 1980, he paid $10,000 to the Research and Productivity Council of Canada to determine what the best ingredients were for a highly absorbent cat litter. By November of that year, it was discovered that a product composed of recycled newspaper would be the most absorbent. Thus, the product name evolved — "Yesterday's News."

For the next three years, Fischel worked on raising the necessary capital to go into business. The total original investment was $1.5 million (Exhibit 1). Of this investment, $255,000 was spent to obtain a building to produce the product, and $500,000 was put toward specialized manufacturing equipment that had the capacity to produce six million 6 lb. bags of cat litter.

In order to compare the product against the competition, an independent laboratory tested "Yesterday's News" against the products of the three large North American producers. The research showed that "Yesterday's News" was between 272 and 390 percent more absorbent than these brands.

Market research was also performed to test consumer perception of the product. In Toronto, 100 homes were given "Yesterday's News" and 100 homes were given a competitor's product (national brand). Questionnaires showed that 75 percent of those using "Yesterday's News" would buy the product, while only 50 percent of those using the competitor's product would buy it. Fischel felt that the positive results were partly a function of the special chemical additives in his product that he claimed killed odor on contact. Similar encouraging results were found in a $100,000 focus group study that Fischel had commissioned in the Greater Boston area. He also offered special discounts to grocery store chains in this area to entice them to carry the product.

When the product reached Maritime grocery stores in August, 1983, at $2.29 to $2.69 for a 6 lb. bag, Fischel was sure that his product was a winner.

## YESTERDAY'S NEWS CAT LITTER

"Yesterday's News" had reached what Fischel felt was its peak in Atlantic Canada with little promotional effort (Exhibit 2). Over the past year, "Yesterday's News" had also been introduced into the U.S. (primarily in the New England states) and now 75 percent of the company's sales came from that country (Exhibit 3).

The majority of sales for "Yesterday's News" were made in the 6 lb. size, packaged in cases of eight bags (48 lbs.). "Yesterday's News" was currently priced as a premium cat litter (average retail selling price: $2.69 in Canada). Variable manufacturing costs for the product were $.50 per bag (including materials, labour, variable factory overhead, and freight).

Despite a strong growth in sales, Celltech faced a second consecutive loss and Fischel believed that now was the time for action. The company had no money left for marketing and depended on short-term financing to cover a $25,000 per month operating loss. Greater volume was needed to ensure the future viability of the firm.

Fischel had recently been able to secure up to $1 million in venture capital from three former business associates. This capital was in the form of equity in Celltech and is what Fischel intended to use to create a future marketing strategy for "Yesterday's News."

## GROWTH OPPORTUNITIES

Fischel considered the province of Ontario to be a viable area for growth. Ontario, the most populous province in Canada, recorded cat litter sales of $8,200,000 in 1984. Fischel was concerned over the high number of generic/private label sales in this market (Exhibit 4) and wondered what effect this would have on his marketing plan. Also, Lowes was very strong in this market. Fischel was encouraged that Ontario grocery stores, on the average, tended to carry only one store brand and one to two other brands in one or two sizes.

A budget of up to $300,000 was set aside for the marketing of the product, if Ontario was chosen as a growth area. Fischel felt that there were three areas in Ontario in which to penetrate: Ottawa; London/Kitchener; and the "Golden Horseshoe" (Oshawa, Toronto, Hamilton) (Exhibit 5). It would cost approximately $10,000 per week to attack any one of these areas with a television campaign. This figure did not include the $45,000 production cost of such a campaign.

Other areas could also be utilized to promote "Yesterday's News." Fischel had considered securing a professional veterinary association endorsement at a cost of $5,000.

A magazine advertisement had been developed (production costs $3,500) to be run in a monthly cat lovers' magazine. The magazine advertisement would be educational and would stress the impressive test results from the comparison of "Yesterday's News" with competitive brands. The magazine had a total paid subscription listing of 25,000 in Ontario and the ads would cost $1,250 per month.

Point-of-purchase advertising could be presented in supermarket chains at a cost of $20,000 per chain. The ads could state whatever message Fischel wanted to get across to the consumers.

Lastly, a 25¢ coupon could be placed in a supermarket chain's weekly flyer (Exhibit 6). Each chain typically distributed flyers to an average of 400,000 homes in this region. The cost to Fischel would be $2,000 per chain per week. Fischel anticipated a redemption rate of 2 percent each time this couponing method was used.

In order to launch this new product, a great deal of capital would be required, not only for advertising, but also for distribution. For example, Canadian supermarket chains typically demanded a product placement fee of $40,000 to $60,000 each. A profile of the major supermarket chains in Ontario is shown in Exhibit 7. Fischel felt he could delay paying the product placement fees for one year, if he offered the supermarket chains some introductory incentives. For example, two or three free truckloads could be offered to entice a chain to carry "Yesterday's News" (approximate cost: $5,500 per truckload). Also, "buy one-get one free" deals were often used over the first two or three months of product introduction. If sales grew as anticipated, the "one for one" could cost $10,000 per month for this Ontario option. The disadvantage of not paying the placement fee right away was that, if the product did not sell quickly upon initial placement, the chain might feel obligated to take the product off the shelf sooner than if the placement fee had been paid from the start.

Supermarket chains received other incentives to carry new products. For example, in Canada, these chains would demand a 30 to 35 percent margin on their retail selling price and plenty of advertising support. The manufacturers would also have to offer the chains two discounts off the manufacturer's selling price: a 10 percent volume discount and a 5 percent co-op advertising discount.

In the past, Celltech had concentrated on the 6 lb. size and maintained a premium selling price ($2.69 RSP). Fischel was considering this same strategy in the future. Alternatively, "Yesterday's News" could be priced at $2.15 (a 20 percent decrease) to place it in the same price range as the 8 lb. generic cat litters. But Fischel felt that the higher price in the 6 lb. size would justify its better performance over an 8 lb. bag of a competitive product. (See Exhibit 8 for competitive prices and product sizing.) Celltech was the only manufacturer of cat litter in the 6 lb. size. If other sizes were offered, Fischel anticipated the same percentage contribution after retailer discounts and broker commissions. Fischel had used a broker to sell the product in the past and planned to maintain this practice in the future. The broker acted only as a commissioned salesman and received an 8 percent commission on the manufacturer's selling price.

**SUMMARY**

Fischel was unsure of whether to tap the Ontario market. He was concerned that this new strategy could put too much strain on the firm. Celltech had a lean management hierarchy (Exhibit 9) with Fischel doing all the sales and marketing and a great deal of the day-to-day decision making. He had recently considered hiring an experienced marketing manager at a cost of nearly $60,000.

Before Fischel went any further, he wanted to reassess the marketing decisions he had already made. He felt that no matter who marketed the product, a proper strategy for "Yesterday's News" should "influence people from all consumer groups." He also felt that this was his last chance to make "Yesterday's News" a viable product. Another poor financial year would certainly dry up any future sources of venture capital and definitely spell the end for Celltech.

### NOTES

1. *Cat Magazine* estimate.
2. Canadian Cat Association.
3. *Cat Magazine* estimate.
4. Celltech estimate.

**EXHIBIT 1**

| Original Investment — Celltech International | |
| --- | --- |
| Venture Capital | $    800,000 |
| DREE (government) grant | 242,000 |
| FBDB (government) loan | 350,000 |
| N.B. government | 120,000 |
| TOTAL | $1,512,000 |

**EXHIBIT 2**
*1984 Market Share —*
*Atlantic Market*

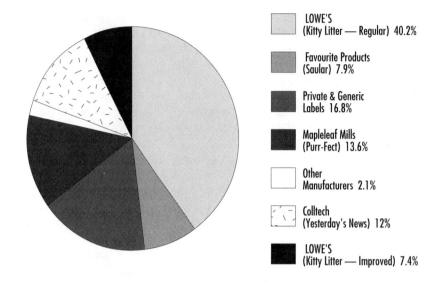

LOWE'S
(Kitty Litter — Regular) 40.2%

Favourite Products
(Saular) 7.9%

Private & Generic
Labels 16.8%

Mapleleaf Mills
(Purr-Fect) 13.6%

Other
Manufacturers 2.1%

Colltech
(Yesterday's News) 12%

LOWE'S
(Kitty Litter — Improved) 7.4%

**EXHIBIT 3**
*Present Sales Area of*
*"Yesterday's News"*

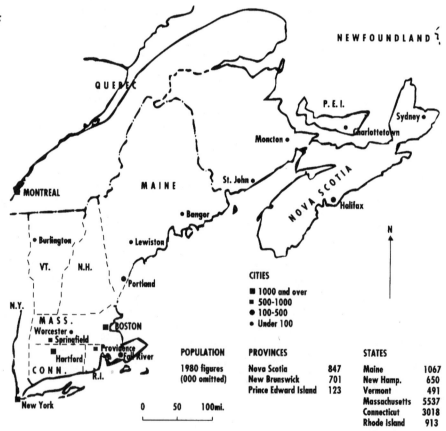

CITIES

■ 1000 and over
■ 500-1000
● 100-500
• Under 100

**POPULATION**

1980 figures
(000 omitted)

**PROVINCES**

| | |
|---|---|
| Nova Scotia | 847 |
| New Brunswick | 701 |
| Prince Edward Island | 123 |

**STATES**

| | |
|---|---|
| Maine | 1067 |
| New Hamp. | 650 |
| Vermont | 491 |
| Massachusetts | 5537 |
| Connecticut | 3018 |
| Rhode Island | 913 |

0   50   100mi.

*Exhibit 4*
*1984 Market Share —*
*Ontario Market*

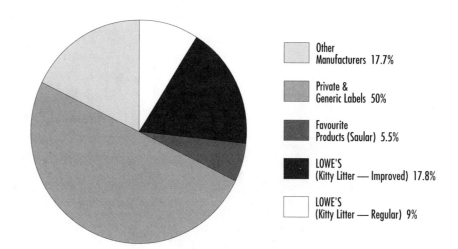

Other
Manufacturers  17.7%

Private &
Generic Labels  50%

Favourite
Products (Saular)  5.5%

LOWE'S
(Kitty Litter — Improved)  17.8%

LOWE'S
(Kitty Litter — Regular)  9%

*Exhibit 5*
*Ontario Market*

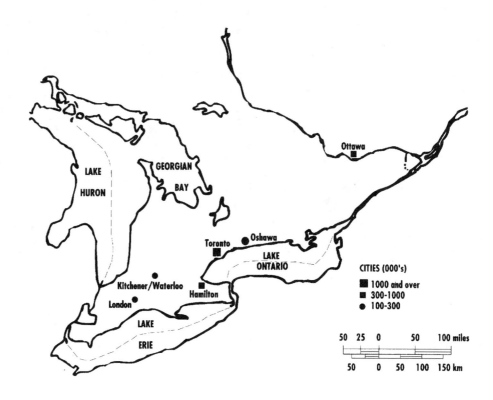

*EXHIBIT 7*

| Market Profile — Ontario Supermarket Chains (1985) | | |
|---|---|---|
| **RETAIL FOOD CHAIN** | **ONTARIO OUTLETS** | **ONTARIO MARKET SHARE**[1] |
| Loblaws companies | 113 | 19% |
| Safeway | 11 | 1% |
| Dominion | 35 | 6% |
| Miracle Food Mart | 76 | 10% |
| A & P | 200 | 12% |
| Food City | 52 | 3% |
| I.G.A. | N/A | 14% |
| Misc. chains | N/A | 4% |
| Misc. independents | N/A | 31% |

1.   Casewriter's estimates.

*EXHIBIT 8*

| Competitors' Pricing and Package Size | | | | |
|---|---|---|---|---|

MARKET AREA: ONTARIO
PERIOD ENDING: DECEMBER 22, 1984

| BRAND | ITEM SIZE (lbs.) | PACK/CASE | AVG PRICE | $ VOLUME |
|---|---|---|---|---|
| Jonny Cat | 10 | 5 | $4.27 | 2,199 |
| Kitty Dri | 10 | 5 | $2.30 | 9,346 |
| Kitty Kit | 10 | 5 | $4.06 | 772 |
| Kitty Pan | 10 | 5 | $2.96 | 294,439 |
| Kitty White | 10 | 5 | $1.86 | 25,159 |
| Litter Green | 10 | 5 | $5.80 | 62,385 |
| Lowes Kitty Litter | 10 | 5 | $2.40 | 93,618 |
| Sani-Cat | 10 | 5 | $1.64 | 16,168 |
| Suzy-Q | 10 | 5 | $2.64 | 293 |
| Treat Em | 10 | 5 | $2.57 | 43,544 |
| Total | | | | $547,923 |

*EXHIBIT 8 (cont'd)*

| BRAND | ITEM SIZE (lbs.) | PACK/CASE | AVG PRICE | $ VOLUME |
|---|---|---|---|---|
| Kitty Pan | 20 | 2 | $5.51 | 3,265 |
| Aristo-Cat | 22 | 2 | $4.40 | 24,728 |
| Cats Pad | 22 | 2 | $3.38 | 25,853 |
| Feeline Favorite | 22 | 2 | $2.30 | 67,299 |
| Lowes Kitty Litter | 22 | 2 | $6.33 | 86,543 |
| Lowes Kitty Litter Impvd | 22 | 2 | $7.03 | 451,374 |
| Saular | 22 | 2 | $5.58 | 144,986 |
| Tidy Tray | 22 | 2 | $4.39 | 66,095 |
| Treat Em | 22 | 2 | $6.23 | 8,225 |
| Generic and priv. label | 20 | — | $4.90 | 2,050,000 |
| Total | | | | $2,928,368 |

| BRAND | ITEM SIZE (lbs.) | PACK/CASE | AVG PRICE | $ VOLUME |
|---|---|---|---|---|
| Jonny Cat | 25 | 1 | $11.99 | 120 |
| Kitty Dri | 25 | 1 | $ 5.16 | 8,611 |
| Kitty Kit | 25 | 1 | $ 9.75 | 136 |
| Kitty White | 25 | 1 | $ 2.77 | 46,516 |
| Lowes Kitty Litter | 25 | 1 | $ 6.47 | 10,781 |
| Suzy-Q | 25 | 1 | $ 5.50 | 39 |
| Total | | | | $66,203 |

| BRAND | ITEM SIZE (lbs.) | PACK/CASE | AVG PRICE | $ VOLUME |
|---|---|---|---|---|
| Kitty Pan | 4 | 5 | $0.86 | 16,859 |
| Litter Green | 4 | 5 | $2.59 | 3,719 |
| Aristo-Kat | 4.41 | 10 | $0.88 | 18,117 |
| Lowes Kitty Litter | 4.41 | 10 | $1.29 | 174,657 |
| Lowes Kitty Litter Impvd | 4.41 | 10 | $1.54 | 59,133 |
| Purr-Fect | 4.41 | 10 | $1.06 | 107,073 |
| Saular | 4.41 | 10 | $1.28 | 43,039 |
| Tidy Tray | 4.41 | 10 | $1.00 | 36,595 |
| Generic and priv. label | 4 | — | $1.05 | 1,025,000 |
| Total | | | | $1,484,192 |

***EXHIBIT 8** (cont'd)*

| BRAND | ITEM SIZE (lbs.) | PACK/CASE | AVG PRICE | $ VOLUME |
|---|---|---|---|---|
| Kitty Dri | 5 | 5 | $1.16 | 4,347 |
| Kitty White | 5 | 5 | $0.99 | 7,629 |
| Lowes Kitty Litter | 5 | 5 | $1.52 | 20,702 |
| Treat Em | 5 | 5 | $1.14 | 49,110 |
| Total | | | | $81,788 |

| BRAND | ITEM SIZE (lbs.) | PACK/CASE | AVG PRICE | $ VOLUME |
|---|---|---|---|---|
| Glamour Kitty | 8 | 5 | $4.06 | 55,408 |
| Aristo-Kat | 8.81 | 5 | $1.51 | 52,461 |
| Cats Pad | 8.81 | 5 | $1.96 | 75,551 |
| Feeline Favorite | 8.81 | 5 | $1.32 | 3,043 |
| Lowes Kitty Litter | 8.81 | 5 | $2.64 | 356,822 |
| Lowes Kitty Litter Impvd | 8.81 | 5 | $2.96 | 963,930 |
| Purr-Fect | 8.81 | 5 | $2.12 | 113,927 |
| Saular | 8.81 | 5 | $2.51 | 270,978 |
| Sitting Pretty Cat Litter | 8.81 | 5 | $3.47 | 74,901 |
| Tidy Tray | 8.81 | 5 | $1.86 | 67,265 |
| Generic and priv. label | 8 | — | $2.15 | 1,025,000 |
| Total | | | | $3,059,286 |

***EXHIBIT 9***
***Organizational Chart***

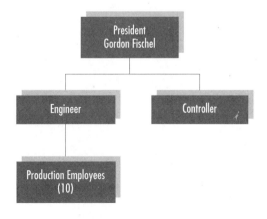

# PART

# AN INTRODUCTION TO OPERATIONS
# MANAGEMENT

Operations is one key to any organization's success. Along with marketing, the operations function, often called production, is where an organization adds value and makes money. You all have experience with operations through your day-to-day life. The goal of operations is to *produce goods and services efficiently and effectively*. To help you develop an effective operating point of view and decision-making skills applicable to most operating contexts, this chapter will explore four fundamental aspects common to any organization:

1. The purpose and basic components of operations,
2. The key tasks that operations managers must manage for their respective organizations to do well,
3. The basic types of operations systems and their management requirements, and
4. The basic tools to diagnose and solve operations problems.

## THE PURPOSE AND BASIC COMPONENTS OF OPERATIONS

### *FUNCTION*

One common way to describe the operations function is the input-transformation-output model shown in Figure 1. According to this model, the organization "purchases" inputs from suppliers, changes them in some way, and then "sells" the outputs to customers. Although the core of operations is the transformation process, the scope of the operations function includes purchasing and often distribution. In addition, all parts of every organization have an operations component. One key message in the sections that follow is that operations is where the action is: it makes things happen.

*FIGURE 1*
*A Model of*
*Operations*

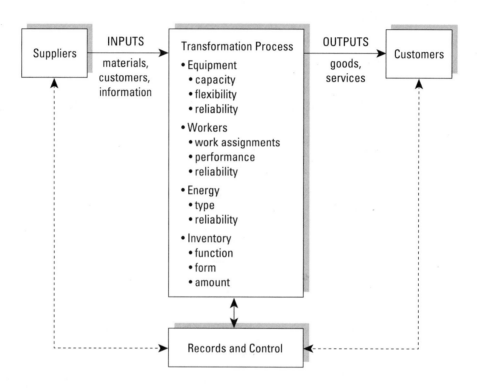

Operations is everywhere, all around each of us every day. Although we see operations every day in such settings as restaurants, hotels, airlines, universities, hospitals, banks, and stores, we normally associate it with mines, factories, and food processing plants, for example. All enterprises perform operations and it is often a critical function key to making money. Exhibit 1 gives some examples.

Exhibit 1 illustrates several points about the model in Figure 1. First, **different organizations process (transform) different types of inputs**. Some enterprises focus on transforming materials, others on transforming customers, and others on transforming information. Although almost every organization transforms a mixture of inputs, one usually dominates. Steel companies concentrate on the first type of input: they transform primarily materials — iron ore, lime, and coal. Dentists, doctors, and universities transform customers (patients or students). Researchers or financial managers transform information. Restaurants transform materials in the kitchen, and customers in the dining room. Invest-

*EXHIBIT 1*

| Examples of Operating Systems | | | |
|---|---|---|---|
| Organization | Inputs | Transformation Process | Outputs |
| Iron mine | iron ore | drilling, blasting, separation, crushing, concentrating | highly concentrated iron oxide, waste rock |
| Steel mill | iron oxide pellets, lime, coal, scrap steel | smelting, pouring, oxygenating, rolling, forming | steel ingots, slabs, sheets |
| Parts manufacturer | sheet steel | pressing, punching, machining, painting, polishing | parts ready to assemble |
| Automobile assembly plant | parts | welding, bolting, riveting, painting, testing | finished automobile |
| Restaurant | foodstuffs, hungry customers | seating, order-taking, drink and food preparation, serving, clean-up, setting table | satisfied customers, waste food |
| University | knowledge, students | analysis, sorting, writing, teaching, counselling, evaluating, planning, gathering data | skilled and knowledgeable graduates, new knowledge |
| Planning rock concert | available dates, necessary activities and required order, estimated times | organizing activities into a network, marshalling resources, scheduling, monitoring progress | completed project on time and on budget |
| Investment management | interest rates, trends, yields, client preferences, network of contacts | data analysis, matching client and portfolio, transactions | wealthy, satisfied clients |
| Personnel department | staff records, performance evaluations, department needs | scheduling, analysis of data, interview, discuss strengths and weaknesses | staff development plan, enhanced resources, satisfied staff |
| Marketing department | records of customer orders and inventory, production schedule, new products | market research, analysis of data, discuss strengths and weaknesses | market plans and incentive systems, successful product launch |

ment managers transform information to make decisions, and transform customers through their conversations and the results of their decisions.

Second, **operations extends to all departments of the enterprise, not just the factory,** and the operations process for such departments can be a significant factor in the company's ability to compete. The accounting department needs a process to transform transactions into the firm's financial records. The marketing department needs a process to capture information from customers. The personnel department needs processes to hire, evaluate, promote, motivate, discipline, and lay off staff.

Third, **one organization's outputs almost always become another organization's inputs**. The iron oxide concentrate produced by the iron mine becomes a major input to the steel mill. In turn, its steel output is purchased by parts manufacturers who produce body panels, wheels, engines, and the like, for sale to automobile assemblers. They sell their finished products to dealers who, in turn, sell them to consumers. Sale to the final user may end the chain, or, as is common in the case of automobiles, there may be active markets in used goods or scrap. Scrap is particularly interesting in this case because a steel company's output may well become one of its own major inputs at some time later when the steel is recycled. To deal with the potential ambiguity, the analyst must carefully define the operations system by deciding where its boundaries are, keeping in mind that, although such boundaries are necessary, they are almost always artificial.

Fourth, **operations links suppliers and customers by adding value for which customers will pay**. Banks buy money from depositors (by paying interest on deposits) and sell it to borrowers (by charging interest on loans). They survive because there is a spread of several percentage points between these two interest rates, and because they provide security, information, and pools of funds unavailable to lenders and borrowers who might interact directly. Real estate brokers bring buyers and sellers together by virtue of their knowledge of the local market. Paper mills link forestry companies to newspapers because of their ability to transform wood into paper.

Fifth, **virtually every process has a number of steps**. The examples in Exhibit 1 tend to be rather large — at the factory or company level. Thus, iron oxide concentrate, limestone, and coal are put in and steel is taken out; thousands of parts are assembled and an automobile is driven away; food is purchased and a meal is prepared. But an automobile assembly plant may have 1,000 work stations, and everyone knows that making a meal involves many steps. Take preparing a breakfast of a boiled egg, coffee, orange juice, and toast, for example. Each of the four items on the menu could be considered as a single step — boil the egg, make the coffee, pour the juice, cook the toast. But, consider the egg boiling step. It, too, can be broken down into a series of separate steps — get out the pot, pour in enough water, get the egg from the refrigerator, add it to the pot of water, put the pot on the stove, turn on the heat, wait, set the timer, and so on. Furthermore, the step of getting out the pot can also be broken down into such steps as walking to the cupboard, reaching forward, grasping the handle, pulling the cupboard door open, locating the pot, reaching in, grasping the handle, and so forth. The level at which you perform such analyses depends entirely on the sorts of decisions you want to make. For kitchen design decisions, a detailed sequence would be useful, but to decide how much to charge for the labour content in such a breakfast, a much broader scope would be appropriate.

Sixth, the model in Figure 1 shows the flow of materials and services. Although this flow is central to any operating process, no process operates completely independently. Decisions must be made: should I start my egg, coffee, juice, or toast first? Should I fry my egg or boil it? How long should I cook it? How well is the process working? These and many more decisions require **information about inputs, outputs, and the process itself,** which must also flow to allow managers to control and evaluate the operation. Figure 1 shows information flows as dotted lines.

## OPERATING SYSTEM COMPONENTS

The transformation process usually involves equipment, people with a range of skills, energy to make it all happen, and inventories of goods to help smooth out the operation. These four elements are the normal components of operations (see Figure 1).

### Equipment

Equipment includes the machinery needed to make production happen: lathes, milling machines, and grinders in machine shops; mixers, stoves, refrigerators, and cash registers in restaurants; aircraft, baggage-handling apparatus, and maintenance equipment in airlines; computers, printers, and automated teller machines in banks. In some operations — for example, a counselling service — there may be little, if any, required equipment. Capacity, flexibility, and reliability are three important features of equipment, and each of these, in turn, has a number of aspects.

**Capacity** has two distinct notions: how much a piece of equipment can hold, and the amount of material, number of customers, or quantity of information that can be processed or produced in a given period of time. Exhibit 2 gives some examples. Note that *capability* is a different notion. One key to understanding these different meanings of capacity is to keep the units straight. Note that the volume examples in Exhibit 2 have single units whereas the speed ones are always expressed as a ratio.

We normally discuss capacity in terms of *theoretical capacity* — what the equipment manufacturer designed and built the unit to do — and *operating capacity* — what happens when the equipment is actually used. The extent to which theoretical capacity is achieved is one measure of the equipment's efficiency. Thus, a class of 62 students (operating capacity) scheduled for a classroom with 75 seats (theoretical capacity), has an equipment efficiency of 62/75 or 82.7 percent. A hamburger grill designed to produce 12 patties every three minutes (or 240 per hour) operating nonstop producing 220 per hour is performing at 91.7 percent (220/240) efficiency.

Why don't we get 100 percent utilization? The reasons vary. In the beer kettle example we may be unable to stir a completely full kettle without spilling some of the contents. Or dents or sensing and stirring devices installed inside the kettle may reduce its effective volume. In the case of hamburger cooking, the operator may have to clean the grill periodically, and must take time to remove cooked patties and replace them with raw ones. These times may not have been considered in calculating theoretical capacity. Usually, operating capacity will be less than theoretical capacity. There are exceptions, however. Workers may speed

*Exhibit 2*

| Types of Capacity | | | |
|---|---|---|---|
| Volume | | Speed | |
| Beer-brewing kettle | 7,000 litres | Bottle capper | 40 bottles per minute |
| Classroom | 75 students | Airliner | 1,000 kilometres per hour |
| Car | 5 people (including driver) | Computer | 100,000 operations per second |
| Elevator | 900 kilograms | Hamburger grill | 12 patties every three minutes |
| | | Worker | 3 forms per hour |
| | | Baseball pitcher | 100 pitches per game |

up machines or change methods to get more than the theoretical capacity. Special equipment and tuning routinely give stock car racers speeds above the manufacturer's rating.

**Flexibility** refers to an operating system's ability to cope with changing circumstances with little penalty in cost, time, effort, or performance. Because flexibility is a multidimensional concept (the word refers simultaneously to many things), use it carefully. It might refer to product range, rates of output, speed of change, and the like. General purpose equipment or skilled workers are usually very flexible. A lathe, for example, can often turn wide ranges of items with different diameters and lengths, and composed of various materials. And a kitchen stove can cook almost anything. An oil refinery, however, is relatively inflexible — it is designed to handle only certain types of crude oil and put out a limited range of petroleum products. A bottling machine may be flexible in its ability to bottle almost any liquid, but inflexible because it can put it in only one size and shape of bottle. Although an automobile assembly plant might be able to produce cars with a wide range of colours and options, it can handle only a single body design and produce efficiently at only one car per minute without major line rebalancing. Labour contracts that spell out detailed job classifications often reduce flexibility by restricting the right to do certain types of work.

**Reliability** refers to the likelihood that a piece of equipment will perform as designed. Some equipment is extremely reliable; the two Voyager spacecraft launched in 1976 to explore the solar system proved to be spectacularly successful: they performed both at much higher levels and much longer than expected. Other equipment never seems to achieve its goals, possibly from a design flaw (as with the Hubble telescope or the early versions of Intel's Pentium computer chip) or from failures of equipment, people, or systems (exemplified by the Chernobyl nuclear reactor or the Cape Breton heavy water plant). High and/or increasing downtime or maintenance costs may indicate a decrease in reliability.

### People

People bring muscles, brains, and interpersonal skills to operations. The above discussion of capacity, flexibility, and reliability also applies to people. Most operations require labour to operate machines, move materials, or perform operating tasks. Computers often require operators; trucks require drivers; full-service restaurants require service staff. Although the use of human muscle is still common, it is increasingly being reduced as more and more tasks become automated or otherwise changed; in many respects people and machines are interchangeable. Factory work, typing, telephone systems, retail banking, sale of small goods, and the transfer of information have changed radically since you were born.

The brains component takes two forms: the worker's ability to evaluate a situation and detect trouble, and his or her ability to think. As muscle tasks become automated, watching tasks become more prevalent. Many workers now watch dials or television or computer monitors, make periodic quality checks, stop the process, and/or make minor adjustments to machines. The thinking component is needed in designing and programming the robot, and in managerial tasks such as planning, controlling, motivating, and making decisions. Even jobs requiring brain power are changing as more and more machines and even whole factories are now fully automated. The managerial job is changing too, as the jobs of workers change and as expert systems automate decision making.

In many services, operations workers interact directly with customers. In such a role, their interpersonal skills are an important determinant of the quality of service provided.

The people component brings the psychological concepts and theories of organizational behaviour face to face with the realities of assigning workers to tasks, assessing performance, and achieving reliability. Operations managers must consider two important aspects in assigning work. First, the managers must know what kinds of work and work sequences are needed to produce a satisfactory good or service. What is the best way to make a hamburger? How would an operations manager make sure that an employee made the hamburger correctly? Job design and methods analysis techniques are tools to ensure that the transformation process is both effective and efficient. At hamburger chains such as McDonald's these sorts of decisions have largely been taken away from the managers of day-to-day restaurant operations by using standard procedures as described in extensive operating manuals.

Second, operations managers need to know the skills and numbers of people required for the various jobs. Recruitment and hiring decisions, training, development programs, and scheduling techniques are useful in properly matching people and jobs. Once a job is staffed, operations managers must obtain the right quality and quantity of output. This part of the job includes assessing machine and labour productivity, and behaviour. Adequate measurement tools are needed, such as production rates, standards, quality levels, and customer satisfaction. Incentive schemes can be useful reinforcers when required performance levels are sought. The work force's reliability is a key to maintaining a smooth link between job assignments and performance. High turnover and absenteeism are signs of low reliability and, likely, low performance. However, lack of reliability can not always be blamed on workers. Management is responsible for designing jobs and for creating a productive work atmosphere that motivates people to do a good job. One recently discovered way to do this, particularly in the service sector, is to allow, indeed expect, front-line workers to make more of their own decisions.

### Energy

Energy is a component of almost any operation. Normally, we don't think very much about it — it is just there. In other cases, however, energy is a major operations factor. Traditionally, our economy developed around energy sources, as many watercourses were exploited to run mills and factories. The number of towns with "Mills" or "Falls" in their name attests to that. The Niagara Falls area, for example, is still a major industrial site. With transportation and electricity now widely available, this argument for site selection has largely disappeared, although in recent times Arvida, Quebec; Kitimat, B.C.; and Bluff, New Zealand, have risen to prominence because of their aluminium smelters. In addition to being relatively remote, these centres share three features: accessibility to large ocean-going vessels; isolation (thousands of kilometres) from the nearest bauxite (aluminium oxide) deposits; and proximity to large hydroelectric facilities. This last feature is no accident. Aluminium smelting requires huge amounts of electricity, and aluminium is thus one substance whose smelters are not located, as with most other kinds of smelting, near the ore body or the markets, but near another significant operations component, electrical energy.

### Inventory

Inventory is an input, a component, and a product of most operating systems. Inventory can be defined as anything purchased or acquired for transformation or resale, or that assists in the transformation of materials into saleable goods. Thus, we can talk about inventories of people, plants, equipment, capacity, or light bulbs. We will, however, restrict our discussion to inventories of items along the material flow shown in Figure 1.

There are three basic kinds of inventory: raw materials, work in process, and finished goods. Wendy's, for example, buys frozen hamburger meat and buns in batches — maybe several days' worth — which it stores as *raw materials inventory*. During a normal day the staff will frequently remove some of the materials from storage and do something to them. For example, they may put 12 hamburger patties on a grill where they cook for a set length of time. Then, the patties sit, waiting for orders from customers. While they are sitting, they are *work-

*in-process inventory* — partially completed units. When a customer orders a hamburger, it is assembled quickly from a number of work-in-process inventories and delivered to the customer. Because Wendy's makes hamburgers to customers' orders (one, two, or three patties, and many combinations of toppings), it does not hold a *finished goods inventory* of hamburgers (although its salad bar items are finished goods). In contrast, McDonald's, whose production process is devoted to making to stock, does carry a small finished hamburger inventory ready for sale when customers order.

Why do organizations have inventory at all? The basic answer is that it is cheaper to have it than not. Inventories both cost and save money — inventory management involves managing these costs. Some of the costs are described in Appendix A. The major benefits can be summed up as helping to smooth the flow of materials, and reduce the costs, in going from the supplier, through the production process and on to the customer.

As shown in Exhibit 3, inventory can serve many functions. A key concept is that just as an inventory item can be raw materials, work-in-process, or finished goods simultaneously (depending on your perspective), it can also serve more than one function at any given time. The key characteristic of *pipeline* or *transit inventory* is that it is moving. If the movement stops, for example, while a valve is changed or the truck driver has lunch, it is no longer purely pipeline inventory; it is still in the pipeline, but it now also has an additional purpose.

All sorts of external (that is, outside the established boundaries of the production system) things can happen to stop the flow of operations. For example, a shipment may be delayed for any number of reasons, customer demand is almost never completely predictable, or customers may demand products even when production is shut down. Inside the plant, a machine may break down or a worker may be absent, both of which disrupt operations. *Buffer inventories* can help operations continue despite these problems. *Decoupling inventories* are in place to separate steps that operate at different rates so that each can work smoothly at its own pace. Decoupling allows each step to be more efficient by keeping them running; neither is affected immediately by a disruption in the other. Continuously moving assembly lines are examples of operations that force each operation to operate at the same rate, or more correctly, to perform each step in the same, usually short, time period paced by the slowest step.

The agricultural and fishing communities are well aware of the build-up of *seasonal inventory* because of well-defined seasons for planting, fertilizing, harvesting, and the like. A special form of seasonal inventory, closely related to buffer stocks, arises from the expectation that something might happen. The key difference between anticipatory and seasonal inventories is that, with the former, events are much less predictable. You might buy beer or sell bonds at a certain time in expectation of price changes. A production manager might anticipate trouble with a certain machine or plan preventive maintenance and build inventory accordingly.

*EXHIBIT 3*

| Functions of Inventory | | | |
|---|---|---|---|
| Function | Rationale | Key Feature | Examples |
| Pipeline or transit | Materials must be transported between two points | It is moving | Oil in a pipeline<br>Ore on ship between mine and smelter<br>Parts moving between two work centres on forklift truck or moving belt |
| Buffer or safety stock | Buffer operation from external uncertainty | External disruption likely | Piles of ore, coal, and limestone at steel mill<br>Finished hamburgers and fries at McDonald's<br>Material between adjacent machines |
| Decoupling | Isolate steps that operate at different rates or patterns | Operations work at different speeds | Chassis between body welding shop (75 cars per hour) and final assembly (60 cars per hour)<br>McDonald's hamburgers between cooking (batches of 12) and customer arrival (reasonably steady stream at much shorter intervals) |
| Seasonal | Production or use has well-defined season or anticipated event | Business activity has definite, predictable peaks and valleys | Harvested apples for sale during winter<br>Salads prepared for lunch peak<br>Texts in book store awaiting start of classes |
| Cycle | Allow operations or transport to function in economical lots | Something is produced, used, or shipped in a "batch" | Truckload of goods for sale<br>Boat load of iron ore for smelting<br>Bins of parts being welded |

The last reason for having inventory is to allow operations to function in economical lots. Whenever a manager decides to buy or make something, he or she will incur an ordering or set-up cost. To avoid these costs, the manager might batch the orders or jobs, creating *cycle inventory*. Appendix A gives some information on how to manage the trade off between the costs of ordering and the costs of holding cycle stock.

Despite the usefulness of inventory, a relatively recent approach to production management called just-in-time (JIT), originating in Japan and discussed in more detail later in this chapter, argues that inventories are not beneficial. The essential argument is that the costs of having inventory are much higher than the costs of not having it. Inventory mostly just sits around costing a lot of money and adding no value of any kind. Do the Japanese live under a completely different set of economic rules? No, but they have found ways to eliminate the reasons for having inventory.

How can these reasons be eliminated? Exhibit 4 gives some examples. Many assembly plants have clusters of supplier plants very close by. Moreover, the whole complex may be near a steel mill and necessary services. This proximity reduces pipeline or transit inventory. Many of an organization's outside uncertainties are related to its supply chains. Parts that are of poor quality will stop

*Exhibit 4*

| Some Ways to Eliminate Inventory | |
| --- | --- |
| Function | Techniques to Reduce Level |
| Pipeline or transit | Locate operations as close to each other as possible<br>Move items between operation steps as fast as possible |
| Buffer or safety stock | Reduce pipeline inventories (and thus pipeline uncertainty)<br>Establish close long-term working relationships with suppliers<br>Ensure high quality material |
| Decoupling | Careful machine design and worker training<br>Accept idle time or use it creatively (possibly for cleaning or job analysis) |
| Seasonal | Work to develop sources of supply and demand that, collectively, extend seasons<br>Develop processing capacity to meet peaks |
| Cycle | Work hard to reduce set-up times |

production, unless sufficient inventory buffers production from the source of bad parts. Reducing these uncertainties helps to reduce buffer stock.

## OPERATIONS TASKS — THE INTEGRATING FUNCTION[1]

The operations tasks are what an organization must do to ensure that its products and/or services are produced to satisfy the customer and allow it to realize its overall objectives. These tasks are much easier to describe than to perform. By now, you should understand that the main operations tasks are transforming inputs into the desired outputs, using the necessary (and available) resources (see Figure 1). In general terms, the goals of the operations tasks are to provide the right product or service, in the right quantity, at the right price, in the right place, at the right time, every time, with an acceptable level of side effects. To understand these activities properly, it is necessary to consider the operating manager's environment. Although the main job of operations managers is transforming inputs, operations is very much an integrating function because operations managers must also interact with managers in other functions.

Although one goal of production is to satisfy customers, marketing is the liaison between production and the firm's external customers. Marketing should help to translate customer needs and wishes into product specifications, forecasts of sales volumes, delivery schedules, and the like. Marketing should also be both aware of, and geared up to sell, what the operations function can produce. Note that in services, the operations and marketing functions tend to merge as customers come into direct contact with production.

A second operations task is managing people. The human resources department is the liaison between operations and its sources of employees. It helps to locate, hire, train, evaluate, and, if necessary, discipline staff; establish personnel policies; keep records; and so on.

Finance connects operations to the firm's treasury. Finance and accounting, often separate departments, should establish financial policies, help operations make investment decisions, measure the costs incurred in operations, and be prepared to provide the funds necessary to support effective production systems. The two departments (particularly accounting) maintain many of the records necessary to perform and measure operations, and are also responsible for sending invoices, and collecting and making payments.

These different departments are all interdependent; not only can operations not function without any of them, but they cannot survive without operations. But, each of the various departments has its own agenda, priorities, and ways of doing things. The operations manager must deal with the inherent conflicts to which these distinctions will give rise in his or her internal environment. In addition, he or she must keep up with changes in the outside world — developments in equipment and ways of making things (technology), new materials, cost changes, and competitive developments, such as changes in capacity by suppliers or competitors.

One way to help to define the operations tasks is to consider operations from a customer's perspective — after all, customers really determine what products and/or services we should provide. Five important customer needs that have significant implications for operations are outlined in Exhibit 5.

**EXHIBIT 5**

| Customer Needs with Some Implications for Operations | |
|---|---|
| Need | Implications |
| Function | Will the product do what the customer needs and wants it to do? |
| Quality | Will the product perform reliably? |
| Quantity | How much product should we make and when? |
| Price | How much will we sell the product for? |
| Service | What services will we provide to accompany the product? |

## FUNCTION

You expect a computer to have certain characteristics, the exact nature of which depends on you. It might be operating speed, working memory, hard drive size, or adaptability. Function depends on design. A computer's failure to run Windows software might be the result of its design. Slide rule manufacturers have disappeared, not because they produced poor-quality slide rules, but because calculators and computers made slide rules unnecessary. The Ford Edsel, home milk delivery, and coal sales for home furnaces failed for similar reasons: customers demanded different product and service designs to perform the different functions required by a changing world.

## QUALITY

When you buy a computer, you want the quality to be high. You do not expect that it will fall apart after a year's use (unless, of course, you have some special, hard use in mind). Quality must be such that the product's functions will perform reliably. Manufacturing affects quality. For example, no matter how good the design, putting a faulty disk drive in a computer will result in a poor-quality finished product.

## QUANTITY

Quantity is an easily understood need. Customers want enough to satisfy their needs. If a rich man wanted to buy compact disc players for each of his five daughters-in-law for Christmas, he would not be satisfied if he could buy only two. Similarly, a university must ensure that it offers enough course sections of sufficient size to enable all its students to take a full load; a city must ensure that it has enough police, fire-fighting, hospital, and library services; and a railroad must see that it has enough space to carry all passengers or freight. Insufficiency in these services can lead to a loss of business to alternative services, or, in the case of public services, to tax revolts or replacement of elected officials. On the other hand, overproducing goods and services results in higher than necessary costs. For operations, quantity demands require attention to customer needs and the timing of those needs.

## PRICE

Price also appears to be a fairly simple idea. Most customers have limited income and are able or willing to spend only a limited amount on any specific product or service. Potential customers who perceive the price to be too high will not buy or will switch to an alternative. However, it is clear that price, particularly that of a single purchase, is not the sole purchase criterion. If it were, courier services, for example, would not exist. Value is a notion that comes closer to the mark. Consumers and organizations often buy more expensive items because they are perceived to be more valuable, providing more function, quality, or quantity per dollar. They might arrive more quickly (courier services), they might last longer (light bulbs), they might be more reliable (solid state electronics), or they may bestow more snob appeal on the buyer (luxury cars).

Although most people usually regard price and value as marketing concerns, these factors have a major effect on operations. Products or services that compete on the basis of low price must be produced at low cost or the organization will not make money. Similarly, those competing at high prices must have high quality or high functional utility to attract customers. Few organizations can manage to produce low cost products or services with a full range of features and high quality.

## SERVICE

Service has many dimensions. One might be a guarantee. Many products, and an increasing number of services, are guaranteed in one form or another. The guarantee is an assurance that if the customer is not satisfied, he or she can expect some recompense — replacement or adjustment of poor-quality parts or workmanship, or perhaps a refund. Service might also include advice on how to operate or maintain a product, financing arrangements, checkups, availability of parts, and provision of qualified labour, and assurance that the manufacturer or service firm will survive the lifetime of the product or service. Once a manufacturer announces that it intends to stop making a product line, purchasers may not be keen to buy one. And who wants to deposit or invest their money in a weak financial institution, obtain a degree from a university that may close, buy a computer with a chip that may give arithmetical errors, even rarely, or buy a ticket from a tour company that faces bankruptcy?

Delivery is yet another facet of service. Delivery has several meanings. Some organizations, such as appliance and furniture stores in the retail sector, deliver purchased goods to customers and use this fact competitively. Insurance salespeople make home visits. Some fitness clubs will send staff members to your home if you wish. However, the once-routine services of doctors who make house calls and grocery stores that deliver now make headlines.

Time is another dimension of delivery. We expect fast response from fire, ambulance, and emergency departments to save lives. We expect newspapers to include the latest news in their current editions. Every manufacturer gets the occasional call from a customer looking for a product in a hurry. Producing on time may be even more important than producing quickly. How useful are snowmobiles delivered to Canadian retailers in April, Christmas cards in February, completed income tax forms after the deadline, or lunch salads at 2:00 p.m.? Many people criticize VIA Rail and Canada Post more because they perceive that they cannot rely on these services' advertised delivery times than for genuine slowness.

Competing on service requires that operations have a delivery system in place that has a lot of flexibility; often excess capacity; equipment, people, and suppliers that are fully competent, reliable, and at least somewhat interchangeable; and intelligent scheduling.

## ACHIEVING THE DESIRED OUTCOMES

Why are we focusing all this attention on customers in a chapter on operations? The answer is in two parts: operations is responsible for supplying goods and services to satisfy specific customer needs, and the viability of the whole enterprise depends on how well this is done. Although well-managed operations can never guarantee corporate success — all functions must be in good shape and well coordinated throughout the company and with the external environment to ensure that — it is fair to say that it is extremely difficult to have good corporate performance if operations is poorly managed. Because operations often accounts for 50 to 70 percent of total costs and employs most of an enterprise's work force, it warrants close attention. Customer needs must be used to set objectives, and operations should be organized to meet them. In most well-run firms, these objectives are set jointly by operations, marketing, and finance.

Function and quality come from the new product development group. The design must be both functional — that is, it must do what the customer wants it to do — and manufacturable. Operations should be involved throughout the product development process. There are many examples of product designs handed to operations ("thrown over the wall"), as though their manufacture were a *fait accompli*, that have turned out to be either impossible or too expensive to make. The result is usually unplanned design compromises or extremely high costs. Early integration can prevent such undesirable outcomes. Throughout the production process, targets should be set and measurements taken to ensure that the product design's quality needs are met.

Sometimes marketing alone translates customer needs into required product quantities; in more progressive companies, operations and other functions will also be involved. The problem is to match the quantity produced with customer demand in any given time period. Both producing too much and producing too little may result in losses.

Firms translate the customer price requirement into a target manufacturing cost, upon which company profits hinge. Thus, operations can be highly cost-oriented and many enterprises establish elaborate systems to measure and control costs to ensure profitable operation.

Organizations transpose customer needs for delivery into operational time targets. They schedule and continually monitor where everything is in the whole operation so that each product will be completed by a certain time. They require information: What is ahead of schedule? Can it be delayed? What is late? Why? What can be done to expedite the items that are behind?

Organizations translate the need for other services much as they do the price need. Because many service aspects have implications for function, quality, quantity, and price, they can be considered as part of these objectives. However, it is not good enough simply to meet only some of these targets, even perfectly. Because the process must be repeatable and improvable, managers must manage operations to ensure that it is in harmony with overall company policies and objectives for continuity of the enterprise. They must also plan both for the short and the long-term. It is not good enough simply to do well today — tomorrow and next year count at least as much. On the other hand, the short-term cannot be ignored. A brilliant long-range plan is useless if the organization does not survive that long.

### EFFECTIVENESS AND EFFICIENCY

The role of the operations manager is to accomplish these tasks as effectively and as efficiently as possible. Exhibit 6 describes and gives some examples of these two concepts. *Effectiveness* is related to quality. Operations is effective if it makes the product as designed, on time. Although a prescribed design is important, many service organizations are demonstrating their effectiveness in satisfying customers by expecting employees to go to whatever lengths are necessary to solve customer problems.

*EXHIBIT 6*

| Effectiveness and Efficiency | |
| --- | --- |
| **Effectiveness** | Doing the right thing: the extent to which an objective is realized |
| ▪ Railroad | Delivering all goods to a destination, within a designated amount of time, without damage, while remaining flexible to changes in future demand |
| ▪ Restaurant | Stocking sufficient goods to meet the published menu, taking customer orders accurately and promptly, preparing the meal as described or asked for by the customer, delivering it within a reasonable period of time, and performing all the necessary service functions politely so that the customer feels welcome and comfortable |
| ▪ Automobile assembly plant | Producing cars to design specifications (high quality) in a reasonable time after the order is placed |
| ▪ Retail store | Clerk who, on his or her own initiative, hires a cab to deliver a forgotten parcel to a customer's home |
| **Efficiency** | Doing things right: producing effectively while minimizing waste (cost, effort, time, etc.) |

*Efficiency* is related to productivity. Operations is efficient if it produces with a minimum of cost, effort, and waste. Effectiveness and efficiency often seem to conflict — you can have one, but only at the expense of the other. In other words, it is possible for an operation to be efficient, but not effective; or, it can be effective, but not efficient. Another possibility is that it might be neither effective nor efficient. Universities that encourage undergraduate classes of 250 students are focusing on efficiency — some academics and students would argue that it comes at the expense of effectiveness. The same institution might well have graduate classes of only five students — in this case the class might be very effective, but cost as much as (or even more than) the 250-student class down the hall.

The ideal, of course, is to be both effective and efficient. Although this goal is not always possible, every organization should strive for it. The relative importance of efficiency and effectiveness depends on the organization's major objectives and required tasks. Effectiveness is usually considered to be much more important than efficiency in courier services; consequently, courier services are relatively expensive. The post office puts more emphasis on efficiency; costs are much lower, but the effectiveness (here measured by delivery speed and variability) suffers. In some cases, efficiency can develop into effectiveness. Many banks originally bought automated banking machines (ABMs) to reduce costs — an efficiency rationale. Recently, however, institutions are adding services to their ABMs to give customers more choice in services — making them more effective.

■
**SECTION**
■
**THREE**
■

## TYPES OF OPERATING PROCESSES AND MANAGERIAL IMPLICATIONS

So far we have talked about operating processes as if they were all the same. Clearly, this is absurd. You have undoubtedly seen or can imagine several different kinds of production processes. But what is the best way to transform inputs into outputs to meet the demands on operations? What is needed to compete? Why would a customer want to buy our product or service rather than one from one of our competitors? How should we classify production processes?

The following sections describe three types of production process along a continuous spectrum as shown in Exhibit 7. In reality, it is difficult to classify a particular production system as clearly one type or another because the differences are not always obvious and some organizations are hybrids because of mixing. Mixing is natural because production facilities may change process type over time. Despite classification problems, however, focusing on these three types is useful because they:

1. stress the need to select a process according to the production tasks to be performed, and

2. represent very different kinds of production processes, each with its own critical characteristics that must be carefully managed.

*EXHIBIT 7*

| Operations Process Types | | | | |
|---|---|---|---|---|
| Project | Job Shop | Batch Flow | Line-Flow | Continuous-Flow |
| Large construction projects | Small metal-working shops | Clothing manufacture | Bottle-filling operations | Oil refineries |
| Repair of large machinery | Management consultancies | Beer brewing | Bottle-making plants | Chemical plants |
| Staging a rock concert | Automobile body shops | University classes | Letter-sorting plants | Pulp mills |
| Organizing a wedding | | | Automobile assembly lines | telecommunications (dedicated lines) |
| | | | | Stock quote systems |

## CONTINUOUS-FLOW AND LINE-FLOW PROCESSES

In a *continuous-flow process*, inputs are transformed into outputs continuously. As Exhibit 7 shows, they are closely akin to *line-flow processes*. The differences between the two are matters of degree; one distinction is that line-flow processes tend to produce discrete units (that is, they can be counted one by one, such as cars or bottles), whereas continuous-flow processes produce products counted in units of measurement (litres of benzene, tonnes of steel). Exhibit 8 shows some important traits of such processes.

**EXHIBIT 8**

| Process Characteristics[1] | | | |
|---|---|---|---|
| | Project | Job Shop and Batch | Line- and Continuous-Flow |
| **Product Characteristics** | | | |
| ▪ mix | special, small range of standards | special to many | standard |
| ▪ designed by | customer | customer and company | company |
| ▪ range | wide | wide | narrow to very narrow |
| ▪ order size | small | small | large to very large |
| ▪ company sells | capability | capability | products |
| ▪ order-winning criteria | delivery, quality, design capability | delivery, quality, design capability | price |
| ▪ qualifying criteria | price | price | quality, design |
| **Process Characteristics** | | | |
| ▪ technology | general purpose | universal to specialized | dedicated |
| ▪ flow pattern | no pattern, often no flow (movement) | jumbled to dominant | rigid |
| ▪ linking process steps | loose | loose to tight | tight to very tight |
| ▪ inventory | mostly work-in-process | raw materials, work-in-process, and finished goods | mostly raw materials and finished goods |
| ▪ notion of capacity | very vague | vague, measured in dollars | clear, measured in physical units |
| ▪ flexibility | high | high | low to inflexible |
| ▪ volumes | very low | low | high to very high |
| ▪ key operations tasks | meet specifications and delivery dates, scheduling, materials management | meet specifications, quality, flexibility in output volume | low cost production, price |

1. Adapted from R.W. Schmenner, *Production/Operations Management: Concepts and Situations*, 4th ed. (New York: Macmillan Publishing Company, 1990), Chapter 1; and T.J. Hill, "Processes: Their Origins and Implications," *Operations Management Review, 8 (2)* (1991), 1–7.

Because all materials in production go through the same steps in the same order, a critical element to be managed is the smoothness of flow in and between the steps. A "break" in production at any place along the line effectively shuts down the whole line. Examples are everywhere: you are in a cafeteria line and someone ahead of you wants to wait for a special serving; you are on a crowded highway when two cars ahead of you collide; a work station on an automobile assembly line runs out of parts; a machine breaks down; a worker has to go to the washroom; one work centre (worker or machine) is slower than the rest. Although the possibilities are endless, the result is the same: operations stop, or at least slow down, in some cases, for a long time.

To keep things moving, managers have to try to foresee some of these problems and take appropriate preventive measures. Rules forbidding special servings, great inventory management procedures, off-line places to put problems, and back-up people and equipment are some possibilities. A major concern in designing continuous-flow or line-flow operations is to make sure that each step takes the same amount of time. This process is called *line balancing* and is designed to control the number and location of *bottlenecks* that occur whenever one step in a connected sequence is slower than the others. Figure 2 provides an example.

For dishwashing on a camping trip, the times in Scenario A may not be a great concern. However, if you were paying the workers, you would pay for idle time. Although the amount might still be trivial in a dishwashing operation, in an assembly operation with 1,000 one-person work stations working 16 hours per day, 5 days per week, 52 weeks per year, and paying each worker $15 per hour, 33 percent idle time would cost $20.8 million per year.

One approach to dealing with this problem is to balance the line, that is, to reduce the idle time to zero. No continuous- or line-flow operation can ever be completely balanced, of course, but it is worth getting the idle time as low as possible. In the dishwashing example, adding a second dryer (Scenario B) would help. Although it would shift the bottleneck to washing, it would reduce drying time to 7.5 seconds per cycle and reduce idle time. Redesigning the drying job might help too. Perhaps the dryer has a poor technique or an awkward layout in which to work. Maybe the washer could also stack, giving a completely balanced two-worker line. A basic technique called *process analysis* is very useful in determining the degree of balance in a process and in planning improvements. We will discuss process analysis and another useful technique, *trade-off analysis*, in Section Four. First, however, we will discuss some additional process types.

## JOB SHOP AND BATCH PROCESSES

In a *job shop* work moves intermittently in batches. *Batch* processes are closely related to job shops. Exhibit 7 gives some examples of both types. Although at

***FIGURE 2***

---

### An Example of an Unbalanced Line

---

Suppose you and some friends are on a camping trip and are washing dishes. The table below shows two scenarios: A, in which one person washes, one dries, and one puts the dry dishes away; and B, in which one person washes, two dry, and one puts the dry dishes away. The process is fairly simple:

| Scenario A: | Scenario B: |
|---|---|
| One washer, one dryer, and one stacker | One washer, two dryers, and one stacker |
| Average production rates (seconds per dish): | Average production rates (seconds per dish): |

| Scenario A | | Scenario B | |
|---|---|---|---|
| Washing | 10 | Washing | 10 |
| Drying | 15 | Drying | 7.5 (15 seconds for each dryer) |
| Stacking | 3 | Stacking | 5 |

| Scenario A | Scenario B |
|---|---|
| Inventory capacity: | Inventory capacity: |
| One or two dishes between each pair of steps | One or two dishes between each pair of steps |
| Pace of the system: | Pace of the system: |
| 4 dishes per minute (drying is the slowest operation in the sequence). With a slow dryer and limited space, the stacker will run out of work and the washer will run out of space to put washed dishes. Consequently, both will be idle for part of the time. | 6 dishes per minute (washing is now the slowest step) |

Time usage (assuming continuous 15-second cycles)

| | Work | Idle | Total |
|---|---|---|---|
| Washer | 40 | 20 | 60 |
| Dryer | 60 | 0 | 60 |
| Stacker | 20 | 40 | 60 |
| Total | 120 | 60 | 180 |

Idle time:   60/180 = 33%

Time usage (assuming continuous 10-second cycles)

| | Work | Idle | Total |
|---|---|---|---|
| Washer | 60 | 0 | 60 |
| Dryer | 90 | 30 | 120 |
| Stacker | 30 | 30 | 60 |
| Total | 180 | 60 | 240 |

Idle time:   60/240 = 25%

---

McDonald's the overall operation is line-flow, the chain *cooks* its hamburgers in batches. Traffic along a freeway moves continuously (at least until volume or an accident interrupts it); traffic lights convert the process into batch flow. McDonald's is an example of mixed processes; traffic flow is an example of a change in process.

Although job shops and batching operations are similar, they are not identical. A key characteristic is their response to customer specifications. A job shop typically performs *custom work in response to a customer order*. Automobile repair shops, for example, work only when they perform the tasks requested by the customer, and can identify the car with the customer at every stage. Individual orders may not be all that complex; the process of tuning an engine does not have to be rethought for every car brought in. A batching operation more likely makes a *standard product line in response to inventory levels*. A restaurant, for example, may have 10 standard dinners and several *à la carte* items. Some items will be prepared to customer order. However, if Irish stew is on special, the chef will likely prepare a batch in advance, based on a demand forecast. The product becomes identified with an individual customer only when it is actually served.

A major feature that distinguishes job shop and batching operations from continuous-flow and line-flow operations is the rigidity of the flow of materials through the transformation process. Line-flow and continuous-flow operations usually have very rigid flow — every unit goes through the same steps, in the same order, and probably at the same rate. In contrast, job shops, in particular, and, to a lesser extent batch operations, exhibit what is called jumbled flow. In these shops, although one flow pattern may dominate, probably no two jobs take exactly the same pathway through the process nor produce the same product. A full-service automobile repair shop may have separate areas for welding, tuning up, and wheel alignment, for example. Some cars may be welded first, then tuned up, then aligned and, finally, given a road test. Others may by-pass welding and wheel alignment. Others may be aligned before being tuned up. Routing depends on scheduling needs or technical requirements — painting is always one of the last operations in a body shop.

Nor is the resource use at each step identical from job to job. Some jobs needing a welding step may require 30 minutes per unit; others using the same welding equipment and staff may need only 30 seconds per unit. The wide range of potential products, customers, volumes, and tasks means that purchasing, inventory planning, workforce planning, and scheduling often cannot be established in isolation from specific customer orders or inventory positions. For many, the trigger that makes things happen is the receipt of a customer order or finished goods inventory dropping to a set level. Only then do all these activities begin to interact. And, without the trigger, nothing happens.

Given the customer's function, quality, quantity, price, and service objectives, the main operations tasks will be to optimize the trade-off between meeting customer needs and maintaining a low-cost operation through high utilization of facilities and low inventories, particularly work-in-process. The operations manager's job, particularly in job shops rather than batching operations, is to juggle conflicting objectives. To get speedy completion, it seems best to process each order through each work centre as soon as it appears. Unfortunately, this policy demands extensive facilities to handle periods of peak demand. These facilities would then be idle during periods of low demand, thus increasing costs. However, if facilities are designed for average demand, peak periods result in backlogs of jobs at various work stations. Batching operations are less exposed to this problem because they schedule production around a finished goods inventory. Furthermore, of course, rapid delivery for one customer may well delay delivery for another.

The jobs must also be scheduled. Because different jobs require different operations, different sequences of operations, and different times for each operation, the scheduling task is very complex. The decision should consider all jobs in the shop, their process requirements, and the current backlog at each work station. Consideration might also be given to orders expected, but not yet received. There are some useful and common, but by no means perfect, scheduling rules. First come first served is a very common one. It is found in all sorts of services — banks, fast food restaurants, retail outlets. Another method gives priority to jobs expected to have the shortest processing time. Express lanes are a common example. Yet another might try to treat urgent cases first. Common examples are hospital emergency departments, and passengers trying to catch a plane about to depart. Still other methods may reward persistent customers. If you want fast service from an automobile repair shop, try sitting and waiting, with your entire family if possible. Some organizations give precedence to large jobs on the grounds that they and the customers are more important financially. Many organizations use judicious combinations of these and other rules.

Quite another problem also arises. One characteristic of a job shop is that it uses general purpose equipment rather than specialized facilities. A single drill press may be used to drill holes of all diameters and depths. Many work centres have to be adjusted differently for each job. This set-up time is unproductive and, in some cases, the cost may be high, with set-up taking several hours or even days. Set-up workers must be paid and, particularly if used at or near capacity, set-up takes a machine out of production with a corresponding opportunity cost. Appendix A shows one way to balance high set-up costs against inventory holding costs. Costs can be reduced by better utilization of facilities if jobs are batched into groups with similar characteristics. A printing press, for example, must be adjusted for different paper sizes and thicknesses, and ink colours. It would make sense to do all printing jobs of the same type in sequence and thus eliminate as many change-overs as possible. Naturally, though, this method will delay delivery time to some customers and complicate scheduling. Another way to reduce set-up time is to use a rational sequence. Thus, ice cream manufacturers always try to move from lighter colours to darker ones because they don't have to clean as carefully as they would going the other way.

The cost of maximizing facilities usage is not just that of customer inconvenience caused by delays. The longer a given part stays in the facility, the larger the work-in-process inventory. In one company that uses batch production to make plumbing products, although the cumulative production time spent making a single part is only one or two hours, parts take eight weeks on average (320 working hours, 1,344 real hours) to go from raw materials to finished goods. Needless to say, the work-in-process inventory is large and costly. For the company producing industrial boilers, it is obvious that the longer the time between the purchase of the steel and the sale of the finished boiler, the greater the financial cost to the company. Similarly, in an automobile repair shop, the longer it takes to complete a task, the greater the garage owner's investment — bills for replacement parts and mechanics' wages must be paid promptly regardless of when the customer pays his or her bill. For job shops with raw materials and finished goods inventories, poor forecasting of demand and materials needs will also increase costs unnecessarily.

Although individual decisions on the optimum batch size, work centre schedule, or size or mix of inventory are difficult and frequent tasks for the job shop manager, they are not the most important ones. Management must watch for changes over time in customer demand regarding the five basic needs (function, quality, quantity, price, and service). As the priority of these demands changes, the manager must be prepared to respond by changing the existing process. This decision is difficult because the changes are subtle and gradual. An automobile repair shop doing a variety of repairs might become known for reliable, fast muffler replacement. The manager might notice that the services most in demand have changed. The shop now has a high portion of muffler jobs and requests for this service are steady. The quantity of these jobs has increased; the expected delivery time is probably shorter than for most jobs; and inefficiencies of scheduling these jobs around larger jobs might well be increasing overall cost. Adjusting the operation from a job shop to one in which at least its muffler jobs are done with line-flow may well be important to future profitability.

## PROJECT PROCESSES

In some cases the market for a product may be very small, possibly only once for a single customer, or the product may be very complex and/or unique. In these situations, a somewhat different approach to production, a *project process*, will be most efficient and effective. Economies of scale and specialization do not apply. The organization is typically "product-dedicated," with the job characteristically being stationary and resources brought to it. Exhibit 7 gives some examples.

In some ways projects resemble job shops in that both handle special custom orders. Projects obtain their unique character from size and complexity. The key cost components are investments in materials and human resources. Thus, early completion is of as much interest to the producer as it is to the customer. The critical task is usually scheduling the various components of the project so that they are finished just as they are needed. The goal is usually to minimize cost by minimizing overall completion time and the investment in the components of the project. A number of methods that identify the project's *critical path* have been developed to help project managers in these tasks. Many commercial computer programs will perform the necessary calculations.

## CHOOSING A PROCESS

The sections that follow relate the type of process to certain product characteristics. Although there are exceptions, observers have noted a strong correlation between process and product. The product characteristics are typical of the product life cycle, which relates changes in product volume and other traits over time. Most products start life as prototypes. They are produced in low volumes, often with radical product changes between one unit and the next, and sold at a premium price. Customers are paying for design features, speed of delivery, and, in many cases, for the producer's ability to customize the design to meet customer needs.

After a product moves through the rapid growth phase to maturity, volume is usually high, the product design has stabilized, and the price has leveled off. The products now compete on such features as price, reliability, quality, and product features. In extreme cases, the product becomes a commodity. These two scenarios, infancy and maturity, are quite different. Consequently, they demand a different approach to operations. Note that although changes in product characteristics should be matched by changes in the process, most organizations cannot afford to change processes frequently; consequently, they may choose to tolerate processes that are not ideal and live with the resulting inefficiencies.

The answer to the question, "What is the best way to make clothes?" can really be answered only by more questions. What type of clothes? Who will buy them? How will they compete? What volume is expected? What features will they have? What quality is needed? After answering these questions (determining what features the product needs), managers are in a position to pick the process. For products early in their life cycles, job shops are typical. Flexibility, design, and quality are important characteristics to the customer, and job shops are ideally set up to provide them. As a product becomes more stable and volume increases, the job shop may well give way to a batching operation, which is less flexible, more price competitive, and more able to produce in volume. At maturity and high volumes, a line-flow or continuous-flow process is most appropriate. In the clothing industry, a large producer of off-the-rack ladies' wear would probably use some form of line-flow process requiring specialized machinery and relatively unskilled labour, possibly from a Third World country. In contrast, a producer of custom clothing, for whom design and quality are paramount and volumes are low, would use a quite different operation. In this case, mechanization would be low, those hired would have to be skilled, and typically, it would be located near the customer. Intermediate product characteristics would demand batching — an intermediate process.

Figure 3 shows the relationship between product and process characteristics. According to this model, successful organizations are found in or near the diagonal band; those found significantly above or below it are uncompetitive. Think about how you would make a line of family cars versus a high-performance race car, or how you would set up a cafeteria as opposed to a *haute cuisine* restaurant.

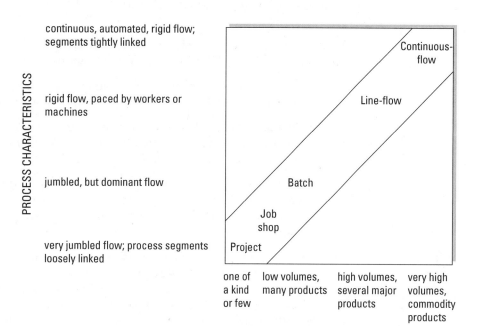

**FIGURE 3**
*The Product-Process Matrix*[1]

1. Adapted from R.H. Hayes and S.C. Wheelwright, "Link Manufacturing Process and Product Life Cycles," *Harvard Business Review, 57*(1) (1979): 133–40.

## OTHER CONSIDERATIONS

To manage an operations system we need to do more than simply choose a suitable process type and change it as the product traits change. The following list gives examples of the sorts of decisions operating managers must make on a day-to-day basis as well as during design and start-up. This chapter's cases and problems will give you more practice in applying the principles of operations and other functions to some of them.

1. *Purchasing.* Do we place a few large orders infrequently or do we order small quantities frequently? (What are your ordering policies for groceries? Why?)

Who should we order from? What relationship should we have with suppliers — arm's length and adversarial, or close and cooperative?

2. *Maintenance.* Should we wait until something needs repair or practise preventive maintenance? (When do you change light bulbs in your home? Should hospital managers use the same rule for their operating theatres?)

3. *Scheduling.* Which jobs get priority — first in, shortest, emergency? How would we schedule an automobile service facility? How far ahead should we plan (planning horizon)?

4. *Subcontracting.* How much should we do ourselves and how much should we pay someone else to do? What should we keep in-house?

5. *Location.* Do we locate near the source of supply, near markets, or somewhere else? (Why are both Dofasco and Stelco in Hamilton, Ontario?)

6. *Layout.* Should our plant be laid out by machine groups, by production steps, for customer convenience, or some other goal? (How would you lay out the equipment in the kitchen of a fast food restaurant?)

7. *Equipment.* Should we rent or buy? Should it be specialized or general purpose? Should it be standard or technologically innovative? (What equipment decisions would you make if you were starting a new gardening and landscaping service?)

8. *Job Design.* Will our workers have very specialized jobs or general ones? Will workers be able to rotate between jobs? (If you were setting up an automobile factory, would you set it up as an assembly line with each worker performing a small task repeatedly, or would you use teams of workers making major portions of the cars together, rather than on an assembly line?)

9. *Research & Development.* Will we do our own or buy someone else's? (Why does Northern Telecom spend so much on R&D?)

Each of these decisions (and many, many more) must consider the production tasks and the firm's internal and external environments. Many choices will be constrained by available company resources; others will be restricted by the type of output desired. Some represent long-term commitments (such as location), others are medium-term (such as equipment investment), and yet others are short-term (such as purchasing policies). Particularly when making major decisions, we must bear in mind both the current circumstances and our anticipation of future developments. Changing major decisions is always expensive and disruptive, sometimes to the point where it cannot be done without threatening the firm's future. Plant location and primary machinery layout decisions are examples of this. One of a university's most important decisions is classroom design. People come and go, but once the bricks and mortar are in place, they tend not to be changed. A classroom designed for lectures to 250 students is unsuitable for case teaching to classes of 70.

## PROCESS AND TRADE-OFF ANALYSES: TWO BASIC ANALYTICAL TOOLS

### *PROCESS ANALYSIS*

A key objective in managing operations processes is ensuring that the units of production proceed through the process as scheduled. In continuous- or line-flow processes, production is usually either on or off, and when it is on, each unit moves along at essentially the same even or level rate. In job shops or batch operations, this is usually not the case. Flow is intermittent, and the rate of any one step can change frequently, leading to bottlenecks. To determine the location of bottlenecks and the degree of process balance, we must perform the key operations tool of process analysis. Typically, it proceeds as follows:

1. Decide what the boundaries of your analysis are. For the questions you want to answer it may be the whole plant, a particular department, a specific machine, or a small sequence on that machine — making one of the many different parts, for example.

2. Make a list of all the steps from the start to the finish of the process in the sequence in which they occur. Include relevant movement, storage, inspection, and transformation steps.

3. Draw a process-flow diagram showing how inputs flow through the sequence of steps. It helps to use a standard notation, such as the one presented in Figure 4.

4. Decide what units of measure you will use for rates, capacities, and inventory levels. Examples are tonnes per hour, boxes per shift, cases, and barrels.

5. Determine the theoretical capacities of each step and the required output of the system. Required output is often based on customer demand, either forecasted or known.

6. Factor in known inefficiencies. Some processes work at 100 percent for a while and then stop completely — possibly for set-ups, preventive maintenance, or cleaning. Others work all the time, but at only a fraction of theoretical capacity.

7. Locate the bottleneck in the process (the step with the slowest operating rate) and the locations of excess capacity and inventory.

8. Determine the effects of production stopping at one of the steps in the production process. How long will it be before adjacent steps (in each direction) are affected? This is usually a function of inventory levels in specific points in the process.

9. What you do next depends on what types of questions you want to address. If you have a line-balancing problem, try to even out the outputs of each step. If you have an overall output problem, determine where to add resources. If the output problem is timing, find out where attention should be directed to smooth out the flow.

**FIGURE 4**
*Process Analysis
Notation*

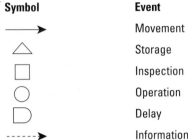

| Symbol | Event |
|---|---|
| → | Movement |
| △ | Storage |
| □ | Inspection |
| ○ | Operation |
| D | Delay |
| ----→ | Information |

As an example, consider dishwashing in the patient dietary services department of a large hospital. (Note that the description that follows is somewhat simplified.) The hospital has 361 beds with an average utilization of 97 percent. Each patient receives three meals per day and uses an average of six dishes per meal, plus associated cutlery. The hospital has enough dishes to satisfy demand for one day. The dishwashing operation employs seven staff members, each of whom works eight hours per day, including 30 minutes for lunch and two 15-minute breaks. The dishes are washed and dried in two 20-year-old machines that take 60 minutes per cycle, including the loading operation.

What can we learn about this process? Figure 5 shows a partial process-flow diagram with the capacities for four of the steps, and the required output. Note that the boundaries are set as the dishwashing operations in this department, excluding cutlery. For units, we have decided to measure the rate in dishes per day. The hospital has an inventory of dishes sufficient for one day's service. Thus, average rates are quite sufficient for our analysis. If it did not have this number of dishes, the exact timing of dish use and return would be much more important and analyzing dishes processed per hour, or even per minute, would be much more appropriate. We do not know of any machine inefficiencies, but know that the workers work for only seven hours per day after breaks are accounted for. The process bottleneck is in the two machine operations (washing and drying) at 6,300 dishes per day (seven hours). In fact, because these two operations take place sequentially in the same machines with no human intervention, they might even be combined in this analysis — unless, of course, we were considering replacing one of them with two machines, one to wash and one to dry. Depending on how the work is scheduled and whether machines must be watched at all times when they are running, the effective work day for machines may be eight hours.

Because the required output is 6,304 dishes per day, we are really tight on overall capacity. How good are the demand and capacity figures? They are close enough to warrant a closer look. In this example, working a small amount of

*FIGURE 5*

| Process Flow for Washing Dishes in a Hospital | | |
|---|---|---|
| Sequence of Steps | Flow Diagram | Rate of Production (Capacity) |
| Dirty dish input from hospital wards | | |
| Storage (raw materials) | ▽ | |
| Hand-scrape, rinse, stack | ① | 8,400 dishes/day (4 people @ 300 dishes/person hour) |
| Storage (work-in-process) | ▽ | |
| Load machine and wash | ② | 6,300 dishes/day (2 machines @ 450 dishes/machine cycle) |
| Machine dry | ③ | 6,300 dishes/day (2 machines @ 450 dishes/machine cycle) |
| Inspect | ☐ | |
| Unload machine and stack | ④ | 7,350 dishes/day (3 people @ 350 dishes/person hour) |
| Storage (finished goods) | ▽ | |
| Deliver clean dishes to dietary | | |

overtime would be a very attractive alternative. However, if capacity were to be increased, it is clear that the first place it should be added is to the washing machines — our bottleneck. The system is not balanced. The worker operations, particularly scraping, rinsing, and stacking, have excess capacity. We might be able to get by with one less worker in this operation. Overall, we need between five and six workers (5.57) at the stated work rates (Exhibit 9). Could we do this by sharing a person between the two worker operations? How good are the work rate and demand figures? How much slack do we want to have to cover contingencies? Is there something else that these workers could do? Questions like these should serve as a signal to management to look more closely. There may be enough money on the line here to make more accurate answers worthwhile. Of course, changing or eliminating jobs would involve the human resources department. The answers to some of these questions will involve a second fundamental operations tool, trade-off analysis.

*EXHIBIT 9*

---

### Calculation of Required Staffing Levels and Demand

---

**Demand**

3 meals per person day x 6 dishes per person meal x 361 person beds x 0.97 persons per bed = 6,304 dishes per day

**Staffing Levels**

| Operation | Capacity (dishes/worker day) | Workers required for 6,304 dishes/day |
|---|---|---|
| Hand-scrape, rinse, stack | 2,100 | 3.00 (6,304/2,100) |
| Unload machine and stack | 2,450 | 2.57 |

---

### TRADE-OFF ANALYSIS

A trade-off arises when you cannot have everything and must make choices. Everyone makes trade-offs every day. Say, for example, that you would like to spend the evening with your friends at a popular pub, but because you would also like to do well on your exam at the end of the week, you decide to spend the evening studying. Or you would like to get into business school and also medicine, but having to choose a limited number of courses forces you to eliminate one option or extend your academic studies. In some cases, the trade-off is black or white — medicine or business. In others, it is progressive — you could study for one, two, or three hours and then go to the pub — with varying costs and benefits. Trade-off analysis helps managers to decide what the "best" compromise is. Like process analysis, trade-off analysis involves a logical step-by-step sequence that will not guarantee success, but may prevent disaster. The steps are:

1. Keep looking for decisions that involve trade-offs — this is a fundamental statement of sound management practice.

2. List the various alternatives open to management.

3. Specify both the costs or disadvantages, and the savings or advantages, of each alternative. This list should include all the qualitative as well as the quantitative information.

4. Try to express as many of the advantages and disadvantages as possible in a common unit. Monetary units are particularly common and useful. Output units and processing rates are also used. This step is not easy and will involve estimates. Determining a monetary value for a qualitative benefit such as better customer service or happier workers is not always possible. One way to begin is to determine how large or small it would have to be before it would make a difference to the decision, thus giving you a feel for how close you have to be.

**5.** Decide on a course of action that you think will give you the largest net gain. This step will necessarily involve a lot of sound managerial judgment because many of the costs and savings will remain qualitative or be very soft.

Let us return to our hospital dishwashing example to see how we can use the logic of trade-off analysis. We found that our process analysis of the dishwashing operation revealed some idle labour time in two of the four steps we identified. Therefore, we may ask: Is there a better way to process the dirty dishes? Can we make the process more efficient and still be as effective in meeting the need to clean just over 6,300 dishes per day? Peaks in demand are apparently not a problem here and dishes are cycled through this process (6,300 clean dishes return as 6,300 dirty dishes — with occasional losses from breakage). Thus, outputs determine inputs, and there is no process need for maintaining excess labour.

For the purpose of illustration, we will consider only two of the many possible alternatives:

**1.** Leave the current system alone (that is, do nothing).
**2.** Reduce the staff on the scraping, rinsing, and stacking operation by one; reassign the work loads of the remaining three people on that operation, plus those on the machine unloading and stacking operation, so that staff perform both operations on a rotating basis; and use varying levels of work-in-process dish inventory levels to allow the labour operations to function independently of the machine operations.

The cost of the first alternative is the quantitative savings of the second alternative — the yearly wages plus benefits of one worker. This may be $24,000. However, laying off a worker and reassigning work does not come cost-free. Staff idle time gives an operation flexibility that may be useful if, for example, one of your machines breaks and washing dishes by hand becomes necessary, or surprise menu changes for a special occasion require seven dishes per patient meal, or a worker is absent. How will the remaining workers react to the new work load? Will fatigue become a problem? Will labour unrest be an issue? As a manager you may feel that these potential problems are major and worth far more than $24,000. Alternatively, you may feel that they are unlikely or will not last long, so that $24,000 saved each year looks like a good deal. Besides, this is a line-flow process for which low cost is likely to be a key objective. Depending on your judgment, you will choose one of the alternatives or continue to investigate others along with their associated trade-offs. In this example, note that departments other than operations are, or should be, involved.

The complexities and challenges of managing this simple example are increased substantially by such questions as:

▪ What are the hospital's policies on purchasing new dishes to replace ones that are broken, lost, or stolen?

- What happens if a washing machine breaks down?
- How are sudden increases or decreases in demand handled?
- What is the best way to schedule the job of picking up dirty dishes from the wards?
- Is too much or too little money invested in the inventory of dishes?
- Should one or two new high-speed dishwashing and drying machines be bought to replace one or both of the existing ones?

Performing a process analysis to gain a good understanding of how a process works and careful consideration of relevant trade-offs will put you in a good position to make operations decisions. Appendix B consists of a number of operations problems that will allow you to practise, using these and other analytical tools to develop your managerial skills.

## THE QUALITY AND PRODUCTIVITY REVOLUTION

Like all fields, operations is constantly developing. The recent past has seen revolutionary changes in attitudes toward quality and in managing quality. These changes affect all aspects of organizations that become part of the quality revolution.

Various approaches to quality are known. In ancient times, quality lay in the hands of artisans and craftsmen — possibly members of a guild — who acted, not only as producers, but also as trainers of apprentices and inspectors of products. This thinking remains with us today in artistic ventures and fields such as accounting, law, and other professional services.

With the advent of the industrial revolution, and particularly the pioneering work of Frederick Taylor and Frank and Lillian Gilbreth in the late 19th and early 20th centuries, which gave rise to scientific management, the need for quality changed. In particular, uniformity and reproducibility became important. The division of labour, under which the individual worker became a specialist responsible for only a small part of the final product, required these traits. This change led to inspection using statistical rules to separate good products (or inputs) from bad ones. Some tests are necessarily destructive or very expensive, leading to the notion of inspecting only a representative sample from a lot as opposed to inspecting every unit. The rules incorporated the notion of the relative costs of accepting a bad product or rejecting a good one.

A fundamental notion behind quality control is that of trying to inspect out bad quality. A logical extension is to try to build it in instead, that is to manage quality as opposed to controlling it. The notion of scientific measurement inherent in sampling and statistical acceptance rules led, in turn, to statistical process control (SPC) by which production steps were measured systematically to identify changes in one or more characteristics of interest. Figure 6 gives an example of how statistical process control can be used.

## FIGURE 6

### An Example of Statistical Process Control

Our brewery has a bottling line with an automatic filling machine that is supposed to fill 900 bottles per minute with 341 millilitres (mL) of beer. We are interested in making sure that the volume is within allowable acceptance limits, perhaps ± 4 mL (that is, a bottle containing between 337 and 345 mL meets our product quality standard). If we underfill the bottles, we break the law, cheat our customers, and potentially attract a lot of unwanted negative publicity. If we overfill, we waste beer and may break bottles. Our bottling machine is capable of filling with a standard deviation[1] ($\sigma$) of 0.5 mL. This means that if the machine is set at 341 mL and in statistical control, it will fill between 340.5 and 341.5 mL (one standard deviation) 68.26 percent of the time and between 339.5 and 342.5 mL (three standard deviations) 99.74 percent of the time. Most experts agree that three standard deviations represents adequate control — there is a probability of only 0.26 percent that a reading outside those control limits has arisen purely by chance. We want to decide whether the filling machine is in control. We measure the volume of beer in filled bottles periodically and plot the results. Measurement might be nondestructive (weighing the filled bottles or measuring the distance from the top of the liquid to the cap) or destructive (pouring the contents into a measuring device). The plotted results might appear as shown in the diagram below, which is an example of what is called an X-bar ($\overline{X}$) chart.

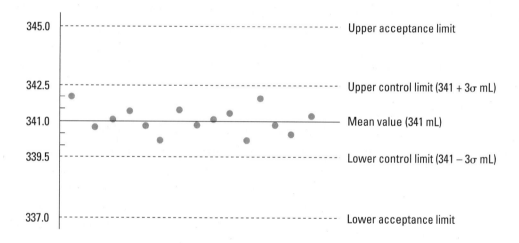

If the points continue to be randomly distributed within the control limits (341 ± 3$\sigma$ mL, that is, from 339.5 to 342.5 mL), we conclude that the filling machine is in statistical control. If they start to wander outside the limits or start to develop nonrandom patterns — for example, all being above or below 341 mL — we would conclude that the machine is no longer in control. In such a case we would most likely seek the cause of the variation and take corrective action to bring the machine back into control. (Note that the machine can be out of statistical control and still produce acceptable product, and vice versa.) The chart shows data for only one attribute, fill volume. We would also want to measure other attributes of beer, such as clarity, colour, taste, chemical composition, pressure, presence of foreign objects in the bottle, and the like. We might use other control charts to do so.

---

**1.** Standard deviation is a measure of dispersion or the width of a distribution around the mean value.

Figure 6 has some interesting features. Data must be collected systematically and rigorously to establish baseline information. It is too late to wait until after a product has failed before looking at machine capabilities. Also, even though quality problems show up in the product, the focus of controlling quality is on the processes that make the product. However, the statistical techniques are too often controlled by a "Quality Control Department," seen by many operations managers and workers as the enemy.

Although SPC is a set of quality improvement techniques, modern total quality management (TQM), as espoused by W. Edwards Deming, Joseph Juran, Philip Crosby, Shigeo Shingo, Genichi Taguchi, Kaoru Ishikawa, Armand Fiegenbaum, and other leaders in the field, broadens the approach in two ways. First, although the term TQM implies a focus on quality, its real goal is to enhance competitive performance in all areas: productivity, costs, market share, and profits, as well as quality. Second, TQM is all-inclusive. It means improving an organization by eliminating waste in its every activity — not only production, but also design, purchasing, inspection, marketing, sales, service, research and development, financial controls, personnel management, and the like. It treats every function as a process, which it sets out to analyze and improve. Although TQM uses several simple SPC tools (such as the $\bar{x}$ chart shown in Figure 6) to diagnose quality problems, TQM is not a set of techniques or even a state — it is a philosophy, an attitude, a never-ending journey. Its unique philosophical underpinning includes:

- quality is *customer driven* — the customer decides what quality is and whether the produced product or service is of high enough quality;
- the environment is *data rich* — we manage by fact and we must collect facts (see Figure 6, as an example);
- *processes are never perfect* — among management's jobs is to identify weaknesses in the process and to improve them — continuously;
- *respond quickly* to problems — therefore, have in place mechanisms to detect trouble and react to it;
- *employees*, particularly low level employees (operators), are among an *organization's most important assets* — therefore, develop and train them, listen to them, involve them;
- *organizations are like families* — develop friendly (although business-like), mutually supporting, partnership relationships with suppliers and customers as members of your family and share information with them freely to reduce uncertainty; and,
- *design quality and error prevention into products and processes.*

These characteristics have some significant implications, some of which are described in Exhibit 10. Because TQM breaks everything down into processes, it recognizes a series of supplier-operator-customer groups linked together in chains. Attention is focused on the links between activities. In such an arrangement, almost all individuals are simultaneously in all three roles. Working in this environment requires cooperation and lateral communication along the chain, both effectively and frequently. The illusive search for perfection leads organizations to "benchmark," that is, improving by seeking and studying the best possible examples of relevant processes, in whatever industry and location they occur. They then use the information to redesign their own processes.

TQM represents dramatic change for many organizations.[2] It is not easy to establish a cooperative culture in a society in which supplier-customer relationships have traditionally been adversarial. However, the benefits are real. TQM producers demand, and get, only acceptable parts and produce only acceptable products. Their close supplier-customer relationship allows them to monitor quality in supplier plants. TQM uses statistics not simply to tell when output has fallen outside the acceptable range, but to analyze variations and defects, and to redesign processes to reduce variability. This implies that decision making for what is unacceptable and what should be done about it is pushed down to individual operators. The changes require an organizational commitment to invest in training, development, and technology to allow change to occur. TQM reverses one 20th century trend: continual job specialization, deskilling, and supervision. Managers often see this change as a personal threat because:

1. their jobs change from gathering information, making decisions, and using incentives and punishments to manage the workforce, to consulting and coaching, and

2. organizations widen their spans of control and reduce layers of management.

The integration achieved through TQM allows the whole organization to focus on a single goal — satisfying customers — links processes and involves top management, indeed everyone, in managing quality. The changes are sufficiently sweeping to alter the very notion of why firms exist. The traditional model sees the *overriding goal* of a firm as maximizing shareholders' wealth by profit maximization. In contrast, TQM views satisfying customers as a firm's prime goal with the effect on shareholder wealth being an *outcome* of customer satisfaction.

The traditional model of a firm views conflict as inevitable — between management and workers, between employees and owners, between one department and another. To align employees' behaviour with those of the firm, the response is to design incentives, sanctions, and (vertical) hierarchical organizational structures. In contrast, TQM tries to meet the long-term interests of shareholders, employees, suppliers, customers, and the like through cooperation achieved by focusing on (horizontal) linked processes leading ultimately to the customer.

With reference to Figure 3, through reduced set-up times, TQM has shifted the attractive band of production from the rigid diagonal shown, toward the lower right-hand corner. It has allowed job shops and batching operations to

*EXHIBIT 10*

| The Traditional Model of the Firm in Contrast to TQM[1] | | |
| --- | --- | --- |
| | Traditional Model | TQM Model |
| Organizational goals | Maximizing shareholder wealth through maximizing profits. | Serving customer needs by supplying goods and services of the highest possible quality. |
| Individual goals | Individuals motivated only by economic goals: maximizing income and minimizing effort. | Individuals motivated by economic, social, and psychological goals relating to personal fulfilment and social acceptance. |
| Time orientation | Static optimization: maximizing the present value of net cash flow by maximizing revenue and minimizing cost. | Dynamic: innovation and continual improvement. |
| Coordination and control | Managers have the expertise to coordinate and direct subordinates. Agency problems necessitate monitoring of subordinates and applying incentives to align objectives. | Employees are trustworthy and are experts in their jobs — hence emphasis on self-management. Employees are capable of coordinating on a voluntary basis. |
| Role of information | Information system matches hierarchical structure: key functions are to support managers' decision making and monitor subordinates. | Open and timely information flows are critical to self-management, horizontal coordination, and a quest for continual improvement. |
| Principles of work design | Productivity maximization by specializing on the basis of comparative advantage. | System-based optimization with emphasis on dynamic performance. |
| Firm boundaries | Clear distinction between markets and firms as governance mechanisms. Firm boundaries determined by transaction costs. | Issues of supplier-customer relations, information flow, and dynamic coordination common to transactions within and between firms. |

1. R.M. Grant, R. Shani, and R. Krishnan, "TQM's Challenge to Management Theory and Practice," *Sloan Management Review* 35 (2), (1994): 25–35.

operate more like line-flow or continuous-flow operations. It represents an attractive, radical departure from traditional North American and European thinking.

## JUST-IN-TIME MANUFACTURING

TQM arose in Japan with just-in-time (JIT) manufacturing. One of the miracles of the last half of the 20th century is the phenomenal rise of Japan from the ashes of World War II to its prominent position among the world's leading nations. Much has been written about the reasons for Japan's success. Conspicuous among them is its TQM approach to operations, arguably its dominant business function. Japanese operations have been called zero inventory (ZI) as well as JIT manufacturing; disgruntled competitors have called them many other names, most of which are unprintable. Just what is JIT all about?

JIT has at least two distinct meanings. Just-in-time literally is taken to mean that a part arrives at a work centre just as it is needed — no sooner and no later. It is exemplified by the *kanban* control system that originated at the Toyota Motor Company, which some believe is the world's best manufacturing company. *Kanban* is Japanese for card, in this case a visible signal authorizing a worker to do something — for example, work on one or a few more parts or move one or a few parts to the next work centre. The rules are simple — no *kanban*, no action. When a machine breaks, or production flow stops for any reason, the flow of *kanban*, and thus production, stops. Because there are only a few *kanban* between any two work centres, the system is very responsive to disruptions. In contrast, in most North American and European systems, workers are expected to work on the next part, if at all possible, and these systems will not stop until workers run out of parts to work on. Because the systems are designed to keep workers occupied, there are always lots of parts and it takes a long time for the system to stop.

What is the advantage of stopping production quickly? Doesn't this lead to lost efficiency? This would be the case, if this were all that happened. But, in Japanese eyes, work stoppages present opportunities to identify and solve real production problems. They also prevent the accumulation of inventories, which cost money and hide opportunities for improvement. If the reason for the stoppage was a poor quality part produced in an earlier operation, you hardly want to keep producing more just to keep workers occupied. The advantages of JIT production have to be balanced against the need for demand stability.

The second idea encompassed by the term just-in-time is the TQM philosophy of continual improvement to operations. In non-TQM plants we often feel that operations, once debugged, are running optimally and that changing things will only cause problems. TQM recognizes that no matter how well something is running, it is never perfect. Under this philosophy, part of everyone's job, including the manager's, is to find waste (production problems) and eliminate it. A useful start is to reduce inventory. Inventory mostly just sits around, costing a lot of money and adding no value of any kind. As we described earlier, JIT operators have found ways to eliminate the reasons for having inventory.

## TQM Recognition

A number of well-known awards recognizing the achievement of TQM proficiency have been established. For over 40 years the Deming Prize has been awarded annually in Japan in a widely watched televised ceremony to recognize quality leaders. The prize was named after W. Edwards Deming, an American statistician who was instrumental in helping the Japanese rebuild after World War II. Since 1988 the United States has awarded the Malcolm Baldrige National Quality Award to promote quality and productivity as essential to successful business strategies.

About the same time as the Baldrige Award was established, the International Organization for Standardization (ISO) developed a family of international standards to guide internal quality management programs and facilitate external quality assurance purposes. ISO is an international agency composed of the national standards bodies of the nearly 100 member countries. ISO's goal is to promote standardization to facilitate international trade. The ISO quality standards, collectively known as ISO9000 (each for a somewhat different situation) are general standards focused not on product specifications, but on management systems, although ISO certification does not dictate a particular management style. As such, they are process standards whose goal is to help organizations achieve quality for their customers continuously. This involves all departments and functions.

After suitable examination, ISO certifies that qualified applicants meet ISO standards. These days it is common to drive by plants displaying posters proudly proclaiming: "ISO9000 Certified." ISO9000 certification is proving to be popular as purchasers, particularly for global acquisitions, increasingly demand that suppliers be certified. Thus, ISO9000 certification affects not only a firm's goods or services output, but also its marketing activities, and its internal management processes.

## Flexibility

**Section**

**Six**

Customers have recently started to demand not more choice but exactly what they want from manufacturers. Typically, they want something different — perhaps in colour, size, flavour, or shape — and they want it fast without a price penalty. The phenomenon has been termed "mass customization," which, needless to say, is more common in some industries than others. In some markets — such as commodities — customers place little value on the possible custom features. Other markets may be restricted by law from customizing.

Here is one example of the sort of thing we are talking about. One small Japanese bicycle manufacturer can produce several million different variations based on model, frame size, colour, etc. The company uses electronic communications to connect the store, where customers are measured, with the factory. It also uses a computer-aided design (CAD) system to design the product. The plant itself, however, is not extensively automated. Although the company promises delivery of custom bicycles within two to three weeks, it can complete them in only 150 minutes (compared to 90 minutes for its standard lines). The custom bicycles sell at a considerable premium above the standard models.

Mass customization differs from providing variety in one important respect: it means economically manufacturing in response to a customer's order instead of trying to meet customer needs through inventory. The requirements of mass customization are both a major challenge and a significant opportunity for manufacturers. The task is to obtain both low cost and flexibility simultaneously. With reference to Figure 3 the question becomes: How can manufacturers combine the traditional scale of line- and continuous-flow processes with the nimbleness of job shops?

There are various ways to deal with this problem. First of all, it pays at the design stage to plan products and/or processes so that customized versions can be built from standard modules. This move can allow rapid creation of the product from standard modules held in an electronic database. It also helps to link all the processes needed to plan, manufacture, and deliver a product as quickly as possible so that customer orders move as quickly as possible from product design, through process planning, to creation and delivery of the product or service.

Another way to increase flexibility is to ensure short supply chains — taken here to include all the steps from your suppliers through to delivery to the customer. It doesn't make much sense to be able to design a product and a process to make it within hours of a customer order if it takes weeks to get the material or to free up capacity in your supply chain. Part of a responsive supply chain is having relatively few steps, low set-up times, and excess capacity.

Many mass customizers dedicate a team to design, produce, and deliver a customer's order. Needless to say, flexibility requires that such teams be established quickly and work together from the start. This implies cooperation, which must be supported by the organization's culture. It also helps to seek and capture customer feedback about both the product and the process. An enterprise can use such information for its own planning, particularly in deciding how to deal with a specific customer in the future.

Lastly, computers can help improve flexibility. The use of computer databases was already alluded to. Virtually anything can be captured in an electronically retrievable form. Coupled with editing capability, product design can be accomplished much more quickly. These days it is not uncommon for hair salons to be able to design a style for you as you sit, watch, and comment. Coupled with modern telecommunications, computers also assist in the transfer of data. It is not uncommon now for designs created in North America to be transferred virtually instantaneously to manufacturers in Southeast Asia, who immediately start manufacture.

Computers are also used in the operating steps themselves. Many buzz words and acronyms are in current use: CAD/CAM, CIM, FMS, robots. These technologies are a form of automation, but differ from other forms of automation by replacing mental labour as well as human physical labour. Thus, a robot can be programmed (trained) to reach for a container, grasp it, lift it, inspect it, place it under a filling device, wait for it to fill, and place it in a pile with other filled containers. A computer-assisted design (CAD) system captures three-dimensional geometry in a machine-readable form. It is the drafting analogue of a word processor. Sophisticated CAD systems can test a design: What happens if we apply a force of a specified magnitude and direction at a specific place on the designed object? What about combinations of forces? At this point the system would more properly be called computer-aided engineering (CAE). CAD coupled directly with a computer-aided manufacturing system (CAD/CAM) allows a designer to sit in front of a computer terminal, design a part, and send the specifications to a manufacturing operation that will make the part. Such a manufacturing centre might have a carousel containing many different types of tools that are picked automatically in sequence according to specifications in computer files. These various levels of automation, flexible manufacturing systems (FMS), and computer-integrated manufacturing (CIM) are increasing levels for automation of mental tasks and a key to increasing manufacturing flexibility.

Computers are also being used in operations planning and control in a technique known as *material requirements planning*, or, more properly, *manufacturing resource planning* (MRP). The main notion behind MRP is that materials and other resources are interconnected rather than independent. Once a fast food restaurant manager has a forecast of the number of hamburgers that will be sold, he or she will know how many hamburger buns (or meat, relish, worker hours, electricity, and so on) will be needed and when to order them, based on established lead times. These values can be calculated based on expected lead times and the demand forecast for hamburgers. This is so because fast food restaurants do not sell these components except as complete hamburgers. They are said to be *dependent demand* items.

MRP's goals are to have the right amount of the right part, in the right place, at the right time, every time; to minimize inventories, especially work-in-process; and to improve customer service by avoiding stock-outs. Note that minimizing inventories and improving customer service are often considered to be conflicting goals. MRP allows a way around this conflict. It requires *accurate* information on inventories, bills of material (a record of exactly how something is made), lead times, and capacities. Advanced MRP systems have modules for accounting, purchasing, and so forth that connect manufacturing to these other functions. Thus, the MRP system is not so much a system to help manage manufacturing, but rather an information system that integrates all functional areas of the organization. Accounting can use it for costing purposes and for preparing bids. Purchasing can use it for information on supplier performance. Marketing can use it for information on when a particular customer's order will be complete, or as an early warning device for orders that will be late. Customers do not like bad news, but if it is inevitable, they prefer to get it early rather than late, because they will then have more options.

MRP can be used by any sort of organization to help control its operations and integrate functions. However, it has yet to penetrate service operations in any meaningful way. Also, within manufacturing, its main use is in batching operations and job shops where lead times are fairly long and the products are discrete (can be counted individually) and complex in that they have many parts, made up through successive levels of subassemblies.

Although MRP and TQM have the same goals, they do differ significantly. JIT production controlled by *kanban* stops quickly after a problem occurs — production is said to be *pulled* through the system. Think about a string attached to a toy. Stop pulling, and the toy stops instantly. In production controlled by MRP, production is *pushed* through the system. Thus, MRP production is relatively insensitive to stoppages in flow unless the MRP program is recalculated. Try stopping a rolling toy by pushing on the string. The aim of MRP is to control the current system using computer programs as tools. In contrast, the aim of TQM is to discover problems in the existing system so that the system can be changed to eliminate the problems.

Referring to Figure 3, although computer systems may be very expensive, computerization in manufacturing can increase flexibility. It can reduce set-up costs per run, making production of small lots of mature products viable (the lower right hand corner).

**SECTION**

**SEVEN**

## CONCLUSION

This chapter was designed to broaden your knowledge of operations situations by discussing four basic aspects of operating systems:

1. The input-transformation-output process and the basic transformation components of equipment, labour, materials, and energy.
2. The key operations tasks of function, quality, quantity, price, and service.
3. The basic process types (continuous-flow and line-flow, batch-flow, job shop, and project) and their management requirements.
4. The two basic operations analysis tools of process and trade-off analysis.

It also dealt with some exciting new developments in operations — ideas on quality and flexibility — and their effect on operating processes.

The chapter was also designed to point out that operations is all around us all the time, and cannot meaningfully be dealt with in isolation from the other functions in the organization. The difficulty and scope of operations problems vary but we believe that you can make a significant start in dealing with these complexities and accepting these challenges with an understanding of the points discussed.

---

## APPENDIX A
### The Costs and Benefits of Holding Inventory

To make any decision to hold or not to hold inventory you must understand the costs associated with both options.

### THE COSTS OF HOLDING INVENTORY

Ironically, the actual cost of items held in inventory is not usually directly relevant to the decision — it is assumed that you will either buy or sell them some time. There are several relevant factors, however.

**Financing.**   Holders of inventory must pay for the money invested in inventory through either debt or equity. A lender, such as a bank, charges interest on loans. Similarly, an investor expects a return on his or her investment in dividends or capital gain. Financing costs are often the largest component of inventory carrying costs.

**Obsolescence.**   There may be some risk that the inventory will lose its value before it is sold. Some seasonal articles, such as Christmas cards, lose their value almost completely after the season is over. Novelty items or ones that have the potential to become a health hazard are similarly risky. In these cases, the inventory may completely lose its value; indeed, in some cases the situation is even worse: the company may have to pay a high cost to dispose of its inventory.

**Shrinkage.**   Inventory might be damaged through improper handling, accident, weather, vermin, theft, or spoilage of perishable items, such as food, drugs, and photographic film.

**Holding.**   These costs are associated with maintaining the storage facilities. Included would be rent, utilities, insurance, storage and handling equipment, taxes, and stockkeepers' wages and benefits. Even if the facilities are owned by the inventory owner, such costs are relevant because the facility could have been used for other purposes — production and rental are two examples.

**Scrap and Rework.**   These costs are associated with detecting poor quality long after the item is made. The delay occurs because it has been sitting in inventory. The costs arise from having to scrap possibly large numbers of units made, but not detected because of the delay. In a busy plant, the scrap costs include opportunity losses associated with products that could have been made and sold if the capacity had not been devoted to producing bad outputs.

**Management.**    Inventory must be planned and managed; records must be kept; lots must be inspected; inventory must be counted; transactions must be accounted for; and equipment must be maintained. These and other costs can be extremely difficult to quantify accurately, but may be substantial.

Some ways to calculate the costs are:

1.    Consider just financing charges. The firm's bank borrowing rate is a reasonable place to start — it may be 13 percent before taxes, for example. This method ignores financing through issuing shares rather than taking out a loan, which itself is hard to quantify, and it completely ignores the other costs that may well cost more than financing.

2.    Calculate specific values for as many costs as possible, usually as a percentage of the total inventory invested. This is both time consuming and difficult. The total cost would be:

$$ICC = AAI \times (C_f + C_o + C_s + C_h + C_{sr} + C_{ma} + C_{mi})$$

where,    $ICC$ = Inventory Carrying Cost        $AAI$ = Average Annual Inventory

$C_f$    = Cost of financing        $C_o$    = Cost of obsolescence

$C_s$    = Cost of shrinkage        $C_h$    = Cost of holding

$C_{sr}$    = Cost of scrap and rework        $C_{ma}$ = Cost of management

$C_{mi}$    = Cost of miscellaneous items

3.    Use a rule of thumb. Over time, a firm may have discovered that the cost of carrying inventory is 30 percent and simply uses this figure in the future. Note, however, that a good rule of thumb for one firm may be totally inappropriate for another. Also, over time, particularly as changes take place, rules of thumb may become inappropriate.

Carrying costs are normally used only when analyzing alternative strategies that involve holding inventory. It is not normally included as a separate item on income statements. They are there, but are included in many other accounts such as interest expense, cost of goods sold, and so on. Inventory might get more attention if it were a separate cost item.

## THE COSTS OF NOT HOLDING INVENTORY

If inventory costs so much to hold, why have any? Despite its costs, inventory also has benefits. The chapter described five reasons for having inventory. A decision not to have inventory essentially says that these reasons are unimportant. Possible results are, of course, shortages or production stoppages. For example, a firm may decide not to maintain an inventory of raw materials, relying instead on the promised delivery dates of various suppliers. If the promised deliveries do not materialize, the equipment, facilities, and labour force may be idle. The firm would then incur a cost by not having raw materials inventory. At short notice, say an hour or two, such as during a power cut, the labour cost could be essentially the full cost of wages because many labour agreements restrict a manager's ability to lay off workers without due notice. An idle plant represents an opportunity cost, which may be high if the plant is fully occupied.

Similarly, a firm's decision not to have finished goods inventory may result in lost sales or backorders (the customer has to wait until the item is available). Back-orders are usually "rush" and entail extra costs for set-ups, customer contact, invoicing, and shipping. A significant cost item is lost customer confidence with the likelihood of lost sales in the future. Like the costs of having inventory, the costs of not having it are real, but hard to determine accurately.

## BALANCING THE COSTS

In the final analysis, the only reason to have inventory is because it costs less to have it than not to have it. If you think you have too much inventory, try reducing it. If you are right, no one will notice. If you are wrong, problems will start to appear. You may solve the problems or reduce their immediate impact by adding more inventory. The "right" level comes from balancing the relevant costs.

For cycle inventories (and *only* for cycle inventories), the trade-off between *variable*[3] set-up or order costs and *variable* holding costs can be made using the economic order quantity (EOQ). Where D is the annual demand (in units), S is the set-up or order cost (in dollars per run), i is the annual carrying cost percentage, C is the cost of an item (in dollars per unit) [and iC is the holding cost per year], ROP is the re-order point (in units), $\bar{d}$ is the average daily demand (in units), and L is the lead time (in days), the EOQ and ROP are:

$$EOQ = \sqrt{\frac{2DS}{iC}} \qquad ROP = \bar{d}L$$

As an example, consider a tire shop that carries several models, a popular one of which has an annual demand of 3,000 (10 per working day). The shop's supplier delivers two days after an order is placed. Every time the shop places an order, the supplier charges it an administrative fee of $25 and the shop incurs a cost of $2 for phone calls and paper work. The shop's own labour is a fixed cost (therefore irrelevant). The tires cost $50 each. Management estimates the carrying cost as 30 percent per year. The EOQ and ROP of this product are:

$$EOQ = \sqrt{\frac{2 \times 300 \times 27}{0.3 \times 50}} = 103.92 \qquad ROP = 10 \times 2 = 20 \text{ units}$$

Thus, it would be reasonable to institute a policy of ordering 104 tires each time an order was placed, and to place an order whenever the amount on hand dropped to 20. Because of the nature of EOQs, placing orders of 100 tires, which would likely be more convenient, would incur only a negligible penalty.

At the EOQ quantity, the annual costs of holding and those of set-up or ordering are equal. The holding costs are the average inventory (EOQ/2) multiplied by the annual holding cost per unit. This is often taken as the cost of a unit multiplied by the holding cost percentage. The order or set-up cost is the cost per order (or set-up) multiplied by the number of set-ups per year (D/EOQ). The annual costs are expressed algebraically as:

$$\text{Holding: } \frac{\text{EOQ}}{2} \times iC \qquad\qquad \text{Ordering (or set-up): } \frac{D}{\text{EOQ}} \times S$$

For the example above, the annual costs are (the small difference is a result of rounding):

$$\text{Holding: } \frac{103.92}{2} \times 0.3 \times 50 = \$779.40 \qquad\qquad \text{Ordering: } \frac{3000}{103.92} \times 27 = \$779.44$$

Although the EOQ model is based on the very unrealistic assumption that everything (demand, costs, lead times, etc.) is known with certainty, the model is very robust. That is, variations do not have dramatic effects. Even if the EOQ assumptions are grossly violated, the model is often a good starting point. And, although you don't have to use it, you do still have to make the order quantity decision. Many variations of the basic EOQ equation have been derived to deal with specific situations in which one or more EOQ assumption is violated.

---

## APPENDIX B
### Operations Questions and Problems[4]

---

1.  Your sandwich-making company has just received two orders for tomorrow. The first, from the local day care, is for 300 peanut butter and jam sandwiches. The second, from the city council, is for 100 roast beef sandwiches.

    a.  Perform a task analysis for each of these customers, supporting your positioning of the variables on the continuum of process types.

    b.  How could you or other managers use this information to make operating decisions?

2.  Give one example of an operation *not in the text* that would efficiently operate under each of the following processes:

    a.  Project

    b.  Job shop

    c. Batch operation

    d. Assembly line

    e. Continuous-flow process

    List the characteristics in your processes that support your classification.

**3.** Jim, the baker, was shaking his head in disgust as he was putting some of the week-old cakes out in the trash. "I just don't understand it," he said, "Last week I sold out of my carrot cakes in only two days. Now I'm throwing half of them out! I must be doing something wrong!"

Jim tried to offer his customers a selection of at least 10 different types of cake at any one time. This selection was changed each week. Because the bakery was closed on Sundays, Jim set this day aside to make enough cakes to last the week. The number of each type baked depended on Jim's estimate. Any unsold cakes at the end of the week were disposed of. Unfortunately, Jim was throwing more and more away, and he was starting to feel this loss in his weekly profits.

    a. Where does Jim's cake production fall on the production process continuum? Support your answer.

    b. Is this the best position? Why or why not?

    c. Advise Jim of at least *two* different options in making his cakes, and state the pros and cons of each.

**4.** Define effectiveness and efficiency. How is each measured? Give some examples of operations with each of the following characteristics:

    a. effective but inefficient

    b. ineffective but efficient

    c. neither effective nor efficient

    d. both effective and efficient

**5.** Classify each of the following examples of inventory by form (raw materials, work-in-process, finished goods) and by function (decoupling, pipeline, and so on):

    a. Sausages in boxes moving along a conveyor to the frozen goods warehouse where they will await shipment to customers.

    b. Passengers walking from the plane from which they have just disembarked to the baggage carousel to wait for baggage.

    c. Spare parts (made in-house) for repair of the machines used in the production of pipeline welding equipment.

    d. Patients waiting in a doctor's office for their scheduled appointments.

    e. Bins of castings awaiting machining in a facility manufacturing plumbing supplies (taps and fixtures).

    f. A large pot containing potatoes peeled and sliced for fries at 11:30 a.m. in a downtown restaurant that caters primarily to the work force of a large office building.

**6.** For the examples in question 5, how could the inventories be reduced to make the operations more like a just-in-time system?

**7.** Competition around the world is heating up rapidly. National borders, indeed nations, are crumbling. Many firms, particularly in the manufacturing sector, are finding that they are not doing very well. Two potential solutions are to invest in computer hardware and software and to adopt a TQM philosophy. What advice would you give manufacturers facing this, and other choices? What are the pros and cons of each general approach?

**8.** In order to satisfy customers, a small manufacturing firm found that over the past several months it had slowly increased the variety of its component parts, lot sizes, and lead times. Discuss the effect such changes to the product line would likely have on the production process.

**9.** The chapter indicates that purchasers are increasingly seeking suppliers with ISO9000 certification. Propose some reasons why purchasers might act this way.

**10.** Refer to Figure 6. Where do you think a brewer might set the fill volume for beer bottles? In addressing this question, consider three possibilities: 341 mL, above 341 mL, or below 341 mL. Give some reasons for choosing each.

**11.** Because of a large increase in demand, Outwest Drillpress was considering expanding its automatic precision drilling operation, for which it charged its customers $30 per hour. The process was automatic except for setting up the controls, placing the part in a jig, and removing it after drilling.

Outwest officials were surprised to find that the cost of this type of equipment had doubled since they had purchased the original machine. The precision driller now cost $109,000, including a $3,000 installation charge. Maintenance on the present machine totalled $2,000 per year and electricity cost $1 per hour. Any new equipment would incur similar expenses. With operator wages costing $15 per hour and a 6,000-hour lifespan on these machines, the company was not sure if it should expand.

As a consultant to Outwest, would you advise them to purchase the new machine?

**12.** A predicted phenomenal surge in the popularity of Leanne's Liquid Beverage would increase weekly demand to 8,000 cases of six 350-mL bottles. The production manager was worried that the process would not be able to handle increased demand.

The mixing operation was capable of producing 3.5 L of Leanne's Liquid Beverage per minute. The bottling machine's effective capacity was 300 bottles per hour. Workers applied labels by hand; each worker could apply labels to 1,920 bottles per day. The capping machine could cap up to 600 bottles per hour. The final machine in the line, the packager, could package 1,600 cases per day. The plant's productive time was eight hours per day, five days per week.

Leanne's production manager informed her that the cost per week of doubling the output at each of the five operations would be:

| | |
|---|---|
| mixing | $ 550 |
| bottling | $1,975 |
| labelling | $1,200 |
| capping | $ 900 |
| packaging | $1,500 |

(Note that each time you increase the output of the bottling machine by 300 bottles per hour, it costs $1,975.)

The current rate of production is 2,000 cases per week. The unit contribution per case is $2.

a. What is the current capacity of this system?

b. Can the current system handle the increased demand?

c. If not, what changes will have to be made?

d. Should Leanne invest in the new equipment? Why or why not?

13. In her home town of Peterborough, Ontario, Vanessa was reviewing the operations of her small business: baskets filled with gift items. Although sales had been up from last year, she remembered several occasions when she had completely stocked out of baskets and was not able to meet the needs of her customers. Sales for the upcoming year were forecasted at 20,000 baskets and varied significantly from week to week. Reviewing some financial data, Vanessa discovered the following costs:

| | |
|---|---|
| cost of gifts placed in the basket | $3.00 |
| cost of the basket | 0.50 |
| direct labour per basket | 0.50 |

Currently, Vanessa carried two weeks' of both raw materials and finished goods inventory at an inventory carrying rate of 20 percent. The baskets sold for $5 each. Vanessa was wondering whether she should increase the finished goods inventory from two weeks to three weeks.

a. Assuming she carries two weeks' worth of both finished goods and raw materials, what will Vanessa's inventory carrying cost be for both next year?

b. How much is she losing with every basket that is *not* sold because of stock-out?

c. What would be the *extra* cost of carrying an additional week of finished goods inventory?

d. Would you advise Vanessa to carry the extra week? Why or why not?

14. Return to the example given near the end of this chapter concerning a hospital dishwashing operation. A manager in the hospital has discovered that disposable dishes can be purchased for about $0.08 each.

a. Would disposable dishes be a viable option?

b. What factors would be important?

c. What other possible solutions warrant investigation?

15. After a tour of the plant, Sue Barnes, the general manager, called Fred Dirkin, foreman of the frame building section in the Sentsun Stereo factory. She said: "What was your section up to this afternoon, Fred? When I walked through, more than half of the workers seemed to be doing nothing. We can't really afford to have workers sitting around idle, you know. And I don't really understand why your section always seems so close to missing your target of 500 frames per hour with all that excess labour. Take a look at it and let me know what gives."

The section, which was responsible for some of the first steps in the stereo production process, employed two types of workers. Nine workers assembled frames; an experienced assembler could produce 60 frames per hour. Fifteen other workers installed heat-sinks (an electrical component). Their job was more complex; installing a heat-sink took an experienced worker about 75 seconds.

Fred wanted to measure the efficiency of each type of worker and prepare his answer for Sue Barnes. He also wanted to ensure that people were not idle the next time she came around.

16. Akbar Taseen, production planner, was trying to decide how long the production runs of his company's popular Q3HD computer diskette should be. The latest annual demand forecast from the marketing department was for 2,150,000 diskettes. Each diskette required $0.18 in materials and $0.05 in direct labour and sold for $0.45. The firm's accountant informed Akbar that its cost of capital was 25 percent. Each time a different diskette model was produced, it took the 10 operators 45 minutes to adjust and check the machines. The labour cost for this time was a total of $190, including benefits. Once running, the production equipment could produce 6,000 diskettes per hour. The plant operated 40 hours per week.

a. Calculate the economic order quantity (EOQ) for Q3HD production.

b. Comment on the usefulness of producing in batches of EOQ size as opposed to producing batches of three days' worth.

## NOTES

1. Based in part on an unpublished note by Professor Michiel R. Leenders of the Western Business School, The University of Western Ontario.

2. Much of this section was derived from: R.M. Grant, R. Shani, and R. Krishnan, "TQM's Challenge to Management Theory and Practice," *Sloan Management Review*, 35 (2), 25-35 (1994).

3. Variable set-up or order costs vary directly with the number of set-ups or orders. Long distance phone charges, stationery, postage, and set-up staff paid on a piece rate are examples. Variable holding costs vary directly with the amount held. Financing costs and insurance are examples. Nonvariable costs are typically fixed charges, such as

labour costs, space charges, etc., allocated to a cost centre and are rarely relevant to economic order quantity calculations.

4. Based in part on a problem set created by J. Cummings, Western Business School, The University of Western Ontario.

# ■■■■ CASES FOR PART 6 ■■■■

**CASE 6.1** Bankruptcy

■

**CASE 6.2** The Brockville Plant

■

**CASE 6.3** The Cat's Pyjamas

■

**CASE 6.4** Dofasco Inc.: Stores and Maintenance Management (A)

■

**CASE 6.5** Fine Footwear Limited (R)

■

**CASE 6.6** Garlic's

■

**CASE 6.7** Hammond Manufacturing Company Limited

■

**CASE 6.8** Introducing New Technology at General Motors

■

**CASE 6.9** No Pants Incorporated

■

**CASE 6.10** Steelway Building Systems

■

**CASE 6.11** The University of Western Ontario Book Store

■

**CASE 6.12** Worldwide Pulp and Paper Ltd.

## C A S E **6.1** BANKRUPTCY

Bernita Graf had just been assigned the new job of production manager — games and toys for the Exemplar Manufacturing Company. For the past seven years, Bernita had worked as a supervisor in another division of Exemplar. Exemplar had several well-established product lines and was beginning to diversify into new areas. Bernita's superior, the general production manager, asked her to work with the new products manager on the latest product, code-named *Bankruptcy*. *Bankruptcy* was a new adult game that the marketing department seemed to think would be an immense success, competing with board games such as *Trivial Pursuit* and *Pictionary*.

An Exemplar staff member, John Duncan, informed Bernita that the basic tasks to be performed were assembling components purchased from other manufacturers. The assembly operations could be performed in any order. In repeated attempts John was able to assemble completed versions of *Bankruptcy* in 15 minutes. He also found that if three workers performed only two assembly operations each, instead of all six, each operation could be completed in half the time. Thus, although one person working alone could produce 32 games a day, a team of three people working together could produce 192 games of *Bankruptcy* per day. Bernita received details on the time requirements and material costs of the various components for each operation as shown in the table on page 515.

All materials could usually be obtained within one week of being ordered. On occasion, materials could take up to two weeks to be delivered. The vice-president of finance recently had sent a memo to managers asking that all inventories be kept at minimum sizes because costs for the company had risen substantially. The vice-president asked to be informed of all investment needs exceeding $40,000.

The community had a good supply of semi-skilled personnel. The starting rate at Exemplar was $8 per hour (including benefits): normal hours were 07:30 to 16:00, with 30 minutes for lunch. Thus, each worker was paid an average of $64 per day. Considering that on average there were 20 working days in a month, this worked out to $1,280 per month. Bernita was told she could hire as many workers as she thought she needed and pay them on whatever basis she wished, so long as she did not exceed the plant average of $12 per hour regular time for semi-skilled labour. Overtime, if used, was calculated at time and a half.

| Assembly Operation | Time Required (Minutes) | | Material Cost |
|---|---|---|---|
| | For One Person Working Alone | For a Three-Person Team | |
| A | 1 | 0.5 | $ 1.00 |
| B | 4 | 2 | 2.50 |
| C | 2 | 1 | 0.50 |
| D | 2 | 1 | 1.00 |
| E | 3 | 1.5 | 5.00 |
| F | 3 | 1.5 | 10.00 |
| | 15 | 7.5 | $ 20.00 |

Bernita was allotted a plant space of 20 x 5 metres and told she could arrange her operations as she saw fit. The department would be charged $48 per square metre annually for the allotted space. Extra space beyond the allotted 100 square metres was also available, but would be charged to her operation at $72 per square metre annually. The raw materials inventory (at $20 per unit) and finished goods inventory (valued at material cost plus labour cost) would require roughly the same volume. Because the boxes were fairly bulky, she could store the equivalent of 60 units of *Bankruptcy* on each square metre of floor space, assuming she piled them as high as possible. John Duncan told Bernita he figured they would need 50 square metres for assembly operations including tables, work stations, lockers, etc. Other fixed manufacturing overhead costs associated with *Bankruptcy* were estimated to be $4,120 per month.

The new products manager told Bernita that the forecasted demand for *Bankruptcy* for at least the first year was 3,600 units per month, with a range from 3,000 to 4,000 in any given month. He stressed that he expected Bernita to avoid stock-outs because *Bankruptcy* would primarily be an impulse purchase, and stock-outs would be very costly. The intended selling price was $25 per unit. Marketing estimated its fixed costs (mostly for packaging design, advertising, and point of purchase displays) at $40,000.

Bernita was also told that one of her suppliers, Hutchison Ltd., had sent in a quotation of $23 per completed unit to produce the year's requirements of *Bankruptcy* for Exemplar. Their quality was not considered as good as Exemplar's, but they were prepared to provide units on any schedule desired. Unfortunately, they added, the delivery time could vary from one to four weeks depending on how busy they were.

### C A S E **6.2** THE BROCKVILLE PLANT

In the Parke-Davis Brockville plant on January 8, 1985, Garry Churchill, a division supervisor, and his quality circle group of the dry manufacturing division of the manufacturing department were reviewing their notes concerning capsule filling and tablet compression. After five months of weekly meetings, the group was wondering what recommendations they should make to the steering committee at the January 31 presentation.

**WARNER-LAMBERT**

Parke-Davis Canada Inc. was a division of Warner-Lambert Canada Inc., which also had five other divisions: Adams Brands Canada Inc., Personal Products, Diagnostic Reagents, Capsugel, and Schick Canada Inc. The Canadian parent company was a subsidiary of the American multinational Warner-Lambert Ltd., which operated many divisions and affiliates including pharmaceuticals, confectionery, personal care products, and medical and scientific instruments. Warner-Lambert Ltd.'s sales for the last four quarters were up 2 percent to $3.2 billion while profits had risen 12 percent to $223.9 million. The increased profitability was attributed to company-wide improvements of production processes, which had resulted in significant cost savings and better product quality.

**PARKE-DAVIS CANADA INC.**

Parke-Davis manufactured pharmaceutical products such as Benylin cough syrup and Sinutab decongestant tablets, and personal care products such as Listerine mouthwash and Efferdent denture cleaner. It also manufactured many prescription and over-the-counter drugs as well.

Production facilities for Parke-Davis were located in Brockville, Ontario, 335 km east of Toronto. The plant employed 280 people and was 200,000 square feet in size. Exhibits 1 and 2 outline a partial organization chart and a partial floor plan. Organization of the plant consisted of six departments: quality assurance, manufacturing, distribution, packaging, engineering and maintenance, and administration (which managed purchasing, production planning and control, finance, and human resources). Under Mr. Trick, manager of the manufacturing department, were four supervisors, each with specific responsibilities: (1) tablet coating, drug and chemical dispensing, sterile manufacturing, and aluminum hydroxide;

(2) liquid manufacturing; (3) capsule filling; and (4) granulation and tablet compression.

The latter two sections fell into the category of dry manufacturing, an area that produced capsules and tablets for prescription and over-the-counter purposes. There were 30 tablet products, which accounted for 285 production runs per year or, in the terminology at Parke-Davis, 285 "cards" per year. Similarly, there were 16 capsule products, which accounted for 200 cards per year. Each card varied in size and could range from 20,000 to 60,000 capsules or tablets. Dry manufacturing held approximately $30,000 worth of work-in-process inventory.

## QUALITY CIRCLES

### The Concept

Quality circles were groups of workers that held regular meetings to discuss production problems and recommend to management ways of improving the overall efficiency and effectiveness. Research had indicated that greater productivity and improved product quality would result if workers had input concerning the production process, work environment, and other related issues.

### Three Quality Circles at Brockville

Warner-Lambert Canada Inc. had planned a company-wide introduction of quality circles. Introduction of quality circles at the Brockville plant had begun in June 1983. After literature outlining general information had been provided to the employees, a seminar was presented that explained how quality circles were to be implemented. The introduction and management of the quality circle program was led by Trick and was fully endorsed by Mr. Reynolds, plant manager.

Volunteers for quality circles were requested and 61 percent of the employees responded favourably. The 30 people selected were divided into three quality circles: manufacturing, packaging, and production planning and control combined with purchasing. Of the 30 selected, six were chosen to be leaders, two per circle. After the six leaders had been trained by Trick during July and August, the groups began meeting in late September and the leaders trained the remaining members until the end of November.

### Manufacturing Department's Quality Circle

Garry Churchill (supervisor of coating, dispensing, sterile manufacturing, and aluminum hydroxide), and Chris Newton (supervisor of granulation and compression) were selected as co-leaders for the quality circle of the manufacturing department. The other two supervisors were not part of the quality circle. The remaining eight members were all workers from the manufacturing department.

Garry Churchill graduated from the University of Toronto in 1975 with a degree in chemistry and physiology. He had worked for a smaller pharmaceutical firm as manufacturing manager before joining Parke-Davis in 1982. Newton had been with Parke-Davis about five years. Prior to this, he had worked with another pharmaceutical company for a few years after graduating from the University of Montreal.

The manufacturing department's quality circle began weekly, one-hour meetings in late September 1983. Churchill and Newton led the training until the end of November. The next three months were spent examining a problem concerning the weight of filled capsules. The circle presented a summary of its training activities and the solution to its first problem on February 21, 1984, to the steering committee.

The steering committee was a group of senior managers who represented a wide cross-section of management talent. The members included: Reynolds, plant manager; Trick, manufacturing manager; Beasley, human resources manager; Becker, production planning and control manager; Taylor, technical services manager; Cuming, capsugel manager; Todd, packaging manager. The role of the steering committee was to evaluate the quality circle's proposals and to implement the proposals if accepted.

For the next presentation on June 26, 1984, the circle worked on minor problems that were similar to the first one solved. As the manufacturing department ceased operations for its annual maintenance shutdown in July, Churchill and Newton considered the group to be working well, since both sets of recommendations had been accepted.

When production resumed in August, Newton formed a second quality circle within manufacturing to examine problems in liquid manufacturing. A second quality circle had also been formed in packaging as this growth was part of the overall plan. Unfortunately, the quality circle formed between production planning and control, and purchasing, encountered difficulties and ceased to exist. Churchill and his quality circle continued to investigate the filling and granulation, and compression areas, from August 7, 1984, until January 8, 1985.

## PRODUCTION PROCESS IN THE DRY MANUFACTURING DEPARTMENT

### Raw Materials Inventory

Raw materials inventory went through four stages before it was ready for production. Initially, it was received and kept in a temporary holding area. Next, a sample was taken and sent to the labs to test for identity, purity, and potency, a process requiring five days. Raw materials inventory that had tested positive was labelled "in quarantine" and remained in the temporary holding area. When a card was scheduled, the raw materials were located and stored in the dispensing room two days prior to production. This operation was performed to ensure that the ingredients to be released into production were correct. Two skilled workers were employed in the dispensing room operations.

### Granulation

During granulation, the dry blending or "mixing" of the powder raw materials occurred. Two highly skilled workers mixed binding ingredients and dyes with the chemicals to make the powder that would be used for tablet compression and capsule filling. The raw materials were removed from the dispensing room and dry blended during a three-hour process in the granulating room. A large mixing bowl type machine combined the ingredients until the desired consistency was formed.

The resulting bulk powder was transferred to granulating storage where it remained for two or three days while samples were tested. The bulk powder was kept in large cardboard drums that were lined with strong plastic bags and stored on skids (pallets) and racks. Retrieval of the correct drum for further processing was difficult because the bulk powder for both tablet compression and capsule filling were stored there. This system resulted in space and identification problems that were time consuming for the operator who had to sort through all the drums. This area was further congested because of storage of the polishing equipment and necessary polishing materials.

**Capsule Filling**

Capsule filling, which was a highly skilled task, began with the set-up of the filling machine. Depending upon the size of the card, one of five filling machines was brought into one of three filling rooms. The set-up took six hours.

The bulk powder to be processed was retrieved from the granulating room and the empty capsules were received from capsule storage. Actual filling took 15 hours and the filled capsules were placed in plastic pails for transport. Filling was delayed by the congestion in the granulating room, and by the crowded corridor between the granulating storage room and filling room, which held empty drums that had not been taken away, empty capsules that had arrived early, and obsolete equipment. It took 10 hours to clean the room and machine at a cost of $57.41 per hour. Samples were sent to the labs for a testing process that took five days, as the capsules were stored in another part of the plant near the packaging department.

The next stage was polishing, which occurred because the filled capsules were coated with bulk powder dust. A fabricating liner and "fun fur" were attached to the inside of a large revolving container. The unpolished capsules were rotated in the container and then "washed" in salt to remove residual powder on capsules. About 20 percent of the cards required polishing, which was done wherever there was space available in the inspection, filling, or granulating rooms. The cost per card was $70 for liners, $40 for fur, and $40 for salt. The polishing process required 8 hours per card of direct labour, and 2.25 hours of indirect labour, costing $57.41 and $23.00 per hour, respectively.

After the polishing had been completed, the capsules were placed on a conveyor that had a light shining from the bottom, and were inspected to identify empty, split, and low-filled capsules. Inspection took 24 hours at an additional cost of $57.41 per hour. Capsules that were not polished were sent straight to inspection after sampling.

The approved capsules were sent to capsule yielding and storage to be weighed. At the yielding stage, the weight of the capsules was taken and compared to the weight of the raw materials that had gone into the system. Yielding, which took two hours, was performed to approximate the number of capsules produced and to ensure that the product had been made correctly from a material weight stand-point. After yielding, a sample was sent to the labs to test purity and potency. After the lab had reported favourably two to four days later, the capsules were sent to packaging and then on to distribution. The polishing, inspection, and yielding operations were lesser skilled tasks.

The throughput time for the average card of capsules processed in the manufacturing department was 29 days. The size of the card (number of capsules) and the type of capsule product affected the length of the throughput time. Churchill thought that this period seemed excessive and was wondering what the expected throughput time was.

**Tablet Compression**

Tablet compression began when one of the four compression rooms had been prepared and the bulk powder had been received from the granulating room. The bulk powder was fed into the machine that stamped the tablets into shape and emptied the tablets into cardboard boxes that cost $0.50 each. A deduster machine was attached to the compressor machine to solve the dust problems similar to those of capsule filling. After tablet compression, about 20 percent of the production runs were covered with a sugar-like coating. This final coating process was a longer and more complex task than the actual tablet compression.

Tablets were yielded after compression by the same person who yielded the capsules. Yielding took place before and after coating for tablets that had been coated, and after compression for tablets that had not been coated. Yielding performed before coating was delayed since the batch size had to be estimated to fit the coating machine. Yielding also took two hours to complete as with capsule filling. If the division of the batch were incorrect, yielding would have to be redone. Samples were taken after yielding, and the card of tablets was labelled "in quarantine." The card of tablets was transferred to the temporary holding area for four days until the positive lab report was received, at which time the card would be sent to packaging and then to distribution. Compression took from 4 to 30 hours, while coating took from 4 to 100 hours to complete.

The tablet yielding area stored bulk powder waiting to be compressed, tablets waiting to be yielded for two days, filled capsules waiting to be inspected, and equipment not in use. It also housed assembled boxes and unassembled cardboard, which were used for transporting tablets and capsules. The compression operators expected the yielding, inspection, and polishing workers to assemble the boxes. If none were ready, the operators waited. Occasionally, they used pails costing $3.29 each that were also stored in the yielding area. The pails could be reused and it was estimated that 300 pails could replace the 35 boxes per card currently consumed.

The throughput time for the average card of tablets processed in the manufacturing department was 21 days, a period that Churchill thought was excessive in this department as well as in capsule filling. The length of time was also dependent upon the size of card and type of tablet product. Exhibit 3 shows the material flow for capsule filling and tablet compression through the dry manufacturing department.

**OPTIONS FOR CHURCHILL'S QUALITY CIRCLE**

A presentation to the steering committee was scheduled for January 31 and, after only three meetings of preparation, the quality circle was wondering what recommendations it should propose. The research revealed several options from which the quality circle could choose for both capsule filling and tablet compression.

**Capsule Filling**

There were three options regarding capsule filling. First, an automatic polishing machine could be purchased for $15,000. Under this option, the material costs for the liners, fur, and salt would be eliminated. In addition, direct labour would not be necessary while the indirect labour would be one-quarter of the original amount per card. Second, instead of performing the polishing operation after the filling operation, the two could be performed simultaneously as an assembly line operation. If this second option were undertaken, the clean-up time would be cut in half and a sampling operation would be eliminated. Third, the inspection time could be reduced by nine hours if it were performed simultaneously with the filling operation. The quality circle had investigated the situation and had concluded that it was possible to do all three operations in one filling room. There were some doubts as to the effectiveness of these latter two options since the granulating storage area and the adjacent corridor were congested. Churchill wondered how the congestion could be relieved in order to make the three options more feasible.

**Tablet Compression**

The two options for tablet compression were designed to minimize the waiting time of tablets in the yielding area. First, the quality circle identified two alternative methods to the current yielding operation of measuring the gross weight of a card. For the first method, five automatic counters costing $450 each could be purchased. These machines would calculate an exact number of tablets produced and eliminate the yielding operation, thus saving $16.25 per hour in labour costs. However, four more dedusters costing $1,200 each would be required. For the second method, a standard weight for each box of tablets could be set that would correspond to a specific number of tablets. The compression operator would record the weight and number of tablets by observing the number of boxes filled.

The quality circle identified two alternative methods for sampling. For the first method, random samples could be taken at various times per day by a product administrator who would be responsible for the transfer and documentation of samples sent to the labs. For the second method, specific samples could be taken at the start, middle, and end of cards by the compression operator.

**THE DECISION**

In addition to the options identified, the quality circle wanted to reduce throughput time. For every percentage decline in throughput time, a corresponding percentage reduction in work-in-process would result. The quality circle wondered what benefits would accrue, since the annual carrying cost of inventory was estimated to be 25 percent.

As the quality circle was discussing what to recommend to the steering committee, Churchill perceived nervousness and apprehension in the group. Although they had made two previous presentations, those recommendations had been minor in comparison to the present discussion of capital expenditures and significant process changes. However, Churchill recognized that decreasing the lab time and making major structural changes were not viable choices, given the quality circle's position. He recalled that their overall mandate was to improve the efficiency without affecting the quality. Therefore, he knew the impact on that, criterion should be assessed at the presentation. He also realized that as leader of the quality circle, he was responsible for ensuring that the group put together an effective presentation.

**EXHIBIT 1**
**The Brockville Plant Partial Organization Chart**

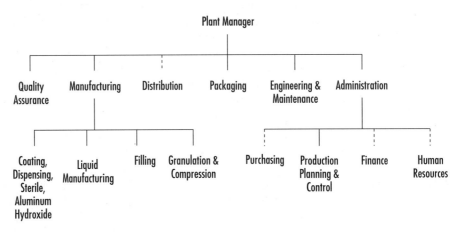

The dotted lines indicate managers who reported to the Parke-Davis head office in Toronto.

**EXHIBIT 2**
**Partial Floor Plan**

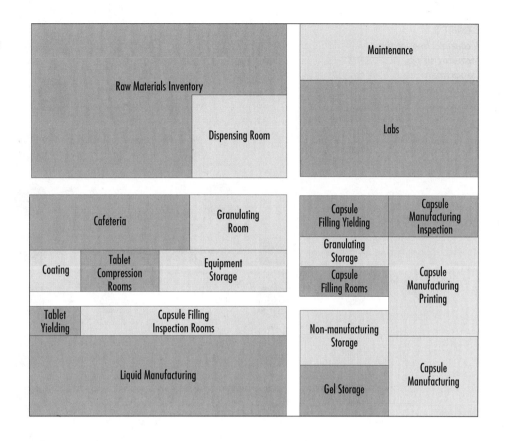

**EXHIBIT 3**
**Material Flow of the**
**Manufacturing**
**Department**

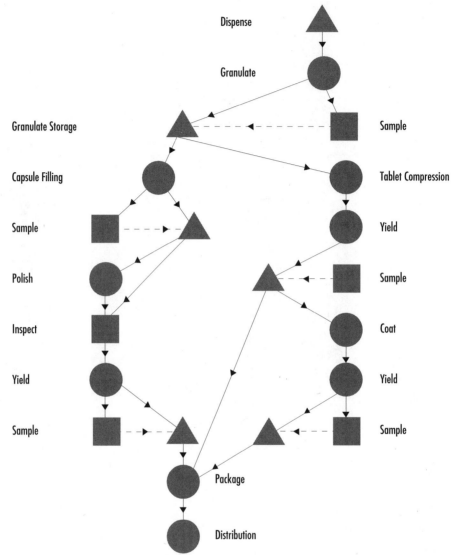

# C A S E   **6.3**   THE CAT'S PYJAMAS

"What's that?"

"It's the cat's pyjamas!" Ollie Fox was pleased with the looks of the tiny nightgown that she had just finished sewing.

"Listen, Ollie, no cat of mine is going to wear pyjamas!" Her husband was obviously unimpressed.

"You don't understand me."

"I don't understand you because I never see you anymore." His tone intimated the beginning of an argument.

She remained unruffled: "Well, I am always here."

"That is irrelevant. I cannot even see the refrigerator anymore under all of this fur. How then, am I supposed to see you, assuming that you are still smaller than the refrigerator?" Things were heating up all right!

Ollie began to bargain: "Very funny! I'll try to do better. In another month I should have this mess cleaned up. I'll even cook you a meal. It's just that I am into some really exciting stuff right now!"

"Fur and cats' pyjamas?" He wasn't mellowing.

She tried to sweeten the deal with dollar signs: "I have been offered this fantastic opportunity to expand sales with a chain of gift shops. Demand could go as high as 60,000 bears. That's about $2,400,000 in sales. We'll be rich!"

"Oh gawd, Ollie, 60,000 pounds of fur will not fit in this kitchen."

"I am moving! Okay?" She was into it deeply now!

"Just great, Ollie, just great! Who gets custody of the cat?"

"As I said earlier, you don't understand me. I have found some industrial space that is renting for about $3,000 a month, so I'll be moving operations. The fur, not me, is moving there. And, for your information, 'the cat's pyjamas' is an expression meaning: 'it's great!' The nightgown is for one of the bears." She thought he looked happier after this disclosure.

Ollie had many decisions to make about the future of her toy bear manufacturing company that was outgrowing her Mississauga home. The potential to expand sales depended on organizing the production of the bears in order to meet demand. Ollie realized that production would have to begin by April 1986 in order to produce enough to meet the Christmas demand. Ollie briefly wondered about the profitability of the expansion. Considering that the product was just a fad, perhaps she should grab what she could while she could. Perhaps she should forget the whole idea and just continue operating on a small scale from her home. It was March 3 and Ollie knew she had to make her decision quickly if she planned to accept the gift shop's order.

Her conversation with her husband had just given her a great idea for a name for her company.

## HISTORY

Originally, Ollie had sewn toy bears for her own children. They were softer and had more expressive faces than ones already available on the market. Whenever she sewed an outfit for the child, she would make an identical version for the bear.

Soon, friends and relatives were asking for the bears. Parents found that they were good for early childhood education in that the buttons, zippers, and strings aided tiny finger coordination. The nightwear for the bears became particularly popular because it seemed to ease the children into the idea of preparing both the bears and themselves for bedtime.

A friend had requested a few bears for sale in the local hospital gift shop. A visitor to the hospital noticed the bears and contacted Ollie to supply his giftware distribution business. He had initially ordered 1,000 bears.

Ollie had advertised for women to sew the bears in their homes. She did all the materials purchases and cutting. The pieces were delivered to the home sewers where they were completely constructed, stuffed, and dressed. Ollie collected, tagged the bears, and prepared them for delivery.

## THE PRODUCT

The three sizes of bears, eighteen-inch, twelve-inch, and eight-inch, were priced to retail for $45.95, $35.95, and $21.95, respectively. Clothes for the bears sold for $5 more. Ollie set her manufacturer's selling price at 40 percent of this retail price.

The bears were an immediate success. Everyone was buying. It was not just young children who were fascinated.

The distributor reported that people were beginning to ask for additional clothing for the bears. Ollie wondered about starting a division to manufacture the bears' clothing only. It could be distributed through the same outlets that sold the bears. The clothes basically fit any similarly sized doll or stuffed animal. Apparently customers chose a bear for its unique facial features and markings. Then they asked the retail clerks to switch the clothing that they liked from one bear to another, if a particular outfit suited their taste. Some people went so far as to ask for custom-made clothing as well as custom-made expressions on the bears' faces.

At her current capacity, Ollie made every effort to fulfill the custom orders at no additional cost. She felt that the six-week lead time for an order was enough deterrent.

Larger custom orders made materials purchases easier. For example, local clubs and institutions had requested several of the bears dressed identically for giveaways and special occasions. These kinds of orders were usually for the eight-inch bear and Ollie felt that she could discount the price because of the economies of larger materials purchases for identically dressed bears.

**MATERIALS**

So far, Ollie was able to purchase materials locally at discount houses where remnants of larger bolts were plentiful. Fur could be purchased for about $8.70 per pound based on the quality and deterioration of the piece. The nature of the remnants dictated that only about 20 bears came from one piece of material. Different materials added to the unique nature of the toys; however, the selection process was time-consuming for Ollie.

On average, the largest bear required 0.75 pounds of fur. The twelve- and eight-inch bears consumed an average of one-half pound of fur. Ollie purchased fur monthly for storage on her premises and there was no limit to local supply.

Ollie had the option of purchasing overseas for about $5 per pound, shipped to her warehouse. The only snag was that the minimum order size was 50,000 pounds for each dye lot that she chose. There was the added complication that the delivered product could be a shade different than the dye swatch that she had chosen from the salesman. Fur would not deteriorate significantly over years of holding in inventory. Panda bears necessitated both white and black fur. Although brown bears constituted approximately 90 percent of previous sales, there was a fair demand for pandas.

Clothing materials could be purchased locally for about $1 per metre. Shipped from overseas, the fabric would cost only $0.50 per metre; however, minimum order quantities were approximately 1,000 metres per fabric. Purchasing clothing materials from overseas would necessitate dressing most of the bears in the same fabric, if not the same design of clothing. She wondered how she could maintain a wide variety of outfits, yet benefit from volume orders. Ollie thought that some sort of jersey material would best suit most of her designs. It now cost about $0.75 per outfit for materials.

**THE MANUFACTURING PROCESS**

The factory was large enough to hold both the warehouse and the manufacturing facilities that would be required. All labour would have to be paid $5 per hour to start.

**Cutting**

Ollie would move the cutting table from her home to the factory. It was really a modified ping-pong table that could be extended to hold 10 metres of cloth at a time. Ollie could cut about 20 outfits of clothes per day herself. Although she had not tried it yet, she realized that she could pile the cloth in layers to increase the capacity of the cutting operation. For example, two layers would double the output from the cutting operation. She wondered how many layers would efficiently meet her demand. In some operations that she had studied, there had been up to 20 layers of cloth per cutting. These operations, however, manufactured the identical design in all 20 layers. The fabric colour or pattern could be different from layer to layer. Ollie had 50 different articles of clothing for the bears, excluding custom designs.

Cutting one layer of fur allowed her to put out pieces for 30 bears per day. She had tried layering the fur for the cutting operation and had found that more than two layers would not work because the fur was too thick. She could redesign the bears in order to increase output; however, the sophisticated look of the bears was compromised. Redesign increased the capacity of both the cutting and the sewing operations by 50 percent.

**Sewing**

Ollie's home sewers could construct between four and six bears per day, on average. The bears were sewn, "finished," and stuffed at home. She had been paying them at the rate of $5 per bear.

The home sewers varied in both the quality and quantity of their output, based on the number of distractions that they encountered in a day. If one of the sewers had a sick child home from school, production was delayed by the length of the illness. Holiday times and special occasions saw a drastic decrease in output. On the other hand, for the very reasons that lowered output, most good sewers preferred to work out of their homes. By staying home, the women eliminated day care costs and were always home to meet older children after school. When the home sewers hurried to make up their weekly production, quality was compromised. This caused problems as Ollie had no time to check quality until she was shipping the bears.

In a factory setting, Ollie believed that each operator could put out no more than 10 bears per day, working on an individual basis. Ollie knew that she could organize a sewing process whereby one sewer attached one piece of the bear only, and then passed the unfinished piece on to the next sewer in the line. This line process would double the rate of output.

The bear's clothes varied in sewing time depending on the number of seams in the design. The clothes were extremely complicated when compared to those from other similar manufacturers. Ollie not only had no time to simplify the designs, but she also believed that the clothes were in large part responsible for the huge success of the bears. Home sewers were paid $2 per outfit and could produce approximately eight outfits per day. By running batches of clothes, the factory could produce about 300 outfits per day with 10 sewers. Industrial sewing machines would cost $2,000 each.

Ollie had decided that home sewers would not be viable for the clothing. Bears could be sewn at home, but the clothing would have to be produced on the premises.

The clothes really presented the largest problem in terms of production. While any bear could wear any outfit, the outfits had to be produced in batches in order to maintain a good mix of shipped bears. If there were 50 separate articles of clothing, then 1,200 bears, in theory, wore the same design. She decided to use a level production schedule and store the finished clothes in available warehouse space. As the bears were shipped, they could be dressed differently from the finished goods inventory.

**Stuffing**

After the bears' outers were sewn, and before they were dressed, they were stuffed with a material that cost about $0.50 per bear. About eight bears per hour could be stuffed by one stuffer.

**Finishing**

There were two finishing processes. The first had to be done right after the heads were sewn. Specially purchased eyes were hand sewn onto the face.

The nose was hand-embroidered and the face was "marked" with scissor cuts and liquid embroidery in order to give each bear unique features. Any expression could be accomplished.

The second finishing process was the embroidering of little paw markings on both the upper and lower extremities of the bear. This meant that each bear had its own "paw print."

Ollie wondered if she could locate the head and paw finishing processes somewhere in the sewing line so that a completely finished (marked and embroidered) bear could be passed to the next sewer. It would be easier to embroider the paws if the extremities were not attached to the body.

The combined finishing processes took 15 minutes to complete by hand. Finishers required no more skill than sewers. Thus, the positions could be rotated for the same salary.

Both finishing processes could be automated by the purchase of a button-hole machine and an embroidering machine. The combined cost of one set of machines (one button-holer and one embroidering machine) was $5,500. With these machines, the finishing processes, including markings and cuttings, would be reduced to five minutes per bear on average. One sewer did both processes, using both machines simultaneously because the machines were programmable to embroider in different patterns.

The number of patterns of embroidering that could be held by the memory in the machines was 15. This factor reduced the uniqueness of the bears to an identical bear in every 15.

### Dressing

Dressing the bears took from 60 seconds to 5 minutes depending on the number and variety of fasteners on the bear's outfit. Ollie felt that this station could also inspect the completed bears and garments.

### SUMMARY

"Wait a minute, Ollie. I have been thinking about this. It's going to take a lot of cash to start this up. You must have lost your mind! I smell rotten bananas!" Her husband had returned from his poker game. No doubt the boys had fed him intravenously with stories of doom!

"That's why I need your help to calculate the costs of this thing. I need to know whether or not I should raise the price of the bears in order to figure out if I should go ahead."

Maybe she could get him involved and interested. After all, he was taking Business some-number-or-other in an evening class at the university. All she had heard about the course so far was that he had this gorgeous instructor who had four children and was absolutely brilliant and very modest to boot.

"I have figured out the things that I need to know. I just don't know how to do the calculations. Where do we start?"

"Ollie dear, bring me the cat and the cat's pyjamas. I have a better idea!"

## C A S E  6.4  DOFASCO INC.: STORES AND MAINTENANCE MANAGEMENT (A)

In 1985, the general foremen of stores and maintenance of Dofasco Inc., Hamilton, Ontario, approached senior management with their concerns about the management of maintenance and related activities in the plant. The senior managers subsequently appointed a task force to investigate inventory control in maintenance, stores, and purchasing. Dofasco's facilities were growing and becoming increasingly complex. The challenge was how to continue to maintain good service to those departments that used the stores and maintenance service, while using resources more efficiently. Outside observers had praised the current system, but some problems were becoming evident. The question was: how could the system be improved?

**BACKGROUND**

Dofasco Steel was a large, fully integrated steel company whose operations extended from mining, through smelting and processing, to production of steel products such as coils, sheets, plates, and galvanized and specialty steels ready for use directly by metal stampers and other manufacturers. Dofasco's steel-making facilities were on a 320-hectare site adjacent to the waterfront in Hamilton. Dofasco was Canada's largest producer of flat-rolled steel and accounted for over 25 percent of Canada's total steel production. In 1984, Dofasco sold 3,319,000 tons of steel for about $1,925 million and earned $180 million. At the end of 1984, Dofasco had $2,100 million of fixed assets ($1,100 million net). The company had just embarked on a $750 million capital investment program designed to modernize the plant and build a continuous casting facility due for completion in 1987.

Since 1979, Dofasco had been growing about 6 percent per year (in sales), but only 0.8 percent per year in tons of steel sold; the main growth had been in the price of steel. Net income had averaged 8 percent of sales. This performance had been achieved through a period of severe recession in the Canadian economy. Management attributed Dofasco's success to its concentration on steel for consumer durables in a highly competitive environment. In 1985, the plant was operating at or near capacity 24 hours per day, seven days per week. Like all steel companies, Dofasco produced more steel than it sold, the balance being scrap, most of which was recycled.

Dofasco's production process set it apart from competitors. Most steel facilities poured molten steel into ingots, which were then cooled and placed in decoupling inventory. These ingots, were subsequently reheated and rolled into finished products. Dofasco's process significantly reduced the decoupling inventory between ingot manufacture and hot rolling because it transported ingots to the hot rolling mill while they were still hot. Dofasco's process managed to save most of the costs of reheating and the holding costs of the decoupling inventory, but required better coordination. Although the company preferred not to, it could use a decoupling inventory, if necessary. The planned continuous casting unit would displace 50 percent of its ingot production because, in essence, molten steel would be poured into one continuous slab that would feed directly into the hot rolling mill.

Dofasco prided itself on its relations with employees and the Hamilton community. The company strongly supported community activities, including the Hamilton Tiger Cats professional football team, and owned a 40-hectare recreation complex for employees. The approximately 12,000 employees were not represented by a union. For years the company's slogan had been: "Our product is steel. Our strength is people."

## MAINTENANCE, STORES, AND PURCHASING

In 1984, maintenance employed 3,500 people, and was estimated to cost over $230 million per year, $99 million of which was for direct maintenance labour, and $60 million for purchases. Maintenance staff carried out routine preventive maintenance and overhauls, as well as repairing inoperative equipment. About 30,000 maintenance jobs were performed per year. The maintenance function held an inventory of $150 million. Inventory data were kept on cards, which were also available in a microfiche format (updated biweekly) so that potential users could check availability, location, etc. Dofasco's maintenance operation had 225,000 such cards, one for each stock-keeping unit of common items. Staff estimated that inventory records were well over 90 percent accurate. Most of the stores sites were open 40 hours per week, but the two or three that held the fast-moving, important items were open at all times. Stores staff had access to closed stores sites in emergencies.

Materials were stored in 15 locations on the Hamilton site and another for large items a few kilometres away. An individual stock-keeping unit was usually held in a single location, but could be in as many as five stores sites at once. Uncommon maintenance requirements were purchased as needed.

Each week plant stores processed 8,500 withdrawal requisitions, 300 returns, 350 employee sales, and 1,500 decontrolled requisitions.

## Ordering

When the inventory of an item reached the pre-established re-order point, plant stores created a purchase requisition (1,100 per week) by photocopying the inventory card and adding order information. Plant stores approved about half of the purchase requisitions directly and sent them to purchasing. The other half were sent to the supervisor of the using department for approval by several people, depending on its value. If there were no problems with the requisition, all approvals could be obtained in four weeks.

However, if questions were asked, information changed, or there were cancellations, the process could be much longer. From time to time a purchase requisition would be misplaced, sometimes for several months, and, occasionally, lost permanently.

*Purchasing*

Upon receipt of an approved purchase requisition, purchasing ordered the item from an approved vendor. Some items were purchased from blanket orders (organized by item family), others required preparation of a purchase order, and still others required price quotations. In the latter case, the price could cause a change in the purchase requisition and thus start a second round of approvals. The growing clerical staff in purchasing processed the purchase orders manually.

*Receiving*

When an item was received at the storeroom, the staff added receiving information to the packing slip and forwarded it to the stores office where the information was added to the inventory card. The packing slip was subsequently forwarded to purchasing, which recorded the receipt and matched it to the relevant invoice to approve payment. Stores handled 2,400 receipts of individual or multiple items per week. Purchasing manually processed 200,000 invoices per year.

*Withdrawals*

As a first step, maintenance staff looked up procedures for each scheduled maintenance job and determined what parts and tools were required. Maintenance staff then looked the parts up on the appropriate microfiche to determine the inventory status of the items and their locations. During the morning of the day the maintenance work was to be done, maintenance staff went to the appropriate store(s) to pick up the items. The stores staff updated the inventory cards. Maintenance staff prepared a stores requisition for the needed parts. This requisition was completed by stores staff, then sent to data processing where the cost was allocated to the using department, and finally sent to finance.

**PROBLEMS**

From their investigation and from talking to others, the task force members realized that, although the current system worked, it was not without problems; some were experienced mainly by one department, whereas others were common across the system.

*Stores*

Stores personnel felt that inventory levels and the associated costs were too high. Long lead times seemed to be a major contributing factor. Management pressure on stores to reduce inventory usually led to reductions in the approximately 30 percent of stocked items that were most easily reduced.

*Maintenance*

The major problem faced by maintenance was the waiting time to get parts from stores. It was not uncommon for maintenance staff to wait at the storeroom for up to an hour while the storeroom staff served other maintenance workers. This problem arose because everyone seemed to arrive at the storerooms at the same times: early in the morning, near coffee break, and after lunch. Although the microfiche system indicated the location of parts, occasionally the storeroom would not have the needed items.

## Purchasing

Purchasing staff felt that they were unable to obtain the best prices because of increasing numbers of orders for small purchase quantities, and because they were not able to forecast, plan, and negotiate as well as they would have liked. Purchasing estimated that with better data and more rational lot sizes, they could reduce prices by about 5 percent.

## Finance

Finance spent considerable resources allocating maintenance costs to Dofasco's various cost centres and classifying stores inventory into various groups. It also had some difficulty keeping track of stores' financial status, including the year-end inventory valuation.

## CONCLUSION

As they thought about all these problems, the task force members wondered if it would make sense to try to capture all the current information in a computer system. They recognized that such a system might overcome many of the problems faced currently, but might also cause several new ones. If Dofasco did computerize its maintenance stores operations, how much might it cost, how much might it save, how should it be implemented, and how long might it take?

## C A S E 6.5   FINE FOOTWEAR LIMITED (R)

In May 1982, Rob Gianni and Joe Perella, co-owners of Fine Footwear Limited, a women's shoe manufacturer located in Toronto, Ontario, were deciding whether or not to increase production in the coming months. They wondered what effect a production increase would have on the production process, the equipment, and the labour force. They also wanted to maintain the quality of their product. In addition, an exclusive women's store had approached Fine Footwear with an offer to purchase high-fashion designer shoes. Perella, Fine Footwear's shoe designer, was excited by the opportunities this contract presented.

**COMPANY BACKGROUND**

The company began in November 1980 when Joe Perella, a shoe designer, and Rob Gianni, a shoe producer, decided to leave the shoe company where they worked and fulfill their dream of owning their own company. Perella recalled their beginnings: "We decided we wanted to have the facilities ready before we approached potential buyers, so after checking about 50 locations, we finally rented a building. At that stage, we had no buyers or orders for our shoes — just a lot of confidence." Financial assistance was obtained through the Federal Business Development Bank and a chartered bank. Twenty-one machines costing a total of $104,940 (see Exhibit 1) were ordered, and sales agents were contacted.

Production began after one worker was employed. Together, the three set out to learn how to use the machines. One thousand pairs of shoes were produced in the first six weeks. In the second and third months, production increased to 2,000 and 3,000 pairs of shoes per month as more workers were hired. As demand grew, production increased until the current monthly level of 12,000 pairs of shoes was reached in April 1982. Sales of over 40,000 pairs of shoes for the year ending December 31, 1981, exceeded $700,000.

**THE PRODUCT**

Fine Footwear Ltd. produced women's dress shoes made of a synthetic material. The company currently sold about 10 different styles of closed-toed shoes in various colours. The average pair of shoes had a retail selling price of approximately $40, a price considered low for women's shoes.

**DESIGNING AND MARKETING**

Since shoes were a clothing accessory, shoe styles closely followed the trends in the clothing industry, and the company was required to produce new styles. To stay abreast of rapidly changing styles, Perella attended trade shows in Europe and followed many trade journals. He noted: "A shoe designer should also be a marketer — he must know what is selling." Accordingly, Perella had close contact with his two sales agents, one who sold in Ontario, and the other in Quebec. The agents received a selling commission of 10 percent on manufacturer's sales, but did not work exclusively for Fine Footwear Ltd.

The company's trade customers consisted of five chain stores, one of which was a very large Canadian retailer that accounted for over half of Fine Footwear's sales. Most chains carried Fine Footwear's shoes under a private brand name, although one large chain also carried a line of Fine Footwear shoes. Sales were fairly steady throughout the year. Orders usually ranged from 500 to 3,000 pairs, with an average order size of 1,500 pairs. Most orders consisted of three different styles of shoes. Some chains ordered regularly each month, some ordered only twice a year, while others ordered at various times throughout the year. It usually took three months from the placing of an order until delivery, but orders could be completed faster if required. A few customers in the past had been upset when the shoes that they had ordered were out of style by the time they were delivered. According to Perella, shoppers looked for a quality product in popular styles to fit their needs at an affordable price.

## LABOUR

The workforce consisted of 33 nonunionized factory employees (mostly female) and one part-time bookkeeper. Keeping employees was sometimes difficult, as some workers would last only one day. New workers started wherever a vacancy occurred in the production process. The highest turnover of new employees occurred on the lasting conveyor line which was also the most complex job. Workers without previous shoemaking experience were usually not able to acquire the skills quickly enough to satisfy Gianni. Yet it was difficult to find experienced workers and expensive to hire them.

The hourly wage rate varied from $3.65 to $8 (averaging $6) depending on the task and the worker's experience. The company was currently operating on a single shift basis of 45 hours per week. Most employees worked this shift from 7:30 to 17:00, Monday to Friday, with half-hour lunches and two 10-minute breaks.[1] Some employees also worked overtime (at one and a half times the regular pay) by working a half-day on Saturdays or by working from 7:00 to 18:00 on some days, as required. Some firms in the industry used full-time second shifts at a wage premium of 25 percent over day wages. At present there were no bonus incentives. Most employees could perform several jobs and were frequently required to do so because of absenteeism. As a result, workers would have to stop working at one station to help with orders at other stations.

## INVENTORY AND SCHEDULING

Once an order was placed by one of the chain stores, materials were ordered, usually from the United States, Italy, or Germany, and arrived four to ten weeks later. Only the most basic raw material (such as soles and heel material) inventories were kept in stock in order to keep the inventory as low as possible. Work-in-process inventory could be found throughout the plant at various stages of assembly. See Exhibit 2 for a diagram of the plant layout. In fact, it seemed as if most of the available floor space in the occupied portion of the plant was taken up with either machinery or work-in-process inventory. Most of this inventory was located on trays and stacked on carts (which held about 50 pairs of shoes) that could be wheeled from operation to operation or was moved around on a conveyor during the lasting operation. (A last was a plastic form in the shape of a foot.) Finished goods (which were shipped f.o.b. factory)[2] were held until the customer arranged for delivery.

After all of the raw materials had arrived for the order, Gianni arranged the production scheduling and tried to balance the line if any bottlenecks developed by moving workers from one area to another. From past experience he was able to determine approximately how long an order would take to complete, and this information was used to arrange a production schedule. Because 10 different styles were offered in a range of colours, many orders were often being worked on at the same time. For example, 11 different orders were currently in various stages of production throughout the factory. From the time work actually started on an order of shoes to the time they were completed, a month usually went by, although a rush order could be completed in one week.

## PRODUCTION PROCESS

Fine Footwear Ltd. produced only women's dress shoes. (Manufacture of men's shoes, running shoes, and other types of shoes required a completely different production process.) The process for this particular type of women's dress shoe involved cutting, preparation, soling and heeling, lasting, and finishing. Shoes were made of two distinct parts, the sole and the upper, which were produced separately and then attached at the lasting operation. A one-page/one-copy production order, made up by Gianni (see Exhibit 3), accompanied each order as it proceeded through the production process.

### Cutting

Two people were involved in the cutting operation, each working on a cutting machine. These machines, acting as "cookie-cutters," could each cut material for about 250 pairs of shoes per day. Soles, linings, and any extra material to be placed on the shoes (such as tassels) were cut from a large sheet of material. The soles were cut to resemble the shape of a footprint, while the lining was cut into the shape of a thick "V." About 40 to 50 soles could be cut from a typical piece of material. If the shapes were cut too far apart (as sometimes occurred), wastage resulted. After cutting, the soles were taken to the soling area, and the lining and tassels were moved to the preparation area. The production order accompanied the lining and tassels.

### Preparation

Twelve people worked on various machines in the preparation area. First of all, a thin piece of reinforcement material was attached to the lining. After these pieces had been pressed together, this flat piece was bent (or "closed") into the shape of a shoe with no bottom to make an "upper." After each upper was folded on the folding machine, the size and lot number were stamped on it. Over a two-day period, this area could produce 1,500 pairs of uppers. Additional reinforcements were attached inside the toe, and then the reinforcements and lining were stitched together on one of the four sewing machines. Any extra material was trimmed and the uppers were sized and placed in containers, ready to be brought to the lasting area. The production order was taped to one of the containers.

### Soling and Heeling

In the soling area the soles were first trimmed around the edges by a trimming machine, then sprayed with black paint and left to dry on a rack. Next the soles were "split" (formed to the shape of the shoe) and cemented with glue. Finally the soles were put in a bin and carried to the press (in the lasting area).

In the heeling area, glue was placed on the tops of the heels (either cut in the factory or bought pre-cut), which were then placed in a rack and taken to the press. With the existing equipment and labour, the soling and heeling area could produce, at most, 520 pairs of soles and heels each day.

### Lasting

It was in the lasting area that the upper, the sole, and the heel became a shoe. Nine operators used nine machines (Exhibit 4) to perform the seven operations in the lasting process. The shoes went through the lasting process in pairs. Each operation, except the drying oven, took on average one minute (including move time) for each pair of shoes because both machine and worker needed the full minute to complete the operation. The lasting operation produced 60 pairs of shoes per work hour. The operation in which the heel and sole were attached to the upper was the one area where the procedure sometimes did not work smoothly. Sometimes the workers could not find the right bins of heels or racks of soles, even though the production order was with the uppers. At other times, the soles and heels had not yet been produced, or were still in the soling and heeling area of the plant.

In the first step, an insole (the inside bottom of the shoe) was stapled onto a last. The insoles were purchased from an outside supplier, while the company owned about 550 pairs of re-usable lasts, each pair costing about $24. Next, a counter (the inner material located at the back of the shoe) was placed in latex glue and cemented to the insole. Then, nails from a nailing machine were placed along the edge of the insole and more glue was applied. Next, the upper was placed over the last, nailed onto the insole, and cement and filler added to ensure a good bond between the two sections. After this process had been completed, the shoes were placed in a slowly rotating oven (which could hold 36 pairs at a time) for 15 minutes in order to dry and shape them. Then the heel and the outer sole, after having been placed in a small heating element to reactivate the cement, were pressed onto the insole. Finally, the last was taken out of the shoe and the final nails were placed in the heel. The shoes were then placed on a cart and wheeled to the finishing area. One worker was responsible for moving the lasts from the end of the line to the beginning of the next process.

*Finishing*

In the finishing area, one person placed a sock lining inside the shoe and performed the final cutting and stapling. Two others then cleaned the shoes, removing any excess glue, and touching them up with colour, if needed. The shoes were taken to a table for final inspection. Finally, they were placed in boxes, which were hand stamped with the size, colour, and customer number, before being closed and placed in the shipping area. See Exhibit 4 for a job breakdown of the workers. The finishing area could handle 2,750 pairs of shoes in a five-day period.

**FUTURE OUTLOOK**

After two years of operation, Gianni and Perella estimated that, with next year's forecasted growth in demand from existing chain store customers, a production level of between 700 and 800 pairs of shoes a day could be warranted; however, they were concerned with becoming too dependent on any one customer. Perella was interested in orders for high fashion shoes that would retail at a price level that was significantly higher than the price of Fine Footwear's current product. Adding these new products to their production line could mean up to 20 orders monthly for exclusive designs, with 50 pairs of shoes per order. Material costs would be substantially higher than those of current shoes. Labour costs would also increase due to the higher quality that this product would demand. In addition, designs would change monthly to meet the demands of high fashion. Perella wanted to try some new designs that were not suitable for their current market.

Because only two-thirds of the 960 square metres of floor space was currently being used, they decided that they had room to expand. However, they realized they might eventually have to add another shift or move to a new location. If daily production were increased to 700 or 800 pairs of shoes, new employees might have to be hired and other production changes required. See Exhibit 5 for cost breakdowns. The owners were also concerned with the effect that an increase in production would have on the quality of their product. Having quickly developed a successful and profitable organization, Gianni and Perella were wondering how to proceed with their plans for expansion.

## NOTES

1. Workers were paid for the two 10-minute breaks but not for the 1/2-hour lunch. This was standard industry practice.

2. f.o.b. = free on board. Supplier delivers goods to a specified point and pays all transport costs to that point. In this case, the point is the supplier's factory loading dock, that is, the buyers had to pay for transportation.

**EXHIBIT 1**
**Equipment Costs**

| | | | |
|---|---|---|---:|
| 2 cutting machines | $13,280 | each | $26,560 |
| Lining, pressing and bending machine | | | 6,500 |
| Folding machine | | | 6,800 |
| 4 sewing machines | 1,120 | each | 4,480 |
| Trimming machine | | | 10,490 |
| Splitting machine | | | 11,500 |
| Heel cutter | | | 3,700 |
| | | | |
| Stapler | 2,300 | | |
| Cement applicator | 4,800 | | |
| Nailing machine | 1,750 | | |
| Cement applicator | 4,800 | | |
| Nailing machine | 1,750 | | |
| Fill machine | 980 | | |
| Oven | 11,420 | | |
| Press | 3,967 | | |
| Nailing machine | 1,750 | | |
| | | | 33,517 |
| | | | |
| Stapler | | | 1,393 |
| | | | $104,940 |

**EXHIBIT 2**
*Plant Layout*

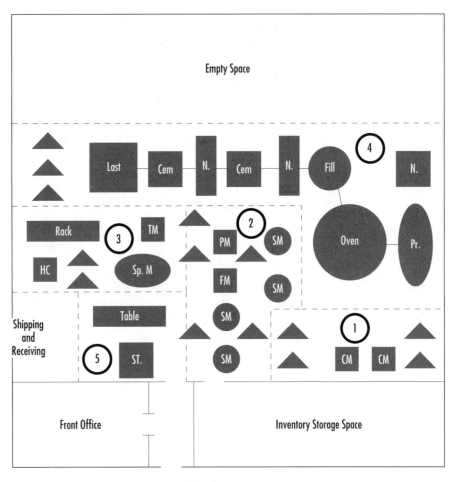

Empty Space

Last Cem N. Cem N. Fill N.

Oven Pr.

Rack TM

HC Sp. M

PM SM

FM SM

SM

CM CM

Table

Shipping and Receiving

ST.

Front Office

Inventory Storage Space

① Cutting Area

② Preparation Area

③ Soling and Heeling Area

④ Lasting Area

⑤ Finishing Area

**Machine Key**

| | |
|---|---|
| CM | CUTTING MACHINES |
| PM | LINING, PRESSING, BENDING MACHINE |
| FM | FOLDING MACHINE |
| SM | SEWING MACHINES |
| TM | TRIMMING MACHINES |
| Sp.M | SPLITTING MACHINE |
| HC | HEEL CUTTER |
| Last | LASTING AND STAPLER |
| Cem | CEMENT APPLICATOR |
| N. | NAILING MACHINE |
| Fill | FILL MACHINE |
| Oven | ROTATING OVEN |
| Pr | PRESS |
| Table | FINISHING TABLE |
| ST | STAPLER AND INSPECTION TABLE |
| △ | WORK-IN-PROCESS INVENTORY |

**EXHIBIT 3**
**Production Order**

Nº **6491**

STYLE NO. __45201__

CUSTOMER _____          DATE __JULY 1/82__

COLOUR __BLACK CALF__                       SOCK STAMP _____

DESCRIPTION __GREY LINING__

| SIZE | 5 | -- | 6 | -- | 7 | -- | 8 | -- | 9 | -- | 10 | TOTAL |
|------|---|----|----|----|----|----|----|----|----|----|----|-------|
| PAIRS | 1 | | 1 | 2 | 3 | 3 | 3 | 2 | 2 | | 1 | 18 |

LAST __452__          SOLE __BLACK__          HEEL __491D__

**EXHIBIT 4**

## Job Breakdown

| Operation | Number of Workers |
|-----------|-------------------|
| ▪ Cutting | ▪  2 workers |
| ▪ Preparation | ▪ 12 workers |
| ▪ Soles and heeling | ▪  2 workers on soles<br>▪  2 workers on heels |
| ▪ Lasting | ▪  1 worker on lasts<br>▪  9 workers on machines |
| ▪ Finishing | ▪  1 worker on socks<br>▪  2 workers on cleaning |
| ▪ Shipping/Receiving Inventory | ▪  1 worker |
| ▪ Boxing/Stapling | ▪  1 worker |
| | 33 workers |

*EXHIBIT 5*

| Cost Sheet | |
|---|---|
| **Labour** | $3.65–$8.00 per hour ($6.00 average) |
| **Material** | $10.15 per pair on average |

| MONTHLY COSTS: | |
|---|---|
| Maintenance, cleaning, repairs | $    480 |
| Factory rent | 3,600 |
| Heat, light, power | 1,200 |
| Bookkeeper | 500 |
| Management salaries (Gianni, Perella) | 4,280 |
| Travel expenses | 2,500 |
| Interest charges | 1,313 |
| Depreciation expenses (10 yr life) | 875 |
| Total monthly costs | $14,748 |

# C A S E 6.6   GARLIC'S

In January 1994, Kathy Burns, owner of Garlic's Restaurant in London, Ontario, had to make some decisions to ensure her first month's high sales figures would translate into long-term success. In particular, she wanted to improve the current dinner reservation system, which she believed was hindering customer service. Burns also wondered if any other changes should be made.

**COMPANY BACKGROUND**

Kathy Burns finished her MBA at the Western Business School in April 1993. Before entering the MBA program, she had worked 10 years in the restaurant and beverage industry, including six years at Western Food Services at the University of Western Ontario. She had always dreamed of owning a restaurant; her dream came true on December 2, 1993, when the doors of Garlic's opened. Garlic's, considered a bistro, focused 60 percent of its menu items on garlic and international cuisine. Burns's vision was to serve excellent food at a reasonable price and provide superior customer service in an informal, comfortable ambience. Her business plan outlined some goals of Garlic's: in the short-term, she wanted to provide customer and employee satisfaction and maintain a 10 percent return on investment; in the long-term, she wanted to grow through expansion to other locations. The restaurant was situated two doors north of the Grand Theatre, London's major theatre, on Richmond Street, in downtown London. London had a population of 315,000 and was located along Highway 401, the major east-west artery through southern Ontario. The city was home to The University of Western Ontario and the head offices of many companies, including Labatt's Brewery and Canada Trust. Richmond Row, approximately eight blocks of Richmond Street from Oxford Street to Queen's Avenue, consisted of many restaurants and retail shops and was generally considered to be the trendy part of town. Burns believed Garlic's close proximity to the theatre would provide a stable dinner crowd and the many office buildings in the downtown core would provide a stable lunch crowd.

**THE GRAND THEATRE**

The Grand Theatre season was from October to May and attracted not only Londoners but also out-of-towners. All evening performances started at 8 p.m. and Wednesday and Saturday matinées started at 2 p.m. Patrons of the theatre had formerly been middle-age with middle to upper income levels, but over the past few years the theatre clientele had changed to reflect the general population. For example, the Grand Theatre produced children's plays as well as provocative productions to mature audiences and targeted students with discounts on ticket prices.

**THE CONSUMER**

Burns offered high quality food combined with a reasonable price to fit with the 1990s customer perception of value. (Garlic's menu is shown in Exhibit 1.) In addition, for a restaurant to be successful it had to combine the food and price with an appealing atmosphere. Various atmospheres ranged from classy and elegant fine dining to lively, relaxed, and casual dining. The atmosphere of Garlic's was considered informal, comfortable, lively, and cosmopolitan. During the day, Garlic's clientele were business people with a one-hour lunch break. Burns noted that some of her business lunch customers also visited Garlic's for dinner. Dinner customers, the majority being the pre-theatre crowd, usually took two hours to dine as they ordered drinks and coffee and, in many cases, ordered dessert. Dinners and lunches represented 70 percent and 30 percent, respectively, of Garlic's sales.

**FOOD PREPARATION AND SERVICING CUSTOMERS**

The food was prepared for anticipated demand. For example, pasta was bought in individual portions, and when an order from the server was brought to the kitchen, the pasta was cooked to order in a spaghetti magic machine. The longest preparation time for any menu item was pizza, which took 10 to 12 minutes. Burns wanted to serve as many customers as possible while still giving the customer an enjoyable experience. Burns believed that an enjoyable experience created word-of-mouth advertising and generated repeat business. Burns's time estimation of a dinner for two is shown in Exhibit 2.

**HIGH SALES IN DECEMBER**

Sales in December totalled $80,000, surpassing optimistic expectations by $24,000. Burns believed that the restaurant's success in December was due to several factors. First, Garlic's was the first new downtown restaurant to open since the Blue Plate had opened in September 1992. (Location of Garlic's and competitors is shown in Exhibit 3.) Second, the location of Garlic's on Richmond Street gave it high visibility, not only to Grand Theatre patrons, but also to walk-by traffic. Third, December is traditionally a busy time of year for restaurants because of the celebratory mood of people. From her 1994 projected income statement, Burns projected fixed costs of $285,000 and a net profit after tax of $79,000, assuming an optimistic sales figure of $600,000. Variable cost was projected at 35 percent of sales.

**THE RESERVATION SYSTEM**

Garlic's used a reservation system that booked all 25 tables. Currently, Burns or any staff member answering the phone recorded the customer's request on the reservation time-table. When a dinner party first arrived at Garlic's, they would either be seated by the host or asked to sit at the bar until their table was ready. There were 12 bar stools to accommodate waiting patrons. Burns described some difficult moments during the dinner hours in December:

> We were pretty much booked solid Thursday, Friday, and Saturday. We had situations in which five people were coming in and we had reserved a table for two people. We had people claiming they had a reservation, but we didn't have anything in our books. We had people showing up Saturday and their reservation in our book was for Friday. As well, we had people complaining that, even though they had booked a week and a half ago, they had terrible seats by the washrooms.

One of Burns's experienced waiters had suggested that Garlic's not reserve tables at 7 p.m. Although 7 p.m. was the most popular time to dine, the next available time the table was vacant, 9 p.m., was too late for people to start dining. In addition to not reserving tables at 7 p.m., Burns thought she should decrease the number of reservations to desirable seating only. Garlic's seating capacity was limited to approximately 80 seats. Changing reservations would be a trial and error approach, and the first step was to decide which seats were undesirable. (Garlic's seating plan is shown in Exhibit 4.)

## OTHER CONSIDERATIONS

During December, Burns gave menus and business cards to customers turned away at the door and encouraged them to phone and make reservations the next time they wished to dine. The menus were rolled with a bow and cost $0.30 each. One thousand business cards cost $189.75. Burns gave out 210 cards and menus in December. She gave menus to potential customers with the hope that they would see the value and return at a later date.

Other options to meet or suppress demand included raising prices or expanding upstairs. If she raised prices, Burns wondered how high to raise them to match the competition. Garlic's nine major competitors and their prices are shown in Exhibit 5. The cost of renovating the upstairs would be about $30,000 and would be ideal to cater to large groups. Garlic's had received many calls from patrons requesting office parties and Burns was unable to accommodate these requests because she wanted Garlic's to be available to the public on a daily basis. The only stairway to the second floor was through the next door neighbour's antique store and Burns would need to solve this problem if she expanded.

There were other concerns. Some customers had complained that the food was not always hot enough when delivered to the table. Burns thought she might need a plate warmer at the cost of $125 and/or a bus person to help in the food delivery. This bus person would work on Thursday, Friday, and Saturday from 5:30 p.m. to 10:30 p.m. and would earn $5.80 per hour.

Burns was unsure which options she should implement, but she knew she wanted to make her first month's high sales totals the first step to long-term success. While Burns, married with two daughters, welcomed the high sales, she wondered how long she could sustain working 90 hours a week.

Yet, in such a competitive market Burns knew she had to ensure customer satisfaction and keep the customers coming back. She commented:

> We've been very successful to date; however, people are curious about new restaurants. I want to ensure Garlic's future and keep our customers returning for many years.

EXHIBIT 1
Garlic's Menu

## MENU

### DIPS & BREADS

**TZATZIKI**
a garlicky cucumber & yogurt dip originally
from Greece . . . . . . . . . . . . . . . . . . . . . . . . . . .$3.95

**CROSTINI**
a baguette topped with a savory mixture of black olives,
pine nuts and garlic, baked in our oven . . . . . . . .$3.95

**BRIE AND GARLIC TOASTS**
roasted garlic and brie spread on a french stick and
melted under the broiler . . . . . . . . . . . . . . . . . . .$4.25

**BAGNO CALDO**
a warm anchovy and garlic dip characteristic
of Northern Italy . . . . . . . . . . . . . . . . . . . . . . . . . . $4.95

**BRUSCHETTA**
tomatoes, fresh herbs and crushed garlic
served warm on a baguette . . . . . . . . . . . . . . . . . . . . $4.50

### SMALL PLATES

**SAKE STEAMED MUSSELS**
12–14 mussels steamed with sake, garlic
and ginger . . . . . . . . . . . . . . . . . . . . . . . . . . . . .$6.95

**FIVE THAI SHRIMP**
with cilantro pesto. . . . . . . . . . . . . . . . . . . . . . . .$5.95

**TRADITIONAL SMOKED SALMON**
cured and smoked in Garlic's kitchen . . . . . . . . .$6.50

**FOUR SPRING ROLLS**
served with our own
apricot-mustard sauce . . . . . . . . . . . . . . . . . . . . . . . . . $3.95

**SUNDRIED TOMATO & BRIE TRIANGLES**
four phyllo pastries served with a
lemon-sage sauce . . . . . . . . . . . . . . . . . . . . . . . . . . . $3.95

### SOUPS

CREAM OF GARLIC SOUP . . . . . . . . . . $2.50

CONCH & GARLIC CHOWDER . . . . . . . . . . . $3.95

### SALADS

**GARLIC'S CAESAR**
with lemony-garlic croutons. . . . . . . . . . . . . . . .$3.75

**GRILLED CHICKEN & SHRIMP SALAD**
with fresh fruit and a raspberry vinaigrette. . . . . .$6.25

**MIXED GREENS SALAD**
with tarragon dressing. . . . . . . . . . . . . . . . . . . . . . . . . $3.95

**CRUSTACEAN CAESAR**
mussels, scallops, shrimps and crab . . . . . . . . . . . . . . $6.95

### FULL PLATES

**GARLIC CRUSTED LOIN OF SPRING LAMB**
with madeira sauce . . . . . . . . . . . . . . . . . . . . . . . . . . . . . . . . . . . . . . . . . . . . . . . . . . . . . . . . . . . . . . . . . $12.95

**BEEF TENDERLOIN**
with oyster mushrooms. . . . . . . . . . . . . . . . . . . . . . . . . . . . . . . . . . . . . . . . . . . . . . . . . . . . . . . . . . . . . . . . . $12.95

**POACHED SALMON**
with red pepper butter. . . . . . . . . . . . . . . . . . . . . . . . . . . . . . . . . . . . . . . . . . . . . . . . . . . . . . . . . . . . . . . . . . $10.95

**BURMESE-STYLE PORK CURRY**
with fresh ginger, rice and our own mango chutney . . . . . . . . . . . . . . . . . . . . . . . . . . . . . . . . . . . . . . . . . . . $9.95

**CHICKEN BREAST**
with roast garlic and rice stuffing and an apricot-mustard sauce . . . . . . . . . . . . . . . . . . . . . . . . . . . . . . . . . . $9.95

FULL PLATES ARE SERVED DAILY FROM 5 P.M. TO 10 P.M.

*Exhibit 1 (cont'd)*

## GOURMET PIZZAS

**SMOKED SALMON**
Smoked salmon with bocconcini and mozzarella cheese, red onions, capers, dill and red peppers . . . . . . . . . . . . . . . $6.95

**CAPACOLA**
Capacola, oyster mushrooms, green peppers, black olives, plum tomatoes, and mozzarella . . . . . . . . . . . . . . . . . . . . $6.25

**PESTO**
Sundried tomatoes, artichoke hearts, grilled eggplant, roasted red peppers, mozzarella and pesto sauce . . . . . . . . . . $5.95

**THREE CHEESE**
Asiago, mozzarella, parmesan cheeses with slices of elephant garlic and tomato . . . . . . . . . . . . . . . . . . . . . . . . . . $5.50

WHEN COOKED, GARLIC NOT ONLY LOSES ITS PUNGENT AROMA AND MUCH OF ITS INTENSE FLAVOR, BUT SOME OF ITS MOLECULES ARE ACTUALLY CONVERTED INTO COMPLEX MOLECULES THAT ARE APPROXIMATELY SIXTY-THREE TIMES SWEETER THAN THOSE OF TABLE SUGAR.

## SANDWICHES

All of our sandwiches are served with Garlic's crispy potatoes.

**SHAVED ALBERTA BEEF**
served on a baguette, au jus. . . . . . . . . . . . . . . . . . . . . . . . . . . . . . . . . . . . . . . . . . . . . . . . . . . . . . . . . . . . . . . . . . $4.95

**GRILLED CHICKEN**
chicken breast, roasted garlic, grilled sweet peppers and swiss cheese served open-faced on a kaiser . . . . . . . . . . . . $5.95

**MAPLE CURED HAM**
shaved ham, grilled peppers and swiss cheese served open-faced on light rye. . . . . . . . . . . . . . . . . . . . . . . . . . . . . $5.95

**SANDWICH OF THE DAY**
ask your server for today's special . . . . . . . . . . . . . . . . . . . . . . . . . . . . . . . . . . . . . . . . . . . . . . . . . . . . . . . . . . . . . $4.50

SANDWICHES ARE SERVED DAILY UNTIL 3 P.M.

CRUSHED GARLIC HAS ABOUT THREE TIMES THE IMPACT OF CHOPPED OR MINCED.

## PASTAS

**SMOKED SALMON FETTUCINI**
Fettucini with smoked salmon in a lemon, garlic and saffron cream sauce . . . . . . . . . . . . . . . . . . . . . . . . . . . . . . . $7.50

**CHICKEN LINGUINI**
Linguini with chicken, snow peas, and sundried tomatoes in a light cream sauce . . . . . . . . . . . . . . . . . . . . . . . . . . $6.95

**EGGPLANT RAVIOLI**
Ravioli stuffed with eggplant served with slivers of crispy onions and drizzled with a lemon-sage sauce . . . . . . . . . $6.25

**ROASTED GARLIC PENNE**
Penne with roasted garlic, peppers, wild mushrooms and black olives, in a basil pesto sauce. . . . . . . . . . . . . . . . . . $6.25

**SEAFOOD FETTUCINI**
Fettucini with jumbo shrimp, scallops and mussels in a tomato sauce . . . . . . . . . . . . . . . . . . . . . . . . . . . . . . . . . . $7.50

**EXHIBIT 1 (cont'd)**

# DESSERTS

ALL OF OUR DESSERTS ARE AVAILABLE IN FULL OR HALF PORTIONS WITH
THE EXCEPTION OF THE ICE DREAMS AND THE CHEESE PLATE.

## FOR CHOCOLATE LOVERS

CHOCOLATE PATE
a slice of Belgian chocolate mousse accompanied by raspberry and passion fruit sauce . . . . . . . . . . . . . . . . . . . . . . . $3.95

TUXEDO SWIRL
a creamy white and dark chocolate filling in a macaroon pastry crust . . . . . . . . . . . . . . . . . . . . . . . . . . . . . . . . . . $3.95

ORANGE CHOCOLATE TORTE
layers of chocolate and white cake with an orange bavarian cream filling . . . . . . . . . . . . . . . . . . . . . . . . . . . . . $3.95

DEATH BY CHOCOLATE
a three layer chocolate cake with creamy icing—imported from Cakewalkers . . . . . . . . . . . . . . . . . . . . . . . . . . . $4.95

## ON THE LIGHTER SIDE

ASSORTED SORBETS AND ICE CREAMS
please ask your server to describe the flavours of the day . . . . . . . . . . . . . . . . . . . . . . . . . . . . . . . . . . . . . . . . . . $1.95

SEASONAL FRANGIPANE
a warm slice of seasonal fruit flan with a crumbly topping . . . . . . . . . . . . . . . . . . . . . . . . . . . . . . . . . . . . . . . . . $3.50

ASSORTED CHEESES & FRESH FRUIT PLATE . . . . . . . . . . . . . . . . . . . . . . . . . . . . . . . . . . . . . . . . . . . . . . . . . . . $4.50

## AND FINALLY ...

PECAN PIE . . . . . . . . . . . . . . . . . . . . . . . . . . . . . . . . . . . . . . . . . . . . . . . . . . . . . . . . . . . . . . . . . . . . . . . . . . . $4.25

CHEESECAKE
New York style with pralines . . . . . . . . . . . . . . . . . . . . . . . . . . . . . . . . . . . . . . . . . . . . . . . . . . . . . . . . . . . . . $4.50

GARLIC ICE CREAM
served with chocolate dipped roast garlic—an adventure worth sampling . . . . . . . . . . . . . . . . . . . . . . . . . . . . . $2.50

## BEVERAGES

| | | | |
|---|---|---|---|
| COFFEE / TEA | $1.50 | CAPPUCCINO | $2.50 |
| MILK | $1.50 | POP | $1.25 |
| JUICE | $1.50 | ESPRESSO | $1.75 |

*Exhibit 2*
*Timing of Dinner*
*for Two*

| Time | Process |
|------|---------|
| 0:00 | guests arrive |
| 0:01 | guests seated with menus |
| 0:04 | water served and drink order taken |
| 0:10 | drinks delivered |
| 0:11 | guests ask questions and order food |
| 0:14 | food order processed in computer |
| 0:22 | appetizers are delivered |
| 0:37 | appetizer dishes are cleared and drink refill offered |
| 0:42 | entrées are delivered |
| 0:46 | server performs quality check |
| 1:02 | entrée plates are cleared |
| 1:05 | dessert menus are delivered and coffee is ordered |
| 1:10 | coffee is delivered and dessert order is taken |
| 1:11 | dessert order processed in computer |
| 1:19 | dessert orders are delivered and coffee is replenished |
| 1:35 | dessert plates are cleared and final coffee is offered |
| 1:40 | bill is delivered |
| 1:45 | bill is processed — change is made or credit card is processed |
| 1:50 | guests leave |

*EXHIBIT 3*
*Map of Competitors*
*— Downtown*
*London*

¹ Garlic's    ³ Piccolo         ⁵ Casey's     ⁷ Joe Kool's    Mykono's Restaurant and Verandah Cafe located
² Blue Plate  ⁴ Strange Angels  ⁶ 99 King      ⁸ Willie's Cafe  a short distance east of the downtown.

**EXHIBIT 4**
*Seating Plan*

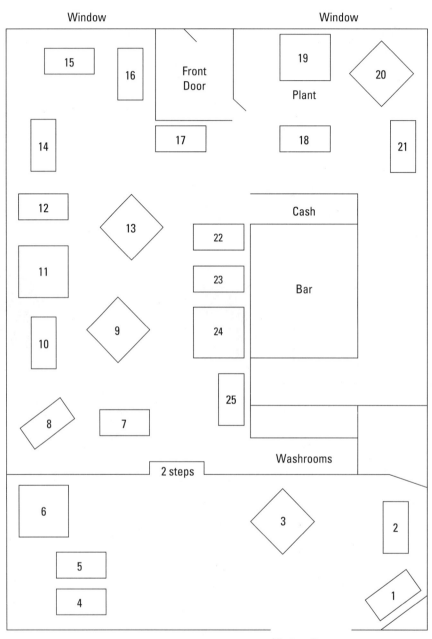

*Exhibit 5*

|  | Competition Price Comparison ($) | | | |
|---|---|---|---|---|
| Restaurant | Appetizer | Lunch | Dinner | Dessert |
| Blue Plate | 2.95 – 5.95 | 4.95 – 6.95 | 4.95 – 6.95 | 3.50 – 4.95 |
| Piccolo | 4.25 – 6.75 | 6.50 – 7.25 | 6.95 – 7.75 | 4.50 – 4.75 |
| Mykonos | 3.15 – 6.95 | 2.65 – 7.65 | 7.95 – 13.95 | |
| Strange Angels | 3.50 – 8.25 | 6.95 – 14.50 | 6.95 – 14.50 | |
| Casey's | 2.49 – 8.99 | 3.99 – 7.49 | 7.99 – 14.99 | 2.99 – 3.99 |
| 99 King | 3.00 – 7.00 | 7.00 – 13.00 | 11.00 – 22.00 | 4.25 – 4.95 |
| Verandah Cafe | | 8.95 | | |
| Joe Kool's | 2.50 – 5.95 | 3.95 – 9.95 | 3.95 – 9.95 | |
| Willies Cafe | 3.25 – 5.45 | 3.25 – 5.25 | N/A | N/A |

1. Fixed price includes appetizer and entrée.

### C A S E  6.7    HAMMOND MANUFACTURING COMPANY LIMITED[1]

Soon after Ron Hansen joined Hammond Manufacturing's Transformer Group as plant manager of the Guelph, Ontario transformer plant in July 1993, he became aware of some materials management problems involving the delivery of transformer enclosures to his plant from Hammond's cabinetry plant, located on the other side of town, about 10 km away. Late deliveries by the cabinetry plant were very frustrating. The resulting production and delivery delays by the transformer plant were unacceptable to customers. Both Mr. Hansen and Pat Evangelisto, plant manager of the cabinetry plant, believed that the main causes of late deliveries were forecasting inaccuracy, frequent changes in customer demand, scheduling techniques, and design changes. The result was wasted resources and lost sales. However, Mr. Hansen and Mr. Evangelisto were more interested in reducing the frequency of late delivery, stock-outs, backorders, and the level of frustration between their plants than in assessing blame for the problems.

**THE COMPANY**    In 1917, the Hammond family established the Hammond Manufacturing Company Limited in Guelph, Ontario, to manufacture electrical transformers for the war effort and other purposes. Although the company had recently issued shares for public trading, the Hammond family still controlled it. Over the years, sales had grown to about $140 million. The company had three operating groups of comparable size, each with its own president and operating executives. The Oil-Filled Transformer Group restricted itself to oil-filled transformers. The Cabinetry Group had a manufacturing plant in the northwest of Guelph and a 9,000 square metre warehouse in Aberfoyle, a small community about five km southeast of the Guelph transformer plant. The company's management offices were located in the Cabinetry Group's plant.

In addition to its Guelph facility, the Transformer Group had manufacturing plants in Waterloo, about 20 km west of Guelph; Walkerton, about 100 km northwest of Guelph; Baraboo, Wisconsin; and Compton, California. It produced a very large assortment of electrical transformers,[2] ranging from the miniature devices used in printed circuits and digital data processing equipment, through those used in small and large electrical appliances, to the huge units used in commercial buildings and by electrical utilities. Although each plant made a different range of transformers, there was some overlap to allow flexibility and redundancy in case of a disaster. The Baraboo, Wisconsin plant had a product line very similar to that of the Guelph plant.

Mr. Hansen's facility in the southwest of Guelph was the largest in the Transformer Group (in terms of sales). It produced six or seven dry transformer product lines (multiple products per line) for commercial applications and buildings. Although they ranged from 3 kVA[3] (weighing about 30 kg) up to 15,000 kVA (weighing 20,000 kg or more), almost all were below 7,500 kVA. One standard product line was 9-750 kVA distribution transformers, each of which was enclosed in heavy sheet-metal that was an integral part of the finished product, with several functions:

- protecting the transformer windings and bus bars carrying electricity;
- protecting the environment from that electricity;
- providing an internal mounting base for the transformer windings;
- providing an external mounting base for the assembled unit; and
- providing punch-out holes of the proper size for the conduits required to connect the transformer electrically to both the electrical source and the building to be served.

The transformer plant purchased about 10 to 15 percent of the metal enclosures produced by the cabinetry plant. The remainder went to other electrical equipment manufacturers, including each of the other Transformer Group plants. In addition, the Guelph transformer plant purchased about 25 percent of its enclosures from outside suppliers. In Mr. Hansen's words: "The cabinetry plant can't always meet our requirements for lead times or special features. It is set up to run high volumes of standard products. However, we get all our distribution transformer enclosures from there." Enclosures represented about 20 percent of the transformer plant's material purchases by value; most of the rest was raw materials rather than semi-finished or work-in-process material. Although the plant purchased other items such as lugs and thermostats, 65 to 75 percent of its material purchases were electrical steel, copper, and aluminum wire, coils, or bar stock. In total, the plant dealt with about 200 suppliers of goods and services.

**FORECASTING AND PRODUCTION PLANNING**

Each October, as part of the company's annual planning activities, the sales staff created forecasts (in dollars) for the next calendar year by product line. The Transformer Group produced 10 to 12 product lines. As the year progressed, the company revised its forecasts for a series of planning meetings. Each quarter, the company's senior managers reviewed progress for the past quarter and the outlook for the remainder of the year. Group and plant staff reviewed performance each month and each week respectively. Basing their decision on the forecasts, the cabinetry and transformer plants planned their production for the next year.

## MATERIALS MOVEMENT

Materials movement for the production of distribution transformers should have been quite simple. The transformer plant received orders for transformers (or a single customized transformer) from the sales department, normally with a required delivery date of two weeks or less. Usually, the raw materials in stock were suitable to begin production as soon as personnel were available. The production process for the transformer consisted of winding the required coils, preparing the core steel, assembling, varnishing, final assembly, and testing. Even for custom units, production normally took five days; if expedited, it could be done in 24 hours. If sufficient numbers of the proper-sized enclosure components were in stock in the transformer plant's inventory, the windings could then be installed, the enclosure assembled, and the order shipped.

The cabinetry plant produced in batches, taking economic order quantities into account. When it received a special order, it revised its schedule. Typically, it produced batches of two of the transformer plant's standard enclosures each week on a rotating basis so that it produced any single enclosure type approximately monthly. When it finished a batch run for the transformer plant, it shipped the product directly to the transformer plant. It distributed products for other customers through its Aberfoyle warehouse.

If the transformer plant's enclosure inventory was too small to fill an order, the plant ordered additional units against the existing standing order with the cabinetry plant for any of the nine standard enclosures. It placed custom orders for nonstandard enclosures.

Normally, the Transformer Group issued purchase orders for about three to four months' supplies of each standard enclosure, to be released in equal monthly lots. The transformer plant tried to keep about two weeks' safety stock of each of the nine standard enclosures. Supplies varied, depending on deliveries from the cabinetry plant and fluctuations in sales from the forecast.

## PROBLEMS WITH THE SYSTEM

Mr. Hansen soon realized that both overall demand and the product mix varied considerably, and that his inventory management people were very busy trying to expedite deliveries from the cabinetry plant. Although Mr. Evangelisto seemed willing to cooperate in eliminating delivery delays, the cabinetry plant was not able to respond quickly to the frequent changes without jeopardizing the existing commitments to its other customers.

Mr. Hansen believed that the cabinetry plant treated its sister plant (the transformer plant) as an internal customer, causing it to be lower on the priority list than its external (or third party) customers. Although neither Mr. Hansen nor Mr. Evangelisto wanted to waste time pointing fingers and assigning blame with respect to the poor delivery service, both men believed that an honest assessment of the major causes of the back-order problems would be a good start to solving their problems. The company had never tried just-in-time delivery coordination between the two plants;

neither plant manager believed they would be ready to attempt such a program for at least three years. In Mr. Hansen's words:

> The cabinetry group is running flat out and there doesn't seem to be any break in sight. Consequently, the time it would take to change the existing system or to shut down to set up for a run of a different part has a real cost. Also, the time from when we place an order until the cabinetry plant completes it is longer than the lead time we have to promise our customers. The cabinetry plant doesn't have flexible manufacturing equipment and is too busy to be flexible with the resources it does have. Because it produces 8,500 stock-keeping units, the problem is far from trivial.

As far as the stock-out situation was concerned, Mr. Hansen believed that Hammond was losing transformer sales because of its inability to deliver by the required delivery date: "The sales staff say we could increase sales by five percent if we could deliver consistently in two weeks." In the distribution transformer business, short lead time response was always a key requirement. Because of the sluggishness of the economy in 1993, the industry had excess capacity, which increased the competition among the players and put further emphasis on short lead times as a key differentiator.

Mr. Hansen was ready to accept nearly any system that would enable him to ship his orders on time. A week-ahead-of-time, just-in-time, or even almost-in-time all appeared to offer improvements over the present system. He found it very frustrating that his own plant could manufacture even custom transformers quickly, but could not put the transformer "in the box" in time to make the sale, simply because it could not acquire "the box" in time.

Mr. Hansen believed that it was not practical to reduce the number of standardized enclosures to four or five. He anticipated problems such as increased transportation charges if small transformers were put in large enclosures, frequent customer requests for the smallest enclosures possible, etc. After several meetings with the key materials management staff from each plant, Messrs. Hansen and Evangelisto had identified the following major causes of the materials flow problems:

- Although sales department aggregate forecasts were usually good, it was not at all unusual for orders for a specific transformer to vary widely from the budget. Consequently, the transformer plant could have a two-to-three-month supply of 75 to 112.5 kVA enclosures available while desperately trying to expedite enclosures for 30 to 45 kVA transformers that were backordered because of unexpected sales of this most popular size.

- Enclosures had a minimum of six pieces (or sides), each of which required metal stamping and some of which required spot welding. The cabinetry plant was much more capital intensive than the transformer plant. Because the stamping press had to be shut down to change dies when production switched from one enclosure to another, both custom orders and expedited orders of standard enclosures by the transformer plant caused serious delays in the delivery of orders by the cabinetry plant. The cabinetry plant not only wasted labour hours for unplanned changeovers, but also lost valuable stamping press running time, delaying subsequent planned production as well.

■ The transformer plant believed that its expediters would cause much less disruption if the cabinetry plant would deliver the orders of standard enclosures on time, thus avoiding the disturbance of unscheduled orders.

■ The cabinetry plant delivered virtually all enclosures unassembled; however, it dealt only in complete sets of (typically six) enclosure components. Although this practice seemed reasonable at first glance, it did cause some problems for a number of reasons. If the transformer plant inadvertently spoiled a few fronts, for example, it was very difficult to regain a balance of enclosure components. Even worse, if a customer would accept five standardized sides, but needed an enclosure with a customized bottom, the transformer plant might have to wait while the cabinetry plant stamped and painted all six components.

## ANTICIPATED DEVELOPMENT

Recently, the Transformer Group had signed a contract with a United States distributor to distribute transformers produced in the Guelph and Baraboo plants. The Transformer Group expected this contract to increase its annual volume significantly, beginning in the fourth quarter of 1993. Mr. Hansen anticipated that the added volume would require several operational changes, in particular, an improved system for enclosure supply management.

Although the additional sales would primarily be standard transformers, packaged in a new standard enclosure (yet to be designed) that would meet all U.S. and Canadian government and safety association requirements, inevitably the new contract would delay production further. In the United States some dry distribution transformers (in addition to oil-filled transformers) were installed outdoors (in areas where winter weather was not a major factor). Consequently, *all* standard enclosures produced after the new contract took effect would have to be coated with baked-on electrical outdoor paint. Each component would have to be coated before final assembly. Because the cabinetry plant was not currently equipped to apply such a coating, in the near future it would have to add an additional production step at a custom painting facility or subcontract out the work. In Mr. Hansen's view, the increased handling, transportation, and areas to lose track of inventory implied in this change would most likely add to the expediting problems and/or increase the allocation of blame for stock-outs and late deliveries. The good news was that colour variations were unlikely to add additional complexity because over 99 percent of the plant's products were one or two standard colours and unadorned with customers' logos or other identifying marks.

## Notes

1. The authors gratefully acknowledge the financial support of the Purchasing Management Association of Canada.

2. A company catalogue defined a transformer as: "an electrical device which by electromagnetic induction transforms electrical energy at one voltage or current to another voltage or current at the same frequency."

3. kVA is the standard abbreviation for the unit kilovolt-amps, formerly known as kilowatts, or kW. A company catalogue defined kVA as: "the output which a transformer can deliver for a specified time at a rated secondary voltage and rated frequency without exceeding the specified temperature rise."

## C A S E  **6.8**  INTRODUCING NEW TECHNOLOGY AT GENERAL MOTORS

In May 1990, John Hare first recognized the opportunity to increase employee efficiency in the hood install operation at General Motors Truck Assembly Plant in Oshawa, Ontario. He believed that an overhead hoist could be used to lift the hood from the monorail carrier over to the trucks passing along the main production line. As process engineer for the truck plant, Mr. Hare was responsible for improving efficiency throughout the production process. An immediate savings in his mind was the elimination of at least one of the four employees involved in the hood install operation.

**THE OSHAWA TRUCK PLANT**

The Oshawa Truck Assembly Plant was the exclusive producer of full-size extended cab pickup trucks for General Motors Corporation (GM) and the American market. The plant was part of GM of Canada's Autoplex Complex, along with two car assembly facilities, and three parts fabrication operations. Combined, these plants employed over 15,000 people, both salaried and hourly rated.

The Truck Assembly Centre encompassed over 2.7 million square feet of floor space and had capacity to produce 215,000 units per year. The plant's 3,000 employees operated on two eight-hour shifts, five days a week, with the capacity of producing 441 units per shift. The facility had been utilized for the production of Chevrolet and GMC trucks since its construction in 1965, but many changes in layout and products had occurred since that time (including the production of buses and heavy duty trucks). In the most recent change-over (1986), state-of-the-art body and paint shops were constructed in an approximately $600 million project, adding one million square feet of floor space. Shop floor automation was enhanced in both of these areas through the introduction of robotics. Also, automatic guided vehicles and an electrified monorail system were implemented, making the truck plant one of the most highly automated vehicle assembly plants in the world.

**THE AUTOMOBILE INDUSTRY**

Despite a significant slowdown in the sale of cars, truck sales managed to maintain a fairly constant growth at approximately 5 percent annually during the 1980s. In December 1990, GM chose to shut down production at both Oshawa car assembly plants for four weeks because of excessive build-up of inventories. The truck plant remained producing at two full shifts. However, as a result of recent economic conditions, the plant eliminated the production of regular cab trucks, which were produced by two "sister" plants in the U.S. As well, the line speed was reduced, bringing the production rate down from 61 to 53 trucks per hour. These combined moves resulted in the reduction of approximately 400 hourly rated employees.

The nature of competition in the automobile industry changed dramatically during the 1980s. The increased competition from foreign manufacturers such as Honda and Nissan created the problem of overcapacity, and the North American producers found themselves fighting to maintain market share. Consequently, sales incentives and competitive pricing were being used to attract customers, resulting in a profit squeeze for the automakers.

One further reaction of some North American producers was to build high-technology production facilities in newly industrialized countries (e.g., Mexico), in an effort to remain internationally competitive. The biggest savings occurred in terms of labour costs. Workers in Mexico received less than $1.50 per hour, compared to the $25 per hour received by North American autoworkers.

The presence of foreign competition was by no means of only short-term concern. The Japanese automakers, who had earned a reputation for building high quality automobiles, were continually establishing themselves in the North American market. By 1990, there were more Japanese models being made in the United States than were imported. It was expected that by 1991, Japanese-owned or -operated assembly plants in U.S. could be producing two million cars and trucks a year.

The challenge was clear. If North American automakers wanted to achieve long-term survival, they were not only going to have to be competitive in price, but also meet the consumers' increasing demand for quality.

**THE SITUATION**

Mr. Hare first became aware of an opportunity to improve efficiency when he noticed the large amount of walking being done by the two hood carriers. After observing the operation for some time, he believed that an overhead hoist, similar to that being used by GM's sister plant in Pontiac, could be implemented to improve employee efficiency.

The entire hood installation procedure currently involved a total of four workers. For a detailed description of their individual tasks and time budgets, see Exhibit 1. The existing procedure required the two hood carriers to lift the hood from the carrier, and carry it over to the truck passing down the main assembly line. The distance carried was approximately eight metres. In addition to this, each had other tasks to perform before returning to retrieve the next hood.

Mr. Hare believed that by introducing an overhead hoist, the hood could be secured and guided to the truck by only one worker. The hoist would use a suction cup device to secure the hood, and would run on pullies to carry it over to the trucks. The single worker would have a small hand control to operate the hoist. Once the hood was above the truck, the two hood secure workers would assist in placing it in the proper position. After the hood was secured, the hoist could be released and taken back to retrieve the next hood. Mr. Hare estimated that it would now take 0.95 minutes for the single operator to perform this task.

Mr. Hare had done some rough drafting, and believed the entire system could be installed at a cost of $85,000. The savings would be a reduction of one production worker. He knew, however, that before this worker could be released, each of the tasks that had to be performed would have to be covered by one of the three remaining workers. The plant paid workers about $55,000 per year. Remembering the goal of the new plant manager of increasing the employee work hours to an average of 55 minutes per hour, Mr. Hare wondered what impact any of these changes would have on this goal. Finally, because implementation of this project would result in the elimination of at least one job per shift, he wondered what reaction he would receive from the union.

| | Job | Task Description | Time |
|---|---|---|---|
| **EXHIBIT 1** *Current Job Descriptions and Times (in minutes)[1] per vehicle* | Hood carry (left) | • obtain hood from carrier — carry hood to truck | 0.42 |
| | | • place rubber bumper inside left fender | 0.14 |
| | | • place plastic clip on front rad support | 0.06 |
| | | • secure harness in clip on inside left fender | 0.08 |
| | | • visual inspection of engine wire — front | 0.10 |
| | | Total Time | 0.80 |
| | Hood carry (right) | • obtain hood from carrier, carry hood to truck | 0.42 |
| | | • press release pedal on floor to advance carriers[2] | 0 |
| | | • place rubber bumper inside right fender | 0.14 |
| | | Total Time | 0.56 |
| | Hood secure (left) | • get tool, check hood hinge for proper width — bend if necessary | 0.16 |
| | | • get two bolts and nuts from bench, return to job | 0.075 |
| | | • secure hood to harness | 0.25 |
| | | • secure hood to hinge | 0.28 |
| | | • visual inspection | 0.10 |
| | | Total Time | 0.865 |
| | Hood secure (right) | • get tool; check hood hinge for proper width — bend if necessary | 0.16 |
| | | • get two bolts and nuts from bench, return to job | 0.075 |
| | | • secure hood to harness | 0.25 |
| | | • secure hood to hinge | 0.28 |
| | | • visual inspection | 0.10 |
| | | Total Time | 0.865 |

1. Times were estimated by the case writer.
2. This operation can be done simultaneously with the above operation; therefore, additional time is not necessary.

# C A S E 6.9 NO PANTS INCORPORATED

In December 1983, Ian Richardson, president of the recently incorporated No Pants Incorporated of London, Ontario, was deciding how to organize the production process for T-shirts. He had to determine the necessary equipment and labour requirements to meet the seasonal demand for the product. Demand varied greatly over the year with the peak period being July to September. Thus, Ian was wondering how he should schedule the manufacture of the T-shirts and the printing operations in order to meet demand. Ian wanted to begin production in January so that he could start taking orders from the elementary and secondary schools, and try to develop the tourist market before the summer season arrived.

**COMPANY BACKGROUND**

No Pants Inc. was formed in December 1983 when Ian Richardson, a recent business graduate of The University of Western Ontario, and Tim Graham, a salesperson for a retail sporting goods store, decided to go into business for themselves. Tim believed that there was room to enter the competitive sportswear market if they could offer a quality product at a lower price. Ian and Tim were able to raise $55,000 through personal savings and family members, and borrowed $20,000 from the Federal Business Development Bank. As well, a $15,000 line of credit was negotiated with a chartered bank for working capital purposes. A building was rented in an industrial mall in South London that would provide ample space for an office and production facilities. Consumer surveys had been undertaken and demand for the first year of operation had been forecasted (see Exhibit 1).

**THE PRODUCT**

No Pants Inc. planned to manufacture and sell T-shirts made of 50 percent cotton and 50 percent polyester with reinforced shoulder seams and cuffs. The shirt would come in blue, green, grey, or white and would have either a full chest crest or a small left chest crest. The T-shirts would retail for $4.95 for adult sizes and $4.50 for children's sizes. Golf shirts would also be sold but not manufactured. They were to be supplied by a manufacturing company in Toronto and delivered to No Pants Inc. without a crest within two weeks. The golf shirts had a left chest pocket and came in the same four colours as the T-shirts. The golf shirts would retail for $9.50 with a small crest. Both shirts would be individually wrapped in plastic and delivered to the consumer in four to six weeks. The garments were priced below competitive retail prices. Sales of golf shirts were expected to represent 55 percent of total sales, while T-shirts would represent 45 percent. The variable costs for making and printing the two types of shirts are shown in Exhibit 2. The estimated monthly operating costs for running the business are also shown in Exhibit 2.

## MARKETING

The target markets were students enrolled in primary and secondary schools and tourists. Students were interested in a low-priced shirt of reasonable quality. They did not mind waiting for delivery as long as the order was on time and consistent with the order's specifications. It was common for schools to have long-standing relationships with one clothing manufacturer if their experiences had been satisfactory. Demand from students would be fairly constant from September through to May.

Tourists desired a shirt with a unique crest that reflected some aspect of their vacation or excursion. They purchased from retailers who sold "tourist merchandise" during the summer and from vendors who sold shirts for special events such as folk festivals. Peak demand for the tourist market would take place from July to September.

To cover Ontario, Ian and Tim planned to hire three sales agents who would receive a straight 10 percent commission. The agents would visit schools and organizers of special events with samples and would assist the purchaser during the ordering process. Advertising would be limited to the Yellow Pages.

## THE PRODUCTION PROCESS

The process for manufacturing the T-shirts was fairly simple and involved four departments: 1) lay, 2) sewing, 3) printing and packaging, and 4) art. Semi-skilled labourers would have to be hired. The average wage would be $4.55 per hour, and the workers would be required to work 7 1/2 hours per day, 5 days per week.

The order was first taken by the salesperson who recorded the product, quantity, colour, delivery date, and printing specifications. When the front office received the order, the quantity required was recorded and at the end of the day a bulk cutting order was sent to the lay department. After the cutting order had been sent, the material was ordered for delivery in one week. The original order form was sent to the art department with the design. When the art department was finished with the design the order form was returned to the office with the corresponding silk screen numbers recorded on it. The order was then filed so that two weeks before it was due the shirts would be pulled from finished stock and printed. The shirts were shipped with an invoice and the customer incurred any delivery expense.

### Lay Department

A "master pattern," which was made of a plastic mould for every size, was used to trace the pattern on the pattern paper. The rolls of material were unrolled and placed in layers on the hand lay machine. During the laying process material with flaws that appeared was cut out to avoid wasting good material and reduce factory seconds. The pattern was coated with adhesive spray to keep it in place while the "straight knife" machine cut through the layers of material along the pattern lines. The shirts were then bundled together in groups of 20 backs, 20 fronts, and 40 sleeves. Four workers were to be employed for this laying process and the estimated capacity would be 520 shirts in four hours. However, the lay department could be operated by one individual at a capacity of 130 shirts in four hours.

The collarette machine was used to cut the trim for the shirt collar and sleeves. The machine cut two-inch wide strips of material and wound them into rolls that could then be transferred easily onto the collarette sewing machine. The collarette could cut enough trim for 500 shirts in a half-hour.

## Sewing Department

The sewer received the bundle of cut material with the pattern on top and a "bundling tag" attached. The tag had detachable tickets with the allotted time for each operation recorded on them. When a sewer completed an operation, she detached the ticket and put it on her time card. Each machine required one worker to operate it. The bundling tickets and time card are shown in Exhibit 3. A list of the sewing operations and the time required on each machine are shown in Exhibit 4.

The serger sewing machine was used on the shoulders and sides of the shirt. It gave a "surgeon-like" stitch that was incredibly strong. The collarette sewing machine ran the rolls of trim through a folder that folded the trim in half as it sewed it on the ends of the sleeves and collar. The hemmer folded the material and sewed it on the inside of the shirt. It also produced a "surgeon-like" stitch that could only be seen as one stitch on the outside and matched the colour of the shirt. When all the sewing was completed the garment was inspected for flaws. The shirts were then folded in piles of 10 and placed in the finished garment inventory ready to be taken to printing. The folding operation was estimated to take 18 seconds per shirt.

## Printing Department

The designated number of shirts was removed from inventory and placed next to the printer with the appropriate silk screens. The printer quickly checked the order form to ensure that he or she had the right colour, quantity, and style of shirt. He or she also checked the screen numbers and the colour of ink. The crest was either printed on the shirt with a four-colour or single-colour machine. The printer lowered the first screen and drew a rubber pad across the face of the screen, forcing the ink through the holes and the pattern or design onto the shirt. The screen was then removed and rotated to the second screen and the second colour. When the second screen was pulled down, locked and aligned with the first colour, the same printing process was repeated. The printer was capable of printing 970 shirts in a four-hour period.

When the full crest was on the shirt, the printer placed it on the dryer conveyor belt. The belt moved the shirt into the electric infrared oven for fifteen seconds in order for the ink to dry properly. Once the shirt reached the end of the dryer it was removed, inspected, folded, and placed in a box, a process that normally took 48 seconds to complete. When the entire order had been completed, it was placed at the shipper's desk for delivery. The dryer itself did not require an operator, but Ian estimated that four people would be needed in the printing and inspection/packaging stations.

**CURRENT SITUATION**   As Ian wandered through the empty building, he realized that equipment would have to be ordered soon if production was to begin in January. Once the equipment was ordered, semi-skilled workers would have to be hired. At this point he was still unsure how much equipment would be required and how many workers would be needed to meet their sales forecast. Ian wondered if the design of the process was correct. He was uncertain about how to design an efficient process that would effectively address the issues of customization and seasonal demand. Exhibit 5 provides the equipment breakdown and costs for available machinery.

He was unsure of the potential profitability of this venture. He was confident in the sales forecast for 1984 and expected demand to increase 30 percent in 1985. However, since the competition was tough and he was not certain of their reaction to his entry into the market, he wanted the initial capital investment in equipment paid back within two years. With these thoughts in mind Ian wondered what decisions he should make.

**EXHIBIT 1**

| Monthly Sales Forecast 1984 | | |
|---|---|---|
| | Volume | |
| Month | T-Shirts | Golf Shirts (not manufactured) |
| January | 1,700 | 2,100 |
| February | 2,400 | 2,900 |
| March | 3,700 | 4,500 |
| April | 4,300 | 5,300 |
| May | 3,500 | 4,300 |
| June | 3,300 | 4,000 |
| July | 8,000 | 9,800 |
| August | 8,600 | 10,500 |
| September | 8,200 | 10,000 |
| October | 4,000 | 4,900 |
| November | 4,200 | 5,100 |
| December | 4,000 | 4,900 |
| Total | 55,900 | 68,300 |

*EXHIBIT 2*

## Estimated Cost Breakdown

### T-Shirt

| | | |
|---|---|---|
| Retail selling price (adult size) | | $4.95 |
| Variable costs: | | |
| Material | $1.91 | |
| Direct labour | 0.54 | |
| Sales commission | 0.50 | |
| Total variable costs | $2.95 | |

### Golf Shirt

| | | |
|---|---|---|
| Retail selling price | | $9.50 |
| Variable costs: | | |
| Material | $6.95 | |
| Direct Labour | 0.16 | |
| Sales commission | 0.95 | |
| Total variable costs | $8.06 | |

## Estimated Monthly Operating Costs

| | |
|---|---|
| Telephone | $ 180 |
| Management salaries (Richardson, Graham) | 3,500 |
| Office salaries | 2,000 |
| Rent | 2,000 |
| Promotion | 250 |
| Utilities | 2,000 |
| Maintenance, supplies, repairs | 440 |
| Interest charges | 270 |
| Total monthly costs | $10,640 |

***EXHIBIT 3***
***Piecework,***
***Timecard,***
***and Bundling***
***Ticket***

| | |
|---|---|
| 1 | |
| VALUE 60 | |
| **98776** | |
| UNITS 20 | |
| 2 | |
| 3 | |
| 4 | |
| 5 | |
| 6 | |
| 7 | |
| 8 | |
| 9 | |
| 10 | |

CLOCK NO. | NAME

JOB CLASS | DATE

### ATTENDANCE TIME

| TOTAL CM WORKED | | OUT |
| OVERTIME CM | | IN |
| REG JOB CLASS CM | | OUT |
| REG JOB CLASS SM | | IN |
| % | | OUT |
| | | IN |

### CLOCKOUT TIME

TC

| CM | | PAY | | | |
|---|---|---|---|---|---|
| NV | TRANS OC | TRANS CC | TT | WAIT | OK |
| MD | DW | SAM | REP | FW | |
| TEACH | INDUS | LABOR | HOT PRESS | PRINT | |
| LAY | INVEN | MISC | ENG | | |
| CM | | SM | | PAY | REASON |

| NV | TRANS OC | TRANS CC | TT | WAIT | OK |
| MD | DW | SAM | REP | FW | |
| TEACH | INDUS | LABOR | HOT PRESS | PRINT | |
| LAY | INVEN | MISC | ENG | | |
| CM | | SM | | PAY | REASON |

| NV | TRANS OC | TRANS CC | TT | WAIT | OK |
| MD | DW | SAM | REP | FW | |
| TEACH | INDUS | LABOR | HOT PRESS | PRINT | |
| LAY | INVEN | MISC | ENG | | |
| CM | | SM | | PAY | REASON |

| NV | TRANS OC | TRANS CC | TT | WAIT | OK |
| MD | DW | SAM | REP | FW | |
| TEACH | INDUS | LABOR | HOT PRESS | PRINT | |
| LAY | INVEN | MISC | ENG | | |
| CM | | SM | | PAY | REASON |

**98776**

**LABEL**
**STYLE**      Adult
               Shirts
**ORDER**

**COLOUR**

Turn, trim
inspect

Hem
bottom

Seam sleeves
and sides

Seam and
close shoulders

Collarette neck
and sleeves

Seam, label
shoulders

| VALUE 61 |
| **98776** |
| UNITS 20 |
| VALUE .37 |
| **98776** |
| UNITS 20 |
| VALUE 1.30 |
| **98776** |
| UNITS 20 |
| VALUE .29 |
| **98776** |
| UNITS 20 |
| VALUE .46 |
| **98776** |
| UNITS 20 |

*Exhibit 4*

| Adult and Youth Shirt Time | |
|---|---|
| **Adult and Youth Shirt Time on Serger** | |
| Operation | Minutes/Shirt |
| 1. Seam, label, and shoulder | 0.60 |
| 2. Seam and close shoulders | 0.29 |
| 3. Seam sleeves and sides | 1.30 |
| | 2.19 |

| Adult and Youth Shirt Time on Hemmer | |
|---|---|
| Operation | Minutes/Shirt |
| Hem bottom | 0.37 |

| Adult and Youth Shirt Time on Collarette Sewing Machine | |
|---|---|
| Operation | Minutes/Shirt |
| Collarette neck and sleeves | 0.46 |

***EXHIBIT 5***

| Department | | Equipment Costs (New and Used) | |
|---|---|---|---|
| Lay (4 workers) | Lay table | $1,343 | |
| | Lay machine | 1,200 | |
| | Cutting knife | 1,625 | |
| | Collarette machine | 485 | |
| | | | $ 4,653 |
| Sewing (1 worker per machine) | Serger sewing machine | $1,600 | |
| | Collarette sewing machine | 2,575 | |
| | Hemmer | 1,875 | |
| | | | $ 6,050 |
| Printing and Packaging (4 workers) | Main dryer | $5,000 | |
| | 4-colour printer | 4,406 | |
| | Hotpress | 560 | |
| | | | $ 9,966 |
| Art | Process camera | $3,879 | |
| | Vacu-Lite table | 1,117 | |
| | Silk screens (100) | 1,455 | |
| | | | $ 6,451 |
| Miscellaneous | Storage racks | $2,245 | $ 2,245 |
| | | | $29,365 |

---

## C A S E 6.10   STEELWAY BUILDING SYSTEMS

Glen White, owner and president of Steelway Building Systems (SBS), was in his office overlooking his production facilities. Lately, the flange line had been taking up a great deal of his thoughts. Mr. White realized that the competitive forces in the industry were changing. He believed that by adding more new technology he would improve his competitive position in the industry, but he wondered which system available to SBS would be the most cost-effective and productive to implement in the flange area.

**STEELWAY BUILDING SYSTEMS**

Steelway, located in Aylmer, Ontario, was incorporated in 1976 by Mr. White. Steelway had gradually expanded its capabilities to the point where it could now manufacture all the necessary components of an entire steel building.

SBS had grown from a one-person operation in 1976 to a company employing up to 100 people in its peak periods. The company was broken into four main areas: sales and customer service, design, production, and administration.

**THE STEEL BUILDING INDUSTRY**

Steel building manufacturers were affected by a number of pressing issues. First, the industry had become highly competitive. A small number of competitors affected SBS directly. Two of these, Canadian Building Systems and Robertson Building Systems, were located within Canada, but were wholly or partly owned by companies from the United States.

Because of the Free Trade Agreement more and more competition was coming directly from the United States. There were approximately four major competitors without Canadian links that had generated strong sales penetration in the Canadian market.

These competitors had already begun to implement automated systems similar to the ones Mr. White had been evaluating for his own plant. If SBS were to survive through the 1990s, it had to keep up with the latest technological trends.

The general economic conditions were also a concern. The increasing value of the Canadian dollar and the recessionary times in 1990–91 had negatively affected the business.

---

**THE PURCHASE PROCESS**

The purchase of a steel building was not as straightforward as it might seem. The end consumer usually contacted a number of local contractors if the need for a new building arose. The contractors each had an already established relationship with a specific steel building manufacturer. The contractors then contacted their steel building manufacturer to get a quote. The contractors gave the end consumer an estimate to complete the construction of the steel building.

Contractors usually dealt with only one steel building manufacturer. For example, a contractor in the London area might deal exclusively with SBS. Another contractor in London dealt exclusively with Robertson Building Systems. SBS worked very hard to develop contractor relationships in many different locations around North America. A company like SBS created all the components for the building, and the contractor assembled the components at the location specified by the end consumer. Exhibit 1 illustrates the variety of projects in which SBS had been involved.

Timely delivery was important to the end consumer. If a grocery store was scheduled to open in May, the building had to arrive and be assembled on time. Just as important as delivery was service, especially the after sales follow up. If there were any problem with the new building, the end consumer had to be able to contact the manufacturer or contractor. At this time SBS's customer service department became very important. Quality was definitely a concern. Mr. White expressed it this way: "If the quality isn't there, you can sometimes get away with it in the short run, but it will catch up to you in the long run."

Contractors were concerned with the delivery, because they had to assemble the building to a set schedule. Quality and price also had to be competitive for SBS to retain the contractor relationship.

**SBS PRODUCTION
Key Success Factors**

Mr. White explained the three key success factors for the manufacture of steel beams in SBS. First, the design had to be accurate and precise. Second, the purchase of the main raw material had to be efficient. It would be ideal to be able to purchase the cheapest steel possible. Third, SBS had to be "a good manufacturer," meaning that it had to be able to obtain the right equipment to process the most efficient material. It needed the ability to cut steel varying in length from a few inches in length up to 60 feet with a tolerance (accuracy) of 1/16 of an inch.

**Beam Production**

Mr. White had introduced CAD/CAM into his plant. CAD/CAM was really two separate pieces of computerization. CAD (computer-assisted (or aided) design) employed computer graphics to create designs of physical objects. SBS used CAD in the design of its steel buildings. Exhibit 2 shows a design of one section of SBS's production area, created using CAD technology.

CAM (computer-assisted (or aided) manufacturing) used computers to control the machinery on the plant floor. One computer could be used to control a number of different operations on the plant floor. CAD/CAM was the integration of the two.

The flange line was the area where flanges and connector plates were manufactured. The area was one part of the total production process for a steel building. Flanges were raised edges that protected the webs. Connector plates were the ends of a beam where other beams were connected to create a building. Exhibit 3 illustrates a steel building frame manufactured by SBS. Exhibit 4 focuses attention on a steel beam that forms part of the entire frame, and illustrates the three components mentioned above (flange, connector plate, and web) in more detail.

The usual process began with raw materials (steel) being shipped to SBS. SBS could use two types of steel. It used sheet steel to produce webs — mini-walls between flanges. Sheet steel was made by primary steel companies, such as Dofasco. The other type of steel, made primarily from scrap steel, was called flat bar. It was melted down by steel mills, such as Lasco. Flat bar was more efficient than sheet steel because it did not have to be cut to width before the flange process began and there was less waste.

### Flange Production

Once the steel was delivered, it was lifted by an overhead crane and placed onto the bar line. Once the flat bar was on the flange line it was manually welded, cut to the appropriate length, and holes were punched in it to facilitate assembly of the frames. Then the flange was manually moved to the next step of the process. The new technology Mr. White was considering adding would eliminate the overhead crane and replace it with a more manageable process.

### Connector Plate Production

The flat bar also had to be cut to length for connector plates, which were considerably shorter than the flanges. The connector plates had to be taken manually from the flange area to the plasma area (see Exhibit 2) for the hole punching step. As a result, there was much more material handling than was necessary. Any of the new processes would eliminate the need to move the connector plates to the plasma area.

The entire flange production and connector plate production process involved a great deal of physical exertion on the part of the people on the shop floor, and the new automated processes could significantly reduce the number of injuries.

Numerous other operations were necessary to complete the production of all the components of the steel building, but the flange and connector plate production was the very first step in the entire process.

### THE PROPOSED SYSTEM

Mr. White believed it was time for SBS to redefine its direction. He explained his reasoning in simple, yet decisive, terms: "I have no choice; it's a matter of do we survive or don't we?"

Mr. White saw the major advantages of changing his current system as the following:

- It would increase the quality of the product because the new computer software would increase production accuracy.

- It would improve customer service because the faster new process would decrease delivery time. Mr. White estimated that an 80 by 120 foot building currently took SBS 40 man-hours to complete. With the new system he estimated that the same building would take only 12 man-hours. As a result, there was an opportunity to decrease the production group by three workers. The people working on the shop floor made approximately $15 per hour (including benefits) and usually worked eight hours a day. These people were considered full-time employees.

- It would decrease the stress on workers because most manual aspects of the operation would be considerably reduced.

- Materials handling would be significantly reduced with any one of these systems installed.

- The estimated materials savings for any of the three options available to Mr. White would be $10,000.

## OPTIONS AVAILABLE TO SBS

Mr. White was considering three options. He had quotes from two separate suppliers: Franklin Manufacturing Company and Washington Manufacturing Company. Alternatively, SBS could assemble the whole system itself from a group of suppliers. Mr. White saw the most critical components of any new system to be accuracy, flexibility (in particular, the ability to cut steel varying widely in length), and compatibility with his current IBM hardware.

## The Franklin Manufacturing Company Quotation

Mr. White had contacted Franklin Manufacturing Company for a quotation to improve SBS's flange line.

The computer component of the system would use a software package compatible with IBM computers. Franklin described it as the world's fastest processor, and the software as highly accurate and reliable. Franklin stated that finished flanges could be from 4 feet to 50 feet in width with a tolerance of plus or minus 1/16 of an inch, meaning that the width could be programmed to within that amount of variance. To reach the capability of cutting lengths to a few inches Franklin would add an extra $100,000 to the price.

Franklin's basic system cost $198,295 and included the following:

- the computer system mentioned above
- welding assembly
- hydraulic press

The delivery period for the basic machine would be 14 to 16 weeks from receipt of the purchase order. If any extra equipment was required (for example, infeed/outfeed equipment), the delivery period would be negotiated.

Purchasing infeed equipment, which fed raw materials (steel) into the press, from Franklin would add an extra $13,750 to the base purchase price. The outfeed equipment, which mechanically pulled the connector plate or flange out of the press, would add an extra $16,285 to the base purchase price. The machinery would be sent to SBS with no start-up assistance. There was a one-year warranty. Mr. White wondered how necessary start-up assistance was.

**The Washington Manufacturing Company Quotation**

Mr. White also had a quote from Washington Manufacturing Company, which used software that it developed itself. SBS might have to purchase a new computer to run the software. No mention was made of tolerances.

The price quoted for this system was $245,800, which included the following:

- infeed equipment
- weld bar assembly — this piece of machinery lifted the steel into position and performed the welding operation
- 350-ton hydraulic press and three-position die set — the press and die set were the heart of the operation where the steel was shaped to create bars which support the rest of the steel building
- outfeed equipment
- start-up assistance — this would include one person for three days to help Steelway assemble and operate the new system

The delivery period was 20 to 24 weeks from receipt of the purchase order; a one-year warranty would apply.

**The Do-It-Yourself Option**

This would entail SBS buying parts of the system from various suppliers and putting the pieces together itself. The do-it-yourself option was attractive because it was relatively inexpensive. Mr. White believed SBS might also be able to make some of the necessary components in its shop. Mr. White realized that this route would take a great deal of time and effort.

One potential pitfall was that if one part of the system was faulty or broke down, the suppliers could blame it on other pieces of equipment from other suppliers. Another pitfall was that the suppliers might think that the in-house assembly of the system lacked the necessary expertise. Exhibit 5 outlines the costs involved in SBS creating its own system. There was also the question of how contractors would react to this change in the Steelway production process.

Mr. White sat with the options spread over his desk. He knew that he had to examine the costs and benefits of each system along with the advantages and disadvantages of the three options. He was also pondering the short-term implications of adding one of these systems to the current production process. He wondered what the priorities should be and what the long-term ramifications would be.

**EXHIBIT 1**
**Examples of**
**SBS Product**
**Line**

**EXHIBIT 2**
**Partial
Production
Area Created
Using CAD
Technology**

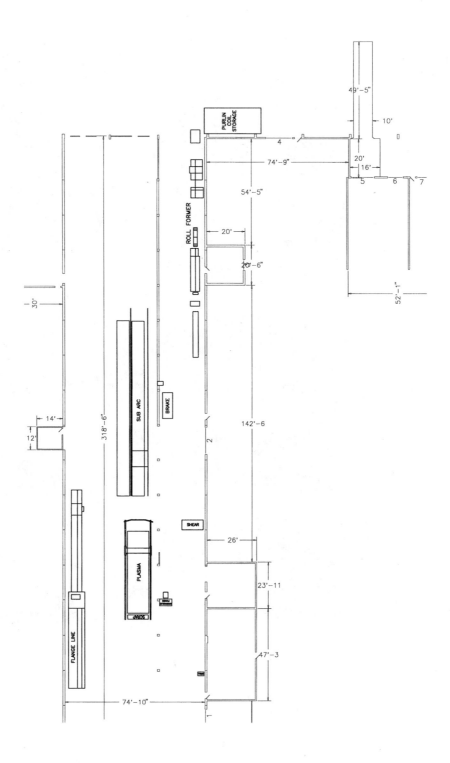

**EXHIBIT 3**
**Steel Building**
**Frame**

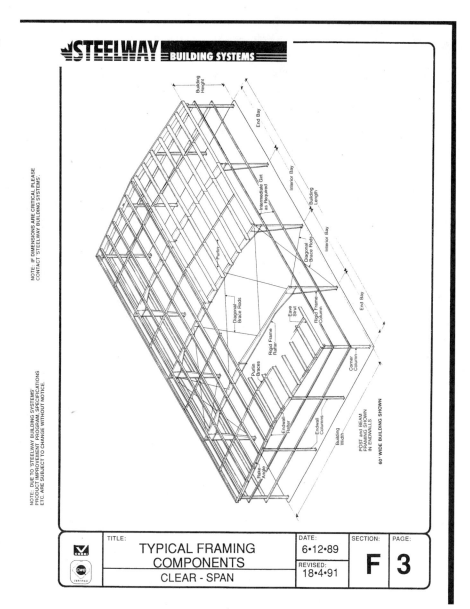

NOTE: IF DIMENSIONS ARE CRITICAL PLEASE
CONTACT 'STEELWAY BUILDING SYSTEMS'.

NOTE:  DUE TO 'STEELWAY BUILDING SYSTEMS'
PRODUCT IMPROVEMENT  PROGRAM, SPECIFICATIONS
ETC. ARE SUBJECT TO CHANGE WITHOUT NOTICE.

Building Height

End Bay

Intermediate Girt as Required

Interior Bay

Building Length

Purlin

Diagonal Brace Rods

Interior Bay

Diagonal Brace Rods

Eave Strut

Rigid Frame Column

End Bay

Rigid Frame Rafter

Purlin Braces

Corner Column

Endwall Rafter

Endwall Columns

Building Width

Rake Angle

POST and BEAM FRAMING SHOWN IN ENDWALLS

60' WIDE BUILDING SHOWN

| TITLE: **TYPICAL FRAMING COMPONENTS** CLEAR - SPAN | DATE: 6•12•89 REVISED: 18•4•91 | SECTION: **F** | PAGE: **3** |

***EXHIBIT 4***
***Close-up of Rigid***
***Frame Column,***
***Illustrates Flange,***
***Web and Connector***
***Plates***

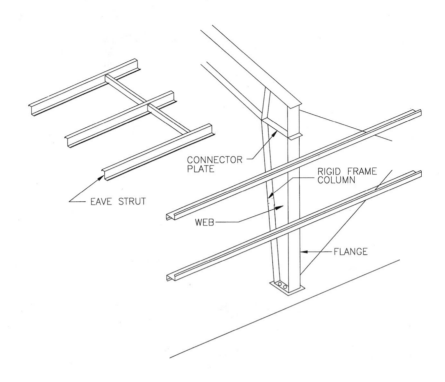

CONNECTOR
PLATE

EAVE STRUT

RIGID FRAME
COLUMN

WEB

FLANGE

*Exhibit 5*

| COSTS OF DO-IT-YOURSELF OPTION | | |
|---|---|---|
| **Flange Line Budget** | | |
| | **Capital Cost** | **Completion Date** |
| Pick and place | $ 5,000 | Apr. 15/91 |
| Input conveyor and centring device | 5,000 | May 15/91 |
| Weld station | 2,000 | May 15/91 |
| Shear[1] | 50,000 | Sept. 30/91 |
| Punch[1] | 50,000 | Sept. 30/91 |
| Output conveyor and stacking | 3,000 | Nov. 30/91 |
| Measuring system[1] | 25,000 | Feb. 15/92 |
| | $140,000 | |

**1.** The solution was still being reviewed for these components. The quoted cost was a maximum; a reduction of up to 30 percent was possible.

## C A S E 6.11 THE UNIVERSITY OF WESTERN ONTARIO BOOK STORE

On April 5, 1993, John Woolsey, director of University Book Store, The University of Western Ontario, was trying to decide how the Book Store should respond to a recent customer survey that had revealed student dissatisfaction with long line ups and the hours of operation. Mr. Woolsey had many options, including the purchase of a retail management system and opening on Saturdays. He wanted to decide which options to pursue before the staff met in one week to begin planning for the annual September rush. Michael Gourley, vice-president administration, had recently been actively encouraging all operating units to adopt total quality service (TQS) in their operations. Mr. Woolsey wondered how its principles might apply to his current decision.

**THE UNIVERSITY OF WESTERN ONTARIO**

The University of Western Ontario (UWO or Western) was located at the north end of London, Ontario, a city of 315,000 located along Highway 401, the major east-west traffic artery through southern Ontario. Western catered to 19,000 full-time and 2,300 part-time undergraduates, and 2,750 graduate students. Three colleges affiliated with UWO, situated within a short distance of the main campus, increased the student population by another 4,000. Like all Ontario universities, Western was facing budgetary constraints. For some years, the Ontario government had reduced funding in response to its fiscal deficits. Western officials believed that fiscal restraint would continue in the foreseeable future; consequently, for the 1993–94 fiscal year (beginning May 1) UWO reduced all operating budgets by 1.6 percent and reduced administrative unit budgets by an additional 0.5 percent. As a result of continued financial restraints, Western had called on its non-operating units (such as the Book Store) to show a profit to support Western's operating budget. In addition, UWO had raised the fees it charged them for administrative support, such as accounting services. These financial concerns came at a time when UWO believed it was at capacity. In addition, the Ontario government would not allow universities to increase tuition fees beyond the authorized seven percent for each of the next two years. Student leaders believed that, with summer jobs hard to find, these increases would be a burden to many students.

## THE UNIVERSITY BOOK STORE

The University Book Store, located in a prominent location in the University Community Centre (UCC), was a full-service facility; it considered students, faculty, staff, and the general public to be its customers. Exhibit 1 shows its layout. Mr. Woolsey believed that the Book Store was typical of those at other North American universities similar in size and nature to UWO. The Book Store was an ancillary operation under the portfolio of Gordon Smiley, assistant vice-president (registrar and student affairs), who in turn reported to Mr. Gourley.

It sold textbooks for all courses on the main campus and in the affiliated colleges, academic reference books, children's books, general books, stationery, and UWO-branded merchandise including clothing, knapsacks, and rings. On average, books returned a gross margin of 21 percent whereas the nonbook merchandise margins were somewhat higher. The Book Store relied on the merchandise sales to offset the high cost of selling textbooks and to meet its financial targets. The sales breakdown was: textbooks, 70 percent; stationery, 7 percent; general books, 13 percent; and merchandise, 10 percent. The store carried approximately 10,000 textbook titles, 30,000 general book titles, 5,000 different student supply items, and a few thousand different units of general merchandise. Mr. Woolsey estimated that each full-time student spent $350 to $700, averaging about $400, on textbooks each year. Exhibit 2 shows the Book Store's return policy.

## TQS PRINCIPLES

Total Quality Service, the principles of which arose in Total Quality Management but which had been modified for service industries, is a management style that imposes a customer-driven culture of continuous improvement within an organization. The principles of TQS include developing and managing processes to serve customers and training employees to become customer focused. Measuring, benchmarking, and seeking feedback from customers and front-line employees are important TQS practices.

## TQS AT UWO

Mr. Gourley came to Western in 1992 as a firm believer in TQS. He believed that UWO's services must be improved to meet customer needs. He often told the story of how his first experience at Western encouraged him to promote TQS:

> The first person I met was a parking attendant, prior to my interview with the university president for my current position. I explained to the attendant that I had been told to come to his booth, as parking arrangements had been made. The attendant replied: "Nobody told me. Nobody tells me anything." I asked if I could park in the lot. He said: "Park over there between the yellow lines." The attendant said he didn't know where the president's office was and that no one had ever told him he needed to know. It was clear to me that this person's job was to police the parking lot. He performed well at that task but I didn't believe anybody should have a poor first impression of this university. Fortunately, I got to

my interview despite the poor signage. I knew Western needed a paradigm shift, not only in parking but in all its services.

As a result of the new TQS focus, training seminars were organized for Western's managers, including Mr. Woolsey. Of the four days, two were spent on an overview of TQS and two on TQS theory.

**JOHN WOOLSEY AND NORM LAVOIE**

John Woolsey graduated from McMaster University with a Bachelor of Commerce degree. Since that time, he had been involved with course materials operations at the correspondence-focused Athabasca University in Edmonton, Alberta. He came to Western in 1988 after managing the book store at Brock University in St. Catharines, Ontario, which had a total of about 9,000 full- and part-time students.

Norm Lavoie, manager of administrative services at the Book Store, would also be heavily involved in any change process. Before coming to UWO in 1990, he had worked at Canada Post's headquarters in retail operations, systems development, and training; before that he had managed the Christmas mail rush at Canada Post in Orillia, Ontario.

**COMPETITION**

No other book store in London matched the Book Store's extensive line of textbooks. However, The University Students' Council operated a used book store in the UCC, which offered used textbooks at discounts of up to 75 per cent. Students also sold used textbooks privately using poster board advertisements throughout the campus. Competition for nontextbook merchandise was more significant. Picadilly (The Pic), a general store located directly across the hall from the Book Store, sold UWO merchandise, stationery, consumer packaged goods, and pharmaceutical products. As well, many stores in the vicinity of the campus sold UWO merchandise.

**THE SEPTEMBER RUSH**

During September, the busiest month of the year, the Book Store completed as many as 10,000 customer transactions in one day. Mr. Woolsey reflected on past Septembers:

Many days it's wall-to-wall people most of the time and very difficult to move. Not only does this congestion make it hard for our customers, but it also puts our staff under a lot of stress. Obviously, it also doesn't help us in stocking the shelves either!

The Book Store's two levels were separated by about one metre vertically; customers entered on the upper level, where they left their bags, etc., and exited from the lower level. Shelving separated and divided the sales areas, and restricted vision. When the Book Store was packed to capacity, security guards limited access, trying to match the entry rate to the exit rate. Once inside, the process was typical of any self-serve retail establishment: customers went to the relevant sections of the store to locate the required items. During the September rush, the Book Store installed a cash register at the entrance to deal with returns. Each year it handled book refunds or credits equivalent to about 6 percent of total book sales; about 51 percent of the year's refunds occurred in the month of September.

**CUSTOMER SURVEYS**

In February of 1992, October of 1992, February of 1993, and March of 1993, the Book Store management had conducted a standard statistically valid and reliable customer survey used in university book stores across North America. From the results, Mr. Woolsey targeted slow checkouts and hours of operations as the most common complaints, which he believed the Book Store could improve. In 1992, during the busiest time of the day during the first week of classes, the Book Store measured waiting times. A staff member gave a time trial form explaining the process to a customer at the end of a line. The staff member recorded the time he or she distributed each numbered form. Upon leaving the store, the customer handed the form to a security guard who recorded the time. The Book Store thanked all participating customers with gifts such as a Western T-shirt. The longest lineup measured was 18 minutes. Mr. Woolsey was uncertain what an acceptable waiting time was and what target waiting time the Book Store should set.

**ANDRÉE BOURGON'S EXPERIENCE**

Andrée Bourgon, a first-year student at Western, commented on her first experience at the Book Store in September 1992:

> It was early afternoon and I decided not to wait in the queue to enter the Book Store. My friend, Bob Wood, and I bought a coffee and waited for the line to diminish. Customers continued to join the line and it wasn't until 45 minutes after I bought that coffee that I saw an opportunity to enter the store without waiting. Once I was in the store I started my hunt to find 11 books, a plastic Western calendar, and a corkboard. It took me approximately 30 minutes to find all the books after asking for directions and finding the different subject areas within the store. It took another 30 minutes to check out. The lineup to check out extended almost the entire length of the store. The line never was at a standstill but continued to move at a slow pace. While I was in line, a few people knocked books off the high stack of books resting in my arms. Bob had to help me hang onto some of the items. We actually felt lucky, as we had estimated it would take two hours to complete buying our books.

**POSSIBLE ACTION**
*Installing a Retail Management System*

Mr. Woolsey was considering purchasing a retail management system. He and his selection committee had spent a considerable amount of time setting specifications and collecting bids from suppliers. Mr. Woolsey knew that the Book Store made purchases of this importance only every 10 to 15 years. It was significant because of the size of the proposed investment, the long-term commitment and training required to use the new hardware and software effectively, and the fact that it would change the way the Book Store did business in some areas. He cited the following situations as examples of the savings and the potential benefits of the system:

> One feature of the retail management system we are looking at is bar code scanning. Currently, a check-out clerk has to enter the price of every

item purchased into a cash register. It takes us an average of two minutes to check a customer out of the store. Queen's University in Kingston, Ontario, uses a bar code scanning system and has the check-out time down to an average of one minute. Also, if we used bar codes, we wouldn't have to put prices on every product we stock. Currently, 30 to 35 percent of one employee's time (at a rate of about $26,000 per year) is spent on this task. However, I think that maintenance on the computer system would offset any salary we could save.

The system's software also promises to provide us with a tremendous amount of customer information, including comprehensive sales data on all our products. As well, it will provide daily information of gross profit and information on product shrinkage. The current system allows us to collect sales data under only two accounts, books and merchandise, and we have to wait until after year-end inventory counts to estimate profit and shrinkage information. Because the new computer system would give us access to the university's main computer, we could process inter-departmental charges electronically instead of sending the business forms to each department like we do now. The new system would also reduce our telecommunication costs by about $3,000 per year because we would need fewer telephone lines to access the university's main frame computer. The system's new printers would also offer us the possibility of quicker credit card authorization.

Our purchasing would also benefit. The faculty member or department for every course provides us with a requisition for all books students will need. Of course, they come from hundreds of publishers. The new system would allow us to consolidate our purchase orders instead of sending a purchase order for each individual faculty requisition. Each year we return 12 percent of the books we purchase to publishers. It takes us the equivalent of one employee month of labour to complete the paperwork. By being able to consolidate, we could save that much and reduce the shipping costs to return books.

The system will also allow us to improve our inventory management. Because the software uses reorder flags, we should have more precise control and thus reduce both inventory overstocking and stock-outs. We might save $15,000 to $16,000 per year on inventory carrying costs.

For three weeks in September it is a real zoo here; we are open from 9:00 a.m. to 9:00 p.m. Monday to Thursday, 9:00 a.m. to 5:30 p.m. Friday, and 11:00 a.m. to 3:30 p.m. Saturday. During that time, we need 20 cashiers for the first two weeks and 18 cashiers for the third week. During the rest of the year, we only need two or three cashiers. We hire the extra cashiers on a temporary basis through an employment firm for $11 per hour. The new system would allow us to reduce our cashier needs by four for each of our busy three weeks.

Although these benefits are quite attractive, I wonder if they make economic sense. I have estimated the necessary investment, annual operating costs, and savings (see Exhibit 3). They are large and if we decide to go ahead there will be no turning back.

| | |
|---|---|
| ***Providing Entertainment*** | The noise level, the image of the Book Store, and complaints from staff and customers concerned Mr. Woolsey. He believed that providing entertainment would make waiting in and around the Book Store more enjoyable, and could increase customers' shopping experience, keep people's minds off the price of the textbooks and the long queues, and thus decrease the number of complaints the Book Store received. Granada, a home entertainment rental company, was willing to loan four televisions to the Book Store in return for the right to distribute literature at the Book Store exit. By tuning into the Much Music station, the Book Store could allow customers to watch music videos while they waited in line. The Intercollegiate Athletics department was also willing to donate the time of a volunteer to play J.W., the Western athletics mascot, who could hand out candy (for about $50 for the month) and otherwise entertain customers. |
| ***Publishing Book Lists During the Summer*** | The Book Store did not provide book lists. However, Mr. Woolsey believed that if it did, students could buy their books earlier, thus reducing the mad rush of textbook sales in September. Such a move would allow students to check prices faster at the used book store and start reading earlier. He estimated that it would cost $1,000 to print the lists and would also involve some staff time to compile the lists using a computer program. He did not know how much suitable software would cost to develop or purchase, and he also wondered where the book lists should be placed if he decided to go ahead with this possibility. One potential location was outside the store. Placing them inside might be better service, but could put an extra burden on staff if they became involved in interpreting student registration information to match textbook needs with specific courses or sections. Currently, staff were ill-equipped for such a role. |
| ***Opening on Saturdays*** | The Book Store opened on Saturdays only during the three-week September peak. Mr. Woolsey wondered if Saturday openings during the rest of the year would make sense. Opening on Saturdays from 10:00 a.m. to 3:00 p.m. would require seven or eight employees at $9 per hour each, plus at least one management staff member at no additional cost. Based on his perceptions, Mr. Woolsey believed that staff would oppose working on Saturdays instead of the customary Monday to Friday schedule. In earlier discussions, some staff had argued that Saturday openings would not increase sales but simply spread them over six days a week instead of five. In 1992–93, the Book Store had decided to stay open until 7:00 p.m. on Wednesday evenings from September to March to serve the part-time evening students who were unable to visit the Book Store during its regular hours. Mr. Woolsey learned that the Book Store could operate on Wednesday evening with only a skeleton staff but had not tracked sales in the evening period. However, he had heard reports of barely trained part-time and student staff struggling with complex systems and trying to offer expert service. He noted: |

Faculty and other customers demand sophisticated answers to their queries on publishing and authors.

Mr. Woolsey wondered if he should evaluate the Saturday opening proposal differently than the Wednesday evening opening.

**Mailing Information to First-Year Students**

Each year since 1990 the Book Store had mailed a brochure to the 5,000 first-year students, at a total cost of $3,500 to 4,000 per year. Students were often shocked when they encountered textbook prices; Mr. Woolsey wanted to decrease this financial surprise by informing students well in advance of the high prices of textbooks, as well as advertising the Book Store and its UWO merchandise. He wanted to re-evaluate the cost of this option against its benefits.

**CONCLUSION**

Mr. Woolsey had many ideas about increasing the quality of service to students and wondered which ideas he should implement to decrease the customers' concerns of long lineups and hours of operations while keeping his costs in line.

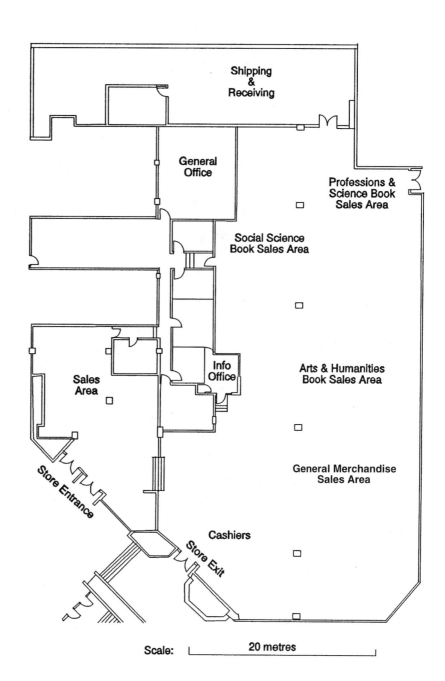

*Exhibit 2*

---

### The Book Store's Return Policy[1]

1. Refunds only within SEVEN DAYS of purchase
2. Cash register receipt must be presented
3. Merchandise must be in mint condition
4. There are no refunds or exchange on used or reduced books
5. Sale merchandise on exchange only

---

**1.** The Book Store informally extended its refund period during September.

Source: Posted publicly in the Book Store.

*Exhibit 3*

---

### Estimated Financial Costs and Benefits of a Retail System

| Year | Initial Investment | Annual Operating Costs | Annual Savings |
|------|--------------------|------------------------|----------------|
| 1 | $270,000[1] | $0 | $0 |
| 2 | 50,000 | 29,000 | 16,000 |
| 3 | 16,000 | 50,000 | 122,000 |
| 4 | 10,000 | 52,000 | 165,000 |
| 5 | 3,000 | 54,000 | 170,000 |

**1.** Made up of: hardware, $167,000; software, $56,000; training, $20,000; and price data conversion, renovation, financing, and miscellaneous costs, $27,000.

Source: Book store files.

# CASE 6.12   WORLDWIDE PULP AND PAPER LTD.

On November 1, 1983, Mike Garfield, the new plant manager of the West Coast Division of Worldwide Pulp and Paper Limited (WPPL), had just received a disturbing telephone call from his superior located at the company's head office. The head office staff had received several complaints from customers supplied by the West Coast Division. These complaints concerned inferior product quality and increasingly late deliveries. Given only two weeks in which to investigate and report back to his superior, Mike Garfield wondered what specifically could be done quickly to improve the overall operating efficiency and effectiveness of the plant.

**THE WEST COAST DIVISION**

The West Coast Division was a manufacturing operation involved in the processing of cut timber (wood) and the production of various paper products. The company's sales and marketing effort was carried out through the head office. Sales orders received by the head office were transmitted via a sophisticated computer communications network to the most "appropriate" plant. Two factors were considered in determining the appropriate plant for the order. First, proximity to the customer was important. The closest plant to the customer was often selected in an attempt to minimize the high transportation costs associated with the industry. Second, and more importantly, most plants were designed to produce only a small range of paper products. Therefore, depending on the type of product ordered, only certain plants were capable of manufacturing products that satisfied the customers' specific requirements.

The West Coast Division plant was a fully integrated operation, in that it produced and processed all of the wood pulp (raw material) it required for its manufacture of paper products. In the simplest terms, the plant or mill was designed to accept cut timber (wood) at one end of the plant, and to ship large rolls or "logs" of paper out of the other end. These large rolls of paper were then transferred to the customer's plant for final processing into finished paper products. A more detailed description of the production process appears later.

**THE CONSUMER**

Although an endless number and variety of paper products were sold at the retail level, the West Coast Division plant supplied companies that produced or used paper products for two basic purposes.

1. Approximately 95 percent of the plant's production was newsprint, used primarily in the production of daily newspapers. End consumers of this product (newspaper readers) thought little of the actual newsprint, unless it was of unusually high or low quality. Only reasonable quality was expected. The newspaper chains, however, were characterized by the marketing staff as extremely price conscious and very concerned about delivery schedules. Recent financial analysis received by Mike Garfield indicated that 98 percent of the West Coast Division's net profit after tax resulted from sales to this segment.

2. The remaining 5 percent of the plant's production was used for specialty writing paper products. This paper was high quality and was produced to widely varying customer specifications. Sales to this segment had begun only two years ago. The marketing staff had identified the specialty writing paper products segment as a small, but poorly serviced, market "niche" or segment. The marketing staff believed that *any* sales, however small, would be a bonus to add to the larger newsprint sales.

   End consumers of these paper products tended to buy infrequently and in small quantities. These consumers were willing to pay a premium price for image or status qualities such as unique sizes, shapes, colours, and textures. Financial records indicated that only 2 percent of net profit after tax resulted from sales to these customers.

   Mike Garfield recalled that although the West Coast Division plant was originally designed primarily for the production of high volume, low-to-medium quality newsprint, machine adjustments could be made to enable the equipment to produce a range of product types. However, this often resulted in shorter, more costly production runs, as a result of significantly increased machine downtime.

## THE PRODUCTION PROCESS

The production process was quite complex at the West Coast plant, but could be simplified into three key components: wood processing, pulp production, and paper production. The total investment in plant and equipment was approximately $350 million (see Exhibit 1 for details).

### Wood Processing

The entire production process began with the receiving of wood logs. Upon receipt, these logs were weighed and sorted by tree species (e.g., spruce, pine, hemlock), and stored separately in an area known as the wood yard. As needed, specific log species were floated in water passageways to two de-barking machines. In the de-barking machines, the tree bark was removed by tumbling the logs against one another vigorously in long de-barking drums.

Once de-barked, the logs were moved to a "chipper" machine. Within several seconds, a large de-barked log was reduced to a pile of wood chips or fragments. The wood chips were then stored in large silos (storage bins). Once again, there were separate silos for different tree species. Separate storage of wood chips by species permitted the controlled mixing of chips into precise combinations or "recipes" required for the particular paper products being produced.

The entire wood processing component of the production process could provide 730 tons of wood chips per hour. Wood processing operated 24 hours per day, 365 days per year.

**Pulp Production**

Pulp, the key raw material for the production of paper, was produced using a complicated chemical process known as the Kraft process. Two tons of wood chips were required to produce one ton of pulp. The Kraft process worked by dissolving the lignin or "glue" that bonds wood fibres together. This "ungluing" was accomplished in two tall pressure-cookers known as digesters, by cooking the wood chips in a chemical solution of caustic soda and sodium sulphide.

Upon leaving the digesters, the digested chips entered a machine known as a blow tank. The blow tank was maintained at a significantly lower pressure than the digesters. This pressure difference caused the wood fibres to "blow apart" as lignin, the bonding glue, was no longer present in the wood fibres. The resulting wood fibre pulp was cleaned and bleached to remove unwanted impurities that might later affect the quality of the paper. The refined pulp remained in temporary storage where chemical additives could be mixed in to further prepare the pulp for paper production.

The pulp production facilities were capable of converting as much as eight million tons of wood chips into about four million tons of pulp per year.

**Paper Production**

The two paper-making machines in the West Coast plant were extremely large and involved an investment of about $75 million each. Each paper-making machine could be used to convert up to 2,250,000 tons of pulp into 2,250,000 tons of paper per year. (One ton of pulp could be converted into approximately one ton of newsprint or specialty paper.) Contribution per ton of newsprint was estimated by the finance department to be $12.

A paper-making machine had a wet end (where the diluted wood fibre pulp entered the process), and a dry end (where the completed paper was wound onto very large rolls or logs of paper). Paper orders of a similar nature were run at the same time to minimize the machine set-up time. Except for this set-up "downtime," the paper-making machines ran as close to 24 hours per day as possible.

The paper-making process was highly complex and required the monitoring of many variables such as temperature, chemical content, and machine speed. In total, approximately 75 technical measurements had to be made every 30 minutes. Currently, about 50 of these measurements were made automatically by computerized process controls. These controls constantly adjusted the machine settings based upon "correct" values as predetermined by the production engineers. The remaining 25 measurements were made by a team of 8 inspection employees. There was a team for each of the three shifts. These workers, all members of the Canadian Paperworkers Union, earned an average of $9.85 per hour.

Mike Garfield recalled a report prepared by the director of computer services indicating that a computer program was available that could enhance the present system so that all 75 measurements could be computer controlled. The report cited increased accuracy and labour savings as the major benefits of such an acquisition. The program would cost $450,000. To Mike, it seemed to be worthwhile, but he wondered why his predecessor hadn't authorized the expenditure.

If machine capacity was at the root of the complaints, Mike knew that a report recently prepared by the production engineers would be most helpful. The report included cost estimates for increasing capacity at various points in the production process. Exhibit 2 provides excerpts from the report.

## THE COMPLAINTS

To better understand the source and cause of the recent complaints, Mike held a meeting with the chief production supervisor, Charlie Robertson. When asked about his understanding of the situation, Charlie responded,

> It's not my fault! It's those idiots in sales/marketing that keep sending me those stupid, small fancy orders ... I don't want them! Never used to get them. My guys are constantly shutting down to make machine adjustments ... by the time the order is completely through the process, we're just beginning to figure the proper settings! ... About those late deliveries, what do you expect? If we keep accepting those special orders, the newsprint just has to wait its turn! Really, Mike, it's *your* problem.

With demand for newsprint expected to increase from 3 million tons of paper in 1983 to 3,680,000 tons in 1984, Mike knew the current complaints might be a sign of worse days ahead. As plant manager, Mike knew he was ultimately responsible for the efficiency and profitability of his plant. With this in mind, he set out to prepare his report to his superior at head office.

## EXHIBIT 1

### Plant and Equipment Investment
### (in millions of dollars)

| | |
|---|---:|
| Paper-making machines | $150 |
| Digesters (2) | 62 |
| Chipper machine | 22 |
| Blow tank | 20 |
| De-barking machines (2) | 16 |
| Storage silos | 14 |
| Low weighing/sorting equipment | 11 |
| Miscellaneous plant/equipment | 55 |
| TOTAL | $350 |

*Exhibit 2*

---

### Capacity Enhancement Cost Study Results

---

1.  **Wood Processing** — $125,000 per increased production of 100,000 tons of wood chips per year, that is, to increase wood chip production by 100,000 tons per year, WPPL must spend approximately $125,000.

2.  **Pulp Production** — $200,000 per increased production of 100,000 tons of wood fibre pulp.

3.  **Paper Production** — $7,500,000 per increased production of 225,000 tons of paper.

---

# PART

# STRATEGIC MANAGEMENT

*"No man is an island, entire of itself; every man is a piece
of the continent, a part of the main ... "*

JOHN DONNE, 17th century poet

Strategic management requires the coordination of all aspects of business into an integrated strategic plan focusing on the company's overall growth and development; in other words, the *positioning* of the firm within the environment and the *balancing* of the business opportunities with corporate resources. The management team[1] or, in some cases, general managers, must spearhead strategy formulation, implementation, and evaluation. To do this effectively, the management team must *continually* assess what business the company should be in and how that company should operate.

Primarily, management should ask itself the following:

1. How effective has the existing strategy been? Has the company adequate resources and skills/competence to implement the existing strategy?

2. How effective will the existing strategy be in the future? Does it adequately exploit the company's distinctive competence and provide a strong competitive advantage to ensure sustainability?

3. How effective would the various proposed strategic alternatives be in the future? Would they exploit environmental opportunities and minimize environmental threats? Could they adequately utilize the company's resources and distinctive competence to ensure a sustainable competitive advantage?[2]

The management team must evaluate all strategic alternatives and implement strategic direction with a focus on the successful integration of the marketing, operations, finance/accounting, and research and development aspects of the business. Management's major responsibility is to make good strategic decisions and provide the necessary leadership and skills/expertise to fulfil successfully the corporation's goals and objectives. These goals, as established by a strategic plan, are achieved within an organization when functional areas, provided with the appropriate skills and resources, are fully integrated with one another and are supported by the organization's employees and management.

■
**SECTION**
■
**ONE**
■

## THE GENERAL MANAGER

The meaning of general management can vary. In a small, one-person business, the chief decision maker is the all-round general manager responsible for long-term planning as well as daily "fire fighting," since there is no delegation of these responsibilities to specialized staff. In larger firms, the general management tasks are essentially the same although more complicated; however, strategic decision making is usually shared by a management team — often through strategy development workshops. The process of decision making is no longer a personal one but a *shared vision* process. In this chapter, the title "general manager" will refer to the decision maker(s) who is (are) primarily responsible for the business or a major unit of the business.

The responsibilities of a general manager are to articulate, implement, and generally define the goals and objectives of the organization. More specifically, the general manager is responsible for:

1. Long-term planning for new products, production/operation processes, new markets, financial flexibility, and organizational changes.
2. Finding, hiring, and training competent middle management teams in functional areas. The management team's goal would be to delegate, coordinate, and facilitate as much responsibility and authority as possible to employees in finance, marketing, operations, and human resources so that time can be spent on the "bigger picture" decisions affecting the company's competitive position within the industry.
3. Ensuring, through personal leadership, that the company's functional departments and their various activities interrelate, coordinate, and strengthen, often through synergy,[3] rather than work at cross-purposes. The general manager's role often consists of being a liaison person or providing direction to ensure that integration and coordination is sought and successfully achieved among these functional areas.
4. The general manager will make decisions that employees are not in a position to make, either because disagreements may arise or because they lack a sufficiently broad perspective on the issues that need to be considered.

In summary, to adequately fulfill this demanding role, the general manager must be able to appraise the company's competencies and its external environment thoroughly and objectively in order to diagnose, interpret, devise, and direct strategic decisions (longer-term goals for the business) and operational decisions (shorter-term specific actions to accomplish shorter-term goals). This must be done with an understanding of all functional areas of business, including their interrelationships and interdependence; a high degree of competence in human resources management is also required.

■
**SECTION**
■
**TWO**
■

## THE STRATEGIC EVALUATION PROCESS

A general manager's major concern is to improve the overall performance of the company. This is done by assessing whether the firm is doing what it should do and whether or not it could be better at what it does. After analyzing the existing opportunities or threats in the external environment and the company's strengths and weaknesses, and determining feasible options for improving performance within the operational capacities of the company, the general manager must devise a future plan for the firm, establishing appropriate corporate goals and objectives. This process of matching the internal capabilities of the firm with external environmental opportunities is called the *formulation of a strategic direction* for the company.

Exhibit 1 describes a strategic evaluation process that can be used by a general manager to review and to critique the external (industry) and internal (company) environments and, if necessary, to lead the process for strategic change. This assessment is a continuous one and dependent, of course, on the speed of change within the industry itself. For example, companies selling computer software will need to regularly assess their external environment, existing market

**EXHIBIT 1**
***The Strategic***
***Evaluation***
***Process***

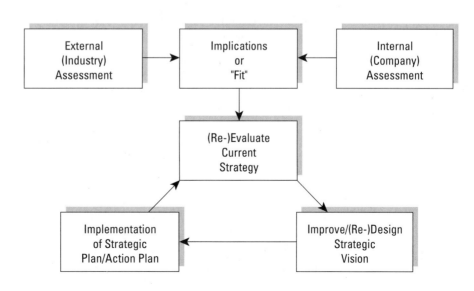

share, and their products' positioning(s) given the continuous acceleration of more complex software package offerings marketed by its competitors. Keeping track of these external changes can minimize the chances of a mismatch between the external environment and the corporation's current strategic direction.

A thorough assessment of the internal and external environments will lead to the identification of specific *implications* such as skills and products needed to compete successfully, changing technological requirements, low-cost requirements, and market niches. By matching the *implications* from the external analysis (changes in the industry, competition, consumer demands, and the environment) with the *implications* of the internal analysis (financial and human resource availability, production/operations capabilities, product sustainability) the general manager is forced to take a "fresh look" at the firm's current corporate "vision" or mission statement. If a change in corporate strategy is necessary, it may require operational and/or structural changes to the way in which the business operates; consequently, the general manager must lead the improvement and redesign of the corporate strategy by *directing* the company's goals and objectives toward this *strategic vision*. This implementation plan (or action plan) should ensure that the current organizational structure, reporting systems, and the appropriate resources are in place to pursue the strategy successfully. Understanding that the process of change within an organization is often not easily attainable is also required — observant managers must recognize the impact of change on the existing corporate culture, values, and beliefs of the employees and the organization.

By regularly monitoring success of the corporate strategy and continuously scrutinizing changes in the industry, management can re-evaluate the company's respective position within that industry to determine if the "fit" is still appropriate or if changes to the company's strategic direction are needed for its survival; consequently, the strategic review process begins again.

Each stage of Exhibit 1 will be presented in detail. The general manager must perform an external analysis, considering the consumer, the competition, and the environment. A corporate, internal assessment will determine the workings of the company in four critical areas: finance, marketing, operations, and human resources. Various stages of corporate development will be discussed, along with basic analytical tools useful in evaluating strategic alternatives, including the valuation of a corporation. Finally, action plan considerations consistent with company goals and objectives will be presented.

## INDUSTRY (EXTERNAL) ANALYSIS

External analysis refers to the assessment of an industry and the environment in which a firm operates. "The existence and magnitude of economic, social, cultural, demographic, geographic, political, governmental, legal, technological, and competitive changes underlie the need for an effective external audit."[4] This analysis is increasing in importance given the continued growth in international markets and international competitors and the changing roles played by governments.

## THE CONSUMER/TRADE

In the marketing chapter, ways of analyzing existing and potential consumer or trade demand characteristics were outlined. By using these techniques, the general manager will arrive at an assessment of:

1. Existing market opportunities — for example, the size and growth rate of a market.

2. The investments and risks associated with the pursuit of new opportunities, such as the cost of an investment in equipment for a product known to have a very short life cycle due to rapid technological advancements.

3. The key success factors (quality, speed of delivery, price, sales, and support services) involved in improving the firm's competitive stance to gain consumer acceptance and to make a profit. The key success factor in door-to-door cosmetic marketing, for example, is a very large, highly motivated sales force; the key success factor in a price competitive, basic commodity industry such as sugar is being a low-cost producer.

These implications will identify the ideal products or services and their appropriate characteristics (price, presentation/packaging, promotion, distribution systems) that best "fit" with the demands of the consumer. Once identified, the general manager can devise a strategy to deliver these products or services in an environment that offers its own risks and opportunities as well as being able to compete successfully with the competition.

## THE COMPETITION

The marketing chapter also discussed the importance of understanding the strengths and weaknesses of the company's major and minor competitors. This analysis of the current competition's existing and potential strengths and weaknesses will point to threats and opportunities. For example, the general manager may discover:

- a gap or niche for a product or service in the marketplace, perhaps as a result of a major competitor announcing a change in strategy. This opportunity may match specific company skills, be easy to introduce, may also not induce, or at least, minimally induce, a competitive reaction;

- competitive trends developing in terms of pricing, marketing, technology, and the number and sophistication of competitors;

- a back-up plan may be needed to help differentiate the company's product or service from that of its competitors. This is a direct attempt to minimize the impact of competitive reactions;

- producing a standardized product at low-cost for price-sensitive consumers would provide the company with a competitive edge;
- the company's current marketing plan may need to be modified as a result of additional information gained from an analysis of the competition. Increased competition from foreign companies may lead a firm to market its product differently. A more specific example of this occurred in the Swiss watch industry:

> When confronted with inexpensive Japanese quartz technology, it was impossible for Swiss companies to compete with the new technology, and some businesses were driven to the brink of collapse. But the industry managed to look at its product as a fashion item rather than merely a high-precision timekeeper. This new outlook revolutionized the industry and the Swatch was born.[5]

Thus, astute general managers monitor the environment in order to identify and take advantage of changes that offer opportunities to their companies.

## ENVIRONMENTAL ANALYSIS

Strategic formulation cannot begin without an environmental analysis of the industry. The marketing chapter discussed ways to examine the social, technological, economic, and political (STEP) trends of importance. Major changes can create fundamental industry change, such as the introduction of robotics to the automotive industry, the introduction of micro-chip processing, the deregulation of the airline industry, or the opening up of Eastern Europe to world markets. Such uncontrollable changes create and destroy major industries and market dominance quickly by offering new opportunities and/or imposing severe constraints. As well, most companies compete in international markets, making strategic implementation more complex because of the numerous business practices and cultural differences. When (re-) defining corporate strategy, the general manager must identify the threats and opportunities from this STEP analysis and lead the firm's strategic direction accordingly.

## CORPORATE (INTERNAL) ANALYSIS

**SECTION**

**FOUR**

Analyzing corporate performance can be difficult as there are so many dimensions to be examined and often not enough information is available. In these circumstances, the general manager will usually begin with a "big picture" approach, gradually becoming more specific as circumstances warrant it. Three basic questions can be asked to help evaluate the company's performance:

1. How well has the company done in terms of resources it had to work with? Resources include the people, financial, marketing, and production resources available to the firm.

2. How well has the company done in terms of its market opportunities? The size of the market, the company's share, and the growth rate will need to be considered.

3. How well has the company done in terms of its overall objectives? Objectives usually include profitability, return on investment, market share, and new product introductions.

A general manager must assess the various activities of the firm and evaluate the strengths and weaknesses in each functional area. It is important to determine why performance in each aspect of the firm was as good as it was and why it was not better. If there was less than satisfactory performance, was it the result of incorrect strategy, poor execution, or a mixture of both? Each of the functional sections described earlier in the text was designed to enable the general manager to do this. For example:

1. In *finance*, management of a company's cash position, analysis of past and projected financial performance, and sources and types of additional funds were discussed. This analysis will point to the company's financial flexibility and to the financial feasibility of implementing a new or existing strategic plan.

2. In *marketing*, understanding and predicting the response of consumers and competitors to changes in a company's product, price, distribution, placement, and promotion policies were studied. Companies now have the technical know-how to quickly react to their competition's offerings. These accelerated competitive reactions can effectively shorten the life cycle of products or eliminate a product's life. Therefore, the *sustainability* of the company's products or services in the marketplace is more tenuous than it ever was.

3. In *operations*, the various processes a company may use to produce goods and services and the techniques to improve its production efficiency and effectiveness were examined. Operations activities often represent the largest part of the firm's employees and capital assets. Properly managed, this function can provide the competitive edge in a company's overall strategy.

4. In *human resources*, ways to understand individuals, groups, and organizations in order to accomplish tasks through the efforts of other people, as well as ways to anticipate employee reaction and leadership styles were reviewed. The existing skills/expertise of employees and the appropriate alignment or "fit" of individual values and goals with the organization's goals and objectives was also reviewed.

A general manager will look at each of these aspects of the overall company to determine corporate strengths and weaknesses. These strengths and weaknesses are best identified by comparing what the company has or does with what is particularly required to succeed in the business being examined (in other words, what are the key success factors in the industry?). The prudent general manager will attempt to build on corporate strengths (often distinctive competencies) and overcome, or at least reduce, its weaknesses.

## IMPROVING THE STRATEGIC VISION

### ANALYTICAL TOOLS AS AIDS IN (RE-)DESIGNING STRATEGY

The general manager may find some basic concepts useful when assessing the merits of various strategic alternatives. This section will discuss the stages of corporate development concept and a few conceptual models.

#### The Stages of Corporate Development[6]

The Stages of Corporate Development Concept outlines the evolution of companies from small, entrepreneurially driven, fairly simple ones to large and complex ones. Three stages are identified in the diagram below:

| Small and Simple | →→→ | Large and Complex |
|---|---|---|
| **STAGE I**<br>one unit<br>"one-man show" | **STAGE II**<br>one unit<br>functionally specialized group | **STAGE III**<br>multi-unit<br>general office and<br>decentralized divisions |

#### Stage I

In Stage I companies, the owner is the manager, making unilateral decisions and maintaining absolute ownership and control. The organization chart is usually simple, with employees reporting directly to the owner-manager. The owner functions as a short-term operator and the proverbial "jack of all trades," "putting out fires" on a daily basis. Resources are often limited, and the company relies heavily on support from suppliers, sales agents, bankers, accountants, and lawyers.

Stage I companies can grow and prosper, often earning enough to support a small management team that will enable them to reach the point of corporate development that marks the transition to Stage II.

#### Stage II

A team of managers with functionally specialized responsibilities characterizes the Stage II company. Complex management teams will be found in a well-developed Stage II firm. All functional units are built around one core business — for example, aluminum — and work together to sell primarily to one end market.

The company's strength lies in its concentration and specialization in one field, but this is also its greatest vulnerability as it tends "... to be weak in coping with basic market changes and the general management problems related to strategic change."[7] Resources can vary; however, Stage II companies are much less reliant on external factors and, consequently, less vulnerable to failure or bankruptcy than Stage I companies. Stage II companies may reach a point where they need to grow by diversifying through product development, mergers, or acquisitions. Successful development of these independent products marks the transition of a Stage II to a Stage III firm.

### Stage III

Stage III corporations are often highly complex, with head offices ultimately controlling several operating divisions, each of which operates like a Stage II firm. Stage III firms focus primarily on the aggressive pursuit and development of further diversification — "both internally via research and development and product development and externally via mergers and acquisitions"[8] — in an effort to develop profit opportunities.

In large Stage III companies, resource availability, including significant cash flows, functional specialization, management depth, and market diversification, seldom, if ever, limits decisions; consequently, a Stage III company is rarely vulnerable to bankruptcy:

> It has great powers to regroup and survive even in the event of such a serious crisis as the complete failure of an entire product division.... Perhaps the most significant weakness of the gigantic Stage III company is that its organization is so large and complex that it tends to become relatively inflexible.[9]

Some authors have extended this model to include a Stage IV. Companies at this stage are typically large, multinationals, which have many products or are made up of many businesses operating in several markets. These companies are well-diversified, decentralized, and may or may not be related; as a result, business strategies and operating decisions are made at the business level as opposed to the corporate level.

A general manager will recognize that both the functions and process of management will differ, based on the corporation's stage of development, and that managing corporate development is critical when corporations are in transition from one stage to another. The management skills necessary to be a strong owner-manager of a Stage I company are very different from those required in Stage III corporations. Both companies will operate and behave differently: for example, an owner-manager of a smaller company who has excellent short-term operating capabilities may not possess the broad management skills involved in human resource/supervision management or management development and style required to be a successful leader in Stage III companies.

An understanding of the stages in corporate development, their characteristics, and the manager's role at each stage will enable the general manager to successfully identify, plan, and direct the implementation of a specific strategy.

### The Product Mission Matrix[10]

This matrix (originally known as the "growth vector") highlights some of the optional strategies available to firms that, generally speaking, are moving from Stage I to Stage II or to firms that are currently at Stage II. As a corporation's products or services mature, it finds it must grow by penetrating existing markets or developing new products for existing markets. Another alternative may be to expand into new markets with the current products or services offered or to enter these new markets with new products. Exhibit 2 illustrates these options:

**EXHIBIT 2**
**The Product Mission Matrix[11]**

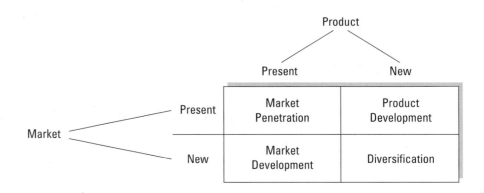

### The Diamond-E Model for Strategic Choice[12]

*Strategy* is the focal point of this model (see Exhibit 3), which positions strategy as the *link through which* the company's internal capabilities are related to the external environment and vice versa. The opportunities and threats presented by the environment (external analysis) determine a firm's strategy and this strategy drives the specific resources needed to compete; conversely, the strengths and weaknesses evident within the firm (management skills, the organizational culture, and resource availability) are related through strategy to the environment. Note the existence of a "two-way street" among corporate resources, management's value systems, organizational content and context, and the firm's strategy. A failure to recognize and to understand these relationships among the firm's functional areas can be detrimental.

Inconsistencies between the strategy and either the external (industry) analysis or the internal (company) analysis pinpoint areas of *risk*, short-term or long-term, facing the firm. It is the general manager's responsibility to assess these risks and to develop reasonable trade-offs between these external and internal,

**EXHIBIT 3**
**The Diamond-E**
**Framework**

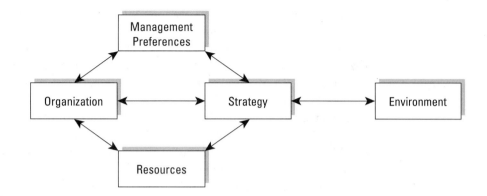

short- and long-term risks. This "balancing act" must be well thought out and understood by management to be successful.

### Segmentation Models

To help understand and characterize the target business environment, it is often useful to develop industry segmentation models that map a firm's current (and potential) competitive positions. Existing or potential customers are mapped into segments of similar, distinctive, demand characteristics; but, of course, none will be identical. This process is a creative one and segmentation models are not to be viewed as precise. However, these models help general managers to conceptually visualize opportunities for focus or expansion, or may pinpoint alternative strategic plans to better position the company's products or services within the target environment.

Any variables or combination considered strategically important can be used for segmentation. Most general managers are familiar with the appropriate distinctive segmentations in their markets, such as size, competitive positions, and technology. Two of these demand characteristics are placed on the "x" and "y" axes of the graph. The company's and its competitors' products or services are then positioned according to these demand characteristics. Once tracked, the strategist can visualize the company's current "fit" within the competitive environment and identify potential "niches."[13]

### The Product Portfolio Matrix[14]

The Boston Consulting Group has labelled and characterized businesses or products in terms of cash generation, into a four-box matrix (see Exhibit 4). Various products, services, or businesses are classified according to market share, profitability, and market growth potential. The four boxes are identified as "stars," "cash cows," "question marks," (sometimes referred to as "wildcat ventures"), and "dogs." Their characteristics are as follows:

**Stars**. These businesses or products currently hold a large portion of market share in high growth markets. Because of their market share dominance and their experience, they (usually) incur lower costs, resulting in higher profitability. The high growth of the market dictates the continued use of large amounts of cash to maintain market share. Therefore, the net cash flow is modest on these businesses or products.

**Cash Cows.** These businesses or products are highly profitable and have a significant percentage of market share, but have little market growth potential left. Many companies utilize the excess cash generated from such products or businesses to improve existing products or to research and develop new ones.

**Question Marks.** These businesses or products are currently not very profitable, mostly due to capturing a smaller market share, but the future growth potential is deemed significant. Given time, question marks could become very profitable if they increase their market share or keep up with the market's growth; however, they will require significant infusions of cash, since they are not currently generating cash for the company.

**Dogs.** These businesses or products have little market share and little potential; they need and provide little cash. An identification of "dogs" would lead decision makers to divest, shut down, or reposition these products or businesses.

This model links market growth and market share with cash flow results. Note the direction of the arrows in Exhibit 4. Solid arrows indicate the movement of cash, whereas dotted arrows represent the desired movement of products/businesses over time from **question marks** to **stars** to **cash cows**. The cash generated from cash cows will often go toward maintenance of market share, for reinvestment in plant capacity, for working capital, or for the question marks and stars, as these are products in a high growth market with the most market growth potential.[15]

It may be useful for strategists to place their products or businesses in these boxes to conceptualize their firm's portfolio offerings at a particular point in time.[16] There may not be enough (or any) stars and/or cash cows to ensure the company's sustainability, or the company may have dogs it should be divesting.

### DEVELOPMENT OF STRATEGIC ALTERNATIVES

Once the general manager has completed a thorough external and internal analysis, using various analytical tools, strategic alternatives can be examined. Some of the fundamental stratagems for consideration are listed below.

1. *Market Penetration.* In stratagem one, the general manager improves the efficiency and effectiveness of resources devoted to the marketing and the production/operations for current products in order to increase the market penetration in current markets and to increase profitability. Marketing efforts will concentrate on creating increased demand for the product or service, based on either tangible characteristics such as differentiating technical fea-

**EXHIBIT 4
The Product
Portfolio
Matrix
(Boston
Consulting
Group)**

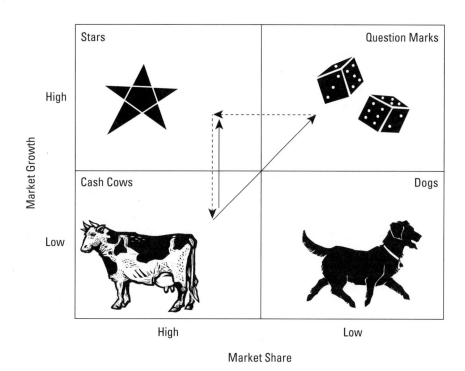

tures and financing, or intangible qualities such as a prestigious image. If we are marketing milk and we want to convince current customers to use more of the company's product or to use it more frequently (market penetration), we might try an overall strategy of suggesting more occasions when drinking milk is appropriate, or find new uses for milk, such as in cooking.

It should be noted that the basis on which differentiation may be pursued and its success varies with the product's life cycle. Early in the life cycle it is easy to differentiate a product based on its unique features, and, perhaps, a more sustainable competitive advantage via patents, copyrights, or brand preference. But:

> In the latter stages of the life cycle, it becomes more difficult to differentiate products in any sustainable way, so many companies focus on reinforcing an established position and using it as the base-point for incremental activities as competitive advantages are usually based on price and cost. Consider, for example, Coca-Cola's brand extensions into Diet Coke and caffeine-free Coke. Without a basic advantage of the long established product to build on, the new initiatives would be relatively meaningless since they would be easy to copy on a purely technical basis. Thus, short of breakthroughs in product development, late cycle competition turns on price and cost.[17]

2. *New Market Development.* In stratagem two, the general manager introduces current products to new markets (geographic areas). New markets may involve expanded sales territories and the development of marketing and

production/operations plans to appeal to new market segments. Sherwin-Williams expanded beyond its retail operations by marketing the Dutch Boy brand of paint products to mass merchants, and the private label, Martin Senow, to individual paint and hardware stores in an effort to increase volume through multiple distribution points.[18]

3. *New Product Development.* In stratagem three, the general manager proposes the development of new products to serve existing markets. In the strategic evaluation process, the general manager may have identified market segments currently poorly served by the firm's competitors' products. For example, a large toy company, highly successful and well-known for manufacturing safe and durable toys, introduced a new product line including baby strollers, playpens, and cribs. This line's products had many "child-proof" and "child friendly" features not currently offered by its competitors, guaranteed the same standards of safety and durability as the toy line, and were researched and developed with the toy firm's existing knowledge of children's behaviour and children's and parents' needs. Prior to the introduction of this new line, the market was dominated by large furniture companies distributing through major retail chains. These same retail chains also carried the toy firm's toy products line. The toy firm's management team had identified a group of consumers who were in need of a product that offered more features and was "user-friendly."

4. *Diversification.* In stratagem four, the general manager proposes the development of new products for new markets. Adding new but related products or services is referred to as *concentric diversification*. Wal-Mart's introduction of hypermarket stores, which combined supermarket and general merchandise at discount prices under one roof, is an example of concentric diversification. Adding new unrelated products or services is referred to as *conglomerate diversification*. Reasons for conglomerate diversification may include saturation of current products in existing markets, antitrust legislation, or an attractive investment opportunity.[19] A major automotive corporation purchasing a large mortgage insurance company is an example of conglomerate diversification.

Sometimes, firms will diversify through acquisitions, when a large firm purchases a smaller firm or vice versa, or mergers, when two firms of comparable size combine into one firm. Acquisitions or mergers can take several forms: joint ventures, alliances, hostile takeovers, and buyouts. When appropriate, the acquisition of needed knowledge and expertise, new products or services, or new markets can provide a firm with rapid growth to gain a competitive edge in the marketplace. Most acquisitions or mergers occur as the result of a need to "round out" a product line or to diversify, leading to less dependence and, therefore, less risk on a single business or industry and/or in an effort to stabilize earnings. For example, a large Canadian brewing company acquired a significant stake in a large Mexican brewery. This investment was intended to capitalize on market opportunities in Mexico, the United States, and Canada.

5. *Integration.* In stratagem five, the general manager may integrate vertically or horizontally. Vertical integration can be either forward, (closer to the final customer), accomplished by developing or acquiring distribution outlets or retailers, or backward (closer to supply sources), achieved by developing or acquiring the firm's suppliers of materials or parts. Most major oil companies are totally vertically integrated, being involved in several stages of the industry supply chain. These companies explore for oil, extract it, refine it into gas and other products, warehouse, distribute, advertise, and market these products to consumers.[20]

Integrating horizontally — buying ownership in or increased control over competitors — is often used as a growth strategy. For example, it is not uncommon for large insurance companies to purchase or buy ownership in their competitors. These acquisitions considerably expand their customer base for selling services and products.

6. *Concentration.* The first five stratagems focus on growth. There may come a time when an enterprise finds it is offering too many products and services across too many markets. Under these circumstances, the general manager will refocus the concentration of effort to areas that offer the greatest chance of sustainable success and profitability. Concentration involves the redeployment or regrouping of resources within the company to current and more profitable products or services. If there are excess resources that cannot be used profitably within the enterprise, disposal of portions of the business is usually appropriate. Large and successful companies, such as McDonald's, have built their reputations pursuing this strategy.[21]

7. *Technological Change.* Although tangential to the above stratagems, technology plays such a critical role in the implementation plan of the alternatives above that it must be considered in the strategic plan. Technology is now being used as the necessary catalyst for corporate *proaction* rather than reaction to the global marketplace. As businesses increasingly operate globally, they are required to organize globally.[22] Many managers believe the wise use of and investment in information technology (telecommunications, data access and storage devices, on-line databases, graphics equipment, software, etc.) is the key to corporate sustainability, as never-ending technological change will improve the speed and quality of product development, lower product costs, and improve accountability and the speed of reporting. The use of this technology will allow the corporation the flexibility it needs to proact during rapid and constant changes to the marketplace, as the example below demonstrates.

> A new generation of software, called Enterprise Support Systems (ESS), is changing the way executives work. ESS provides information from every nook and cranny of an organization. The UCS Group, the $300-million retailing arm of Imasco Ltd. known as United Cigar Stores, is finding out just how useful an ESS can be. Every day any of its 30 senior or middle managers can log onto its system and check sales at any of its 476 stores. A marketing executive might pull up a weekly or monthly sales

summary and check it against the company's business plan. If sales are off target, he can then "drill down" through the data to find the division, region or district where sales are slackening. He can cross-reference by store type or by product line to see if, perhaps, it's cigarette sales at hotel locations in Ontario that are causing the problem. He can even search by promotion, to find out, for example, if a two-pack cigarette discounting program is dragging down revenue instead of boosting it.[23]

## EVALUATING STRATEGIC ALTERNATIVES

When examining strategic alternatives, it may be necessary to estimate a company's value. There are three basic ways in which this may be done: capitalization of earnings, net book value, and economic appraisal. One or all of these methods can be used in valuing a business.

### Capitalization of Earnings

This method uses a price/earnings multiple that is applied against expected earnings. Price/earnings multiples observed for the common stocks in the same industry on public stock exchanges can form the base for estimating an appropriate multiple. The multiple is affected by growth expectations (the higher the growth rate, the higher the multiple), by risk (the higher the risk, the lower the multiple), and by the debt proportion (the higher proportion debt is of the total capital structure, the lower the multiple).

### Net Book Value

Net book value involves simply subtracting the total liabilities from the total assets to arrive at "net book value." This method does not account for the prevailing market value of the firm's assets, nor for intangible asset investment. Sometimes analysts subtract intangible assets from total assets before deducting liabilities because the value of intangible assets is so ephemeral. For acquisitions and concentration, overall company valuation is important. If owners wish to sell all or part of their business, they need to know what their selling price should be. Investors look at the potential earnings of the firm to maximize their returns on their stocks.

### Economic Appraisals

Economic appraisals are often done by a city or municipality for tax reasons or by a lender for collateral purposes. Lenders favour this method over book value. For example, land may appear on the books at its original cost of $105,000. A real estate company may determine through an appraisal, however, that the market value of this land at the time of appraisal was $245,000. Appraisals may be based on replacement value or liquidation value. Consider a machine for filling bottles. To buy a new one to perform the same function may cost $100,000, but if the current machine were sold, especially if buyers knew we were anxious to be rid of it, only $40,000 might be received. In other words, the economic value placed on a firm's assets depends largely on the reason for valuation and the circumstances of the firm. Assets are nearly always worth more if the firm is considered an ongoing business than if it is about to be liquidated. To arrive at net economic value of the equity, liabilities are deducted from the sum of the asset appraisals.

**SECTION**

**SIX**

## IMPLEMENTING THE STRATEGIC PLAN

As different strategic alternatives are generated, evaluated, and ranked, the general manager must be cognizant of the skills and resources required to implement each of these strategies within the appropriate and necessary time frame. There will likely be differences in the degree of risk associated with each of these alternatives and differences in the expected payoffs to the company; these differences are what make strategy formulation difficult and interesting.

A solid and thorough analysis of the strategic alternatives will enable the general manager to formulate an action plan relatively easily: the action plan should practically "drop out" of the analysis. Such a plan should answer the following questions:

1. What needs to be done? Is financing needed? Are capital acquisitions/additional resources necessary? What product/service, price, promotion, and distribution channels will be used? Will job descriptions/employee requirements change?

2. When will the implementation begin? (Include an implementation date and a time horizon.)

3. Who has the responsibility and authority to implement the plan? Which organizational level and which individuals should be involved?

4. How will results be measured? (Computers can enhance the strategic evaluation process by generating a variety of strategy evaluation reports for different corporate levels and types of managers.)

5. How will results be measured in terms of compensation or promotion? What are the rewards/punishments?

The action plan must be consistent with the firm's corporate goals and objectives. It is the general manager's job to ensure that the functional areas — such as finance, marketing, operations, and human resources — fit together into an integrated whole, constituting the overall corporate strategic action plan. In other words, the general manager must provide structure and processes. This includes the need to assess and change, if necessary, the organizational structure, and the ways it operates, along with establishing long-term corporate goals and objectives that are attainable, provide direction, and reveal priorities consistent with the chosen strategy. For example, if a firm's new goal is toward product development, the research and development department must have the necessary financial resources (for technological support) and employee skills/expertise to fulfill this goal. These goals and objectives may include the following:

- the current and potential resources (financial, physical, human, and technological) and skills of the organization, including the organization's strengths and weaknesses
- industry knowledge (consumer segmentation, competitive strengths and weaknesses, environmental threats and opportunities)
- the company's current and future products or services, and their current and future competitive dimensions, such as price, quality, delivery, and service

It is often necessary to consider trade-offs among objectives, when it is only possible to achieve one objective at the expense of another. For example, consider the following trade-offs:

- Short-term profits versus long-term growth
- Profit margins versus competitive position
- Penetration of existing markets versus development of new markets
- Related versus unrelated new opportunities as a source of long-term growth

In summary, one very useful way to assess an idea for change is to compare the projected results of that change with the projected results without that change; in other words, to project the firm's performance first under a "no change" scenario and then compare that with the "change" scenarios. Another good test is to try to persuade a sceptical person that the plan of action makes sense. As a general manager, you should be able to explain both *what to do specifically and why it is worth doing.*

## CONCLUSION

General managers should systematically formulate, implement, and evaluate the strategic direction of the firm. It is essential that the general manager review the firm's strategies, as they can become obsolete. This process entails a thorough analysis of the external (industry) and the internal (company) environments, and a *matching* of the external threats and opportunities with the internal strengths and weaknesses, that is, *a comparison between what the company has or does with what is specifically required to succeed in its industry.* Ideally, this "fit" will include a sustainable competitive advantage for the firm.

Astute general managers recognize the importance of clearly stating the new strategic direction in the corporate vision. The firm's long-term and short-term goals and objectives should be consistent with this vision and be communicated clearly at the corporate management and organizational levels so as to provide no ambiguity. All strategic plans should include the monitoring of results. Measuring individual and organizational performance requires the utilization of solid accounting functions and reliable reporting systems, such as financial statements, market share reports, and ROI calculations, which must be in place to evaluate the plan's relative success and to aid in the analysis and corrective action of issues or problems.

A thorough and complete strategic analysis and implementation plan may not be sufficient; many strategists believe that companies must also be able to anticipate change and to proact as well as to react quickly and decisively to the market place. Therefore, general managers need to improve the organization's speed and flexibility; that is, for the firm to have strategic competence it must be nimble and adaptive to changes in strategy. This process of continuous re-evaluation drives the firm's management team to regularly reappraise the firm's current strategy in light of industry and corporate change.

## NOTES

1. Boards of directors are becoming more involved in an organization's strategic management than ever before as they are being held more accountable for the firm's operations.

2. "A *sustainable competitive advantage* is an advantage that is difficult to imitate by competitors and, consequently, leads to higher-than-average organizational performance over a long time period. It exists even after competitors have done everything they can to imitate it." Jeffrey S. Harrison and Caron H. St. John, *Strategic Management of Organizations and Stakeholders. Theory and Cases.* (Minneapolis: West Publishing Company, 1994), p. 16.

3. The combined effect of minds that exceeds the sum of their individual effects.

4. Fred R. David, *Strategic Management*, 2nd ed. (Columbus, Ohio: Merrill Publishing Company, 1989), p. 120

5. Kathryn Dorrell, "Comedy Shows Companies How to Improvise," *Western News*, January 20, 1994, p. 12.

6. Adapted from Donald H. Thain, "Stages of Corporate Development," *The Business Quarterly*, Winter, 1969.

7. Ibid., p. 6.

8. Ibid., p. 7.

9. Ibid., p. 8.

10. H.I. Ansoff, *The New Corporate Strategy*, (New York: John Wiley & Sons, 1987), Chapter 6.

11. Ibid., Chapter 6.

12. Joseph N. Fry and J. Peter Killing, *Strategic Analysis and Action*, 3rd ed. (Scarborough, Ontario: Prentice Hall Canada, Inc., 1995), p. 49–63.

13. Fry and Killing, *Strategic Analysis and Action*, 1st ed., pp. 81–84.

14. Product Portfolio Matrix, @ 1970, The Boston Consulting Group, Inc. Perspectives No. 66.

15. Fry and Killing, *Strategic Analysis and Action*, 3rd ed., p. 225.

16. It should be noted that not all products/businesses will fit neatly into this matrix.

17. Fry and Killing, *Strategic Analysis and Action*, p. 131.

18. Amy Feldman, "The House That Jack Rebuilt," *Forbes*, April 25, 1994, pp. 91–94.

19. David, *Strategic Management*, p. 69.

20. Harrison and St. John, *Strategic Management of Organizations and Stakeholders*, p. 123.

21. Ibid., p. 181.

22. Rich Karlgaard, "Percy Barnevik," *Forbes ASAP*, 1994/95.

23. Mark Stevenson, "He Sees All He Knows All," *Canadian Business*, Spring 1994, pp. 31–35.

# ■ ■ ■ ■  CASES FOR PART 7  ■ ■ ■ ■

**CASE 7.1** Blackshop Bistro

■

**CASE 7.2** The Body Shop Canada

■

**CASE 7.3** Filter Plus

■

**CASE 7.4** The Greek Cosmobob

■

**CASE 7.5** Mail-Order in Canada

■

**CASE 7.6** Medical Services Limited (A)

■

**CASE 7.7** Mondetta Everywear

■

**CASE 7.8** Rampac Distributors

■

**CASE 7.9** A Strategic Plan for Midtown Hospital

■

**CASE 7.10** SWO Service

■

**CASE 7.11** Telemus Electronic Systems Inc.

## C A S E 7.1   BLACKSHOP BISTRO

In November 1991, Alec Cerny was discussing a business opportunity with his father, Jan, who owned Blackshop Bistro in Cambridge, Ontario. The current facility offered little opportunity for sales growth. Jan proposed to relocate and expand their family business into a small business development nearby. Alec knew that such a move would have significant implications for the company's current strategy as well as for operations, marketing, finances, and human resources. Jan wrapped up their conversation:

> Well, Alec, I would really like to have a bigger place and I think this is an attractive opportunity. But I won't go ahead unless you agree. Why don't you use some of that stuff they have been teaching you at business school? What do you think?

Alec realized that a restaurant on the scale proposed would allow him to stay in the family business and use some of his newly acquired skills if he wanted to. On the other hand, if Blackshop Bistro did not expand, there would be no position open for him. He wanted to make a decision and to be able to present his father with a solid action plan as soon as possible. The developer needed an answer within the next two weeks. Alec knew that if he decided not to proceed, his father would ask him for some realistic options.

**CAMBRIDGE, ONTARIO**

Cambridge, Ontario, was about 100 km southwest of Toronto, adjacent to Kitchener. Highway 401, a multilane divided highway that served as the major traffic artery through southern Ontario, ran through the northern part of Cambridge. About 575,000 people lived within 40 km of Cambridge. The main communities were Kitchener-Waterloo, 240,000; Guelph, 109,000; and Brantford, 94,000; as well as Cambridge itself, 95,000. Slightly farther away were the cities of Woodstock, 30,000; Burlington, 139,000; and Hamilton, 320,000. Cambridge was easily accessible to all these communities by road. Exhibit 1 shows maps of the area. The municipalities of Galt, Preston, and Hespeler had been established in the early 19th century to take advantage of the water power offered by the Grand River and its tributary, the Speed River, which flowed through Cambridge. On January 1, 1973, the three municipalities and parts of Waterloo and North Dumfries Townships amalgamated under the name Cambridge. The enlarged city still reflected its origins: it had three main districts, with Galt as the largest, clustered along the rivers and separated by less developed areas. The Kitchener-Waterloo and Cambridge area was a major Ontario industrial centre and home to many manufacturing and service firms. It boasted a large multicultural pool of skilled and semi-skilled labour, particularly those of German, Italian, and Portuguese descent. Although the direct economic importance of water power had long since disappeared, the rivers continued to affect traffic flow in the area.

The population of the Kitchener, Waterloo, and Cambridge communities was growing at about twice the growth rate for Canada as a whole.[1] Its per capita income and retail sales figures were about 8 percent above and 2 percent below the respective Canadian averages.[2] The average household in the area had 2.8 people[3] and spent about $1,665 per year on restaurant meals.[4]

## THE CERNY FAMILY

Jan Cerny was born and raised in Czechoslovakia where he spent his youth helping his parents operate the family restaurant. He dreamed of opening his own restaurant or hotel. The Soviet army shattered such aspirations in August 1968, when it invaded Czechoslovakia to repress the reforms introduced by leader Alexander Dubček. Because he had to support his wife, Eva, and their 16-month-old son, Alec, Jan remained in Czechoslovakia operating a local hotel. In 1980, Jan and his family, which now included their second son, John, who had been born in 1971, escaped to Austria and eventually arrived in Canada.

## BLACKSHOP BISTRO

After having worked three years at restaurants in London and Cambridge, Jan acquired financing, and in 1983 opened Blackshop Restaurant in a 100-year-old house that he had renovated. He hoped to provide his family with a stable business for the future. The idea behind the restaurant was that of an old blacksmith shop, hence the company's name. Jan chose dark decor to augment this theme and used antiques to create a sense of history. The restaurant always played recorded classical music to create an atmosphere of intimacy. The menu featured a combination of ethnic Czechoslovakian cuisine and dishes that Jan had seen served in Canadian restaurants in which he had worked, and included seafood, beef, and chicken. The concept proved to be very attractive to Cambridge residents. The restaurant enjoyed a busy first year with sales of just over $175,000. Jan hired an additional waiter and a dishwasher to make operations run more smoothly.

However, the concept eventually lost its lustre. Czechoslovakian food was greasy and heavy, characteristics that conflicted with the 1980s' trend toward healthy and sensible meals. As a result, revenues leveled off. In response, the Cernys removed the Czechoslovakian food from the menu in 1986. Except for this change, the menu remained largely intact.

In 1988, revenues leveled off again for no apparent reason. Jan raised prices only to see revenues drop. After consulting his staff, he realized that the menu needed to be more North American. He hired a new chef and introduced new, lighter menu items to reflect French and Italian influences in main courses, appetizers, desserts, and beverages; consequently, business improved again.

The Christmas period in 1988 was slow, and in 1989 revenues again began to stagnate. That year Jan spent some time in hospital and Alec entered the Western Business School at the University of Western Ontario, in London. However, because of his father's illness, Alec returned home for a few months to run the restaurant. When Jan returned from the hospital in the spring of 1990, he, Alec, and Shafiq Rao, one of Alec's childhood friends, who was Blackshop Restaurant's waiter, initiated additional changes to the concept of the restaurant. They renovated the facility internally by raising the lighting level, removing the metal decor, painting the interior in bright colours, and using peach-coloured table cloths, and enlivened the atmosphere by introducing recorded jazz as background music. A new name, Blackshop Bistro, as well as a lighter menu reflecting Australian and Californian influences, accompanied these changes. Despite the changes, the Cernys were able to retain the facility's family atmosphere and consistently high quality food and service. Jan believed that this reputation was key to his business's success. Once again, sales returned to their former levels. Exhibit 2 shows complete menus and wine lists from 1991.

Alec believed that the restaurant had not been well organized at first, owing largely to his father's limited knowledge of business in Canada. However, the small size of the staff allowed the restaurant to survive. Alec worked as a busboy and waiter for tips alone. Although the restaurant did well enough to support the family, it did not do well enough to provide a secure future nor to save for a new venture. Beginning in 1989, after six years of making ends meet, Jan began to look for a way out. In September 1990, Alec returned to the Western Business School from which he was scheduled to graduate in June 1992.

**Current Operations**

Blackshop Bistro was truly a family-run operation. Jan acted as the waiter and oversaw all operations. His wife, Eva, a dietician, did all the bookkeeping and helped out the chef who had immigrated from Czechoslovakia in 1989. Their younger son, John, was a certified chef and was considering entering the University of Guelph's Hotel and Food Administration program. Both sons helped out on evenings and weekends.

Alec believed that the cuisine at Blackshop Bistro was top quality and priced at a premium. In late 1991, the average price for a full course meal was $15 per person at lunch, and $40 per person at dinner. He commented:

> We are by no means a cheap meal out. Our reputation is for excellent but expensive food. Middle-class customers consider us to be a restaurant suitable for special occasions. Only well-off people become regular clients. This really reduces the size of our market. Customers won't just walk in for a light meal or a cocktail. They would feel intimidated.

Although change had been slow in Blackshop Bistro's early history, more recently the Cernys had adjusted their lunch and dinner menus every six to eight months to reflect changing customer demands and to offer variety to their very loyal clientele. Jan was proud of his efforts to consult his customers. He believed that this effort proved essential in recognizing problems early. Alec explained:

> You have to keep changing in this business. This encompasses many aspects, including decor, menus, specials, music. You don't want to run the risk of your customers getting bored. If they don't enjoy the product, you can be sure that they'll tell two friends, and so on.

Blackshop Bistro, which relied heavily on word-of-mouth advertising and did little additional marketing, soon developed a strong base of loyal customers. At least 40 regular customers frequented the restaurant on a weekly or biweekly basis. The economy was booming and Blackshop Bistro was successful. Exhibit 3 shows a review from the press, and Exhibit 4 shows some financial information.

Providing good service was the priority among Blackshop Bistro's staff of one chef, two waiters, and two dishwashers. They emphasized friendliness and efficiency, rather than pretentiousness. Jan hired only expert staff. The waiters and dishwashers received minimum wage — standard practice in the restaurant industry. The restaurant paid the chef an average wage. However, because the chef had limited ability in English and had no Canadian certification papers, Alec realized that his alternative opportunities were limited. Jan believed that customers appreciated the familiarity of having the same person serving them time after time, and thus, that high turnover caused poor service and inconsistent quality.

The main business district in the Galt section of Cambridge lay east of the Grand River between Park Hill Road and Warnock Street, on the right hand side of the map shown in Exhibit 5. Blackshop Bistro was on Ainslie Street on the northern edge of this district, in a one-floor house of about 71.5 square metres for which the Cernys paid an annual lease of $204.50 (1991) per square metre. The original lease specified annual rent increases of 10 percent; the Cernys expected further increases at the same rate. The building was at the back of the lot behind a real estate office. Ainslie Street was one way (north) and had a corner just south of the restaurant. The recessed location of the restaurant and the characteristics of Ainslie Street made the restaurant difficult to see. The lot had about 12 parking spaces available for Blackshop use, some of which were used by employees. Parking was not allowed on either Ainslie Street or Park Hill Road. There was a major grocery store immediately across Ainslie Street from the restaurant; it had complained to the Cernys about restaurant staff and patrons using its parking lot.

The restaurant had 32 seats. It was open for lunch from 11:30 a.m. until 2:00 p.m., Tuesday to Friday, and for dinner from 5:00 p.m. until 9:30 p.m., Tuesday to Saturday. The average table of two-four people took one hour for lunch and 2 to 2.5 hours for dinner. Blackshop Bistro remained open until the last customer left, even if it was after 9:30 p.m. Although customers did not require reservations for either lunch or dinner, the restaurant recommended that customers have them. Lately, seats had often been heavily booked two weeks in advance for Friday and Saturday nights; the necessity of reservations on weekends ensured profitable business but deterred walk-in customers. Because the restaurant was small, the tables were too close together for business people to conduct business. The restaurant was not available for parties of more than 10. Blackshop Bistro was unable to meet the demand for this service, which was significant, especially around Christmas.

## Dinner Ordering Process

The process was typical of full-service restaurants. When customers arrived, a staff member greeted them at the door, hung up their coats, escorted them to a table, and seated them. The waiter brought them menus and bread, described the daily specials, and took their drink orders. While the customers decided what food to order, the waiter filled the drink orders. This process usually took around 10 minutes. Most customers ordered appetizers as well as a main meal. The waiter took the appetizer orders to the kitchen, where the chef spent between five and eight minutes preparing them. The waiter took the appetizers to the customers' table, where they were consumed usually in 10 to 12 minutes. The waiter then returned to the kitchen and said "pick-up," which signalled the cooks to begin preparing the main meal. Following the preparation time of 7 to 10 minutes, the meals were served, and consumed in about 15 minutes. After clearing these dishes, the waiter offered customers coffee and dessert. When the customers had finished their meal, the waiter brought the bill, which the customers paid at the table. The process was similar at lunch, but faster.

## THE RESTAURANT MARKET

Alec believed that Blackshop Bistro was a fine-dining restaurant whose customers wanted top quality food and service, but in a relaxed environment. Although most of their clientele were business and affluent people in the Cambridge area, the Cernys knew that some customers came from Kitchener-Waterloo, Guelph, Brantford, and other communities within 40 km of Cambridge.

The Restaurant and Food Association identified five industry segments, based on differences in price and quality:

| Segment | Quality | Price | Portion of Restaurant Spending[5] |
|---|---|---|---|
| fine | high | high | 3% |
| casual | medium-high | medium | 15 |
| family-style | medium | low-medium | 13 |
| fast food | low-medium | low | 55 |
| convenience | low | low | 14 |

**THE COMPETITION**     Alec discussed Blackshop Bistro's competitors:

> We have three main competitors in the fine-dining segment. Two of them are right near us [see Exhibit 5]; the other one is farther away. Scallions has about 40 seats and is very similar to us. Two Italian brothers operate it. They are great chefs and take pride in knowing their customers, but they seem to lack business sense. Their home-made food is good and their prices are similar to ours. However, I think their service is inconsistent and they don't pay enough attention to their surroundings. It seems to look dirty.
>
> The Cambridge Mill is our most expensive competitor. Its average cheque is about $25 per person for lunch and $45 per person for dinner, but the quality of the food is inconsistent. It has 75 seats and a private room for 150 and offers its customers a beautiful view overlooking the Grand River. Jan was offered the Mill when it was in receivership in 1990. When we looked at the figures, we found that rent, including the parking lot, was running at $10,000 per month. We would have needed annual sales of $1.5 million just to survive.
>
> Twelve years ago Graystones was the best and the only classy restaurant in Cambridge. However, it didn't move with the times and now has a reputation for being old-fashioned, stuffy, and expensive. It has about 50 seats but no banquet facilities. Although it has brought its prices down to about the same level as ours, it can't seem to shake its reputation. Graystones is located at the far end of the main street through the Preston section of Cambridge, some five km northwest of here near the Speed River, not far south of the 401.
>
> Another nearby competitor is Café 13, but it is in the casual dining segment. It has great atmosphere and fair prices. An average dinner cheque is about $20 per person. Its owner is a very good businessman who promotes his business heavily. It is the only restaurant in town with some class to which you can go just to have a drink. Although I don't think its food is very good, it is edible — there are no surprises. I think it is Cambridge's most successful restaurant.

**THE PROPOSAL**     Recently, Jan had felt less motivated to continue Blackshop Bistro's current operations. He also wanted higher profits to prepare for an early retirement. Because of these factors and the high demand for Blackshop Bistro's service, Jan hoped to expand the company's operations. The current lease agreement was due to expire in October 1993. The landlord would not agree to Blackshop Bistro's expanding the current facility; consequently, Jan began looking for other opportunities.

In November 1991, John Lammer, a developer from the neighbouring city of Guelph, approached Jan. John was erecting a 1,100-square metre, two-floor building on Hobson Street at the corner of Park Hill Road. John Lammer's design called for an elegant natural stone building of a style similar to the historic 150-year-old buildings common in the area. He wanted a prosperous restaurant in the building and strongly believed that Jan would be a success. The project was due for completion in April 1992, just five months away.

The location was about 400 metres across the Grand River (via the Park Hill Road bridge) from Blackshop Bistro. It was on the edge of a residential area about a 15-minute walk from the centre of Cambridge's main business district. Although the building would abut on the Grand River, views of the river and the dam at that site would be restricted to the building's upper floors. Hobson Street was scheduled to become a main thoroughfare connecting Cambridge with Kitchener-Waterloo.

The new restaurant could occupy up to 315 square metres, which would accommodate a lounge with 20 seats, a bar with 10 stools, a dining room with 65 seats, and a banquet room with 80 to 100 seats. The new lease would cost $162 per square metre annually. In Jan's opinion the leasehold improvements, shown in Exhibit 6, would be generous. The restaurant would also have the first right of refusal on the entire second floor until December 1992. Property and business taxes would be about $25,000 per year, a significant increase from the current level of about $1,500. Alec estimated that the annual costs of the proposed expansion would include: food and beverages, 33 percent of sales; labour, 30 to 35 percent; interest, $13,500; depreciation on new equipment, $23,300; all other operating costs (except rent, property taxes, and advertising), $55,000.

The building would have 40 parking spots that Blackshop Bistro could use. In addition, customers would have access to a free city-owned, 120-parking spot lot just across Hobson Street. The building would allow the Bistro to broaden its service offerings. It could have a banquet room suitable for Christmas parties, wedding receptions, and other group functions. The front lounge and bar could have a fireplace and serve as a pleasant area for customers waiting for a table in the dining room. The lounge would also allow Blackshop Bistro to offer a menu with lighter meals for customers who did not want a full-course meal.

Because of the option offered, the building also allowed for ample potential growth. Alec believed that expanding to the second floor could offer advantages such as a river view and an opportunity to add a conference room and a banquet room should demand exist. Shafiq, on the other hand believed such a location would prove to be troublesome:

> My experience working at the Cambridge Mill has opened my eyes to second floor locations. Turnover of tables is slower as people spend more time watching the river, especially if it is flowing slowly, or if people are fishing or something. The river sets the pace of the whole meal!

**THE DECISION**

Alec didn't have much time to decide what to do and report to his father. Because Blackshop Bistro's reputation and its strong base of loyal customers were valuable, he did not want to damage either of these elements. Alec also wanted to preserve the company's family-oriented service concept and worried about the implications of trying to implement it on a larger scale. He expressed his views:

I am concerned about a lot of things. I am not sure that our current market niche is large enough for this possible expansion. The ethnic groups in this community traditionally don't eat out often. We might have to go after another target in the future. I wonder if there is one. We should be helped out by local trends. Lots of restaurants are leaving downtown Kitchener. Their move north to Waterloo makes Cambridge more attractive to people coming from the south end of Kitchener or off Highway 401.

At Western I took a course in service management. The professor described service concepts as the core of what the service is all about — the answer to the question: "What business are we in?" He elaborated by saying that you had to think carefully about the marketing mix — product, place, price, and promotion — and, particularly for services, how the process would work, what characteristics the servers and customers should have, and what the place would look like. He believed that a good concept was one that had a consistent marketing mix and was aimed at meeting the needs of an identified target market. It makes sense. Now I have to figure out what our concept should be.

If we did go after another group, I wonder what changes would be necessary to our current concept so it would appeal to a larger market? And, what effect would those changes have on our current clients?

If I decide to support the proposal, I will need a thorough plan of action. What operational, staffing, and marketing concerns will I have to consider? I guess we should start by looking at our name. Should it remain Blackshop Bistro? Or, should it go back to Restaurant? Perhaps we should change the Blackshop name too.

If a chain opened a restaurant of the calibre we are thinking about, it would probably spend $350,000 on start-up costs. I think if we did a lot of the work ourselves, we could probably cut that figure in half. But that is still a lot of money. Where and how can the family get access to such a sum? My father could probably invest up to $10,000 personally, but no one in the family could come up with much more.

If we were to offer banquet room services, what factors would we have to consider? It seems to me that anyone could make money from banquet facilities in peak periods such as Christmas. The secret is to do well in the slack periods too. What would be required to make it fly?

I also think about the second floor. It would offer a nice view. The ground floor has no view at all. On the other hand, as Shafiq says, a view could screw up our process. If we don't take the second floor and want it later, there is no way it will be available. If we take both floors, we will have a lot of tables to sell and I am not sure we could afford it. And the second floor is only one timing issue. Our current lease doesn't run out until October 1993. What should we do about that?

The last thing I want to do is to ruin a good thing and destroy the business my father and the rest of us have worked so hard to establish. We have a nice "family" atmosphere here that certainly includes all our staff and extends to our regular customers as well. I am not sure it will be easy to maintain that if we grow. Growth might reduce quality, too, although if we had two chefs instead of one we would be able to extend our hours. What do I have to do to ensure the success of the potential venture? I am involved in the restaurant now and I don't want to work on Bay Street, but I am not sure I or my brother, John, wants to make a career out of being a restaurateur. I could usually do a decent job on the cases we analyzed at university, but now the dollars are real and the stakes are personally high. I wonder what I should do.

Alec had two weeks to assess the opportunities that the developer was offering his family's business, and to determine Blackshop's, and his own, future.

## NOTES

1. E.J. Graham, ed., *Canadian Markets* (Toronto: Financial Post Publications, 1991).

2. *Canada's Postal Markets 1990: A Source of Business and Consumer Demographics and Buying by FSA* (Toronto: Compusearch Market and Social Research Ltd., and Financial Post Information Service, 1990).

3. Ibid.

4. Ibid.

5. The Canadian Restaurant and Food Association and Crest Canada, 1990.

**EXHIBIT 1**
**Maps of a Portion of Southern Ontario**

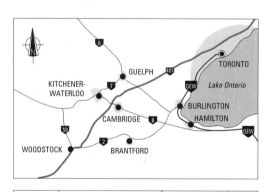

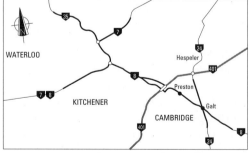

***EXHIBIT 2***
***Menus Offered by***
***Blackshop Bistro***

## DINNER
### AT THE BLACKSHOP BISTRO

**COLD APPETIZERS**

SMOKED SALMON WITH CAPERS, ONIONS, LEMON AND DILL MAYONNAISE
   SAUCE $6.00
BABY SHRIMP COCKTAIL ON FRESH LETTUCE WITH ROSE-MARIE SAUCE $6.70
BOCCONCINI CHEESE WITH MARINATED RED ONIONS AND TOMATO $6.50
ASSORTED GREENS WITH ORANGE AND SCALLION DRESSING $4.00
GREEK SALAD • NEW AT THE BLACKSHOP, JUST ARRIVED FROM ATHENS! $4.95
CAESAR SALAD $4.50      SMALL $3.50      WITH SMOKED SALMON $7.90

**HOT APPETIZERS**

ESCARGOTS IN GARLIC, RED WINE AND BUTTER. "A VAMPIRE'S NIGHTMARE" $6.90
FRESH MUSSELS IN TOMATO SAUCE WITH GARLIC AND BRANDY $6.90
WENCESLAUS CHEESE LIGHTLY BREADED AND SERVED WITH
   TARTAR SAUCE $5.50
SOUP OF THE EVENING $3.50

**ENTREES**

BLACKSHOP PEPPERSTEAK • N.Y. SIRLOIN ROLLED IN BLACK CRUSHED PEPPER,
"GOOD THINGS NEVER CHANGE," ON THE MENU SINCE 1983
    REGULAR CUT $18.90      SMALL CUT $13.90
FILLET OF BEEF TENDERLOIN WITH BERNAISE "BACK BY DEMAND" $18.90
GRILLED ESCALOPE OF CHICKEN WITH GINGER AND MANGO CHUTNEY $14.50
VEAL SCALLOPINI IN CREAM SAUCE WITH GARLIC, WHITE WINE AND GREEN
   PEPPERCORNS $15.90
VIENNA SCHNITZEL LIGHTLY BREADED AND SHALLOW FRIED $11.50
ROASTED NEW ZEALAND RACK OF LAMB, LIGHTLY BREADED WITH DIJON,
   GARLIC AND TARRAGON      FULL RACK $22.90       HALF RACK $15.90
DAILY PASTA WITH TOMATO SAUCE, BASIL AND JULIENNE OF VEGETABLES $9.90
FILLET OF SOLE WITH PIQUANT CREOLE SAUCE $12.50

GST AND PST APPLICABLE

*EXHIBIT 2 (cont'd)*

### LUNCH
### AT THE BLACKSHOP BISTRO

**SALADS**

ASSORTED GREENS WITH ORANGE AND SCALLION DRESSING $4.50

CAESAR SALAD $4.90    SMALL $3.70    WITH SMOKED SALMON $7.90

WARM BLACKSHOP SALAD • BREAST OF CHICKEN ON A BED OF MIXED
GREENS WITH ORANGE AND SCALLION DRESSING $8.60

GREEK SALAD • NEW AT BLACKSHOP, JUST ARRIVED FROM ATHENS $5.50

**OPEN FACE SANDWICHES**

SMOKED SALMON WITH ONIONS, LEMON, DILL MAYONNAISE ON DARK
BREAD $7.90

REAL CRABMEAT SALAD WITH LEMON ON FRENCH STICK BREAD $8.90

COMBINATION—HAVE THEM BOTH—SMOKED SALMON AND CRABMEAT
$8.50

N.Y. STEAK SANDWICH ON THE GRILL, SERVED WITH CAESAR SALAD $9.00

ADD SOUP TO ANY SANDWICH OR SALAD $2.00 • SOUP ONLY $3.50

**HOT ENTREES**

GRILLED BONELESS BREAST OF CHICKEN WITH MANGO-GINGER CHUTNEY
$8.50

VIENNA SCHNITZEL LIGHTLY BREADED, SHALLOW FRIED $7.90

DELFT BLUE VEAL SCALLOPINI WITH PIQUANT CREOLE SAUCE $9.90

BLACKSHOP PEPPERSTEAK • "SOMETHINGS NEVER CHANGE," ON THE
MENU SINCE 1983 $11.90

FRESH MUSSELS IN TOMATO SAUCE WITH BRANDY, GARLIC AND
OREGANO $8.90

FILLET OF SOLE IN PARSLEY AND HERB BATTER WITH LIME BUTTER $7.50

• ALL ENTREES INCLUDE SOUP OR SALAD AND FRESH VEGETABLES.

PST AND GST APPLICABLE

*EXHIBIT 2 (cont'd)*

## Blackshop Bistro's White Vintage

| | |
|---|---:|
| Lindemans (91) Semillon-Chardonnay (Australia) | $17.00 |
| Jacob's Creek (91) Semillon-Chardonnay (South-East Australia) | $17.50 |
| Glen Ellen (90) Reserve, Sonoma Valley (California) | $18.00 |
| Glen Ellen (90) Chardonnay, Sonoma Valley (California) | $20.00 |
| Cave D'Obernai (89) Riesling, Vin d'Alsace (France) | $21.50 |
| Lindemans (91) Chardonnay, Bin 65 (South-East Australia) | $22.00 |
| Houghton (90) Chenin Blanc, Wildflower Ridge (Australia) | $22.00 |
| Wente Bros (90) Chardonnay, Central Coast (California) | $22.00 |
| Inniskillin (89) Chardonnay, Niagara (Canada) | $22.50 |
| Chartron La Fleur (90) Entre-Deux-Mers (France) | $23.00 |
| Monterey Vineyard (90) Chardonnay, Monterey (California) | $23.50 |
| Pierre Sparr (90) Pinot Blanc Reserve d'Alsace (France) | $24.00 |
| Della Staffa (89) Chardonnay (Italy) | $24.50 |
| Wyndham Estate (89) Chardonnay (Australia) | $25.00 |
| Lajolie (89) Chardonnay Vin de Pay's 0 (France) | $25.00 |
| Louis Latour (91) Chardonnay Coteaux d'Ardeche (France) | $25.00 |
| Dry Creek (89) Fume Blanc, Sonoma County (California) | $26.00 |
| Leasingham (90) Chardonnay, Clare Valley (Australia) | $26.50 |
| Rudesheimer Rosengarten (89) Spatlese (Germany) | $27.00 |
| Hardy's Siegersdorf (90) Chardonnay (Australia) | $27.00 |
| Fetzer (90) Sundial Chardonnay, Redwood Valley (California) | $28.00 |
| Wolf Blass (90) Oak Chardonnay (Australia) | $28.00 |
| Latour (90) Chardonnay, Bourgogne (France) | $32.00 |

SPARKLING WINES

| | |
|---|---:|
| Codorniu Brut Classico, Sparkling Wine (Spain) | $25.00 |
| Martini & Rossi Asti Spumante, Sparkling Wine (Italy) | $27.00 |
| Cordon Rouge, G.H. Mumm, Brut Champagne (France) | $55.00 |

HOUSE WINE

L'Epayrie, France

Glass     $4.50          1/2 Litre   $11.00          Litre     $20.00

GST & PST Not Included

*EXHIBIT 2 (cont'd)*

### Blackshop Bistro's Red Vintage

| | |
|---|---|
| Anjou Villages (89) (France) | $17.00 |
| Lindemans (89) Shiraz-Cabernet Sauvignon (Australia) | $18.00 |
| Cruse (89) Bordeaux (France) | $19.00 |
| Walnut Crest (88) Merlot, Rapel (Chile) | $19.00 |
| Santa Carolina (85) Reserve Cabernet Sauvignon (Chile) | $20.00 |
| Montecillo (87) Rioja Vina Cumbrero (Spain) | $21.00 |
| Vina Carmen (88) Cabernet Sauvignon, Maipo (Chile) | $22.00 |
| Chateau Bellevue la Foret (90) (France) | $22.00 |
| Carrascal (85) Mendoza, Cabernet, Merlot, Malbec (Argentina) | $23.00 |
| Mildara (88) Hermitage Coonawara (Australia) | $24.50 |
| Chateau des Charmes (87) Cabernet, Franc, Merlot (Canada) | $25.00 |
| Monterey Vineyard (88) Cabernet Sauvignon (California) | $26.50 |
| Hungerford Hill (87) Cabernet Sauvignon (Australia) | $27.00 |
| J. Lohr Estates (87) Paso Robles Cabernet (California) | $27.50 |
| Geyser Peak (87) Cabernet Sauvignon Alexander Valley (California) | $28.00 |
| Bouchard Aine & Fils (89) Beaujolais Superior (France) | $28.00 |
| Gattinara (82) Nebbiolo (Italy) | $29.00 |
| Berberana (83) Reserva, Rioja (Spain) | $31.00 |
| Jekel Vineyard (85) Cabernet Sauvignon, Greenfield (California) | $31.00 |
| Wolf Blass (87) Cabernet Sauvignon, Yellow Label (Australia) | $32.00 |
| Cuvaison Zinfandel (87) Napa Valley (California) | $35.00 |
| Mitchell (89) Shiraz Clare Valley (Australia) | $36.00 |
| Paul J. Aine (89) Crozes Hermitage (France) | $37.00 |
| Chateau La Garde (86) Graves Leognan (France) | $38.00 |

HOUSE WINE

L'Epayrie, France

| | | | | | |
|---|---|---|---|---|---|
| Glass | $4.50 | 1/2 Litre | $11.00 | Litre | $20.00 |

GST & PST Not Included

Source: Company files.

**EXHIBIT 3**
**A Press Review on**
**Blackshop Bistro**

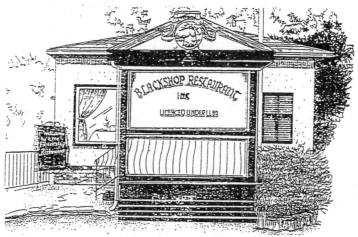

Ken Ledbetter

# The Blackshop sets standards for the others

The Blackshop Restaurant in Cambridge continues to be one of the more pleasant dining spots I've had the pleasure of eating in, and it continues to serve some of the best food this area has to offer. .

It's been doing so for five years now, feeding people who know about it a variety of foods that are cooked and served to near perfection, time and time again. I've never been the least bit disappointed when I've eaten there, and I haven't heard of anyone who has.

It's small and unpretentious (30 seats), but quite comfortable and attractive. It's so inconspicuous that it's almost lost — tucked behind a realtor's office and a pine furniture store on Ainslie Street. A lot of people may drive by it every day without even knowing that it's there.

But it's a three-star restaurant, and I think it would receive that kind of rating in anybody's book. It's less elegant than Graystones (the other three-star restaurant in Cambridge) and doesn't offer diners quite the same degree of choice, but the food itself may be a little better, especially the Caesar salad and the pepper steak.

For under $80, two people can have a scrumptious four-course dinner with a bottle of vintage wine. The food is fresh, prepared with considerable tenderness in the Blackshop kitchen and beautifully presented. Although some of the flavors and aromas are delightfully unusual, everything I've ever had there has been blessed with a most exquisite taste.

There's a cook inside the Blackshop kitchen who knows food — knows how to buy it, how to cook it, how to put it on a plate. And more than that — knows what to put with what, from garlic creamed with cucumber to pernod in espresso to shrimp and smoked salmon in the finest Caesar salad I've ever had.

Just thinking of the food there makes me drool. And eating at the Blackshop makes me even more convinced than ever that genuine three-star quality and consistency are most often found in restaurants that are small. What lets these little bistros rise above the others is that everything takes place under the watchful eyes of people who know what they're doing and who care.

How else to explain the wonderful dinners that the Blackshop serves? Complimentary fresh brown bread and fantastic home-made pate are served with drinks. Diners have a choice of soups, one chilled the other hot — mushroom and potato, for example, or a smooth and delicate cold peach soup.

Sometimes the Blackshop serves fresh oysters, as large and slick and succulent as anyone can find, with a sauce that's very much alive and with tabasco on the side (like in New Orleans, like in other exotic oyster bars that are usually far from home).

Other appetizers include various combinations of seafood and avocado, smoked salmon with onions and capers in a palate-priming dill sauce, escargots and deep-fried cauliflower. All are heady and delicious and they look it, too. I wouldn't call them works of art (they aren't contrived or "cute"). They simply look like food that's fresh and appetizing. They look like food that's good to eat.

The Blackshop serves fine steaks, a rack of lamb, broiled tiger shrimp with pernod sauce, provimi veal, baked salmon and orange roughy. The pepper steak has had a generous amount of pepper pounded in (quite a different entree from a steak that's simply smothered in a peppercorn sauce). The lamb sometimes is served de-boned, so tender that it almost melts.

Entrees come with a variety of fresh vegetables, delicately seasoned and not overcooked. Some restaurants don't even bother with fresh vegetables anymore, and those that do serve only one or two. But at the Blackshop, I can always count on four or five: yellow beans and peppers, broccoli and carrots plus potatoes — truck gardening at its best, served on a nice warm plate.

The wine list varies with the season or with the availability of particular labels (sometimes it's simply a matter of the government's best price). But the cellar always has a fair selection in the $20 to $25 range.

What really kicks a Blackshop meal another notch or two beyond the ordinary, however, is the hot palatchinki that's offered for dessert. Fine crepes are stuffed with fruit and doused with grand marnier and chocolate sauce. Even people who are full find they can eat them all. They eat them with a cup of what the Blackshop calls "funny espresso" or with the area's finest cappuccino.

Few restaurants anywhere serve better food. A friend of mine (to give one fair example) ate shark in San Diego years ago, so good he dreamed about it. For five years he'd been searching for some just as good. He even tried at home — tried to grill a shark steak to perfection. But it never turned out quite as juicy, never quite as tender or delicious.

He finally found it at the Blackshop, a late-summer special that reduced him for a good 10 minutes to a mass of quivering flesh. "Is it as good as San Diego?" His teeth and eyes continued flashing as he sighed. "It's even better." He celebrated with a second brandy, then gave the car keys to his wife who drove him home.

The Blackshop Restaurant, 121 Ainslie St. N. in Cambridge, serves lunch from Tuesday to Friday and dinner from Tuesday to Saturday. Since it's small, I'd make a reservation several days ahead.

Source: *Kitchener-Waterloo Record*, September 29, 1988, p. C18.

*Exhibit 4*

| Financial Statements for Blackshop Bistro | | | | |
|---|---|---|---|---|
| | **1990** | | **1991** | |
| Sales | $262,814 | 100% | $265,674 | 100% |
| Cost of sales | | | | |
|    Purchases | 96,902 | 36.9 | 99,434 | 37.4 |
|    Wages and benefits | 96,758 | 36.8 | 101,354 | 38.2 |
|      TOTAL | $193,660 | 73.7 | $200,788 | 75.6 |
| Gross margin | 69,154 | 26.3 | 64,886 | 24.4 |
| Operating expenses | | | | |
|    Rent | 12,242 | 4.7 | 14,624 | 5.5 |
|    Advertising and promotion | 3,188 | 1.2 | 2,957 | 1.1 |
|    Bank charges and interest | 7,324 | 2.8 | 6,411 | 2.4 |
|    Depreciation and amortization | 6,740 | 2.6 | 5,029 | 1.9 |
|    Utilities | 4,710 | 1.8 | 5,487 | 2.1 |
|    Other expenses | 24,174 | 9.2 | 26,641 | 10.0 |
|      TOTAL[1] | $58,378 | 22.2 | $61,149 | 23.0 |
| Net income before tax | 10,776 | 4.1 | 3,737 | 1.4 |
| Income taxes (recoverable) | 851 | 0.3 | (577) | (0.2) |
| Net income | $9,925 | 3.8 | $4,314 | 1.6 |
| Deficit (beginning) | $31,577 | | $21,652 | |
| Deficit (ending) | $21,652 | | $17,338 | |

1. Some totals may not add exactly due to rounding.

***EXHIBIT 4** (cont'd)*

| Balance Sheet as of January 31 | | |
|---|---|---|
| | **1990** | **1991** |
| ASSETS | | |
| Current | | |
| Cash | $      0 | $ 2,292 |
| Inventories | 10,000 | 11,000 |
| Income taxes recoverable | 0 | 577 |
| Prepaid expenses | 1,717 | 1,034 |
| TOTAL | $11,717 | $14,903 |
| Fixed | | |
| Equipment | 30,075 | 30,525 |
| Leasehold improvements | 25,251 | 25,251 |
| Vehicle | 16,000 | 16,000 |
| TOTAL | $71,326 | $71,776 |
| Less: accumulated depreciation and amortization | 51,164 | 56,193 |
| TOTAL | $20,162 | $15,583 |
| TOTAL ASSETS | $31,879 | $30,486 |
| LIABILITIES | | |
| Current | | |
| Bank overdraft | $    981 | $      0 |
| Bank loan | 2,000 | 0 |
| Accounts payable | 11,186 | 16,857 |
| Income taxes payable | 851 | 0 |
| Current portion of long-term debt | 14,125 | 15,724 |
| TOTAL | $29,143 | $32,581 |
| Non-current portion of long-term debt | 11,151 | 12,726 |
| Due to shareholders | 13,227 | 2,507 |
| Shareholders' deficit | | |
| Stated capital[2] | 10 | 10 |
| Deficit | 21,652 | 17,338 |
| TOTAL | $21,642 | $17,328 |
| TOTAL LIABILITIES AND SHAREHOLDERS' DEFICIT | $31,879 | $30,486 |

**2.** Authorized and issued: 100 common shares without par value.

Source: Company files.

*Exhibit 5*
*Map of Downtown*
*Cambridge (GALT)*

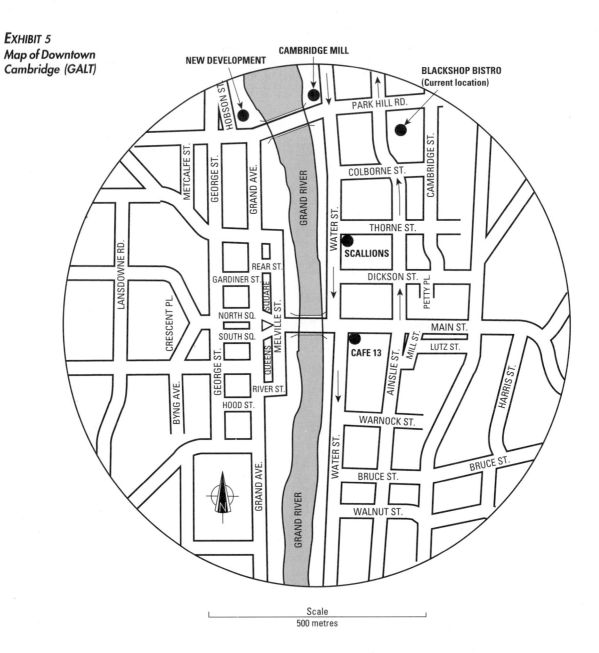

Scale
500 metres

***EXHIBIT 6***
***Summary of Leasing***
***Proposal for 20 Hobson***
***Street Commercial***
***Complex Ground Floor***
***Restaurant Space***

SPACE INFORMATION:

- total leased area is 315 square metres
- rent is $162 per square metre net-net[1] or $4,250 per month
- taxes are anticipated to be approximately $32 per square metre
- all common area expenses are included

LEASEHOLD IMPROVEMENTS INCLUDED:

- complete heating and air-conditioning system
- kitchen exhaust fan and make-up air system
- all ceramic flooring in kitchen and bathrooms
- complete bar with refrigeration
- complete gas-burning fireplace
- all electrical rough-ins and basic wiring
- an electrical service sufficient to accommodate the kitchen equipment and fixtures
- plumbing for all washrooms, including fixtures
- all engineering and architectural fees related to the interior design, seating and lighting plan, and kitchen layout
- all partition walls, doors, hardware, and locks
- fluorescent lighting for kitchen and bathrooms
- prime-coat-finished drywall walls and ceilings

LEASEHOLD COSTS:

- all light fixtures except as above
- walk-in cooler
- stainless steel hood and $CO_2$ system
- tables and chairs, including booths and flower planters
- carpet for dining areas and flooring for all storage, office, and staff rooms
- the balance of the decorating and interior improvements

1.   Net-net means that all common area costs, such as snow removal and outside work, are included in the rent.

Source: Company files.

## C A S E 7.2   THE BODY SHOP CANADA

"You're not the kind of franchise applicant we usually get," said Harry Rob-ertson, company lawyer for the Body Shop Canada, as he opened his meet-ing with potential franchisee Richard Paul. "I suppose we'll find out whether that's an advantage or disadvantage," replied Mr. Paul. Mr. Robert-son's comment had taken Mr. Paul by surprise, and though he was pleased with his response, the comment had produced a sinking feeling in the pit of his stomach.

**RICHARD PAUL**

Mr. Paul, age 36, was about to graduate from the M.B.A. program at the University of Western Ontario. His employment background included a stint as a high-school business education teacher and seven years of retail management. He had managed independent stores and also had managed for one of Canada's national department store chains.

He had investigated a number of job possibilities, but had received no offers and was still unclear about the direction he wished to follow. His strengths appeared to lie in the marketing and human resources area. He had little interest in joining a major retail company: "I've been on that tread-mill before," he said. He felt that whatever his eventual career choice would be, he wanted to do "something that will make some difference to me and to others." The idea of working for himself was appealing: "At least I'd be sweating to put money in my own pocket."

While perusing the job advertisements in the *Globe and Mail*, Canada's "national newspaper," he came across one placed by the Body Shop Can-ada. The notice stated that the company had a number of operating stores available for franchise, including locations in City A and City B. Mr. Paul was aware of the company's enormous international success and was sur-prised to discover that franchises might be available. Furthermore, he had never known the Body Shop Canada to advertise for franchisees.

**THE BODY SHOP**

The Body Shop was the brain-child of Anita Roddick, a forward-thinking Briton with a strong commitment to an ideal.[1] The company offered conven-tional consumer products with a twist: it sold only naturally based products and disdained its competitors' exaggerated product claims. In fact, it did no advertising at all. The company positioned itself as a champion of social responsibility and activism. It promoted holistic health, environmental responsibility, charitable acts, Third World development, women's issues, and other causes. It generated considerable publicity for itself by these means.

In the 14 years since its founding, one little store had grown into a chain of over 450 stores located in 37 countries world-wide. In Canada there were 72 shops — 56 franchised and 16 corporate owned.

The Body Shop Canada stores, averaging about 100 square metres, were in prime retail locations, either on main shopping arteries or in malls. Stores sold only proprietary products, always at "list prices." There were no sales and there was no discounting. The line consisted of nearly 400 items that could be purchased at every store or ordered from stores through the mail. All stores were of similar appearance: they were decorated in identical colour schemes, with displays, fixtures, and even window displays standardized from store to store across the country. Customers tended to be loyal, even fanatical, in their support of the company. Once someone became a customer, he or she would probably not purchase a competitor's product again.

## THE INITIAL CONTACT

Mr. Paul was well aware of the success record of franchise operations, and of this one in particular. In fact, he had just attended a conference where a major national retailer had spoken of the Body Shop Canada in glowing terms! However, he had never given serious consideration to purchasing a franchise. He thought that for someone with imagination and good business sense, a franchise would be far too restrictive. However, with a "what have I got to lose?" mentality, he wrote to the address listed in the advertisement and asked for more information. Within a week he received a reply, on recycled paper.

## FRANCHISE INFORMATION

The package that arrived in the mail contained 35 pages of information about the company and its operations. The presentation seemed almost amateur, with much of the material obviously photocopied. Nonetheless, Mr. Paul took a night off from analyzing cases to study the documents. The material consisted of:

- Company background            8 pages
- Environmental issues           15 pages
- Information on the franchise agreement    3 pages
- Financial data                6 pages
- List of current franchisees        3 pages

The synopsis of the franchise agreement outlined the standard elements of a franchise agreement and included the following, additional facts:

- the Body Shop Canada would lease the premise and sublet it to the franchisee;

- the franchisee must operate the business and be in the store at least 40 hours per week;
- the franchisee must purchase the complete product line;
- the franchisee must retain effective ownership and control;
- any sale of the franchise to a new franchisee must be approved by the franchisor;
- the franchisor may terminate the franchise if the franchisee fails to operate within the law or fails to carry on business as prescribed by the franchise agreement; and
- no royalty fees would be paid except a monthly administration fee of $200, and a promotion and publicity fee of 2 percent of gross sales.

Costs to start a new franchise were estimated as:

| | |
|---|---:|
| Franchise fee | $15,000 |
| Fixtures | 100,000–120,000 |
| Design fee | 5,000 |
| Opening inventory | 90,000–110,000 |
| Legal fees | 5,000 |
| First and last month's rent | 5,000–6,000 |
| Training accommodation costs* | 0–5,000 |
| Site selection | 6,000 |
| Public relations** | 0–3,000 |
| Management aptitude tests*** | 900 |
| Total | $226,900–$257,900 |

\*   Potential franchisees must attend a seven-week training program in Toronto at their own expense. At the end of the course they must pass an exam before being awarded a franchise.

\*\*   This fee would depend on whether the Body Shop had an existing store in the market.

\*\*\*  The Body Shop Canada was phasing out its management aptitude test. At the time of this case the test was used only to choose between two applicants who were otherwise tied.

Mr. Paul estimated that he could come up with about $125,000 himself. He would have to finance the inventory and part of the fixtures through a bank loan. Given the excellent track record of the Body Shop Canada and his experience and qualifications, Mr. Paul believed he would have no trouble borrowing the necessary capital from a bank. Using the company's sales and operating projections, he created pro forma financial statements for the first two years. Exhibit 1 shows the statements.[2] Mr. Paul thought that the numbers looked promising and that it was worth devoting additional time, even at the expense of preparing cases, to find out more about the Body Shop Canada.

**MR. PAUL'S PLAN**

If buying a franchise for the Body Shop Canada made sense, then why not try to buy two? Mr. Paul's education and personality combined to make him ambitious. He had examined the list of franchisees and realized that 13 of them had multiple stores. One couple owned five!

Mr. Paul reasoned that there would be economies of scale for a multi-store operation because some of the start-up costs and operating expenses would be no higher than for a single store operation. Would he have enough capital? Would he be able to secure competent management to operate on a broader scale? Both problems seemed resolved after discussions with two close friends.

His two friends, both women, were tremendously enthusiastic about the possibility of becoming involved with the Body Shop Canada. Both said they would quit their current jobs at a moment's notice and would want to purchase a minority equity position, probably 10 to 15 percent of the store they managed. Mr. Paul was certain the two women would be ideal managers and business partners. Their equity holdings would provide him with additional capital and them with a strong incentive to work hard. If worse came to worst, he would be in a strong position to buy them out in the future.

Mr. Paul thought that the best organizational structure would be to create a holding company with him as a sole owner, and for the company to enter into separate partnership agreements with each of the women. Each partnership would hold one store. He revised his pro forma statements (see Exhibit 2).

Mr. Paul was thrilled with the projected results. He believed that he had used a conservative set of assumptions and that even under these conditions he could expect to eliminate all debt within three years. Even if there were zero sales growth after the second year he could expect after-tax earnings in the area of $150,000. That night he completed the formal application for a franchise and began to dream....

**THE OPTION OF BUYING EXISTING FRANCHISES**

In the course of his investigations, Mr. Paul had been able to discover more about the two existing locations available for franchise. The store located in City A was already a franchise operation. The current owner had been experiencing personal problems and was keen to sell the business. The store was small, only 40 square metres, but was favourably located in the best mall in the city. Many people described the location as the only good retail location in the city. A friend who lived in City A expressed some small concern that the store had not always been well managed, sometimes appearing to be poorly staffed and inadequately stocked.

The City B store was corporately owned and was being offered as part of a plan by the parent company to divest itself of all corporate stores (except for some in Vancouver and Toronto). It was one of three outlets in City B and was located in one of the newest malls in an area surrounded by up-scale housing and extensive development. A major university was less than five km away, and plans were under way to expand the mall by some 70 stores within two years. The Body Shop Canada had recently been moved to a better location within the mall and almost doubled in size to about 80 square metres.

Mr. Paul felt certain that sales in these stores would be well above the levels projected for start-up operations, but had no way to determine by how much. The locations really interested him. He owned a house in City B and he would be happy to stay. One of his two potential partners also lived there, and the other had recently moved to City A, near the United States border. The Body Shop's Canadian operation had the right to expand into the virgin territory of several United States border states, including the one nearest to City A. Growth prospects seemed unlimited! It appeared to be a perfect fit. The only question was how much of a premium the on-going operations would command.

About 10 days after completing the franchise application, Mr. Paul received a phone call from the Body Shop Canada inviting him to go to Toronto for a meeting with Harry Robertson. Mr. Paul felt he had already passed a major hurdle because the franchise application had required extensive personal and financial information. If the company wanted to meet him, he must be an acceptable candidate. On a beautiful spring day he pulled into the parking lot of the Body Shop Canada head office, full of excitement at the prospect of what was about to unfold.

## THE MEETING

Mr. Robertson described the typical Body Shop Canada franchisee: "female 35 to 45, married with school age/adolescent children, limited formal education, and crazy about the Body Shop. Anyway, none of our franchisees have M.B.A. degrees!" Mr. Paul realized he had a fight on his hands. "It seems to me you have a view of what M.B.As are like, that they're all fanatical, hard-nosed, money-hungry tyrants," said Mr. Paul. "I don't think that's fair, any more than it would be fair to say that all lawyers are alike."

This comment seemed to break some of the ice. But if the relationship between the two men had begun to thaw, the discussion that ensued and the information that surfaced over the next hour did nothing to cheer Mr. Paul. His plan had obviously been a pipe-dream.

Mr. Robertson was adamant on a number of points. The Body Shop Canada would not grant multiple franchises to a new franchisee; the company first wanted franchisees to demonstrate their potential to handle more than one outlet. The franchisee must personally work in the store full-time. Although many Body Shop Canada franchises were held by partnerships, the company was cautious; it was particularly wary of nonoperating financial partners. If the company did acquiesce, it would want absolute discretion over the content of the agreement. "We want operators, not investors."

Mr. Paul pressed for information about the City A and City B stores. The news on these fronts was no better. Goodwill charges would be about $125,000 for City A and $250,000 for City B! Expected sales for the two stores for 1990 were $600,000 and $750,000, respectively. Apparently, volume at the City B had increased 66 percent since its relocation. City A sales were up 33 percent over the previous year.

The meeting ended on an amicable note with Mr. Paul promising to let Mr. Robertson know within two weeks whether he was interested in proceeding. If the answer was "yes," Mr. Robertson would consider whether to place Mr. Paul on a short-list of candidates. The short-list would be subjected to a 12-hour battery of interviews and then placed in a store for a week. After the trial, both parties would decide whether to commence training. The Body Shop Canada would not award the franchise until after training had been completed. However, even at this advanced stage, the franchisor could still reject the potential franchisee and leave him or her without recourse.

**THE DECISION**

When Mr. Paul returned home from Toronto his immediate instinct was to rush to his computer to create new pro forma statements, but before doing so he thought it would be helpful to note down his options and his concerns. See Exhibit 3 for his notes.

Mr. Paul knew he had a tough problem on his hands. He decided to produce pro forma statements along the lines of his first projections. He had fairly accurate percentage cost data that Mr. Roberston had provided for the existing stores. He wanted to compare performance for each of the existing operations to a start-up, assuming each was operated as a single entity by a sole proprietor. Exhibit 4 contains the statements.

Mr. Paul had some important questions to consider beyond the financial analysis. Could he see himself inside an 80-square-metre store for the next 10 years? Could Mr. Robertson be persuaded to compromise? After all, how many people could fit his ideal profile of someone with the right balance of spiritual devotion to the Body Shop Canada's philosophy, business acumen, and access to the required capital of around $250,000? Was there anything Mr. Paul had missed in his analysis? Somehow this was going to be a lot more difficult than doing a case. This was his life!

## NOTES

1. For a recent history of the Body Shop, see Ms Roddick's book *Body and Soul* (London: Ebury Press, 1991).

2. The company made no provision for profit sharing among nonmanagement level employees. Mr. Paul's decision to allocate 10 percent of store gross profit for this purpose was consistent with his business philosophy.

**EXHIBIT 1**

| Pro Forma Statements for a Single Franchise | | | | | |
|---|---|---|---|---|---|
| **CAPITAL COSTS** | **MINIMUM** | **MAXIMUM** | | **YEAR 1** | **YEAR 2** |
| Franchise fee | $ 15,000 | $ 15,000 | Sales | $475,000 | $617,500 |
| Fixtures | 100,000 | 120,000 | Cost of goods sold | 247,000 | 321,100 |
| Design fee | 5,000 | 5,000 | GROSS PROFIT | $228,000 | $296,400 |
| Legal documentation | 5,000 | 5,000 | | | |
| Site selection | 6,000 | 6,000 | Rent | 42,000 | 49,400 |
| Management test[1] | 900 | 900 | Salaries | 65,000 | 68,250 |
| TOTAL | $131,900 | $151,900 | Common area | 9,600 | 10,080 |
| | | | Publicity and advertising | 9,500 | 9,975 |
| ONE TIME COSTS | | | Insurance | 1,200 | 1,260 |
| | | | Business taxes | 1,200 | 1,260 |
| Public relations fee | 0 | 3,000 | Telephone | 900 | 945 |
| Last month's rent | 2,500 | 3,500 | Travel | 1,500 | 1,575 |
| Training costs | 2,500 | 5,000 | Service charge | 2,400 | 2,520 |
| Opening inventory[2] | 60,000 | 60,000 | | | |
| Legal and incorporation | 2,000 | 2,000 | OPERATING PROFIT | $ 94,700 | $151,135 |
| TOTAL | $ 67,000 | $ 73,500 | | | |
| | | | Profit share | 9,470 | 15,114 |
| CAPITAL REQUIRED | $198,900 | $225,400 | Debt charge | 13,073 | 13,073 |
| | | | Depreciation | 22,000 | 17,600 |
| EQUITY (Mr. Paul) | $125,000 | $125,000 | | | |
| | | | INCOME BEFORE TAX | $ 50,157 | $105,348 |
| LOAN | $ 73,900 | $100,400 | One-time costs | 10,250 | 0 |
| | | | Income tax | 19,156 | 50,568 |
| | | | NET PROFIT | $ 20,751 | $ 54,780 |
| | | | | | |
| | | | CASH FLOW | $ 42,751 | $ 72,380 |

**Assumptions:**
Loan @ 15%
Income tax @ 48%
Inflation @ 5%
Sales growth @ 30%
Operator/Manager's base salary $24,000
No debt re-payment

1. The Body Shop Canada was phasing out its management aptitude test. At the time of this case the test was used only to choose between two applicants who where otherwise tied.
2. $60,000 of the opening inventory had to be paid for C.O.D.; the balance and future shipments were Net 30.

***EXHIBIT 2***

| Pro Forma Statements for Two Stores | | | | | |
|---|---|---|---|---|---|
| **CAPITAL COSTS** | **MINIMUM** | **MAXIMUM** | | **YEAR 1** | **YEAR 2** |
| Franchise fee | $ 30,000 | $ 30,000 | Sales | $950,000 | $1,235,000 |
| Fixtures | 200,000 | 240,000 | Cost of goods sold | 494,000 | 642,200 |
| Design fee | 10,000 | 10,000 | GROSS PROFIT | $456,000 | $ 592,800 |
| Legal documentation | 5,000 | 5,000 | | | |
| Site selection | 12,000 | 12,000 | Rent | 84,000 | 98,800 |
| Management test[1] | 900 | 900 | Salaries | 130,000 | 136,500 |
| TOTAL | $257,900 | $297,900 | Common area | 19,200 | 20,160 |
| | | | Publicity and advertising | 19,000 | 19,950 |
| ONE TIME COSTS | | | Insurance | 2,400 | 2,520 |
| | | | Business taxes | 2,400 | 2,520 |
| Public relations fee | 3,000 | 6,000 | Telephone | 1,800 | 1,890 |
| Last month's rent | 5,000 | 7,500 | Travel | 1,500 | 1,575 |
| Training costs | 5,000 | 10,000 | Service charge | 4,800 | 5,040 |
| Opening inventory[2] | 120,000 | 120,000 | | | |
| Legal and incorporation | 2,000 | 2,000 | OPERATING PROFIT | $190,900 | $ 303,845 |
| TOTAL | $135,000 | $145,000 | | | |
| | | | Profit share | 19,090 | 30,385 |
| CAPITAL REQUIRED | 392,900 | $442,900 | Debt charge | 37,935 | 0 |
| | | | Depreciation | 44,000 | 35,200 |
| EQUITY (Mr. Paul) | $125,000 | $125,000 | | | |
| | | | INCOME BEFORE TAX | $ 89,875 | $ 238,260 |
| EQUITY (Partners) | $ 40,000 | $ 40,000 | One-time costs | 20,000 | 0 |
| | | | Income tax | 33,540 | 114,365 |
| LOAN | $227,900 | $277,900 | NET PROFIT | $ 36,335 | $ 123,895 |
| | | | | | |
| | | | CASH FLOW | $ 80,335 | $ 159,095 |

**Assumptions:**

Loan @ 15%

Income tax @ 48%

Inflation @ 5%

Sales growth @ 30%

Operator/Manager's base salary $24,000

No debt re-payment

1. The Body Shop Canada was phasing out its management aptitude test. At the time of this case the test was used only to choose between two applicants who where otherwise tied.
2. $60,000 of the opening inventory had to be paid for C.O.D.; the balance and future shipments were Net 30.

*EXHIBIT 3*
*Mr. Paul's Notes*

**Options**

1. Forget the whole thing.
2. Try to get a new franchise.
3. Buy City A.
4. Buy City B.
5. Try to find a way to buy both stores.

**Concerns**

1. Are either of the operating stores worth the asking price?
2. How hard would it be to get a bank loan to finance goodwill?
3. If I proceed, should I try a partnership or go it alone?
4. Roberston says when corporate stores become franchised sales increase at least 30 percent overnight. Is that realistic?
5. Robertson says City A should be moved within the mall if a bigger site becomes available. That would mean more sales but another $125,000 for new fixtures. Could I afford that?
6. If the Body Shop Canada proceeds with its plan to open four stores in the United States near City A this year, how will City A's sales be affected?
7. Do I need to consider the Canada–United States Free Trade Agreement in my projections?
8. If City B is up 66 percent so far this year, is it reasonable to expect that growth to continue over the whole year?
9. Would construction at City B hurt sales?

*EXHIBIT 4*

| Pro Forma Statements for Existing Operations | | | | | |
|---|---|---|---|---|---|
| **CAPITAL COSTS** | **CITY A** | **CITY B** | | **CITY A YEAR 1[1]** | **CITY B YEAR 1[1]** |
| Franchise fee | $ 15,000 | $ 15,000 | Sales | $600,000 | $750,000 |
| Fixtures | 60,000 | 120,000 | Cost of goods sold | 312,000 | 390,000 |
| Goodwill | 125,000 | 250,000 | GROSS PROFIT | $288,000 | $360,000 |
| Legal documentation | 3,000 | 3,000 | | | |
| Management test[2] | 900 | 900 | Rent | 48,000 | 60,000 |
| TOTAL | $203,900 | $388,900 | Salaries | 90,000 | 112,500 |
| | | | Publicity and advertising | 12,000 | 15,000 |
| ONE TIME COSTS | | | Insurance | 1,200 | 1,200 |
| | | | Business taxes | 1,200 | 1,200 |
| Inventory[3] | 90,000 | 90,000 | Telephone | 2,000 | 1,800 |
| Last month's rent | 4,067 | 5,083 | Travel | 1,800 | 1,500 |
| Training costs | 3,750 | 3,750 | Service charge | 2,400 | 2,400 |
| Legal and incorporation | 2,000 | 2,000 | | | |
| TOTAL | $ 99,817 | $100,833 | OPERATING PROFIT | $129,400 | $164,400 |
| | | | | | |
| CAPITAL REQUIRED | $303,717 | $489,733 | Profit share | 12,940 | 16,440 |
| | | | Debt charge | 26,807 | 54,710 |
| AVAILABLE | $125,000 | $125,000 | Depreciation | 12,000 | 24,000 |
| | | | | | |
| LOAN | $178,717 | $364,733 | INCOME BEFORE TAX | $ 77,653 | 69,250 |
| | | | One-time costs | 9,817 | 10,833 |
| | | | Income tax | 32,561 | 28,040 |
| | | | NET PROFIT | $ 35,275 | $ 30,377 |
| | | | | | |
| | | | CASH FLOW | $ 47,275 | $ 54,377 |

**Assumptions:**
Loan @ 15%
Income tax @ 48%
Inflation @ 5%
Sales growth @ 30%
Operator/Manager's base salary $24,000
No debt re-payment

1. Based on current sales.
2. The Body Shop Canada was phasing out its management aptitude test. At the time of this case the test was used only to choose between two applicants who were otherwise tied.
3. The entire store inventory must be paid for up front.

*EXHIBIT 4 (cont'd)*

| | City A Year 2 | City B Year 2 | City A Year 2 | City B Year 2 | City A Year 2 | City B Year 2 |
| --- | --- | --- | --- | --- | --- | --- |
| | **Pessimistic** | **Pessimistic** | **Expected** | **Expected** | **Optimistic** | **Optimistic** |
| Sales | 600,000 | 750,000 | 690,000 | 862,500 | 798,000 | 997,500 |
| C.O.G.S. | 312,000 | 390,000 | 358,800 | 448,500 | 414,960 | 518,700 |
| Gross profit | 288,000 | 360,000 | 331,200 | 414,000 | 383,040 | 478,800 |
| Rent | 48,000 | 60,000 | 55,200 | 69,000 | 63,840 | 79,800 |
| Salaries | 90,000 | 112,500 | 90,000 | 112,500 | 90,000 | 112,500 |
| Pub. and adv. | 12,000 | 15,000 | 13,800 | 17,250 | 15,960 | 19,950 |
| Insurance | 1,200 | 1,200 | 1,200 | 1,200 | 1,200 | 1,200 |
| Business taxes | 1,200 | 1,200 | 1,200 | 1,200 | 1,200 | 1,200 |
| Telephone | 2,000 | 1,800 | 2,000 | 1,800 | 2,000 | 1,800 |
| Travel | 1,800 | 1,500 | 1,800 | 1,500 | 1,800 | 1,500 |
| Service Charge | 2,400 | 2,400 | 2,400 | 2,400 | 2,400 | 2,400 |
| OP. PROFIT | 129,400 | 164,400 | 163,600 | 207,150 | 204,640 | 258,450 |
| | | | | | | |
| Profit share | 12,940 | 16,440 | 16,360 | 20,715 | 20,464 | 25,845 |
| Debt charge | 26,807 | 54,710 | 26,807 | 54,710 | 26,807 | 54,710 |
| Depreciation | 8,160 | 19,200 | 8,160 | 19,200 | 8,160 | 19,200 |
| INC. BEF. TAX | 81,493 | 74,050 | 112,273 | 112,525 | 149,209 | 158,695 |
| One-time costs | 0 | 0 | 0 | 0 | 0 | 0 |
| Income tax | 39,116 | 35,544 | 53,891 | 54,012 | 71,620 | 76,174 |
| NET PROFIT | 42,377 | 38,506 | 58,382 | 58,513 | 77,589 | 85,521 |
| | | | | | | |
| CASH FLOW | 50,537 | 57,706 | 66,542 | 77,713 | 85,749 | 101,721 |

## C A S E 7.3   FILTER PLUS

In early January 1989, Sara Rice, vice-president of marketing for Filter Plus, a small Canadian manufacturer of air filters for passenger cars and light trucks, was assessing how she would handle a request by one of the company's largest customers, a U.S. retailer, to lower prices on Filter Plus's air filter lines. This customer's total purchases currently accounted for 30 percent of the company's total retail air filter sales. Sara faced a tough decision because the company's current pricing to the U.S. retailer for its line of air filters was very close to cost for some product sizes and also resulted in negative contributions for some lines. Therefore, lowering the price could result in more negative contribution margins. Yet, she did not want to lose such a large and valuable account.

**SUMMARY OF THE CANADIAN AFTERMARKET FOR FILTRATION PRODUCTS[1]**

1. The air and oil filter markets were stable and mature. These industries were based on high volumes and were characterized by intense price competition.

2. Three large multinational firms dominated the market. These firms were strongly committed to this subsector of the industry.

3. Canadian operations were controlled by their American parents, but Canada did have strong manufacturing capabilities.

4. Parts proliferation was becoming an increasing problem as vehicle manufacturers designed model-specific filters. There were 400 to 500 different stock keeping units (SKUs). SKUs represented the number of different car air filters on the market. For example, filters differ by car model, year, and size.

5. Some smaller players had established niche markets.

6. Filters were a high demand, disposable commodity with recognizable brand names.

**FILTRATION INDUSTRY**

In Canada, in 1988, there were approximately 12 million passenger cars and light trucks registered. On average, car and light truck owners changed their air filters .8 times per year. This was known as the usage factor or incidence of repair frequency.

The filtration industry consisted of three segments: retail/do-it-yourself consumer, commercial/mechanic-installed, and original equipment manufacturers (OEMs). The automotive aftermarket included the first two segments. *The 1988 Car Maintenance in Canada Report*[2] stated that mechanics replaced 57.3 percent of the air filters that were installed on passenger cars and light trucks in Canada during the 12-month period from November 1987 to October 1988. Do-it-yourselfers replaced the remaining 42.7 percent of air filters. Passenger cars accounted for 82.6 percent of vehicles, and light trucks accounted for 17.4 percent of vehicles in which air filters were replaced. Ontario had the largest regional market share for the replacement of air filters at 35.3 percent followed by Quebec with 26 percent, the Prairie Provinces with 20.2 percent, British Columbia with 11.1 percent, and the Atlantic Provinces with 7.4 percent. Men were responsible for making the decision to have the air filter replaced on their vehicles 75.6 percent of the time, while women were responsible for the remaining 24.4 percent of the time.

## Players in the Canadian Market

Fram, Hayes-Dana, and Purolator were the three main manufacturers that, according to industry sources, had a relatively equal share of 70 to 80 percent of the Canadian air filter market. As the big three air filter competitors were U.S. multinationals, production in Canada was based on company objectives generally established by the American parent.

In order to achieve economies of scale, the big three tried to concentrate their production. Subsequently, different facilities would produce specific product lines for both the Canadian and U.S. markets. Consequently, some of the Canadian manufacturing capacity was used to produce product lines for export to the U.S.

The remaining 20 to 30 percent of the Canadian air filter market was supplied by a number of smaller Canadian and U.S. companies. Approximately 55 to 65 percent of all product lines for sale in Canada, according to industry sources, were manufactured in Canadian facilities. However, the share of imported cars continued to grow and, therefore, they would slowly capture more of the market.

## Market Trends

The air filter replacement market was stable. The number of filters replaced annually had been constant for the last few years. However, with smaller engine components and the near-universal adoption of electronic fuel injection in newer-model cars and light trucks, the traditional round air filter was being replaced by space-saving panel air filters. Since the smaller filters had still to do the same amount of work, the product had become more efficient in design and absorption. Due to its less visible location and increased difficulty of accessibility, industry sources feared that although the filter was no harder to replace, do-it-yourselfers would be more negligent in its replacement.

In addition, the potential existed to educate consumers of the need to change filters more frequently and thereby to increase the market substantially.

**Retail/Do-It-Yourself Consumer**

The market consisted of both round filters, which were large and easily changed, and the technologically more advanced panel filters. Panel filters, incorporating the latest in absorption technology, were much smaller filters that were unique to each engine model. Such proliferation of filters had forced the retailers to carry a wide selection to match the make, model, and size of the car. Retail prices ranged from $4.50 to $35 per unit.

Retailers believed that customers could not differentiate between products; therefore, their buying decision would be based on price and availability. Consequently, retailers typically carried only one house brand.

Consumers who were do-it-yourselfers and bought their replacement air filters at retail outlets were of a younger age profile than the customers who used service outlets to replace this product. The installation of an air filter was an easy task for consumers who were familiar with their vehicles; however, it was not generally a priority item. Instead, consumers replaced their air filter during regular maintenance of their cars.

According to *The 1988 Car Maintenance in Canada Report*, Canadian Tire accounted for the largest market share of the Canadian retail outlets with 60.4 percent, followed by auto parts stores with 16.8 percent, new car dealers with 7.2 percent, discount/department stores with 5.7 percent, and the remaining retail outlets with 9.7 percent.

Distribution for this segment went from the manufacturer to a wholesaler, to the retailer. Margins in this segment were 20 percent for the manufacturer, 30 percent for the wholesaler, and 35 percent for the retailer, resulting in an average retail selling price of $5.37 per unit. The large retailers acted as wholesalers for their stores; for example, Canadian Tire's head office would buy from the manufacturer and then increase the price to receive a 30 percent margin before it sold to its stores.

**Commercial/ Mechanic Installed**

According to *The 1988 Car Maintenance in Canada Report*, new car dealers accounted for the largest market share of Canadian service outlets with a 32.2 percent market share, followed by service stations with 25.9 percent, independent repair shops with 14.7 percent, Canadian Tire with 9.8 percent, and the remaining outlets with 17.9 percent.

Distribution of air filters generally followed the traditional path from manufacturer to warehouse distributor to jobber to service outlet. High volume purchasers, such as specialty service repair, were more likely to bypass channels and buy directly from the manufacturer. The respective margins were 35 percent for the manufacturer, 30 percent for the wholesaler, and 30 percent for the jobber. The service centers would then mark up the product by 10 percent. The resulting average selling price to the consumer was $6.74 per unit.

These service outlets usually carried only one national brand. Typically, changing an air filter would be part of a tune-up. Subsequently, the labour cost would be included in the total tune-up cost.

## OEM

The OEM segment consisted of car manufacturers. These companies bought directly from the manufacturer. The parameters of this segment were undefined.

## FILTER PLUS

Filter Plus was a private company. Corporate objectives included providing a quality product and excellent service. The company was able to secure a market niche through aggressive selling and low costs.

## Product

Filter Plus produced and marketed a complete line of replaceable air filter products. The different product lines and sizes had varying margins. Filter Plus's sales for 1988 were $810,000, of which 70 percent was in the retail market, 27 percent was in the mechanic-installed market, and 3 percent in the OEM market.

## Distribution

The trade channel for the retail segment was direct to the customer via one of the management team. These accounts were easy to manage because they involved contact with only one buyer per chain. Retail chains typically provided an in-house distribution facility to facilitate volume purchasing benefits from Filter Plus. Subsequently, Filter Plus shipped orders to the retailers' distribution centres in Ontario. The large U.S. retailer received its orders at its distribution centre in Columbus, Ohio.

Retailers placed orders early in the spring and Filter Plus had to accommodate the seasonal ordering patterns. A maximum of three brief meetings would be all Filter Plus would have to sell its product line for the upcoming year.

Filter Plus used wholesale distributors to reach the commercial segment. The wholesaler would then sell to jobbers[3] who would sell to service centers. Direct purchasing did occur, but to a small extent only. The non-retail industry was very efficient at the wholesale level; however, it was more work managing these accounts because of the large number of wholesalers. Filter Plus estimated the annual costs of hiring a salesperson to be $75,000 to $100,000.

The channel for OEMs was either direct to the client or through a distributor. This last segment represented a very small portion of Filter Plus's sales and was not actively sought.

## THE CURRENT SITUATION

In 1986, Filter Plus had actively gone after the large U.S. retailer account for many reasons, including the credibility it would provide because the company would be able to use the retailer's name as a reference, as well as the opportunity to increase its sales volume. Filter Plus's strategy with the U.S. retailer's account had been to initially price lower to build a relationship and then, once a solid reputation was established, to raise prices. Subsequently, Filter Plus's margin was reduced to 18.4 percent from the industry norm of 20 percent for the retail market. Its average manufacturing costs remained at $1.95 per unit, consisting of 74 percent material costs, 10.5 percent labour costs, and 15.5 percent freight and U.S. brokerage fees. In addition, the low-valued Canadian dollar in 1986 provided a favourable position for exports to the U.S.

The U.S. retailer's latest request directly conflicted with this strategy. In fact, it had requested that Filter Plus somehow lower its costs and then pass the savings on to the U.S. retailer by decreasing Filter Plus's selling price.

**STRATEGIC ALTERNATIVES**

Sara investigated the filter production process and the financial records and determined a few potential alternatives:

1. Decrease Filter Plus's selling price to the U.S. retailer by 10 percent.

   a. Attain a 5 percent decrease in raw material costs from suppliers.

   b. Change the packaging and lower material and labour costs by 3 percent per individual unit.

2. Proceed with alternative 1 and then negotiate an agreement with the U.S. retailer, so that Filter Plus would sell only the product lines which provide a positive contribution (see Exhibit 1).

3. Stop selling to the U.S. retailer and try to increase sales in other Canadian markets.

4. Do nothing — communicate to the U.S. retailer that Filter Plus would be unable to lower prices.

Sara discovered that packaging costs could be lowered by increasing the size of the boxes sent to retailers to contain 12 rather than 6 packages. The resulting material and labour savings would decrease these variable costs by 3 percent each. However, Filter Plus would have to convert all of its production in order to realize these savings.

If alternative 1 was carried out, Sara wondered how the new U.S. retailer's selling price would compare to the previous $5.25 per unit. In addition, Sara wondered how Filter Plus's new total contribution would compare to 1988's total contribution from the U.S. retailer account.

Alternative 3 required a thorough analysis of Filter Plus's current Canadian market, as well as the industry. In evaluating this alternative, Sara wanted to determine Filter Plus's market-share of the Canadian air filter automotive aftermarket in 1988.

Finally, Sara wondered if her fourth alternative was feasible.

Sara knew that she faced a difficult decision. Her decision was further complicated by the stronger Canadian dollar in early 1989. She was eager to select a viable strategy to respond to the U.S. retailer's request.

#### NOTES

1. Source: Des Rosiers Automotive Research Inc.
2. Automotive Industries Association of Canada.
3. A jobber is an automotive parts retailer.

*Exhibit 1*

| Sample from the U.S. Retailer Account for December 1988 in Canadian Dollars | | |
|---|---|---|
| **Product Line** | **Volume in Units** | **Unit Contribution** |
| 1 | 300 | $0.05 |
| 2 | 780 | −$0.20 |
| 3 | 1,080 | $0.70 |
| 4 | 225 | $0.03 |
| 5 | 137 | −$0.25 |

This represents some of the product lines supplied to the U.S. retailer.

# C A S E 7.4   THE GREEK COSMOBOB

In early February 1983 Mr. Cosmo Panetta, owner of Cosmo's Restaurants Ltd. in Niagara Falls, Ontario, felt that some important decisions had to be made about the future of the family business. Panetta realized the benefits of opening a third drive-in/take-out restaurant, but his current thoughts revolved around the restaurant's best selling product — the Cosmobob. Originally an in-house product, in September 1982 Cosmo's Restaurants began producing the Cosmobob for other restaurants. The results of that decision had been very encouraging, and by February 1983 the demand for the product had outgrown the restaurant's production facilities. Mr. Panetta knew that it was time to determine a future strategy for the family business, but with only $10,000 available before having to turn to a bank, he was also concerned about the financial requirements of any future plans.

## THE FOOD INDUSTRY

In 1968, 20 cents of each family food dollar was being spent away from home. In 1978, that figure soared to 36 cents and, according to industry predictions, the figure should reach 50 cents in the mid-1980s. Both general merchandise and food service entities have benefited from changing economic and demographic factors. During 1978, there were hundreds of food processors vying for a share of the $22.4 billion Canadian food market. These food processors were either marketing their products to the food service market, or to the home consumer, via retail grocery outlets.

### The Food Service Market

The food service market covered all foods eaten away from home. This broad spectrum included: schools, hospitals, prisons, nursing homes, as well as hotels, motels, and restaurants of all types. In 1978, Canadians ate 41 billion meals, of which 12 billion or about 29 percent were eaten away from home. In the away-from-home market, 92 percent of the meals were eaten in institutions, where the consumer had little choice of where or what to eat. Hotels and restaurants served at least 960 million meals, representing the remaining 8 percent of the total market for meals away from home. Fast food service accounted for 80 percent of the hotel and restaurant dollar volume.

In the food service market, whether the operation was an institution, a hotel, or a restaurant, the major cost, in both food and labour, of any meal was the entrée. As the entrée was the main part of the meal, its quality was of primary importance to the customer. There were four basic food service systems for delivering an entrée. First, there was the conventional food system where food of all types was purchased raw and was totally processed on the premises shortly before serving. The semi-conventional food system eliminated some food preparation by purchasing pre-proportioned meat cuts, frozen vegetables, and desserts, and some prepared salads. The "ready" foods system produced pre-cooked frozen entrées on the premises for use later on.

Finally, there was the total convenience system, which purchased 90 to 95 percent of all food items in the convenience form, including entrées, from outside commercial suppliers. Since food production was eliminated, direct food production personnel were replaced by less-skilled people who prepared the meal simply by heating the product. The benefits derived from total convenience foods were: uniformity in quality and cost of the product; a reduction in initial capital costs because less floor space and less equipment were needed; and a reduction in the need to find qualified help as fewer positions needed to be filled. It was expected that, by 1990, one-fourth of all hotels and restaurants would use solely full convenience foods and the other three-quarters would have doubled their usage of convenience foods. Because 80 percent of the sales volume in most restaurants took place during only 20 percent of the day, the use of convenience foods contributed to efficient service during peak periods, permitting faster customer turnover and, hence, increased sales volume.

All Food Services products were distributed either through food wholesalers or directly by the food manufacturer. Food wholesalers such as Hickeson-Langs, Signet Foods, Chef Foods, Loeb, and National Grocers had large warehouses located throughout Canada and distributed thousands of manufacturers' products. Small restaurants and hotels usually opted for the simplicity of dealing with only one food wholesaler. Large institutional accounts were visited weekly, by a sales representative from each food wholesaler. The institution would submit a quote sheet outlining the products required for the following week. When the quotes were completed by the wholesaler, the institution would choose the food wholesalers with the best price, and the best brand for each product. Institutional buyers required unscheduled delivery to satisfy their requirements, while the smaller buyers were on a regular delivery pattern. The food wholesalers offered both groups 2 percent/10 net 30 purchase terms.

Food manufacturers that did not use wholesalers were either under contract for product supply, such as most dairy companies were, or they had a truckdriver/salesperson that made regular calls for their narrow product line. For the smaller restaurant accounts, seven-day purchase terms were usually established. However, institutional buyers demanded more liberal purchase terms, which often strained the working capital needs of the food manufacturer.

**The Grocery Retailing Market**

The retail grocery business in Canada was characterized by strong competition. Exhibit 1 shows a market profile of the larger supermarket chains. Many of the changes in retailing during the past few years have resulted from the efforts of retailers to tailor their product selection, prices, services, and other store characteristics to meet the needs of consumers within their marketing area better than their nearest competitor.

Economic changes have contributed most to the evolution of grocery retailing. The food industry has responded to these changes by creating vast arrays of refrigerated and frozen foods, convenience items, and improved housekeeping aids, in addition to existing staple goods. Consumers have readily adapted to supermarket concepts, while at the same time supporting the local neighbourhood convenience store to satisfy interim shopping needs.

Food processors, the food industry, and the retail grocers took advantage of trends in consumer tastes and preferences. The market for delicatessen and fast food products, such as prepared and cured meats, sandwiches, entrées, salads, and specialty cheeses, was strong and likely to continue growing. Successful retailers became attuned to the need for different types of outlets, different product mixes, and different merchandising approaches to serve the needs of the widely varying market segments. Typical supermarkets offered approximately 15,000 items.

As a result of their vast distribution network and customer acceptance, grocery retailers have developed a powerful base for dealing with food processors and food manufacturers. New product introduction was definitely an area where retailers held the upper hand. Creative promotion was the key to getting retailer cooperation with the manufacturer. A $20,000 placement fee per product per supermarket chain, plus standard industry price discounts, samples, free food allowances, and cooperative advertising were all needed to develop retail chain acceptance of a new product. Trade promotion could run as high as 15 percent of the manufacturer's selling price. Once those costs were incurred, the manufacturer would need to develop promotional techniques that would generate consumer acceptance of the product. Consumer promotion for an established food product ranged between $80,000 and $500,000 per year, with the launch year somewhat higher.

**THE PANETTA FAMILY**

Cosmo Panetta was 58 years of age. Mr. Panetta, his wife Josephine and their eldest son, Joe, immigrated to Niagara Falls, Canada, from Greece in 1958. For two years Panetta worked in Northern Ontario mines as a labourer, before returning home to his family for a job with the City of Niagara Falls, in 1960. In 1968, Mr. Panetta used personal savings and a small loan from his brother-in-law to purchase a small variety store. It had always been Panetta's dream to establish a family business, and the variety store seemed to be a good place to start. Panetta worked at the store 18 hours per day, with his son Joe assisting him as a stockboy. Josephine Panetta spent her time at home, caring for their younger sons Frank and Andy. In 1970, the variety store was demolished and a new variety store, with a four-room motel, was erected on the same site. By 1975, both Joe and Frank were helping their father in the store. Neither of the boys was academically inclined, and both sons indicated the desire to make the family business their livelihood.

In 1975, a convenience store chain purchased the variety store from Panetta for $150,000. With the proceeds from the sale, and a small bank loan, Panetta purchased an existing drive-in restaurant, which was renovated and renamed Cosmo's Drive-in. Panetta purchased a second drive-in/take-out restaurant in 1979. The restaurants were operated by Cosmo and Joe, with Joe's wife Cindy, Frank, and the youngest son, Andy, helping out with miscellaneous kitchen work. Both restaurants were open 15 hours per day, seven days a week and used mostly part-time help. Mr. Panetta maintained that a good location, high product quality, and a fair price were the necessary ingredients for a successful restaurant business. The business was incorporated in 1979. A small bookkeeping firm was retained to handle the company's books and accounting needs.

## COSMO'S RESTAURANTS

### The Concept

Cosmo's Drive-in was really a combination drive-in and take-out establishment. The restaurant prepared and sold wrapped meals of specific foods for consumption away from the premises, or in a seating area. Cosmo's concentrated on a limited menu of fast food items, such as: hamburgers, hot dogs, chicken, fish, french fries, onion rings, and beverages. Cost-conscious consumers were continually attracted to Cosmo's because of the good food and the perceived value for their money, resulting from the efficient and standardized operations.

Cosmo's Restaurants resembled the Harvey's drive-in restaurant concept. The buildings and equipment had been structured for specific purposes and production systems were developed for an efficient product flow. When a customer arrived at the inside counter, he or she placed an order and paid the cashier. The cook made and assembled the order, while the cashier prepared and placed the drinks. The whole process took approximately two minutes.

Although, to some extent, the concept of limited selection had been retained to preserve efficiency, some highly successful new products had been developed and introduced to give drive-in/take-out restaurants a competitive edge. One of the most widespread methods of diversifying menus was for companies which had previously served mainly hamburgers to introduce various specialty sandwiches. The more popular specialty sandwiches included: chicken, steak, roast beef, fish, ham, and cheese. A few chains were also trying pork and veal preparations. Cosmo's, for example, created and developed the pork-based Cosmobob. The introduction of salad bars in some fast-food restaurants had probably been the most important factor in improving the industry's nutrition image. A few fast food establishments also produced light gourmet food such as quiches, soups, and fruit-based desserts. A significant new product in the fast food industry was alcoholic beverages. Licensing fast food establishments to serve alcohol was continually occurring in the industry. Other than introducing the Cosmobob, however, Cosmo's had not undertaken menu diversification.

## The Niagara Falls Market

The city of Niagara Falls had a population exceeding 70,000 and was located in Southern Ontario, 100 km south of Toronto, at the United States border. Each year, over 12 million visitors were attracted to the famous natural wonder of the world. Most of the tourism occurred from June to August.

Niagara Falls boasted a strong hotel, motel, and restaurant industry to handle the annual influx of visitors. Most of the tourist accommodation was located on Lundy's Lane and in the Clifton Hill area. Exhibit 2 provides information on Niagara Falls. Famous international restaurants and hotels in Niagara Falls included the Sheraton Brock Hotel, the Casa D'oro Restaurant, the Capri Restaurant, and the Hungarian Tavern. The city also had a significant number of franchised hotel establishments such as Howard Johnson's and Best Western Hotels. The franchised restaurants were mostly of the fast food variety: McDonald's, Burger King, Wendy's, Harvey's, Arthur Treachers, etc. These outlets were very busy in the summer and moderately busy during the rest of the year.

## Cosmo's Restaurants Operations

Cosmo's Restaurants had two locations in Niagara Falls by 1979. The first location was opened on Lundy's Lane, four miles from the Falls and the Clifton Hill area. That section of Lundy's Lane was known by local residents as "the fast food strip" since most fast food chains were located in that area. The second restaurant was located on Thorold Stone Road, a main industrial thoroughfare. Cosmo Panetta managed the Thorold Stone Road outlet, and Joe Panetta the Lundy's Lane restaurant.

There were two to six employees on duty at each outlet at any one time. The size of the staff could be expanded or contracted to meet demand. The units expected 50 percent of their business between 12 noon and 2 p.m. Another 30 percent occurred between 5 and 7 p.m. The remainder was evenly distributed throughout the day. It was estimated that the level of business on Sunday was only half of what might be expected on the other days of the week. An average bill for a customer would be $3.44.

Cosmo's Restaurant had grown to $240,000 in assets in 1982 and almost $600,000 in sales. Exhibits 3 and 4 show income statements and balance sheets for Cosmo's Restaurants operations. Exhibit 5 outlines selected ratios for Cosmo's Restaurants and other fast food establishments.

Cosmo's Restaurants were popular with visitors to Niagara Falls and with local residents. The restaurants were most celebrated for the Cosmobob. The widespread popularity of the Cosmobob was attributed to the product's consistent quality, which was widely broadcasted by in-restaurant promotions, over the local radio and through newspaper advertising. In 1982, the Cosmobob accounted for 35 percent of the Thorold Stone Road restaurant's sales and 30 percent for the Lundy's Lane outlet.

**THE COSMOBOB**

In 1979, Mr. Panetta began developing the Cosmobob, a product he felt had potential for mass-market introduction and development. The Cosmobob was a portion-controlled food product that consisted of small cubes of pork that were seasoned and mounted on a bamboo skewer. Exhibit 6 shows the Cosmobob ready to be served. Souvlaki was the generic name of the Greek Cosmobob. Some people referred to the product as shishkabob. However, since some restaurants did not produce good quality souvlaki, the generic product's image was inconsistent. For this reason, Panetta chose the unique Cosmobob name for the fairly well-known Greek souvlaki.

Mr. Panetta believed that the major attributes of the Cosmobob were its consistent size and quality and the food preparation savings resulting from volume production. These features would guarantee higher, more stable gross margins for the product, as well as developing a consistent superior quality souvlaki for the consumer. Prior to serving, the Cosmobob was cooked, rolled in warm pita bread, where the skewer was removed, and then garnished with the Cosmobob sauce, onions, tomato, and pickle. The Cosmobob was also served with rice and vegetable. Exhibit 7 outlines the presentation and preparation of the Cosmobob.

In September 1982 Panetta decided to try to manufacture the Cosmobob on a large scale and sell it to area restaurants and institutions. A 150-square foot area in the backroom of the Thorold Stone Road restaurant was used for production. The room was concrete block, and not insulated, thereby providing the necessary cool production facility. Minor facility upgrading was completed for the room to pass local health inspection. The restaurant had limited freezing facilities, so arrangements were made to store the finished product at a Niagara Falls icehouse. The icehouse charged $200 per month for their unused area.

Three people were initially hired on a part-time basis. One worker cut the pork in cubes, seasoned the pork with dry spice, and let it set for two days. The other two workers would skew the seasoned pork in 50-gram portions, vacuum-pack 10 portions per package, box 6 packages per case, and ship the cases to the icehouse. Labour was paid $4.50 per hour. Exhibit 8 provides data on labour productivity for producing the Cosmobob at the end of December.

Mr. Panetta and his son Frank introduced and attempted to sell the product to restaurants and institutions in the 100 km corridor from Fort Erie to Hamilton, Ontario. Sales visits included preparation and serving demonstrations of the Cosmobob. Panetta felt that it was necessary to create demand before any of the 18 Ontario food wholesalers would consider carrying the product. The Cosmobob sold for $24.48 per case. Initial acceptance was strong, and Panetta sensed some lucrative extra revenue from his fairly modest investment. Fast food restaurants that purchased the Cosmobob would serve it on pita bread with Cosmobob sauce and garnish, and sell the product for $1.25. Restaurants that served the Cosmobob on rice or noodles sold the dinner entrée for as much as $8.95. Sales of the Cosmobob went from 100 cases in each of September and October to 400 cases in November and close to 600 cases in December. In December, production staff was increased to six people and, by February, the backroom facilities had reached their capacity for both in-house and external orders and could not handle an increased level of demand. Exhibit 9 outlines operating results associated with the Cosmobob until the end of December. The variable cost per case was $15.60 at that time.

**FUTURE OPPORTUNITIES**

In February 1983 Panetta was approached by a commercial developer who was seeking a fast food operation to locate in a new Victoria Avenue mall (Exhibit 2). The mall, which was scheduled to open in June 1983, was located on Victoria Avenue between the Clifton Hill tourist area and Queen Street, the Niagara Falls business district. The list of mall tenants included a convenience milk store, a hair styling salon, a flower shop, and a dry cleaner. The developer felt that approximately 500 cars would visit the mall on an average day.

Rent at the mall was set at $800 per month. Panetta was expected to sign a 20-year lease, calling for annual rent increases of inflation plus 1 percent. The lease could be broken any time after five years by paying the penalty clause of full rent for one-half the remaining years on the contract. Panetta thought that the location had good potential, and while sales would originally be about 60 percent of the Thorold Stone Road sales, that outlet's sales could be matched in two years. He further estimated that $5,000 in leasehold improvements would be necessary, as well as $25,000 in equipment, but that a check with vendors would provide more accurate figures.

Panetta's thoughts were also with the Cosmobob. Delighted with the product's early success, Panetta realized that it was time to define the Cosmobob's role in the family business. The backroom production facilities were cramped for space, and the icehouse freezing arrangement caused problems with shipping. Any strategy which would cause sales to increase would require new production facilities to produce the Cosmobob. In February, Panetta was aware of two potential sites.

One site was an old mushroom factory in Grimsby, Ontario. Grimsby was located between Toronto and Niagara Falls. Rental charges for the factory were $1,000 per month for the first year lease. The rent would be raised by 15 percent in each subsequent year. The lease also gave the tenant a $150,000 purchase option along with the first right of refusal[1] to any change in ownership. Facilities improvements for the mushroom factory, in order to meet provincial health standards, would cost $50,000 to $60,000. This amount would cover the cost of refrigerating the work area, and of building a walk-in cooler. All food processed for sale in Ontario was required to adhere to provincial health standards.

The second option was an old dairy plant in Niagara Falls. The dairy had a refrigerated work area and prefabricated freezer units. To meet provincial health standards, miscellaneous leasehold improvements that would cost $15,000 were needed. The tenant was expected to sign a three-year lease, with rent at $1,000 per month for the first six months, $1,200 per month for the next six months, $1,500 in year two and $1,700 in year three.

The building was appraised at $225,000 and the lease would include the first right of refusal with a $200,000 purchase option. Panetta preferred the Niagara Falls location if the Cosmobob was introduced on a large scale, because lower capital costs would get the plant operational, and a Niagara Falls location would permit him to use existing labour.

Panetta figured that it would cost $15,000 to $20,000 extra for either of the buildings to pass federal government inspection. These changes would include paving the parking lots, installing stainless steel racks, sealing all wall and floor cracks, and various other techniques to control bacteria. Federal inspection was necessary for products to be sold in more than one province. Equipping a plant with weigh scales, trays, knives, packaging equipment, etc., would cost approximately $40,000, although operations could start up with one-half that amount. Labour needs would also have to be determined, but would likely depend on product demand.

Panetta felt that a decision to pursue the Cosmobob would require a clear marketing plan. The company could attempt to establish a customer base in the food services market either on a provincial or national scale. This would require the company to either establish its own salesforce to visit the various restaurants and/or institutions or to arrange for food wholesalers to distribute the Cosmobob to those outlets. A salesperson would have to be paid at least $15,000 per year and would incur $5,000 in expenses. Hickeson-Langs, a food wholesaler with distribution in both the Ontario and national market, had already approached Panetta about obtaining the right to distribute the Cosmobob. Hickeson-Langs requested a 20 percent margin on their purchase price. If a food wholesaler was selected, Panetta wondered if the Cosmobob could be sold as a single product. In the Niagara Falls area, it was the Cosmobob concept, with pita bread and Cosmobob sauce, that was sold to local establishments. Since either pita bread or the sauce was not available in all Ontario markets, a decision on whether or not to carry those products would have to be made. Cosmobob sauce was made once a month and the pita bread was purchased from a local bakery and repackaged. The bookkeeper indicated that additional working capital would be required to cover approximately 22 days of receivables and four weeks of inventory. Payments on most accounts payable would have to be made in seven days.

A second marketing approach was the possibility of distributing the Cosmobob to the home user through supermarket chains. This market was larger than the food services market, and there was no existing "ready to serve" souvlaki available to the home user. Panetta realized that, although the market was large, federal inspection would be required if the Cosmobob was introduced nationally and that a great deal of promotion would be necessary. Supermarket chains would expect a 20 percent margin on retail selling price, good promotion support, and guaranteed delivery.

**CONCLUSION**

As Panetta sat back to review his possible courses of action, he knew that whatever strategy was chosen would have to be in the best interests of his wife and sons. He realized that marketing and production changes involved in any decision would have to be operational, but that the most difficult task would be to estimate the financial requirements and feasibility of the chosen strategy.

## NOTES

1. First right of refusal gives Cosmo Panetta priority over any third-party offer to purchase the building by paying the $150,000 purchase option price.

**EXHIBIT 1**

### The Greek Cosmobob
### Market Profile of Selected Canadian Supermarket Chains (1981)

| Retail Food Chain | Canadian Market Share | Ontario Outlets | Ontario Market Share |
|---|---|---|---|
| Loblaws Companies | 17% | 135 | 23% |
| Provigo | 14% | N/A | N/A |
| Safeway | 11% | 26 | 3% |
| Dominion | 11% | 219 | 36% |
| Steinberg (Miracle Food Mart) | 10% | 73 | 10.5% |
| Food City | 6% | 47 | 8% |
| A & P | 3% | 114 | 6% |

Source: *Business Quarterly,* Winter 1982, p. 54.

***EXHIBIT 2***
***Partial Map of***
***Niagara Falls***

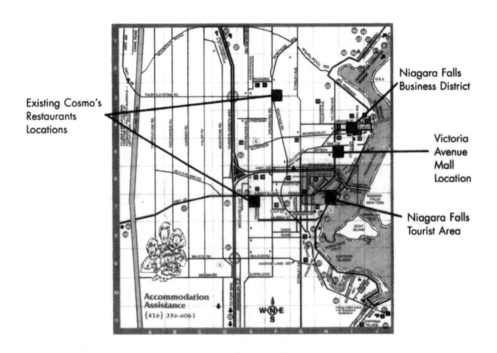

Existing Cosmo's
Restaurants
Locations

Niagara Falls
Business District

Victoria
Avenue
Mall
Location

Niagara Falls
Tourist Area

*EXHIBIT 3*

| | Thorold Stone Road Outlet | | Lundy's Lane | |
|---|---|---|---|---|
| **The Greek Cosmobob**<br>**Cosmo's Restaurants Ltd.**<br>**Income Statements**<br>**for the Years Ending December 31, 1981, 1982** | | | | |
| | **1981** | **1982** | **1981** | **1982** |
| Sales | $251,177 | $268,753 | $281,813 | $312,431 |
| Cost of goods sold: | | | | |
| Food costs | 88,921 | 97,289 | 100,607 | 112,475 |
| Paper costs | 14,819 | 16,125 | 16,345 | 18,433 |
| Wages and salaries | 82,386 | 88,688 | 92,998 | 103,727 |
| Other production costs | 8,038 | 8,869 | 8,173 | 9,373 |
| Total cost of goods sold | 194,104 | 210,971 | 218,123 | 244,008 |
| Gross profit | 57,073 | 57,782 | 63,690 | 68,423 |
| Operating expenses: | | | | |
| Advertising and promotion | 7,535 | 8,063 | 8,454 | 9,685 |
| Maintenance and repairs | 3,014 | 3,225 | 3,382 | 3,749 |
| Utilities | 13,061 | 13,975 | 13,527 | 14,684 |
| Administrative expenses | 3,200 | 3,700 | 3,600 | 4,100 |
| Depreciation expense | 5,931 | 5,946 | 6,189 | 6,204 |
| Other expenses<br>(including interest) | 7,535 | 8,063 | 7,891 | 9,061 |
| Total operating expenses | 40,276 | 42,972 | 43,043 | 47,483 |
| Net profit before tax | $16,797 | $14,810 | $20,647 | $20,940 |

*Exhibit 4*

|  | The Greek Cosmobob<br>Cosmo's Restaurants Ltd.<br>Balance Sheet<br>as at December 31, 1981, 1982 | |
| --- | --- | --- |
|  | **1981** | **1982** |
| ASSETS | | |
| Current assets | | |
|    Cash | $ 4,629 | $ 6,573 |
|    Accounts receivable | 12,288 | 14 530 |
|    Inventories | 11,909 | 13,902 |
|    Prepaid expenses | 2,142 | 2,356 |
| Total current assets | 30,968 | 37,361 |
| Fixed assets | | |
|    Land | 85,000 | 85,000 |
|    Buildings (cost) | 140,000 | 146,123 |
| Less accumulated depreciation | | |
|    Buildings[1] | 39,200 | 44,800 |
|    Net buildings | 100,800 | 101,323 |
|    Equipment | 65,200 | 68,500 |
| Less accumulated depreciation | | |
|    Equipment[2] | 45,640 | 52,160 |
|    Net equipment | 19,560 | 16,340 |
| Total fixed assets | 205,360 | 202,663 |
| Total assets | 236,328 | 240,024 |
| LIABILITIES AND EQUITY | | |
| Current liabilities | | |
|    Notes payable to bank | 10,000 | 5,000 |
|    Accounts payable | 37,787 | 45,498 |
|    Accrued expenses payable | 1,963 | 1,026 |
|    Current portion long-term debt | 1,000 | 1,000 |
| Total current liabilities | 50,750 | 52,524 |
| Long-term debt (net of current portion) | 21,000 | 15,000 |
| Total liabilities | 71,750 | 67,524 |
| Shareholder's equity | | |
|    Common stock, Cosmo and Josephine Panetta | 100,000 | 100,000 |
|    Retained earnings | 65,578 | 72,500 |
| Total shareholder's equity | 165,578 | 172,500 |
| Total liabilities and shareholder's equity | $236,328 | $240,024 |

**1.** Buildings were depreciated "straight line" over 20 years.
**2.** Equipment and leasehold improvements were depreciated "straight line" over 10 years.

EXHIBIT 5

| | The Greek Cosmobob Financial Ratios | | | | | |
|---|---|---|---|---|---|---|
| | Thorold Stone Road | | Lundy's Lane | | Burger King[1] | McDonalds[1] |
| | 1981 | 1982 | 1981 | 1982 | (1980) | (1980) |
| PROFITABILITY | | | | | | |
| Sales | 100.0% | 100.0% | 100.0% | 100.0% | 100.0% | 100.0% |
| Cost of goods sold: | | | | | | |
|     Food | 35.8 | 36.2 | 35.7 | 36.0 | 32.9 | 33.4 |
|     Paper | 5.9 | 6.0 | 5.8 | 5.9 | 3.6 | 4.5 |
|     Wages and salaries | 32.8 | 33.0 | 33.0 | 33.2 | 27.2 | 25.8 |
|     Other | 3.2 | 3.3 | 2.9 | 3.0 | 3.2 | — |
| Cost of goods sold | 77.7 | 78.5 | 77.4 | 78.1 | 66.9 | 63.7 |
| Gross profit | 22.3 | 21.5 | 22.6 | 21.9 | 33.1 | 36.3 |
| Operating expenses | | | | | | |
|     Advertising and promotion | 3.0 | 3.0 | 3.0 | 3.1 | 5.6 | 5.2 |
|     Maintenance and repairs | 1.2 | 1.2 | 1.2 | 1.2 | — | 1.3 |
|     Utilities | 5.2 | 5.2 | 4.8 | 4.7 | 4.8 | 2.8 |
|     Administrative | 1.3 | 1.4 | 1.3 | 1.3 | — | 1.7 |
|     Depreciation | 2.4 | 2.2 | 2.2 | 2.0 | — | — |
|     Other expenses | 3.0 | 3.0 | 2.8 | 2.9 | 3.0 | 7.0 |
|     Rent | — | — | — | — | 9.0 | 9.8 |
| Total operating expenses | 16.0 | 16.0 | 15.3 | 15.2 | 22.4 | 27.8 |
| Net profit before tax | 6.7 | 5.5 | 7.3 | 6.7 | 10.7 | 8.5 |
| LIQUIDITY | | | | | | |
|     Current ratio | .61:1 | .71:1 | | | | |
|     Acid test | .33/1 | .40/1 | | | | |
| EFFICIENCY | | | | | | |
|     Age of accounts receivable | 8.4 days | 9.1 days | | | | |
|     Age of inventory | 10.5 days | 11.2 days | | | | |
|     Age of payables | 58.2 days | 63.2 days | | | | |
| STABILITY | | | | | | |
|     Net worth/Total assets | 70% | 72% | | | | |
| GROWTH | | 1981–82 | | | | |
|     Sales | | 9.0% | | | | |
|     Net Profit | | (4.5%) | | | | |
|     Assets | | 1.6% | | | | |
|     Equity | | 4.2% | | | | |

1. Source: W. Earl Sasser, *Management of Service Operations.*

***EXHIBIT 6***
***The Cosmobob***

**EXHIBIT 7**
*The Cosmobob's Preparation and Presentation*

- The Cosmobob can be cooked on griddle, broiler, charcoal pit, barbecue, or microwave.

- When cooking on griddle or microwave, Cosmobobs must be covered with a lid at all times.

- When cooking, flatten Cosmobobs with palm of hand to increase cooking surface and heat conductivity and to speed up cooking.

- To sear meat, place on cooking surface for one or two minutes each side to lock in juices and keep meat from drying out.

- Once Cosmobobs have been seared, they can be wrapped in foil (shiny side in) to be cooked to serve as required. Holding time of pre-cooked Cosmobobs is approximately 24 hours, if refrigerated after cooling at room temperature.

- The Cosmobob is seasoned with herbs and spices but no salt. Good for no-sodium diets, ideal for hospitals or institutions where this is important.

- We do suggest using lemon and salt on Cosmobobs after cooking to bring out flavour — tastes great!

- To make Cosmobob-Schnitzels, flatten meat with meat hammer (rough side), roll in *all purpose flour*, dip in whole beaten egg (do not add milk or water to eggs as they may add sour flavour), roll in coarse unseasoned bread crumbs. Fry in corn oil for better flavour and no greasy taste. Set temperature at 375 degrees F and place breaded Cosmobobs in hot oil; when juices rise on top, turn over and finish cooking, approx. 6 to 7 minutes. Do not deep fry.

- The Cosmobob is a very versatile food product and can be served in many ways, on rice or noodles with a sauce and wedge of lemon, as a lunch or dinner item, or alone as a bar or finger food item, plain or schnitzeled. Great with fries or baked potatoes. Good on pita bread with Cosmobob Sauce and garnish. Any way you like it, simply delicious!

- Being high quality and portion controlled is by far the most important advantage. Food cost is controlled and consumer affordability is maintained.

**EXHIBIT 8**

| The Greek Cosmobob Labour Productivity Data | |
|---|---|
| **Job and Function** | **Cases per Employee per day** |
| Cutter: trim, debone, and cube pork; season cubes | 50 cases |
| Skewer: weigh pork, insert cubes onto bamboo skewers | 10 cases |
| Packer: pack, seal, flash freeze, and box Cosmobobs | 100 cases |

*Exhibit 9*

| Unaudited Operating Results for the Cosmobob (1982) | | | | |
|---|---|---|---|---|
| | September | October | November | December |
| Volume | 100 cases | 100 cases | 400 cases | 600 cases |
| Sales | $2,488 | $2,448 | $9,792 | $14,688 |
| Cost of goods sold: | | | | |
| Meat and packaging | 930 | 930 | 3,720 | 5,580 |
| Labour | 640 | 540 | 1,872 | 2,808 |
| Other production costs | 162 | 162 | 648 | 972 |
| Total cost of goods sold | 1,732 | 1,632 | 6,240 | 9,360 |
| Gross profit | 756 | 816 | 3,552 | 5,328 |
| Operating expense: | | | | |
| Administrative expenses[1] | 250 | 325 | 500 | 820 |
| Selling expenses[2] | 850 | 1,205 | 2,025 | 2,370 |
| Other operating expenses[3] | 500 | 1,000 | 125 | 70 |
| Total operating expenses | 1,600 | 2,530 | 2,650 | 3,260 |
| Operating profit | (844) | (1,714) | 902 | 2,068 |

1. Panetta expected $10,000 per year administrative expenses if the Cosmobob was produced on a large scale.
2. These expenses were incurred by Cosmo and Frank while selling the Cosmobob. A full-time salesperson would have to be paid at least $15,000 per year and would incur $5,000 per year in expenses.
3. Other expenses referred to miscellaneous start-up costs. Panetta felt that these costs would not exceed $5,000 if the Cosmobob was produced on a large scale.

### C A S E 7.5   MAIL-ORDER IN CANADA

On April 10, 1991, Linda King, an Honours Business Administration student at U.W.O., put the finishing touches on a 50-page business plan that she had prepared for a course entitled New Enterprise Management. Her report proposed the opening of a retail lingerie and leisure wear store in London, Ontario, modeled after the highly successful Victoria's Secret in the United States. To increase awareness of the products and company name, she proposed introducing the venture with a mail-order catalogue. It was this area about which Linda was most enthusiastic, and she was now wondering how she could go about breaking into the Canadian mail-order and lingerie market.

**THE LINGERIE AND LEISURE WEAR MARKET**

Lingerie can be defined as "women's underwear and nightclothes made of lace, silk, nylon, etc." This broad category includes underwear, brassieres, undershirts, teddies, nighties, and pyjamas. Leisure wear includes all other casual night clothes and lounge wear, night shirts, long-johns, flannel pyjamas, bathrobes, and slippers. Lingerie and leisure wear products can be categorized by briefs, sleep-wear, and lounge-wear.

Lingerie and leisure wear can be found in retail boutiques, department stores, and through mail-order catalogues. Currently, the latter make up an insignificant part of the Canadian market. Although the retail industry has suffered over the last few years, there have been some positive signs for specialty stores, which include specialty lingerie stores. Over the last five years, sales at women's stores have grown significantly. Between 1986 and 1990, sales in the category of "intimate apparel" have grown consistently. Between 1989 and 1990, sales growth was 14.7 percent.

The industry is expected to grow at an average of 6 percent for the next 5 to 10 years. Underwear is the most popular women's wear item. Imports of women's underwear in 1990 totalled 13 million pairs, and the total Canadian production is estimated at about 13.5 to 15 million pairs per year.

**THE LINGERIE CONSUMER**

Lingerie consumers are considered to be women aged 16 and over. Within Canada there are approximately 5.2 million such women who purchase two to three items of bras and underwear every year. These women purchase items for personal consumption or to be given as a gift. Lingerie is purchased all year round, with seasonal fluctuations over the holiday season in December and the summer months. Most women who purchase the more adventurous items prefer to shop in malls where they can blend into traffic inconspicuously.

## THE LONDON MARKET

London, Ontario, is located about 160 km southwest of Toronto, easily accessed by the MacDonald-Cartier Freeway (Highway 401). With a metropolitan population in excess of 300,000, London is nationally known as "the Forest City" for its tree-lined streets. Many of the small towns surrounding the city (Exeter, Ilderton, Lucan, Grand Bend, Ailsa Craig, Parkhill, Thorndale, and St. Thomas) utilize London's many services and conveniences. Residents from as far away as Sarnia, Goderich, and Stratford (a 70-km radius) frequently make the journey to London for shopping and other amenities.

The economy of the city could be characterized as stable, white collar, and mainly service-based. Unemployment was lower than the national average while individual personal income was 9 percent above the national average. With a higher personal disposable income than most Canadian cities, London boasted more retail shopping space per capita than any other city in North America.[1]

## COMPETITION

Janet Alexander currently operates two stores in the London area. These stores carry brand name items such as Voguebra, Warners, and Lejaby. The product line includes lingerie and sleep-wear.

Lingerie Elisse is another local competitor targeting the quality conscious consumer. The products it offers are similar to those of Janet Alexander and are supplied by Canadian manufacturers. Its London location has been open since 1989, but they have a more established store in Markham, Ontario.

La Vie En Rose is the only national competitor. With 19 stores across Canada, it is the second largest Canadian lingerie retailer in 5 provinces . Its stores are located in both malls and street-front boutiques. The image of quality is achieved through its elegant store atmosphere. No difference in product quality was observed between this store and the previously mentioned ones.

Frederick's of Hollywood is a major U.S. lingerie retailer. Frederick's began as a mail-order company and added the retail units once the name was established. As of 1988, mail-order made up 40 percent of Frederick's sales and 60 percent of the company's profits. Frederick's stores have had trouble establishing themselves in the market because consumers have tended to purchase their items as jokes or novelties. This chain has had extreme difficulty shaking this image and has yet to break into the everyday underwear market.

Victoria's Secret offers a wide variety of lingerie and leisure wear products that are perceived to be superior in quality and value to anything currently offered in Canada. It is owned by a larger U.S. retailer, The Limited. Victoria's Secret also operates a very extensive mail-order business.

## THE CLOTHING MAIL-ORDER INDUSTRY

The mail-order industry is a division of a marketing technique called direct marketing. Direct marketing involves selling products directly to the consumer via mail advertisements, catalogues, phone solicitation, or T.V. sales (i.e., the home shopping network). Mail-order is the most popular of these options. Mail-order involves having a catalogue delivered to the residence of a consumer. The catalogue describes product features, shows pictures of the products being sold, details their prices, availability, and order process. Typical products sold through the mail include books, appliances, clothing, shoes, audio items, and camping gear. The order process can take several forms. The most popular one is an agent marketing system, which has successfully been employed by Avon Cosmetics. This system provides backup sales people who make house calls to deliver the catalogue and then follow up calls to collect the customers' orders. Another common method of ordering from a catalogue requires customers to place their orders over the phone direct to the company via a 1-800 phone number.

Offering products through a mail-order catalogue presents the potential for national awareness. It also provides the advantage of achieving quantity discounts from manufacturers sooner than would be available using a solely retail operation. A mail-order business can be started with a smaller capital investment than is required to open a retail store. This kind of customer service can create lifetime customers. Mail-order also offers some challenges. First, Canada has the largest number of malls and department stores per capita in North America. This offers the consumer many alternative places to shop. Second, Canadians tend to be more conservative than their neighbours south of the border. Third, the climate and changing seasons mean a constantly changing product line, which requires a fast turnover of merchandise.

## THE MAIL-ORDER CONSUMER

Although the majority of mail-order is unsolicited, it is carefully targeted toward those whom the company considers to be potential customers. Clothing mail-order consumers are considered to be individuals aged 18 to 30. The market can be segmented based on past mail-order purchase history. Someone who has shopped mail-order would already have a good understanding of how the system works, have different shopping habits, and would also be less averse to risk. The individual who has never shopped mail-order should not be ignored, however, since this segment makes up the majority of the Canadian market.

### Have Bought Through Mail-Order

Those who have bought clothing through mail-order before and have been satisfied with the outcome will not have to be convinced of its merits. These consumers have likely shopped through some of the more established mail-order companies and will be used to prompt delivery and excellent service.

These individuals likely have a relative who lives in the United States or live themselves within 200 km of the U.S. border. Many of the mail-order items bought in Canada are a result of catalogues filtering across from the U.S. These consumers tend to be adventurous and willing to "take a chance" on a product. These individuals do not have a lot of time on their hands to browse through conventional malls to look for a certain product. Furthermore, they tend to have a higher discretionary income to spend on indulgent items for themselves. Consumers that are sold on this method of shopping usually cite its convenience and flexibility as well as the variety of available products as its main advantages. Flexibility refers to the time of day in which they can shop. It is not unusual to have 24 hour per day service. Customers are not constrained by the usual 10 a.m. to 6 p.m. store hours.

**Have Never Shopped Mail-Order**

This segment consists of those who have never been given the opportunity, and those who have never taken the chance. The most common excuses for resistance to mail-order are that you can't touch the material to feel its quality, you can't try items on, and you experience a hassle in returning a product that doesn't fit. These consumers tend to be more risk-averse than someone who is willing to try mail-order and would sooner go without the product than risk unnecessary disappointment.

**THE NEW VENTURE PROPOSAL**

The original report proposed opening a retail store that would offer an alternative to the traditional marketing of lingerie. The concept intended to create an elegant atmosphere that would draw the consumer into the store on impulse, rather than out of necessity. This atmosphere would be achieved by placing emphasis on the store front, layout, fixtures, and lighting to create a real "shopping experience." The sales at the retail store would be supplemented by a mail-order catalogue. The products to be sold included ladies' sleep-wear, hosiery, underwear, bras, robes, toiletries, accessories, and men's wear.

After considerable thought, Linda thought it might be best to start the business with just the mail-order division. This would help to promote awareness of the products and store name, while keeping costs low.

**Mail-Order Distribution**

The process would begin by mailing the catalogue to the target consumer.

The production of the catalogue would be contracted out to a printing company called Charterhouse Printing Services (CPS). CPS estimated a cost of $4,650 for 2,000 catalogues. The catalogues would be 8 1/2″ x 11″ in size with 28 pages including the cover. Photography would be supplied free of charge from a friend who was studying at the Ontario College of Art. Depending on the target consumer group, there would be two possible methods of catalogue distribution. Canada Post admail delivery service would be used for national distribution, and an independent agency called Star Mail-Ibax would be used for any deliveries within London (Exhibits 1 and 2).

A successful mail-order depends on the consumer group targeted. In order to reach the "has shopped mail-order" segment, Linda could call a list broker and purchase a list of all women aged 18 to 30 who have subscribed to mail-order catalogues in the past. Lists cost $100 for every 1,000 names. The list is then sent in the form of address labels, which can be placed directly on the catalogue. Using a list broker allows national distribution since names from across Canada are included.

Since there would be no list available for the "never shopped mail-order" segment, a cold-call strategy would have to be used. Because this method would require a lot more effort, Linda decided to use London as a test market. Linda discovered that Statistics Canada published demographic data on the households in London. Combined with a postal code map of the city, this information would help to pinpoint an area of the city that would be most responsive to a mail-order lingerie catalogue (Exhibits 3A and 3B).

Once the customers received the catalogue they would be free to browse through at their leisure. When they decided upon the products they would like to purchase, they could place their orders via a 1-800 phone number. To provide 24 hour per day service, an answering machine would have to be purchased. The information gained over the phone would include the item number, colour, size, customer address, and method of payment (only Visa or Mastercard would be accepted).

Upon receipt of the order all the relevant customer information would be inputted into a database. The supplier would then be called and the merchandise ordered. In order to maintain good service for the customers, a one-week lead time from the suppliers between placement and receipt of the order would be necessary. This way the customers would receive their orders within 10 days. The average order size per week from the supplier was expected to be 5 kg. When the products were received, they would be mailed out to the customer. Canada Post's Priority Courier would be employed for delivery. Each delivery per household was not expected to exceed 1 kg. The Priority Courier costs are $1.40 for delivery of up to 5 kg within London and $4.70 for 1 kg within Canada. These costs would be paid by the customer.

### Supplier Sourcing

Production of the products would be contracted out to lingerie manufacturers. Two manufacturers were currently being considered, one in Canada and one in Hong Kong. The candidate would be chosen based on the ability to meet design and delivery requirements at the lowest cost.

When importing goods from Hong Kong, the production process becomes slightly more complicated and time-consuming, but the potential cost savings can justify the effort. One of the biggest costs involved in dealing with overseas manufacturers is the trip to Hong Kong to see the quality of their work before placing the initial order. Ordering from Hong Kong requires a longer lead time as it is necessary to account for the delivery. The time involved from the point of order to receipt of the product runs between four and six months. Linda wondered what effect this would have on the mail-order process. All payment to these manufacturers must be made with a letter of credit, which involves a banking fee and interest cost.

Of several Hong Kong manufacturers, Linda had narrowed her choice down to Oodways International Limited. They had been the most helpful in replying to requests for product lists and cost data information. Oodways' terms of delivery were 75 days after receipt of the letter of credit. They also specified minimum orders of 300 items. Average manufacturer's selling price was expected to be $10 for briefs, $25 for sleep-wear, and $40 for lounge-wear.

The Canadian manufacturer, Delicate Lingerie, was based in Montreal. They required credit terms of 30 days and had a returns policy for accepting returns due to an error in shipment or defective merchandise. All claims for returns must be made within five days of receipt of goods. The delivery terms were quite different from Oodways. Fall delivery took place from June 1 through October 25; winter delivery was from October 15 through November 15. Average manufacturer's selling price was expected to be $12 for briefs, $21 for sleep-wear items, and $31 for lounge-wear.

## Mail-Order Costs

The mail-order business would be run out of the basement of a friend's house in London, and would not require a lot of time commitment after the initial start-up. The same product lines would be sold through the mail-order and the "atmosphere" could be achieved through quality photography and layout of the catalogue.

Most of the costs for the mail-order operation would be fixed. These included rent at $400 per month for the use of the basement office in London, an answering machine for $217.35, catalogue production, catalogue distribution, the 1-800 number at $1,880 for 55 hours of calls plus an additional $32 per hour for an additional 50 hours, $1,500 for a computer and database program, advertising and promotion and, finally, the salaries for the personnel who would operate the division. The operation would require one full-time employee to answer phone orders and another part-time employee to provide support for order processing. The full-time employee would earn a salary of $18,000 per year, while the part-time employee would earn $7 per hour. Other miscellaneous expenses were expected to total $3,000 in the first year. The charges for accepting Visa and Mastercard would be 4 percent of sales, which would be treated as a variable cost.

## Retail Store

The retail store would require a large investment of both time and money in the start-up months. Masonville Mall was chosen as a potential location for the retail store. It is estimated that 60 percent of mall traffic consists of women aged 25 to 40 with above-average disposable income levels. A research survey conducted in 1989 indicated that in 1991 $24 million would be spent on women's wear. Mall management projected that its primary market would grow an average of 7 percent over the next 10 years, and with the recent mall expansion, they expected to capture more consumer spending.

The same supplier chosen for the mail-order division would be secured for the retail store.

Rent would be $4,375 per month, and capital costs covering store fixtures and decor were expected to be $25,000. An advertising budget of $15,000 was set for the first year. Salaries and wages would be $2,900 per month, covering the salary of one full-time manager and three part-time workers. Other miscellaneous expenses should total $6,000.

**Combined Strategy**

The final strategy would be to open the retail store and mail-order business simultaneously. The mail-order division would start off selling merchandise identical to that which was sold in the store. The mail-order business might be nation-wide or restricted to London, depending on which target market is chosen.

It was expected that briefs would account for approximately 60 percent of all sales, sleep-wear 25 percent of sales, with the remainder of sales coming from lounge-wear. Total sales for the retail store in the first full year of operation were expected to reach $150,000. Sales for the mail-order division were expected to reach $50,000. Margin on cost of 42 percent was projected for all briefs, 50 percent for sleep-wear, and 48 percent for lounge-wear.

**Advertising and Promotion**

Linda was not sure how much she would have to spend on advertising and promotion. She maintained that an effective distribution of the catalogue for the mail-order concept should serve as good advertising. "But what about everyone who's not on your mailing list?" a friend questioned. "An ad in a newspaper or magazine could include information on how to get a catalogue mailed to you, if you are not in the London area." Linda wondered if this was a valid point.

Several advertising options were available to solve this problem. A newspaper ad could be taken out in the mail-order section of either the *Globe and Mail*, the *Toronto Star*, or the *London Free Press* (see Exhibit 4). Linda liked this idea and remembered reading that Tilley Endurables started out with an ad in a newspaper, and had since turned out to be quite a success story. The average cost of a magazine ad in Canadian homemaker magazines runs at $2,000 for a full-page ad.

**Other Considerations**

Linda was confident that she could secure bank financing of $65,000 for the first year of operations. She could only afford to put in $10,000 from personal savings; two classmates had offered to match this amount in exchange for partnerships in the company.

In August, Linda was going to start a full-time job with a management consultant firm in Toronto, so she would not have a lot of time available to spend on the venture.

Linda was hoping eventually to reach the goal of $500,000 in sales. This was a milestone she had set for herself and she wondered how long it would take to reach it. She also wanted to achieve a return on investment of 15 percent over five years.

**FINAL CONSIDERATIONS**

Can the Canadian market support a lingerie mail-order catalogue and retail store? This was the question Linda was pondering. She was relatively risk-averse, and did not want to get in over her head.

Linda understood that establishing a retail and/or mail-order company in Canada would pose a great many challenges in the start-up months. It still had to be decided whether or not to open the retail store, develop a mail-order business, or do both at the same time. In addition to that, she had to decide which consumer segment to target for the mail-order division, how to attract them, and where to source the product (domestic or abroad). All this and she had yet to decide upon a name for the company!

### NOTES

1. *Canadian Markets 1993*, 67th ed. (Toronto: The *Financial Post Data Group*, 1993, and *Statistics Canada, 1993*). Excerpted from *The Ugly Dog Pizza Company*, April 1995.

---

**EXHIBIT 1**

### Canada Post Admail Rates

Single Mailing Volume Rates (Residential Delivery Only)[1]

Customers mailing large volume Single Mailings of Printed Matter may qualify for volume discount rates as outlined below.

| VOLUME PER MAILING | Premium Rates (Standard Items) | | Economy Rates (Nonstandard Items) | |
|---|---|---|---|---|
| | 0–50 g | over 50 g | 0–50 g | over 50 g |
| 5,000 | 7.1c | 4.8c + 46c/kg | 6.6c | 4.5c + 42c/kg |
| 10,000 | 7.0 | 4.8 + 44 | 6.5 | 4.4 + 42 |
| 20,000 | 6.9 | 4.7 + 44 | 6.4 | 4.3 + 42 |
| 30,000 | 6.8 | 4.6 + 44 | 6.2 | 4.2 + 40 |
| 40,000 | 6.7 | 4.5 + 44 | 6.1 | 4.1 + 40 |
| 50,000 | 6.6 | 4.5 + 42 | 5.9 | 4.0 + 38 |
| 100,000 | 6.5 | 4.4 + 42 | 5.8 | 4.0 + 36 |

All volume rates apply to items deposited at the office of delivery. Customers wishing to have Canada Post forward items to any other delivery office(s) may do so for an additional transportation fee of $4 per 1,000 items ($0.004 per piece).

---

1. Compliments of Canada Post.

*EXHIBIT 2*

| Costs of Catalogue Distribution |
| --- |

Star Mail-Ibax — Independent Admail Delivery Service

|  | 2,500 units — 9,999 units (minimum order: 2,500 units) |
|---|---|
|  | $40 for every 1,000 |
| or | 4.0 cents per unit (1 catalogue) |
|  | 10,000 units — 19,999 units |
|  | $34 for every 1,000 |
| or | 3.4 cents per unit |
|  | 20,000 units — 99,999 units |
|  | $31 for every 1,000 |
| or | 3.1 cents per unit |

*EXHIBIT 3A*

## Demographic and Income Data for Postal Code Areas, 1988[1]

| Area | All Taxfilers % By Age | | | | | Taxfilers Reporting Total Income % With Income Greater Than | | | | | | |
|---|---|---|---|---|---|---|---|---|---|---|---|---|
| London, Canada | Number | <25 | 25-44 | 45-64 | >64 | Number | $15,000 | $25,000 | $35,000 | $50,000 | $75,000 | $100,000 |
| N5V - 1 | 14,175 | 20 | 48 | 27 | 6 | 14,125 | 57 | 34 | 16 | 3 | 0 | X |
| N5W - 1 | 16,675 | 17 | 43 | 27 | 14 | 16,600 | 55 | 29 | 13 | 3 | 0 | X |
| N5X - 1 | 10,125 | 17 | 45 | 29 | 9 | 10,100 | 67 | 48 | 33 | 17 | 5 | 3 |
| N5Y - 1 | 20,500 | 20 | 46 | 22 | 13 | 20,400 | 53 | 29 | 14 | 4 | 1 | 0 |
| N5Z - 1 | 14,775 | 17 | 48 | 23 | 11 | 14,700 | 54 | 28 | 12 | 3 | 0 | X |
| N6A - 1 | 7,825 | 17 | 40 | 22 | 21 | 7,800 | 61 | 40 | 26 | 14 | 6 | 4 |
| N6A4B5-RR | 200 | 14 | 43 | 29 | 14 | 200 | 63 | 38 | 25 | X | X | X |
| N6A4B6-RR | 275 | 17 | 33 | 33 | 17 | 275 | 64 | 45 | 27 | 18 | 9 | X |
| N6A4B7-RR | 225 | 11 | 44 | 33 | X | 225 | 56 | 44 | 22 | 11 | X | X |
| N6A4B8-RR | 375 | 20 | 33 | 33 | 13 | 375 | 60 | 33 | 20 | X | X | X |
| N6A4B9-RR | 325 | 17 | 33 | 33 | 17 | 325 | 69 | 46 | 31 | 15 | X | X |
| N6A4C1-RR | 200 | 13 | 38 | 38 | 13 | 200 | 50 | 38 | 13 | X | X | X |
| N6A4C2-RR | 300 | 18 | 45 | 27 | 9 | 300 | 58 | 33 | 17 | X | X | X |
| N6A4C3-RR | 450 | 17 | 44 | 28 | 11 | 450 | 61 | 39 | 22 | 6 | 2 | 1 |
| N6C - 1 | 21,725 | 16 | 49 | 22 | 14 | 21,675 | 63 | 39 | 21 | 8 | 2 | 1 |
| N6E - 1 | 16,850 | 19 | 59 | 17 | 4 | 16,800 | 60 | 36 | 19 | 4 | 0 | 0 |
| N6G - 1 | 14,025 | 17 | 52 | 23 | 8 | 13,975 | 61 | 43 | 28 | 13 | 5 | 3 |
| N6H - 1 | 16,775 | 15 | 35 | 25 | 25 | 16,750 | 62 | 39 | 23 | 11 | 3 | 2 |
| N6J - 1 | 17,350 | 17 | 44 | 26 | 13 | 17,300 | 60 | 36 | 20 | 8 | 2 | 1 |
| N6K - 1 | 14,825 | 16 | 45 | 26 | 13 | 14,800 | 65 | 46 | 31 | 16 | 5 | 3 |
| OTHER | 2,950 | 13 | 32 | 18 | 37 | 2,959 | 55 | 36 | 22 | 13 | 6 | 3 |

1. Statistics Canada Catalogue No. 17-202, Issue 1990, pp. 170–73, Table #1. Reproduced with permission of the Minister of Supply and Services Canada, 1992.

*Exhibit 3B*
*City of London*

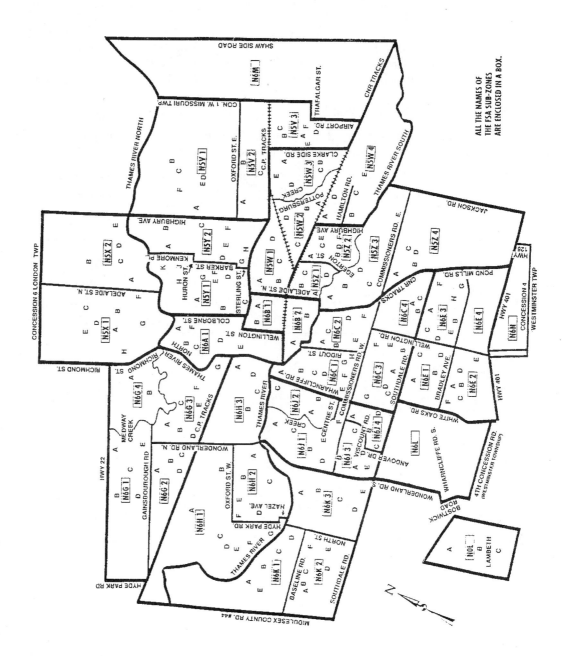

Sheldon's Retail Directory by the United States and Canada, 1991.
Reproduced with permission from Phelon, Sheldon & Marsar, Inc.

*EXHIBIT 4*
*Advertising Cost*
*Data*

Toronto Star

Costs listed are for approximately 1/8 of a page (2 1/16 inches by 4 inches).

|  | Circulation | Cost | Readership |
|---|---|---|---|
| Mon–Fri | 550,000 | $ 874/day | 1.6–1.8 million/day |
| Saturday | 850,000 | $1,076/day | 2.6 million/day |
| Sunday | 540,000 | $ 687/day | 1.3 million/day |

Globe and Mail

Costs listed for 2 1/16 by 3 3/8 inch, the smallest size of ad available. For a larger ad, double both dimension and price.

|  | Circulation | Cost | Readership |
|---|---|---|---|
| Mon–Sat | 330,000 | $1,554/6 days + GST | 1 million/day |

London Free Press

Costs listed for an 1/8 of a page.

|  | Circulation | Cost | Readership |
|---|---|---|---|
| Mon–Thurs and Sat | 125,610 | $967/day | N/A |
| Friday | 136,633 | $967/day | N/A |

# C A S E 7.6   MEDICAL SERVICES LIMITED (A)

Mary Fletcher sat at her desk in Kingston. She had managed to get some quiet time to ponder the future of her company. Perhaps she should grow? Or consolidate? There were several options available and Mary had gathered some information to help make the decision, which she felt was critical at this stage of the company's development. She wondered if there were any other possibilities that could be explored.

**THE MARKET**

The focus on the Health Care Market over the past few years has been attributed to the fact that Canada's population is aging. In 1901, only 5 percent of the population was 65 and over. In 1986, this proportion had grown to 10 percent. The over-65 segment was projected to grow at a greater rate than the rest of the population and would represent nearly 14 percent by the year 2000.

An aging population and a shift from a predominantly institutional model of health care to a model that encompassed alternative services enabling the sick and elderly to be cared for in a noninstitutional environment created a challenging health service market. The diverse client base for this type of health care included various local and provincial government agencies as well as hospitals, nursing homes, retirement homes, and group homes.

The total long-term care system amounted to $2 billion. It was divided as follows: 12,000 Chronic Care beds (39 percent), Nursing Homes (NH) and Home For The Aged (HFA) beds (38 percent), and In-Home/Community Services (23 percent). The latter was considered to be the fastest growing segment of the market. Industry growth rate had been in the order of 20 to 25 percent over the past five years and was expected to continue with increasing emphasis on care outside the normal hospital-care concept.

Incentives and disincentives to shift resources to out-patient and community services were now receiving much more attention. This was due to rising costs within hospital systems and the desire to give hospitals more flexibility to trade off programs and services within their budgets in line with community needs.

**MARY FLETCHER**

Mary was the oldest of six children. After finishing high school, she enrolled directly into a Registered Nursing Program. Her husband (Mary married in her third year of nursing) went to Case Western University in Cleveland, Ohio, and Mary nursed in a Surgical Intensive Care Unit at Mt. Sinai Hospital in Cleveland, right in the heart of the black ghettos just shortly after the race riots. Within six months, Mary was appointed head nurse on "nights."

After a year and a half she became pregnant and health problems forced a return to Kingston. Back in Canada after giving birth, she went to work in a dialysis and transplant unit. Nursing at this stage seemed rather boring but the high tech area was intriguing. Mary ended up teaching people and their spouses how to dialyse at home, including the safety factors. This was her first entry into the home care market, looking after people in their own homes, helping them to look after themselves. The cost savings were significant.

As head nurse in the Home Dialysis Unit, she was approached by an American company that sold artificial kidneys, for a sales position in Ontario. Mary was the first woman ever hired for a sales position in this particular company. Although hired as a specialist for Ontario, she would travel all over Canada, United States, and Europe.

She was at a transition point in her career:

> I went from being a nurse who wanted to work Monday to Friday, 8 to 4, to becoming a person who thought: "The harder I work the more money I am going to make." I liked the prestige. I liked the recognition and it became very much a challenge to take this task and really do something! I made a lot of money.

It also gave her a great feeling of independence.

The next move satisfied her desire to stay closer to home. Mary was hired by Caretenders, a home-health division of a large nursing home company, and turned the division around in one year from losing $10,000 per month to making $100,000 per year. She was promoted to regional manager, and then took over a new division of the company. Shortly thereafter, she was promoted to vice-president of marketing for Canada and the United States. This meant building a sales force across Canada and developing marketing programs.

The nursing home company was purchased by a national insurance company that decided to cut "uncertain" divisions. At this point, Mary was persuaded to resurrect an old marketing plan and go into partnership with a former vice-president of the nursing home company. She invested her life savings and was back in the home-care business. This meant a move from Toronto back home to Kingston.

It was a tough start, competing with large national and regional home-care companies such as Upjohn, Comcare, Red Cross, and other commercial home-making services. It also meant providing professional nursing and medical services. The company was renamed Medical Services Limited.

**THE COMPANY**   The company was divided into three divisions:

1. *Private Home Care* — services were paid through private insurance plans, Blue Cross, or an employee's Greenshield. Whenever a doctor made a referral, or when friends or family applied, the company did an assessment of what was needed. Medical Services called the physician and worked under his or her direction. An insurance company or the client was billed for RN, RNA, Nurse's Aide, or Homemaker services.

2. *Institutional Staffing* — done either under negotiated contract for services provided or for relief — clients called on an as-needed basis. The company competed very effectively, mainly on service (price was usually the same as its competitors).

3. *Government* — the Ministry of Health or Ministry of Community and Social Services funded the program and purchased the service under contract with Medicare.

When the partners' nursing homes needed staffing, the company expanded beyond Kingston. Satellite centres were set up.

**LATER DEVELOPMENTS**   When the majority partner demanded that medical services from the company be provided to his nursing homes at cost, so that a maximum return to the nursing home would be assured, disagreements resulted. Mary was forced to buy out the partner.

Mary managed on her own from 1984 to 1986, building the company and trying to develop a management team. As Medical Services Limited's reputation spread, further expansion outside Kingston became necessary. Capital was sorely needed. A new partnership, formed with a large private nursing home/retirement company, appeared to be an ideal marriage. The nursing home/retirement company had an excellent management team, a good reputation, and a desire to expand its own retirement/nursing home business into the health-care business. The best route for expansion seemed to be by acquisitions of smaller medical-care companies. One acquisition was soon completed and several others were under consideration.

A rude awakening came within six months. While having lunch with a friend, Mary discovered that her parent company, Retirement Lodges Inc., was for sale. This was confirmed. Even the president who had persuaded Mary to merge did not know of the plans. Apparently, the owners had experienced real-estate troubles in Western Canada and decided to sell the company.

**PRESENT SITUATION**   Foresight had prompted Mary to include in her purchase agreement a clause that allowed her first right of refusal on the shares of Medical Services Limited should any unusual situation arise.

Given half a chance, the company could grow but capital would still be needed. Medical Services Limited's growth to date was reflected in the financial statements shown in Exhibits 1 and 2.

In her office, Mary considered her options and the future of the company she had created. In fact, at this stage Mary *was* the company. In order to buy back the shares in her company, she could mortgage her house again. She could look to her competition to buy out Medical Services Limited and permit her to run it. Perhaps there was money in the medical profession? Venture capitalists? Perhaps she should let any new owners of Retirement Lodges Inc. buy her out and she could then walk away from it all. Mary wondered if there were any other possibilities.

*EXHIBIT 1*

| CONSOLIDATED STATEMENT OF EARNINGS | | | |
|---|---|---|---|
| Years Ending December 31 (000s) | | | |
| | **1987** | **1986** | **1985** |
| Revenue | $1927[1] | $1216 | $ 812 |
| Direct costs: | | | |
| Wages | 1167 | 742 | 503 |
| Benefits | 143 | 88 | 69 |
| | $1310 | $ 830 | $ 572 |
| Gross profit | 617 | 386 | 240 |
| General and administrative expenses: | | | |
| Administrative salaries and benefits | 295 | 152 | 114 |
| Office expenses | 99 | 64 | 44 |
| Office supplies | 37 | 10 | 8 |
| Advertising | 69 | 30 | 22 |
| Training | 5 | 5 | 3 |
| Professional fees | 21 | 12 | 5 |
| Depreciation and amortization | 9 | 3 | 1 |
| Interest | 8 | 5 | 5 |
| Bad debts | 2 | 1 | 1 |
| Insurance and bank charges | 5 | 5 | 4 |
| | $ 550 | $ 287 | $ 207 |
| Earnings before income taxes | 67 | 99 | 33 |
| Income taxes | 38 | 56 | 6 |
| Net earnings | $ 29 | $ 43 | $ 27 |

1. The increase in expenses from 1986 to 1987 was due to the start-up of two new locations: one in late 1986 and the other in early 1987.

*EXHIBIT 2*

| CONSOLIDATED STATEMENT OF RETAINED EARNINGS | | | |
|---|---|---|---|
| Years Ending December 31 (000s) | | | |
| | 1987 | 1986 | 1985 |
| Retained earnings, beginning of year | $56 | $28 | $21 |
| Net earnings | 29 | 43 | 27 |
| | $85 | $71 | $48 |
| Dividends on common shares | 0 | 13 | 17 |
| Dividend distribution tax | 0 | 2 | 3 |
| | $0 | $15 | $20 |
| Retained earnings, end of year | $85 | $56 | $28 |

*EXHIBIT 3*

## CONSOLIDATED BALANCE SHEET

### Years Ending December 31
(000s)

| | 1987 | 1986 | 1985 |
|---|---|---|---|
| **Assets** | | | |
| Current assets: | | | |
| Cash | $ 15 | $145 | $ 5 |
| Accounts receivable, less allowance for doubtful accounts[1] | 233 | 175 | 88 |
| Prepaid expenses | 29 | 8 | 6 |
| Due from shareholder | 0 | 1 | 0 |
| Total current assets | $277 | $329 | $ 99 |
| | | | |
| Furniture and equipment, at cost | $ 46 | $ 16 | $ 9 |
| Less accumulated depreciation | 11 | 4 | 1 |
| | $ 35 | $ 12 | $ 8 |
| | | | |
| Incorporation costs, at cost | $ 5 | $ 5 | $ 4 |
| Licence, at cost | 10 | 0 | 0 |
| Goodwill, at cost, less accumulated amortization | 14 | 16 | 0 |
| TOTAL ASSETS | $341 | $362 | $111 |
| | | | |
| **Liabilities and shareholders' equity** | | | |
| Current liabilities: | | | |
| Bank loan | $ 0 | $ 0 | $ 15 |
| Accounts payable and accrued liabilities | 117 | 127 | 62 |
| Advance from parent company | 84 | 76 | 0 |
| Income taxes payable | 5 | 53 | 6 |
| Total current liabilities | $206 | $256 | $ 83 |
| Shareholders' equity: | | | |
| Capital stock: | | | |
| Preference shares without par value | | | |
| Authorized — unlimited; issued and outstanding — none | | | |
| Common shares without par value. Authorized — unlimited; issued and outstanding — 148 shares (1985 — 130) | $50 | $50 | 0 |
| | $ 50 | $ 50 | $ 0 |
| Retained earnings | 85 | 56 | 28 |
| | $135 | $106 | $ 28 |
| | | | |
| TOTAL LIABILITIES and SHAREHOLDER'S EQUITY | $341 | $362 | $111 |

1. $3,000 for 1987; $1,000 for 1986 and 1985.

*EXHIBIT 4*

| | Ratios | | |
|---|---|---|---|
| | **1987** | **1986** | **1985** |
| PROFITABILITY | | | |
| Sales | 100% | 100% | 100% |
| Cost of goods sold | 68.0% | 68.3% | 70.5% |
| Gross profit | 32.0% | 31.7% | 29.5% |
| Total expenses | 28.5% | 23.6% | 25.5% |
| Net profit | 1.5% | 3.5% | 3.3% |
| | | | |
| LIQUIDITY | | | |
| Current ratio | 1.35 | 1.4 | 1.34 |
| Working capital | $71,000 | $106,000 | $ 28,000 |
| | | | |
| STABILITY | | | |
| Age receivables[1] | 44 days | 52.5 days | 39.6 days |
| Age inventory | — | — | — |
| Age payables[2] | 32.6 days | 55.9 days | 39.6 days |
| | | | |
| Return on investment | 24.0% | 64.1% | 96.4% |
| | | | |
| Net worth/total assets | 39.6% | 29.3% | 25.2% |
| | | | |
| Interest coverage | 9.4 times | 20.8 times | 7.6 times |
| | | | |
| GROWTH | | | |
| Revenues | 58.5% | 49.8% | — |
| Assets | (5.8)% | 22.6% | — |
| Profit | (32.6)% | 59.3% | — |
| Equity | 27.4% | 164.0% | — |

1. 365 day per year for ratio calculations.
2. Assumption: beginning inventory = ending inventory.

## C A S E 7.7   MONDETTA EVERYWEAR

In June 1992, the office of Mondetta Clothing Company in Winnipeg, Manitoba, was alive with activity as Mondetta's four owners and their support staff were busy at work. In the company's meeting room, samples were being examined for the upcoming fall fashion line, while in the back warehouse, new clothing shipments were being sorted. After several years of rapid growth in the Canadian casual-wear industry, Mondetta's managers were committed to making their company a success through further market penetration. They wondered whether they should continue to solidify clothing sales in Canada or proceed with their desire to expand into the American and, eventually, the European markets. In order to make a reasonable decision, each expansion alternative would require careful examination of market and industry data as well as the company's ability to handle another phase of increased growth.

**COMPANY BACKGROUND**

Mondetta Clothing Company was founded as a partnership in Winnipeg, Manitoba, by brothers Ash and Prashant Modha, and Raj and Amit Bahl. The brothers were close friends who started by operating a small business selling cards and stationery while studying at university. In 1987, they decided to offer local casual-wear buyers unique fashions by designing and manufacturing a line of beachwear and casual pants. Working out of their families' basement, they managed product designs, production, marketing, and distribution and were rewarded with $10,000 in sales in that year.

Winnipeg, the capital of Manitoba, is located on the #1 Trans Canada Highway at the crossroads between Eastern and Western Canada, with direct connections to the United States. Winnipeg boasts a metropolitan population of approximately 650,000 and is the largest distribution centre between Vancouver and Toronto. Winnipeg is the financial centre of Western Canada and remains the headquarters for Canada's grain industry. Manufacturing rounds out the city's economy of which the garment industry is a key sector, exporting products around the world.

During the following two summers, the company's casual cotton pants, shorts, and tops were sold outside the city from a booth at Winnipeg's popular Grand Beach. In 1988, its sales grew to $25,000 and reached $125,000 by 1989. As the Mondetta name proceeded to gain exposure in the Winnipeg market, the brothers were awarded the Small Business Achiever Award by

Winnipeg's *Uptown Magazine*, as well as other distinguished industry and media honours. In May 1990, after most of them had completed their undergraduate studies, they incorporated the business and started full-time company operations. Soon Mondetta expanded from a few Winnipeg retail stores to more than 350 outlets across Canada, with sales beyond $2.4 million. The company's financial statements are presented in Exhibits 1, 2, and 3.

## MONDETTA EVERYWEAR

Mondetta's most popular items were their "flagshirts," sweatshirts adorned with the flags of world countries. The name Mondetta was based on a play of French words for "small world" and the focus of the collection was the high quality appliqué and embroidery on cotton clothing. The company's styles were targeted to the socially or politically concerned man, woman, or young adult who enjoyed superior quality casual- or street-wear.

## THE CASUAL-WEAR AND STREET-WEAR MARKET

Mondetta catered to a market that bordered between casual- and street-wear, and which could be classified as trendy wear. There were numerous types of casual-wear products in the rapidly changing Canadian apparel market. Regular or mainstream casual-wear consisted of similar clothing styles that could easily be found in any department or chain store. Street-wear included casual clothing that appealed to more unique and diverse tastes. Trendy-wear shoppers generally desired clothing that offered them something different from what was available in most regular stores. They specifically searched for eye-catching products and often purchased from companies with an established brand name reputation.

The casual- and street-wear market was more easily divided into two age groups: older and younger buyers. The older casual-wear consumer was above 30 years old and wanted a product made of high quality materials with superior graphics designs. Younger customers aged 13 to 30 looked mainly for quality through an established brand name. Although younger consumers were highly influenced by fashion trends, the price of the apparel nonetheless remained an important consideration in their buying process. Word of mouth and the visual appearance of the clothing also influenced both consumer groups, who approached trendy-wear stores to find the hottest new clothing available. Consequently, innovative clothing companies often started their businesses by selling clothing to trend-setting stores in hopes that their products would create a new fashion craze. Once a trend had been created, product visibility and sales were increased through movement into the mainstream clothing stores.

## THE CANADIAN TRADE ENVIRONMENT

In the casual- and street-wear market, the graphics design either led to rapid product acceptance or rejection. Thus, retailers were hesitant to take on new products since rejection forced them to mark down prices in order to dispose of unwanted inventories. To protect themselves, retailers looked for product quality and fit within their stores, as well as for the visual graphics appeal of the clothing. In addition, they usually made a small trial order to test the product's saleability before ordering in larger quantities.

Since the Canadian apparel market was dominated by a limited number of large department and chain stores, clothing companies tried to sell their products through their own sales representatives or independent agents at the most advantageous prices available. Some casual- and street-wear firms also sold to local independent or specialty stores.

Department stores such as Eaton's, the Bay, and Sears were generally less flexible and entrepreneurial than other retail outlets and relied on more tightly controlled planning of operations. Department stores purchased clothing (based on product type) from central or regional buying offices through designated buyers. Some department stores also specifically allocated budgets for the exploration of goods from local companies to match merchandise with local demand. In order to get placement in a department store, clothing company representatives had to approach the appropriate buying officer. For casual- and street-wear, this officer was more likely to be the men's or ladies' wear buyer.

Department store demands were usually very high. Most expected signed contracts specifying desired prices, mark-ups, volume discounts, and early payment discounts. Mark-ups on cost for casual wear were close to 50 percent, while volume and early payment discounts ranged between 3 and 5 percent each. Although product distribution was usually allocated per store location by the clothing firm, products had to be sent to the department store's central warehouse before being shipped to designated store outlets. This system resulted in an additional 2 percent warehousing discount. Some department stores also demanded a 1 to 2 percent advertising discount. The resulting 9 to 14 percent worth of discounts allowed Canadian department stores to sell products at a lower price than other retailers, thereby creating the perception that department stores sold discount low quality clothing.

The chain store network was divided into regional chains that serviced either Western or Eastern Canada and national chains. Chain stores were more stable and credit-worthy than independent stores and had more purchasing power than the department stores. Chain stores expected a 55 percent product mark-up as well as a 2 percent warehousing discount. Early payment terms were 3 percent in 10 days net 60 days. Most chain stores offered relatively little product advertising and relied on in-store displays and word-of-mouth to attract customers. The need to approach only one or two buying offices for each chain offered the provision of wide geographic distribution with less selling effort than required for the independent stores.

Independent store owners usually managed one or, at most, two local stores in a city or town. Some independents were considered to be local trend setters, while others were followers who copied the trend makers after product exposure had been created. Purchases were performed from one location, usually the store itself, using fashion trend information. Many independents were considered to be poor credit risks due to their limited financial resources, unstable management, and variable clientele. Even though placement in an independent store appeared risky, it was an important channel for brand name and trend creation. The most successful independents distinguished themselves through their management style and the establishment of their own reputation, visibility, and local market niche. Since independent stores generally did not have the ability to purchase in large quantities, volume and early payment discounts were not granted. Payment terms to producers were 30 to 60 days with a 50 percent mark-up to retail customers.

## THE AMERICAN TRADE ENVIRONMENT

American trade dynamics differed from Canadian dynamics in several ways. First, the discount image of Canadian department stores made independent and chain stores hesitant to take on products originally featured in a department store. In the United States, department stores such as Bloomingdales, Macy's, and Nordstroms were perceived as leaders in the fashion industry. Therefore, initial placement in these stores created a fashion trend that the independent and chain stores were willing to endorse. Second, the American market was dominated by numerous strong retail stores and apparel companies that were more aggressive and demanding than their conservative Canadian counterparts. Third, highly diverse consumer tastes and the desire for more bold and flashy items resulted in an intensely competitive retail environment. These factors and the specific demands of American retailers are outlined in Exhibit 4.

The American apparel industry was also undergoing a period of change and restructuring. By 1989, discount stores and mail-order firms had gained market share at the expense of specialty department and chain stores. In fact, discounters replaced department stores as the largest retail segment. Another trend in the American apparel industry was the formation of close, interdependent relationships between retailer and supplier based upon a joint commitment to mutual profitability through in-store boutiques. In addition, in order to improve efficiency and lower costs, retailers were making efforts to narrow their supplier structure with larger commitments and bigger orders.

## THE COMPETITION

Competitors in the casual-wear industry sold similar products (jeans, sweatshirts, and T-shirts) adorned with their brand names in retail chain, department, and independent stores throughout Canada and the United States. Because competing products were normally placed side-by-side in the store, sales depended more on brand name and reputation rather than product differentiation. Top industry names were Guess Jeans, Buffalo Jeans, and B.U.M. Equipment and were all associated with large American and European firms. The success of these companies was due to the creation of a highly visible media hype focused on brand name and product promotion. Brand names were also heavily promoted in well-known fashion and trend-setting magazines such as *Vogue, Rolling Stone*, and *GQ*. Guess and B.U.M.

were also beginning to license themselves in the European market. Buffalo Jeans was a European label licensed in Canada. Through licensing, a European manufacturer had the right to produce and sell approved designs using a clothing's brand name and logo.

The management style among smaller Canadian apparel firms could be characterized as entrepreneurial. Owners, supported by informally organized executive staffs, performed all the functions required in the day-to-day operations of the business. Some of the medium- and larger-sized firms had started to rely on the specialized skills of their management teams to bring a more corporate approach to executive decision making. Nevertheless, many apparel firms were averse to the long-term strategic reinvestment of profits and tended to concentrate on short-term operation decisions rather than the development of long-term business planning and market positioning.

The fragmentation and volatility of market conditions as well as the entrepreneurial management nature made financial institutions hesitant to extend long-term financing to apparel firms. A number of companies had tried to reorganize their financial positions by becoming public companies. However, this strategy appeared unsuccessful due to the poor performance of share offerings in public exchanges.

Exhibit 5 presents an overview of major international apparel markets and producers as well as their main strengths and weaknesses. The United Kingdom, Germany, France, and Italy were perceived as leaders in the European and international fashion industries. Countries such as China, Hong Kong, Singapore, and the Philippines were well known for their ability to provide high quality products using cheaper labour. The Canadian apparel market, once a stable market, faced increased competitive pressure from these low-cost imports and, by 1989, imports had increased at rates in excess of Canadian market growth despite protective import restraints. As a result, apparel firms faced greater pressure to rationalize and restructure their operations.

Exports were not a major influence in the apparel industry's overall sales performance. In 1989, sales to the United States accounted for approximately 85 percent of Canada's apparel export shipments. Canada's competition in foreign markets was primarily from European producers. Among the products exhibiting the best performance record were ladies' designer fashions, winter outerwear, some types of men's fine clothing, children's wear, and occupational apparel. In the European and American high fashion markets, country of origin was less important than factors such as quality, style, and price, particularly in the medium- to higher-price ranges.

**THE ENVIRONMENT**    The casual- and street-wear market was highly volatile and vulnerable to changing fashion trends, lifestyles, and leisure activities. Sometimes, a popular trend enticed companies to saturate the market, a move which eventually led to the deterioration of the trend. During recessionary periods, apparel companies generally experienced reduced demand for their products. However, since trendy-wear sales were highly dependent on the intensity of the latest trend, it was difficult to relate sales to poor business conditions.

Increased opportunities for Canadian apparel firms to enter the large American market were becoming available due to the gradual reduction of trade tariffs under the recent Canada/U.S. Free Trade Agreement. However, Canadian companies wishing to export to the United States faced many established competitors. In addition, their flexibility was reduced due to a requirement to place 50 percent Canadian content in their goods. As a general rule, apparel made from third-country fabrics was not eligible for duty-free treatment under the agreement. Freer trade with the United States also prompted several large American retailers to expand into Canada, thereby increasing competition for the Canadian consumer. By June 1992, North American Free Trade talks with Mexico were well underway and an agreement was expected to be reached before the end of 1992.

Currency fluctuations appeared to have little impact on export competitiveness with the United States. On the other hand, the devaluation of the Canadian dollar relative to European currencies over the past two years had sparked renewed interest by Canadian manufacturers in the European market. However, in Europe the duty-free movement of goods among European community countries, strong competition from European designer labels, and the aggressive marketing of private-label manufacturers hindered Canada's apparel trade in this market.

Technological systems were becoming more advanced and useful to both producers and retailers. The computerization of sales and inventory data allowed companies to keep informed of rapidly changing market conditions in order to improve their market position and service to customers. Some retailers made arrangements with suppliers to transmit orders by computer when a minimum inventory level was reached. These "quick response" systems created better relationships between retailer and supplier and provided apparel firms with the flexibility to switch from one style or product to another as profitable market opportunities were discovered. In Canada, sophisticated response systems were still relatively unknown to retailers, while in the United States, large chain stores were more experienced in the use of quick response systems. Although American department stores had no sophisticated systems in place, they were starting to plan for the future installation of new technology.

## MONDETTA'S CURRENT STRATEGY

Mondetta's strategy focused around product exclusivity rather than market saturation. This was achieved through careful selection of industry sales agents and retailers for clothing promotion. In 1989 and early 1990, Mondetta clothing was sold throughout Western Canada in high quality regional and national chain stores and local independent stores. Since heavy price discounting by department stores compromised Mondetta's high quality exclusive image, department store sales were restricted to Eaton's in Winnipeg. In late 1991, after the establishment of Western Canadian sales, Mondetta expanded into Ontario, Quebec, and the Maritimes. Management's sales goal for the 1992 fiscal year was $5 to $6 million, which they hoped to achieve through increased national and international market penetration.

## Finance

Although monthly cash flow forecasts based on pre-booked orders were prepared, the frequent opening of new accounts resulted in completely different cash requirements than those projected. This situation was beginning to strain Mondetta's $250,000 line of credit for inventory financing. While government incentives to support small business were available to companies that promoted local employment, poor economic conditions in 1992 and the company's young age made government agencies hesitant to provide funds. Banks were also afraid to lend funds to what they labelled as "here today, gone tomorrow" businesses. This feeling was created by the recent bankruptcy of several highly successful Winnipeg clothing companies that were owned and operated by young managers.

In order to deal with a difficult cash situation, Mondetta operated by customer order. This system enabled the company to match receivables with payables while carefully managing supply relationships to ensure timely payments. Management hoped that a new computerized system for accounting, purchase orders, production, marketing, and receivables would assist with the development of strict cash management plans.

## Marketing

Mondetta's most popular logos, "Mondetta Everywear" and "The Spirit of Unification," were company trademarks. Traditionally, the two fashion lines (spring and fall) focused on the theme of international awareness and globalization. Exhibit 6 outlines Mondetta's production timeline for 1992. In 1993, the company hoped to sell four fashion lines (one per season) that placed more emphasis on the Mondetta name instead of flags.

Mondetta's managers tried to foster a mystique cult following and to avoid market saturation by restricting their products to a limited number of superior quality stores. To create visibility for its flagshirts, the company employed industry agents who targeted trendy name-setting stores in each location before distributing to the high quality chain stores. Agents received a 10 percent commission on the Mondetta selling price (industry commissions ranged from 8 to 12 percent). Marketing communications consisted mainly of press exposure, word-of-mouth, and the graphics appeal of the clothing. In Winnipeg, Mondetta clothing was also displayed on transit shelters.

The brothers participated in two semi-annual trade shows hosted by Salon International. Trade shows created product visibility and were attended by numerous retail sales agents and buyers. The spring/summer show was held during February in Montreal while the fall/winter show was held during August in Toronto. A trade show booth cost approximately $20,000, with a space cost of $5,000. Travelling and on-site expenses resulted in a total cost of $30,000 per show.

Mondetta's major customers were Bootlegger (nation-wide), Below the Belt and Off the Wall (western regional chains), and Eaton's in Winnipeg.

Approximately 40 percent of the company's sales volume resulted from these accounts. Exhibit 7 compares Mondetta's Canadian sales with those of the Canadian apparel industry. Western Canadian sales comprised 80 percent of the company's business with 18 percent in Ontario and only 2 percent in Quebec and the Maritimes. Canadian retail apparel sales in 1991 were around 37 percent in Ontario, 34 percent in Quebec and the Maritimes, and 29 percent in Western Canada.

## Competition

Nationally, Mondetta clothing was placed side by side with other established brand name products such as Guess Jeans, Request, and Pepe Jeans. However, the companies selling these labels had wider retail distribution networks in both Canada and the United States.

In Winnipeg, an independent company called Passport International had recently opened a retail outlet next to Eaton's downtown store. Passport's designs were identical to Mondetta's with the exception of the logo, and the clothing was also sold at a lower price. For example, Mondetta's highly successful flagshirt, which retailed for $79.95, was sold for $64.99 in Passport. Passport also offered customized flags of any country compared to Mondetta's 45 flags. Although Passport was made of lower quality materials, customers wanting a Mondetta but not being able to afford one generally turned to Passport for their designs. Passport International was rumoured to be opening a new location in Toronto's Fairview Mall by Fall 1992.

## Operations

The apparel design either led to rapid product acceptance or rejection, thus making it the first and most crucial step in the production process. Other major steps in apparel manufacture were material sourcing, pattern making, fabric cutting, sewing, and finishing. When Mondetta first began operations, the brothers sourced their own materials and transported them to the manufacturer to cut, make, trim, and finish the product. This method created numerous problems and often resulted in inconsistent quality, as they continuously researched, purchased, and stored inventories of shirt materials, embroidery thread, and coloured flag patches. This purchase process not only consumed a considerable amount of management time, but it also required elaborate inventory controls and vast amounts of storage space. To alleviate the situation, management started to rely on their producers to source and produce clothing materials based on their specified quality standards. As a result, the brothers had more time to concentrate on company operations and design.

During the first two years of operations, Mondetta clothing was produced in Winnipeg by 8 to 10 medium-sized clothing manufacturers. However, when the product's quick success raised producer demands, unit labour and material costs escalated, forcing management to search for offshore manufacturers in order to reduce production costs and increase production capacity. An agent was subsequently secured for Hong Kong through some well established industry contacts. Although offshore production created periodic quality control problems, the cost of wasted production was much less than the cost of local production. Exhibit 8 outlines Canadian production costs of the company's T-shirt and sweatshirts. Exhibit 9 presents a cost comparison of local versus offshore production of the company's T-shirts and indicates a 20 percent savings on every T-shirt produced abroad.

By 1992, approximately 40 percent of Mondetta's product line was produced in Hong Kong. While both local and offshore manufacturers had the capacity to produce approximately 10,000 T-shirts per month, shipment time for overseas production took an additional month. To avoid sales forecast misjudgments, Mondetta relied on pre-booked orders to trigger production, with an additional 20 to 25 percent buffer inventory built into each order.

Imports from Hong Kong were highly dependent on a quota system whereby the Canadian government allowed a maximum number of goods to be imported annually from Hong Kong, based on product type and category. After the appropriate quota had been determined, the Hong Kong government divided it among manufacturers who produced goods for Canadian companies. This system placed the burden on the manufacturer to find adequate quota to supply the desired amount requested by the Canadian importer. If quota was unavailable, the manufacturer had to purchase the desired amount from a quota market before beginning production.

### Human Resources

Mondetta Clothing Company was managed by Ash, Prashant, Raj, and Amit. The company also employed a customer service representative and a support staff of four people. Ash Modha, Mondetta's president and chief executive officer, was 23 years old and had just completed a Bachelor of Arts in Economics from the University of Manitoba. His brother, Prashant, aged 25, had completed a Bachelor of Science in Chemistry in 1988 and received a Master of Business Administration degree from the University of Manitoba in June 1991. Raj Bahl, also 25 years of age, had a Bachelor of Arts degree in Applied Economics from the University of Manitoba. His brother, Amit, attended the University of Winnipeg but chose to work instead.

The company had no structured hierarchy and the brothers operated in an informal team-oriented atmosphere. Internal communications and reporting structures were also not formally specified. Traditionally, day-to-day operations were completed by the most experienced and available person. Major operating decisions were given deliberate individual consideration before a consensus was reached. During crisis situations, decisions were made quickly after careful consideration of available alternatives.

Although responsibilities were not formally segmented, increased growth had started to create a more divisionalized approach to management. Ash and Raj were primarily responsible for the company's fashion designs. Ash also managed the company's production requirements, while Raj was responsible for marketing and salesforce management. Prashant monitored the company's financial operations and Amit organized distribution, shipping, and receiving.

**FUTURE STRATEGY**

The four brothers were committed to the company's growth and were considering several growth opportunities such as expansion into the United States, further penetration into Eastern Canada, and licensing in western Europe.

**Expand to the United States**

The nature of the apparel industry demanded that management approach their American entry with caution in order to avoid unmanageable rapid product acceptance or damaging product rejection. First, management had to consider which areas of the country to target. Exhibit 10 outlines American apparel consumption by region. Largely populated areas with the highest apparel consumption were the eastern states, while the northwestern states more closely resembled the Canadian market. In addition, the appropriate distribution channels and distribution strategy for market penetration and trend creation had to be determined. A geographic segmentation map of the United States and a breakdown of American department stores per region is presented in Exhibit 11.

The brothers also needed to determine suitable product selection and market penetration strategies. Since production in Manitoba would be insufficient for demand, apparel would have to be shipped directly from Hong Kong to the United States, requiring quota negotiations similar to those for Canada. The company's popular flagshirts and flag T-shirts could be made available for sale, as well as its new product line, which focused on the Mondetta name. Sales agent commissions would be approximately 10 percent of Mondetta's selling price and American retailers would likely demand a 50 to 60 percent product mark-up on cost. Some chains would also try to negotiate buy back options or replacement of nonselling styles and volume discounts. Annual travelling and other expenses were estimated around $5,000 to $10,000 (Canadian), while annual trade show expenses would be $25,000 for the summer Magic Show in Las Vegas. The Magic Show was one the largest trade shows in America, attracting 52,000 agents, buyers, and retailers.

American sales growth could not expand beyond $500,000 in the first year due to Mondetta's limited ability to handle rapid international growth. Profit margins would be similar to those earned in Canada since losses on export duties would likely be recovered with the currency exchange.

**Continue Penetration into Eastern Canada**

Consumer acceptance of Mondetta clothing in Eastern Canada, particularly in Quebec, appeared slower than in Western Canada. Mondetta's managers believed that slow sales in Quebec were due to poor product visibility created by inexperienced sales agents. In addition, retail sales in Quebec were controlled by large powerful buying groups. Established relationships with the buyers of these groups would be essential to product acceptance.

Although the company was experiencing healthy growth in Ontario, the Mondetta name was still relatively unknown in a large potential market. Management's biggest concern was Passport International's expansion to Toronto's Fairview Mall where Mondetta was also sold. If necessary, mall advertising and billboards would cost approximately $6,800 for six months.

Other marketing communications could also be used to speed up product exposure in both Ontario and Quebec. Economical advertisements such as point of purchase ads would cost approximately $25,000 per year. A Mondetta fashion catalogue could also be printed and distributed at an annual cost of $10,000 to $15,000. Advertising in the French version of *Elle* fashion magazine in Quebec would cost $7,000 per issue. Management wondered which forms of advertising should be purchased in Eastern Canada, and what sales level would be required to break even.

### Pursue Licensing in Europe

Successful name licensing could create new product demand and expand brand name exposure in both the United States and western Europe. Many well-known names such as Guess Jeans and Buffalo Jeans were already licensed. Guess Jeans already had 22 licences across the world while Buffalo was licensed in major European centres.

Through licensing, another company would be granted exclusive rights to manufacture, promote, distribute, and sell products using the Mondetta name with Mondetta designs or approved designs. The major advantage of licensing was widespread market penetration with minimal capital and financing requirements. There were also several risks. First, finding appropriate licensees could be difficult due to the required product specifications, quality, and commitment. Second, licensees could demand that Mondetta handle the majority of product advertising. Third, a licensee could copy Mondetta's sample designs and sell clothing under a new brand name. The brothers hoped that careful selection of licensees would reduce the risks and were planning to attract licensees for kidswear, shoes, and women's wear while continuing their main fashion designs and product lines.

The average licence agreement was usually three years. During the three-year term, the licensee would be required to pay a nonrefundable initial licence fee as well as an annual licence fee. Initial and annual fees could range from $10,000 to $1,000,000 depending on the size and reputation of the licensee. Management hoped major licensees would generate $2 to $3 million in sales during their first year of operations. In each and every calendar year throughout the term, licensees would have to spend an average of 6 percent of sales to advertise and promote the apparel. In addition, a royalty of 8 to 10 percent of sales would be owed to Mondetta. Mondetta would also incur lawyers' fees and trademark costs for different geographic areas. For example, Canadian trademarks for "Mondetta Everywear" and "The Spirit of Unification" each cost approximately $1,500.

### DECISIONS

Clearly, the task of determining where to take Mondetta Clothing Company was not an easy one. While the company's rapid market acceptance appeared to promise greater success in the future, further market penetration demanded careful consideration of alternatives before making the appropriate strategic decisions.

*Exhibit 1*

|  | STATEMENT OF OPERATIONS (For the Year Ended April 30) | | |
|---|---|---|---|
|  | **1990**[1] | **1991** | **1992** |
| Total revenue | $ 104,896 | $ 247,970 | $2,436,644 |
| Cost of goods sold | 75,506 | 178,543 | 1,863,427 |
| Gross profit | $ 29,390 | $ 69,427 | $ 573,217 |
| Operating expenses: | | | |
| Accounting and legal | 2,649 | 2,699 | 7,732 |
| Advertising and promotion | 1,224 | 8,964 | 29,135 |
| Bank charges and interest | 3,198 | 8,762 | 14,726 |
| Bad debts | 3,702 | 4,031 | 21,735 |
| Depreciation and amortization | 0 | 2,504 | 9,038 |
| Factoring commissions | 0 | 920 | 52,006 |
| Insurance | 0 | 593 | 810 |
| Leases and equipment | 265 | 1,398 | 8,498 |
| Management bonus | 0 | 0 | 110,400 |
| Miscellaneous | 307 | 1,531 | 1,328 |
| Printing and stationery | 695 | 1,167 | 9,055 |
| Parking | 0 | 207 | 46 |
| Property and business tax | 0 | 822 | 1,276 |
| Rent | 1,288 | 9,246 | 12,696 |
| Repairs and maintenance | 0 | 182 | 528 |
| Salaries and benefits | 1,437 | 29,005 | 75,339 |
| Telephone | 1,136 | 6,516 | 12,091 |
| Travel and entertainment | 1,693 | 7,974 | 14,731 |
| Utilities | 0 | 477 | 970 |
| Total operating expenses | $ 17,594 | $ 86,998 | $ 382,140 |
| Earning (loss) before tax | $ 11,796 | $ (17,571) | $ 191,077 |
| Income taxes | 0 | 0 | 43,517 |
| Income tax reduction resulting from loss carry forward | 0 | 0 | 3,864 |
| Net earnings (loss) | $ 11,796 | $ (17,571) | $ 151,424 |

1. For the period covered by this date the organization was a partnership. The firm was incorporated May 1, 1990.

*EXHIBIT 2*

| | BALANCE SHEET (As of April 30) | | |
|---|---|---|---|
| | 4-month period 1990 | 1991 | 1992 |
| **ASSETS** | | | |
| Current assets: | | | |
| Accounts receivable | $ 76,473 | $ 72,789 | $ 875,641 |
| Inventories | 38,780 | 54,961 | 433,653 |
| Prepaid expenses | 1,472 | 1,794 | 3,752 |
| Total current assets | $116,725 | $129,544 | $1,313,046 |
| | | | |
| Fixed assets: | | | |
| Equipment and leasehold improvements | 0 | 13,583 | 53,895 |
| Accumulated depreciation | 0 | 2,306 | 10,982 |
| Fixed assets (net) | 0 | $11,277 | $42,913 |
| | | | |
| Other assets | 0 | 3,588 | 6,593 |
| | | | |
| TOTAL ASSETS | $ 116,725 | $ 144,409 | $1,362,552 |
| | | | |
| **LIABILITIES:** | | | |
| Current liabilities: | | | |
| Bank overdraft | $ 1,539 | $ 14,041 | $ 57,936 |
| Bank loan | 41,400 | 58,880 | 185,840 |
| Accounts payable | 27,585 | 62,676 | 790,847 |
| Bonus payable | 0 | 0 | 110,400 |
| Income taxes payable | 0 | 0 | 39,653 |
| Total current liabilities | $70,524 | $135,597 | $1,184,676 |
| | | | |
| Long-term liabilities: | | | |
| Note payable | 34,049 | 7,820 | 0 |
| Payable to shareholders | 0 | 18,379 | 22,218 |
| Total long-term liabilities | $34,049 | $26,199 | $22,218 |
| | | | |
| **SHAREHOLDERS' EQUITY:** | | | |
| Share capital | N/A | 184 | 21,804 |
| Retained earnings | 12,152 | (17,571) | 133,854 |
| Total equity | $12,152 | $(17,387) | $155,658 |
| | | | |
| TOTAL LIABILITIES AND SHAREHOLDER'S EQUITY | $ 116,725 | $ 144,409 | $1,362,552 |

*Exhibit 3*

| RATIO SHEET | | | |
|---|---|---|---|
| | **1990** | **1991** | **1992** |
| PROFITABILITY | | | |
| Total revenue | 100.0% | 100.0% | 100.0% |
| Cost of sales | 72.0% | 72.0% | 76.5% |
| Gross margin | 28.0% | 28.0% | 23.5% |
| | | | |
| Operating expenses: | | | |
| Accounting and legal | 2.5% | 1.1% | 0.3% |
| Advertising and promotion | 1.2% | 3.6% | 1.2% |
| Bank charges and interest | 3.0% | 3.5% | 0.6% |
| Bad debts | 3.5% | 1.6% | 0.9% |
| Depreciation and amortization | 0.0% | 1.0% | 0.4% |
| Factoring commissions | 0.0% | 0.4% | 2.1% |
| Insurance | 0.0% | 0.2% | 0.0% |
| Leases and equipment | 0.3% | 0.6% | 0.3% |
| Management bonus | 0.0% | 0.0% | 4.5% |
| Miscellaneous | 0.3% | 0.6% | 0.1% |
| Printing and stationery | 0.7% | 0.5% | 0.4% |
| Parking | 0.0% | 0.1% | 0.0% |
| Property and business tax | 0.0% | 0.3% | 0.1% |
| Rent | 1.2% | 3.7% | 0.5% |
| Repairs and maintenance | 0.0% | 0.1% | 0.0% |
| Salaries and benefits | 1.4% | 11.7% | 3.1% |
| Telephone | 1.1% | 2.6% | 0.5% |
| Travel and entertainment | 1.6% | 3.2% | 0.6% |
| Utilities | 0.0% | 0.2% | 0.0% |
| Total operating expenses | 16.8% | 35.1% | 15.7% |
| | | | |
| Earning (loss) before tax | 11.2% | –7.1% | 7.8% |
| Income tax | 0.0% | 0.0% | 1.6% |
| Net earnings (loss) | 11.2% | –7.1% | 6.2% |
| | | | |
| LIQUIDITY | | | |
| Current ratio | 1.66 | 0.96 | 1.11 |
| Acid test | 1.11 | 0.55 | 0.74 |
| Working capital | $46,201 | $(6,053) | $128,370 |
| | | | |
| EFFICIENCY | | | |
| Age of accounts receivable | 266 | 107 | 131 |
| Age of inventory | 187 | 0 | 0 |
| Age of payables | 133 | 117 | 129 |
| | | | |
| STABILITY | | | |
| Net worth/total assets | 10% | –12% | 11% |
| Interest coverage | 4.7 | –1.0 | 14.5 |
| | | | |
| GROWTH | | **1990–91** | **1991–92** |
| Sales | | 136.4% | 882.6% |
| Net Income | | –249.0% | — |
| Assets | | 23.7% | 843.5% |

*EXHIBIT 4*

## American Retail Channel Profiles by Store Type[1]

| | Department Stores | Chain Stores | Specialty Stores | Independent Stores |
|---|---|---|---|---|
| **Market Flows** | • have their own private label programs<br>• want unique and exciting fashions to service customer needs<br>• medium quality/medium price<br>• high volume | • wide geographic distribution<br>• medium volume<br>• diversity and uniqueness<br>• fit in the store<br>• right goods at right price<br>• look for brand names<br>• country of origin less important | • highly prestigious names (Neiman Marcus, Sak's, Tiffany's)<br>• considered to be in world of fashion and luxury<br>• great notoriety<br>• variable volume<br>• unique designs<br>• very high quality/high price | • small (1–2 stores)<br>• competitive pressure<br>• in-depth customer knowledge<br>• unique styles<br>• high quality/high price<br>• low volume |
| **Sales Force and Relationships** | • can suddenly drop suppliers<br>• not loyal, will depend on sales performance and profitability | • prefer long-term cooperative relationships | • want exclusivity<br>• less loyal to suppliers<br>• will drop suppliers that fail to meet performance goals<br>• market trade shows are key for establishing contacts and selecting products | • personal/flexible service<br>• value long-term relationship<br>• trust |
| **Merchandising and Packaging** | want:<br>• attractive return policies<br>• shared mark-downs<br>• 48–52% mark-up<br>• early payment discounts 8%<br>• volume discounts 4–5%<br>• co-op advertising 2–3% | want:<br>• 45–50% mark-up<br>• early payment discounts up to 8%<br>• volume discounts 1–2%<br>• co-op advertising 2–3%<br>• 90-day terms | want:<br>• liberal return policies<br>• no risk product testing<br>• shared mark-downs<br>• 50–60% mark-up<br>• early payment discounts 6–8%<br>• volume discounts 2–5%<br>• co-op advertising 2–3% | • limited financial resources to finance inventory<br>• rapid refills<br>• 50–60% mark-up |
| **Distribution Concerns** | • centralized distribution centres<br>• may request customized store orders<br>• want on-time delivery<br>• value exclusivity | | • centralized distribution centres<br>• customized store orders may be requested<br>• value exclusivity | • value on-time delivery |
| **Electronic Linkage** | • behind, but starting to get more sophisticated | • sophisticated response and inventory systems | • few linkages in place | • no sophisticated procedures in place<br>• electronic cash registers for inventory management |

1. Preparing for Free Trade: Apparel Retailing in the United States. Reproduced with permission from Industry, Science and Technology Canada.

***Exhibit 5***
***The International***
***Apparel Market[1]***

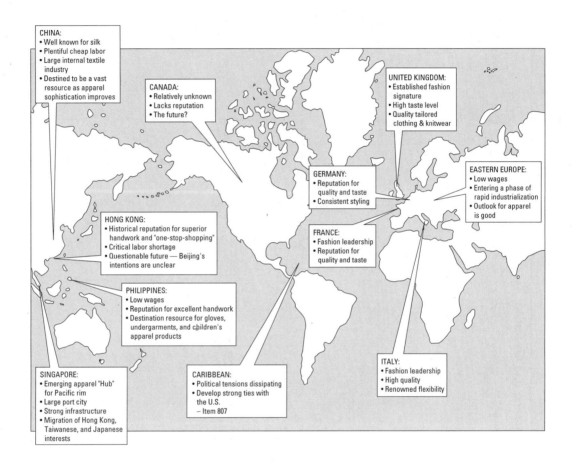

CHINA:
• Well known for silk
• Plentiful cheap labor
• Large internal textile industry
• Destined to be a vast resource as apparel sophistication improves

CANADA:
• Relatively unknown
• Lacks reputation
• The future?

UNITED KINGDOM:
• Established fashion signature
• High taste level
• Quality tailored clothing & knitwear

GERMANY:
• Reputation for quality and taste
• Consistent styling

EASTERN EUROPE:
• Low wages
• Entering a phase of rapid industrialization
• Outlook for apparel is good

HONG KONG:
• Historical reputation for superior handwork and "one-stop-shopping"
• Critical labor shortage
• Questionable future — Beijing's intentions are unclear

FRANCE:
• Fashion leadership
• Reputation for quality and taste

PHILIPPINES:
• Low wages
• Reputation for excellent handwork
• Destination resource for gloves, undergarments, and children's apparel products

ITALY:
• Fashion leadership
• High quality
• Renowned flexibility

SINGAPORE:
• Emerging apparel "Hub" for Pacific rim
• Large port city
• Strong infrastructure
• Migration of Hong Kong, Taiwanese, and Japanese interests

CARIBBEAN:
• Political tensions dissipating
• Develop strong ties with the U.S.
  – Item 807

**1.**   Apparel Retailing in the United States.

*EXHIBIT 6*

## Production and Operations Time for 1992

| | Jan. | Feb. | March | April | May | June | July | Aug. | Sept. | Oct. | Nov. | Dec. |
|---|---|---|---|---|---|---|---|---|---|---|---|---|
| | ▪ finalize and complete fall 1992 designs and product line | ▪ deliver orders taken in Oct/Nov 1991 | ▪ continue spring shipments | ▪ finish spring shipments | ▪ finalize and complete spring 1992 designs and product line | | ▪ begin shipment of fall orders | ▪ attend trade show in Toronto for spring line | ▪ process orders for spring 1993 | ▪ continue order processing for spring 1992 | ▪ continue spring line production | |
| | | ▪ attend trade show in Montreal for fall line | ▪ take and process orders for the fall fashion line | ▪ cut-off for fall orders in the third week | ▪ ship, repeat orders for spring 1992 | | | ▪ continue shipment of fall fashion line | ▪ continue shipment of fall fashion line | ▪ spring line production begins | ▪ finish fall shipments | ▪ ship repeat orders to fall 1992 |
| | | ▪ begin shipment of spring fashion line | | ▪ fall line production begins in fourth week | ▪ continue production of fall 1992 line | | | | | ▪ design and complete summer 1992 fashion line[1] | | |

1. By 1993 fiscal year, the company will move from the design and manufacture of Spring and Fall fashion lines to Spring, Summer, Fall and Winter lines.

*Exhibit 7*

| PERCENTAGE OF RETAIL APPAREL SALES IN CANADA | | |
|---|---|---|
| **Region** | **Canada[1]** | **Mondetta** |
| Quebec and Maritimes | 33.9% | 2.0% |
| Ontario | 37.3% | 18.0% |
| Manitoba/Saskatchewan | 6.5% | 20.0% |
| Alberta/British Columbia | 22.2% | 60.0% |
| Yukon/Northwest Territories | 0.1% | 0.0% |

1.  Canadian sales data do not include department stores.

Source:  Statistics Canada, Catalogue No. 63-005, December 1991.

*Exhibit 8*

| PRODUCTION COSTS OF SELECTED PRODUCTS | |
|---|---|
| **World Flag Shirts** | |
| Manufacturing cost | $19.50 |
| Applique | $7.80–$10.40 |
| Labels, tags | .26 |
| Total cost | $27.56–$30.16 |
| **World Flag T-Shirts** | |
| Manufacturing cost | $4.88 |
| Embroidery | 6.83 |
| Bag, tag, labels | .78 |
| Total cost | $12.49 |
| **Call Letter Sweatshirt** | |
| Manufacturing cost | $20.93 |
| Embroidery | 10.73 |
| Labels | .26 |
| Total costs | $31.92 |

*EXHIBIT 9*

### COMPARISON OF LOCAL VERSUS OVERSEAS COSTS OF WORLD BASEBALL JERSEY

|  | Overseas | Local |
|---|---|---|
| Manufacturing costs | $19.83 | $31.85 |
| Customs duties (25% of cost) | 4.96 | 0 |
| Shipping costs to Winnipeg | .39 | 0 |
|  | $25.18 | $31.85 |
| Commissions (10% of Mondetta selling price) | 4.00 | 4.00 |
| Total cost | $29.73 | $37.05 |
| Mondetta selling price | $40.00 | $40.00 |
| Retail selling price (50% mark-up) | $60.00 | $60.00 |

*EXHIBIT 10*
**American Apparel Consumption by Region**

Source: U.S. and Canadian Governments.

**EXHIBIT 11**
**American Department Stores Segmented by Geographic Location[1]**

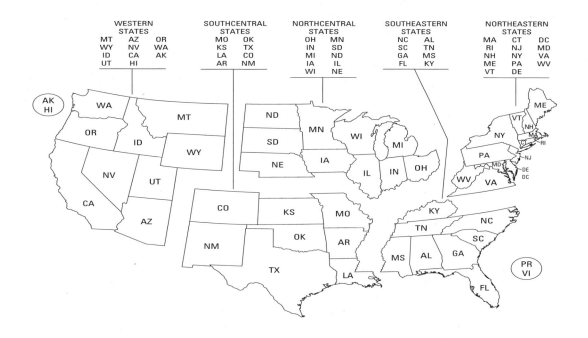

| Region | WS | SCS | NCS | SES | NES | Total |
|---|---|---|---|---|---|---|
| Bloomingdales | 0 | 0 | 1 | 4 | 10 | 15 |
| Bullocks | 22 | 2 | 0 | 0 | 0 | 24 |
| Macy's East | 0 | 4 | 0 | 21 | 46 | 71 |
| Macy's West | 26 | 0 | 0 | 0 | 0 | 26 |
| Macy's South | 0 | 10 | 0 | 15 | 0 | 25 |
| Lord & Taylor | | | | | majority | 49 |
| Nordstroms | 27 | 0 | 3 | 0 | 25 | 55 |
| Hechts | 0 | 0 | 0 | 0 | 43 | 43 |
| Marshall Field | 0 | 2 | 22 | 0 | 0 | 24 |

**1.** Sheldon's Retail Directory by the United States and Canada, 1991. Reproduced with permission from Phelon, Sheldon & Marsar, Inc.

# C A S E 7.8 RAMPAC DISTRIBUTORS

It was late March 1993 when Michael Wexler found himself contemplating the future of his business distributing household paper products and cleaning supplies in Montreal. Several decisions had to be made that could drastically alter the operations of his summer company. These decisions included three ways to expand (enlarge the salesforce, target a new market, and pursue a franchise program) and three ways to change the nature of the venture (launch an environmental line, distribute nonperishable foods, and reduce delivery quantities). Underlying all of these was the possibility of selling the business and pursuing an opportunity with a multinational corporation.

**BACKGROUND**

RAMPAC Distributors was registered in 1989 as a partnership between Robert Bard and Michael Wexler, two college students in Montreal, Canada, a city of three million people. The name of the company was an acronym that stood for **R**obert **A**nd **M**ichael's **Pa**per **C**ompany. The two youths had no significant business experience or financial assets but had a desire to run their own business. After they examined the assets available to them (Michael's mother's station wagon and extra warehouse space from Rob's father), they decided on a distribution or delivery business. The partners proposed to deliver paper products to households and companies. They hoped that corporate business could be won with superior prices, given their lack of overhead. Similarly, they thought that retail business could be achieved by offering a delivery service that stores did not offer, and by selling bulk quantities (i.e., sufficient for a household for six months to one year).

**THE INITIAL MONTHS**

There were two key tasks in starting the business: finding suppliers and generating sales. Every paper goods company in the Yellow Pages was contacted and asked for a quotation to supply RAMPAC. The first quotations were at prices higher than retail, as suppliers sensed the inexperience of the owners who did not know the jargon of the industry (i.e., sizes, formats, brands, qualities, terms, and volumes). Initial quotations were as high as $42 per bulk case. After gaining familiarity with the business and being less than truthful about the age of the business and expected volumes, first purchases were negotiated at $24 per bulk case. Over the next four years, as volumes grew and management developed buying skills, prices were haggled down as low as $9 per bulk case.

During the first three months, business was very slow. Commercial accounts took much longer to acquire than expected. When the summer came, Bard wanted to travel for two months. Since the venture had already strained their friendship, and it would have been unfair to build a partnership alone, Wexler purchased Bard's half of the business for $300. Operating alone, Wexler spent the majority of his time soliciting households, selling door-to-door for 16 weeks straight. He would present a customer (usually the lady of the house) with a listing of his products and prices and explain the business concept (see Exhibit 1). If an order was not received, he would follow up at the door again within three days, and possibly phone after one week. The business grew steadily as a customer base of over 300 customers was developed.

The commercial side of the business, which received only minor attention, floundered for two reasons in Wexler's opinion. First, cleaning supplies seemed to be of minor concern to most businesses; hence, cold callers were quickly dismissed. Second, making contacts and bypassing red tape took months. Wexler was going away to university in the fall and believed he did not have enough time to secure and service commercial accounts during the school year.

### THE SECOND YEAR — A FOCUS ON SERVICE

In selling door-to-door, Wexler noticed that the customers who ordered were not price-sensitive. This was surprising to him since price was the traditional competitive dimension in paper products in the grocery business. Apparently, customers liked the idea of not having to continuously replenish these paper supplies and carry bulk goods from the store. He decided to "price what the market will bear," so prices were increased substantially, such that many items were more expensive than in local supermarkets. RAMPAC's new emphasis was quality, convenience, and service.

A typical order began with a salesperson offering to meet with the customer at any time and place (i.e., lunch break at work or evening at home). While details could easily be discussed over the phone, this measure helped to develop loyalty to the business and demonstrated concern for the customer's needs. The salespeople were extremely well trained with regard to product knowledge, i.e., detergent effectiveness for various fabrics, microwavability of different brands of plastic wrap, and other queries product labels didn't usually cover.

Wexler stressed that every order was special, hence no special requests were refused. This included finding nonstandard bag sizes for discontinued garbage pails, importing a stain remover not sold in Canada, delivering dog food, seeking product information from manufacturers, and taking returns of items not sold by RAMPAC.

Delivery was available whenever the customer wanted, including immediately after placing the order, on the weekend, or at 7 a.m. before going to work. The previous summer, RAMPAC had limited its inventory needs by ordering from suppliers only after accumulating several customer orders. Delivery time from RAMPAC to the customer had averaged four days. The second summer saw increased inventory levels.

When an order was delivered, the delivery person insisted on carrying all boxes to a basement or storage area. He or she then unpacked items, explained features, and ensured satisfaction. All products were of the highest quality. The softest tissues, strongest garbage bags, stickiest plastic wrap, etc. If a customer was for any reason dissatisfied, (legitimately or not, in Wexler's opinion), a full refund was given apologetically without asking for return of the goods.

**EXPANSION OF PRODUCTS, PROFITS, AND CUSTOMERS**

Over time, the profits of the business expanded for three reasons according to Wexler: increased profit per case, greater volume per customer, and more customers. These ends were pursued in different ways.

1. **Profit Per Case**

Initially, the contribution margin averaged 26 percent of selling price, whereas the average grocery store achieved a gross margin less than 21 percent (see Exhibit 2). With a new focus on service, margins were increased from 26 percent to 42 percent of selling price, without negatively affecting sales. The increased margins allowed RAMPAC to be very generous with customers in the return policy and satisfaction effort.

2. **Volume Per Customer**

The first flyer listed only paper products, about eight items and 13 SKUs (stock keeping units, i.e., unique items by brand and size). This range was expanded to include cleaning products, 17 items with 50 SKUs (see Exhibit 3). These products were as well received by customers as the paper products, effectively doubling sales per customer. Also, as customers reordered (85 to 90 percent repeat rate over a year), they increased the number of products purchased as their appreciation for the concept and their confidence in the quality and service grew. The average order size grew from $60 in 1989, to $105 in 1990, to $200 in 1991.

In the summer of 1991, the product line was further extended to include soft drinks and mineral water, also bulky items that consumers stock. This addition was very successful, as the quantity of these items consumed by a family over one year is tremendous. As a final means to increase sales from the established customer base, small volume customers (three cases or less) were lured with a "10 percent off" strategy. After receiving an order for X number of cases, and ensuring that the customer wanted nothing else, the salesperson would inform the customer that there was an "opportunity for additional savings, because any cases in addition to X are 10 percent off." As well, any customer who ordered fewer items than had been purchased the previous year was enticed to order more by offering 10 percent off any growth in order size. These techniques almost always worked; the nature of the product range was such that there were inevitably other goods offered that the customer could use but had not ordered because they didn't consume sufficient quantities to pursue in bulk or wanted to limit the order size. Presented with the discount proposal, they usually seized the opportunity. While extra cases added to an order had 25 percent lower contribution, they were seen as incremental sales that would not have been otherwise achieved.

### 3. Number of Customers

*Salesforce*

To expand the customer base, several sales people were recruited to target areas of the city that had not yet been solicited. They were lured by basic job posting at the Canada Summer Employment Centre and the summer employment offices of McGill and Concordia universities. Also, a notice was posted at two CEGEPs, the Quebec equivalent to Ontario Grades 12 and 13 (see Exhibit 4). Successful applicants were hired exclusively on commission. They were trained by Mr. Wexler about the business concept, the products offered, and the selling techniques that were most effective. Their commission was a flat $8 per case to avoid complexity. This remuneration was very meaningful, as the average salesperson could sell four cases per hour when going door-to-door. Delivery time (the person who sold the goods delivered them as well) was then unpaid. While this initiative increased the customer base by approximately 20 percent, the results were seen as disappointing. Few people applied, apparently due to a stigma associated with door-to-door sales and a reluctance to work exclusively on commission. Many who tried the job disliked having to work evenings, the key selling time when people are home. Others could not tolerate the volatility of sales, earning $250 one evening and nothing the next two. Finally, some salespeople who were initially very successful selling to family, friends, and neighbours became discouraged when sales to the general public did not keep pace. Incentive schemes, including RAMPAC T-shirts, RAMPAC logo watches, business cards, and sales level bonus payments, were ineffective since the problem with the program was not a lack of tangible reward. Of 20 salespeople who were hired and trained over three summers, only three were considered "successful" in management's estimation.

*Advertising*

The first advertising campaign began in 1990. Flyers were distributed through Canada Post to several thousand households. This was complemented by local newspaper advertising (see Exhibit 5) in four weekly community papers that had circulation of about 4,000 homes each. The response to these programs was difficult to measure, and they were deemed unsuccessful. The direct response rate was less than two calls per thousand people reached. The indirect benefit of the increased name awareness when potential customers were approached at the door was not accurately determined. Despite the newspaper's claim that the ads had to be run several times to achieve any results, the program was discontinued.

**COMPETITION**

When the business started, there was a void in the paper products delivery business because the largest supplier had ceased to serve households, targeting the commercial market exclusively. When approached by RAMPAC, those former household customers were eager to try bulk delivery and were familiar with the process.

Many new companies entered the industry to compete directly with RAMPAC. Usually, these were started by students, attracted by both the opportunity to sell their time and the lack of start-up capital required. Most used a flyer listing similar products but sometimes undercutting RAMPAC on price (see Exhibit 6). The flyers varied: some handwritten, some professionally produced, some just a letter to introduce the business. Most of these ventures did not exist two years after starting for a variety of reasons: owners found other summer jobs, the new business was unsuccessful as a result of poor management decisions (e.g., selling poor quality goods), and difficulties penetrating upscale areas of the city where RAMPAC was firmly established.

This competition affected RAMPAC in several ways. A competitor that satisfied customers with good quality products and service but was not in business one year later served to create a household favourable to bulk delivery, and RAMPAC was often the beneficiary of this sentiment. Alternatively, a company that delivered poor quality products and service served to negatively taint customers' opinion of the bulk delivery concept for a long time. Few RAMPAC customers were actually lost to competitors, because satisfaction levels were strong, price was not the basis of competition, and the market was big enough to support several companies without crossing paths.

There were two forms of indirect competition: grocery stores and warehouse stores such as Club Price. The fundamental difference between the product offered by these outlets and that provided by RAMPAC was delivery, a critical part of the package of benefits surrounding the purchase.

The problem encountered in competing against grocery stores was their famous loss leader sales.[1] Cleaning products were often used to build store traffic; the most commonly promoted loss leader was paper towels, which would be sold as low as $0.59 (the regular price was $1.19). If a customer cited this low price to a salesperson, his or her response would be something like this: "Loss leader items usually have a quantity limit of three. The rest of the year, purchases are made at the full price. RAMPAC sells a bulk quantity at a better than normal price, resulting in savings over the full year and preventing you from running out. While it would be conceivable to get all your groceries at loss leader prices, it is not practical to run around to hundreds of different stores with each discounting different goods. The grocer offers these prices to get you into the store to buy other items at full price." However, as a result of this competition, RAMPAC offered customers one item at a loss leader price, on a minimum order of five items.

Grocery stores also tried to provide delivery convenience. Some stores offered to deliver a customer's order for a flat fee of $5. Wexler felt that this did not catch on for several reasons: the customer still had to come to the store and select items; time of delivery was unspecific; the delivery fee, which was not built into the price, was a deterrent; and the delivery offer was never publicized.

The grand opening of Club Price in Montreal was of greater concern to Wexler. Like RAMPAC, Club Price offered consistently discounted prices and bulk quantities. However, the Club Price shopping experience included many unpleasant aspects that RAMPAC eliminated. These included searching for a parking spot, walking a significant distance from the car to the store, pushing around jumbo carriages or flatbed carts, struggling within huge crowds on weekends, waiting in line up to two hours (Saturday afternoon), pushing a heavily loaded carriage all the way back to the car, loading the goods into the car, and then unloading and carrying them again at home. Wexler was worried that Club Price would change its concept and offer delivery. This anxiety was substantiated by a customer survey that he encountered in the store, seeking opinion on delivery features. (He often browsed the store and was kicked out swiftly for writing down prices.)

Club Price sold many categories of products, such as food, cleaning products, clothing, and automotive supplies, such that RAMPAC could not offer itself as a complete alternative. By using RAMPAC, however, a customer could reduce the volume of goods purchased in each outing and the frequency of visits. As well, RAMPAC offered personalized service, greater variety in cleaning products, depth within a specific product category, and better quality products.

The growing popularity of Club Price did have a negative impact on sales, although the magnitude was uncertain because RAMPAC itself was growing so quickly. In Wexler's estimation, this loss of business was not because RAMPAC's selling proposition was relatively inferior. Constantly in contact with customers, he was of the opinion that less than 10 percent valued the additional cost savings above the superior variety and convenience he felt RAMPAC offered. However, it was evidently easier for customers to include cleaning products in the Club Price purchase than to remember to call RAMPAC. In order to combat this phenomenon, he stamped all RAMPAC boxes with a phone number to call when supplies were almost finished, and he was about to distribute fridge magnets.

**THE FUTURE**

Over several years, RAMPAC built up a significant customer base (350 regulars). The quality of products and service offered seemed to ensure the future stream of sales and a phenomenally high repeat rate. Mailing list software had been purchased and was being used to allow personalized contact with all customers (see Exhibit 7), a list of whom was carefully guarded. Upon graduation from the H.B.A. program at the University of Western

Ontario, Mr. Wexler was considering several options for the future of the business.

1. **Expansion Under Current Format**

   Three possibilities were considered to expand the business under the current format:

   a) *Hire more salespeople* to achieve greater penetration in the areas of the city already served. While 350 customers was sizable, it was insufficient to justify operating the business all year, and was certainly only a fraction of the potential customers that could be converted to the RAMPAC concept. With 2 percent of all anglophones in Montreal considered affluent, Wexler thought there were many more sales opportunities.

   b) *Target a new market* to boost sales. Francophone Montrealers comprised 85 percent of the city's population, but had not been targeted due to uncertainties about cultural differences that might affect their propensity to embrace the concept.

   c) *Set up a franchise program.* Experiments with this had been moderately successful in the past. Two of Wexler's friends had tried the concept in Brampton and Cambridge, Ontario. Both had earned good returns for the time and money invested. Wexler had initiated contact with Student Supplies, a paper products franchise business that operated throughout Canada but not in Montreal. After discussion with the owner, Wexler was offered the opportunity to run the entire Canadian organization for the upcoming summer.

2. **Modify the Current Format**

   Three possibilities were considered to change the nature of the business:

   a) *Launch an environmentally friendly line of products.* A company run by students had already introduced such a line, but was not aggressively advertising it. Initial contacts with the manufacturer indicated that there were environmentally friendly substitutes available for RAMPAC's entire product line, at prices less than the original products. However, their quality was inferior if not outright poor. Wexler was unsure whether a "green line" would have to be targeted toward a different customer group, whether it was hypocritical to sell both lines of goods, and how people would react to an environmental marketing approach.

   b) *Sell nonperishable food products, including canned, boxed, and powder foods.*

   c) *Deliver smaller quantities of goods more frequently and offer credit terms.*

3. **Sell the business**

   With exciting job offers from several companies, Wexler wondered if it was time to sell the business and embrace corporate life. He was unsure of the value of the business, and how he might go about selling it.

## NOTES

1. A loss leader is a product at or below cost in order to attract customers to the store. The item is usually heavily advertised and placed at a prominent end-of-aisle position. While some shoppers come to the store only to purchase that item, most also buy several other products, which, for the retailer, justifies the discounted merchandise.

*Exhibit 1*
*Rampac Distributors*
*Products List*

# LES DISTRIBUTEURS
# *RAMPAC*
## DISTRIBUTORS

## A STUDENT ENTERPRISE

GARBAGE BAGS (250 bags)
Regular.................................................................. $31.20
Heavy Duty............................................................ $33.10
Garden Bags (Super strong, 100 giant bags)............. $33.10

KITCHEN CATCHERS (500 bags)
White Bags............................................................. $32.80

CLING WRAP (Borden)
11" X 2500"........................................................ $36.40

ALUMINUM FOIL (Alcan Plus or Reynolds Industrial)
300cm x 200m..................................................... $34.50
45cm x 100m....................................................... $34.50

TOILET PAPER (48 Rolls)
2 ply: Facelle Royale (320 sheets) ......................... $34.90
1 ply: White Swan (1000 sheets) ........................... $34.90

PAPER TOWELS (Facelle Royale 2 ply)
Jumbo size (24 rolls x 100 sheets) ......................... $34.60

FACIAL TISSUE (Facelle Royale)
36 boxes 100 sheets 2 ply .................................... $32.30

NAPKINS
Lunch: Scott 180 x 9 packages .............................. $32.20
Dinner: Duni 3 ply (500)........................................ $39.10

## QUALITY - CONVENIENCE - SERVICE

For more information or to plan an order, please call
Michael Wexler at 486-2055
Pour plus d'information ou pour commander, telephoner
Michael Wexler a 486-2055
Rampac will beat the price of any competitor.

*EXHIBIT 2*

| Financial Results of a Typical Canadian Supermarket 1990 | | |
|---|---|---|
| **Income Statement** | | % |
| Sales | | 100.00 |
| Cost of goods sold | | 79.33 |
| Gross margin | | 20.67 |
| Administrative expense | 1.61 | |
| Accounting and data processing | 0.40 | |
| Buying and merchandising | 0.27 | |
| Interest expense | 0.62 | |
| Occupancy (rent, maintenance, utilities) | 4.73 | |
| Advertising and promotion | 0.93 | |
| Wages and benefits | 9.92 | |
| Handling and delivering expense | 0.79 | |
| Other operating expenses | 1.23 | |
| Total operating expenses | | 20.50 |
| Operating income | | 0.17 |
| Other income | | 0.59 |
| Profit before tax | | 0.76 |
| Income taxes | | 0.19 |
| Net profit after tax | | 0.57 |

Source: Canadian Grocer Model; Net Profit from Retail Council Food Survey, 1990.

*Exhibit 3*

---

**Rampac Distributors Cleaning Products Extension**[1]

---

**Cleaning Products**

Please note: "H" is the price for one-half the listed quantity.

| Fabric softeners: | Bounce | (600) | 63.90 H: 39.70 | sheets |
|---|---|---|---|---|
| | Downy | (600) | 59.80 H: 38.40 | sheets |
| | Downy | (4x4L) | 42.10 H: 29.20 | liquid |
| | Snuggle | (2x8L) | 38.20 H: 27.60 | liquid |
| | | | | |
| Laundry detergent: | All | (15kg) | 49.00 | powder |
| | Arctic Power | (20kg) | 59.30 H: 38.50 | powder |
| | Family Tree | (18kg) | 35.10 | powder |
| | Tide | (20kg) | 65.90 H: 39.70 | powder |
| | Tide | (4x4L) | 56.90 H: 36.90 | liquid |
| | Wisk | (2x8L) | 53.10 H: 34.80 | liquid |
| | | | | |
| Dishwasher detergent: | Cascade | (6x3.5kg) | 48.70 H: 32.30 | powder |
| | Electrasol | (4x4.5kg) | 48.70 H: 32.30 | powder |
| | | | | |
| Dish washing soap: | Palmolive | (4x4L) | 49.40 H: 33.10 | liquid |
| | | | | |
| Bleach: | Javex | (6x3.6L) | 29.70 H: 22.20 | liquid |
| | Javex for UnB | (20L) | 43.10 H: 29.20 | powder |
| | Javex 2 | (6x3.6L) | 46.10 H: 31.70 | liquid |
| | | | | |
| Cleaning products: | Windex | (4x5L) | 43.40 H: 29.70 | refill |
| | Fantastic | (4x5L) | 51.20 H: 33.60 | refill |
| | Spray N' Wash | (4x5L) | 57.20 H: 36.60 | refill |
| | Pledge | (6x500g) | 39.50 H: 27.10 | cans |
| | Vim | (6x1L) | 38.60 | |
| | Mr. Clean | (4x4L) | 51.80 H: 33.90 | |
| | Spic N' Span | (4x4L) | 57.20 H: 27.00 | |
| | Pinesol | 4x4L | 55.70 H: 36.10 | |
| | Comet | (24x600g) | 39.20 H: 27.80 | |
| | Ajax | (48x400g) | 44.80 H: 31.00 | |
| | Lysol | 8x450g | 43.30 H: 29.80 | |
| | Ivory Liquid | (2x4L) | 39.80 H: 28.30 | refill |
| | J-Cloths | (200) | 41.00 H: 28.00 | |
| | | | | |
| Ziploc food bags: | Freezer | (1201g ÷ 75md) | 31.60 | |
| | Sandwich | (1200) | 38.70 H: 27.80 | |
| | | | | |
| Soft drinks: | 72 cans | (3 types max.) | 38.60 (÷dep) most brands | |
| | Evian | (72 small) | 44.90 (24 large) 39.80 | |
| | Perrier | (72 small) | 55.90 (24 large) 39.80 | |

| Also Available: | Any brand or household product not listed, Styrofoam cups, plastic and paper plates, and baking chocolate! |
|---|---|

---

1.  Reduced from actual flyer size.

*EXHIBIT 4*
*Rampac Distributors'*
*Posting to Recruit*
*Salespeople*

---

Opportunity for employment with

**RAMPAC DISTRIBUTING**
613 Victoria Ave.
Westmount, Quebec
Tel. # 486-2055

INFORMATION ON BEING A SALESPERSON FOR RAMPAC DISTRIBUTING

WHAT WE SELL: Household paper products and cleaning supplies, including garbage bags, Kitchen Catchers, Saran Wrap, aluminum foil, toilet paper, paper towels, facial tissue, napkins, fabric softeners, laundry and dish detergents, and most cleaning products. As well, we sell soft drinks, mineral water, and Ziploc bags. All products are sold in bulk quantities (i.e., larger than can be purchased in stores) to save the consumer time and money.

WHO WE SELL TO: Mostly individual households, with some businesses as well.

HOW WE SELL: Sales are initiated through door-to-door canvassing, and contacts through parents, relatives, friends, etc.

INDIVIDUAL INVESTMENT REQUIRED: None.

POTENTIAL EARNINGS: Unlimited. Salary will be based fully on generous commission on each item sold. Salespeople will earn $8 on each "case" (standard bulk quantity of a good) sold. The average salesperson consistently sells approximately four cases per hour, earning $32 per hour. A full explanation of the commission system is available from any RAMPAC representative.

YOUR OBLIGATION TO RAMPAC AFTER HIRING: Once hired, RAMPAC asks that you maintain a minimum level of selling each week, usually around 20 cases.

WHAT RAMPAC WILL DO FOR YOU: RAMPAC manages invoicing, purchasing, inventory, and running the business. It will deliver for you as well, for a portion of the commission. If you have access to a car, then you can choose to deliver yourself. In that case, all you need to do is pick up the products you sell from the RAMPAC outlet conveniently located in Westmount.

ADVANTAGES TO CONSIDER: As a salesperson, you can choose when to work and when not to. You control your own hours and have no boss watching over you. The average salesperson will work about half as many hours as his or her friends, but earn nearly twice as much!!

If you are interested in selling or seek more information, please do not hesitate to call Michael Wexler at 486-2055.

Salespeople will be interviewed and hired starting May 5.

**EXHIBIT 5**
***Rampac Distributors' Newspaper Advertisement***

**TIRED OF RUNNING OUT?**

RAMPAC DISTRIBUTORS

Provides convenient FREE DELIVERY of household paper products and cleaning supplies

- Garbage Bags
- Paper Towels
- Food Wrap
- Toilet Paper
- Detergents
- and much more

SAVE TIME AND MONEY
by ordering
QUALITY name brand products in bulk

Call 486-2055 Michael Wexler
*A Student Enterprise*

*Exhibit 6*

---

**Competitor's Flyer, "Student Kitchen Supply Sales"[1]**

---

# STUDENT KITCHEN SUPPLY SALES

ARI: 484-6699
BILL: 738-4078

TO PLACE AN ORDER
OR FOR ANY INFORMATION

$PRICES$

|  | GROCERY STORE (tax included) | OURS |
|---|---|---|
| GARBAGE BAGS (INDUSTRIAL) | | |
| 26" x 36" → standard size (250 BAGS) | $76.03 | 38.00 |
| 35" x 50" → "giant size" (200 BAGS) | 99.92 | 45.00 |
| 20" x 22" → kitchen size (500 BAGS) wht. | 54.27 | 33.00 |
| ALUMINUM FOIL | | |
| ALCAN OR REYNOLDS 12" X 650 ft. | | |
| 18" x 328 ft. | 42.51 | 29.00 |
| PLASTIC WRAP | | |
| BORDEN'S (2000 ft.) | 44.01 | 25.00 |
| FACIAL TISSUE (36 BOXES/CASE) | | |
| FACELLE (100 TISSUES/BOX @ 66¢ each) | | |
| 2 PLY | 35.97 | 24.00 |
| BATHROOM TISSUE (48 ROLLS/CASE) | | |
| COTTONELLE (400 SHEETS/ROLL) | 37.41 | 33.00 |
| PERKINS DECOR (320 SHEETS/ROLL) | 29.65 | 24.00 |
| 2 PLY | | |
| KITCHEN TOWELS | | |
| SCOT TOWELS (24 ROLLS X 90 SHEETS) | 33.88 | 28.00 |
| 2 PLY | | |
| SCOTT DINNER NAPKINS (600) | 41.75 | 21.00 |

| ZIPLOC BAGS: | SMALL | MEDIUM | LARGE |
|---|---|---|---|
| (300 bags) | 15.00 | 19.50 | 21.00 |

# FREE DELIVERY!! TAX INCLUDED!!!

---

1.  Reduced from actual flyer size.

*EXHIBIT 7*
*Rampac Distributors'*
*Personal Letters to*
*Customers*

August 7, 1990

Dear 1~,

As a valued customer of RAMPAC DISTRIBUTORS, I am writing to inform you that I will be returning to the University of Western Ontario on September 1.

I would like to suggest that you place an order now to stock up for the winter season. I have enclosed a RAMPAC flyer for your convenience. For those customers who ordered in May or June, you will notice a substantial increase in the range of products available.

Thank you for your support. I look forward to serving you again next summer.

Sincerely,


Michael Wexler

---

May 1, 1991

Dear 1~,

As a valued customer, I am writing to inform you that RAMPAC DISTRIBUTORS has returned to full operation for the months of May and June. I am most anxious to supply you with a wide range of paper and household products. Most prices are lower than last year, delivery is free, and accommodating service is provided with a smile. Please read the enclosed RAMPAC flyer and call me to place an order. I look forward to hearing from you.

Sincerely,


Michael Wexler

### C A S E 7.9   A STRATEGIC PLAN FOR MIDTOWN HOSPITAL

In March 1989, Dick Martin, executive director of Midtown Hospital, Ontario, Canada, sat down to plan recommendations for the district health council. Fiscal year end was close, and each department in the hospital had submitted its budget needs for the next year. Martin knew he would not be able to fulfil all of the departments' requests. Recently, health-care expenditures were scrutinized to an unprecedented extent by stakeholders in the province of Ontario's public health-care system. In fact, he could present only two proposals for budget increases (from among those submitted) to the district health council. He would be lucky to receive just one.

**THE HEALTH CARE INDUSTRY**

Ontario, the largest province in Canada, offered a fully funded health-care plan, called the Ontario Health Insurance Plan (OHIP), to its nine million residents. In 1988, Ontario disbursed one-third of its entire budget, almost $13 billion, to deliver this health-care system. Within the next 20 years, the number of Ontarians aged 65 and over would double, a fact that would place further stress on the budget for health care, because incidence of disease[1] increased with age.

With taxes steadily rising, the Ontario government was under considerable pressure by its residents to establish a better managed health-care system, one that would maintain the province's high standard of health care into the year 2000, and simultaneously control costs.

**Ontario Hospitals — Costs**

Gross operating costs for public hospitals increased by 9.64 percent from 1987 to 1988 bringing the total cost up to $6,416,790,386. Of this, the Ministry of Health was responsible for just under 80 percent of financing. See Table 1 for a breakdown of major ministry expenditures.

Table 1: Daily Per Patient Cost for Hospital Care

|  | 1987 | 1988 |
|---|---|---|
| Cost per diem for in-patient care | $294.24 | $318.18 (this represents an 8.1% increase) |

The costs in Table 1 represent averages only. The daily acute-care cost for a patient at Toronto's Sick Children's Hospital was $927.96 In other hospitals, the costs were as low as $218.00. The per diem cost of providing acute care, $344.34, was roughly double that of a day of chronic care, $169.18.

## Ontario Hospitals — Funding

Provincial and federal governments received much of their revenue through taxes and, in turn, disbursed payments to all sectors, including health care.

Since 1969, Ontario's public hospitals had been funded primarily on a global budgeting system. Under this system, hospitals received a global envelope of funds, adjusted each year for inflation, new programs, and growth, with no automatic settlement made at the end of the year (that is, if the funds were not spent, the remainder was not recovered). This system of funding was simple to manage; however, it also contributed to a "spend it or lose it" mentality.

Many hospitals operated on a deficit basis and projected that additional funds were required to maintain effective operations. Yet, Canada spent more per capita on health care than any other country in the world with a national health-care system, despite the fact that it had one of the youngest populations in the western world.

Private hospitals were funded by a similar method, called a modified global system. Under this method, global funding was approved at the beginning of the year. The allocation to private hospitals was based on the previous year's allocated amount plus a percentage increase to cover inflation in wages and prices. Unlike the public hospital's global system, any unspent monies were recovered at the end of the year, and any overspending was absorbed by the hospital. Included in this system of funding for private hospitals was an allowance for a 6.5 percent return on investment for the equity holders, based on audited statements.

In 1989, health care cost an average of $2,394 for each Ontario resident. Given existing trends, it was projected that by the year 2011 this figure would increase to $6,125.

In 1987, chronic-care patients accounted for 25 percent of total hospital patient days. In many instances, these patients occupied the more expensive acute-care beds. A study completed in 1987 concluded that 25 percent of those patients in chronic-care beds should have been somewhere else. These patients could have been placed outside of public institutions in alternatives for care like the Home Care Program and other community-based services.

## Physicians — The Gateway to the System

Most Ontario physicians were paid on a fee-for-service (FFS) basis, under the Ontario Health Insurance Plan (OHIP). Each time a physician provided a service to a patient, he or she received a standard, predetermined fee. Each year the government of Ontario met with the Ontario Medical Association (OMA) to negotiate the standardized fee for each consultative, diagnostic, and therapeutic service provided.

In essence, Ontario supported a publicly funded system that paid health-care providers to deliver services. Over 90 percent of physicians were self-employed, and over 90 percent of hospitals were public, nonprofit organizations. Usage of Ontario's hospitals was, for the most part, regulated by physicians.

Thirty percent of the provincial budget for health care, or $3,628.2 million, was paid to physicians in 1987–88 on a fee-for-service basis. Fee-for-service also applied to most physician services provided to patients in hospitals. Almost 34 percent of the monies paid to physicians under OHIP was spent on services that physicians provided to patients in hospitals.

In 1987–88, there were 91.9 million claims for fees by physicians. This number of claims translated into 9.95 claims per patient (claimant). The previous year, there had been 85 million claims or 9.25 claims per patient. The increase in claims between the two years was attributable to:

- an effective price increase of 7.7 percent
- a population increase of 1.73 percent
- a residual increase (consisting of increases in physician and practitioner supply and use) of 4.21 percent

Table 2: Average Cost and Services Per Claim (SPC)

|  | 1987–88 | SPC | 1986–87 | SPC | % Increase |
|---|---|---|---|---|---|
| Medical | $38.38 | 2.4 | $35.59 | 2.4 | $7.80 |
| Dental | $281.22 | 2.4 | $222.19 | 2.4 | $26.60 |

Table 3: Average Per Capita Cost

|  | 1987–88 |  | 1986–87 |  | % Increase |
|---|---|---|---|---|---|
| Medical | $363.43 |  | $318.80 |  | $14.00 |
| Dental | $.79 |  | $0.71 |  | $11.30 |

**The Ontario Medical Association (OMA)**

Ontario in 1888 was vastly different than it was in 1988. There were 15 general hospitals: four in Toronto, two each in Guelph, Kingston, and Ottawa, and one each in Hamilton, London, Ottawa, Pembroke, and St. Catharines. Toronto also had a home for incurables. There were five mental hospitals situated in Hamilton, Kingston, London, Orillia, and Toronto. For the majority of the 1,700 practising physicians the home was the place where babies were delivered, fractures were reduced and immobilized, the sick were nursed, and heroic surgery was performed.

The initiative to establish a provincial association for doctors (OMA) came from a need for the pooling of knowledge, resources, and experiences, so that their patients might be given better medical care.[2] In 1988, membership in the Ontario Medical Association was 17,067 physicians — a ten-fold increase over the 108 years since its inception. The mandate of the OMA had changed considerably, too.

In particular, the OMA outlined goals for the improvement of its public image (somewhat damaged by a doctors' strike in 1986) and goals for positive dialogue between the OMA and government.

In recent years the OMA established committees to deal with a more complicated society:

- task force on AIDS was established to increase awareness by physicians and to provide advice and expertise to the OMA;

- committee on Child Welfare identified issues for increased awareness such as eating disorders in adolescents and literacy. Issue topics included child abuse, day care, nutrition, adoption, poverty (and the health of children), and the child welfare system;

- committee on women's health issues reviewed the OMA's existing mechanisms of identifying health problems specific to women, of advising the OMA on current research into gender-specific biological factors, and to address the psychosocial and cultural experiences of being a woman in contemporary society.

*Facilities*

As of March 31, 1989, the majority of Ontario's health-care facilities were devoted to treating patients with acute diseases. Publicly funded hospitals provided the bulk of services. Private hospitals were generally much smaller than public ones and located primarily in rural areas. Most offered long-term chronic care to elderly members of the community.

Table 4: Summary of Ontario Hospitals' Bed Capacities

|  | Number of Hospitals | Total Number of Beds |
|---|---|---|
| Public hospitals | 223 | 54,014 |
| Private hospitals | 16 | 718 |
| Federal hospitals and nursing stations | 16 | 504 |
| TOTAL | 255 | 55,236* |

*There were 5.6 hospital beds available for every 1,000 Ontario residents. The majority of facilities were devoted to treating patients with acute diseases. Public hospitals provided the bulk of service.

Statistics showed that although acute-care patients made up the majority of cases received and treated, their hospital stay was much shorter. Thus, they did not account for an equally large portion of bed occupancy. Of the 1,389,659 patients received last year, 97 percent required acute care. The

Table 5: Types of Beds Per 1,000 Residents

| Types of Beds per 1,000 People | Number of Beds per 1,000 People | Percentage of Total |
|---|---|---|
| Beds for use in Acute Care | 4.1 | 73% |
| Beds for use in Chronic Care | 1.3 | 23% |
| Beds for other use | 0.2 | 3% |
| TOTAL | 5.6 | 99% |

Table 6: Occupancy Rates for the Period April 1/87 to March 31/88 (based on both public and private hospitals)

| | | Increase over last year (%) |
|---|---|---|
| Patients received | 1,389,659 | 1.1 % |
| Days of care given | 16,208,521 | 0.9 % |
| Average length of stay | 11.7 days | no change |
| Days used for acute care | 71% | |
| Days used for chronic care | 25.2% | |
| Days used for other care | 3.8 % | |

breakdown for average length of stay and bed occupancy rates for both acute and chronic care patients is shown in Table 6.

The above statistics gave rise to an average accupancy rate of 87.6 percent. In 1987, 59,012 staffed beds were available. The average number of patients treated in the same year was 51,695; thus, 51,695 patients ÷ 59,012 staffed beds × 100% = 87.6 percent.

The average length of stay for chronic-care patients had increased by 11.4 percent over the past six years, bringing the average length of stay for chronic-care patients to 264.8 days. Outpatient emergency visits increased by 19.8 percent over the same six-year period. Full-time staff increased by 6.4 percent, while part-time staff rose by 42.3 percent.

Other trends in hospital care are given in Exhibit 2.

**Hospital Staff**

Over the previous five years, total part-time and full-time staff had grown approximately 4 percent annually.

Table 7: Paid Staff and Total Hours Worked

| Description | Number |
|---|---|
| Full-time employees | 106,583  persons |
| Part-time employees | 54,786  persons |
| Total paid hours of work | 251,993,000  hours |

Total paid hours increased at a much faster rate than the days of care given (i.e., 13.5 percent versus 4.9 percent) over the same time period. There were two alternative explanations for this inequity: either hospital employees had become less efficient, or more sophisticated technology (requiring more tests, treatments, or care per patient) resulted in more paid hours.

**The Home Care Program**

The Home Care Program, introduced in 1968, provided in-home services to both chronic and acute patients. It was administered through 38 local home-care programs across the province. Most of the services provided to clients were purchased by the program from independent agencies such as the Victorian Order of Nurses (VON), Red Cross, and other private commercial agencies.

Home care was divided into two main areas: the *acute program* (introduced in 1968) offered short-term, medically oriented services intended to lead to rehabilitation; the *chronic program* (introduced in 1970) offered services on a longer-term basis. Chronic home-care assistance focused on maintenance rather than medically centred services. Clients admitted to chronic home care were likely to have limited rehabilitation capabilities. Their need for care might extend from several months to many years.

The chronic-care program had contributed significantly to growth in usage of home care, to the increase in average length of stay, and to program spending. Spending increased substantially following the introduction of the chronic program.

The top three primary diagnoses accounting for new cases admitted to home care were in descending order: cerebrovascular disease, diabetes mellitus, and ischemic heart disease. Between 1978 and 1988, cerebrovascular disease, diabetes mellitus, and heart disease case admissions increased 135 percent, 175 percent, and 911 percent, respectively. These diagnostic categories represented chronic disease conditions.

To be eligible for home care, clients had to be insured under the Ontario Health Insurance Plan (OHIP) and supervised by an attending physician. The patient's medical condition had to be such that adequate treatment could be provided at home. The patient was to be in need of at least one of the professional services: nursing, physiotherapy, occupational therapy, or speech therapy. The residential environment had to be suitable for the provision of the required care and the patient's family or other appropriate persons had to be willing and able to participate in the program, as required. Finally, the patient's needs had to be such that they could not be met on an out-patient basis.[3]

The Home Care Program's objectives were "to provide, on a visiting basis, professional health and support services to acute and chronic patients in a home environment as an alternative to institutional care and to ensure the provision of health support services in the school setting."

The 38 existing local programs were administered by four different types of agencies: local boards of health (public health units accounted for 29 of the 38 programs), regional municipal governments, hospitals, and Victorian Order of Nurses, plus one free-standing structure (Metro Toronto operated under a free-standing board).

In addition to the acute and chronic programs that represented the core elements of service, Home Care's Programs included:

*The School Health Program* was introduced in 1984 and gave local home-care programs responsibility for providing eligible direct health-care services to certain children in schools.

*The Integrated Homemaker Program* was introduced at six local sites in May 1986 and was since expanded to 18 sites. This program was funded and directed by the Ministry of Community and Social Services, although it was administered locally by home-care programs. It provided homemaker and meals benefits only and, therefore, did not require that professional services be a condition of program eligibility.

*The Assistive Devices Program (ADP)* was introduced by the Ministry of Health in 1982 and had progressively expanded in scope since then. Local home-care programs played a key role in the delivery of this program. The ADP provided to eligible clients a benefit payment (usually 75 percent) for designated equipment.

*The Ontario Drug Benefit Program (ODB)* was a drug program for which all home-care clients were eligible. Under the ODB Formulary, a list of drugs eligible for benefits was identified. If a home-care client was prescribed drugs that were not contained in the formulary, special authorizations for payment were obtained from the ODB by local Home Care Programs.

The development of home care had been characterized by piecemeal introduction of new service components, offered across the province in a gradual manner. There was no overall strategic plan or framework for guiding these developments, assessing their appropriateness, or determining their effectiveness.

The number of acute patients using home care increased by 63 percent from 1978 to 1987. The numbers of chronic cases increased by 1,221 percent. The average length of stay for all programs (acute, chronic, and school) increased from 34 days in 1978 to 75 days in 1988. Still, only 2.2 percent of the province's population used the service.

The greatest percentage of people served by home care was in the age groups 75+. The need for services (percentage served) increased dramatically in the population aged 60 to 64. The only other group with a comparable increase in level of use was the four-year-old and under group.

The population of Ontario aged 65 and over increased 32 percent between 1976 and 1985. The entire population increased by 5 percent during these same years. Between the years 1986 and 2006, the entire population of Ontario was expected to grow by 14.1 percent; however, the population aged 65 and over would increase by 50.2 percent because the baby boom was about to enter that age group. During those same years, the population 75 and over would increase by 81.4 percent.

**Home Care Program — Costs**

Spending on the Home Care Program went from $13.3 million in fiscal 1975–76 to $245 million in fiscal 1987–88. Throughout much of this period, growth in expenditures reflected the progressive implementation of the program across the province.

Between 1984 and 1987, program expenditures increased by 92 percent. During this same period, program caseload increased by 28 percent. The program was not introduced in metropolitan Toronto until 1984.

**Home Care Program — Funding**

The Home Care Coordinator from the Ministry of Health was responsible for approving the budgets of local programs within the provincial allocation. In 1988–89, the target for local programs was provided with a 5 percent allowance for growth of utilization and a 4.5 percent increase to cover inflation. Local program officials considered that these small increases meant the ministry had effectively capped program expenditures.

**ISSUES FACING THE CURRENT HEALTH CARE SYSTEM IN ONTARIO**
**Control**

Costs of health care were at present growing faster than the provincial economy. The existing system provided no incentives for controlling costs or efficiencies. There was a lack of bottom-up responsibility because pressure for cost control did not reach the grass roots where cost actually occurred. As a consequence of OHIP coverage, consumers were not compelled to operate under tight constraints and, therefore, had little incentive for keeping costs down or searching out the most cost efficient care.

A report of the Ontario Health Review Panel (June 1987) proposed key issues for health care in Ontario:

> Ontario has not focused sufficient attention on the role of the individual in health and health care. In other words, we do not have a clear understanding of the proper balance between the contributions of the individual to good health and health care and the contributions of health care providers and government.

In addressing the growing gap between demand for services and supply of resources, the report focused on the responsibilities of the individual to an extent that the individual would be empowered to exercise informed choices (e.g., the management of child birth, death with dignity, and consent to psychiatric care) about one's own health and the health options in the community. The panel was careful to point out that it did not support policies or attitudes that blamed the victim for being sick or that would lead to further inequities of health care between rich and poor.

Ontario's residents are becoming increasingly aware of and interested in the positive results of healthful lifestyle choices in such areas as diet, alcohol and tobacco consumption, exercise, and stress management. Policy should support individual choices in these areas, and recognize that positive change in individual behaviour is more likely when steps are taken to make change more convenient and socially acceptable.

Among the suggested action to support healthful choices by the individual were:

- restriction of smoking in the workplace
- early passage of worker and community right-to-know legislation regarding hazardous materials used, produced, or disposed in Ontario
- development of specific programs, such as the campaign to reduce impaired driving, that involve more than one level of government and more than one ministry
- strengthened health curriculum in schools
- basic health information prepared on various diseases, disorders, treatments, environmental hazards, and lifestyle choices

***Planning Systems***

Within the system there was too much independent planning among regions. Many communities were driven to self-sufficiency, demanding their own equipment, most of which was very expensive. Some hospitals competed with others in the same region. The obvious result was a duplication of services and a lack of rationalization.

In addition, this lack of rationalization resulted in an inequity of service. For example, greater resources were deployed in southern and urban Ontario, as opposed to the northern and rural areas.

Within the global system of funding, hospitals received budget increases through growth and expansion of services. As a result, each hospital was driven to spend more money on introducing new systems with little acknowledgement of limited resources.

In May 1989, the Premier's Council on Health Strategy issued a report that addressed the pressures for change in the health-care system and offered some recommendations for the future.

The report recommended a modified global funding arrangement for hospitals, suggesting a "case-mix" approach — funding that would recognize differences in various hospitals' particular caseload types. Local differences or specializations would be taken into consideration, giving hospitals greater flexibility to trade off programs and services within their budgets and in line with community needs. The report proposed to involve physicians in the budgeting process.

The report also recommended a review of previous (ministry) plans that would have added 4,000 beds to the hospital system. Instead, the report stated that other mechanisms (community-based services, extended care, duplication or potential rationalization with neighbouring hospitals, and health status indicators of the client population) should be studied before any capital funds were expended for new beds.

The report supported moves to strengthen community health services as an equal partner in the provision of health care. Community services were seen as intrinsically more responsive to individual and local needs. Funding for community services was specified as a redirection of existing resources.

**Institutionally Based System**

The great majority of funding was currently awarded to institutions. As outlined earlier, this was one of the most expensive types of care. In many cases, alternative community-based programs were more appropriate and less costly.

There was evidence of inappropriate use of both acute and long-term beds with unnecessary admissions and unnecessarily long lengths of stay. An overconcentration of health-care resources existed in the institutional-care sector, hospitals, and chronic-care facilities. The Health Review Panel (June 1987) suggested hospital-organized home care to facilitate earlier discharges and to divert patients from unnecessary hospital admission.

**Technological, Political, and Social Trends**

Although improvements in technology had rendered a higher standard of health care, they carried a heavy price tag. As well, an increasing number of doctors were sued for malpractice. As a result, doctors started to practise defensive medicine: assigning additional tests and therapy, laden with newer technologies, to be "on the safe side."

Finally, as mentioned previously, the number of persons aged 65 and over was expected to double within the next 20 years. Coupled with this trend was an increased life expectancy (see Exhibit 3), and a breakdown of the extended family meant that the elderly who were no longer supported by relatives, needed alternative care facilities.

**Consumer Expectations**

Ontario residents were becoming more vigilant about determinants of health and health importance. Although this trend was a positive one, it also created higher expectations of the health-care system.

The Report from the Ontario Health Review Panel (June 1987) suggested that:

> Health-care providers are experiencing unprecedented expectations from the individual patient for the highest quality care which is both comprehensive and accessible. On the one hand, the concern of government is to contain the large portion of provincial expenditures directed to health; government must respond to pressures for expansion of the health budget to accommodate higher utilization, new technology and more hospital inpatient facilities, particularly for long-term care.

The panel offered some innovative funding approaches to provide incentives that placed greater emphasis on care in ambulatory and community settings. For example, premiums were suggested for professionals who performed procedures on an outpatient basis. Premiums for physicians who provided regular office hours on evenings and weekends were suggested (in an effort to relieve the burden on hospital emergency departments).

The panel also suggested penalties for hospitals and physicians when patients admitted to hospitals for diagnostic evaluation or surgery did not undergo the procedure by the second day of their stay. Penalties were suggested for hospitals and physicians where the patient exceeded the expected length of hospital stay for a professionally selected list of diagnostic categories.

The panel suggested capitation as an approach to payment of healthcare providers. Capitation would provide for fixed fees to the physician. The fee would be a prepayment for the health services that an individual might consume during a given period. Although capitation payments would not be related to the amount of services that the patient would use during that period, the payment could be varied according to risk criteria such as age and health status. The panel expressed the belief that capitation would provide an incentive for physicians to emphasize preventative medicine.

As part of the enhanced community services, the report suggested a change in the curricula of the traditional professions. Health policy, promotion, and prevention were cited as core to the curricula of providers and planners of health care.

**Basis of Payment**

Under the current system, doctors and hospitals received monies under two different methods. Hospitals had pre-established global funding, while doctors received fee-for-service payments. With no limit placed on doctors' fees, it was possible for an imbalance to occur if doctors' fees exceeded budgeted amounts.

The Premier's Council on Health Strategy pointed out that OHIP payments to physicians and other practitioners quadrupled in a 10-year period from $900 million in 1977–78 to $3.6 billion in 1987–88 — and that this growth range of 15 percent per annum far exceeded the growth rate of the provincial economy. The report endorsed a more mixed (fee-for-service, capitation, and salary) reimbursement for physicians.

The report stated that an increase in physician supply was a major contributor to rising Ontario Health Insurance expenditures. As well, it pointed to a continuing increase in the number of services provided per physician.

**Health Service Organizations**

A Health Service Organization (HSO) was a system under which physicians were funded on a per capita basis (not a fee-for-service basis) for each patient served. In 1986, 180,000 Ontario residents — about 2 percent of the population — were served through HSOs.

For comparative purposes, the dominant example of a prepayment system was the American model, the Health Maintenance Organization (HMO). The broadest and most philosophical difference between an HMO and an HSO was that HMOs were independent organizations, competing for consumers/clients in a pluralistic health-care marketplace. HSOs, however, were simply a method of payment to physicians within a universal health insurance plan that was administered and financed by government.

An HSO was a form of payment, an HMO was a unit, a hospital, or a portion of a hospital in which the physicians were paid by salary or capitation. An HMO was responsible professionally to the patient and contracted financially to the patient or his employer. As a rule, an HMO contract was made by employer groups with a doctor, a group of doctors, or a hospital. Physicians were paid a salary.

The opinion of the OMA was that existing HSOs had not been carefully evaluated, with respect to cost or to efficiency. However, the impetus behind HSOs was considerable, fuelled by politicians and health-care economists. The impetus was largely fiscal, though sometimes veiled behind conjecture on improvements in the preventative aspects of medicine.

**The Public Debate**   With a budget deficit of $1 billion, the province of Ontario concentrated on reducing physicians' fees, which was one of the fastest growing of its budget items. In 1988, the province increased fees for physicians by only 1.75 percent even though outside negotiators recommended a 3.4 percent rise.

Media reports on Ontario's 223 public hospitals gave them tarnished reputations. Hospitals wanted to polish their image as well-managed health-care providers. Public satisfaction with hospitals had dropped 8 percentage points in the past year. Research showed that almost half of the people polled said they were not confident about getting quick access to high technology procedures.

Studies by the Ontario Medical Association and the Canadian Medical Association uncovered severe staff shortages in several specialities, including neonatology, psychiatry, general surgery, and laboratory medicine.

Dr. Carole Guzman, president of the OMA, summarized the issues for the next decade:

> We are healthy because health care is accessible, and universal. No individual in this province is denied medical care because he or she cannot afford it .... But the system is under great social, economic and political pressures .... Our health-care system must meet the needs of everyone in society while, at the same time, not impose an unacceptable burden on the public purse....

**MIDTOWN HOSPITAL**   Midtown Hospital was a 200-bed community facility offering medical, surgical, critical, paediatric, obstetrical (child delivery), and chronic care to the population it served. The hospital was located approximately 30 minutes' travelling time from a major medical and teaching centre with extensive facilities in all ranges of medical service.

Residents around Midtown Hospital were happy to know that their families' health-care needs could be provided at the local hospital, particularly when there was an extended illness.

With expenses totalling $19.9 million in fiscal 1989, Midtown Hospital was anticipating a freeze on all expenditures. Alternative solutions, like cutbacks in some areas to favour others, would become necessary if any major changes to the existing system were to take place. The board of governors expected a small increase, for inflation only, from the provincial government.

The mix of chronic and acute beds was currently similar to that in every other hospital in Ontario. At Midtown Hospital, the major patient service used was general medicine. Sixty-five percent of all patients, excluding newborns, were general medicine patients. General medicine considered the treatment of more common illnesses, and described care given to persons not falling under one of the three other groups: surgery, obstetrics and paediatrics.

Ministry of Health bed-to-population guidelines for chronic care were allocated on a county-wide basis. Currently, the ministry projected an increased need of 15 percent in chronic beds by 1990.

The majority of physicians who utilized the facilities at the hospital were from family practice (22 family practitioners in total). All of the specialties, excluding obstetrics/gynaecology, ophthalmology, and otolaryngology, were covered by one specialist each. Consulting and courtesy physicians from neighbouring centres augmented the hospital's professional base.

**Department Proposals**   Because of increased patient loads in Midtown's emergency department, the department manager had requested additional beds for emergency care. There was space available in the existing emergency facility; however, expenditures for staff (especially in the evening hours) would have to be increased, and the "quiet" space allocated for the physician on call would have to be used as an assessment room. This latter fact had caused quite a stir among local physicians who were required to "staff" the emergency department 24 hours per day. The physicians previously devised a call schedule that was changed periodically and amicably according to their needs.

Surgery had requested some new equipment that would accommodate more ear, nose, and throat (ENT) procedures. The equipment purchase could be accommodated within the existing budget; however, pre- and post-surgical care would require additional staff.

The nursing director had requested some salary increases above and beyond normal allocations for inflation. She had explained her request on the basis of the difficulty of obtaining qualified help. Most of the registered nurses in the area preferred to commute to higher paying positions at the larger centre (30 minutes away). The remaining qualified RNs in the area were prone to part-time work while they raised families. It was particularly difficult to staff weekends and evenings.

One of the hospital's board members had suggested the establishment of an out-patient clinic, attached to the hospital and staffed from 8:00 a.m. to midnight. The out-patient clinic would be similar to an emergency facility, but would not include much of the expensive, high technology equipment found in most emergency units. Those patients whose injuries did not require the use of emergency equipment could be treated in this out-patient clinic, thus freeing up the emergency facilities for those truly requiring them.

Martin needed to decide a strategic plan to present to the district health council. The decisions he would make today required assessment of the kinds of facilities that would be needed at Midtown over the next decade. Finally, while he remained cognizant of the multiple pressures on the provincial health-care system, his first loyalty was to the needs of Midtown's community.

## NOTES

1. For the purpose of this document, "disease" will be divided into two broad categories: acute and chronic. *Acute Disease:* refers to disease characterized by severe symptoms and a relatively short duration. *Chronic Disease:* refers to a disease that develops slowly and persists for a long period of time, often the remainder of the lifetime of a patient.

2. Glenn Sawyer M.D., *The First 100 Years*, Ontario Medical Association, 1981.

3. Treated on a daily basis at a hospital with no overnight stay.

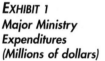

***EXHIBIT 1***
***Major Ministry***
***Expenditures***
***(Millions of dollars)***

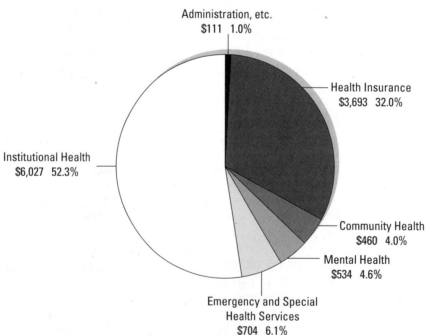

Administration, etc.
$111   1.0%

Health Insurance
$3,693   32.0%

Institutional Health
$6,027   52.3%

Community Health
$460   4.0%

Mental Health
$534   4.6%

Emergency and Special
Health Services
$704   6.1%

**EXHIBIT 2**
**Trends in Public Hospital Care**

| All Public Hospitals in Ontario | End of Reporting Period | | | | | |
|---|---|---|---|---|---|---|
| | 1987/88 | 1986/87 | 1985/86 | 1984/85 | 1983/84 | 1982/83 |
| Rated Beds | 54,014 | 53,920 | 53,563 | 52,916 | 52,517 | 52,506 |
| Approved Beds | 50,861 | 50,466 | 50,130 | 49,481 | 48,973 | 48,762 |
| Beds Staffed and in Operation | 49,832 | 49,658 | 49,333 | 48,815 | 48,373 | 47,943 |
| Number of Adults and Children | | | | | | |
| Admissions | 1,331,769 | 1,319,177 | 1,310,031 | 1,305,119 | 1,291,536 | 1,285,799 |
| Discharges and Deaths | 1,334,418 | 1,316,052 | 1,310,761 | 1,302,927 | 1,291,055 | 1,288,500 |
| Patients Under Care (1) | 1,377,483 | 1,361,763 | 1,353,344 | 1,346,240 | 1,332,199 | 1,329,233 |
| Total Patient Days (Adults and Children) | | | | | | |
| of Discharges and Deaths (2) | 15,749,169 | 15,319,501 | 15,149,493 | 14,939,024 | 14,597,551 | 14,711,676 |
| of Care Given During Year (3) | 15,966,889 | 15,783,137 | 15,602,341 | 15,497,698 | 15,330,073 | 15,219,209 |
| Average Length of Stay of Patients Discharged or Died | | | | | | |
| Acute | 8.7 | 8.7 | 8.7 | 8.7 | 8.7 | 8.7 |
| General Rehabilitation | 37.0 | 37.4 | 36.0 | 37.3 | 37.0 | 37.3 |
| Special Rehabilitation | 46.7 | 46.9 | 46.5 | 44.4 | 45.7 | 45.0 |
| Chronic | 264.8 | 263.5 | 263.2 | 252.8 | 240.5 | 237.6 |
| Psychiatric (4) | 32.7 | 31.2 | 32.0 | 31.3 | 30.7 | 30.1 |
| Alcohol and Drug Addiction (5) | 28.5 | 26.4 | 26.7 | 32.3 | 30.1 | 28.0 |
| Total | 11.8 | 11.6 | 11.6 | 11.5 | 11.3 | 11.4 |
| Number of Diagnostic Radiological Examinations | | | | | | |
| Done by Hospital | 6,616,879 | 6,324,526 | 6,065,167 | 5,899,968 | 5,628,716 | 5,461,638 |
| Done by Other Agencies | 48,775 | 48,689 | 45,877 | 40,414 | 31,088 | 26,201 |
| Total | 6,665,654 | 6,373,215 | 6,111,044 | 5,940,382 | 5,659,804 | 5,487,839 |
| Total Units of Laboratory Services Performed in Hospitals | | | | | | |
| In-patients | 285,113,896 | 285,087,489 | 286,633,336 | 379,495,633 | 379,876,203 | 379,861,160 |
| Out-patients | 174,292,294 | 164,607,226 | 162,880,996 | 189,398,258 | 180,032,034 | 174,987,915 |
| Referred-in | 55,175,370 | 51,202,636 | 51,767,934 | 61,160,875 | 59,872,218 | 58,631,531 |
| Routine Health | 96,514,801 | 94,264,268 | 94,854,207 | 113,682,069 | 116,144,713 | 114,672,227 |
| Total Out-patient Emergency Visits | 6,015,198 | 5,780,246 | 5,424,378 | 5,296,247 | 5,122,479 | 5,021,413 |
| Total Staff and Employees of Hospitals at End of Reporting Period | | | | | | |
| Full-time | 106,533 | 104,966 | 102,596 | 100,364 | 99,732 | 99,705 |
| Part-time | 54,786 | 51,770 | 48,152 | 44,694 | 41,632 | 39,161 |
| Total Paid Hours of Work | 251,993,304 | 244,765,121 | 236,887,945 | 230,905,103 | 225,951,895 | 222,086,549 |

(1) Discharges and deaths plus patients in-residence at end of period.
(2) Days of discharges and deaths are all the days which have accrued to the separations that occurred within the reporting year, from their dates of admission. These days will include days from a prior year(s) but will not include days for patients in-residence at the end of the reporting period.
(3) Days of care given during reporting period to discharges and deaths and patients in-residence at end of period.
(4) Refers to Clarke Institute and Sudbury Algoma Hospital.
(5) Refers to Donwood Institute only.

*EXHIBIT 3*

---

### POPULATION TRENDS IN ONTARIO

The following charts outline some of the trends that have occurred in Ontario's population over the past years:

| Year | % population > 65 | Average Age |
|------|-------------------|-------------|
| 1976 | 8.9 | 28.59 |
| 1981 | 10.1 | — |
| 1982 | 9.7 | 31.0 |
| 1983 | 10.4 | 31.4 |
| 1984 | 10.5 | 31.7 |
| 1985 | 10.7 | 32.0 |
| 1986 | 11.0 | 32.3 |
| 1987 | 11.1 | 32.5 |
| 1995 | 11.0 | 33.2 |
| 2000* | 11.1 | 34.5 |

The above chart shows a steady increase in the average age of Ontario residents. Furthermore, as shown on the chart below, people are beginning to enjoy longer lives, and this trend is expected to continue in the future.

Table 8: Life Expectancy

| Year | Male | Female |
|------|------|--------|
| 1976 | 69.89 | 77.43 |
| 2000* | 70.62 | 79.15 |

* Projected by Statistics Canada.

# C A S E 7.10   SWO SERVICE

Dave Airey and George Albinson left their second annual retreat wondering in what direction to take their Mississauga-based company. It was August 1991, and the recession did not seem to be improving. However, they had sealed two major sales that would contribute $88,000 in cash over the next six months. A decision, whether to sell or expand the business, would be required soon.

**BACKGROUND SUMMARY**

SWO was a small software firm formed as a 50/50 partnership by Dave Airey and George Albinson in 1984. The firm specialized in accounting and inventory software packages for distribution firms in the Toronto area. It used exclusively a programming language called PICK, which was well-known for its ability to manipulate large amounts of data.

Dave had extensive programming experience, had worked for several software firms in the past, and wanted to work for himself. George worked in a refinery in Sarnia, had saved a substantial amount of money, and wanted to open a business. In 1984, they agreed to start a software business, where Dave would invest his know-how and George his money to start the firm.

The first six years were extremely volatile. They started with a base of two customers and built up a software package. The strategy was to sell the first few installations cheaply, and then sell the rest for a higher price after the "bugs were out."

They had been fairly successful with the strategy. The company developed a software package that was highly praised by its customers. Hardware suppliers felt initially that it was one of the best PICK systems on the market.

However, the firm found itself pulled in different directions by its customers. Its program was constantly being upgraded and changed with each new customer. The customers still demanded a low cost product, and many product alterations. This led to the majority of sales in software service, but occasionally a big hardware and software sale would occur. It also led to wide fluctuations in profitability. The company made large profits when it sold software packages, but lost money on their ongoing service.

SWO had an extremely difficult year in 1991. These difficulties arose primarily from the poor shape of the economy. There were also unrelated internal problems.

## THE SOFTWARE INDUSTRY FOR DISTRIBUTORS

The distributor market was divided into three categories based primarily on the size of the customer. Needs of the different segments varied greatly. Needs also differed from customer to customer, especially for the larger distributors.

### Small Distributors

There were thousands of these operations all over Toronto. They sold everything from lamps to rice, and had less than $2 million in sales each. The companies were most often owner-operated, and the owners were eager to talk about software. The primary need of these consumers was an accounting package to handle their payables and receivables. They could not afford the service costs of adapting their software, although they often wanted alterations. The majority of these businesses bought off-the-shelf software like ACCPAC. Their knowledge of packages was limited to word-of-mouth reputation and in-store promotions.

### Mid-sized Distributors

These firms were mainly owner-operated; however, they also had professional management staff. They often had greater needs for their software, so that off-the-shelf packages were not sophisticated enough. Their primary need was for a good inventory control system that was tied into their accounting package.

These firms demanded sophisticated service for their package. They often wanted design modifications, and immediate service for day-to-day problems. They had a better knowledge of software, and had often had at least one bad experience with a cheap package. As a result, they did not like paying for service, but would do so.

There were a wide variety of businesses in this segment. Their sales ranged from $2 million to $20 million. At this size, they knew their competition. They often saw their computer system as their competitive advantage, and did not want their competitors to obtain a similar package. They expected their software firm to know their business and their needs. The packages were purchased by both experienced and inexperienced staff. The majority of product information came from word-of-mouth and testimonials from satisfied customers. There were approximately one thousand distributors of this size in the Toronto area.

### Large Distributors

These distributors had sales over $20 million, and demanded much of their software suppliers. They expected and were willing to pay for 24-hour service. The software had to be fully integrated and able to handle the diverse and specific requirements of the company. Large distributors often purchased packages specifically designed for their company. They also insisted that the package could not be used by any other company.

Distributors of this size could demand a lot of their software supplier. They expected perks such as a 1–800 number or permanent on-site programmers for service. These companies would spend a million dollars or more on a system. The system represented a key part of the business, and the supplier had to be dependable and experienced. The purchase decision was usually made by a company board on the recommendation of consultants or by company experts. The purchase decision was usually a long, involved process, that could extend more than two years. There were several hundred distributors of this size in the Toronto area.

## COMPETITION

Competition in the software industry was stiff. Any programmer with a basic program could set up shop in his or her house and start a business. These cottage industry programmers put pressure on prices in the industry. They also hurt the reputation of the industry. Often, these small shop software houses would sell flawed software at a cheap price. Since most distributors did not have the ability to tell the difference between good and bad software, this resulted in many small and medium-sized distributors distrusting software houses. Distributors often commented that software houses overpromised and underdelivered.

The lower end of the market for small businesses was mostly taken up by one-person shops and off-the-shelf packages. The cost of these packages was usually around $600 to $4,000, with very limited after-sale service. ACCPAC was the industry leader in this segment. It had a large portion of the North American market, and many accountants recommended this package to small distributors. ACCPAC often trained accountants and consultants on its system for free, to encourage the use of the package.

The mid-range of the market was splintered. Off-the-shelf packages did not do well, due to the more sophisticated needs of the clients. There was an infinite variety of software and hardware combinations in this segment; the combination of hardware and software was the key to success. Many of the problems faced by the distributors were related to incompatibilities between software and hardware. Successful competitors developed relationships with one or two hardware manufacturers. This allowed better systems and better support.

In this segment, the range of prices for a system was $10,000 to $200,000. The product features and level of service depended on the price. The challenge to the software house was to convince the distributors that they needed to invest in order to get the software they needed. This was difficult, given the small margins in the distribution industry, and the number of low-priced packages that promised to do the same things. Software firms used a combination of direct mail, hardware supplier referrals, consultant and accountant referrals, and customer testimonials to promote their products.

Competition for the large distributors was fierce, though limited to a few competitors. These competitors were usually wings of accounting firms or divisions of large hardware manufacturers. Large distributors limited their business to these suppliers due to their need for stability. The cost of a system was usually $500,000 or more. Arthur Andersen and IBM were two of the leading competitors in the segment. These firms were well financed and had extensive expertise.

## TRADE IN THE COMPUTER INDUSTRY

The majority of software sales also included hardware sales. The sale could be initiated either by the hardware firm or the software house. Usually, small and medium-sized software houses developed a relationship with one or two hardware suppliers. The relationship was based on the mutual exchange of business and trust. The software house did not want hardware that made its product look bad, and the hardware firm did not want software to make its hardware look bad. As a result, these relationships took time, and were limited to established software firms.

Software houses often received a 30 percent margin on the hardware they sold. However, the hardware firms did not provide good credit terms. The majority of system deals involved a leasing company. Leasing companies bought the hardware from the hardware firm and paid the software house a commission. They then leased the equipment and sometimes the software to the distributor. This changed the system cost into an annual payment instead of an upfront investment for a cash-strapped distributor.

## EXTERNAL FACTORS

Several factors affected the industry. A primary factor was the economy, which had been in a recession for over two years. Although a recovery was said to be under way, the economy was sluggish. Numerous distributors had gone out of business, and those that had not were pushing their payables. There was little or no purchase of new systems.

However, computer systems were continuing to be more critical to the already competitive distribution industry. Many distributors attributed their ability to survive to their competitive advantage in their system. Distributors realized that better inventory and accounts management was the key to success.

Politically, the federal government had initiated the GST (Goods and Services Tax) two years earlier. This complex value-added tax on business had prompted many companies to computerize in order to manage the process. The government was also keen to expand the computer industry. As a result, there were several programs that would subsidize wages and help firms cover the cost of training their employees.

## INTERNAL ANALYSIS

SWO had two primary sources of income: system sales and ongoing service revenue. These sources had not, however, provided SWO with a stable base of income. In years when SWO made two or three system sales, the company made a good profit. The money was then used to develop a new facet of the product. See Exhibits 1, 2, 3, 4, and 5 for the financial statements for the past three years.

**System Sales**

System sales, in particular, were a "hit or miss" proposition. The two system sales that SWO had just concluded were two years in the making. Hours and hours of time were required to establish relationships with the customers. Dave had done the majority of the sales work to date; however, he did not enjoy it. He found cold calls on new customers extremely difficult, and only liked to talk to small distributors because they were chatty.

Recently, SWO had tried to improve its sales effort. Nine months ago, the company had hired a salesman who was the brother of a marketing consultant they had used. He had not generated any sales yet, but was good at mailings and cold calls on potential customers.

SWO tried several marketing blitzes. It targeted distributors that were similar to its current customers. The company felt that its knowledge of their business areas would help it gain new customers. However, it had limited success. Dave did not have the time to follow up on the letters, and George, who was in Sarnia, did not either. The new salesman had some success in this area; however, he did not know enough about the system to fully follow up.

Further, current customers were reluctant to help SWO sell the product to their competitors. They would only recommend the product to potential customers who were not direct threats. For example, SWO was able to use its computer parts client to get a computer parts distributor in Niagara Falls. Unfortunately, SWO was unable to service this new client quickly enough, and lost the account.

The brightest spot in marketing was the new relationship with Data General. SWO had attempted several relationships with hardware firms in the past. All had failed. Either the hardware firm was too undependable and SWO terminated the relationship, or the hardware firm was not interested in SWO. This was the first respectable hardware firm that had indicated a desire to develop a relationship with SWO. Data General sales reps had already given SWO some good sales leads, and had helped to close its latest sale. SWO, in turn, was promoting Data General equipment to its customers, who seemed to find it reliable and affordable.

**Ongoing Service Revenue**

This area of the company had suffered greatly in recent times. The company charged firms by the hour for service; however, it charged below market rates. Dave believed that SWO had to charge less because its customers could not afford regular rates. George felt that the company was currently charging less than the cost of its people.

SWO had two technicians who did the majority of its service work. Dave also did some of this work on a part-time basis. SWO had another technician whom the customers liked because she explained things well. However, she was let go when revenues declined in 1990. She was not as technically strong as the other two, although she got better reviews from customers.

George often wondered if the existing staff knew how to make customers happy. He often heard that customers became very happy when small screen displays were changed, and did not appreciate when complex programming tasks were completed. The firm currently did no proactive customer development. The overwhelming amount of customer service work was done at the customer's request.

**SWO's Current Customer Base**

The SWO customer base included a business forms distributor, a computer parts distributor, and 10 small distributors. Their two new medium-sized customers were an electrical parts distributor and a popcorn distributor. Currently, the business forms distributor was almost bankrupt, and the computer parts distributor was unhappy with SWO's service. The small distributors provided steady income, but also caused numerous receivable problems. Also, some major companies used SWO programmers for assistance, but did not have SWO software.

**FINANCES AT SWO**

SWO was currently fully funded by investments made by the shareholders. George had invested over $100,000 over the years, $20,000 just recently. Dave had invested $40,000 plus receiving a salary far below what he could have received as a corporate programmer. The two men debated the amounts that they invested at the retreat, but then decided it really didn't matter.

The banks would not loan SWO any money because it had no assets to speak of, and software firms were not good risks. George had to use personal lines of credit to get the firm money. However, he now wanted to get this money out to pay the bank back.

George calculated that the monthly expenses of the company were $16,000, and that the monthly service revenue was $10,000. The shortfall was covered by George's cash injections. Cash flow remained a major concern for the company.

These financial difficulties were compounded by a complex financial management system. SWO was in the process of moving its books off ACCPAC on George's computer in Sarnia, onto its own system in Mississauga. However, Dave did not fully understand how the system was to work for SWO and lacked time to do the entries. George preferred to have the financials on his computer, but agreed to put it in Mississauga so that Dave could better understand the company's finances.

A lack of consistent data entry also meant that SWO was poor at collecting its receivables. Receivables were often not entered into the computer until weeks after a job was done. They were then billed weeks later, and finally chased after by George if they were more than three months past due. However, George's full-time job in Sarnia made it difficult for him to put much time into this process.

**FUTURE OPPORTUNITIES**

The two recent sales had pumped new hope into the company. Both George and Dave wanted the company to do well and grow. However, neither one of them was willing to put much more money into it. The cash from these sales would be the last chance for SWO to break the cycle of boom and bust. The only other option was sell the business and get out as much money as they could.

**Expanding the Business**

Dave and George were uncertain of how to proceed on this course. They knew that several key areas of the company needed help. The expansion of the business would require a detailed and well-executed marketing plan.

They felt that with the right marketing assistance SWO could hope for $400,000 worth of systems sales with a 75 percent margin. This sales figure would be on top of regular service sales. Sales could go as high as $800,000 or as low as $250,000 depending on the success of the marketing effort. This success would depend greatly on the people SWO hired.

Dave felt that the company's greatest need was for a system analyst. This would be particularly important with the two new installations of the SWO system coming up in the fall. He knew that he would be too busy managing the company and looking after current customers to do this work. The cost of a system analyst would be approximately $45,000. Dave had chosen a dependable analyst for this position who could start right away.

On the other hand, George felt that the company needed a general manager most. This person would run day-to-day operations and coordinate the sales effort. The majority of people qualified to do a good job in this area would want a stake in the company. George figured that the company would have to provide a $36,000 salary and offer 30 percent of the company. George felt that if the person did the job well, after a three-month trial run, he or she could then be offered a third of the company.

Dave thought that they only needed a sales manager. He felt that he could run the company in time. He was still having difficulty understanding the finance side, but was sure he would learn as he went along. George also had difficulty with the idea of giving up control of the company, but had decided that they did not have a choice. He had been interviewing several candidates, and thought he had found one who would fit the bill.

They agreed that they also needed a full-time receptionist. SWO needed to have someone in the office to take calls and to input the receivables to the computer; this employee would cost $27,000. They also felt that they should invest some money in training their current staff, who had not had any formal training in almost a year.

Exhibit 6 presents a preliminary revised organization chart to accommodate their expansion plans for SWO.

**Selling the Business**

This option was not one that Dave and George were excited about; however, it needed to be investigated. They realized that the only real tangible assets of the company were the customer base and the software.

As there were not many software houses currently using a PICK system for distributors, the customer base would be valued differently by different software houses. There would likely be a bid on a multiple of the service earnings for the customer base. The software would not likely be worth much more than this. In addition, the receivables from the two new sales could not be collected until the systems were installed.

*EXHIBIT 1*

| | **INCOME STATEMENT** For the Years Ending April 30 ($000s) | | |
| --- | --- | --- | --- |
| | **1991** | **1990** | **1989** |
| Income | $354 | $248 | $437 |
| Cost of goods sold | 81 | 48 | 141 |
| Gross profit | 273 | 200 | 296 |
| Expenses: | | | |
| Advertising and promotion | 2 | 0 | 0 |
| Bad debt | 28 | 21 | 15 |
| Consulting | 14 | 7 | 0 |
| Depreciation | 5 | 5 | 6 |
| Loan interest | 14 | 12 | 4 |
| Maintenance and repair | 3 | 8 | 4 |
| Miscellaneous | 12 | 12 | 20 |
| Office and computer supplies | 8 | 6 | 11 |
| Rent | 15 | 13 | 4 |
| Software expense — research | 0 | 5 | 8 |
| Telephone | 11 | 12 | 12 |
| Travel | 3 | 6 | 5 |
| Wages | 158 | 162 | 183 |
| Vehicle lease | 9 | 7 | 8 |
| | 282 | 276 | 280 |
| Net income (loss) (note 4) | ($ 98) | ($ 76) | $ 13 |

*Exhibit 2*

| | | | |
|---|---|---|---|
| **STATEMENT OF RETAINED EARNINGS**<br>**For the Years Ending April 30**<br>**($000s)** | | | |
| | **1991** | **1990** | **1989** |
| Accumulated earnings (deficit) —<br>  Beginning of year | ($64) | $12 | ($ 1) |
| Net income (loss) | (8) | (76) | 13 |
| Accumulated (deficit) — End of year | ($72) | ($64) | $12 |

*EXHIBIT 3*

| | BALANCE SHEET[1] As at April 30 ($000s) | | |
|---|---|---|---|
| | **1991** | **1990** | **1989** |
| ASSETS | | | |
| Current assets: | | | |
| Bank | $ 23 | $ 25 | $ 0 |
| Accounts receivable (net of allowance of $14,200; $6,000 in 1990) | 55 | 57 | 111 |
| Inventory (note 1 and 5) | 53 | 45 | 6 |
| | $131 | $126 | $118 |
| Fixed assets: (note 1) | | | |
| Computers | 18 | 18 | 18 |
| Office equipment | 18 | 18 | 16 |
| Software | 19 | 18 | 18 |
| | $ 54 | $ 53 | $ 51 |
| Less accumulated depreciation | (40) | (36) | 31 |
| | $ 14 | $ 17 | $ 21 |
| Other assets: | | | |
| Incorporation costs | | | 1 |
| TOTAL ASSETS | $145 | $144 | $140 |
| LIABILITIES AND SHAREHOLDERS' EQUITY | | | |
| Current liabilities: | | | |
| Bank overdraft (note 2) | $ 0 | $ 0 | $ 5 |
| Accounts payable and accruals | 36 | 15 | 14 |
| Taxes payable | 0 | 0 | 4 |
| Deferred revenue (note 5) | 36 | 36 | 0 |
| | $ 72 | $ 51 | $ 23 |
| Long-term liabilities: | | | |
| Lease payable | 1 | 2 | 4 |
| Other loans (note 3) | 144 | 154 | 101 |
| | $217 | $208 | $104 |
| Shareholders' equity: | | | |
| Retained earnings (deficit) | (72) | (64) | 12 |
| TOTAL LIABILITIES AND SHAREHOLDERS' EQUITY | $145 | $144 | $140 |

1. Totals may vary due to rounding of figures.

*EXHIBIT 4*

---

## NOTES TO FINANCIAL STATEMENTS
### As at April 30
### ($000s)

---

### 1. ACCOUNTING POLICIES:

The accounting policies of the Company are in accordance with generally accepted accounting principles.

Inventory:  The Inventory is recorded at the lower of cost and net realizable value (note 5).

Depreciation:  Depreciation is calculated using the following methods and rates:

| | |
|---|---|
| Office equipment | 20 percent declining balance |
| Software | 100 percent straight line |
| Hardware | 30 percent declining balance |

Income Taxes: The Company follows the tax allocation basis of accounting for income taxes, whereby tax provisions are based on accounting income, and taxes relating to timing differences between accounting and taxable income are deferred.

### 2. BANK OVERDRAFT:

The bank overdraft results from cheques that were written but not cashed.

### 3. OTHER LOANS:

The other loans are due to a shareholder and other related people.  Interest on these loans consists of a reimbursement to the shareholder for interest paid on a personal bank loan whose proceeds were reloaned to the Company at interest of various rates approximating 10 percent.

| | 1991 | 1990 | 1989 |
|---|---|---|---|
| Shareholder | $105 | $ 98 | $83 |
| Shareholder | 33 | 38 | 0 |
| Shareholder's mother | 7 | 8 | 8 |
| Shareholder's brother | 0 | 10 | 10 |
| | $144 | $154 | $101 |

### 4. LOSS CARRY FORWARD:

The company has a loss carry forward of $73 ($70 in 1990), which may be used to reduce taxable income in future years.  This loss carry forward expires as follows:

| | |
|---|---|
| 1997 | $70 |
| 1998 | 3 |
| | $ 73 |

In addition, the company has written more depreciation that it has claimed for tax purposes in the amount of $10 ($6 in 1990).  This amount can also be used to reduce taxable income in future years.

### 5. REVISION TO EARLIER STATEMENTS:

Subsequent to the publication of the statements, management discovered that certain prices of inventory that had previously been recorded as cost of sales had, in fact, never been transferred to the customer despite the fact that payment had been received.  As a result of ongoing discussions with the customer management has determined that the inventory may not be accepted by the customer.  As a result, these statements have been revised to reflect deferred revenue of $36 and decreased cost of sales of $36.  The effect of this revision on the income and retained earnings of the company is nil.

***EXHIBIT 5***

| | Ratio Analysis<br>For the Years Ending April 30<br>($000s) | | |
| --- | --- | --- | --- |
| | **1991** | **1990** | **1989** |
| PROFITABILITY | | | |
| Sales | 100% | 100% | 100% |
| Cost of goods sold | 22.9% | 19.3% | 32.3% |
| Gross profit | 77.1% | 80.7% | 67.7% |
| EXPENSES | | | |
| Advertising and promotion | 0.4% | 0.1% | 0.1% |
| Bad debt | 7.8% | 8.4% | 3.4% |
| Consulting | 4.0% | 2.6% | 0.0% |
| Depreciation | 1.3% | 2.1% | 1.4% |
| Loan interest | 3.9% | 4.7% | 0.9% |
| Maintenance | 0.9% | 3.3% | 0.8% |
| Miscellaneous | 3.5% | 4.7% | 4.5% |
| Office and computer supplies | 2.2% | 2.4% | 2.6% |
| Rent | 4.3% | 5.1% | 2.8% |
| Software expenses R&D | 0.0% | 2.2% | 1.8% |
| Telephone | 3.0% | 4.9% | 2.8% |
| Travel | 0.8% | 2.6% | 1.2% |
| Wages | 44.6% | 65.4% | 41.8% |
| Vehicle lease | 2.5% | 2.8% | 1.8% |
| Net income (Loss) | −2.2% | −30.7% | 2.8% |
| LIQUIDITY | | | |
| Current ratio | 1.8:1 | 2.5:1 | 5.1:1 |
| Acid test | 1.1:1 | 1.6:1 | 4.8:1 |
| EFFICIENCY | | | |
| Age of accounts receivable | 56.9 | 83.7 | 92.7 |
| Age of inventory | 240.1 | 339.6 | 16.6 |
| Age of payables | 160.7 | 113.5 | 36.2 |
| STABILITY | | | |
| Net worth/total assets | 0% | 0% | 8.0% |
| GROWTH | **1991–90** | **1990–89** | |
| Sales | 48% | −76.3% | |
| Net profit | 880% | −603% | |
| Assets | 1% | 3% | |
| Equity | −12% | −543% | |

**EXHIBIT 6**
*SWO Organizational Chart*

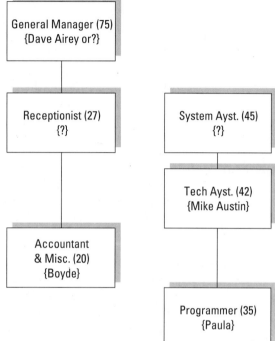

( ) – Salary in 000s
{ } – Person for spot

## C A S E 7.11   TELEMUS ELECTRONIC SYSTEMS INC.

In late 1990, Ron Benn, chairman and controller of Telemus Electronic Systems Inc., considered the outlook of the company. Telemus was a defence electronics company located in Ottawa, Canada. Without a suitable buyer, Telemus lacked the funds required to continue as a going concern. Ron pondered the future, recognizing the urgency of the situation.

**TELEMUS'S PRODUCT AREAS**

Telemus competed for contracts in the rapidly changing field of defence electronics. Its three main products were frequency dividers, digital radio frequency memory units, and radar warning receivers flight line test sets. The company also produced other products and had developed several other training and test sets.

**Frequency Dividers**

Frequency dividers were tiny electronic components used in radar and radio-frequency to break down and analyze incoming signals. In 1984, Telemus's trademarked frequency divider, the "Halver," was at the front edge of technology. By 1986, technology that rivalled the Halver had been developed in Japan. As competition grew and the market became limited, prices fell from $3,000 to $2,000 to $600 per unit. Halvers became a low-margin, high-volume business and Telemus lacked the distribution network and infrastructure to compete effectively. Telemus did continue to produce the Halver in limited quantities.

**Digital Radio Frequency Memory Units**

Digital radio frequency memory units (DRFMs) were high-speed recording, storage and playback devices, used to protect aircraft and ships from radar guided missiles. The DRFM captured an incoming missile's radar signals, temporarily stored them, and re-echoed them with varying delays. The false echo hid the aircraft or ship from the missile by creating a false electronic target. DRFMs were priced in the $200,000 (U.S.) range.

Telemus's DRFM sampled radar signals faster than any substitute. The DRFM was never patented, in part because it was difficult to determine whether it had been copied.

**Radar Warning Receivers Flight Line Test Sets**

Radar warning receivers (RWRs) were military "fuzzbusters" used to warn pilots of threatening radar activity. These receivers employed specific software libraries to identify the exact type of radar threat encountered. The RWR flight line test set was used to test an aircraft's RWR system to ensure that it was operating properly. With its $50,000 (U.S.) to $75,000 (U.S.) price tag, the RWR flight line test set had better international potential than the higher-priced DRFM.

Telemus's RWR flight line test set was the most capable unit of its type on the market and could ultimately capitalize on the test needs of an estimated 20,000 military aircraft carrying RWR equipment in the noncommunist world. Four Telemus RWRs had been sold to the Canadian government.

**Other Training and Test Sets**

Training and test set devices were not used on board a military aircraft. Rather, they were used to test a pilot's reactions by simulating the frequencies of oncoming missiles and radar. Telemus was one of a few firms in the world with active contracts in this increasingly important area.

Telemus's DRFM Test Set was used by the U.S. Navy; the U.S. Air Force had considered it. Another Telemus product, the ESM flight line test set, had received rave reviews from the Department of National Defence in Canada.

**Other Products**

Telemus obtained a $500,000 contract with the Canadian Navy for the electronic counter measures unit (ECMU), which was built around the DRFM. Telemus spent $750,000 fulfilling the contract. Telemus's success in this market was limited by the Navy's previous commitment to outfit up to 20 ships with a Dutch product. Other similar, one-time contracts saw Telemus sink substantial funds into products which the company could not effectively market or where specifications could not be met.

**THE MARKET FOR DEFENCE ELECTRONICS**

A defence electronics firm could sell either directly to a country's defence department or indirectly, through a contractor that sold to the defence department. This placed smaller firms like Telemus in the interesting position of competing with their customers for contracts. While smaller contracts attracted fewer bids, those in excess of $250,000 attracted many bidders of varying sizes.

Defence contractors ranged in size. The larger competitors' strengths included substantial financial resources, security of supply, and existing, working products. A huge competitor might employ as many as 10,000 employees. Smaller firms, while lacking the project management skills and financial resources of the larger competitors, tended to compensate with greater innovative abilities.

In its early years, Telemus targeted only the Canadian market, through the Department of National Defence (DND). From 1984 to 1990, DND accounted for at least two-thirds of Telemus's revenues. A huge, one-time contract to Teledyne CME in the U.S. made up 10 to 15 percent of sales, and other foreign customers contributed the remainder.

**Canadian Customers**

The Department of National Defence processed contracts slowly, so that the contract winner had to wait a long time before the first cheque was received. Once the winner was announced and contract specifications were finalized, that company had to commence work immediately in order to meet the fixed delivery deadline. Payment was received 30 days after invoices were submitted.

Canadian contracts were tied heavily to the federal government's fiscal year, where year-end was March 31. During February and March, when departments spent the remainder of their budgets, business was generally good.

In 1991–92, the Canadian government was expected to spend $2 million on RWR test sets and DRFM training systems alone. Similar training system and RWR needs in foreign countries could easily double or triple this figure.

### Foreign Customers

The market for defence electronics was worldwide. The American market for DRFMs was as large as $10 to $15 million per year.

American sales could be achieved through large contractors such as Teledyne and Datacom. These companies, in turn, sold to the U.S. defence department. Telemus sold in the U.S. only through Teledyne, which sold to the U.S. Department of Defence, and through Datacom, which contracted DRFM training devices for the U.S. Navy.

Telemus sold Halvers to customers in countries including India and Italy.

### Bidding for Contracts

In many cases, contracts were written so that few companies could fulfill them. It seemed that the best way to win a contract was to help write its specifications. In Ron's words, "If you assist your customers in defining their needs, then you've got an inside track." At the same time, it was possible to spend a lot of time and money writing proposals.

Prices were determined when a customer decided what its budget was; the bidder designed a project to meet it.

### Competition

The market for Halvers was huge; on a given contract, hundreds of companies would bid. For DRFMs, there were only four or five suppliers in the world. Telemus was considered "the DRFM house for Canada." Besides the DRFM producers in the U.S., Telemus found competitors in foreign markets, where Telemus was often considered too small to compete. Only three companies in the world provided DRFM test and training equipment.

Canadian defence contractors included MEL Defence Systems Ltd., Lockheed Canada, and Canadian Astronautics Limited (CAL). In its 1988 fiscal year, CAL had achieved sales of $25 million. Both MEL and Lockheed were subsidiaries of much larger companies.

Competition took place in meeting specifications. Price became more important as margins fell. The buying process was long, with a company often selling a customer a product that did not yet exist.

**EXTERNAL FACTORS SURROUNDING THE DEFENCE ELECTRONICS INDUSTRY**

While the defence industry flourished during the Cold War of the 1980s, the 1989 fall of communism in the Soviet Union left defence spending a much lower priority for most first-world countries.

Electronic Warfare (EW) was considered important to national security by most advanced nations. Many nations developed EW systems themselves and restricted access to foreign competitors. For example, the United States purchased only made-in-America products. Canada was one of the only countries that bought "ready-made" defence electronics. On the other hand, training and test sets were competed for openly and without major restrictions to foreign competitors. Used solely for training purposes, they were not considered to be of strategic importance.

On a local level, the recent failure of a large, Ottawa-based defence contractor led to a loan review by local banks. The banks were no longer interested in lending to firms in the defence industry unless the company was in strong financial condition.

**COMPANY HISTORY**

In 1984, two Department of National Defence scientists approached two Ottawa businessmen with the idea behind Telemus Electronic Systems. The scientists had developed a prototype version of a frequency divider that they wished to market. Telemus began operations with $2 million in cash; the investment was earmarked to move the Halver from the laboratory bench to the marketplace. The four founders had put up a total of $50,000; the remainder was contributed by five venture capitalists.[1]

After continuing net losses, most of the $2 million investment was consumed and the Halver had not met sales expectations. By 1986, the Halver had achieved less than 25 percent of projected sales. Research contracts for the Canadian government kept the company afloat; Telemus doubled its sales expectations in this area.

From 1985 to 1988, the four founders left Telemus. In 1987, it was predicted that Telemus would declare bankruptcy. Michael Gale, the new president, modified Telemus's focus so that it relied less on Halvers and more on other product areas. Ron Benn came to Telemus in August 1988, filling the controller position. In 1990, Ron became chairman of the board and Mark Cloutier took over the role of president.

Company president Michael Gale had attempted to lead Telemus into the international scene. By 1986, Telemus had found significant off-shore demand, which did not replace but offset the total reliance on the Canadian market. Ron Benn and Mark Cloutier's strategy was that "you had to sell internationally to make it and you had to be a niche player."

**INTERNAL ORGANIZATION**

Marketing was carried out by the president and business unit managers, who were responsible for generating sales for their own units. (See Exhibit 1 for an organizational chart.) None of these men had formal marketing training. Some specification sheets were mailed out, but most marketing involved "knocking on doors." At times, Telemus managers exhibited a lack of focus and a lack of understanding of the customer's decision-making process. It was often necessary to convince a chain of people of the merits of a product because the technology was a component of a much larger system.

From 1984 to 1990, Telemus did not turn a profit. (See Exhibits 2, 3, and 4 for selected financial results.) Telemus was on firm but fair terms with its bank. In mid-December 1989, Telemus was advised that the bank would not entertain any further loan requests. By July 1990, immediate danger from the bank had passed, although it was clear that it would continue to monitor the Telemus account very carefully.

Cash-flow problems resulted from 10 percent holdbacks.[2] These holdbacks often ran well beyond the delivery of the contract and were difficult to get a release on until the customer determined that the product had met specifications. For a cash-strapped business such as Telemus, these delays were problematic.

As a result of its poor cash position, Telemus delayed payment to some of its creditors and suppliers. Most suppliers were unhappy with Telemus's lengthy payment terms. In July 1990, Telemus was two months in arrears on its rent, but negotiated payment terms with the building owner.

Production was scheduled according to contracts due. The majority of products were designed and built at Telemus. Most employees were very talented, holding exceptional engineering skills in specialty defence electronics and electronic warfare in particular.

In a project-oriented company, it was normal for the number of employees to vary. In 1989, the average number of full-time technical staff was 23.5; the company had reached a high of 35 employees in 1987–88. Layoffs of varying size took place in 1987, 1988, 1989, and 1990. People accepted the layoffs, in general. They knew their jobs were tied to the company's ability to win a contract. The technical staff often just left, while the support staff were caught in between.

At Telemus, bid prices were handled by the employees who would work on the contract. Prices were devised from estimated materials and labour requirements, with an appropriate mark-up for overhead costs. The estimating process was the same for all bids, although private customers yielded a higher mark-up than government contracts.

When Telemus technical staff were not on time or on budget, the employee was given a chance, even the second or third time it happened. Unlike competing firms, Telemus managers tried to determine what had caused the problem and correct it. It was difficult to hold employees responsible when they were building to specifications that had never before been met.

## THE FUTURE OF TELEMUS

From 1987 on, Telemus desperately sought a parent company with an interest in the group's technology and business areas. It was hoped that the parent would acquire the intellectual and physical assets of Telemus and hire its employees.

A local partner would allow Telemus to penetrate the defence departments outside Canada. Since Telemus's technology had to be integrated into a larger system, Telemus officers sought customers designing such systems as potential buyers. For example, Florida-based Datacom was a major supplier to the U.S. Navy. In order to continue supplying the Navy, Datacom might be asked to ensure its sources by buying out such suppliers as Telemus.

In early 1990, the Receiver Division was sold to Canadian Astronautics Limited for $50,000 cash. The sale was designed to help focus the company on DRFMs. The payroll was cut by three employees. At this time, the bank reminded Telemus that the search for new equity or some form of external guarantee of its loans was critical.

Telemus received three or four offers. In 1988, Michael Gale received a lucrative offer from an American firm for $1.3 million. The offer was withdrawn at the last minute.

## CONCLUSION

Ron Benn realized that time was running out. Telemus could not go to the bank for any more money, yet the company had many pressing financial obligations to meet. Ron pondered the options available to Telemus Electronic Systems Inc.; he would report to the board of directors as soon as a feasible alternative was determined.

## NOTES

1. Venture capitalists provide investments in a firm in exchange for an ownership stake and influence over the firm.
2. Holdbacks were monies withheld from each invoice until completion of the contract.

**EXHIBIT 1**
*Telemus Electronic Systems Inc. Organizational Chart*

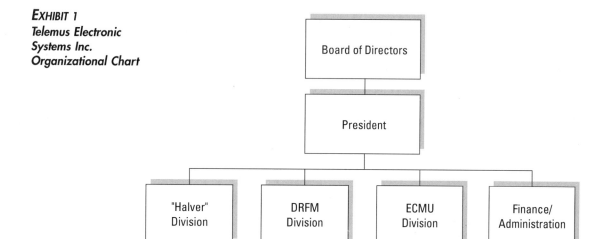

***EXHIBIT 2***

| | TELEMUS ELECTRONIC SYSTEMS INC.<br>STATEMENT OF INCOME<br>For the Year Ending December 31 | | |
|---|---|---|---|
| | 1990<br>(9 months) | 1989 | 1988 |
| REVENUES | $1,238,450 | $1,479,867 | $1,724,746 |
| OPERATING EXPENSES | | | |
| Research and development expenses | 799,468 | 757,783 | 1,149,040 |
| General and administrative expenses | 468,643 | 690,894 | 732,845 |
| Marketing | 0 | 81,130 | 125,102 |
| Depreciation and amortization | 71,286 | 100,741 | 96,689 |
| Interest expense | 54,531 | 69,279 | 42,000 |
| Total operating expenses | $1,393,928 | $1,699,827 | $2,145,676 |
| LOSS FROM OPERATIONS | $(155,478) | $(219,960) | $(420,930) |
| Interest income | 2,134 | 2,314 | 6,417 |
| Severance payments of former employees | | | 79,687 |
| NET LOSS FOR THE PERIOD | $(153,344) | $(217,646) | $(494,200) |

*EXHIBIT 3*

| TELEMUS ELECTRONIC SYSTEMS INC.<br>BALANCE SHEET<br>As at December 31 | | | |
|---|---|---|---|
| | **1990<br>(9 months)** | **1989** | **1988** |
| ASSETS | | | |
| Current assets | | | |
| Accounts receivable | $ 410,250 | $ 468,284 | $ 557,497 |
| Investment tax credits | | | |
| Recoverable | 270,000 | 331,837 | 390,005 |
| Inventory | 221,402 | 281,768 | 381,107 |
| Prepaid expense | 25,513 | 5,950 | 8,700 |
| Total current assets | $ 927,165 | $1,087,839 | $1,337,309 |
| Net fixed assets | 461,722 | 550,051 | 551,081 |
| Other assets | 8,539 | 8,539 | 9,457 |
| TOTAL ASSETS | $1,397,426 | $1,646,429 | $1,897,847 |
| LIABILITIES | | | |
| Current liabilities | | | |
| Due to bank | $ 141,789 | $ 197,526 | $ 102,032 |
| Accounts payable and accruals | 370,172 | 389,735 | 511,621 |
| EODC export development loan | 255,938 | 213,750 | 213,750 |
| Current portion of long-term debt | 75,000 | 61,518 | 50,000 |
| Total current liabilities | $ 842,899 | $ 862,529 | $ 877,403 |
| Long term debt[1] | 166,767 | 217,749 | 236,667 |
| TOTAL LIABILITIES | $1,009,666 | $1,080,278 | $1,114,070 |
| SHAREHOLDERS' EQUITY | | | |
| Share capital[2] | $2,000,410 | $2,000,388 | $2,000,268 |
| Deficit | (1,612,650) | (1,434,237) | (1,216,591) |
| TOTAL EQUITY | $ 387,760 | $ 566,151 | $ 783,777 |
| TOTAL LIABILITIES AND EQUITY | $1,397,426 | $1,646,429 | $1,897,847 |

**1.** Loan requirements demanded that Telemus's net worth not drop below $500,000.
**2.** Share capital above the initial $2,000,000 resulted from employee stock options.

*Exhibit 4*

| | | | |
|---|---|---|---|
| **TELEMUS ELECTRONIC SYSTEMS INC.** Selected Ratios | | | |
| | **1990 (9 months)** | **1989** | **1988** |
| PROFITABILITY | | | |
| REVENUES | 100.0 | 100.0 | 100.0 |
| OPERATING EXPENSES | | | |
| Research and development expenses | 64.6 | 51.2 | 66.6 |
| General and administrative expenses | 37.8 | 46.7 | 42.5 |
| Marketing | 0.0 | 5.5 | 7.3 |
| Depreciation and amortization | 5.8 | 6.8 | 5.6 |
| Interest expense | 4.4 | 4.7 | 2.4 |
| Total operating expenses | 112.6 | 114.9 | 124.4 |
| LOSS FROM OPERATIONS | −12.6 | −14.9 | −24.4 |
| NET LOSS FOR THE PERIOD | −12.3 | −14.7 | −24.0 |
| | | | |
| STABILITY | | | |
| Net worth : total assets | 27.7 | 34.4 | 41.3 |
| | | | |
| LIQUIDITY | | | |
| Current ratio | 1.10 | 1.26 | 1.52 |
| Acid test | 0.81 | 0.93 | 1.08 |
| Working capital | $84,266 | $225,310 | $459,906 |
| | | | |
| EFFICIENCY | | | |
| Age of accounts receivable in days of sales | 90.8 | 115.5 | 118.0 |
| | | | |
| GROWTH | | | |
| | **1990–91** | **1989–90** | |
| Sales | 11.6 | −14.2 | |
| Assets | −15.1 | −13.2 | |
| Equity | −31.5 | −27.8 | |

## To the owner of this book

We hope that you have enjoyed *Introduction to Business Decision Making, Text and Cases,* fifth edition, and we would like to know as much about your experiences with this text as you would care to offer. Only through your comments and those of others can we learn how to make this a better text for future readers.

School _____     Your instructor's name _____

Course _____     Was the text required? _____     Recommended? _____

**1.** What did you like the most about *Introduction to Business Decision Making?*

_____

_____

_____

**2.** How useful was this text for your course?

_____

_____

_____

**3.** Do you have any recommendations for ways to improve the next edition of this text?

_____

_____

_____

**4.** In the space below or in a separate letter, please write any other comments you have about the book. (For example, please feel free to comment on reading level, writing style, terminology, design features, and learning aids.)

_____

_____

_____

_____

### Optional

Your name _____     Date _____

May Nelson Canada quote you, either in promotion for *Introduction to Business Decision Making* or in future publishing ventures?

Yes _____     No _____

*Thanks!*

PLEASE TAPE SHUT. DO NOT STAPLE.

TAPE SHUT

TAPE SHUT

- - - - - - - FOLD HERE - - - - - - -

**Nelson**

**MAIL POSTE**

Canada Post Corporation
Société canadienne des postes

| Postage paid | Port payé |
|---|---|
| if mailed in Canada | si posté au Canada |
| **Business Reply** | **Réponse d'affaires** |

**0066102399** **01**

0066102399-M1K5G4-BR01

NELSON CANADA
MARKET AND PRODUCT DEVELOPMENT
PO BOX 60225 STN BRM B
TORONTO ON M7Y 2H1

TAPE SHUT

TAPE SHUT